Marketing

Marketing

Paul Baines,
Chris Fill,
and Kelly Page

OXFORD
UNIVERSITY PRESS

OXFORD
UNIVERSITY PRESS

Great Clarendon Street, Oxford OX2 6DP

Oxford University Press is a department of the University of Oxford.
It furthers the University's objective of excellence in research, scholarship,
and education by publishing worldwide in

Oxford New York

Auckland Cape Town Dar es Salaam Hong Kong Karachi
Kuala Lumpur Madrid Melbourne Mexico City Nairobi
New Delhi Shanghai Taipei Toronto

With offices in

Argentina Austria Brazil Chile Czech Republic France Greece
Guatemala Hungary Italy Japan Poland Portugal Singapore
South Korea Switzerland Thailand Turkey Ukraine Vietnam

Oxford is a registered trade mark of Oxford University Press
in the UK and in certain other countries

Published in the United States
by Oxford University Press Inc., New York

British Library Cataloguing in Publication Data

Data available

Library of Congress Cataloging in Publication Data
Baines, Paul, 1973–
Marketing / Paul Baines, Chris Fill, and Kelly Page.
p. cm.
Includes index.
ISBN 978–0–19–929043–7
1. Marketing.   I. Fill, Chris.   II. Page, Kelly, 1974–   III. Title.
HF5415.B26 2008
658.8—dc22
2008003363

Typeset in 9.7/13pt Slimbach by Graphicraft Limited, Hong Kong
Printed in Italy
on acid-free paper by L.E.G.O. S.p.A

ISBN 978–0–19–929043–7

3 5 7 9 10 8 6 4 2

'To Ning, for your generous love and cheeky nature'

Paul Baines

'To Karen, for our 33 years since Warwick'

Chris Fill

'To Mum and Dad, for showing me the road less travelled
and believing in me on every path.'

Kelly Page

Contents

List of Case Insights   ix

List of Market Insights   x

Author Profiles   xiii

Acknowledgements   xiv

Preface   xvii

Walk-Through of Textbook Features   xx

Walk-Through of the Online Resource Centre   xxii

Walk-Through of DVD Resources   xxiv

List of Academic Insights   xxvi

List of Online Cases   xxvii

Part 1: Marketing Fundamentals   1

  1 Marketing Principles and Society   2

  2 The Marketing Environment   48

  3 Marketing Psychology and Consumer Buying Behaviour   90

  4 Marketing Research and Marketing Information Systems   134

Part 2: Principles of Marketing Management   173

  5 Marketing Strategy   174

  6 Market Segmentation and Positioning   214

  7 Market Development and International Marketing   264

  8 Marketing Implementation and Control   314

Part 3: The Marketing Mix Principle   351

  9 Products, Services, and Branding Decisions   352

  10 Price Decisions   390

  11 An Introduction to Marketing Communications   428

  12 Marketing Communications: Tools and Techniques   468

  13 Managing Marketing Communications: Strategy, Planning,
     and Implementation   508

  14 Channel Management and Retailing   548

Part 4: Principles of Relational Marketing   **587**

  15 Services Marketing and Non-Profit Marketing   588
  16 Business-to-Business Marketing   626
  17 Relationship Marketing   670

Part 5: Contemporary Marketing Practice   **715**

  18 New Technology and Marketing   716
  19 Postmodern Marketing   756
  20 Marketing Ethics   788

Glossary   829
Index   851

List of Case Insights

RM plc	3
Michelin Tyres	49
Tyrrells Potato Chips	91
Bunnyfoot	135
Innocent Drinks	175
Stagecoach	215
Oxford Instruments plc	265
Molly Maid	315
Royal Philips Electronics	353
P&O Ferries	391
British Airways London Eye	429
ZSL London Zoo	469
Pergo Flooring	509
Ekinoks	549
Radisson SAS	589
Reed Smith	627
AA	671
The National Trust	717
Livity	757
The Co-operative Bank	789

List of Market Insights

1.1   Have FABs Lost their Fizz?   16
1.2   Low-Cost Airlines: Cutting out the Middlemen   19
1.3   Singapore Airlines: Styling a Classy Service   24
1.4   The Body Shop Sells to L'Oréal: Will its Customers Mind?   27
1.5   The Clean and Mean Toyota Prius   37
1.6   Fairtrade: Clean Conscience for Consumers and Fair Deal for Farmers?   41
2.1   Thanks a Million Bernie!   54
2.2   'It's Good to Talk', but Cheaper via the Internet   60
2.3   Regulating Advertising in the UK: Flora pro.activ   63
2.4   Who Ate All the Bars?   67
2.5   European Rivals in the Sky   78
2.6   Drinking the Fruits of a Balanced Portfolio   82
3.1   Diffusion of Consumer Durables in Spain   96
3.2   Peugeot: Taking the Pain out of Purchase   103
3.3   The British Conservative Party: 'Nasty' or Nice?   106
3.4   L'Oréal: Because He's Worth It   117
3.5   Champagne Brands: Still the Society Drink?   122
3.6   The Rise of Ethnic Brands in Britain: When your Name Means Business   127
4.1   Dyson: What to Do When your Research Sucks!   138
4.2   Evaluating Comprehension Levels for a Public Information Campaign:
      Example of a Market Research Brief   142
4.3   What is One Thinking? Public Attitudes towards the British Monarchy   150
4.4   Guinness Drinking: The Irish Way?   151
4.5   The Final Destination Thrillogy: Testing a Film to Death   158
4.6   You Are What You Eat? Tesco's Use of EPOS Data to Profile its Customers   163
5.1   Vodafone: Talking Strategies   180
5.2   Challenging and Competitive Games   185
5.3   Shell: What to Do When the Future is Murky   189
5.4   Printing a Competitive Advantage   197
5.5   Colgate Fights Back   203
6.1   A Tale of Two Approaches   220
6.2   Political Failure to Segment   229
6.3   Slap it On, All Over   233
6.4   Fluid Service Flows!   242
6.5   Silverjet Circles the Business Flyer   245
6.6   Repositioning the Yorkie bar   257
7.1   H&M Heads East   274
7.2   Global Beer: What's on Tap?   277
7.3   The Multinational on Show   281
7.4   Coca-Cola and International Market Opportunity   284
7.5   Transforming China   289
7.6   UK Cultural Training in Aviva's Call Centres   294

7.7	It's All Goody's in Greece	305
8.1	Pret À Manger: Marketing with a Smile	318
8.2	Tesco's Outsourcing of Customer Analytics: As Appetizing as it Looks?	323
8.3	Clydesdale: Banking on TEAM Values	327
8.4	*The Blair Witch Project*: Frighteningly Good Marketing Effectiveness	339
8.5	British Airways: Flying High Again	339
8.6	Luxottica Eyes the Chinese Market	342
9.1	Customer Experiences at Disney	355
9.2	Very Special Cars	361
9.3	China Mobile Rings Lots of Bells	366
9.4	Developing Viagra	372
9.5	Elastic Brands?	381
9.6	Redesigning Sunny D	385
10.1	GSK Drug Pricing: Fair or Foul?	399
10.2	Sunglass Hut: Framing its Prices	402
10.3	Tesco's Value Pricing Approach	410
10.4	Soap Wars in India	412
10.5	Vertu: Pricey or Priceless?	414
10.6	English Higher Education: How Much for a Degree?	417
11.1	Heineken, Not Shaken and Not Stirred	432
11.2	Bottled, Iced, and Refreshed	436
11.3	Opinionated Ice Creamers	440
11.4	Engaging with Urban Youth Audiences	443
11.5	Call-to-Action against the Government	455
11.6	Culturally Driven Flaxseed	459
11.7	Promoting Brands at Ramadan	461
12.1	Virgin Media Announce Themselves	474
12.2	PR Taking Off	481
12.3	Direct Contacts at the Airport	484
12.4	Direct Mixing for Boots No. 7	490
12.5	Social Networking Media	496
13.1	Supermarkets' use of Pull Strategies	514
13.2	Profile Strategies at Shell	517
13.3	Competitive Drinking in Asia	523
13.4	Getting it All Together	526
13.5	All Change at the Agency	534
13.6	Digital Manoeuvres	539
14.1	Motorola Reaches out in India	552
14.2	Red Bull Grows Wings	556
14.3	Fast Fashion	561
14.4	BigBarn Keeps it Local	565
14.5	Tuning into iTunes	580
15.1	Nearly Pure Products and Services	592
15.2	The Hilton Blueprint	594
15.3	Variable Recovery Services	597
15.4	Promoting Group Service	603
15.5	Servicing Queues	606
15.6	Enterprising Leisure	620

16.1	Fluctuating Demand for Computers	631
16.2	Dealing in Motorbikes	635
16.3	Grouping to Buy Health Supplies	638
16.4	Influencing the Influencers	649
16.5	Collaborative Packaging	657
16.6	Airways to Sales Heaven	661
16.7	Anyone for Tennis?	664
17.1	BASF Chemicals Mean Value	674
17.2	Electrical Exchanges	678
17.3	Cisco Bring Added Value	683
17.4	Acquiring Customers the Direct Way	689
17.5	Nectar Brings Sweet Rewards	694
17.6	Bagging Points at Tesco	696
17.7	Channel Experts Build Knowledge	702
17.8	Talking to Customers at Carphone Warehouse	707
18.1	Creating Community with MySpace!	722
18.2	Getting Creative with YouTube	726
18.3	Toyota Keeps it Real!	731
18.4	Play with your Brand!	734
18.5	It's Only Human!	739
19.1	Who's Watching Whom? *Big Brother* and the Birth of Reality Television	761
19.2	Back to the Future: The Royal Enfield Bullet Electra	764
19.3	Marketing in the Community: Ebay.com	766
19.4	The Tribe of Harley-Davidson	768
19.5	Opposites Attract: Flowerbomb	775
19.6	Guinness: Deconstructing the Black Stuff	777
19.7	Walkers Crisps and Carbon Labelling: Trick or Treat?	781
20.1	Doing the 'Right' Thing?	802
20.2	Durex: A Touchy-Feely Subject	810
20.3	Ford and Bridgestone/Firestone: Tyre Blowout—Whose Fault is it Anyway?	812
20.4	ExxonMobil: Statement on Bribery and Corruption	818
20.5	Corporate Disasters: Accidental or Irresponsible?	820
20.6	CSR at Tata: Are Community Initiatives Good for Business?	822

Paul Baines is Senior Lecturer in Marketing and Course Director, MSc in Strategic Marketing, at Cranfield School of Management, Cranfield University. Paul is the (co)-author of numerous journal articles, books, and book chapters on marketing, particularly for political parties and candidates. Paul is an experienced author whose publications include books on PR and strategy. Paul's marketing consultancy projects have included work for a number of organizations including a high-profile football club, a large aerospace maintenance company, a national charity, an advertising agency, and an examination board. His previous experience in marketing spans business development, sales, and market research, particularly in higher education, and the toys, stationery, and fancy goods sectors. From 2006–2008, Paul was a non-executive director of North London Limited, the sub-regional development agency.

Chris Fill is Principal Lecturer in Marketing and Strategic Management at the University of Portsmouth. Much of his research to date has centred on aspects of integrated marketing communications, corporate identity, and associated branding issues. He has written a number of books, including the most recently published fourth edition of his internationally recognized textbook *Marketing Communications*. In addition to teaching both marketing communications and business-to-business marketing at undergraduate and postgraduate levels, he undertakes consultancy assignments for public and private sector organizations. He is also Senior Examiner for the Chartered Institute of Marketing, responsible for the Marketing Communications module. He speaks regularly on marketing communications issues. Prior to his academic career, Chris enjoyed a successful marketing and commercial career with a variety of international organizations.

Kelly Page is a Lecturer in Marketing and Strategy at Cardiff Business School. Her research focuses on the psychology of human–technology interaction, electronic technology adoption, and the evolution of electronic marketing activities. Her lecturing activities include undergraduate, masters, and executive education programmes in the UK, Europe, and Australia on Marketing Research, Marketing Communications, and Electronic and Interactive Marketing. Kelly has delivered MBA marketing modules for ALBA Graduate Business School (Greece) and APESMA Management Education (now Chiefly Business School) (Australia), and is an alumna of the University of New South Wales (Australia). Her marketing experience is grounded on commercial marketing research and contracts in electronic marketing spanning FMCGs, technology, and the public sector.

Acknowledgements

Modern textbooks and their bells-and-whistles websites are substantial projects, resulting from the sweat and toil of a great number of people not just in their design, development, and production, but in the sales, marketing, and distribution of them. As a result, there have been a great many people who have contributed to this particular book and its Online Resource Centre and DVD; some of those people we outline below and many others we don't, but whose contributions should be acknowledged anonymously nonetheless.

We would like to thank our colleagues at Cranfield School of Management, Cardiff Business School, and the Portsmouth Business School for their support, discussions, and general input. We would like to thank John Egan at Middlesex University Business School for his contribution to the design of the initial format and outline of the book. Because of their input in the early stages of the development of three of the chapters, we would like to thank Sir Robert Worcester, founder of MORI (now Ipsos MORI), Professor Bodo Schlegelmilch of the University of Vienna, and Professor Richard Elliot of the University of Bath, for allowing us to interview them on the topics of market research, marketing ethics, and ethnography.

As with any large textbook project, this work is the result of a co-production between the academic authors and Oxford University Press editors and staff. We would particularly like to thank Sacha Cook, Editor-in-Chief, for persuading us to take on such a gargantuan project in the first instance. The contributions of the Development Editors have been fundamental: thanks to Jane Clayton for her help in the design stage and initial development phase of the text and particularly the design of the Online Resource Centre; thanks to Lucy Hyde for her contribution in organizing and collating the fairly substantial reviewer feedback at multiple stages and the efforts she went to in aiding the authors to attain a particular tone and focus to the text; and finally on the development side, we must also thank Francesca Griffin, particularly for her input into the development of the Online Resource Centre, for her efforts in organizing the academic and practitioner lecturettes and on one occasion for her tireless devotion, even going so far as to interview one of the practitioners to make sure the authors had the material necessary to produce the Case Insight at the beginning of the chapter! As a result, the editing process has ensured that our text is now focused on both lecturers' needs (in teaching marketing) and students' needs (in learning about marketing). Thomas Sigel, a freelancer, was of enormous help in soliciting and organizing the input of many of the companies and practitioners that are exemplified in the text.

We would like to thank Helen Tyas, Production Editor, for her role in shaping the final design of the book and bringing it out on schedule with the help of the design team, Charlotte Dobbs, Naomi Clark, and Simon Witter. Thanks also to James Tomalin for his excellent video production work. As marketers we know it's of no use producing something unless our customers, students, and lecturers want to use it and so we recognize the efforts of the marketing team, Sophie Oldacres, Marianne Lightowler, and Andy Halliday, in developing and implementing an innovative marketing plan for this project. Finally, thanks also to Fiona Goodall and Denny Einav for their editorial help in relation to the cases and materials in the Online Resource Centre.

The design for the book was initially developed from the six anonymous university lecturer participants of a focus group, who had kindly agreed to meet at OUP offices to discuss what was needed in a new marketing textbook. We would particularly like to thank them for their support.

The authors and publishers would like to thank the following people, for their comments and reviews throughout the process of developing the text and the Online Resource Centre:

Geraldine Cohen, *Brunel University*
John Egan, *Middlesex University*
Fiona Ellis-Chadwick, *Loughborough University*
Malcolm Goodman, *Durham University*
Michael Harker, *University of Strathclyde*
Nnamdi Madichie, *University of East London Business School*
Alice Maltby, *University of the West of England, Bristol*
Tony McGuinness, *Aberystwyth University*
Richard Meek, *Lancaster University*
Nina Michaelidou, *University of Birmingham*
Janice Moorhouse, *Thames Valley University*
Chris Rock, *University of Greenwich*
Lorna Stevens, *University of Ulster*
Paul Trott, *University of Portsmouth*
Prakash Vel, *University of Wollongong, Dubai?*
Peter Waterhouse, *University of Bedfordshire*
Peter Williams, *Leeds Metropolitan University*
Matthew Wood, *University of Brighton*
Helen Woodruffe-Burton, *University of Cumbria.*

Thanks also to those reviewers who chose to remain anonymous. The publishers would be pleased to clear permission with any copyright holders that we have inadvertently failed, or been unable to, contact.

Preface

Welcome to *Marketing*. You may be wondering: **'why should I buy this marketing text-book?'** The simple answer is that marketing lecturers told us you needed a new one! The longer answer is that our focus group research, and university marketing lecturer expert reviewers, indicated to us that you need:

* A more concise, less daunting (but still rigorous) book that offers you real value for money;
* An inspirational text that you can really engage with, taking your experience of marketing as a starting point;
* To be able to gain insights into what marketing practitioners actually do and the decisions they have to make;
* A book that recognizes the need to go further than the traditional 4Ps approach and reflect on newer perspectives, covering both classical and modern theories of marketing;
* Help with identifying, locating, and reading seminal papers; and
* To be taught marketing in a more creative and visual way.

Marketing has been conceived to fully meet these needs. What's more, it is the first truly integrated print and electronic learning package for introductory marketing modules. It comprises a textbook packed with learning features, combining authority with a lively and engaging writing style together with a diverse range of electronic resources matched perfectly to the content of the textbook, available on the book's Online Resource Centre.

The purpose of this package is to bring contemporary marketing perspectives to life for students new to the concept of marketing, and for it to be motivational, creative, applied, and highly relevant to you.

Marketing starts with the basic concepts from classical marketing perspectives and contrasts these with newer perspectives from the relational and service-based schools of marketing, helping you develop your knowledge and understanding of marketing. On the Online Resource Centre we also provide you with web-based research activities, abstracts from seminal papers, study guidelines, multiple choice questions, and a flashcard glossary to help you broaden and reinforce your own learning.

We aim to provide powerful learning insights into marketing theory and practice, through a series of 'Insight' features—Case, Market, and Research Insights. *Marketing* is for life, purchased at level 1 or 2, or as pre-course reading for a Masters programme, but retained and referred to throughout the course of your marketing or business degree. We hope you enjoy the journey!

Who Should Use This Book?

The main audiences for this book are:

* Undergraduate students in universities and colleges of Higher and Further Education, who are taught in English, around the world. The case material and the examples

within the text are deliberately global and international in scale so that international students can benefit from the text.

- Postgraduate students on MBA and MSc/MA courses with a strong marketing component will find this text invaluable, particularly because of the cases adopted within the text.

How to Use This Textbook

This text aims to enhance your learning as part of a university course in marketing. It can act as a 'book for life' in the sense that it will also operate as a reference book for you on marketing matters, during your career in business.

Generally, we only learn what is meaningful to us. Consequently, we have tried to make your learning fun and meaningful by including a multitude of real-life cases. If there is a seminal article associated with a particular concept, try to get hold of the article through your university's electronic library resources and read it. Reflect on your own experience if possible around the concept you are studying.

Above all, recognize that you are not on your own in your learning: you have your tutor, your classmates, and us to help you learn about marketing.

This textbook includes not only explanatory material and examples on the nature of marketing concepts, but also a holistic learning system designed to aid you, as part of your university course, to develop your understanding through reading the text. Work through the examples in the text and the review questions, read the seminal articles that have defined a particular sub-discipline in marketing, and use the learning material on the Online Resource Centre. This textbook aims to be reader-focused, designed to help you learn marketing for yourself.

Most of you will operate either a surface or a deep approach to learning. With the former you are simply trying to memorize lists of information, whereas with the latter you are actively assimilating, theorizing about, and *understanding* the information. With a surface-learning approach, you can run into trouble when example problems learnt are presented in different contexts. You may have simply memorized the procedure without understanding the actual problem. Deep approaches to learning are related to higher quality educational outcomes and better grades, and the process is more enjoyable. To help you pursue a deep approach to learning, we strongly suggest that you actually do the exercises associated with the text and interact with the online material if you want to improve your understanding and your course performance.

Honey and Mumford's Learning Style Questionnaire

Honey and Mumford (1986) developed a Learning Style Questionnaire that divides learners into four categories based on which aspect of Kolb's learning process they perform best at. Completion of the questionnaire, available at a reasonable price as a 40-item questionnaire at www.peterhoney.com, provides you with scores on each of the following four categories to allow you to determine your dominant learning style. The four styles are:

1) **Activists**—where this style is dominant, you learn better through involvement in new experiences through concrete experience. You learn better by doing.

2) **Reflectors**—where this style is dominant, you are more likely to consider experiences in hindsight and from a variety of perspectives and rationalize these experiences. You learn better by reflecting.

3) **Theorists**—where this style is dominant, you develop understanding of situations and information by developing an abstract theoretical framework for understanding. You learn better by theorizing.

4) **Pragmatists**—where this style is dominant, you learn better by understanding what works best in what circumstances in practice. You learn through practice.

Analysis of your learning style will allow you to determine how you learn the most at the moment, and will give you pointers as to what other approaches to learning you might want to adopt to balance how you develop. You may already have completed a Learning Style Questionnaire at the beginning of your course and so know which learning styles you need to develop.

We believe most textbooks are designed to particularly develop the theorist learning style. Review-type questions also enhance the reflector learning style. However, in this text, we also aim to develop the pragmatist component of your learning style by providing you with Case Insights, by showing you material in which marketing practitioners discuss real-life problems with which they had to deal. Finally, we ask end-of-chapter discussion questions which require you to work in teams and on your own to develop your activist learning style.

We aim to enhance your learning by providing an integrated marketing learning system, incorporating the key components that you need to understand the core marketing principles. In this respect, we hope not only that this text and its associated Online Resource Centre will facilitate and enhance your learning, making it fun along the way, but that you will find it useful to use this text and, refer back to it, throughout your student and life experiences of marketing.

Remember, learning should be fun as well as challenging. Good luck!

> Chapter-Opening Features

Learning Outcomes

After reading this chapter, you will be able to:

✔ Define the marketing concept.

✔ Explain how marketing has developed over the twentieth century.

✔ Describe the three major contexts of marketing application, i.e.

CASE INSIGHT

Innocent Drinks market their smoothies in a highly innovative way. What strategies will they use to market their new water/juice drinks? We speak to Dan Germain, Head of Creative at Innocent, to find out more.

Dan Germain for Innocent Drinks

Innocent Drinks make smoothies, drinks made from pure whole crushed fruit, with no preservatives, colouring, or nasty additives. They're sold in little bottles and big cartons, all of which feature trademark innocent fun and games on the back of the pack. Innocent effectively developed a whole new drinks sector, one that many experts at the start said could not be done. Innocent is now a £100 million business.

In 1999 Innocent's three co-founders had a great product, lots of enthusiasm, but no experience of running a business, no customers, and no turnover. To help get started we made a few smoothies and sold them at a small music festival. We asked our customers to place their empty cups in a 'yes' or 'no' bin to vote whether the three of us should give up our jobs and make smoothies full-time. At the end of the weekend, the 'yes' bin was full and so we quit our jobs the next

day, spent several months finding the necessary finance and started a company that is now doubling its profits every year.

> We asked our customers to place their
> empty cups in a 'yes' or 'no' bin to vote
> whether the three of us should give up
> our jobs and make smoothies full-time

It has not all been plain sailing, as initially distributors refused to stock our drinks. Innocent's response was to load up a van and take the drinks to delicatessens and health food shops in Notting Hill. As a form of introduction we said, 'we're a local juice company that's just started up, here's four boxes for free, stick them on your shelves and if they sell give us a ring'. Out of the 50 shops reached, 45 wanted more. We then

Introduction

What selection process did you go through to decide which university course you were going to study? How do you decide which restaurant to which movie to see, and why? Have you ever considered why and how things? In this chapter, we explore consumer buying behaviour.

Learning Outcomes

Each chapter opens with a bulleted outline of the main concepts and ideas. These serve as helpful signposts to what you can expect to learn from each chapter.

Case Insights

Based on interviews with practitioners from a range of companies, the Case Insights describe real-life marketing challenges. Hearing about practitioners' experiences will help you to contextualize the chapter you are about to read; once you have finished the chapter, the first discussion question links back to the Case Insight and invites you to decide how you would approach the situation if you were involved in the case yourself.

Introduction

The chapter introduction clearly explains the topics to follow and offers a 'way in' to the chapter.

> In-Text Features

MARKET INSIGHT 7.5

Transforming China

RESEARCH INSIGHT 8.5

To take your learning further, you might wish to read this influential book.

Ries, A., and Trout, J. (2006), *Positioning: The Battle for your Mind*, London: Mc

Al Ries and Jack Trout's book, first published in 1981, remains the bible of ad defined what they called 'positioning' not as what you do to a product to ma customers, but what you do to the mind of the prospect. Positioning, therefo rather than an inside-out thinking approach.

Market Insight

The book is filled with many real-life examples which apply the marketing theory being discussed to a well-known product or brand. Each Market Insight feature is accompanied by questions to assist you in your critical thinking and to guide your analysis of the case.

Research Insights

Integrated in the chapter text are annotated further reading suggestions. These Research Insights signpost seminal journal articles and books that have defined the subject. Reading these will help you to broaden your understanding of the topics covered in each chapter.

> End-of-Chapter Features

Chapter Summary

To consolidate your learning, the key points from this chapter are summarized belo

- Explain the nature and characteristics of products and describe the product/s spectrum.

    A product encompasses all the tangible and intangible attributes related not just physical goods but also to services, ideas, people, places, experiences, and even a of these various elements. Anything that can be offered for use and consumptio in exchange for money or some other form of value, is referred to as a product

Review Questions

1 How does marketing implementation fit into the strategic marketing planning

2 How many different forms of marketing organization do we outline in this cha

3 What are the key features of successful marketing teams?

Discussion Questions

1 Having read the Case Insight at the beginning of this chapter, how would you advise Innocent Drinks to develop their brand?

2 Find three examples of mission statements and associated organizational goals. Then, using these examples, discuss the value of formulating a mission statement and the benefits that are likely to arise from setting organizational-level goals.

3 If the external environment is uncontrollable and markets are changing their shape and characteristics increasingly quickly, there seems little point in developing a strategic marketing plan. Discuss the value of formulating marketing strategies and

References

Allison, K. (2006), 'Apple recall deepens Sony battery crisis', *Financial Times*, 24 August, availabl www.ft.com/cms/s/c2eab782-3394-11db-981f-0000779e2340,_i_rssPage=6700d4e4-6714-11 a650-0000779e2340.html, accessed December 2007.

Ambler, T, and Vakratsas, D. (1998), 'Why not let the agency decide the advertising', *Market Lea* 1 (Spring), 32–7.

Ampuero, O., and Vila, N. (2006), 'Consumer perceptions of product packaging', *Journal of*

Chapter Summary

The key points of the chapter are outlined and summarized in a form that helps fix them in your mind. This feature enables you to assess your readiness to progress to the next chapter topic and also serves as a useful revision tool.

Review Questions

At the end of every chapter, a suite of carefully devised review questions has been provided to help you assess your understanding of central themes.

Discussion Questions

A series of discussion questions has also been provided at the end of every chapter to help you develop skills in analysis and debate, and to work as part of a team to complete short tasks and demonstrate your understanding of core concepts.

References

To take your learning even further, consider reading the original articles and books in the wider reference list provided to find out more about the issues raised within each chapter topic.

> Key Terms and Glossary

Key trends affecting information provision activities as a result of new logy include **audience fragmentation**, **channel convergence**, and inte **integrated marketing communications (IMC)**:

Audience fragmentation—Market and audiences sizes are breaking up a ting smaller due to the increased number of media channels now available, the complexity of media and technology audience usage behaviour.

Channel convergence—Media channels are converging in that cha

Glossary

accessory equipment goods these support the key operational processes and activities of the organization.

account managers agency personnel who are responsible for representing the interests of the

relationship between str opportunities.

anthropology the scier and recording, the beha animals.

Key terms are highlighted in blue where they first appear in each chapter to help fix them in your mind and to allow easy navigation of the chapters both when you encounter the subject for the first time and in your revision. Key terms and their definitions are also collated into a substantial glossary at the end of the book.

www.oxfordtextbooks.co.uk/orc/baines/

The **Online Resource Centre (ORC)** comprises resources for both **lecturers** and **students**.

> Lecturer Resources

Lecture Slides

This resource comprises a suite of customizable lecture slides in Microsoft PowerPoint (.ppt) that accompany each chapter and provide a succinct visual presentation of the core marketing theories and concepts as discussed in each chapter.

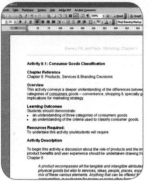

Tutorial Activities

The tutorial activities encompass a suite of hands-on class activities arranged by chapter. The tutorial activities have been designed to assist lecturers in the delivery of their module through interactive activities that reinforce practical marketing skills and aid students in the application of their learning to a range of new marketing situations. The activities have been designed for in-class seminar and tutorial environments with some adaptation possible for online discussion environments and homework activities. Example activities include mystery shopping expeditions, secondary data treasure hunts, taste testing, product packaging and labelling design, advertising creation, concept testing, and team/class games.

Answers to Discussion Questions

At the end of each chapter, the authors have provided a series of discussion questions that can be used for in-class discussion, group activities, and subject revision. This resource includes suggested answer guides for these questions, to aid the lecturer in the design and development of the subject's delivery.

Online Case Studies

The book is accompanied by a bank of twenty online cases (1000–1500 words each) comprising detailed 'marketing in action' stories linked back to the chapter text. These cases are designed to reinforce students' understanding of particular chapter themes and to encourage them to undertake more involved situational analyses of marketing scenarios. Each case study is accompanied by three critical thinking questions and solutions.

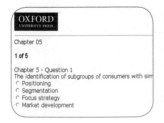

Test Bank

This is an interactive resource containing multiple choice and essay questions to be used by lecturers for assessment purposes. The purpose of the multiple choice questions is to test students' definitive understanding of specific marketing concepts. The purpose of the essay questions is to encourage students to synthesize their cumulative knowledge and demonstrate their understanding of each chapter's concepts and theories and the linkages between them.

> Student Resources

Internet Activities

This resource comprises a suite of stimulating and interactive online activities arranged by chapter to guide you in practising your online research skills and engaging with examples of marketing practice online. The purpose of this resource is to assist you with your assignments and to enable you to engage in self-directed learning and understanding of marketing in practice.

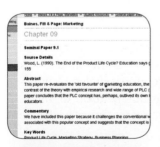

Web Links

This resource comprises a suite of annotated web links, designed to point you in the direction of marketing-related sites to assist you with your coursework and your general understanding of marketing. Examples include links to industry associations, company websites, and online marketing information resources which are helpful in keeping you informed of the latest developments in marketing practice.

Multiple Choice Questions

This resource comprises a bank of interactive multiple choice questions arranged by chapter. These self-marking questions give you instant feedback, and provide page references to the textbook to help you focus on areas which need further study. The questions are designed to reinforce your understanding of marketing through frequent and cumulative revision and to assist with independent self-study.

Seminal Paper Links

Throughout the textbook reference is made to seminal academic papers that can assist you in the further development of your understanding of a particular concept or theory that has been introduced. Organized by chapter, this resource provides links to these seminal papers, available on the types of electronic databases subscribed to by most universities worldwide.

Flashcard Glossary

Learning the jargon associated with the range of topics in marketing can be a challenge, so these online flashcards have been designed to help you understand and memorize the key terms used in the book. Click through the randomized definitions and see if you can identify which key term they are describing. You can even download them to your iPod for revision on the move!

> DVD

The DVD comprises a suite of resources for lecturers to supplement their in-class and online module delivery with the aim of enriching the student experience through the use of interactive and multimedia resources.

1. Marketing Resource Bank
2. Guest Lecturer Videos
3. Practitioner Interviews (for chapter Case Insights)

1 Marketing Resource Bank

The Marketing Resource Bank comprises a suite of interactive and multimedia marketing tools and examples of marketing practice that have been sourced from a wide range of businesses, industries, and country contexts. These include examples of integrated marketing communications campaigns, TV advertisements, cinema trailers, webcasts, marketing briefs, press packs, documentary previews, podcasts, viral marketing, and corporate marketing.

The purpose of the Marketing Resource Bank is to provide lecturers with a diverse repository of marketing illustrations and practical examples that can be dropped into lectures, seminars, and/or online discussions to inspire and educate students on marketing in practice. The Marketing Resource Bank has been designed to illustrate and contextualize key theoretical concepts throughout each chapter, with each resource accompanied by a paragraph of commentary.

A regularly updated Marketing Resource Directory of links to marketing tools can also be found on the Lecturer's Online Resource Centre as a supplement to this Marketing Resource Bank.

2 Academic Insights (Guest Lecturette Videos)

In these short guest lectures, leading academics provide their perspective on every chapter topic. Show these in class to introduce your students to a particular topic in marketing and enthuse them about the subject you are about to cover. PowerPoint slides are interspersed with the 'talking heads' to ensure students grasp the key points.

3 Practitioner Insights (practitioner interviews for chapter Case Insights)

In these short ten minute videoed interviews, the practitioners explain how they actually dealt with the marketing challenge outlined in the Case Insights. Once students have read each Case Insight and chapter, and formulated a strategy for dealing with the marketing challenge themselves, the lecturer can show them the video in class: thus completing the learning loop. (In a few cases, the videoed interview has been replaced with a written 'answer' to the problem outlined where practitioners were, for practical reasons, unavailable for interview.)

List of Academic Insights (Guest Lectures)

Chapter	Academic	Title
1	Professor Michael Saren, School of Management, University of Leicester	Why is it Important to be Critical in Marketing?
2	Dr Paul Baines, Cranfield School of Management, Cranfield University	Why Analyzing the Marketing Environment is the Key to Marketing Success
3	Professor Jagdish Sheth, Emory University, USA	The Consumer Buying Psyche
4	Dr Kelly Page, Cardiff Business School	How the World's Best Companies use Market Research Effectively
5	Professor Nigel Piercy, Warwick Business School	The Rhetoric and Realities of Marketing Strategy
6	Gareth Smith, Loughborough University Business School	Market Positioning and the UK Automobile Industry
7	Professor Stan Paliwoda, University of Strathclyde	Do Global Consumers Really Exist?
8	Professor Malcolm McDonald, Cranfield School of Management, Cranfield University	Why Some Marketing Programmes Fail and Others Do Not
9	Dr Stuart Roper, Manchester Business School	A Brief History of Branding
10	Tom Chapman, University of Portsmouth	Pricing: Marketing's Forgotten Holy Grail
11	Chris Fill, University of Portsmouth	The Changing Nature of Marketing Communications
12	Beth Rogers, University of Portsmouth	Issues in Sales Management and Planning
	Professor Dennis Sandler, Pace University, USA	Planning and Implementing a Marketing and Communications Campaign (Ambush Marketing)
13	John Egan, Middlesex University Business School	To Integrate or not to Integrate your Marketing Communications?
14	Dr Fiona Ellis-Chadwick, Loughborough	How IT has Transformed Retail Marketing
15	Professor Christine Ennew, Nottingham University Business School	The Importance of Quality and Experience in Services Marketing
16	Professor Caroline Tynan, Nottingham University Business School	Managing Buyer–Seller Interactions to Achieve Marketing Success
17	Professor Hugh Wilson, Cranfield School of Management, Cranfield University	Actioning Customer Insight: The 6 'I's of CRM
18	Dr Mairead Brady, Trinity College Dublin	New Technology and Marketing
19	Dr Pamela Odih, Goldsmiths, University of London	Advertising and Postmodern Consumer Culture
20	Chris Fill, University of Portsmouth	Why Ethics in Marketing is More Important than ever Before

List of Online Cases

Chapter	Contributor	Title
1	Dr Paul Baines, Cranfield School of Management, Cranfield University	CIM: The Problem of 'Marketing' Marketing
2	Dr Phil Harris, University of Otago, New Zealand	The Self-Regulation and Development of the Chemical Industry in Europe
3	Lorna Stevens, University of Ulster	Red Magazine: Women Consumers, Lifestyle Trends, and the New Zeitgeist
4	Dr Paul Baines, Cranfield School of Management, Cranfield University	Writing Research Proposals: The Case of PolMedia
5	Dr Paul Hughes, Loughborough University and Professor Robert Morgan, Cardiff Business School	Blackberry: Lessons in Strategic Positioning
6	Professor Malcolm McDonald, Cranfield School of Management, Cranfield University	GlobalTech: Service Segmentation
7	Dr Kelly Page, Cardiff Business School	Cargill: Localization in the Chinese Food Market
8	Dr Charles Dennis, Brunel University	Promoting the Promoters: Outdoor Advertising of JC Decaux
9	Professor Simon Knox, Dr Paul Baines, Cranfield School of Management, Cranfield University and Gary Smith, Rolls Royce	Building the 7E7: NPD at Boeing
10	Tom Chapman, University of Portsmouth	Apple Inc: The Significance of 'iPricing'
11	Martin Evans, Cardiff Business School	Dr and the Ghostly Persuaders: Multi-Step Flows of Communication in Medical Markets
12	Dr Yasmin Sekhon, University of Bournemouth	Talking to Heidi: Choosing the Right Communications Mix
13	Dr Yasmin Sekhon, University of Bournemouth	Planning to Sell Waterbeds: Aqua Style Waterbeds' Strategic Planning
14	Professor Leigh Sparks, University of Stirling	Seven-Eleven Japan: 'Life Infrastructure'
15	Dr Steve Oakes, University of Liverpool	Lewington's: Designing the Department Store Musicscape by Zone—How Music Influences Consumers in Service Environments
16	Beth Rogers, University of Portsmouth	The Personal Touch: How Dal Maschio Sales Engineers Deliver Value to Customers
17	John Egan, Middlesex University Business School	When the Relationship is Over: The Case of Disney and McDonald's
18	Dr Kelly Page, Cardiff Business School	Facebook: A New Chapter in Social Connectivity
19	Professor Stephen Brown, University of Ulster	Titanic: The Unsinkable Brand
20	Iain Davies, Cranfield School of Management, Cranfield University	Who to Work With: Ethical Dilemmas at Day/ Divine Chocolate Company

Part 1

Marketing Fundamentals

Part 1 introduces the fundamentals you need to know about marketing: marketing in society, the marketing environment, psychology, consumer behaviour, and market research.

Part 1: Marketing Fundamentals

1 Marketing Principles and Society
2 The Marketing Environment
3 Marketing Psychology and Consumer Buying Behaviour
4 Marketing Research and Marketing Information Systems

Part 2: Principles of Marketing Management

5 Marketing Strategy
6 Market Segmentation and Positioning
7 Market Development and International Marketing
8 Marketing implementation and Control

Part 3: The Marketing Mix Principle

9 Products, Services, and Branding Decisions
10 Price Decisions
11 An Introduction to Marketing Communications
12 Marketing Communications: Tools and Techniques
13 Managing Marketing Communications: Strategy, Planning, and Implementation
14 Channel Management and Retailing

Part 4: Principles of Relational Marketing

15 Services Marketing and Non-Profit Marketing
16 Business-to-Business Marketing
17 Relationship Marketing

Part 5: Contemporary Marketing Practice

18 New Technology and Marketing
19 Postmodern Marketing
20 Marketing Ethics

Marketing Principles and Society

There is more similarity in the marketing challenge of selling a precious painting by Degas and a frosted mug of root beer than you ever thought possible.

A. Alfred Taubman

Learning Outcomes

After reading this chapter, you will be able to:

✔ Define the marketing concept.

✔ Explain how marketing has developed over the twentieth century.

✔ Describe the three major contexts of marketing application, i.e. consumer goods, business to business, and services marketing.

✔ Understand the contribution marketing makes to society.

✔ Assess critically the impact marketing has on society.

RM plc was formed in 1973 in the UK but now has offices in the US, India, and Australia. Aside from its commercial success, how does it treat customers and contribute to society more generally? We speak to Fiona McLean to find out more.

Fiona McLean for RM plc

Founded by Mike Fischer and Mike O'Regan, RM plc is focused on the development of information and communication technology (ICT) products and services in education.

Its vision is to improve the life-chances of children worldwide by providing the best educational ICT for teaching and learning. It's not just about supplying computers and software for schools, colleges, and universities, it's also about understanding that education should be transformational and life-changing for learners.

> *Education should be transformational and life-changing for learners.*

From the beginning, we concentrated on making industry-standard technologies accessible in an educational environment. Since 1987, every new system introduced by RM has been compatible with industry standards. We've formed long-term partnerships with educationalists and learning technology companies to deliver genuine learning productivity, as schools, colleges, and universities have demanded, and we've achieved market leadership in our sector.

We provide a web-based email service to schools called EasyMail Plus. In 2007, we became aware that the number of spam emails coming into schools was increasing dramatically. Up until recently, we blocked approximately 75% of incoming mail as spam i.e., 10 million messages per week. And the problem was increasing.

Between 21–27 May 2007, we blocked somewhere in the region of 94% of all incoming email as spam, i.e., 23.4 million messages in one week alone. With RM providing web-based email and calendar services for over 7,500 schools and managing almost 9,000 mailboxes,

spam was becoming a serious problem. Login times were seriously affected. By the 1 March, a login time of 1 second had risen to 70 seconds. So, we implemented earlier-than-planned upgrades.

Unfortunately, this caused a power failure on our server and back-up servers, leading to 8 disk drive failures and subsequent data loss. The timing couldn't have been worse. Schools were in the middle of their end-of-year reports to their funding bodies. Four hundred million files, equivalent to 2.4 terabytes of data, and the accounts of almost 1 million users had to be restored, taking an entire week.

This looked disastrous for RM. Email is mission-critical to schools. Heads and the senior management teams use email all the time and schools were in the middle of government quality inspections recruiting staff for the following academic year.

If you were faced with a customer service failure of this type, what would you do?

RM supply computers and software for schools, colleges, and universities.

Introduction

How have companies marketed their products to you in the past? Consider the drinks you buy, the sports teams you follow, the music you listen to, and the holidays you take. Why did you decide to buy these products? Each one has been marketed to you to cater for a particular need that you have at a particular time. Consider how the product was distributed to you. What component parts is it made of? What contribution does each of these products make to society? How useful are these products really? Are other better versions of these products available which meet your needs and the needs of society better? These are just some of the questions that marketers might ask themselves when designing, developing, and delivering products to the **customer** and determining whether or not the customer's wants and needs have been met.

In this chapter, we develop our understanding of marketing principles and marketing's impact upon society by defining marketing, comparing and contrasting definitions from the American, British, and French contexts. We consider the origins and development of marketing, throughout the twentieth century. We explore how marketing is different in the consumer (B2C), business-to-business (B2B), and services marketing sectors. The core principles of marketing, incorporating the marketing mix, the principle of marketing exchange, **market orientation**, and **relationship marketing**, are all considered. How marketing impacts upon society is also detailed and, finally, we explore the need to reflect on marketing critically, as both marketers and consumers, by considering its impact upon society from both positive and negative perspectives. In short, in this chapter, we cover the basics of marketing, providing you with a thorough grounding in the principles, and so that you can understand the rest of the book!

What is Marketing?

Consider your own already fairly vast experience of being marketed to throughout your own life. So far, you have probably been subjected to millions of marketing communications messages, bought many hundreds of thousands of products and services, been involved in thousands of customer service telephone calls, and visited tens of thousands of shops, supermarkets, and retail outlets. And that's probably by the time you've hit your late teens! You're already a pretty experienced customer, so you've experienced one side of the marketing exchange already. Our role as authors is to explain how professionals do the other side of marketing. In other words, how to market products to customers. Remember most customers are just like you and will be just as discriminating as you are when buying goods. If they don't like the product, they won't buy it.

In order to explain how we go about marketing goods and services to customers, we must first describe exactly what marketing is. There are numerous definitions of marketing but we present three of these for easy reference in Table 1.1.

Table 1.1

Definitions of
marketing

Defining institution/author	Definition
The Chartered Institute of Marketing (CIM)	'The management process of anticipating, identifying and satisfying customer requirements profitably' (CIM, 2001).
The American Marketing Association (AMA)	'Marketing is the activity, set of institutions, and processes for creating communicating, delivering, and exchanging offerings that have value for customers, clients, partners, and society at large' (AMA, 2007).
A French perspective	*'Le marketing est l'effort d'adaptation des organisations à des marchés concurrentiels, pour influencer en leur faveur le comportement de leurs publics, par une offre dont la valeur perçue est durablement supérieure à celle des concurrents',* which broadly translates as 'Marketing is the endeavour of adapting organizations to their competitive markets in order to influence, in their favour, the behaviour of their publics, with an offer whose perceived value is durably superior to that of the competition' (Lendrevie, Lévy, and Lindon, 2006).

The **CIM** and **AMA** definitions recognize marketing as a 'management process' and an 'activity' although, in reality, many firms organize marketing as a discrete department rather than across all departments (Sheth and Sisodia, 2005). The CIM and AMA definitions are similar in that they stress the importance of considering the customer, of determining their requirements, or needs. The CIM definition refers to customer 'requirements' and the AMA to 'delivering **value**'. The French definition by contrast refers to the need to develop an offer of superior value. Neither the AMA or CIM definition refers explicitly to products. The French definition explicitly discusses an 'offer'. It is now widely recognized in marketing that customer requirements are delivered through offerings whether these are products, services, or ideas or some combination of the three.

The CIM definition discusses anticipating and identifying needs and the American Marketing Association discusses 'creating...offerings that have value for customers...'. Both definitions recognize the need for marketers to undertake environmental scanning activity (see Chapter 2) and marketing research (see Chapter 4) to satisfy customers, and in the long term, to anticipate customers' needs.

The French definition talks of influencing the behaviour of publics, rather than customers, recognizing the wider remit of marketing in modern society. The challenge, according to the French definition, is to develop an offering which is 'durably superior' to that of the competition. This definition therefore explicitly recognizes the importance of market segmentation and **positioning** concepts (see Chapter 6).

The CIM definition recognizes that marketing is a process with a profit motive, although it does not explicitly state whether or not this is for financial profit, or some other form of profit, e.g. of gain in society, as in the case of a charity.

The current AMA definition is clearer about this, by arguing that marketing is a process undertaken to benefit 'clients, partners, and society at large' as targets for marketing activity.

The previous AMA definition was amended in 2004 from 'the process of planning and executing the conception, pricing, promotion and distribution of ideas, goods and services to create exchange and satisfy individual and organisational objectives' (AMA, 1985). The amendment outlined above recognizes the importance of customers and customer relationships rather more than the previous definition, which emphasized the 4Ps, of product, place, price, and promotion, which we consider further later on.

What we can clearly see with these definitions is how the concept of marketing has changed over the years, from transactional concepts like pricing, promotion, and distribution to relationship concepts such as the importance of customer trust, risk, and commitment.

What's the Difference between Customers and Consumers?

We've discussed that you probably have lots of experience as a customer already. But what is a customer? And what is the difference between a customer and a **consumer**?

A customer is a buyer, a purchaser, a patron, a client, or a shopper. A customer is someone who buys from a shop, a website, a business, and, increasingly, another customer, e.g. Ebay or Amazon exchange. The difference between a customer and a consumer is that while a customer purchases or obtains a product, service, or idea, a consumer uses it (or eats it in the case of food).

To illustrate the example, consider the marketing degree or marketing course you are enrolled on, assuming you are using this book as an aid to learning on the course. Did you pay your course fees yourself? Or did your parents pay them for you? Or did someone else pay for them? If you did pay the fees yourself, you are the customer. If someone else paid for them, they are the customer. But you make use of, and study for, the degree or course. So you are the consumer.

Another example is Yoplait's Frubes, the fruity yoghurt tubes product-designed to make fruit and yoghurt more accessible to children. In this case, the customer is the chief shopper, the mother/father, or guardian, and the consumer is the child. The customer and consumer can be the same person, e.g. the girl buying the cinema tickets for herself and her boyfriend online to see the next big blockbuster movie is both the customer and consumer, but her boyfriend is only a consumer, unless she was with him and they bought the tickets at a kiosk.

The Marketing Process

Now we know what a customer and a consumer is, how are customers and consumers marketed to? As a process, marketing comprises four phases of activity, which

Yoplait's Frubes: the fruity yoghurt tubes product-designed to make fruit and yoghurt more accessible to children

Yoplait Dairy Crest

we've called the 4Ds here. Each phase of activity is a component in the process of creating value for the customer. Each of these phases is outlined as follows:

1 The design phase, where companies and organizations, identify and anticipate customer and consumer needs and design the product offering around their needs to create value for the customer.

2 The development phase, where companies and organizations develop products, services, and ideas which meet those needs and deliver the intended value,

3 The delivery phase, where companies and organizations distribute those products, services, and ideas to their customers and consumers and customers receive the product offering and the value created.

4 The determination phase, where companies determine whether or not what the customers receive really fits their needs or not and if not design or redesign the product until it does fit their needs and provide the customer with real value (or the organization goes out of business).

The process is cyclical, as in Figure 1.1, and initially begins at the determination phase. There is a feedback loop to determine whether or not the products, services, or ideas in reality meet the customers' and consumers' needs. These processes are influenced by, and dependent upon, **society** and are regulated by **government**. (See Chapter 2 for more discussion on how government and society influence marketing activity.)

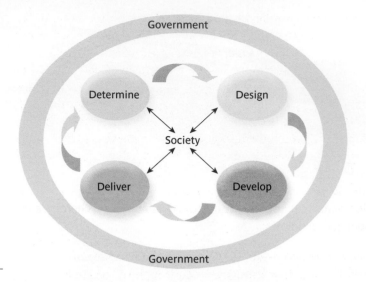

Figure 1.1
The 4Ds: Marketing as value creation process

Marketing: Ancient or Brand New?

So far it sounds as if marketing is a relatively new technique but you might be surprised to learn that marketing as a coherent approach to business has been around since the early 1920s. But it is difficult to pinpoint exactly when marketing was born! Most marketing texts present the development of marketing as a four-stage sequence in the twentieth century, as follows:

1 Production period, 1890s–1920s—characterized by a focus on physical production and supply, where demand exceeded supply, there was little competition, and the range of products was limited. This phase took place after the industrial revolution.

2 Sales period, 1920s–1950s—characterized by a focus on personal selling supported by market research and advertising. This phase took place after the First World War.

3 Marketing period, 1950s–1980s—characterized by a more advanced focus on the customer's needs. This phase took place after the Second World War.

4 Societal marketing period, 1980s to present—characterized by a stronger focus on social and ethical concerns in marketing. This phase is taking place during the 'information revolution' of the late twentieth century (Enright, 2002).

Enright (2002) criticizes the above timeline, arguing that there was good evidence of mass consumption in England in the seventeenth and eighteenth centuries, and the operations of guildsmen and entrepreneurs in the sixteenth- and eighteenth-century markets, as well as a strong market for insurance from the early eighteenth century.

So while some marketing historians regard marketing as an invention of the twentieth century (Keith, 1960), others regard marketing as a process that has evolved over a much longer period of time, without any production era ever having existed at all. Soap firms, for example, were advertising in the late nineteenth century in the UK, USA, and Germany (Fullerton, 1988). The idea that marketing did not develop until the 1950s is probably wrong when we consider that self-service supermarkets developed in America from the 1930s, and products were increasingly developed based on the process of what was then called 'consumer engineering', where products were designed and redesigned, using research, to meet customer needs (Fullerton, 1988).

Marketing as a discipline has developed through the influence of practitioners, and through developments in the areas of industrial economics, psychology, sociology, and anthropology, as follows:

- *Industrial economics influences*—our knowledge of the matching of supply and demand, within industries, owes much to the development of the discipline of microeconomics. For instance, the economic concepts of perfect competition and the matching of supply and demand underlie the marketing concept, particularly in relation to the concepts of the price at which goods are sold and the quantity distributed (see Chapter 10) and the nature of business-to-business marketing (see Chapter 16). Theories of income distribution, scale of operation, monopoly, competition, and finance facilities all come from economics (Bartels, 1951). Nevertheless, the influence of economics over marketing is declining over time (Howard *et al.*, 1991).

- *Psychological influences*—our knowledge of consumer behaviour comes principally from psychology, particularly motivational research (see Chapter 4) in relation to consumer attitudes, perceptions, motivations, and information processing (Holden and Holden, 1998), as well as our understanding of persuasion, consumer personality, and customer satisfaction (Bartels, 1951). Understanding buyer psychology is of fundamental importance to the marketing function. Since marketing is about understanding customers' needs, we must place ourselves in the mindset of our customer if we are to properly understand their needs.

- *Sociological influences*—our knowledge of how groups of people behave comes mainly from sociology, with insights into areas such as how people from similar gender and age groups behave (demographics), how people in different social positions within society behave (class), why we do things in the way that we do (motivation), general ways that groups behave (customs), and culture (Bartels, 1951, 1959). Our understanding of what society thinks as a whole (i.e. public opinion), and how we influence the way people think and to adopt our perspective (propaganda), have all informed market research practice.

- *Anthropological influences*—our debt to **social anthropology** increases more and more as we use qualitative market research approaches such as **ethnography** and **observation** to research consumer behaviour (see Chapters 4 and 19), particularly the behaviour of sub-groups (e.g. like beer drinkers or motorcyclists).

Differences between Sales and Marketing

When we are new to marketing, we may well ask: what is the difference between selling and marketing? If we consider the four stages in the development of marketing as outlined above, we would say that marketing has developed from sales.

But perhaps a more comprehensive answer is that sales emphasizes the process of 'product push', by creating distribution incentives for both salespeople and customers to make exchanges which may or may not benefit the customer in the long term (see Chapter 16 for more on sales management).

Marketing on the other hand is more focused on creating 'product pull', or demand, amongst customers and consumers, and the offering is designed and redesigned through customer and consumer input, through research, to meet their longer-term needs. Marketing activity is geared around understanding and communicating to the customer to design, develop, deliver, and determine the value in the product offering whereas sales is organized principally around enhancing the distribution of the companies' products once the product offering has already been designed. Sales departments are mostly concerned with the delivery part of the value creation process. However, sales as a function does and should have inputs to the design phase (through information from sales representatives), the development phase (particularly in test marketing, see Chapter 4), and the determination phase, where their often informal knowledge of customers' needs is important in the marketing process (as we see later in the section on market orientation).

While marketing activities principally act to stimulate demand, sales activities are designed to principally stimulate supply. In this sense, marketing is clearly a more sustainable approach to business, if we assume that keeping customers and consumers happy leads to business profitability or organizational success. Table 1.2 provides a basic summary of these differences.

Table 1.2
Differences between marketing and sales

Marketing	Sales
Tends towards long-term satisfaction of customer needs	Tends towards short-term satisfaction of customer needs; part of the value delivery process as opposed to designing and development of customer value processes
Tends to greater input into customer design of offering (co-creation)	Tends to lesser input into customer design of offering (co-creation)
Tends to high focus on stimulation of demand	Tends to low focus on stimulation of demand, more focused on meeting existing demand

What Do Marketers Do?

To answer this question, the British government's Department for Education and Skills set up the Marketing and Sales Standards Setting Board (MSSSB) to work with relevant stakeholders to map out how the marketing function operates. Their consultation indicated that the job covered eight functions areas as indicated in Figure 1.2, each of which is interlinked with stakeholder requirements. Marketers at different levels within the organization will undertake different components of these functions at different levels. Generally, the senior marketer or marketing director will guide and direct these functions, while the marketing manager will manage them, the marketing executive will undertake the actions necessary to fulfil these functions, and the marketing assistant will support the marketing executive (CIM, 2005).

Just as society is constantly changing, so the marketing profession is constantly changing, and marketing's place within the business profession and society more generally is often criticized. While doctors, teachers, and judges are generally held in high respect (Worcester, 2005), marketing practitioners tend to be held in low respect (Bartels, 1983; Kotler, 2006). According to renowned US scholars Jagdish Sheth and Rajendra Sisodia, to reform marketing practice we need to:

• Make marketing a corporate staff function so that it operates across departments, and is strategic, as are the finance, information technology, legal, and human resource management functions.

• Ensure that the head of the marketing function reports directly to the chief executive officer (CEO).

• Rename the head of corporate marketing the chief customer officer (CCO).

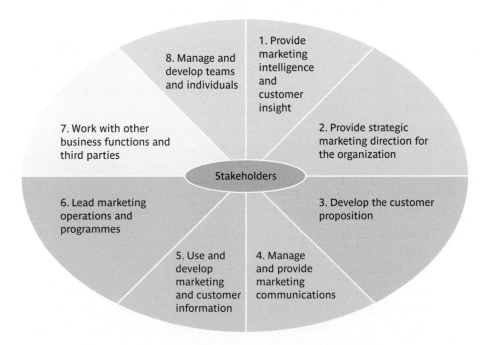

Figure 1.2
A functional map for marketing

Source: The Marketing and Sales Standards Setting Body (2006). Reproduced with the kind permission of Dr Chahid Fourali, Head of MSSSB.

- Provide marketing with capital expenditure budgets in addition to operating expenditure budgets so that the marketing function can make major capital investments, e.g. in customer acquisition and retention technologies (e.g. CRM projects), building and plant, and other capital items.

- Ensure that the marketing function controls the functions of branding, key account management, and business development.

- Ensure that the marketing function manages external suppliers such as market research, advertising, and public relations agencies.

- Set up, within the public limited company, a board-level standing committee, on which senior marketers sit, comparable to audit, compensation, and governance committees (Sheth and Sisodia, 2006).

The Principal Principles of Marketing

Despite around a hundred years of study and thousands of years of practice, there are few true *scientific* principles of marketing. We know this is not what you wanted to hear but unfortunately it's true. But don't be demoralized. We do still know an awful lot about marketing in general.

Over sixty years ago, Robert Bartels said, 'there exists neither a clearly identified body of marketing principles nor general agreement as to what a principle is' (Bartels, 1944). He suggested at that time that there might be principles associated with the following, which should be further investigated:

- Markets—what are the elements of exchange?

- Marketing functions—how do they operate under different circumstances, so how is marketing affected by context?

- Institutions—how is marketing affected by geography, history, economy, society, and so on?

- Distributive channels—how do market conditions and policies impact upon the establishment of distributive channels?

- Operating costs—what are the relationships between distribution costs and policies of market selectivity (or what we would now call market segmentation)?

Bartels (1951) stated in a discussion of whether or not marketing is an art or science that only two marketing generalizations exist as follows:

1 As [a consumer's] income increases, the percentage of income spent for food decreases; for rent, fuel, and light remains the same; for clothing remains the same; and for sundries [miscellaneous items] increases (Engels' Law).

2 Two cities attract retail trade from an intermediary city or town in the vicinity of the breaking point (the 50 per cent point), approximately in direct proportion to the populations of the two cities and in inverse proportion to

the square of the distance from these two cities to the intermediate town (Reilly's Law of Retail Gravitation).

Clearly, things have changed since Engels produced his 'Law', especially since we now tend to buy our accommodation rather than renting it, and food is relatively less expensive than it was 60–80 years ago, so it is debatable as to whether or not the first 'Law' still applies.

On the second 'Law', the point is that when you are locating your store, for example, if you are working in the site location department for a major supermarket, you should locate your store near the larger of the major population centres, and as close to them as possible. Again this might sound obvious as a general principle but Reilly's Law allows retailers to determine with some degree of precision exactly where that location might be. Nowadays multiple retail grocers, such as Carrefour in France, Tesco in UK, Coles in Australia, and Lotus in Thailand, might use complex mathematical formulae (e.g. algorithms) to determine where to locate their supermarkets, often purchasing land and developing suitable properties rather than converting existing business premises where they find a particularly valuable location.

In the race for a scientific approach to marketing, several prominent US academics became strong proponents for developing a 'General Theory of Marketing', which would explain the fundamental nature of marketing (Bartels, 1968; Hunt, 1971, 1983). Currently, we are still searching for this Holy Grail of marketing theory. Nevertheless, we have moved closer to achieving it. Hunt (1983) suggested that to understand the phenomenon of marketing more completely, we must first understand the following:

- The behaviour of buyers aimed at consummating exchanges answering such questions as: why do which buyers purchase what they do, where they do, when they do, and how they do?

- The behaviour of sellers aimed at consummating exchanges answering such questions as: why do which sellers price, promote, and distribute what they do, where they do, when they do, and how they do?

- The institutional framework (e.g. government, society, and so on) aimed at consummating/facilitating exchanges answering such questions as: why do which kinds of institutions develop to engage in what kinds of functions or activities to consummate and/or facilitate exchanges, when will these institutions develop, where will they develop, and how will they develop?

- The consequences on society of the behaviours of buyers, sellers, and the institutional framework directed at consummating/facilitating exchanges answering such questions as: why do which kinds of buyers, behaviours of buyers, behaviour of sellers, and institutions have what kinds of consequences on society, when they do, where they do, and how they do?

The listing above indicates how marketing involves a series of highly complex interactions between individuals, organizations, society, and government and that we know only a little about how marketing really works in theory, never mind in practice. But, we can make some more generalizations about marketing. According to Leone and Shultz (1980), these include the following:

- Generalization 1: Advertising has a direct and positive influence on total industry (market) sales. Put another way, all advertising done at industry level serves to increase sales within that industry.

- Generalization 2: Selective advertising has a direct and positive influence on individual company (brand) sales. Put another way, advertising undertaken by a company tends to increase the sales of the particular brand for which it was spent.

- Generalization 3: The **elasticity** of selective advertising on company (brand) sales is low (inelastic). Put another way, for frequently purchased goods, advertising has only a very limited effect in raising sales.

- Generalization 4: Increasing store shelf space (display) has a positive impact on sales of **non-staple** grocery items. For example, products bought on impulse (e.g. ice cream, chocolate bars) rather than those that are planned purchases, less important but perhaps more luxurious types of goods (e.g. gravy mixes, cooking sauces). Put another way, for impulse goods, the more shelf space you give an item the more likely you are to sell it.

- Generalization 5: Distribution, defined by the number of outlets, has a positive influence on company sales (market share). Put another way, setting up more retail locations has a positive influence on sales.

As we are beginning to see, marketing techniques are not generally developed in a scientific sense. We cannot accurately describe in a scientific sense or predict the behaviour of consumers, customers, and producers according to some pre-defined formulae. At least, not yet anyway.

However, there are some general concepts that help managers frame their actions as they develop their marketing plans and undertake marketing tactics. We cover these concepts next in the chronological order in which they were developed including the marketing mix for products (4Ps) in the 1950s/1960s, the concept of exchange in marketing in the 1970s, the marketing mix for services (7Ps) in the 1980s, **market orientation** developed in the 1990s, and **relationship marketing** developed mainly in the 1990s.

The Marketing Mix and the 4Ps

What are the responsibilities of the marketing manager? To outline these, Neil Borden developed the concept of the **marketing mix** in his teaching at Harvard University in the 1950s, although he did not formally write the theory up until 1964. The idea came from the notion that the marketing manager was a 'mixer of ingredients', a chef who concocted a unique marketing recipe to fit the requirements of the customers' needs at any particular time.

The emphasis was on the creative fashioning of a mix of marketing procedures and policies to produce the profitable enterprise (see Market Insight 1.1). He composed a twelve-item list of elements (with sub-items, not reproduced here) which the manufacturer should consider when developing their marketing mix policies and procedures, as follows:

To take your learning further, you might wish to read this influential paper.

Borden, N. H. (1964), 'The concept of the marketing mix', *Journal of Advertising Research*, 4, 2 – 7.

Perhaps the most famous concept in marketing, this easy-to-read early article explains how marketing managers act as 'mixers of ingredients' in developing their brand policies and programmes. The concept of the marketing mix, popularized as the 4Ps, remains very popular even today, although the advent of relationship marketing has challenged the impersonal notion of marketers as manipulators of marketing policies, and focused more on the need to develop long-term interpersonal relationships with customers (see Chapter 17).

1 Product planning;

2 Pricing;

3 Branding;

4 Channels of distribution;

5 Personal selling;

6 Advertising;

7 Promotions;

8 Packaging;

9 Display;

10 Servicing;

11 Physical handing; and

12 Fact finding and analysis (Borden, 1964).

This useful, though not exhaustive, list was simplified and amended by Eugene McCarthy (1960), to the more memorable but rigid 4Ps as follows (see Figure 1.3):

1 Product—e.g. the offering and how it meets the customer's need, its packaging and labelling (see Chapter 9);

2 Place (distribution)—e.g. the way in which the product meets customers' needs (see Chapter 14);

3 Price—e.g. the cost to the customer, and the cost plus profit to the seller (see Chapter 10); and

4 Promotion—e.g. how the product's benefits and features are conveyed to the potential buyer (see Chapters 11–13).

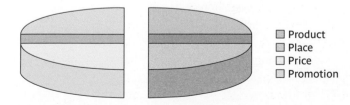

☐ Product
☐ Place
☐ Price
☐ Promotion

Figure 1.3
The 4Ps of the marketing mix

Have FABs Lost their Fizz?

The UK market for flavoured alcoholic beverages (FABs) was valued at £1.3 billion, about €2 bn, in 2004. But the market had been in decline over the period between 2002 and 2004, seeing double digit decline at 18%. This downward spiral is set to continue with the market reaching £887 m (€1.3 bn) by value at 2005 prices. The problem is that customers are getting older, meaning there are fewer 18–34 year olds, they are trading up to the more expensively priced cocktails, made in situ rather than pre-packed, and flavoured alcoholic beverages are perhaps simply no longer 'cool'. Table 1.3 outlines the marketing mix for alcohol manufacturing companies when marketing FABs.

Table 1.3
The marketing mix for UK flavoured alcoholic beverage companies

Marketing aspect	UK flavoured alcoholic beverages industry
Basic customer need	To enjoy an alcoholic drink, to enjoy good times with our partners, friends, and significant others, and to enjoy time out from our worries and concerns in a safe manner.
Target market	Large domestic market, focused at both the on-trade (i.e. pubs and clubs) and off-trade (e.g. supermarkets and off-licences) and the 18–44 year old target consumer. Need to ensure product is not taken up by underage drinkers.
Product	A wide range of flavours available delivered in 27.5 cl bottles, multi-packs of 27.5 cl and larger 70 cl bottles. Companies attempt to protect their product from imitation by other companies through branding activities. The top five brands by estimated size of market share in 2005 include: Diageo's Smirnoff Ice (29%), Beverage Brand's WKD (24%), Bacardi-Martini's Bacardi Breezer (12%), Coor's Reef (7%), and Halewood International's Red Square (6%) (Mintel, 2005).
Price	Priced to compete with wine, lager, and cider but more expensive given the amount of alcohol by volume when compared with many of the substitute brands. Significant pressure on price expected over period of 2005–10 through supermarket discounting in what is a highly competitive market, likely to see decline in sales by value although not by volume (Mintel, 2005).
Principal promotional tools	These are highly regulated but include: (1) personal selling to pubs and bars, supermarkets, and off-licences, (2) sales promotions and sampling activities, (3) point-of-sale material in off-licences and in pubs and bars, (4) TV, cinema, radio, and ambient (i.e. outdoor) advertising, (5) internet, with games, competition, and chat forums. But alcohol industry self-regulated by the Portman Group which sets guidelines on how companies should advertise their products.
Distribution	Supply chain incorporates distribution to pubs/clubs, hotels/restaurants (on-trade) and supermarkets and off-licences (off-trade) (Mintel, 2005).

The competition is on amongst the drinks manufacturers to develop the next generation of flavoured alcoholic beverages to spice up the night lives of their target audience. The question is what new products will they have to develop to maintain their target consumers?

Source: Mintel (2005).

1 Alcoholic beverage companies are not allowed to promote youth lifestyles in their advertising promotions or suggest that alcohol enhances sexual prowess, or that alcoholic drinks are key to social success. Why do you think this is?

2 There has been increasing concern by government that young people are binge-drinking. Should alcoholic beverage manufacturers do more to ensure responsible drinking? How do they do this?

3 How can alcoholic beverage manufacturers use the 4Ps to revive the market for FABs?

The intention was to create a simpler framework around which managers could develop their planning. Although there was some recognition that all of these elements might be interlinked (e.g. promotion based on the price paid by the consumer), such interplay between these mix components was not taken into account by McCarthy's framework. (See Market Insight 1.1 for an example of how to apply the 4Ps to the marketing of FABs.)

Although some commentators have argued that the 4Ps framework is of very limited use, we include it here because managers still use the framework extensively when devising their product plans.

Marketing as Exchange

Earlier, we talked about marketing as a four-stage process of designing, developing, delivering, and determining value for the customer. But marketing is a two-way process. It's not just about the marketing organization doing all the work. The customer also has a strong input. In fact, not only must they specify how we might satisfy their needs as marketers, because marketers are not mind-readers, but they must also pay for the product or service.

Around the middle of the 1970s, there was increasing belief that the underlying phenomenon in marketing related to the exchange process between buyers and sellers and associated supply chain intermediaries. Exchange relationships might not only be economic, e.g. a consumer buying groceries, but social as well, e.g. the service undertaken by the social worker on behalf of society paid for by government (Bagozzi, 1975). This recognition of the importance of the underlying relationship within marketing has led to the broadening of the concept of marketing and the relationship marketing school of marketing (which we consider in more detail in Chapter 17).

There are three main types of buyer–seller exchanges in marketing. Figure 1.4 outlines these two-way (**dyadic**) exchanges as follows:

1 In the first exchange type, the exchange takes place between the fire service who protect the general public from fire and provide emergency planning

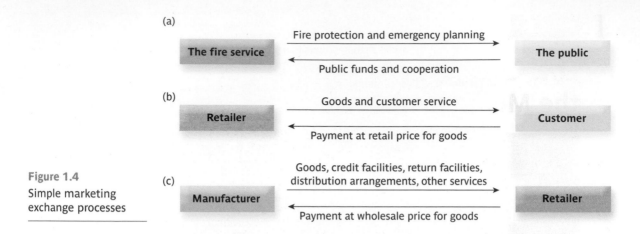

(a)

The fire service → Fire protection and emergency planning → The public

The fire service ← Public funds and cooperation ← The public

(b)

Retailer → Goods and customer service → Customer

Retailer ← Payment at retail price for goods ← Customer

(c)

Manufacturer → Goods, credit facilities, return facilities, distribution arrangements, other services → Retailer

Manufacturer ← Payment at wholesale price for goods ← Retailer

Figure 1.4
Simple marketing exchange processes

activity and services, and the public who support them in return, sometimes politically through signing petitions to keep them in service in a particular locale, and especially through their national and local taxes, depending on the country we are talking about.

2 In the second exchange type, the one we are probably more familiar with as consumers, we enter a shop, say H&M—the Swedish fashion outlet—and purchase the necessary goods by paying for these with money or by credit/debit card.

3 In the third type of exchange, we have a manufacturer, and a retailer. Here, the retailer (e.g. London's Hamleys toyshop) purchases goods from the manufacturer (e.g. Mattel) through a credit facility, e.g. payment in 30 days, and expects any damaged goods to be returnable, and wants the goods delivered on certain types of pallets at a certain height, within a particular time limit. In return, the retailer undertakes to pay a wholesale (i.e. trade discounted) price.

However, few exchanges in marketing are really this simple. They might well involve lots of other individual transactions and may involve multiple combinations. For example, (2) and (3) can be combined to indicate a (very) simple supply chain for, say, a toy manufacturer selling through to shops who sell on to the general public, their customers. Understanding exactly how our exchanges take place between the various members of the supply chain allows us to understand where we are, and are not, adding value to the customer experience.

Extended Marketing Mix for Services: The 7Ps

We can imagine from the discussion above about marketing exchanges that what is exchanged in a service context (e.g. purchasing a holiday) is different from a product context (e.g. buying a DVD). By the end of the 1970s, it was recognized that the traditional 4Ps approach to marketing planning based on physical products, e.g. salt, CDs, alcoholic drinks, was not particularly useful for either the physical product offering with a strong service component, e.g. laptop computers with extended warranty, or services with little or no physical component, e.g. spa

Low-Cost Airlines: Cutting out the Middlemen

EasyJet flies to airports with lower landing charges to keep customer costs down

EasyJet

In the European low-cost airline market, airlines (e.g. Ryanair and EasyJet as the pioneers) recognized that they could cut out the travel agents, who acted to 'collect' customers in large volumes for the airlines, if the low-cost carriers could deal with the airline passengers directly themselves in sufficient volumes. To do this, they decided to:

- Reach passengers through the internet;

- Fly to airports with lower landing charges and directly to specific points, rather than flying out to hubs, e.g. Chicago O'Hare or London Heathrow, and then onward elsewhere;

- Lower the baggage allowance to reduce weight carried to increase fuel efficiency; and

- Limit the food stored and the number of cabin crew required to service the passengers. (See Figure 1.5.)

The first model (Figure 1.5a) represents the national airline carriers, mainly pre-2001 before they started to sell their own tickets online, trim their services, and reduce their number of routes, e.g. Lufthansa, Air France, and British Airways. The second model (Figure 1.5b) represents the low-cost carriers, e.g. EasyJet, Wizzair. How might this model look for the airline which you are most familiar with?

By analysing these kinds of marketing exchanges we can see where the value might lie in the transaction. For example, a problem could arise if the airline passengers are not provided with the kind of service that they expect to receive in both of the above cases. If passengers believe that they receive a poor-quality service, this has an effect on the airline brand and on whether or not customers repurchase tickets. The key consideration for the low-cost airlines is ensuring that in cutting out the middlemen (i.e. the travel agents), they don't also cut out all the value that the middlemen once provided to the airline passenger (e.g. choice of levels of service).

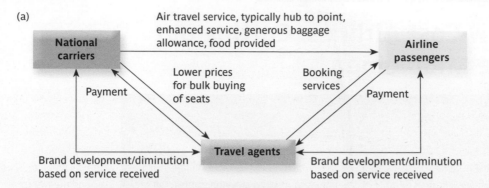

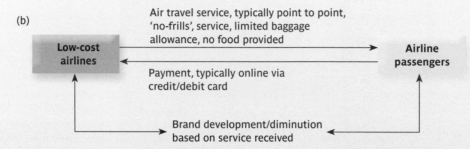

Figure 1.5 Marketing exchange processes in the European airline industry

1 Do you think low-cost airlines provide a valued service for the airline passenger or do you think they have taken the no-frills concept too far?

2 As the third party (or middleman), how should travel agents try to reclaim their relationships with holidaymakers flying by air? What other services do they need to offer to lure us back?

3 Think of as many other products or services where we use a third party (middleman) to deliver products or services to us as you can. Do you think it would be advantageous for those companies to deal with us directly?

and massage, hairdressing, sports spectatorship. (We consider the differences between services and physical goods marketing in greater detail in Chapter 15.)

To illustrate how marketing needed to market services differently, two American scholars, Booms and Bitner (1981), incorporated a further 3Ps into the marketing mix as follows (see Figure 1.6):

1 Physical evidence—to emphasize that the tangible components of services were strategically important since customers used these to infer what the quality of the service might be, e.g. potential university students often assess whether or not they want to attend a university and a particular course by requesting a copy of brochures and course outlines or by visiting the campus.

2 Process—because service delivery cannot be separated from the customer consumption process, we include process because of the need to manage

To take your learning furhter, you might wish to read this influential paper.

Bagozzi, R. P. (1975), 'Marketing as exchange', *Journal of Marketing*, 39 (October), 32–9.

An important article which outlined how the key consideration in marketing is the satisfaction of exchange relationships, setting the scene for widespread acceptance of social marketing methods and accelerating the search for a general theory of marketing, particularly through marketing relationships. Bagozzi wanted to answer such questions as how do people and organizations satisfy their needs through exchange? Why do some marketing exchanges last and others fail? What is an equitable exchange? How should we go about analysing marketing exchanges? And is the exchange concept equally applicable to all societies around the world?

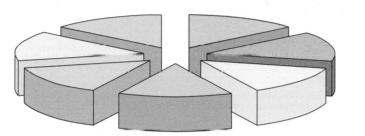

☐ Product
☐ Place
☐ Price
☐ Promotion
☐ Physical Evidence
☐ People
☐ Process

Figure 1.6
The amended marketing mix for services: the 7Ps

customer expectations, interaction, and satisfaction. When processes are standardized, it is easier to manage customer expectations, e.g. DHL International GmbH, the German international express, overland transport, and air freight company, is a master at producing a standardized menu of service options, e.g. track and trace delivery services, which are remarkably consistent around the world.

3 People—included to emphasize that services are delivered by customer service personnel, sometimes experts and often professionals who interact with the customer sometimes in an intimate manner (e.g. healthcare services, spa treatments). How they interact with customers, and how satisfied customers are as a result, is of strategic importance.

To see how the extended mix, the physical evidence, people, and process components work consider how they are used in the airline industry. For instance, the process component of the services marketing mix within the airline sector has been revolutionized through internet ticket booking and web check-in services. The traditional middleman, the travel agency, has had to radically alter its customer proposition as the major national carriers (e.g. Air France, United Airlines, British Airways) offer their services directly by internet to compete with a new class of lower-cost airlines also offering their services direct to the public via the internet at substantially lower prices (see Market Insight 1.2). The travel agencies have put their own services online, customizing their holiday offerings in a bid to differentiate their services from the airlines and add value for the customer, offering better deals on insurance, identifying best flight connections, providing advice on best airlines, and offering affiliate hotel deals (Saren, 2006).

Table 1.5

Types of products and services

Sector type	Nature of product		
	Tangible	**Hybrid**[a]	**Intangible**
Business to business	• Components/raw materials suppliers (e.g. chemical supplier, Clariant, cement manufacturer LaFarge) • Finished goods for wholesale/retail trade (e.g. the toy manufacturer, Mattel, car manufacturer Ford)	• IT systems developers (e.g. Oracle) • Recruitment services (e.g. Adecco)	• Accounting services (e.g. Grant Thornton) • Corporate advisory (e.g. KPMG)
Business to consumer	• Multiple retail grocery (e.g. Carrefour, Tesco) • Fast-moving consumer goods (e.g. L'Oréal, Nike)	• Telecommunication services (e.g. Orange, Sony Ericsson) • Universities (e.g. Harvard, Oxford)	• Airline industry (e.g. Singapore International Airlines, Lufthansa) • Financial services (e.g. Citibank, HSBC)

[a] Hybrid refers to a product with a strong mixture of goods and service components.

Marketing techniques need to be adapted to the specific sector in which they are used (Blois, 1974). The context, whether it is industrial (e.g. business to business), consumer (e.g. retail), or services based (e.g. either business-to-business services like accountancy or business-to-business products like component manufacturers), has an impact upon the marketing tools and techniques that we need to use. Table 1.5 provides examples of business-to-business and business-to-consumer products with different degrees of **tangibility** and **intangibility**, i.e. the extent of the product's physical nature. The table shows the existence of a hybrid category of product, which comprises offerings with the tangible characteristics of products and the intangible characteristics of services. However, the reality is that no single product or service is completely tangible product or intangible service. It may principally be product or service, but all offerings combine some elements of the two. We discuss the intangible nature of services in Chapter 15.

Having identified three unique contexts of marketing, consumer goods, industrial (business to business), and services, we discuss how each of these contexts affects how we undertake marketing activity.

The Consumer Goods Perspective

Bucklin (1963) defined consumer goods as either convenience goods (purchased frequently with minimum effort), shopping goods (purchased selectively based on suitability, quality, price, and style), and speciality goods (purchased highly selective because only that product was capable of meeting a specific need). Examples of consumer goods industries might include the retail car market, the luxury goods market, and multiple retail grocery. Examples of companies operating in this sector might include the American automobile manufacturer Ford, the French fashion house Louis Vuitton Moët Hennessey (LVMH), and ASDA Wal-Mart, the British/American supermarket chain.

The consumer goods perspective of marketing has been the dominant concept in the history and study of marketing to date. The concept is concerned with ideas of the 'marketing mix' and the 4Ps. The consumer goods perspective, borrowing heavily from neoclassical economics, assumes there are comparatively few suppliers within a particular industry, all rivals for the **aggregated demand** (i.e. demand totalled at the population level rather than at the individual level). In fast-moving consumer goods markets (FMCG), the price at which a good is sold is clearly defined. The product exchanged is tangible (i.e. has physical form) and exchanged between buyer and seller through retail distribution outlets. Consumption takes place at a later and different point in time, with demand stimulated through the 'promotional mix', i.e. advertising, personal selling, direct marketing, and public relations (see Chapter 12).

The focus of marketing in this context is how to facilitate the rapid exchange of goods, the effectiveness of the marketing in determining the match between supplier offering and customer demand, and efficiency in managing the distribution of the product through the supply chain. Of particular importance in the consumer goods marketing context are the principles and practice of retailing (see Chapter 10), since this is the principal means by which customers acquire their consumer goods. In retailing, the marketer should focus on:

- Ensuring the retail outlet is properly located in an appropriate place which customers can easily access;

- Whether the product range should be wide (e.g. as in a hypermarket) or narrow (e.g. as in a **category killer** like the online retailer Amazon or the British home improvement company B&Q);

- Whether to lease the retail outlet or to purchase it;

- How to organize the retail outlet's **atmospherics** (i.e. the ambience);

- How to position the store in the minds of consumers (see Chapter 12 for further discussion of the concept of positioning); and

- Product replenishment and inventory management.

Because of the need to stimulate demand from consumers, focus is placed on the importance of advertising (see Chapter 12) to stimulate demand and market research (see Chapter 4) to determine how to develop appropriate consumer products and how they are received by the consumers once they've launched into the marketplace. More recently, the internet and other digital mechanisms have greatly increased the way in which customers receive information about their goods and by which retailers reorder goods and services from their suppliers. (We cover the impact of new technologies on marketing in further detail in Chapter 18.)

The Consumer Services Perspective

The services perspective in marketing is organized around the idea that markets are increasingly characterized not by physical goods but by intangible services. Around the late 1970s and early 1980s, there was recognition that the standard goods marketing approach was ill-suited to the marketing of services. Services marketing thinkers suggested that the intangible, performance-dependent, nature of services substantially affected the way they should be marketed (Shostack, 1977). There was a focus on the quality of service offered as a result (Grönroos, 1984), as well as a focus on the difference between customer perceptions of actual service quality and their expectations of service quality (Parasuraman, Zeithaml, and Berry, 1985). Service industries are generally seen to have five important differentiating characteristics, as shown in Table 1.6.

Some commentators have questioned the use of the product analogy altogether in services marketing (Grönroos, 1998; Vargo and Lusch, 2004). Quite simply, they argue that there are significant differences and similarities between goods and services as follows. Services:

- Cannot be protected by patent;
- Do not make use of packaging;
- Lack a physical display; and
- Cannot be demonstrated in the same way.

Others have argued that there are major similarities, including the need to:

- Work at full capacity;
- Develop trade and service marks;
- Use promotional media;
- Use personal selling techniques; and
- The approach to pricing based on cost and value (Judd, 1968).

The Business to Business Perspective

Many marketing textbooks overemphasize consumer goods marketing and do not pay adequate attention to industrial/organizational marketing. Concepts of competition are particularly relevant in this context since firms are competing against one another for custom. Theories centred on how companies develop competitive advantage based on their development of resources (the resource-based view), rather than how they manage external threats and opportunities, originate from economic theory. The notion of **product differentiation**, creating small differences in product characteristics to serve a wider market, was a strategy first considered in microeconomic theory. The corresponding theory in marketing—**market segmentation**—was not developed until the mid-1950s (Smith, 1956). (We cover the concept of market segmentation further in Chapter 6.)

Business-to-business marketing is essentially different from consumer marketing because the customer is a business rather than an individual household, or chief

Table 1.6 The five characteristics of service products

Service characteristic	Explanation
Intangibility	Services have no few physical cues for the customer to judge the offering they receive. Therefore service organizations attempt to 'tangibilise the intangible' (Levitt, 1981), by enhancing the physical environment by introducing service guarantees; by producing brochures, leaflets, and pamphlets; or by obtaining service quality kitemarks (e.g. AACSB or EQUIS accreditation in American and European business school higher education).
Inseparability	Production and consumption are inseparable in service markets, encouraging the need to facilitate complex producer–customer interactions, e.g. the singing and performance of a band in a pop concert (production) occurs at the same time as the audience receives the music and atmosphere created (consumption). There is a need to manage carefully relationships between clients and their customers, managing their expectations of the quality of the service that they receive at the point that they receive it.
Variability	The quality and standard of service products varies depending on the individual customer and the service provider. As the customer is involved in the production process at the time of consumption, what marketers refer to as co-production, it can be difficult to monitor and control service production to ensure consistent service standards. There is a need to control and set up systems to maintain a consistent standard of service quality and ensure service quality meets customers' minimum expected standards, e.g. Kwik-Fit, the British automotive maintenance company, stresses the need to achieve 'customer delight'.
Perishability	Services cannot be stored and consumed at a later date, unless they are recorded, e.g. as information services and entertainment are on digital media. If we purchase gym membership on an annual or monthly membership, and we do not use the facilities of the gym during these periods, that time is lost. Service-based businesses must maximize how much their facilities are used through yield management. They do this by offering discounts for services delivered at specific times (e.g. airline tickets for off-peak periods, or cinema tickets for daytime movie shows). There is a therefore a need to use price, part-time labour, and demand to maximize income.
Non-ownership	Customers cannot own the service they receive because ownership is not transferred from the seller to the buyer as it is with a tangible good. This can be less beneficial because there is a lessser need for a company to give refunds or make amends if a service is not properly delivered than might be the case with a company selling tangible goods, especially one with a clear returns policy (e.g. Marks and Spencer or H&M in Europe). However, many product-based companies are now marketing goods on a lease or temporary basis (e.g. car manufacturers selling contract hire cars, Rolls Royce selling aero engine leases, so-called 'power by the hour'), and so are essentially offering a goods rental service.

shopper, for example. Business-to-business marketing requires marketers to deal with more sophisticated customers who may buy in volume, as part of a decision-making unit (with other buyers and technicians), who are trained to buy/procure professionally, and who are rewarded for buying the right products and services at the right price (see Chapter 16).

Much business-to-business marketing activity revolves around the need to develop strong prospects for your company's products and services and ensure effective supply chain management operations to develop the market for a business-to-business product and to ensure it is delivered appropriately. Because buyers typically purchase in large volumes of product or complex 'bundles' of services (e.g. customized IT software solutions sold by the German company SAP), tight specifications are usually produced by them with which suppliers must comply. Buyers try to ensure that they obtain the best supplier possible by offering suppliers a temporary exclusive franchise for a set period of time through a bidding process, which is of course substantially different from the set of circumstances that faces the average retail customer, for example.

In public sector markets, the **procurement** process (i.e. purchasing) is bound by strict legal guidelines for product and service contracts valued over a set amount. This process creates substantial rivalry with firms often submitting bids which they cannot then fulfil either because they've underpriced themselves, or because they've over-promised what they can deliver; a phenomenon known as the 'winner's curse' since the winning company ends up servicing an unprofitable contract (Fleisher and Bensoussan, 2004).

The emphasis in business-to-business markets is strongly focused on the development and building of mutually satisfying relationships based on commitment and trust (Morgan and Hunt, 1994) to win the contract in the first place and henceforth to deliver it to the customer's specifications. However, building relationships between buyers and suppliers while important is also impacted by whether or not a firm delivers on its promises. Such delivery of promises is in part linked to the **logistics** function (i.e. warehousing, inventory management, delivery) of the firm, be it product or service focused. Consequently, business-to-business marketers can create a competitive advantage if they develop a strong linkage between the marketing and logistics functions, developing a strong customer service proposition on the following items:

- Reduction in order cycle times;
- Simple accurate invoicing procedures;
- Consistent and reliable delivery;
- Simple and effective claims procedures;
- Availability of inventory;
- Good condition of goods and effective service delivery;
- Few order size constraints or limited customization of services;
- Effective and planned salesperson visits;
- Convenient ordering systems and provision of order status information;
- Flexible delivery times; and
- Strong after-sales support (Christopher, 1986).

What Impact Does Marketing Have on Society?

Now that we've got some idea of the complexity of how marketing operates, if we consider how much the marketing industry contributes to society in any one country, we will probably be amazed. Wilkie and Moore (1999) describe the complexities of how the 'aggregate marketing system' works using the example of how marketing brings all the ingredients of a breakfast to households in America.

Consider the individual ingredients of a typical American breakfast, for example, coffee or tea, together with pancakes and syrup (and the necessary ingredients required here), the cups and plates to contain the food, the hotplate or grill to heat the food, and so on. The aggregate marketing system is awesome when reflected on in this way. We should remember that there are over 270 million people in the USA, with over 100 million households (Wilkie and Moore, 1999), each of which is brought its own unique mixture of products and services which come together to form an individual breakfast for any one particular person. Broadly, the system in most countries around the world works reasonably well. We're not all generally starving and we don't have to ration our food to preserve the amount we eat to be fair to others. Of course, there are certain countries in Africa, North Korea, and parts of China, for example, where people are dying of hunger, but these countries often experience imperfections in supply and demand because of political (e.g. war, dictatorship, famine) and environmental circumstances (e.g. drought). Marketing plays an important role in developing and transforming society. Consider how some of the products outlined in Table 1.7 have affected your own life (see also Market Insights 1.5 and 1.6).

What would we do without these products in today's world? In each case, we enjoy the use of these products because innovative individuals and companies designed, developed, and delivered these products to us, as consumers. Take the tin can for storing food, for example. We couldn't conceive of not having this device now and yet it is only around 200 years old. Prior to that food was stored in earthenware pots and was spoilt at a much faster rate. Could you imagine ketchup not existing? It was brought to us by Heinz but based on an ancient Chinese fish sauce recipe called *ketsiap*! Of course in each of these cases, the invention outlined below has been an extraordinary success. But the aggregate marketing system not only serves to bring consumers those products and services which truly meet their needs, it also serves to stop the failures from getting through as well. The aggregate marketing system serves to impede products because they don't meet consumer needs. So, it serves a number of benefits to society including the following:

- The promotion and delivery of desired products and services;
- The provision of a forum for market learning (we can see what does and what doesn't get through the system);
- The stimulation of market demand;
- The offering of a wide scope for choice of products and services by offering a close/customized fit with consumer needs;
- Facilitates purchases (or acquisitions generally, for example if no payment is made directly as in the case of public services);
- Saves times and promotes efficiency in customer requirement matching;
- Brings new products and services, and improvements, to market to meet latent and unserved needs; and
- Seeks customer satisfaction for repeat purchases (Wilkie and Moore, 1999).

Table 1.7 Some modern consumer products and their dates of invention

Consumer product	Product attribute	Consumer need	Inventors/pioneers[a]	Year of invention
Tin can (for storing food)	Metallic food storage device	Allowed traditionally perishable food to be stored for longer periods of time	Hall and Dorkin, UK	1810
Ketchup (from the Chinese word *ketsiap*)	A food condiment, derived from the Chinese fish-based sauce, *ketsiap*, but adapted for Western taste, using tomatoes	Designed to improve the consumer's enjoyment of their food by improving the taste, and reducing the dryness of some foodstuffs	F & J. Heinz Co., USA	1876
Diesel-fuelled internal combustion engine	An engine with an efficiency of 75% (meaning that 75% of the energy produced was used to power the engine) as opposed to 10% for the steam engines of the day	Enabled independent craftsmen to compete with large industry	Rudolph Diesel, Germany	1892
Breakfast cereals	Cereals which when added to milk provided a healthy meal	Quick and easy to prepare foodstuff which was rapidly adopted as a breakfast meal	W. K. Kellogg Foundation, USA	1906
Television	Transmission of moving images	Information, entertainment, and education	Baird Television Development Company, UK/Telefunken, Germany	1929/1932
Microwave oven	Heating device for use in kitchen	Allows rapid heating of foodstuffs, saving time and labour. Particularly useful for frozen food meals	Raytheon Company, USA	1946
Consumer credit card	Allowed user to purchase products and services without paying in cash at time of original purchase	Convenience of not having to pay immediately and provision of credit for a set period of time	Diner's Club, USA	1950
Velcro fasteners	An ingenious hook and fastening device inspired by the technology used for transport by seed pods in nature. Named based on French velour (velvet) and crochet (small hook)	A simple means to fasten two items together, without permanently fastening, and which allows easy separation	George de Mestral/Velcro Industries, Switzerland	1955
Artificial sweeteners	Xylitol, as the sweetener is known, is used to sweeten food products such as sugar-free chewing gum and toothpastes	It sweetens food products without damaging our teeth	Cultor, Finland	1969
Rubik's Cube	A six-sided (cubic) toy puzzle with nine-coloured squares on each side	The need for intellectual stimulation	Tibor Laczi and Erno Rubik/Consumex (Hungarian State Trading Co.)	1975
Karaoke sing-along system	A TV system linked to music player, with words of music tracks displayed on screen allows a person with a microphone to sing to a track's musical background	Designed to entertain small groups in house parties and large groups of individuals at venues who typically enjoy singing themselves and listening to others, or laughing at their friends' efforts	Roberto del Rosario/Trebel Music Corporation, The Philippines	1975
Personal computer	Machine which allows users to play electronic games, perform calculations, and write word-processed documents and other applications	Time-saving device simplifying complex writing/arithmetic tasks, offering recreational possibilities i.e. game playing	International Business Machines (IBM), USA	1980
Portable digital music player	A device for storing and playing digital music files	The ability to listen to high-quality music wherever and whenever we like, by carrying a small portable device	Apple Computer, USA	2001

[a] The named companies are not always the inventors *per se*; often they acquired the patents from the inventor and were so licensed to produce and distribute the invention.

Sources: Various including: www.inventors.about.com, manufacturers' websites.

To take your learning further, you might wish to read this influential paper.

Wilkie, W. L., and Moore, E. S. (1999), 'Marketing's contributions to society', *Journal of Marketing*, 63 (Special Issue), 198–218.

This is a ground-breaking article, describing how marketing operates as an aggregated system within society. The article explains how marketing impacts upon, and contributes to, society by considering how products and services flow through society, contributing both positively and negatively to individual well-being and the economy. The article concludes that the marketing system adapts and changes to the needs of modern society but broadly contributes greatly to it.

MARKET INSIGHT 1.5

The Clean and Mean Toyota Prius

The race is now well and truly on to produce the **Wünderkind** of the car industry, an all-singing, all-dancing, good-looking electric car. Silent and pollution free, with engineering underpinned by green technologies, the car must not compromise on performance, looks, or handling. The change has come about because of greater public concern, and the need for European legislation concerning vehicle fuel emissions, to combat global warming. Since car drivers are collectively a major user of oil, to power their cars, a shift to electric seems obvious. Problems with oil supply in the Middle East, since the OPEC crises of the 1970s, have worsened the situation.

But battery-powered cars have had a poor history. In Britain in 1984, Sir Clive Sinclair launched a battery-assisted tricycle, the Sinclair C5, with a top speed of 15 mph, but was met with public contempt. Sinclair Vehicles, which developed the concept in partnership with Lotus and Hoover, collapsed after sales of only 17,000 vehicles. Electric wasn't cool enough. Until Toyota Motor introduced a new concept in green car technology, the hybrid Toyota Prius in 1997, combining a petrol engine with an electric battery. The car performs at similar speeds to a traditional car, but with greater fuel economy. It uses the petrol engine when it needs high performance and the battery when it doesn't. Substantially improved since, the Prius has sold over 270,000 units in 23 countries. The Prius 1.5 model, launched in the UK, with the tagline 'mean but green', goes 0–62 mph in 10.9 seconds, with a fuel economy of 67.3 miles per gallon, and is priced from £18 k (€27 k). Other companies like Honda, Ford, and Chevrolet have all followed suit. The problem for Toyota is how do they persuade existing motorists to part with their petrol engine Nissan, Honda, or BMWs and buy a Toyota hybrid?

Sources: Dale (1985); Toyota (2006).

1 Why do you think it has taken so long to develop the cleaner car? Why is it not completely electric?

2 What has been the secret of the Toyota Prius' marketing success? How are consumer needs and attitudes in society shifting in the twenty-first century?

3 Can you think of any other well-known products or services which have taken advantage of our society's movement towards stronger environmental values? What are they?

Nevertheless, the marketing function within society does not always serve the good (see Chapter 20). Marketing is frequently criticized for doing precisely the opposite. Marketing is charged with being unethical in nature, and manipulative, and creating wants and needs when none previously existed (Packard, 1960).

The Critical Marketing Perspective

Because marketing's contributions to society are not necessary all good, it is important that we develop a critical approach. This is not only to allow us to constantly evaluate and re-evaluate marketing, to improve it, but also to ensure that it remains a useful concept to us, so that marketing continues to operate in a desirable manner within society. While the aggregate marketing system distributes life-saving medicines, food, and important utilities, e.g. heat and light, it also distributes alcohol, tobacco, and gambling products, for example. These are products that we might regard as dangerous to our health and well-being. Of course, in many cultures around the world, people enjoy drinking, smoking, and gambling. However, we are fooling ourselves, especially if we use these to excess, if we think we are really satisfying our own needs and not causing ourselves harm.

Unless told otherwise by government, the aggregate marketing system would distribute anything. Were prostitution and soft drugs, such as cannabis, made legal in Britain, the aggregate marketing system would distribute them. It already does this in the Netherlands, for instance, where these practices are no longer illegal. In that sense the aggregate marketing system in itself is inherently *amoral*, i.e. without morals. Not *immoral*, which means designed to harm, but amoral, designed without any care as to whether it harms or not. The system is only made moral by the decisions made by government and other institutional actors who may act upon and regulate the aggregate marketing system.

Some might consider that the very ideology of marketing is rooted in big business, mass consumer sovereignty, and excess supply over demand and ever-increasing consumption (Brownlie and Saren, 1992). In other words, we are consuming far too much and marketing companies are to blame for it! This argument mooted at the very start of the 1990s was far-sighted for its time, and has developed some considerable backing in the 2000s, with governments around the world working to regulate e.g. the fast food industry to ensure that they deliver a healthy product to the marketplace (see Chapter 2 for further discussion of the fast food industry and the changing market environment). Consider: what else are we over-consuming because of marketers? There are many other controversies in marketing, some of which include the following:

- What is a fair price for companies and organizations in wealthier countries to pay suppliers in poorer countries (see Market Insight 1.6)?
- Where is the line between persuading customers and manipulating customers to purchase products, services, and ideas? Is some marketing promotion consequently really corporate propaganda?
- To what extent should the goods, services, and ideas of one country be marketed over the goods, services, and ideas of another country? What are the cultural implications?

(opposite)
The Prius 1.5 model, launched by Toyota in the UK with the tagline 'mean but green'

Toyota/Michael Rausch

- How much should we consume of any one particular good, service, or idea? When should governments step in to limit consumption?

- Are some groups more susceptible than others to certain types of marketing promotion? If they are, at what point and how should they be protected?

- Are some producers or buyer groups more powerful than others and what impact, if any, does this have upon society?

- Does the aggregate marketing system itself advantage some groups over others and what are the implications for society?

A critical approach to marketing can help us to further understand the nature of marketing knowledge. In fact, we would do well to try to understand marketing from the critical perspective as a natural approach to learning about, and understanding the nature of, marketing. 'Marketing can then be learned from the many varieties of market that exist rather than concentrating on branded, mass consumption products in developed economies' (Easton, 2002), as marketing is so often portrayed. Adopting a critical approach to understanding marketing serves us well, and is in keeping with how managers actually learn the discipline in practice (Easton, 2002). Critiquing marketing helps to consider:

- How marketing knowledge is developed and the extent to which this is based on our contemporary social world. For example, much of current marketing knowledge is based on American practice and research. What implications does this have for the rest of the world?

- How do the historical and cultural conditions in which we operate, as consumers, and as students of marketing, impact on how we see marketing as a discipline?

- The need for continuous re-examination of the categories and frameworks that we use to understand marketing.

- How marketing can benefit from other intellectual perspectives, e.g. social anthropology, social psychology (see Burton, 2001).

In this chapter, we have aimed to explore marketing from the perspective of how it interacts and has developed in society. We see marketing as a force within society in itself, as a form of virus because of the way in which it replicates itself (Gladwell, 2002). We consider marketing as a management process, operating as a holistic process, within and outside the firm or organization that is using it. Of course, it is currently fashionable, and perhaps always was, to criticize marketing and, **capitalism** in particular (Packard, 1960; Klein, 1999). But the move from a production-led to a consumer-led society within many societies (Western or not) has undoubtedly arisen because of marketing, as the following quote illustrates:

'The power of market forces and that of marketing to virtually shape every aspect of a society's mores [customs], attitudes and culture should not be under-estimated. Used wisely and with restraint, marketing can harness and channel the vast energies of the free market system for the good of consumers, corporations and for society as a whole. Used recklessly, it can cause significant harm to all those entities. Thus, marketing is like a potent drug with potentially serious side effects' (Sheth and Sisodia, 2005).

Fairtrade: Clean Conscience for Consumers and Fair Deal for Farmers?

The Fairtrade certification system has been applied to a number of commodity items including fruit

Fairtrade

The Fairtrade mark

Fairtrade

Fairtrade Labelling Organisations International (FLO) is an umbrella organization of twenty labelling initiatives and producer networks that represents Fairtrade-certified producer organizations in Africa, Asia, and South America. In the UK, the Fairtrade Foundation is the labelling initiative that licenses the Fairtrade mark to products that meet international Fairtrade standards. FLO's mission is to ensure the economic independence and empowerment of producer organizations and their members, through Fairtrade certification by:

• Setting international standards in Fairtrade certification;

• Supporting producers in using Fairtrade product labelling as effectively as possible; and

• Raising awareness for the fair trade movement generally.

Through long-term trading relationships, Fairtrade-certified producers benefit from economic stability and improved livelihoods. The additional Fairtrade social premium payment is used by producers to invest in social, economic, or environmental development projects such as technical assistance for infrastructure development, communication system development, improved healthcare and education, and skill development for their cooperative members and families.

The Fairtrade certification system has been applied to a variety of agricultural commodity items, including fruits, honey, cotton, nuts, tea, and wine. The scheme operates across fifteen European countries, as well as in Australasia, North America, Mexico, and Japan. And clearly the consumer approves as well because by 2005, global sales in Fairtrade products totalled around €1.1 billion (FLO International, 2006). The question is: are consumers prepared to pay the generally higher prices that they have to pay for products with the Fairtrade mark than non-labelled products?

Source: www.fairtrade.net.

1 Why has the Fairtrade mark become so important in recent times?

2 Are consumers really prepared to pay the higher prices for a cleaner conscience? Why do you think this is?

3 Have you bought a Fairtrade-labelled product recently? If not, why haven't you purchased such an item?

Chapter Summary

To consolidate your learning, the key points from this chapter are summarized below:

- Define the marketing concept.

  Marketing is the process by which organizations anticipate and satisfy their customers' needs to both parties' benefit. It involves mutual exchange of benefits but over the last twenty years, the marketing concept has increasingly been amended to recognize the importance of the long-term customer relationship to an organization rather than a simple transactional focus.

- Explain how marketing has developed over the twentieth century.

  While some writers have suggested a simple production era, sales era, marketing era development for marketing over the twentieth century, others recognize that marketing has long existed in different forms in different countries. Nevertheless, there is an increasing recognition that marketing is a more systematic organizational activity through market research, and sophisticated promotional activity, than it ever was. There is increasingly a move towards the recognition of the need for companies and organizations to behave responsibly in relation to society.

- Describe the three major contexts of marketing application, i.e. consumer goods, business-to-business, and services marketing.

  Marketing is often divided into the above three types, recognizing that marketing activities are designed based on the context in which an organization operates. The consumer goods marketing approach has been the dominant one stressing the 4Ps and the marketing mix. Business-to-business marketing tends to focus more on principles of relationship marketing, particularly those required in bringing together members of a supply chain. Services marketing stresses the intangible nature of the product, the need to manage customer expectation, and levels of service quality.

- Understand the contribution marketing makes to society.

  The aggregate marketing system delivers us, as consumers and citizens, a wide array of products and services, either directly, or indirectly through business markets, to serve our needs and wants. There is much that is positive about the aggregate marketing system and it has served to improve the standard of living of many around the world.

- Assess critically the impact marketing has on society.

  However, the aggregate marketing system has its faults, by also allowing the promotion and distribution of products and services which may be inherently bad for us, and the over-consumption of things which in moderation are good for us. Understanding why we think about marketing in the way that we do is helpful in understanding both the true nature of marketing and how marketing can aid society. We suggest adopting a critical marketing perspective as a natural approach to learning marketing. As society is changing, new critical approaches to marketing are increasingly developing (e.g. the Fairtrade movement).

 Visit the **Online Resource Centre** that accompanies this book to read more information relating to the marketing environment: www.oxfordtextbooks.co.uk/orc/baines/

? Review Questions

1 How do we define the marketing concept?

2 How do the American Marketing Association and the Chartered Institute of Marketing definitions of marketing differ?

3 How has marketing developed over the twentieth century?

4 What is the marketing mix?

5 How does Bagozzi define marketing exchange?

6 What is the difference between sales and marketing?

7 What are the three major contexts of marketing application?

8 What are the five characteristics of services marketing?

9 What contribution does marketing make to society?

10 How should the aggregate marketing system operate within society?

? Discussion Questions

1 Having read the Case Insight at the beginning of this chapter, how would you advise RM plc to react to the situation of not being able to provide their customers with the service that they had promised to provide but were unable to?

2 Read the section on the marketing mix within the chapter and draw up marketing mixes for the following organizations:

(a) A Hollywood movie studio releasing a blockbuster film and the cinema audience.

(b) A travel agency specializing in luxury holidays and their wealthy clientele.

(c) Apple, as makers of the iPod, its network of distribution outlets, and the end user.

(d) A chemical company supplying fertilizers to farmers.

3 Outline simple marketing exchange processes for the following buyer–seller relationships:

(a) The relationship between a toy company salesperson and the owner of a retail outlet.

(b) The relationship between a pop band of your choice and its audience.

(c) The relationship between an online dating agency and its subscribers.

4 What are the attributes of the product offer, and consumer needs associated with those attributes, for the following product offers:

(a) Retail bank current accounts?

(b) A spa offering massage, facial treatment, aromatherapy, and detox services?

(c) The Mont Blanc pen?

(d) A celebrity magazine like *Hello!* (*Ola*, etc.) or *OK*?

(e) Watching a football match live in a sports stadium?

📖 References

American Marketing Association (AMA) (1985), 'The definition of marketing', *Marketing News*, 1 March, p. 2.

——(2004), 'Code of ethics: ethical norms and values for marketers', available at www.marketingpower.com/content435.php, accessed 3 August 2006.

——(2007), 'Definition of marketing', available at www.marketingpower.com/mg-dictionary.php?SearchFor=marketing&Searched=1, accessed 30 December 2007.

Bagozzi, R. P. (1975), 'Marketing as exchange', *Journal of Marketing*, 39, 4 (October), 32–9.

Bartels, R. D. W. (1944), 'Marketing principles', *Journal of Marketing*, 9, 2 (October), 151–8.

——(1951), 'Can marketing be a science?', *Journal of Marketing*, 15, 3, 319–28.

——(1959), 'Sociologists and marketologists', *Journal of Marketing*, October, 37–40.

——(1968), 'The general theory of marketing', *Journal of Marketing*, 32 (January), 29–33.

——(1983), 'Is marketing defaulting its responsibilities?', *Journal of Marketing*, 47 (Fall), 32–5.

BBC News (2006), 'Body Shop agrees L'Oréal takeover', 17 March, available at news.bbc.co.uk, accessed 3 June 2007.

Blois, K. J. (1974), 'The marketing of services: an approach', *European Journal of Marketing*, 8, 2, 137–45.

Booms, B. H., and Bitner, M. J. (1981), 'Marketing strategies and organisation structures for service firms', in J. H. Donnelly and W. R. George (eds.), *Marketing of Services*, Chicago: AMA Proceedings Series, 48.

Borden, N. H. (1964), 'The concept of the marketing mix', *Journal of Advertising Research*, 4, 2–7.

Brownlie, D., and Saren, M. (1992), 'The four Ps of the marketing concept: prescriptive, polemical, permanent, and problematic', *European Journal of Marketing*, 26, 4, 34–47.

Bucklin, L. P. (1963), 'Retail strategy and the classification of consumer goods', *Journal of Marketing*, January, 51–6.

Burton, D. (2001), 'Critical marketing theory: the blueprint?', *European Journal of Marketing*, 35, 5/6, 722–43.

Christopher, M. (1986), 'Reaching the customer: strategies for marketing and customer service', *Journal of Marketing Management*, 2, 1, 63–71.

CIM (2001), 'Marketing', Glossary, available at www.cim.co.uk, accessed 14 September 2007.

——(2005), 'Professional marketing standards: a guide for employers', available at www.cim.co.uk/mediastore/ProfMarketingStandards/ProfessionalMarketingStandards05_web.pdf, accessed 14 September 2007.

Dale, R. (1985), *The Sinclair Story*, Ely: Fern House Books.

Day, G. S (1994), 'The capabilities of market-driven organisations', *Journal of Marketing*, 58, 3, 37–52.

Easton, G. (2002), 'Marketing: a critical realist approach', *Journal of Business Research*, 55, 103–9.

Economist (2001), 'Crisp and even', *The Economist*, 20 December.

Enright, M. (2002), 'Marketing and conflicting dates for its emergence: Hotchkiss, Bartels and the fifties school of alternative accounts', *Journal of Marketing Management*, 18, 445–61.

Euromonitor (2005), *Passenger Cars, ATVs, RVs, and Pick-ups in the UK*, 1 October, London: Euromonitor plc.

Fleisher, C. S., and Bensoussan, B. E. (2002), *Strategic and Competitive Analysis*, Englewood Cliffs, NJ: Prentice-Hall.

FLO International (2006), *Annual Reports 2000–2005*, Bonn: Fairtrade Labelling Organisations, available at www.fairtrade.net, accessed 3 June 2007.

Fullerton, R. A. (1988), 'How modern is modern marketing? Marketing's evolution and the myth of the "Production Era"', *Journal of Marketing*, 52 (January), 108–25.

Gladwell, M. (2002), *The Tipping Point: How Little Things Can Make a Big Difference*, London: Abacus Books.

Grönroos, C. (1984), 'A service quality model and its marketing implications', *European Journal of Marketing*, 18, 4, 36–44.

——(1994), 'From marketing mix to relationship marketing: towards a paradigm shift in marketing', *Management Decision*, 32, 2, 4–20.

——(1998), 'Marketing services: a case of a missing product', *Journal of Business and Industrial Marketing*, 13, 4/5, 322–38.

Gummesson, E. (1987), 'The new marketing: developing long term interactive relationships', *Long Range Planning*, 20, 4, 10–20.

——(1991), 'Marketing revisited: the crucial role of the part-time marketers', *European Journal of Marketing*, 25, 2, 60–7.

Holden, A. C., and Holden, L. (1998), 'Marketing history: illuminating marketing's clandestine subdiscipline', *Psychology and Marketing*, 15, 2, 117–23.

Howard, D. G., Savins, D. M., Howell, W., and Ryans, J. K., Jr (1991), 'The evolution of marketing theory in the United States and Europe', *European Journal of Marketing*, 25, 2, 7–16.

Hunt, S. D. (1971), 'The morphology of theory and the general theory of marketing', *Journal of Marketing*, April, 65–8.

Hunt, S. D. (1983), 'General theories and fundamental explananda of marketing', *Journal of Marketing*, 47, 4 (Fall), 9–17.

Judd, R. C. (1968), 'Similarities and differences in product and service retailing', *Journal of Retailing*, 43, 4, 1–9.

Keith, R. J. (1960), 'The marketing revolution', *Journal of Marketing*, 24 (January), 35–8.

Klein, N. (1999), *No Logo*, London: Flamingo.

Kohli, A. K., and Jaworski, B. J. (1990), 'Market orientation: the construct, research propositions and managerial implications', *Journal of Marketing*, 54 (April), 1–18.

Kotler, P. (2006), 'Ethical lapses of marketers', in J. N. Sheth and R. J. Sisodia (eds.), *Does Marketing Need Reform: Fresh Perspectives on the Future*, Armonk, NY: M. E. Sharpe, chapter 17.

Levitt, T. (1981), 'Marketing intangible products and product intangibles', *Harvard Business Review*, 59 (May–June), 94–102.

Lendrevie, J., Lévy, J., and Lindon, D. (2006), *Mercator: Théorie et pratique du marketing*, 8th edn., Paris: Dunod.

Leone, R. P., and Shultz, R. L. (1980), 'A study of marketing generalisations', *Journal of Marketing*, 44 (Winter), 10–18.

McCarthy, E. J. (1960), *Basic Marketing*, Homewood, Ill.: Irwin.

Marketing and Sales Standards Setting Board (2006), *Developing World-Class Standards for the Marketing Profession*, March, available at www.msssb.org/marketing/, accessed 3 August 2006.

Mintel (2005), *Flavoured Alcoholic Beverages—UK—October 2005*, London: Mintel, available at www.mintel.com.

Morgan. R. M., and Hunt, S. D. (1994), 'The commitment–trust theory of relationship marketing', *Journal of Marketing*, 58, 3 (July), 20–38.

Narver, J. C., and Slater, S. F. (1990), 'The effect of a market orientation on business profitability', *Journal of Marketing*, October, 20–35.

OED online (2006), 'Customer', *Oxford English Dictionary Online*, www.oxfordreference.com, accessed 31 July 2006.

Packard, V. O. (1960), *The Hidden Persuaders*, Harmondsworth: Penguin Books.

Parasuraman, A., Berry, L. L., and Zeithaml, V. A. (1985), 'A conceptual model of service quality and its implications for further research', *Journal of Marketing*, 49 (Fall), 41–50.

Payne, A. (1993), *The Essence of Services Marketing*, Hemel Hempstead: Prentice-Hall.

Regan, W. J. (1963), 'The service revolution', *Journal of Marketing*, 27, 57–62.

Reichheld, F. F., and Sasser Jr., W. E. (1990), 'Zero defections: quality comes to services', *Harvard Business Review*, September–October, 105–11.

Saren, M. (2006), *Marketing Graffiti: The View from the Street*, Oxford: Butterworth-Heinemann.

Sheth, J. N., and Sisodia, R. J. (2005), 'A dangerous divergence: marketing and society', *Journal of Public Policy and Marketing*, 24, 1, 160–2.

————(2006), 'How to reform marketing', in J. N. Sheth and R. J. Sisodia (eds.), *Does Marketing Need Reform: Fresh Perspectives on the Future*, Armonk, NY: M. E. Sharpe, chapter 20.

Shostack, G. L. (1977), 'Breaking free from product marketing', *Journal of Marketing*, 41 (April), 73–8.

Slater, S. F., and Narver, J. C. (1994), 'Market orientation, customer value and superior performance', *Business Horizons*, March–April, 22–7.

Smith, W. R. (1956), 'Product differentiation and market segmentation as alternative marketing strategies', *Journal of Marketing*, July, 3–8.

Toyota (2006), *Hybrid Synergy Drive*, available at www.hybridsynergydrive.com/en/top.html, accessed 31 July 2006.

Vargo, S. L., and Lusch, R. F. (2004), 'Evolving to a new service dominant logic for marketing', *Journal of Marketing*, 68 (January), 1–17.

Wall Street Journal (2001), 'Cost of developing drugs found to rise', 3 December.

Webster, F. E., Jr. (1992), 'The changing role of marketing in the corporation', *Journal of Marketing*, 56 (October), 1–17.

Wilkie, W. L., and Moore, E. S. (1999), 'Marketing's contributions to society', *Journal of Marketing*, 63 (Special Issue), 198–218.

Worcester, R. M. (2005), 'Trust is what this election is about', *Worcester's Weblog for epolitix.com*, 26 April, available at www.ipsos-mori.com/publications/rmw/ep050426.shtml, accessed 3 August 2006.

2

The Marketing Environment

A wise man also fears a weak enemy.
Publilius Sirius (*c.* 100 BC)

Learning Outcomes

After reading this chapter, you will be able to:

✔ Identify and define the three key areas of the marketing environment.

✔ Describe the key characteristics associated with the marketing environment.

✔ Explain PESTLE analysis and show how it is used to understand the external environment.

✔ Explain the environmental scanning process.

✔ Analyse the performance environment using an appropriate model.

✔ Understand the importance of analysing an organization's internal environment and identify the key resources and capabilities.

Michelin Tyres has been established for over a century and is now active in more than 170 countries. How does it keep abreast of the marketing environment? We speak to Helen Tattersall to find out more.

Helen Tattersall for Michelin Tyres

The Michelin Tyre Company Ltd, first incorporated in 1905, was set up in 1889 by two brothers, André and Edouard Michelin. Now active in more than 170 countries, Michelin operates across all continents of the world, manufacturing and selling tyres for all kinds of vehicles, publishing maps and guides, and operating specialist digital services. Most people recognize our world famous mascot, Bibendum, 'The Michelin man', looking good considering his age! My own division is concerned with tyres made for heavy goods vehicles over 3.5 tonnes, including trucks, coaches, and buses. In the UK and the Republic of Ireland, we have an extensive sales force supporting thousands of tyre distributors, from tyres used in cars and trucks, to those used in specialist industrial and earthmoving equipment.

To conduct environmental scanning, we adopt several approaches. We use joint panels with key national and regional trade journals, conducting telephone questionnaires with customers on challenges, issues, and developments in the haulage industry. Our sales force in the UK and Ireland is responsible for collecting market intelligence, especially on competitors' actions and products.

- *Our sales force is responsible for*
- *collecting market intelligence, especially*
- *on competitors' actions and products.*

We work with the Road Haulage Association and the Freight Transport Association, which offers us a chance to mix with customers in a non-selling environment, and we belong to the EuroPool organization, an independent body which acts on behalf of all European tyre manufacturers. Here, we declare our

sales on a monthly basis and they send back to us details of our market share. In addition, we conduct our own annual surveys with distribution partners (including ATS Euromaster—a Michelin group company—and independent tyre dealers). We use the results of these surveys to track industry market shares with sales revenues. Finally, we analyse and test competitors' tyre products at our research and development centre.

Our scanning activity has picked up lots of challenges, for example rising fuel costs, changes in haulage patterns due to an increase in internet shopping, new legislation around driving and emission standards, and changing patterns of labour with the increase in Eastern European drivers (often bringing with them their cheaper fuel). However, the biggest challenge that we have experienced in the last 4 or 5 years is the strong competition from cheap imported tyre manufacturers from emerging economies in the east, including India, China, and Korea. These new tyre brands sell very cheaply because of the low manufacturing and labour costs in these countries. Although we knew these brands were coming, we were very surprised by how rapidly customers adopted them.

If you were faced with unexpected competition of this type, what would you do?

Introduction

Have you ever wondered how organizations adapt to the changing business environment? How do companies keep up with the changes in politics, markets, and economics? What process do they use to try to anticipate changes in technologies? How do they determine what will impact on their businesses and what will not? We aim to answer these and other questions in this chapter.

The environment in which all organizations operate, whether they be commercial, charities, government, or the public sector, is never static, never entirely predictable, and has the capacity to influence the markets in which organizations operate. The environment changes and continues to change in response to a variety of factors. In this chapter we examine the nature of the environment in which marketing is conducted, determine environment-related issues, and as a result provide a context in which we can develop marketing strategies, as explored further in Chapter 5.

The marketing environment is best understood by considering the degree to which an organization can influence the various forces acting on it. The external environment, for example, consists of the political, social, and technological influences, and organizations have relatively little influence on each of these. The performance environment consists of the competitors, suppliers, and indirect service providers who shape the way an organization achieves its objectives. Here, organizations have a much stronger level of influence. The internal environment concerns the resources, processes, and polices an organization manages in order that it can attempt to achieve its goals. These elements can be influenced directly by an organization. Each of these three marketing environments is discussed in this chapter (see Figure 2.1).

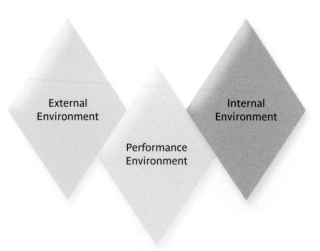

Figure 2.1
The three marketing environments

Understanding the External Environment

The external environment is characterized in two main ways. The first is that the elements do not have an immediate impact on the performance of an organization, although they might do in the longer term. The second is that although the elements can influence an organization, it is not possible to control them. This suggests that the level of risk attached to the external environment is potentially high.

In order to make sense of the external environment we use a framework known as PESTLE. This is by far the easiest and one of the most popular frameworks with which to examine the external environment. This technique was formerly referred to as PEST analysis but the recent rise in concern and awareness attached to ecological and climatic issues has impacted on most organizations. **PESTLE** therefore stands for the Political, Economic, Social, Technological, Legal, and Ecological environments, as shown as Figure 2.2.

The Political Environment

When we conduct environmental scanning programmes, we consider the firm or organization's political environment. Although the legal environment relates to the laws and regulations associated with consumers and business practices, the political environment relates to the period of interaction between business, society, and government before those laws are enacted, when they are still being formed, or are in dispute. So, political environmental analysis is a critical phase in environmental scanning because companies can then detect potential legal and regulatory changes in their industries and so they have a chance to impede, influence, and alter that legislation. In most corporate and marketing strategy textbooks, particularly the older ones, we teach that the **political environment**

Figure 2.2
The external marketing environment

is largely uncontrollable, that the marketing manager has very limited impact on this particular environment. However, this is not always the case. There are circumstances when an organization, or an industry coalition, can affect legislation in its own favour, or at the very least respond more flexibly to changes in legislation than its competitors. There is increasingly an understanding that business–government relations, properly undertaken, can be a source of **sustainable competitive advantage**. In other words, organizations can outperform other organizations over time if they can manage their relationships with government and regulatory bodies better than their competitors (Hillman, Keim, and Schuler, 2004). (See Market Insight 2.1 for an example of a business–government relations campaign.)

Because legislation is such a technical area, and often written in technical legal language, few firms have the capability to understand and influence legislation without employing specialists. In such circumstances, special industry lobbyists are hired for the following reasons:

- To represent clients to government decision makers;
- To provide strategic advice to clients on how to design their campaigns; and
- To provide administrative support for their clients (Moloney and Jordan, 1996).

Companies or organizations often make the decision to influence governments in collaboration with other organizations, either through industry or trade bodies or together with other large companies in their industry. For example, Japanese automotive manufacturers Nissan and Honda lobbied the EU to recognize cars assembled in the UK largely from Japanese parts to be European in the early 1990s to offset import quotas on certain Japanese goods (see Kewley, 2002). There have been many successful examples of other lobbying campaigns, for instance, that of the Shopping Hours Reform Council (SHRC), consisting mainly of large supermarket chains, who managed to lobby the then Conservative government to make Sunday trading legal in July 1994 (Harris, Gardner, and Vetter, 1999). Nevertheless, there are six key ways in which marketers might conduct business–government relations in various countries as shown below:

- Lobbyist firms, with key industry knowledge, can be engaged either permanently or as needed.
- Public relations consultancies, e.g. Weber Shandwick, can be commissioned for their political services, often having MPs or others with a high degree of political influence serving as directors and/or advisers.
- A politician may be paid a fee to give political advice on matters of importance to an organization, where this is legal within that particular jurisdiction, and that politician is not serving directly within the government in question on the same portfolio as that they are advising on.
- An in-house public relations manager might handle government relations directly.
- An industry association might be contacted to lobby on behalf of members (e.g. in the European financial services industry, groups include the Banking Federation of the EU, the European Savings Bank Group, and the European Association of Co-operative Banks).

- A politician may be invited directly to join the board of directors, board of trustees, or board of advisers of an organization to aid the company develop its business–government relations, e.g. the Carlyle Group, a Washington DC-based private equity investment firm, hired the British former prime minister Sir John Major for this purpose. (Sir John Major no longer works for Carlyle.)

Working with parliaments, civil servants, and governments in different countries provides serious difficulties particularly where a company or organization has limited knowledge of the market. In addition, successive governments seldom work in the same way either, and so there is usually a learning curve at the start of the electoral cycle in any jurisdiction. Generally, when conducting a public affairs campaign, it is important to:

- Identify and prioritize the issues at hand (commercial and political).
- Develop contacts with the appropriate officials in the relevant government, commission, or parliamentary departments.
- Design a planning and contacts 'grid' which outlines which **stakeholders** need to be contacted over what issues by which dates.
- Identify key politicians and other interested parties.
- Read, and try to influence, the press over the issues on which you are campaigning (Morris, 2001).

The Economic Environment

Companies and organizations have to develop an understanding of the economic environment in which they operate and trade. This is not least because a country's economic circumstances have an impact on what economists term factor prices within a particular industry for a particular firm or organization. These factors could include raw material, labour, building and other capital costs, or indeed any other input to a business. The external environment of a firm is affected, but not exclusively, by the following items:

- Wage inflation—how much wages increase on an annual basis in a particular sector will depend on the supply of labour in that sector. Where there is scarcity of supply, wages usually increase (e.g. doctors).
- Price inflation—how much consumers pay for goods and services is dependent on the rate of supply of those goods and services. Where there is a scarcity of supply, there is usually an increase in the price of that consumer good or service (e.g. petrol in the 2000s).
- **Gross domestic product** per capita—this is the combined output of goods and services in a particular nation and is a useful measure for determining relative wealth between countries when comparisons are calculated per member of the population (GDP per capita at purchasing power parity, see paragraph below).
- Income, sales, and corporation taxes—these taxes, typically operating in all countries around the world usually at different levels, substantially affect how we market goods and services.

Changes in technology particularly affect high-technology industries, where firms must decide whether they wish to dominate that market by pushing their own particular technology standards, and especially where new technology renders existing standards obsolete (e.g. the MP3 player and the tape and vinyl record manufacturing industries). In the pharmaceutical industry, changes in technology could lead to new product formulations adopting differing delivery mechanisms (for example, Britain's Powderject Pharmaceuticals plc (now acquired by the Chiron Corporation) developed a needleless vaccine injection delivery system using proprietary gas propulsion technology. Pilkington glass became a global manufacturer of glass and glazing products after it developed a system of glass production which lowered its costs and increased the quality of its products (the 'float glass' process invented by Sir Alastair Pilkington in 1952), and then licensed its technology worldwide.

As marketers scanning the technological environment, we are particularly interested in research and development trends, particularly those of our competitors. Strategies to ascertain these can involve regular searches of patent registration, trademarks, and copyright assignations as well as maintaining a general interest in technological and scientific advances to determine their potential impact on product and service redesign. Firms' actions vis-à-vis one another are shaped by technological opportunity within the technological environment (Wilson, 1977). For example, in the pharmaceutical and chemical industries, companies have for a long time developed new compounds based on modifications of compounds registered for patents by their competitors in a process known as '**reverse engineering**'.

But the reverse engineering principle does not solely operate within these industries. Companies in other industries frequently develop new product and service formulations based on their competitors' products and services, in what is often known as a 'me-too' or imitation marketing strategy. In fact such imitation

The award-winning Jubilee Library in Brighton's regenerated city square makes use of the Pilkington Planar frameless structural glazing system

Pilkington Group Ltd

lies at the heart of the inability of firms to turn their technological advances into sustainable competitive advantages (Rao, 2005). The problem is that as soon as they introduce a new product or service variant it is quickly copied. The trick is to *continually* introduce new products and services, and to stay as close to the consumer as possible. (See Market Insight 2.2 for an example of technological innovation in the telecommunication industry.)

The difficulty for most firms is how to determine whether or not to invest in radical new technologies, since the potential benefits are far from clear at the outset. Fear of obsolescence is usually a greater incentive to invest in new technologies than the lure of enhancement of existing products and services (Chandy, Prabhu, and Antia, 2003). Companies are particularly concerned about the impact of technological changes on their product and service lifecycles. However, innovation becomes a necessary condition in the strategic marketing decision making of high-technology firms. For less technology-intensive firms, innovation of some form, whether it is process or product/service focused or at least rapid adoption of new product/service variants based on competitors' offerings, is still usually necessary in order to stay ahead of the competition.

The Legal Environment

In the USA, perhaps the most important legislative changes in recent times include the Sarbanes–Oxley Act 2002, which stipulates new regulations on corporate governance and provides more stringent controls over how accurately companies report their finances, as a result of financial scandals involving gross inflation of revenues by companies such as WorldCom, Inc. and Enron Corporation. This change in legislation has also affected companies in other countries around the world. Since reported revenues affect stock market share prices, these companies inflated their share prices by artificially raising their revenues. Needless to say, once the markets discovered their errors, the companies' reputations were irreparably damaged and both companies have since been liquidated and stopped trading as a result. But changes in legislation and regulation also provide a company with potential new business, as the section on trade blocs in Chapter 7 outlines.

We can see that the legal environment covers every aspect of an organization's business. Laws and regulation are enacted in most countries ranging from the transparency of pricing, the prevention of restrictive trade practices, minimum wages and business taxes, product safety, good practice in packaging and labelling, the abuse of a dominant market position, to codes of practice in advertising, to take just a small selection.

Product Safety, Packaging, and Labelling

In the European Union, product safety is covered by the General Product Safety Directive to protect consumer health and safety both for member states within the EU, and importers from third-party countries to the EU or their EU agent representatives (see Chapter 9 for more on product decisions). Where products pose serious risks to consumer health, the European Commission can take action, imposing fines and criminal sentences for those contravening the Directive. The

'It's Good to Talk', but Cheaper via the Internet

Voice-over-internet protocol technology allows internet users to talk with one another through their existing broadband connection. It allows speech between two computers by 'packet switching' voice conversation as digital data at one end of the conversation, sending the packets through the internet connection, and decoding the packets at the other end back into voice conversation, sufficiently quickly so that neither caller hears any silence, delay, or noise.

In the UK, there were 34 million fixed line subscribers in 2005, down slightly from 35.6 m in 2001, at least partly because of the advent of VOIP technology. By 2005, internet telecommunication connections had reached 16.3 million, up 33% between 2001 and 2005. Although VOIP technology has been around as long as the internet has, no one had yet offered a service of sufficiently good quality, and the existing fixed line providers, e.g. BT in the UK, France Telecom, and AT&T in the USA, have had little incentive to cannibalize their own markets by offering the much cheaper internet telephony service. But the tide may finally have turned.

Since Skype made available its internet communication software and began offering free calls between its users on the internet in 2003, its ability to attract users has been phenomenal. Ebay was so impressed with the software that it bought Skype in October 2005 for $2.6 bn, to allow users of its auction website to communicate with each other. But Skype also offers relatively cheap, paid-for services for calling from Skype to landline and mobile phones (SkypeOut) and receiving calls from such phones (SkypeIn). By mid-2007 it had amassed over 220 million registered users.

Skype are not the only players in town: Vonage, Google, Yahoo!, and Microsoft's MSN have all launched VOIP services. The question is how long will it take before all calls are made over the internet?

Sources: Mintel (2007); Kharif (2006).

1 Why has it taken so long for VOIP technology to become available to the average user?

2 Why has the service not yet become the standard approach to telephony despite being free to use for internet-to-internet calls?

3 Why have the fixed line telephone companies been so slow to roll out their own VOIP services?

General Product Safety Directive does not cover food safety; this is subject to another EU Directive, Regulation (EC) No. 178/2002 of the European Parliament and of the Council, which establishes a European Food Safety Authority, and a set of regulations covering food safety. As a company operating in these sectors, it is important to keep up with changes in legislation. Failure to do so could jeopardize the business.

In the most extreme cases, such as occurred in Britain when British beef became infected with BSE (bovine spongiform encephalopathy), the European Commission can ban all trade in a particular foodstuff both for export and domestic consumption. Japan has long banned the import of certain British and American beef products because they does not correspond with their own exact standards.

The EU banned British beef from 1996 until 1999 for European consumption and did not grant an export licence outside the EU until a decade later, in 2006. Similar problems have occurred before e.g. the detection of avian bird flu, first isolated in Guangdong Province in China in the 2000s. Because the circumstances tend to change over each epidemic, food safety regulations and practices also change to keep up. There has been an increase in food labelling schemes providing country-of-origin information. In the food industry, the practice is to clearly label the product to track it from 'gate to plate' indicating, in the case of meat, where it has originated from.

There are frequently sets of regulations specific to certain industries where product safety has special significance. For instance, in the UK toy industry, regulation is covered by the Toys (Safety) Regulations 1995, which are corresponding regulations to the European Toy Safety Directive, and which stipulate that all toys which comply with European Commission minimum safety standards on toys must bear the CE mark. In Britain, the British Toy and Hobby Association have a more stringent set of toy safety standards and produce their own labelling, the Lion Mark, to indicate compliance with these standards. Standards are different in other countries outside the EU.

In the pharmaceutical industry, regulations govern testing, approval, manufacturing, labelling, and the marketing of drugs. Most countries also place restrictions on the prices that pharmaceutical companies can charge for drugs, and so in Japan, price regulations are stipulated for individual products, while in the UK, strict controls are placed on the overall profitability of products supplied by a specific company to the National Health Service, under the Pharmaceutical Price Regulation Scheme until 2010. Companies that develop cosmetics and fragrances are required to comply with legislative measures designed to protect the cosmetic user and so need to ensure that products remain cosmetics and are not reclassified under different regulations, for instance, those related to medicines, which makes innovation within the cosmetic industry more difficult (Gower, 2005). In Britain, eggs carrying the lion mark conform to strict safety standards including vaccination against Salmonella Enteritidis.

Generally, in the EU, product labelling regulation tends to relate to recycling of packaging and waste to ensure it complies with environmental regulations. In the USA, packaging and labelling regulations are more concerned with fair practice and ensuring that packaging does not contain misleading advertising statements.

Wages and Taxes

Laws and regulation with regard to minimum wages offered to employees differ dependent on the country of operation. In the UK, a national minimum wage did not come into being until then Prime Minister Blair joined Britain to the EU's employment regulations in 1999—introducing minimum wage levels for workers of certain ages. In 2006, the minimum wage in Britain was set at a substantially higher level than in the USA. Companies operating in foreign countries need to be aware of employment legislation related to wage levels or risk both infringing the law and reaping the relevant legal and financial penalties, and/or facing reputational damage when the international media picks up the story and disseminates it through the press to the general public.

Table 2.1 Top fifteen chocolate confectionery brands in Great Britain

Chocolate product	Brand owner	Sales 2004 period (£m rounded)	Sales 2005 period (£m rounded)	Change 2004/5 (actual)
Cadbury Dairy Milk	Cadbury Schweppes	320.2	317.5	−0.8%
Galaxy	Masterfoods	126.2	137.5	+8.9%
Maltesers	Masterfoods	128.6	127.4	−0.9%
Mars	Masterfoods	103.1	97.0	−5.9%
Cadbury Flake	Cadbury Schweppes	56.4	70.3	+24.5%
Kit Kat	Nestlé	91.4	69.9	−24.0%
Celebrations	Masterfoods	73.9	69.4	−6.1%
Cadbury Roses	Cadbury Schweppes	58.1	68.8	+18.4%
Quality Street	Nestlé	65.1	68.4	+5.1%
Aero	Nestlé	49.5	63.5	+28.4%
Snickers	Masterfoods	54.9	51.2	−6.9%
Cadbury Buttons	Cadbury Schweppes	49.1	49.9	+1.6%
Milky Bar	Nestlé	49.6	49.7	+0.2%
Ferrero Rocher	Ferrero USA, Inc.	46.2	48.8	+5.6%
Cadbury Crème Egg	Cadbury Schweppes	53.3	46.0	−13.6%

Source: Benady (2006); manufacturers' websites. Reproduced with the kind permission of *Marketing Week*.

1 If you were CEO of Britain's largest chocolate manufacturer, Cadbury Schweppes, how would you develop the market for chocolate treats while continuing to act as a socially responsible company?

2 How would you organize the marketing function so that you were kept in touch with the latest market, customer and competitor information?

3 How do you reconcile the fact that carbon labelling inherently suggests reduction in consumption while advertising in itself suggests more consumption? Is this a trick or a treat?

use it to develop their own competitive strategies. It is important to assess how this movement towards greener and sustainable marketing is affecting your own industry to ensure that your company is either not adversely affected by these changes (e.g. by non-compliance with regulatory change such as packaging) or can take advantage of the opportunities (e.g. a haulage company taking advantage of hybrid lorries using engines which run on a combination of energy produced by petrol combustion and electricity production to lower energy costs).

Information about each of these sub-environments needs to be gathered in order that an assessment can be made about the potential impact on the organization. All organizations need to watch all PESTLE elements but some may be of particular importance. For example, pharmaceutical organizations such as GlaxoSmithKline monitor legal and regulatory developments (e.g. labelling, patents, and testing), the Environment Agency monitors political and ecological changes (e.g. flood plains for housing developments), road haulage companies should watch for any changes that impact on transport development (e.g. congestion charging, diesel duty, toll roads), whilst music distributors should watch for changes in technology and associated social and cultural developments (e.g. MP3 players and mobile music, downloading and the Napster case).

Environmental Scanning

In order to understand how the elements in the external environment are changing it is necessary for organizations to put in place methods and processes to inform them of developments. A key process is environmental scanning.

According to Aguilar (1967), **environmental scanning** is the process of gathering information about a company's external events and relationships, in order to assist top management in its decision making, and so develop its future course of action. It can be regarded as the internal communication of external information about issues that may potentially influence an organization's decision-making process, focusing on the identification of emerging issues, situations, and potential threats in the external environment (Albright, 2004). Environmental scanning is an important component of the strategic marketing planning process (see Chapter 5). The development of an organization's strategic options is dependent on first determining the opportunities and threats in the environment and auditing an organization's resources.

We gather information in environmental scanning exercises using company reports, newspapers, industry reports and magazines, government reports, and marketing intelligence reports (e.g. those published by Datamonitor, Euromonitor, and Mintel). In addition, 'soft' personal sources of information obtained through networking are also important such as contacts at trade fairs, particularly for competitive, and legal and regulatory information. Such verbal, personal sources of information can be critical in fast-changing environments (May, Stewart, and Sweo, 2000) when reports from government, industry, or specific businesses have yet to be written and disseminated.

Conversely, small manufacturing companies, for example, tend to scan three important areas of information in environmental scanning activities which, according to Beal (2000) include:

- *Customer and competitor information*—including competitors' prices, competitors' new product introductions, competitors' advertising/promotional programmes, competitors' entry into new markets and new product technologies, customers' buying habits, customers' product preferences, customers' demands and desires.

- *Company resources and capabilities*—including company's R&D capabilities and resources, company's advertising and promotions resources, company's sales capabilities/resources, company's financial capabilities/resources, company's management capabilities/resources.

- *Suppliers of labour and funds*—including availability of external financing, availability of labour, and new manufacturing technologies.

For larger companies, or small companies operating in global environments, because of the increased complexity, there is an even greater need to undertake effective environmental scanning exercises. Thus, firms successfully operating in international markets were more likely to find information on export opportunities through information from secondary sources and from market research exercises. They tended to monitor their competitors' export performance, involvement in exporting, and their export intention, and they were more likely to monitor changes in technology, in products, in economic conditions, and in socio-political conditions (Lim, Sharkey, and Kim, 1996).

The process through which companies scan the marketing environment typically involves three stages (see Figure 2.4). In Stage 1, the focus is principally, but not exclusively, on data gathering. In Stage 2, the focus is principally, but not exclusively, on interpreting the data gathered in a process of environmental interpretation/analysis, and in the final stage, the focus is principally, but not exclusively, on strategy formulation.

In each of the key scanning stages, there is some activity in each of the other two areas so that the three processes dominate a particular stage but are present in each one. So, in Stage 1, we might spend 60 per cent of our time gathering data, 20 per cent of our time undertaking environment analysis/evaluation, and the

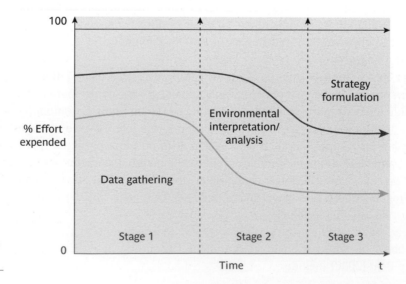

Figure 2.4

The environmental scanning process

Source: Adapted from O'Connell and Zimmerman (1979). Reproduced with the kind permission of *California Management Review*.

remaining 20 per cent of our time on strategy formulation. In Stage 2, we spend more time relatively on undertaking the environment analysis/evaluation, and in Stage 3, we spend more time relatively on strategy formulation. Environmental scanning is an activity which must be built into the strategy development and formulation process if it is to impact upon company decision making and help firms outperform their competitors by better adapting to their environment.

Although the process seems relatively straightforward, and simply a matter of collecting the 'right' information, barriers to effective environmental scanning occur because it is difficult to determine what the 'right' information actually is. In addition, data gathering can be time-consuming. In such cases, the information gathered ceases to provide a useful input to strategic marketing decision making. In addition, multinational corporations may see opportunities and desire organizational change, and collect the right data, to take advantage of those opportunities, but fail to actually undertake such opportunities because of **switching costs** and organizational inertia related to production, sourcing, and other business operations. In a transatlantic survey of European and American companies in the late 1970s (O'Connell and Zimmerman, 1979), American executives reported the following frustrations in their environmental scanning exercises:

- Inability to move faster;
- Managerial inhibitions related to pessimistic discussions;
- Conflict between the desire for stability and the reality of constant change;
- Missed opportunities due to poor timing; and
- Motivation of the management team to discuss the issues.

European executives reported the following frustrations:

- Inability to organize for environmental scanning;
- Difficulty of matching individual executive beliefs with detectable trends;
- Delay between external developments and their interpretation of them;
- Difficulty in applying a systematic approach; and
- Problems in finding relevant information in the exercise.

Most commentators on environmental scanning assume that managers take advantage of environmental changes in a reactive manner rather than actually

RESEARCH INSIGHT 2.1

To take your learning further, you might wish to read this influential paper.

Levitt, T. (1960), 'Marketing myopia', *Harvard Business Review*, July – August, 45 – 56.

This is, perhaps the most famous and celebrated article ever written on marketing. It has twice been reprinted in the *Harvard Business Review*. The central thesis of the article, as true today as it was in the 1960s, is that companies must monitor change in the external environment and keep abreast of their customers' needs or they risk decline.

bringing about environmental change for their own gain. There are competing views on how organizations interact and react with their environment and their adaptability to it. Nevertheless, it is important for us to recognize that 'managers of a firm cannot simply stand outside the structure and activity within their industry, sector or market and adjust themselves to the trends they observe there; their actions make the trends' (Brownlie, 1994).

Understanding the Performance Environment

The performance environment consists of those organizations that either directly or indirectly influence an organization's operational performance. There are three main types:

- Those companies that compete against the organization in the pursuit of its objectives.

- Those companies that supply raw materials, goods, and services and those that add value as distributors, dealers, and retailers, further down the marketing channel. These organizations have the potential to directly influence the performance of the organization by adding value through production, assembly, and distribution of products prior to reaching the end user.

- Those companies that have the potential to *indirectly* influence the performance of the organization in the pursuit of its objectives. These organizations often supply services such as consultancy, financial services, or marketing research or communication agencies.

Analysis of the performance environment is undertaken so that an organization can adapt to a better position, relative to that of its stakeholders and competitors, in particular. These adjustments are made as circumstances develop and/or in anticipation of environmental and performance conditions. The performance environment encompasses not just competitors but also suppliers and other organizations such as distributors, who all contribute to the industry value chain.

Knowledge about the performance arena allows organizations to choose how and where to operate and compete, given limited resources. Knowledge allows adaption and development in complex and increasingly turbulent markets. Conditions vary from industry to industry. Some are full of potential and growth opportunities, such as cruise holidays, Fairtrade food, and the online travel and gaming industries, whilst others are in decline or at best stagnating, for example high street music stores and car manufacturing. Rivalry may be on an international, national, regional, or local basis. The source and strength of competitive forces will vary so that a strong organization operating in an 'unattractive' industry may have difficulty in achieving an acceptable performance. Weaker organizations, however, operating in 'attractive' environments, may record consistently good performances.

Analysing Industries

An industry is composed of various firms who market similar products and services. According to Porter (1979) it is important to review the 'competitive' environment within an industry and to identify the major competitive forces as this can help assess their impact upon an organization's present and future competitive positions.

There are a number of variables that help determine how attractive an industry is and which shape the longer-term profitability for the different companies that make up the industry. Think of industries such as shipbuilding, cars, coal, and steel where levels of profitability have been weak and hence unattractive to prospective new entrants. Now think of industries such as new media, oil, banking, and supermarkets where levels of profitability have been astonishingly high. The competitive pressures in all these markets vary quite considerably but there are enough similarities to establish an analytical framework to gauge the nature and intensity of competition. Porter suggests that competition in an industry is a composite of five main competitive forces. These are the level of threat that new competitors will enter the market, the threat posed by substitute products, and the bargaining power of both buyers and suppliers. These in turn affect the fifth force, the intensity of rivalry between the current competitors. Porter called these variables the Five Forces of Competitive Industry Analysis (see Figure 2.5).

As a general rule, the more intense the rivalry between the industry players, the lower will be their overall performance. On the other hand, the lower the rivalry the greater will be the performance of the industry players.

Porter's model is useful because it helps to expose the competitive forces in operation in an industry and can lead to an assessment of the strength of each of the forces. The collective impact determines what competition is like in the market. As a general rule, the stronger the competitive forces the lower the profitability in a market. An organization needs to determine a competitive approach that will allow it to influence the industry's competitive rules, protect it from competitive forces as much as possible, and give it a strong position from which to compete.

New Entrants

Industries are seldom static. Companies enter and exit industries all the time. EasyJet—the budget European airline company—entered the European airline market after the European Commission deregulated it, along with other companies such as Ireland's Ryanair, and the Dutch airline KLM launched Buzz, although it subsequently sold this to Ryanair. These new smaller budget operators have competed effectively with the national carriers of Europe, e.g. British Airways, Lufthansa, KLM, and Air France, by lowering their costs. Another example is the UK beverage industry, with the entrance of energy drink manufacturers such as Red Bull and fruit smoothie makers PJ Smoothies and Innocent Drinks. These relatively new companies are now competing head-on with industry stalwarts Pepsico, Coca-Cola, and GlaxoSmithKline's Lucozade, probably the original energy drink in the UK beverage market.

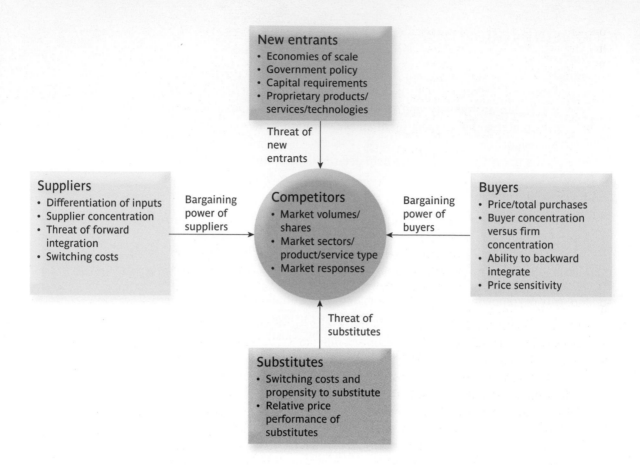

Figure 2.5 Industry analysis: Porter's five forces

Source: Adapted from Porter (1979). Reproduced with the kind permission of Harvard Business School Publishing.

When examining an industry, we consider whether economies of scale are required to operate successfully within it. For instance, motor manufacturing in the UK requires significant investment in plant and machinery. Unfortunately, since British labour costs are also high and foreign direct investment incentives (e.g. government development grants) are not as lucrative as they once were, many British-based motor manufacturers have now moved their manufacturing facilities to Eastern Europe and Far Eastern countries. New entrants may be restricted through government and regulatory policy or they may well be frozen out of an industry because of the capital requirements necessary to set up business. For example, in the oil and gas industry, huge sums of capital are required not only to fund exploration activities but also to fund the extraction and refining operations.

Companies may be locked out of a market because companies within that market are operating using proprietary products/services or technologies, e.g. the pharmaceutical industry where patents protect companies' investments in new medicines. The cost of a typical new patented drug at the turn of the twenty-first century was around $800 million in R&D costs alone—before marketing and other commercial costs—taking on average around twelve years from invention through to commercial launch (Wall Street Journal, 2001). Few companies can compete in such a market since the set-up and ongoing R&D costs are very large. One strategic response in the industry was a wave of consolidation in the late 1990s (i.e. mergers and alliances) as pharmaceutical companies tried to build critical mass in R&D, marketing, and distribution. Examples included GSK, from the merger of Glaxo Wellcome plc and SmithKline Beecham plc in 2000, AstraZeneca from the merger of Sweden's Astra AB and Britain's Zeneca plc in 1999, and Novartis, created from the merger of two Swiss pharmaceutical companies Sandoz and Ciba-Geigy in 1996.

Substitutes

In any industry, there are usually substitute products and services that perform the same function or meet similar customer needs. Levitt (1960) warned that many companies fail to recognize the competitive threat from newly developing products and services. He cites the American railroad industry's refusal to see the competitive threat arising from the development of the automobile and airline industries in the transport sector.

Sometimes, however, substitute products and services are produced by companies that we might not think are likely to become competitors, e.g. Scottish Power set up Scottish Telecom (now called THUS plc) in 1994 by hanging fibre optic cables along its electricity (i.e. pylon) network in competition with British Telecom, mainly in Scotland at that time, and others in the fixed line telephony market.

As telecommunications markets continue to converge (i.e. move together) with the development of broadband internet services, we now see a variety of different companies operating in the same competitive marketspace e.g. Orange, BT, AOL, Time Warner, and many others. With the development of VOIP (voice over internet protocol), an internet telecommunication voice transmission standard, fixed line telecommunications is already becoming a commodity and firms operating in the area will increasing look to develop value-added services such as online TV (content-on-demand), interactive gaming, and web conferencing services. In 2006, Ebay Inc.—the online auction powerhouse—purchased Skype, the free online communication service, so that it could enhance its auction services by allowing auctioneers and buyers to talk to one another. However, this same competence also allows Ebay Inc. to offer telecommunications services more generally.

At the moment, most countries' fixed line operators are still holding on to the vast majority of their subscribers even though much cheaper alternatives are beginning to appear in the market (e.g. cable, internet, fusion telephone plans incorporating mobile and fixed lines). It takes time for consumers to become aware of new product and service possibilities and obtain the necessary information to allow them to make a decision over whether or not to switch to an alternative offering (see Chapters 3 and 18). Consumers consider the switching costs associated with such a decision, which in turn affects their propensity to substitute the product or service for another offering. They consider the relative price performance of one offering over another. For example, if we decide we wish to travel from Amsterdam to Paris, we can fly from Schipol airport to Charles de Gaulle airport, take the train, or drive (or hire a car and drive if we don't have one). We would consider the relative price differences (the flight is likely to be the most expensive but not always) and we would also factor into this decision how comfortable and convenient these different journeys were hypo-thetically before we finally make our choice. In analysing our place within an industry, it is fundamental that we consider what alternative product and service offerings exist in the marketplace which also meet, to a greater or lesser extent, our customers' needs.

Buyers

Companies should ask themselves how much of their sales go to one individual company. This is an important question because if one buying company purchases a large volume of product from the supplying company, as car manufacturers do from steel suppliers, it is likely to be able to demand price concessions (price/total purchases) when there are lots of competing suppliers in the marketplace relative to the proportion of buyers (buyer concentration versus firm concentration). Buyers may also decide to increase their bargaining power through **backward integration**. For instance, a company is said to have backward integrated when it moves into manufacturing the products or services it previously bought from its suppliers. Tesco—the British multiple retail grocer now operating in thirteen markets outside the UK—also sells financial services including debt and credit services to its customers, which it previously would have purchased from Visa and MasterCard merchant operators. Since customers have tended to pay for many years now using credit/debit cards rather than cash, Tesco has lowered its transaction costs by setting up its own credit/debit services. Nevertheless, for the other suppliers in a market, it means that they effectively have a new entrant into the market and hence a new competitor. Another factor impacting upon a buyer's bargaining power is how price sensitive that particular company is (see Chapter 10). Dependent on their own trading circumstances, some companies may be more price sensitive than others. If they are more price sensitive and there are lots of competing suppliers, you may well lose their business. Most companies try to enhance other factors associated with an offering (e.g. after-sales service, product/service customization) to try to reduce a client company's **price sensitivity**. When analysing an industry, we should understand the bargaining power that buyers have with their suppliers since this can impact upon the price charged and the volumes sold or total revenue earned.

Suppliers

In analysing a particular industry, we should determine how suppliers oper-ate within a particular industry and the extent of their bargaining power. For instance, if a small number of suppliers operate within an industry with a large number of competitors, the suppliers have the stronger bargaining advantage. Conversely, in an industry where there are a large number of suppliers with few competing companies, the buying companies have the bargaining advantage. We should also consider whether or not the suppliers are providing unique compon-ents, products, services which may enhance their bargaining situation. In some industries, suppliers increase their market dominance by forward integrating (e.g. a toy manufacturer setting up a retail outlet to sell its own products). Forward integration not only allows a company to control its own supply chains better but also allows it to sell at lower prices, thereby increasing sales vis-à-vis competitors and profit from increased retail sales as well. Equally, if companies face high switching costs, economic, resource, and time costs associated with using another supplier, then a supplier has stronger bargaining power as a result with that particular company.

Competitors

To analyse an industry, we develop an outline of which companies are operating within that particular industry. For example, in the UK cosmetic sector, the market leading cosmetic manufacturers include: Avon European Holdings Ltd, Estée Lauder Cosmetics Ltd, L'Oréal (UK) Ltd, Procter & Gamble Ltd, the Unilever Group, and large retailers such as Boots Group plc, The Body Shop International plc, and Superdrug Stores plc. In undertaking a competitor analysis we outline each company's structure (e.g. details of the main holding company, the individual business unit, any changes in ownership), current and future developments (these can often be gleaned from reading company prospectuses, websites and industry reports), and the company's latest financial results. We would be interested in calculating the market volumes and shares for each competitor, since market share is a key indication of company profitability and return on investment (Buzzell, Gale, and Sultan, 1975). (See also Market Insight 2.5 for the changing competitive landscape in the European airline industry.)

In analysing the competitors within an industry, we are interested in different types of goods and services that competitors offer in different market sectors. Clark and Montgomery (1999) call this process of identification of competitors the supply-based approach because it considers those firms who supply the same sorts of goods and services as your own firm. However, they identify another approach to competitor identification which they term the demand-based approach, identifying competitors based on customer attitudes and behaviour. Firms with similar offerings, as perceived by the customer, are regarded as competitors.

We are also interested in measuring market responses to any new strategy developments that our company initiates. While this might seem obvious, research indicates that companies do not tend to consider their competitors' strategies (what the authors call 'strategic competitive reasoning'), except occasionally in relation to pricing strategy, perhaps because—due to the substantial uncertainties involved in second-guessing competitors' reactions—they do not feel it is worth the effort (Montgomery, Moore, and Urbany, 2005). Generally, managers tended to name relatively few competitors, and needed to focus more on competitors as determined by customer requirements, reconsidering who their competitors were from time to time (Clark and Montgomery, 1999).

Critical Success Factors

In addition to undertaking industry analyses, it is important that we understand 'the rules of the game': in other words, how companies in an industry have to operate to survive and succeed. Typically, these 'rules' are unwritten. They can be regarded as critical success factors defined as 'the limited number of areas

European Rivals in the Sky

After deregulation of the European airlines industry in 1987, the industry changed substantially with the entrance and exit of low-cost carriers such as the successful Ryanair and EasyJet and the less successful Buzz (which was set up by KLM but subsequently bought by Ryanair) and Debonair (which went bust almost immediately). Since the early success of Ryanair and EasyJet, a whole host of companies have set up including GermanWings in Germany and WhizzAir from Hungary. Existing competitors within the market, such as Air France, Lufthansa, and British Airways, lost market share in the short-haul airline market as the low-cost carriers quite literally flew away with their business.

Low-cost airlines possess the competitive advantage of operating at significantly lower costs than their larger national counterparts, and since they entered the market have maintained their low-cost advantage, partly by operating lower wage costs, using flexible employment contracts, and far quicker airport turnaround times. Landing charge costs have been cut by flying to and from provincial, regional airports, e.g. EasyJet used Torp outside Oslo in Norway, Stansted near Cambridge in the UK, and Ciampino outside Rome in Italy. The low-cost airlines reduced channel marketing spend by cutting their reliance on travel agents, using the internet to generate customer traffic instead.

Business models also changed as the low-cost carriers emphasized very high load factors, no-frills services (including extra charges for baggage, meals, and other services), and in some cases the use of second-hand aircraft. National carriers have fought back by lowering their own cost structures and renouncing flight slots at airports on less profitable routes, e.g. as BA did in its Size and Shape Review in 2002, although it only returned to profitability in 2006 after eight years of successive losses on its short-haul operations.

Source: Done (2006).

1 What was the original barrier to entry for competitors to the EU short-haul airline market?

2 How did low-cost carriers alter the relationships between buyers and suppliers to airline companies operating in the short-haul airline market?

3 How strong is the threat of entry from new low-cost operators within the short-haul airline marketplace?

---

in which results, if they are satisfactory, will ensure successful competitive performance for the organisation' (Rochart, 1979) or as 'factors inside and outside the company which must be identified and reckoned with because they support or threaten the achievement of company objectives, or even the existence of the company' (Ferguson and Dickinson, 1982). In analysing the market for banking services, Chen (1999) suggests that there are four critical success factors, incorporating the following:

- Bank operations management—incorporating staff politeness, management ability of the bank manager, the speed of business handling, computerization capability, asset and liability management capability, and internal auditing and control capability.

- Bank marketing—incorporating the development of long-term relationship with customers, deposit acquisition, competitor analysis, and provision of staff incentivization.

RESEARCH INSIGHT 2.2

To take your learning further, you might wish to read this influential paper.

Porter, M. E. (1979), 'How competitive forces shape strategy', *Harvard Business Review*, 57, 2 (March – April), 137 – 45.

This paper was Porter's first public presentation of his ideas about industry analysis. They were subsequently reproduced in his book *Competitive Strategy: Techniques for Analysing Industries and Competitors*, published the following year by The Free Press of New York, and which has become the seminal work on industry analysis.

- Developing banking trademarks—incorporating bank reputation and image, bank location, and the size of the bank's branch retail network.
- Financial market management—incorporating the quantity and contents of service items, and taking advantage of government deregulation policy and the prosperous stock and securities markets (Chen, 1999).

Understanding the Internal Environment

An analysis of the internal environment of an organization is concerned with understanding and evaluating the capabilities and potential of the products, systems, human, marketing, and financial resources. An analysis of an organization's resources should not focus on the relative strength and weakness of a particular resource, but look at the absolute nature of the resource itself. As Thompson (1990) suggests, 'Resources are not strong or weak merely because they exist . . . their value depends upon how they are being managed, controlled and used.'

Attention here is given to two main elements, products and finance.

Product Portfolio Analysis

When managing a collection or portfolio of products, it is important to appreciate that understanding the performance of an individual product can often fail to give the appropriate insight. What is really important is an understanding about the relative performance of products. By creating a balance of old, mature, established, growing, and very new products, there is a better chance of delivering profits now and at some point in the future, when the current products cease to be attractive and, of course, profitable.

One of the popular methods for assessing the variety of businesses/products that an organization has involves the creation of a two-dimensional graphical picture of the comparative strategic positions. This technique is referred to as a product portfolio or portfolio matrix. The Boston Consulting Group (BCG) developed the

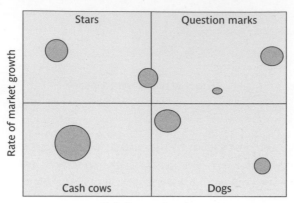

Figure 2.6
The Boston Box

Source: Reprinted from B. Hedley, 'Strategy and the business portfolio', *Long Range Planning*, 10, 1, 12. © 1977, with permission from Elsevier.

original idea and their matrix—the **Boston Box**, shown at Figure 2.6—is based on two key variables, market growth and relative market share (i.e. market share as a percentage of the share of the product's largest competitor, expressed as a fraction). Thus, a relative share of 0.8 means that the product achieves 80 per cent of the sales of the market leader's sales volume (or value, depending on which measure is used). This is not the strongest competitive position but not a weak position either. A relative market share of 1 means that the company shares market leadership with a competitor with an equal share. A relative market share of 2 means that the company has twice the market share of the nearest competitor.

In Figure 2.7, the vertical axis refers to the rate of market growth and the horizontal axis refers to a product's market strength, as measured by relative market share (as described above). The size of the circles represents the sales revenue generated by the product. Relative market share is generally regarded as high when you are the market leader (i.e. the relative market share is 1 or greater). Determining whether or not market growth rate is high or low is more problematic and depends on the industry to some extent. In some industries, a market growth rate of 5 per cent might be regarded as high, wheras in others this might be 10 per cent. The benchmark between high and low is however often taken to be 10 per cent.

Question marks (also known as 'problem children') are products that exist in growing markets but have low market share. As a result there is negative cash flow and they are unprofitable. Stars are most probably market leaders but their growth has to be financed through fairly heavy levels of investment. Cash cows on the other hand exist in fairly stable, low-growth markets and require little ongoing investment. Their very high market share draws both positive cash flows and high levels of profitability. Dogs experience low growth, low market share, and generate negative cash flows. These indicators suggest that many of them are operating in declining markets and they have no real long-term future. Divestment need not occur just because of low share. In March 2007, Procter & Gamble decided to leave the paper business, and this involved selling off Bounty, their kitchen roll brand, and Charmin, their toilet tissue brand. They sold the business because of falling performance and because they did not see how they could achieve number 1 or 2 position in the different paper markets. Instead, they sold the business to the main rivals, SCA (Godsell, 2007).

Portfolio analysis is an important analytical tool as it draws attention to the cash flow and investment characteristics of each of a firm's products and indicates

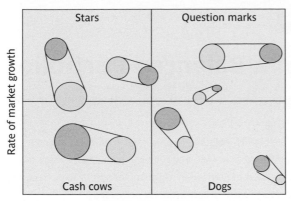

Figure 2.7
Present and future positions in the BCG matrix

Source: Reprinted from B. Hedley, 'Strategy and the business portfolio', *Long Range Planning*, 10, 1, 12. © 1977, with permission from Elsevier.

how financial resources can be manoeuvred to attain optimal strategic performance over the long term. Essentially, excess cash generated by cash cows should be utilized to develop question marks and stars, which are unable to support themselves. This enables stars to become cash cows and self-supporting. Dogs should only be retained as long as they contribute to positive cash flow and do not restrict the use of assets and resources elsewhere in the business. Once they do they should be divested or ejected from the portfolio.

By plotting all of a company's products onto the grid it becomes visually easy to appreciate just how well balanced the product portfolio is. An unbalanced portfolio would be one that has too many products clustered in one or two quadrants. Where products are distributed equally, or at least are not clustered in any one area, and where market shares and cash flows equate with their market position, it is said that the portfolio is financially healthy and well balanced.

By analysing the product portfolio in this way it becomes possible to project possible strategies and their outcomes. These are shown in Figure 2.7.

Portfolio Issues

Portfolio analysis is an important guide to strategic development, if only because it forces answers to questions such as:

● How fast will the market grow?

● What will be our market share?

RESEARCH INSIGHT 2.3

To take your learning further, you might wish to read this influential paper.

Day, G. (1977), 'Diagnosing the product portfolio', *Journal of Marketing*, April, 29–38.

Day outlines in this very readable article how managers should evaluate the relative performance of products within a portfolio in order to develop appropriate marketing strategies. He concludes that portfolio analysis is a useful guide—but not substitute—for strategy development.

Drinking the Fruits of a Balanced Portfolio

Britvic is the UK's second biggest soft drinks manufacturer with many of its brands positioned as number 1 or 2 in their respective sub-categories.

Britvic's product portfolio includes stills and carbonates brands, including Robinson's, Pepsi, 7 Up, Drench, Tango, J$_2$O, Britvic, Fruit Shoot, R. White's, and Pennine Spring to name a few. Britivic has tried to develop the breadth and depth of its portfolio so that it can target consumer demand in all the major soft drinks categories, through all relevant distribution channels, and across a wide range of consumption occasions.

Britvic has a successful long-standing relationship with Pepsico that was renewed in 2004 for a further fifteen years. This relationship gives Britvic the exclusive right to distribute the Pepsi and 7 Up brands in Great Britain and access to all new carbonated drinks developed by Pepsico for distribution in Great Britain.

The breadth of Britvic's 'balanced' portfolio of market-leading brands, the existing customer relationships, and its scale of operations provide Britvic with a solid base for growth. Britvic believes that in order to achieve the company's objectives it places great emphasis on the portfolio and the need to develop it through innovation to meet evolving consumer preferences. Its marketing strategy will continue to focus on driving brand

J$_2$O is one of Britvic's drinks brands

Britvic Soft Drinks

awareness around its major growth products through advertising and promotion and using its distribution network to further increase availability of its products.

1 How might Britvic maintain its portfolio in the light of strong competition from its rivals? Are there other types of soft drink brands that it could acquire?

2 How might use of the internet help Britvic achieve its marketing goals?

3 The phrase 'consumption occasions' was used in the Market Insight. Can you think of three different occasions when Robinson's or Pepsi might be the preferred drink?

- What investment will be required?
- How can a balanced portfolio be created from this point? (See also Market Insight 2.6.)

However, the questions posed and the answers generated through use of the Boston Box do not produce marketing strategies. As with all analytical tools and methodologies, the BCG provides strategic indicators, not solutions. It is management's task to consider information from a variety of sources and then make decisions based upon their judgement.

Financial Analysis

One of the most important tools for measuring the performance and strength of an organization is financial analysis. This is often the first (and regrettably only) tool managers use when reviewing performance. This form of analysis is useful to managers as it provides a means of measuring the performance of current strategies with those of the past. Finance and benchmarking techniques also allow measurement of an organization's performance against competitors. Suppliers can also use financial data to measure risk, as it can help them to decide whether to start or continue trading with a customer. Finally, investors use financial analysis to help examine the recent and potential performance of an organization and the level of risk.

The reason to undertake an internal financial analysis is to determine the level of financial resource available to support and sustain marketing strategies. This is not necessarily a matter of just setting a budget. It is a financial appraisal that helps to shape the direction and intensity of marketing strategy. For example, a growth strategy based on product development is unlikely to be successful if there are insufficient resources to fund R&D, product development, and to launch into new markets.

Marketing Audit

In order to make sense of all the information that has been collected, considered, and analysed during the strategic market analysis part of the marketing strategy

| Environmental audit—external and performance environments |
| Marketing strategy audit—mission, goals, strategy |
| Marketing organization audit—structure, personnel |
| Marketing systems audit—information, planning, and control systems |
| Marketing function audits—products, services, prices, distribution, promotion |

Figure 2.8
Dimensions of a
marketing audit

process, a marketing audit is normally undertaken. Just as a financial audit considers the financial health of an organization, so the marketing audit considers its marketing health. In particular, it brings together views about the three environments. First, it considers the external opportunities and threats, where management have little or no control. Second, it considers the nature, characteristics, and any changes occurring within the performance environment, where management have partial influence. Third, the audit reviews the quality and potential of the organization's products, marketing systems, resources, and capabilities, as part of the internal environment, where there is full control. The topics normally undertaken as part of the marketing audit are shown at Figure 2.8.

The audit covers the marketing environment, an organization's objectives and strategies, its marketing programmes and performance, plus the organization itself and the relevant marketing systems and procedures. The reason for undertaking a marketing audit is that it brings together critical information, identifies weaknesses in order that they can be corrected, and provides a platform on which to build marketing strategy.

The marketing audit can be undertaken either by an internal team, led by a senior manager, or if a more objective interpretation is desired, an outside consultant can be used. Whoever conducts the audit it should be undertaken on a regular, annual basis and be regarded as a positive activity that can feed into marketing strategy. Marketing audits should not be instigated in response to a crisis but undertaken on a regular, annual basis.

Chapter Summary

To consolidate your learning, the key points from this chapter are summarized below:

- Identify and define the three key areas of the marketing environment.

  The marketing environment incorporates the external environment, the performance environment, and the internal environment. The external environment incorporates macroenvironmental factors which are largely uncontrollable and which an organization generally cannot influence. The performance environment incorporates key factors within an industry which impact upon strategic decision making. The internal environment is controllable and is the principal means, through its resource base, by which an organization influences its strategy.

- Describe the key characteristics associated with the marketing environment.

    The external environment consists of the political, social, and technological influences, and organizations have relatively little influence on each of these. The performance environment consists of the competitors, suppliers, and indirect service providers who shape the way an organization achieves its objectives. Here, organizations have a much stronger level of influence. The internal environment concerns the resources, processes, and policies an organization manages in order that it can attempt to achieve its goals. These elements can be influenced directly by an organization.

- Explain PESTLE analysis and show how it is used to understand the external environment.

    We considered the various components of the external marketing environment in detail using the PESTLE acronym which includes the following factors: political, economic, socio-cultural, technological, legal, and ecological. It is important to note that some of these factors are more important than others in any particular industry. We use the acronym to identify possible factors which may impact upon any particular organization.

- Explain the environmental scanning process.

    The environmental scanning process consists of the data-gathering phase, the environmental interpretation/analysis phase, and the strategy formulation phase. The three processes are interlinked but over time, more attention is focused on each one more than the others so that at the end of the process, greater effort is expended on using knowledge gleaned from the external and competitive environments to formulate strategy.

- Analyse the performance environment using an appropriate model.

    The most common technique used to analyse the performance environment is Porter's Five Forces Model of Competitive Analysis. He concludes that the more intense the rivalry between the industry players, the lower will be their overall performance. On the other hand, the lower the rivalry the greater will be the performance of the industry players. Porter's Five Forces comprise (1) suppliers, (2) buyers, (3) new entrants, (4) competitors, and (5) substitutes.

- Understand the importance of analysing an organization's internal environment and identify the key resources and capabilities.

    An organization's principal resources relate to the product portfolio that it carries and the financial resources at its disposal. We use product portfolio analysis, specifically the Boston Box, to help us determine whether products are stars, dogs, question marks, or cash cows, each category of which provides differing levels of cash flow and resource requirements to develop. It is important to undertake a marketing audit as a preliminary measure in order to allow proper development of marketing strategy.

 Visit the **Online Resource Centre** that accompanies this book to read more information relating to the marketing environment: www.oxfordtextbooks.co.uk/orc/baines/

❓ Review Questions

1. What are the three main marketing environments?

2. What are the three stages of the environmental scanning process?

3. How might changes in the political environment affect marketing strategy?

4. How might changes in the economic environment affect marketing strategy?

5. How might changes in the socio-cultural environment affect marketing strategy?

6. How might changes in the technological environment affect marketing strategy?

7. How might changes in the legal environment affect marketing strategy?

8. How might changes in the ecological environment affect marketing strategy?

9. What are Porter's Five Forces?

10. What is product portfolio analysis and why is it useful?

❓ Discussion Questions

1. Having read the Case Insight at the beginning of this chapter, how would you advise Michelin Tyres to react to the rapid uptake of cheap imported Indian and Chinese tyres in the UK market? What strategy would you recommend?

2. Read the Market Insight 2.4 Who Ate All the Bars? example. Search the internet for further information on the obesity debate, and answer the following questions:

   (a) What changes have taken place in the external environment that have brought about the obesity debate?

   (b) How should Cadbury Schweppes ensure that they keep up to date with trends in consumer lifestyles, government legislation, and competitor new product development?

   (c) What strategies in relation to product development and promotion could Cadbury Schweppes adopt to ensure that they maintain their market dominance in the chocolate countline market?

   (d) Why do you think Cadbury's recently acquired the organic chocolate maker Green and Black's?

3. Undertake an environmental analysis using PESTLE, by surfing the internet for appropriate information and by using available market research reports, for each of the following markets:

   (a) The pharmaceutical market (e.g. you might be Pfizer, GlaxoSmithKline, Novartis, or AstraZeneca).

   (b) The telecommunications market (e.g. you might be Orange, NTT (Nippon Telegraph and Telecom), British Telecom (BT), China Telecom, or AT&T (American Telegraph and Telecom).

   (c) The financial services market for retail banking (e.g. you might be Citibank, Banco Santander, HSBC).

4 Analyse the ecological marketing environment for the multiple retail grocery industry in a country of your choice. Look specifically at socio-cultural patterns and trends in eating habits. You may surf the internet for appropriate documents and market intelligence material to help you develop your arguments.

5 Read the Market Insight 2.4 Who Ate All the Bars? example. Using the data in Table 2.1, identify the relative market shares of the various products in this market. Calculate the market growth rate by determining the difference in sales between 2004 and 2005 for the top fifteen brands overall. Then draw up a Boston Box to illustrate the product portfolio for this market for each of the key companies and their brands.

References

Abrams, F., and Butler, K. (1997), 'How Blair's ear was bent by the king of Formula One', *The Independent*, Thursday, 6 November, section 7.

Aguilar, F. Y. (1967), *Scanning the Business Environment*, New York: Macmillan.

Albright, K. S. (2004), 'Environmental scanning: radar for success', *Information Management Journal*, May–June, 38–45.

ASA (2006), 'Non-broadcast Adjudication: Unilever Bestfoods UK Ltd and Flora pro.active', London: Advertising Standards Authority, available at www.asa.org.uk/asa/adjudications/non_broadcast/Adjudication+Details.htm?Adjudication id=41460.

Baxter, S. (2006), 'Hispanics nudge US population to 300 m', *Sunday Times*, 9 July, 23.

Beal, R. M. (2000), 'Competing effectively: environmental scanning, competitive strategy, and organisational performance in small manufacturing firms', *Journal of Small Business Administration*, January, 27–47.

Benady, D. (2006), 'Wonky at the choc factory', *Marketing Week*, 9 March.

Blackwell, G. (2007), 'The Skype's the limit', *Canadian Business*, 12 February, 10–12.

Brownlie, D. (1994), 'Organising for environmental scanning: orthodoxies and reformations', *Journal of Marketing Management*, 10, 703–22.

Business Insights (2006), *Innovation in Natural and Organic Food and Drinks*, May, accessed at www.bi-interactive.com/index.aspx.

Buzzell, R. D., Gale, B. T., and Sultan, R. G. M (1975), 'Market share—a key to profitability', *Harvard Business Review*, January–February, 97–106.

Chandy, R. K., Prabhu, J. C., and Antia, K. D. (2003), 'What will the future bring? Dominance. technology expectations and radical innovation', *Journal of Marketing*, 67 (July), 1–18.

Chen, T.-Y. (1999), 'Critical success factors for various strategies in the banking industry', *International Journal of Bank Marketing*, 17, 2, 83–91.

Clark, B. H., and Montgomery, D. B. (1999), 'Managerial identification of competitors', *Journal of Marketing*, July, 67–83.

DoH (2004), 'Choosing Health: Making Healthy Choices Easier', *White Paper, Cm 6374*, London: The Stationery Office.

Done, K. (2006), 'BA finds the right size and shape', *Financial Times*, 19 May.

Ferguson, C. R., and Dickinson, R. (1982), 'Critical success factors for directors in the eighties', *Business Horizons*, May–June, 14–18.

Godsell, M. (2007), 'Not number one, not interested', *Marketing*, 21 March, 18.

Gower, I. (ed.) (2005), *Cosmetics and Fragrances Market Report 2005*, London: Keynote Limited.

Harris, P., Gardner, H., and Vetter, N. (1999), '"Goods over God" lobbying and political marketing: a case study of the campaign by the Shopping Hours Reform Council to change Sunday trading laws in Britain', in B. I. Newman (ed.), *Handbook of Political Marketing*, London: Sage Publications.

Health Canada (1999), *Information Research on Labelling*, Quebec, available at www.hc-sc.gc.ca.

Hillman, A., Keim, G. D., and Schuler, D. (2004), 'Corporate political activity: a review and research agenda', *Journal of Management*, 30, 6, 837–57.

Kewley, S. (2002), 'Japanese lobbying in the EU', in R. Pedler (ed.), *European Union Lobbying*, Basingstoke: Palgrave Press.

Kharif, O. (2006), 'Bad vibes of VOIP', *Independent on Sunday*, 12 February, 9.

Lawrence, P. (1993), 'Developments in European Business in the 1990S: the Single European Market in context', *Journal of Marketing Management*, 9, 3–9.

Levitt, T. (1960), 'Marketing myopia', *Harvard Business Review*, July–August, 45–56.

Lim, J.-S., Sharkey, T. W., and Kim, K. I. (1996), 'Competitive environmental scanning and export involvement: an initial enquiry', *International Marketing Review*, 13, 1, 65–80.

Ling, J. (2006), 'Going anywhere exotic?', *The Marketer*, July–August, 25.

May, R. C., Stewart, W. H. Jr., and Sweo, R. (2000), 'Environmental scanning behaviour in a transitional economy: evidence from Russia', *Academy of Management Journal*, 43, 3, 403–27.

Mintel (2007), *Telecoms Retailing—UK*, May, London: Mintel International Group, available at www.mintel.com, accessed 17 June 2007.

Moloney, K., and Jordan, G. (1996), 'Why companies hire lobbyists', *Service Industries Journal*, 16, 2, 242–58.

Montgomery, D. B., Moore, M. C., and Urbany, J. E. (2005), 'Reasoning about competitive reactions: evidence from executives', *Marketing Science*, 24, 1, 138–49.

Morris, P. (2001), 'Dealing with Whitehall and Westminster', Hawkesmere Seminar on Lobbying, Berners Hotel, London, 4 April.

Murray, S. (2006), 'Confusion reigns over labelling', *Financial Times*, Special Report on Responsible Business, 2.

O'Connell, J. J., and Zimmerman, J. W. (1979), 'Scanning the international environment', *California Management Review*, 22, 2, 15–23.

Orsato, R. J. (2006), 'Competitive environmental strategies: when does it pay to be green?', *California Management Review*, 48, 2 (Winter), 127–43.

Porter, M. (1979), 'How competitive forces shape strategy', *Harvard Business Review*, March–April.

Rao, P. M. (2005), 'Sustaining competitive advantage in a high-technology environment: a strategic marketing perspective', *Advances in Competitiveness Research*, 13, 1, 33–47.

Rochart, J. F. (1982), 'Chief executives define their own data needs', *Harvard Business Review*, March–April, 81–92.

Sclater, I. (2005), 'The digital dimension', *The Marketer*, May, 22–3.

Snoddy, R. (2006), 'Brands face £70bn pink conundrum', *Marketing* (UK), 15 February.

Tempest, M. (2002), 'New claims over Ecclestone links', *The Guardian*, 15 April.

Thompson, K. M. (1990), *The Employee Revolution: Corporate Internal Marketing*, London: Pitman.

UN Population Division (2005), *World Population Prospects: The 2004 Revision*, available at www.un.org/esa/population/publications/WPP2004/wpp2004.htm, accessed 22 July 2006.

Valdiserri, T. (2002), 'Pink market needs respect', *Precision Marketing*, 8 March.

Wall Street Journal (2001), 'Cost of developing drugs found to rise', 3 December.

Webster, P. (2002), 'How Blair aide made the first move to win Ecclestone's £1m', *The Times*, 15 April, 1.

Wilson, R. W. (1977), 'The effect of technological environment and product rivalry on R&D effort and licensing of inventions', *Review of Economics and Statistics*, 59, 2 (May), 171–9.

3

Marketing Psychology and Consumer Buying Behaviour

The only way to know how customers see your business is to look at it through their eyes.

Daniel R. Scroggin, CEO, TGI Friday's Inc.

Learning Outcomes

After reading this chapter, you will be able to:

✔ Understand how consumers respond to the diffusion of innovations.

✔ Explain the consumer product acquisition process.

✔ Explain the processes involved in human perception, learning, and memory in relation to consumer choice.

✔ Understand the importance of personality and motivation in consumer behaviour.

✔ Describe opinions, attitudes, and values and how they relate to consumer behaviour.

✔ Explain how reference groups influence consumer behaviour.

Tyrrells Potato Chips produce the more sophisticated crisp and sell it at a premium price with the promise of quality. We speak to Will Chase to find out more.

Will Chase for Tyrrells Potato Chips

Tyrrells Potato Chips was launched in 2002, after potato farmer William Chase decided to branch out into the premium chip world. Having previously been a struggling potato farmer, growing potatoes for a number of different retailers, he decided to travel abroad to learn more about the crisp-making business, to return to Herefordshire to set up on his own farm.

Fuelled by a desire to get closer to the end customer, William set about developing the more sophisticated crisp. He sliced the potatoes more thickly, so that they maintained their original taste and natural juices and kept their natural starches. This meant they absorb less oil, and the Tyrrells Potato Chip was born. They are enjoyed by the discerning buyer and bought at a premium price to reflect their superior quality and flavour.

With increased education and a growing concern about the rising levels of obesity, standard crisp sales have slowed over the last five years, so Will Chase was facing a challenge. Help was at hand: although the traditional market for crisps was in decline, premium crisps were on the up—in 2002 they represented 21% but were now increasing to 29% of the market volume. In addition to this, the demographic of the crisp eater was changing: women were beginning to munch on low-fat crisps balancing out the male–female split (Mintel, 2007).

Indeed, we have managed to revamp the image of crisps as being 'cheap and greasy', attracting a large number of 'ABC1' consumers (i.e. managerial and clerical workers), in contrast to the traditional crisp buyers who tended to come from socio-economic groups C2 and D (i.e. semi-clerical and unskilled manual workers). We were pulling in a wealthier purchaser who was older and well versed in ethics and environmental issues.

Since its launch in 2002 Tyrrells has developed a trade customer base of over 4,000 independent retail customers including prestigious food retailers like Harrods, Fortnum & Masons, and Selfridges. This network has been developed through direct sales by a small sales force who pride themselves on building a personal relationship with each of their customers. We offer in-store tastings when new flavours come out and keep in touch with a quarterly newsletter too.

An advert for Tyrrells Potato Chips

Tyrrells Potato Chips

: *Tyrrells is on a winning streak.*

Tyrrells is on a winning streak. With a premium product and a growing market share, and increasing demand, we face a difficult decision now, on how to grow the business whilst retaining the unique selling point of being a local Herefordshire farmer.

Tyrrells Potato Chips sell into all socio-economic groups, but are more attractive to the wealthier consumer. How would you use your knowledge of consumer buying behaviour in this market to grow the business across a wider range of socio-economic groups?

Introduction

What selection process did you go through to decide which university marketing course you were going to study? How do you decide which restaurant to go to, or which movie to see, and why? Have you ever considered why and how we buy things? In this chapter, we explore consumer buying behaviour.

We consider business-to-business buying behaviour (how companies buy things from other companies) in Chapter 16, because business-to-business buying behaviour is so different because of its context. We consider cognitions (thoughts), **perceptions** (how we see things), and learning (how we memorize techniques and knowledge). These are processes which are fundamental in explaining how consumers think and learn about products and brands. As consumers, we are always learning. Learning about goods and services is no different from learning about concepts in general. Consider how we find out about a new product launch, e.g. the iPod. We don't just know about it intuitively, we have to learn about how it differs from existing music player systems; its relative benefits and disadvantages in terms of product features, price, and where it is available.

We discuss the concepts of personality and motivation to help you understand how these psychological concepts affect how we buy. We also discuss opinions, attitudes, and values, to give you an introductory understanding of how we are persuaded by **reference groups**. These are important considerations in marketing because goods and services are often designed to appeal to particular types of people. Banks target their personal accounts at us based on our personalities and motivations. Fast-moving consumer goods companies constantly bombard us with images of celebrity endorsers, who act as our reference groups for a wide variety of goods and services. Marketing comes alive when it is interlinked into the fabric of our social lives. Finally, we consider how **social class**, lifestyles, and our stage in the lifecycle influences consumer behaviour.

Consumer Behaviour: Operational versus Socio-Psychological

The rise in importance of consumption began shortly after the 1950s, as citizens in countries around the world began to prosper in relative peace after the Second World War, and the industrial companies who were part of the war effort turned their attention from producing military equipment and supplies to producing consumer and industrial goods. At this time, consumers (e.g. the cinema-goer or the holidaymaker) were generally thought to be rational beings, according to **neoclassical economics** theory, individually maximizing their satisfaction (what economists call **utility**), based on a cost–benefit analysis of price and availability. The consumer was thought to be carefully measuring whether or not the benefits of a good or service, in terms of its functional values, outweighed its costs.

This point is illustrated by considering an example from the Soviet Union (Russia, pre-1990). In such a strictly regulated, planned economy, products were produced

RESEARCH INSIGHT 3.1

To take your learning further, you might wish to read this influential paper.

Holbrook, M. B., and Hirschman, E. C. (1982), 'The experiential aspects of consumption: consumer fantasies, feelings and fun', *Journal of Consumer Research*, 9, 132–40.

This influential article reconsidered how we perceive consumer behaviour, moving marketing thought away from the idea that customer behaviour is purely rational and towards a greater understanding of the irrational content of consumer decision making including the importance of our feelings and fantasies, and whether or not we were having fun. The authors developed a useful model contrasting the differences between the information-processing (i.e. rational) and the experiential view (i.e. irrational) perspectives of consumer behaviour.

to meet basic functional needs. Nevertheless, consumers sought out televisions with specific factory numbers, produced in certain factories in certain regions or countries, because they were more reliable and produced better pictures. So, even when a country's government tries to squeeze out human desires, those desires to possess, and possess the best of what is available, continue anyway. These could be termed operational buying motives and are linked to rational purchasing decisions derived from physical performance of the product (Udell, 1964).

By contrast, in modern-day Europe, people are more likely to indulge socio-psychological buying motives. These are linked to irrational buying motives and stem from a buyer's social and psychological interpretation of the product and its performance. Consider our motivations to purchase particular types of music, for example. Let's take the example of Madonna's latest release. A CD is not bought because of what it is. After all, it's just an optical disc or MP3 file. Nor is the box in which it comes particularly useful, except to provide us with information about the disc when we are deciding to buy it or not. The insert on the other hand may be useful once the item is bought because it may contain some details about our pop princess and the tracks on the album. Instead, we are likely to buy her album not because of what it is, but what the music represents to us. In other words, we buy the music because of how it makes us feel (e.g. happy, sad, elated). Perhaps we associate that music with a particular boyfriend, girlfriend, or partner, experience, time, or way of being. We may also buy the music because of what it represents to us (e.g. coolness, fun), a quality which is dependent on how significant others (e.g. our friends) also feel about the music.

Diffusion Theory

Although we know that consumers may buy using both operational and socio-psychological motives when purchasing, not all customers adopt new products at the same speed or time. Their different attitude to risk, their level of education,

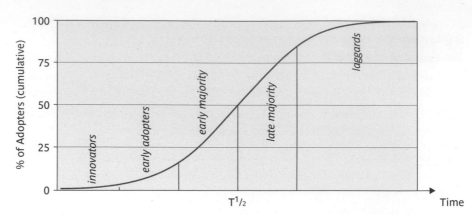

experience, education, and needs, means that different groups of customers adopt new products at different and varying speeds. The rate at which a market adopts an innovation is referred to as the process of diffusion (Rogers, 1962). According to Rogers, there are five categories of adopters (see Figure 3.1) as follows:

- **Innovators**: These are an important group because they are required to kick-start the adoption process. These people like new ideas, are often well educated, young, confident, and financially strong. This means they are more likely to take risks associated with new products. Being an innovator in one product category, such as photography, does not mean they are an innovator in other categories. Innovative attitudes and behaviour can be specific to one or two areas of interest.

- **Early Adopters**: This group are characterized by the high percentage of opinion leaders. These people are very important for speeding the adoption process. Consequently marketing communications need to be targeted at these people who in turn will use word-of-mouth communications to spread information. Although early adopters prefer to let innovators take all the risks, they enjoy being at the leading edge of innovation, tend to be younger than any other group, and above average in education. Other than innovators, this group takes more publications and consults more salespeople than all others.

- **Early Majority**: The main characteristic of this group is that they are more risk averse than the previous two groups. This group requires reassurance that the product works and has been proven in the market. They are above average in terms of age, education, social status, and income. Unlike the early adopters, they tend to wait for prices to fall and prefer more informal sources of information and are often prompted into purchase by other people who have already purchased.

- **Late Majority**: These people are sceptical of new ideas and only adopt new products because of social or economic factors. They take few publications and are below average in education, social status, and income.

- **Laggards**: This group of people are suspicious of all new ideas and their opinions are very hard to change. Of all the groups, laggards have the lowest income, social status, and education and take a long time to adopt an innovation, if at all.

Rogers illustrated how innovators generally represent 2.5 per cent of the buying population, early adopters around 13.5 per cent, early majority around 34 per cent, late majority 34 per cent, and laggards 16 per cent. His theory was subsequently validated by other researchers (see Bass, 1969). The rate of diffusion, according to Gatignon and Robertson (1985), is a function of (1) the speed at which sales occur (2) the pattern of diffusion as expressed in the shape of the curve, and (3) the size of the market. This means that diffusion does not occur at a constant or predictable speed, that it may be fast or slow. One of the tasks of marketing communications is to speed the process so that the return on the investment necessary to develop the innovation is achieved as quickly and as efficiently as possible.

Marketing managers need to ensure that these variables are considered when attempting to understand and predict the diffusion process. However, it is likely that a promotional campaign targeted at innovators and the early majority, and geared to stimulating word-of-mouth communications, will be more successful than if these variables are ignored.

In his best-selling book *The Tipping Point*, journalist Malcolm Gladwell (2002) compares the diffusion of goods, services, and ideas to an epidemic, spreading like a virus. He points out the important role of three categories of people who help the diffusion process.

- 'Mavens' (see Feick and Price, 1987)—who have a voracious appetite for product and service information, passing this to others within a community;
- 'Connectors'—whose social networks are extensive, bringing people within a community together; and
- 'Salesmen'—who specialize in persuading people to adopt new goods, services, and ideas.

The difficulty in marketing is identifying these important groups of people. Increasingly, companies are using word-of-mouth marketing techniques to promote goods and services, particularly through blogs and websites where a selection of consumers are provided with free samples and asked to write their experiences on user websites. (See Market Insight 3.1 for a case study of the diffusion process in Zaragoza, Spain.)

RESEARCH INSIGHT 3.2

To take your learning further, you might wish to read this influential book.

Rogers, E. M. (1962), *Diffusion of Innovations*, New York: Free Press.

An insightful book describing how consumers respond to the release of new products. While innovators are eager to try new goods, services, and ideas and tend to be risk takers, early adopters tend to be more linked into the social system and slightly less risk taking in their personalities. The early majority group are more deliberative, purchasing innovations only after substantial consideration. The late majority group are even more sceptical and risk averse, purchasing innovations only when necessary. Finally, laggards, the most socially conservative and risk-averse group of all, represent those who are traditional and suspicious of new ideas and change.

Diffusion of Consumer Durables in Spain

In a study undertaken to evaluate the acceptance and diffusion of consumer durables in Zaragoza in Spain, researchers found rates of adoption differed for selected consumer durables (see Table 3.1). For example, different proportions of consumers bought refrigerators, washing machines, dishwashers, ovens, vitroceramic hobs, and microwave ovens at different times.

Table 3.1 Adoption of consumer durables in Zaragoza, Spain

Products	Innovators	Early adopters	Adoption timeline (yrs)	Early majority	Adoption timeline (yrs)	Late majority	Adoption timeline (yrs)	Laggards	Adoption timeline (yrs)
Refrigerator	1.7%	7.3%	4.2	33.3%	10.0	33.3%	10.0	24.4%	24.2
Washing machine	1.3%	7.2%	5.2	33.5%	13.2	33.5%	13.2	24.5%	31.6
Dishwasher	0.4%	18.7%	11.3	29.6%	6.2	29.6%	6.2	21.7%	23.7
Oven	1.1%	14.8%	7.6	30.8%	7.2	30.8%	7.2	22.5%	22.0
Vitroceramic hob	0.4%	20.0%	6.4	29.1%	2.5	29.1%	2.5	21.4%	11.4
Microwave oven	0.7%	19.2%	5.3	29.3%	2.4	29.3%	2.4	21.5%	10.1

Source: Martinez, Polo, and Flavian (1998). Reproduced with the kind permission of Emerald Group Publishing Ltd.

We define innovators as those consumers who buy a product as soon as it becomes available. Often people within this group have pre-ordered the product, where this is possible. If it's not, they tend to be the very first people in the queue!

What this study indicated is how the diffusion process was more rapid for products such as the vitroceramic hob, the dishwasher, and the microwave oven even though there was a relatively slow introduction period compared with the refrigerator and the washing machine. This study in the Spanish market provides evidence for the importance of advertising and publicity early on in the launch of new consumer durable goods. Generating word of mouth becomes important over time as consumers socialize each other into purchasing new products.

Source: Martinez, Polo, and Flavian (1998).

1 Why do you think more people are in the innovator category for refrigerators than are in the innovator category for dishwashers?

2 Consider your own purchasing behaviour of high-technology goods. Are you an innovator, early adopter, or in the early majority or late majority for most items that you purchase?

3 What would you expect the diffusion adoption timeline to be for Apple's iPod product? Why do you think this?

Product Acquisition

We know that buyers have different approaches to buying new goods and services, fitting into different categories of buying type based on the length of time a product has been available on the market, but what is going on in their minds, individually, in deciding whether or not to buy—or in the case of a not-for-profit consumer acquire—a particular good or service?

The first question is how do products (i.e. both goods and services) move from producers to consumers? Initially, scholars presented a partial theory of marketing which outlined how finished goods (e.g. footballs) are developed from their raw materials (e.g. leather, stitches) through a process of transactions between buyer and seller, called **transvections**, through the supply chain. For example, in a simplified process we might see the leather sold by a farmer as cow skin to a leather manufacturer who dries, cures, and colours it, before selling it on to a football manufacturer who then stitches it, and then perhaps sells it on to a sporting good wholesaler/exporter.

In this example, transactions relate to all the individual relationships between various buyers and sellers as the raw materials are transformed into a product. The transvection relates to the sequence of transactions, seen from the seller's perspective all the way through the supply chain process. Alderson and Martin's (1965) theory of transactions and transvections focused marketing for the first time on the buyer–seller relationship. Since this theory was first put forward, simpler models of buying behaviour which focus more on the consumer's perspective have been developed, which we consider next.

The Consumer Product Acquisition Process

The consumer product acquisition process consists of six distinct stages (see Figure 3.2). The model outlined in this figure is particularly useful because it highlights the importance, and indicates the distinctiveness, of the product selection and re-evaluation phases in the process. We use the term acquisition rather than purchase in this instance because not all products are paid for, in financial terms, e.g. not-for-profit environments. Consider the example of a government providing free higher education to its citizens (e.g. Germany, Scotland). In Figure 3.2, we see that the buying process is iterative, because each stage can lead back to any of the previous stages in the process or move forward to the next stage in the process.

Motive Development

The model begins when we decide we need to acquire a product. This involves the initial recognition that some sort of problem needs solving. In order to begin to solve the problem, we must first become aware of if. So, for example, when you realized that you needed a book for your marketing course, you acquired this one. Your motive to buy a book developed as you realized you needed something to supplement the lectures you received on your course. But how did you buy it and what thought processes did you go through?

To take your learning further, you might wish to read this influential book.

Howard, J. A., and Sheth, J. N. (1969), *The Theory of Buyer Behavior*, New York: John Wiley and Sons.

Howard and Sheth's theory of the buyer behaviour process provided original and powerful insights into the psychology of the buying process by considering how learning theory can be applied to consumer behaviour. The buyer behaviour process consists of stimulus inputs (e.g. price, quality, service, and social settings) which feed into a perceptual process where the inputs are received and considered, and which then interact with a person's **attitudes** and motives and existing **choice criteria**. This may or may not lead to purchase **intention**, and other outputs, including changes in attention given to the product, extent to which the consumer understands what the brand stands for (**brand comprehension**), and their attitude towards the brand (whether they like it or not).

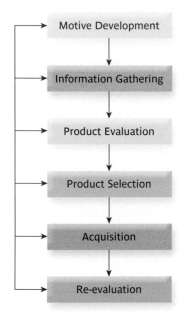

Figure 3.2
The consumer product acquisition process

Another example might be a female consumer who decides that she needs to buy a new dress for a party, or because she's grown tired of the old one, or because she thinks it's out of fashion, or to cheer herself up, or for a special occasion (e.g. engagement or hen party), or a whole host of other reasons.

Information Gathering

The next stage in the process requires us to look for alternative ways of solving our problems. In the case of the dress buyer, she might ask herself where she bought her last dress, how much dresses generally cost, what the different retail outlets are that sell dresses, and where they are located. She might also ask herself where she normally buys party dresses, what kinds of party dresses are in fashion at the moment, perhaps where there are sales on at present, and which store staff treat her best when she visits them.

Our search for a solution to solve our problem may be active, an **overt search**, or passive, in other words, we are open to ways of solving our problem but we are not actively looking for information to help us (Howard and Sheth, 1969). The search for information may be internal (in other words, we consider what we already know about the problem we have and the products we might buy to solve our problem) or external (we don't know enough about our problem and so we seek advice or supplementary information to help us decide).

Product Evaluation

Once we feel that we have all the information that we need to make a decision, we evaluate the products. But first we must determine the criteria we will use to rank the various products. These might be rational (e.g. based on cost) or irrational (e.g. based on desire). For example, the lady buying the party dress might ask herself which shop is the best value for money and which is the most fashionable retailer.

A consumer is said to have an **evoked set** of products in mind when they come to evaluate which particular product, brand, or service they want to solve their particular problem. So an evoked set for a consumer looking for a party dress might include Zara, Monsoon, Jigsaw, H&M, Mango (MNG elsewhere in the world), or Mexx, for instance. The more upmarket buyer might visit Anne Klein, DKNY, Gucci, Yves St Laurent, and Ferragamo, for instance.

Product Selection

In most cases, the product that we eventually select is the one that we evaluate as fitting our needs best beforehand. However, we might decide on a particular product away from where we buy or acquire it. For example, we might decide we want a haircut at one particular stylist but change our choice because the appointment we want is not available at the time we want. In the case of the lady buying a party dress, she may have checked the stock of a shop online and made her selection then but when she turned up at the retailer to try it on, the dress she wanted was not available and so she decides on an alternative there and then at the point of purchase. Thus, product selection is actually a separate stage in the product acquisition process, distinct from product evaluation, because there are times when we must re-evaluate what we buy or acquire because what we want is not available, for one reason or another.

Acquisition

Once selection has taken place, different approaches to product acquisition might exist. For example, what we want may be a routine purchase, e.g. a can of Coke

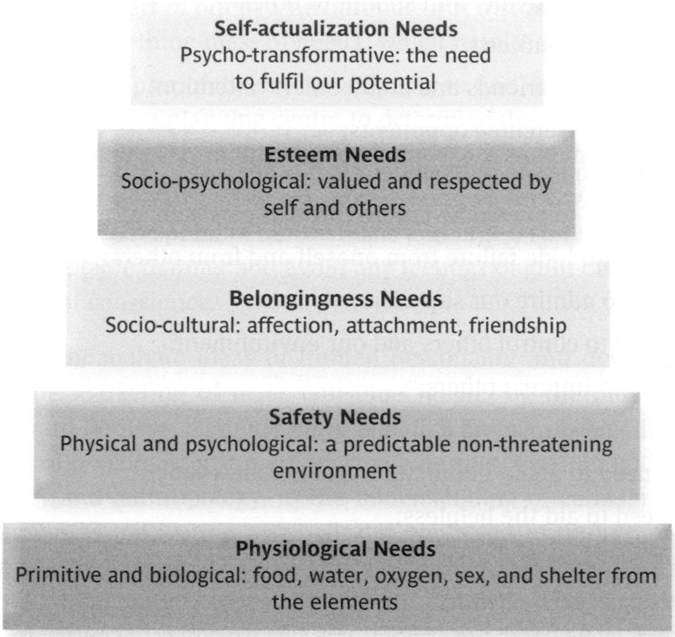

Self-actualization Needs
Psycho-transformative: the need
to fulfil our potential

Esteem Needs
Socio-psychological: valued and respected by
self and others

Belongingness Needs
Socio-cultural: affection, attachment, friendship

Safety Needs
Physical and psychological: a predictable non-threatening
environment

Physiological Needs
Primitive and biological: food, water, oxygen, sex, and shelter from
the elements

Figure 3.4
Maslow's hierarchy
of human needs

Source: Adapted from
Maslow (1943) with the kind
permission of John Wiley &
Sons Ltd.

According to Maslow, we seek to satisfy our lower-order physiological needs first, before our safety needs, before our belongingness needs, our esteem needs, and finally our need for self-actualization. Although there is little research evidence to confirm Maslow's hierarchy, the concept does possess logical simplicity, and seems obvious, which makes it a useful tool in understanding how we prioritize our own human needs. Clearly, in contemporary (Western) societies, products and services tend to be focused on solving consumer needs in the esteem and self-actualization categories, since the needs in other categories are already provided for the vast proportion of citizens in these countries. However, in the poorer parts of sub-Saharan Africa, products and services may well operate for the majority of citizens at the level of solving safety and belongingness needs. The implications for marketers are that products and services aimed at the mass market in Africa for products and services in the self-actualization category (e.g. higher education, long-haul travel) are likely to fail. Note, however, that this does not mean there are not market segments with this need. Quite the opposite: clearly, there are groups of people in sub-Saharan Africa whose income allows them to enjoy these very products and services.

There is still debate about whether a buyer of products and services is primarily motivated by rational (as outlined by Howard and Sheth, 1969) or irrational motives. Holbrook, Lehman, and O'Shaughnessy (1986) started to consider irrational motives when they suggested that our wants could be latent, passive, or active and were related to both intrinsic and extrinsic reasons, as follows:

• Latent—needs are hidden, our subject is unaware of his or her need;

• Passive—the costs of acquisition exceed, for the moment, the expected satisfaction derived from acquisition; and

- Active—the subject is both aware of their needs and expects perceived benefits to exceed the likely costs of acquisition.

According to Holbrook, Lehman, and O'Shaughnessy (1986), when our needs are active they can arise either through **habit**, or through a process of choosing a brand which the authors call **picking**. Picking is the process of deliberative selection of a product or service from amongst a repertoire of acceptable alternatives even though the consumer believes the alternatives to be essentially identical in their ability to satisfy his or her need. It can be motivated by intrinsic or extrinsic evaluations (or both). An intrinsic evaluation occurs because a consumer likes a product, and represents no reasons beyond anticipated pleasure. On the other hand, an extrinsic evaluation might occur because a friend mentioned that it was a 'cool' product. An extrinsic evaluation could also entail conscious cost–benefit analyses. The authors suggest that our extrinsic reasons for purchase can be subdivided into five categories which include the following:

- Economic—concerned with expenditure of money, time, and effort spent in purchasing and consuming a product or service.
- Technical—concerned with the product's perceived quality of performance in the anticipated usage situation.
- Social—concerned with the extent to which a purchase will enhance a person's feelings of esteem, personal worth in relation to others (cf. Maslow's hierarchy), including the keeping up with the Joneses effect and general adherence to group norms and effects (see next section).
- Legalistic—concerned with what are perceived to be the legitimate demands of others (e.g. buying on behalf of a company, or for a child or spouse).
- Adaptive—concerned with imitating others, seeking expert advice (e.g. from consumer websites or industry or consumer magazines), or by relying on a particular company or brand's reputation in cases of uncertain or limited purchasing information.

The latter of these reasons, the adaptive, is a form of social learning (see earlier section). As far as the marketer is concerned, it is important to determine which of these reasons operate and in what rank order when consumers purchase a good or service. Economists refer to the concept of **price elasticity of demand** to determine how demand is affected when price is increased or decreased. However, concepts of time and effort elasticity of demand are also in operation. For example, to what extent do people switch their shopping habits from one supermarket to another on the basis of the queues that they find when they come to pay for their goods? Some buyers may perceive the technical components of a product or service as being of more importance than others. For example, the buyer of a Porsche 911 Carrera may buy it either for its beautiful aesthetic design, its sloping curves, and aerodynamic body, or for its incredible engine performance (0–100 kmh/62 mph in 5 seconds, top speed 177 mph/285 kmh). Equally, the social aspects associated with visiting a gym might be an important component in getting and staying fit for some gym members, particularly where they are relying on group activities such as yoga, boxercise, and circuit training.

Self-Concept Approach

There is an increasing belief amongst marketing researchers that people buy goods and services for the brand that they represent and its relation to the buyers' perception of their own self-concept or personality. In other words, we buy brands which we feel resemble the same or similar characteristics to how we perceive ourselves. In a study of the luxury goods market, Dubois and Duquesne (1993) demonstrated how buyers of luxury goods typically divided into one of two categories, as follows:

- Those that made their purchases principally on product quality, aesthetic design, and excellence of service, motivated by the desire to impress others, ability to pay high prices, and the ostentatious display of their wealth.

- Those that bought luxury goods for what they symbolize, purchasing luxury goods because they represent an extreme form of the expression of their own values.

The Prada advert, from the iconic Italian fashion house, provides an example of an advert aiming to appeal to the young female consumer through the projection of urban(e) chic, decadence, bohemian values, cool and unfettered sexuality.

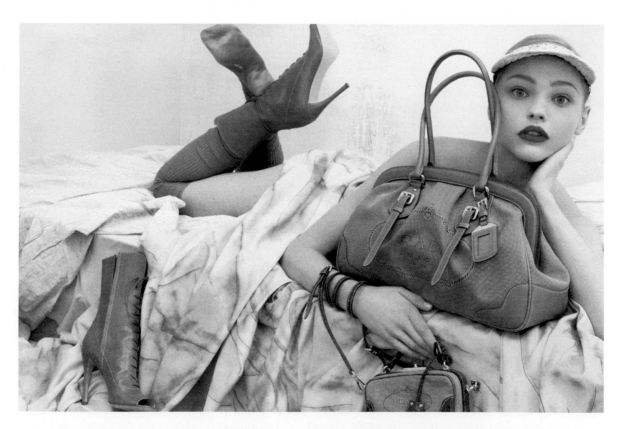

The Prada advertising campaign for the Spring/Summer 2006 Collection

Steven Meisel/Prada

Perhaps the best example of how consumers buy products based on their own self-concepts is through an analysis of self-giving behaviour (Mick and DeMoss, 1990). Gift giving has long been understood as a common phenomenon, arising particularly within families and between friends (as well as work colleagues from within and between companies). It is a highly symbolic form of communication connoting love (e.g. Valentine's and Mother's/Father's Days), congratulations (e.g. wedding presents), regret (e.g. the flowers purchased by an overworking man for his wife), and dominance (e.g. clothes bought by a spouse to change the look of the other person). Self-giving, on the other hand, arises from different motivations, such as to reward oneself, to be nice to oneself, to cheer oneself up, to fulfil a need, and to celebrate. There is clearly a link between the purchase of

L'Oréal: Because He's Worth It

L'Oréal Paris, the French cosmetic giant, has long understood the importance of selling cosmetics as a form of self-gift. The company is involved in developing many cosmetic beauty care products, ranging from skin care, hair care, and hair colouring to make-up and styling products, marketed under famous brand names including Elsève, Studio-Line, and Dermo-Expertise. To further extend the luxurious feel of its products, L'Oréal employs the expertise of top beauty specialists, make-up artists, hair colourists, and dermatologists, including James Kaliardos for make-up and Christophe Robin for colouring, when developing its ranges.

Famous for its 'Because I'm worth it' tagline originally invented by McCann Erickson in 1967, L'Oréal has recently changed its tagline to 'Because you're worth it'. The company emphasizes its self-indulgence advertising theme embodying Parisian beauty by using some of the world's most glamorous women, including Andie MacDowell, Eva Longoria, Milla Jovovich, and Oscar-winning actress Charlize Theron. Women are therefore purchasing the L'Oréal Paris brand because they want to feel glamorous and special themselves.

More recently, L'Oréal Paris has recognized that women may not be the only gender that want to pamper and preen themselves. It seems that there is a group of 'metrosexual' men who are quite prepared to buy and use cosmetic products although their habits seem to differ based on age and nationality. Younger men are the most likely to buy L'Oréal's 'Men Expert' product range. In Europe, 24% of men under 30 years of age use skincare products. In Japan, this rises to 30% of men under 30 years of age, and in South Korea, over 80% of young men in the same age group use skincare products. With a market that grew by 11% in 2005, it's no wonder L'Oréal Paris thinks he's worth it, even if he doesn't himself.

Sources: Manning-Schaffel (2006); Baines, Egan, and Jefkins (2004).

1 Why do you think men, particularly young men, are now more likely to use skincare products?

2 How do you think men's skincare products need to be positioned to be successful? How do men perceive them at the moment, do you think?

3 Consider your own perceptions of men's skincare products. If you are a man: have you ever bought any men or women's skincare products in the past? Would you in the future, as it becomes increasingly common? If you are a woman: has a male friend or partner you know ever bought any men or women's skincare products in the past? What were your perceptions on hearing of this behaviour?

clothing as a self-gift, i.e. a special purchase, rather than a typical purchase, and a consumer's self-concept (see Market Insight 3.4 for the expanding market in men's cosmetics as a form of self-gift). An extreme example of when people purchase products to build their self-concept, although it tends to work in the short term and damages longer-term self-concept perceptions, is when consumers indulge in compulsive consumer behaviour (e.g. shopping, gambling).

The Importance of Social Contexts

Although our own personality and other characteristics have an impact upon how we choose to think and consume products, so the opinions, attitudes, and values of others have an affect on how we consume. In other words, our own internal perspective is not only determined by our own thoughts and personality structures but by the input of others. So, other people have an effect on our opinions, attitudes, and values. In order to understand how this takes place, we must first define these three psychological features.

Opinions, Attitudes, and Values

Opinions can be described as the quick responses we might give to opinion poll questions about current issues or instant responses to questions from friends. They are typically held with limited conviction partly because we have often not yet formed or fully developed an underlying attitude on this issue or item. So an opinion might be what we think of the latest advertising campaign, for instance, for a high-profile brand. Attitudes, by comparison, are held with a greater degree of conviction, held over a longer duration, and are much more likely to influence behaviour. **Values** are held even more strongly than attitudes and underpin our attitudinal and behavioural systems. Values tend to be linked to our conscience, developed through the familial socialization process, through cultures and subcultures, our religious influences, and are frequently formed in early childhood.

It is important for the marketer to understand the difference between these three different mental states. Opinions tend to be **cognitive** (i.e. based on thoughts). Attitudes are what psychologists call **affective**, in that they are linked to our emotional states. Finally, psychologists refer to values as **conative**. They are linked to our motivations and behaviour. It is important to recognize that, although we sometimes have a specific attitude towards something, we do not always follow it in terms of our behaviour. In other words, we may want to give up smoking but we can't. Or we may want to be more fashionable in our dress sense but we don't try any new styles.

Group Influence

Consumers learn naturally through imitation. They learn, for instance, by observing and copying their parents, and friends, and significant others generally, as we discussed earlier. As consumers we may consider our opinions, attitudes, values, and behaviour patterns in relation to those of our reference groups. Reference groups are those groups 'that the individual tends to use as an anchor point for evaluating his/her own beliefs and attitudes. A reference group may be positive; i.e. the individual patterns his or her own beliefs and behaviour to be congruent with those of the group, or it can be negative' (AMA, 2007), in which the individual does not model his or her own behaviour patterns to be congruent with the group.

Nevertheless, if a consumer feels his or her freedom to choose is being threatened, they may react against this intervention. So, a consumer whose decision alternative is blocked, partially or wholly, will become increasingly motivated to go against that specific decision alternative through rebellious behaviour (Clee and Wicklund, 1980). For example, the 'tweenage' daughter (aged between 10 and 12 years old) who is told by her father not to buy short skirts may very well continue to do so while the rebellious teenage son continues drinking against his mother's advice. This form of negative group influence occurs because of **psychological reactance**.

In this section, we consider how consumer behaviour is affected particularly by social class and life cycle, although the reader should recognize that many other forms of group membership exist which impact upon how we consume (aggregated buying behaviour, or market segmentation, is considered further, both from the consumer and industrial contexts, in Chapter 6).

With reference to how we perceive and use products and services, Bargh and Chartrand (1999) state that consumers' assumptions about an individual's behaviour, based on identified group membership, become automated if they are frequently and consistently made. This represents a form of social learning. For instance, an American male consumer might continue to purchase Crest toothpaste because this was the brand he was taught to use by his parents while a French beverage consumer might drink Orangina religiously because that is what their parents provided for them as children.

The link between a consumer and a particular reference group depends on how closely the consumer associates with the particular reference group. Where they do associate closely, the attachment to the brand is also often assumed. For example, consumers identifying with the skateboarding genre might wear Airwalk trainers because the skateboarding crowd generally wear Airwalk trainers.

Message receipt is also affected by peer group pressure, through word of mouth whether intended or otherwise. Members of groups tend to conform to a group norm, enhancing the self-image of the recipient and increasing the feeling of group identity and belongingness. This principle works in Harley-Davidson's favour, for instance, since it allows them to both socialize new bikers into using their brand and persuade existing bikers to retain their brand when they require a new motorbike.

Consumers may have their own cultures and subcultures, which impact upon how a particular marketing message may be received (see Chapter 19 for more discussion of how marketing and culture interact). Some marketing messages might incorporate **celebrity endorsement** appeals, e.g. through popular culture role models, who have influence over the target consumer group. Pepsi has made use of major pop artists over the years, including Michael Jackson, Madonna, and Britney Spears, to advertise its brands, particularly at young people, its target market. Police, the sunglasses brand, has used Bruce Willis, George Clooney, and David Beckham to persuade consumers to wear their brand of glasses. Marketing campaigns frequently leverage the persuasive power of reference group membership through word-of-mouth campaigns, particularly in the internet age, where consumers discuss product and service experiences in chatrooms and on (web)blogs. The producers of the film *The Blair Witch Project* initially marketed the film at minimal cost through their website, using only viral marketing techniques (see Chapter 18). Word-of-mouth communication is particularly powerful as we tend to trust our friends' and colleagues' opinions. For example, in the British funeral business (Mintel, 2002), on average around 4 in 10 (39 per cent) people identify a funeral director when a loved one dies based on whether they are local or near, 3 in 10 (26 per cent) based on advice from friends/family, 2 in 10 (23 per cent) based on previous experience with a funeral director, and 2 in 10 people (17 per cent) use a well-known brand. However, amongst 15–34 year olds, this proportion jumps to around 5 in 10 (15–24 years old: 49%; 25–34 years old: 45%) as they seek advice from others because of their own perceived lack of knowledge.

Social Grade

In marketing, the term 'social grade' refers to a system of classification of consumers based on their socio-economic grouping. 'Social grade' was originally developed for the IPA National Readership Survey (NRS) in the 1950s, and was subsequently adopted by JICNARS (the Joint Industry Committee for National Readership Surveys) on its formation on 1968. Social grade is a means of classifying the population by the type of work they do. This was originally based on the occupation of the head of household (the member of the household who owns the accommodation or is responsible for the rent), but since 1992 it has been based on the occupation of the chief income earner (the member of the household with the largest income). NRS Ltd (the successor to JICNARS) continues to provide social grade population estimates, not only for the National Readership Survey, but also for a number of other major industry surveys. These population estimates are obtained from the Survey's interviews with a representative sample of some 36,000 adults every year, and are based on detailed information about the occupation of the chief income earner (see Table 3.2).

There is a widely held belief that consumers make purchases based on their socio-economic position within society. (Market Insight 3.5 looks at champagne drinking and social class.)

Social grading scales provide an indication of a particular consumer's position in society. This approach has long been criticized, on the basis that it must have changed significantly over the years as Britain, and most other Western nations, has moved from a manufacturing base to a service economy. There has been an increase in middle-class consumers, as a result, but nevertheless the NRS classification approach is still widely used by market research agencies because of its simplicity. Social grade continues to provide an effective demographic tool for advertising planning, and it is still extensively used by advertisers, advertising agencies, and media owners. Frequently, researchers combine the grades into two, ABC1 and C2DE, and three categories, AB and C1C2 and DE.

Table 3.2
JICNARS social
grading scale

Social grade	Social status	Occupational status	Population estimate, Great Britain, age 15+ (1976) (%)	Population estimate, Great Britain, age 15+ (2006) (%)
A	Upper middle class	Professionals, chief executives, and senior managers with a large number of dependent staff	2.1	4
B	Middle class	Intermediate, managerial, administrative, or professional	9.8	21.9
C1	Lower middle class	Supervisory, clerical and non-manual administrative, lower managerial or early professional (e.g. junior white-collar workers based in offices)	23.6	29.0
C2	Skilled working class	Skilled manual workers	32.4	20.7
D	Working class	Semi- and unskilled manual workers	21.9	16.2
E	Those at lowest levels of subsistence	Unemployed and casual workers, pensioners or widowers with no income other than that provided by state	10.2	8.1

Source: National Readership Survey. Reproduced with the kind permission of the National Readership Survey.

An American system of social grading was developed by anthropologist William Lloyd Warner in 1960, which divided their society into the following upper-, middle-, and lower-class categories:

- **Upper-upper class:** 'Old money'. The aristocracy. Born with, and inherited, wealth.

- **Lower-upper class:** 'New money'. A group termed the *nouveaux riches* and those that achieve wealth during their lifetimes through their own endeavours.

- **Upper-middle class:** Professionals and managers (i.e. doctors, architects, solicitors, corporate executives).

- **Lower-middle class:** White-collar non-manual workers.

- **Upper-lower class:** Blue-collar manual workers.

- **Lower-lower class:** Unskilled manual workers and the unemployed.

Champagne Brands: Still the Society Drink?

Champagne, the sparkling wine originating from the Champagne region of France, has long been the drink of choice at weddings and on other special occasions in the UK but is most often drunk at home by Britons and occasionally in restaurants and at the more upmarket pubs. Just five brands account for 68% of total sales by value in the UK market including Moët et Chandon, Lanson, Veuve Clicquot, Laurent-Perrier, and Bollinger.

Because of its relatively high cost, social class can be applied to the analysis of consumer behaviour of champagne drinkers. The motivations for drinking by the different social classes become clear. The professional and managerial class (AB) tend to be conservative champagne drinkers, drinking in moderation and at home, while clerical and administrative workers (C1) are more likely to focus on quality, willing to pay

The Bollinger brand of champagne

Bollinger

Table 3.3 UK champagne consumers by buying type and social class

Social class	Quality-conscious (%)	Price-conscious (%)	Excessive drinkers (%)	Conservative drinkers (%)
AB	30.4	16.1	17.7	35.8
C1	30.0	21.7	23.1	25.1
C2	21.3	28.3	30.1	20.3
D	22.5	33.1	27.3	17.1
E	13.3	36.3	24.8	25.6

Source: Mintel (2004). Reproduced with the kind permission of Mintel.

extra and splashing out on meals in restaurants. In contrast, the skilled manual workers category (C2) tend to drink excessively to get drunk and comprise only slightly more men than women. Non-skilled manual workers (D), the unemployed, and those on benefits (E) unsurprisingly tend to be price-conscious in their champagne consumption behaviour (see Table 3.3).

Around 28% of British adults drink champagne, representing a significant market by volume and the second highest proportion of champagne drinkers after the French (unsurprisingly), while only 17% of Germans and 9% of the Spanish drink champagne. However, less than 17% of British adults drink champagne out of home (i.e. in restaurants or in more upmarket pubs). Those that do are only slightly more likely to be women than men and are significantly more likely to be under 35 years of age. In fact, the 20–24-year-old age group were likely to be over represented when asked whether or not they had drunk a bottle in the previous month.

Individual brands work hard at maintaining their upmarket image. For example, Moët et Chandon have sponsored London Fashion Week, Lanson was the 2006 FIFA World Cup official champagne, and Veuve Clicquot have sponsored the Gold Cup of the British Open Polo Championship.

Source: Mintel (2006b).

1 Why do you think champagne consumption differs by social class?

2 Why do you think the unskilled manual workers group are most likely to drink to excess?

3 Why do you think out-of-home champagne drinking appeals particularly to the younger age group?

While there are clearly differences in type of job conducted and the material wealth of each group, Martineau (1958) has suggested that there are also clear psychological differences between the middle, i.e. ABC1, and the lower classes, i.e. C2DE (see Table 3.4).

Nevertheless, segmenting consumers using the class grading system is increasingly criticized as it is recognized particularly by practitioners that more and more people in Britain work in office-based environments (ABC1) rather than in manual or unskilled professions (C2DE) as Britain's industrial structure shifts from being product dominant to being service dominant (see Chapter 1). As a

Table 3.4

Martineau's class differences by psychological outlook

Middle class	Lower class
1 Pointed to the future	Pointed to the present and the past
2 Viewpoint embraces a long expanse of time	Lives and thinks in a short expanse of time
3 More urban identification	More rural in identification
4 Stresses rationality	Non-rational essentially
5 Has a well-structured sense of the universe	Vague and unclear structuring of the world
6 Horizons vastly extended or not limited	Horizons sharply defined and limited
7 Greater sense of choice making	Limited sense of choice making
8 Self-confident, willing to take risks	Very much concerned with security and insecurity
9 Immaterial and abstract in thinking	Concrete and perceptive in thinking
10 See themselves as part of national happenings	World revolves around family and body

Source: Martineau (1958).

result, the social-class segmentation approach is becoming less able to discriminate between different group behaviours (see Chapter 6 on market segmentation).

Life cycle

While the ACORN approach to consumer categorization by group is based on postcode data (i.e. zip code in USA), based on the notion that people living in particular areas live the same kinds of lifestyles, it can equally be hypothesized that people in the same stages of life purchase and consume similar kinds of products and so, to some extent, it turns out to be. In research undertaken in America in the 1960s, Wells and Gubar (1966) determined that there were nine categories of lifecycle stage in a consumer's life, from leaving home to living as a solitary survivor, i.e. without a spouse. In contemporary society, perhaps more so in the Western world (Occident) than the Eastern (Orient), the lifecycle concept might need a degree of readjustment to take into account that fewer people are getting married, and at a later age, than they were in the 1960s, and increasingly there is a move by couples towards cohabiting.

Most market research agencies routinely measure attitudes and purchasing patterns based on stage in the lifecycle to determine differences among lifecycle groups. As Table 3.5 indicates, there is a difference in the type of goods and

Table 3.5 The lifecycle concept

Bachelor stage; young single people not living with parents/ guardians	Newly married or long-term co-habiting; young, no children	Full nest I; youngest children under 6	Full nest II; youngest children 6 or over	Full nest III; older married couples with dependent children	Empty nest I; older married couples, no children living at home, chief income earner or both in work	Empty nest II; older married couples, no children living at home, chief income earner or both retired	Solitary survivor, in work	Solitary survivor, retired
Few financial burdens. Fashion opinion leaders. Recreation oriented. Buy: basic kitchen equipment, basic furniture, cars, package and long-haul holidays, education.	Better off financially since dual wages. High purchase rate of consumer durables. Buy: cars, refrigerators, package holidays.	Home purchasing at peak. Low level of savings. Buy: washer dryers, TV, baby food and related products, vitamins, toys.	Financial position better. Sometimes both parents in work. Buy: larger-sized family food packages, cleaning materials, pianos, child-minding services.	Financial position better still. Both parents more likely to be in work. Some children will have part-time jobs. High average purchase of consumer durables. Buy: better home ware and furniture products, magazines, and non-essential home appliances.	Home ownership at peak. Most satisfied with savings and financial position. Interested in travel, recreation, self-education. More likely to give gifts and make charitable contributions. Less interested in new products. Buy: luxurious holidays, eating out, home improvements.	Drastic cut in household income. More likely to stay at home. Buy: medical appliances and private healthcare, products which help sleep, digestion.		Same medical needs as other retired group; drastic cut in income. Buy: household staples, cruise holidays, nursing home services, funeral plans.

Source: Adapted from Wells and Gubar (1966). Published by American Marketing Association.

Advert for
a Saga cruise

Saga Holidays Ltd

services purchased as a result with solitary survivors far more likely to purchase funeral plans, nursing home care, and cruise holidays, and bachelors more likely to spend their income on package and long-haul holidays and educational service products, for instance.

Ethnic Groups

In an increasingly globalized society, increasing interest has been placed in how we market goods and services to ethnic groups within particular populations. Since these groups can often be quite large and have their own unique customs, they represent an opportunity either to build a niche (ethnic) market or to consolidate an existing market, i.e. by appealing to a new set of consumers in addition to the old. In the USA, the Hispanic population—principally, but not solely, immigrants from Mexico—and the Black population together represent a sizeable proportion of the total population. Companies frequently market goods and services in Spanish to the Hispanic population although there is evidence that doing so, particularly for high-involvement service brands, is of limited effect (Torres and Briggs, 2005). In other words, when determining whether or not to purchase from a particular service provider is highly involved (e.g. a solicitor's

The Rise of Ethnic Brands in Britain: When your Name Means Business

In the UK, Muslims represent around 2% of the population or around 1 million people. Increasingly, we are beginning to see brands aimed more at Muslim customers. For example, GlaxoSmithKline, the pharmaceutical giant, recently announced that Ribena—the juice drink—is **halal** and HSBC, the British-based banking group, offers Islamic (Sharia-law compliant) insurance. The Qibla brand of cola was launched in the UK by a group of Muslim entrepreneurs as an alternative to Coca-Cola, in a deliberate attempt to gain customers amongst Muslims disaffected with America as a result of the War in Iraq, using the strapline 'Live your life your way, Liberate your taste'. L'Oréal quickly recognized the development of the ethnic trend, launching the Dark and Lovely personal care brand for Afro-Caribbeans, capturing 23.5% of the market share by 2003.

Part of the problem is that ethnic groups are relatively hard to research and, although they sometimes cluster in particular residential locations, they are also more difficult (in terms of profitability, effectiveness) to reach by traditional marketing media. One data management company, Experian, has launched a software package called Ethnic Origins, developed in association with ACORN developer Richard Webber, which allows the ethnic origin of an individual to be determined on the basis of their name. With over a million Asian Indians, around three-quarters of a million Pakistanis, over a million Black African and Afro-Caribbeans, and over a quarter of a million Chinese in the UK population, it is little wonder that companies are starting to wake up to the ethnic marketing opportunities.

Sources: Jenkins (2002); Stones (2004); Kleinmann (2003); Kilby (2005); Tiltman (2007).

1 Do you think that targeting ethnic products exclusively to ethnic groups could cause racial tensions with the non-ethnic population within a country?

2 What kinds of goods and services do you think are best developed for an ethnic audience?

3 What goods and services could be offered specifically to the UK Chinese population?

services), the Hispanic consumer focuses more on other criteria to determine whether they can meet their needs. Other European countries also have sizeable ethnic populations: for example, in France there is a large Black African population and in Germany a large Turkish community exists. In Dubai, in the United Arab Emirates, a large community of expatriates (i.e. people from other countries) exists, particularly from India. These groups within a country represent a potential opportunity for the marketer, if they are sizeable enough to be profitable and have similar needs. Market Insight 3.6 looks further at products marketed at ethnic groups.

Chapter Summary

To consolidate your learning, the key points from this chapter are summarized below:

- Explain the consumer product acquisition process.

  Consumer buying behaviour has both rational and irrational components although rational theories have dominated the marketing literature until the present. Although there are a variety of models of consumer buying behaviour, the consumer product acquisition model is perhaps the simplest to understand, stressing how the consumer goes through six key stages in the product acquisition process including motive development, information gathering, product evaluation, product selection, acquisition, and re-evaluation.

- Understand how consumers respond to the diffusion of innovations.

  Consumers respond differently to the diffusion of innovations. According to research by Rogers (1962), when an innovative product is launched onto the market, a small group of buyers known as innovators will instantly purchase it, followed, after time, by early adopters, then by the early majority of buyers, then the late majority of buyers, followed lastly by the laggards. Consequently, when developing marketing strategy, it is important to recognize that different tactics are required to persuade the different customer groups to take up a particular product or service at the different stages.

- Explain the processes involved in human perception, learning, and memory in relation to consumer choice.

  The human perception, learning, and memory processes involved in consumer choice are complex. Marketers should ensure when designing advertising, when developing distribution strategies, when designing new goods and services, and other marketing tactics, that they (repeatedly) explain this information to consumers in order for them to engage with the information and then subsequently retain it, if it is to influence their buying decisions.

- Understand the importance of personality and motivation in consumer behaviour.

  People are motivated in their consumer behaviour differently dependent on their personalities and, to some extent, how they feel their personality fits with a particular brand of product or service. Murray's (1938) trait theory is useful in helping us understand our needs as consumers. Maslow's (1943) seminal work on human needs is also particularly relevant in understanding how we are motivated to satisfy our five basic desires, ranging from physiological, safety, belongingness, and esteem through to self-actualization needs.

- Describe opinions, attitudes, and values and how they relate to consumer behaviour.

  Opinions are relatively unstable positions that people take in relation to an issue or assessment of something. Attitudes are more strongly held and are more likely to be linked to our behaviour. Values are more strongly held still and are linked to our conscience.

- Explain how reference groups influence consumer behaviour.

  Reference groups including such role models as parents, entertainers, and athletes have an important socializing influence on our consumption behaviour, particularly in adolescence. However, where we live, what social class we come from, what stage of the lifecycle where in, and which ethnic group we belong to, all have an impact on our behaviour as consumers.

 Visit the **Online Resource Centre** that accompanies this book to read more information relating to marketing psychology and consumer buying behaviour: www.oxfordtextbooks.co.uk/orc/baines/

? Review Questions

1 What is the process consumers go through when buying goods and services?

2 What is cognitive dissonance and how does it relate to consumer behaviour?

3 How do customers generally respond to the diffusion of new goods and services?

4 How are the psychological concepts of perception, learning, and memory relevant to our understanding of consumer choice?

5 How are concepts of personality relevant to our understanding of consumer behaviour?

6 How are concepts of motivation relevant to our understanding of consumer behaviour?

7 What are opinions, attitudes, and values and how do they relate to consumer behaviour?

8 What reference groups do you belong to?

9 How do reference groups influence consumer behaviour?

? Discussion Questions

1 Having read the Case Insight at the beginning of this chapter, how would you advise Tyrrells Potato Chips to continue to develop its customer base amongst customers from the higher social grading scale, without changing its perception of originating from a local Herefordshire farmer?

2 Describe the product acquisition process you might go through to obtain the following products in terms of the consumer product acquisition model shown in Figure 3.2:

(a) Chocolate countline product, e.g. Snickers or Cadbury's Dairy Milk;

(b) Long-haul flight to a sunny destination from your home country;

(c) Laptop to help you write the essays and group work for your undergraduate marketing course;

(d) Washing machine;

(e) A householder receiving refuse collection services from the local council (paid for indirectly through local council taxes).

3 A company has developed a holographic television system, called the Claro TV, which projects 3D images onto a transparent screen. A limited number of holographic TVs were made available at the exclusive London-based department store Harrods in 2005, with the whopping price of £25,000. Use your knowledge of Rogers' Theory of Diffusion and adopter categories for new innovations to explain how you might encourage people to buy such a television system.

4 Using Murray's Trait approach to personality, outline what needs we might be satisfying when consuming each of the following items:

(a) Cigarettes;

(b) Action films;

(c) A candlelit dinner for two;

(d) A visit to a historic temple/mosque/church.

5 What kinds of celebrity endorsers have you noticed companies using in their advertising to persuade you to adopt the following products?

(a) Sports apparel;

(b) Packets of crisps;

(c) Luxurious watches;

(d) Beverages;

(e) Sunglasses.

📖 References

Alba, J. W., and Hutchinson, J. W. (2000), 'Knowledge calibration: what consumers know and what they think they know', *Journal of Consumer Research*, 27, 123–56.

Alderson, W., and Martin, M. W. (1965), 'Toward a formal theory of transactions and transvections', *Journal of Marketing Research*, 2 (May), 117–27.

AMA (2007), *Dictionary of Marketing Terms*, available at www.marketingpower.com, accessed 10 June 2007.

Anon. (2005), 'Heineken to buy Russian beer firm', 6 May 2005, available at http://news.bbc.co.uk/2/hi/business/4520401.stm, accessed 12 February 2006.

Baines, P., Egan, J., and Jefkins, F. (2004), *Public Relations: Contemporary Issues and Techniques*, Oxford: Butterworth-Heinemann.

Bandura, A. (1977), *Social Learning Theory*, Englewood Cliffs, NJ: Prentice-Hall.

Bargh, J. A., and Chartrand, T. L. (1999), 'The unbearable automaticity of being', *American Psychologist*, 57, 7 (July), 462–79.

Bass, F. M. (1969), 'A new product growth model for consumer durables', *Management Science*, 15 (January), 215–27.

BBC (2002), 'Century of the self part 1: happiness machines', aired Monday, 29 April, BBC4, London: British Broadcasting Corporation.

Belk, R. W. (1995), 'Studies in the new consumer behaviour', in D. Miller (ed.), *Acknowledging Consumption*, London: Routledge, 58–95.

Bettinghaus, E. P., and Cody, M. J. (1994), *Persuasive Communication*, 5 edn., London: Harcourt Brace Publishers.

Bettman, J. R. (1979), 'Memory factors in consumer choice: a review', *Journal of Marketing*, 43 (Spring), 37–53.

Clee, M. A., and Wicklund, R. A. (1980), 'Consumer behaviour and psychological reactance', *Journal of Consumer Research*, 6, 389–405.

Collins, L., and Montgomery, C. (1969), 'The origins of motivational research', *British Journal of Marketing*, 13, 2 (Summer), 103–13.

Cova, B. (1997), 'Community and consumption: toward a definition of the "linking value" of products or services', *European Journal of Marketing*, 31, 3/4, 297–316.

Dichter, E. (1964), *The Handbook of Consumer Motivation: The Psychology of the World of Objects*, London: McGraw-Hill.

Dittmar, H. (1992), *The Social Psychology of Material Possessions*, Hemel Hempstead: Harvester Wheatsheaf.

Dubois, B. (2000), *Understanding the Consumer: A European Perspective*, London: FT/Prentice-Hall.

—— and Duquesne, P. (1993), 'The market for luxury goods: income versus culture', *European Journal of Marketing*, 27, 1, 35–44.

Elliot, R. (1997), 'Existential consumption and irrational desire', *European Journal of Marketing*, 31, 3–4, 285–96.

Feick, L. F., and Price, L. (1987), 'The market maven: a diffuser of marketplace information', *Journal of Marketing*, 51 (January), 83–97.

Festinger, L. (1957), *A Theory of Cognitive Dissonance*, Palo Alto, Calif.: Stanford University Press.

Firat, A. F. (2005), 'Meridian thinking in marketing: a comment on Cova', *Marketing Theory*, 5, 2, 215–19.

——Dholakia, N., and Ventakesh, A. (1995), 'Marketing in a postmodern world', *European Journal of Marketing*, 29, 1, 239–67.

——and Shultz II, C. J. (1997), 'From segmentation to fragmentation: markets and modern marketing strategy in the postmodern era', *European Journal of Marketing*, 31, 3–4, 183–207.

Freud, S. (1927), *The Ego and the Id*, Richmond: Hogarth Press.

Gabriel, I., and Lang, T. (1995), *The Unmanageable Consumer: Contemporary Consumption and its Fragmentations*, London: Sage.

Gatignon, H., and Robertson, T. S. (1985), 'A propositional inventory for new diffusion research', *Journal of Consumer Research*, 11, 4 (March), 849–67.

Gladwell, M. (2002), *The Tipping Point: How Little Things Can Make a Big Difference*, Boston: Little and Brown.

Holbrook, M. B., and Hirschmann, E. C. (1982), 'The experiential aspects of consumption: consumer fantasies, feelings and fun', *Journal of Consumer Research*, 9 (September), 132–40.

——Lehmann, D. R., and O'Shaughnessy, J. (1986), 'Using versus choosing: the relationship of the consumption experience to reasons for purchasing', *European Journal of Marketing*, 20, 8, 49–62.

Howard, J. A., and Sheth, J. N. (1969), *The Theory of Buyer Behavior*, New York: John Wiley and Sons.

Jenkins, P. (2002), *The Next Christendom: The Coming of Global Christianity*, Oxford: Oxford University Press, 94–104.

Johnson, E. J., and Russo, J. E. (1978), 'The organisation of product information in memory identified by recall times', in K. Hunt (ed.), *Advances in Consumer Research*, vol. V, Chicago: Association for Consumer Research, 79–86.

Johnson, R. M. (1971), 'Market segmentation: a strategic management tool', *Journal of Marketing Research*, 8, 13–18.

Kilby, N. (2005), 'Beauty should be skin deep', *Marketing Week*, 19 May, 36–7.

Kleinmann, M. (2003), 'Qibla-Cola backs anti-Western UK launch with £2m', *Marketing*, 24 April.

Kotler, P. (1965), 'Behavioral models for analyzing buyers', *Journal of Marketing*, 29 (October), 37–45.

Manning-Schaffel, V. (2006), 'Metrosexuals: a well-groomed market?', 22 May, available at www.brandchannel.com, accessed 8 June 2007.

Martin, C. A., and Bush, A. J. (2000), 'Do role models influence teenagers' purchase intentions and behavior?', *Journal of Consumer Marketing*, 17, 5, 441–54.

Martineau, P. (1958), 'Social classes and spending behaviour', *Journal of Marketing*, October, 121–30.

Martinez, E., Polo, Y., and Flavian, C. (1998), 'The acceptance and diffusion of new consumer durables: differences between first and last adopters', *Journal of Consumer Marketing*, 15, 4, 323–42.

Maslow, A. H. (1943), 'A theory of motivation', *Psychological Review*, 50, 370–96.

Mick, D. G., and DeMoss, M. (1990), 'To me from me: a descriptive phenomenology of self-gifts', *Advances in Consumer Research*, 17, 677–82.

Mindak, W. A. (1961), 'Fitting the semantic differential to the marketing problem', *Journal of Marketing*, 25 (April), 29–33.

Mintel (2002), 'Funeral Business—UK', September, London: Mintel International Group Ltd, available at www.mintel.com, accessed December 2007.

——(2004), 'Champagne—UK', March, London: Mintel International Group Ltd, available at www.mintel.com, accessed December 2007.

——(2006a), 'Cars—UK', October, London: Mintel International Group Ltd, available at www.mintel.com, accessed December 2007.

——(2006b), 'Champagne and Sparkling Wines—UK', March, London: Mintel International Group Ltd, available at www.mintel.com, accessed December 2007.

——(2007), 'Crisps and Snacks—UK', May, London: Mintel International Group Ltd, available at www.mintel.com, accessed December 2007.

Moschis, G. P., and Churchill, G. A., Jr. (1978), 'Consumer socialisation: a theoretical and empirical analysis', *Journal of Marketing Research*, 15 (November), 599–609.

Murray, H. A. (1938), *Explorations in Personality*, New York: Oxford University Press.

Orange, R. (2005), 'Putin calls time on Russia's vodka industry', *Sunday Business* (UK), 6 February.

Rogers, E. M. (1962), *Diffusion of Innovations*, New York: Free Press.

Skinner, B. F. (1954), 'The Science of Learning and the Art of Teaching', *Harvard Educational Review*, 24, 88–97.

Stones, J. (2004), 'Are companies set to embrace Islam?', *Marketing Week*, 19 August, 22.

Tiltman, D. (2007), 'Ethnic Britain', *Marketing*, 18 April.

Torres, I. M., and Briggs, E. (2005), 'Does Hispanic targeted advertising work for services', *Journal of Services Marketing*, 19, 3, 150–7.

Udell, J. G. (1964), 'A new approach to consumer motivation', *Journal of Retailing*, Winter, 6–10.

Union of Russian Brewers (2005), 'Russian beer market will increase by 5–7% in 2005', available at www.beer-union.com, accessed 12 February 2006.

Wells, W. D., and Gubar, G. (1966), 'Life cycle concept in marketing research', *Journal of Marketing Research*, 3 (November), 355–63.

Worcester, R. M., Mortimore, R., and Baines, P. (2005), *Explaining Labour's Landslip*, London: Politicos Publishing.

4

Marketing Research and Marketing Information Systems

Not everything that can be counted counts, and not everything that counts can be counted.

Albert Einstein

Learning Outcomes

After reading this chapter, you will be able to:

✔ Define the terms market research and marketing research.

✔ Explain the role marketing research plays in the decision-making process of a business and the types of research that might be conducted.

✔ Explain the importance of competitive intelligence and marketing information systems.

✔ Recognize the importance of ethics and the adoption of a code of conduct when undertaking marketing research.

✔ Understand the concept of equivalence in relation to obtaining comparable data.

✔ Describe the process of coordinating international marketing research.

The Bunnyfoot agency conducts market research to help its clients understand their customers. We speak to Sarah Ronald to find out more.

Sarah Ronald for Bunnyfoot

Eye-tracking services enable us to test the design and copy in adverts, websites, forms and product packaging, games, billboard, and mobile devices in a natural and realistic way. Non-invasive eye tracking highlights what people engage with, read, attend to, recall, and the impression that's left. It also helps to understand the nature of the engagement; whether it is positive, negative, cognitively demanding, and what degree of interest is generated.

- *engaging with users with the right*
- *research techniques...gives deep*
- *insights into consumers' personal*
- *preferences*

From eye-tracking data, we can infer the typical behaviour of a broadly based and highly divergent user group. Eye tracking shows the attention distribution on a website or a product, allowing us to draw conclusions about searching behaviour, or which elements attract attention and more often which are not perceived at all. So, engaging with users with the right research techniques helps to answer the question of how usable a system or product is and gives deep insights into consumers' personal preferences in comparison with competitors' offerings, regarding content, colour, design, and shape, for example.

When a large financial organization approached us for help, they had less than 4% conversion of web visitors to sales, a high volume of complaints, high-volume service

calls, and the website was not being used as an effective self-service or marketing platform. It was really flat, with limited control, and the content was lifted straight from offline communication packages.

Our target was to provide the customer insight necessary to allow the client to improve customer conversion, increase site stickiness (i.e. time spent on the site by the customer), and reduce the volume of complaints and service calls. The problem for us was to develop a suitable research approach to help identify areas of the site which could be improved to create the right overall experience and interaction for the target customer base.

If you were creating the research programme for the financial services client to help them improve their online offering, what would you do?

Introduction

What's the most persuasive ad you've seen recently? How do companies make such useful products? Most of us take it for granted that great companies make great products, because of intuition, and that's why they're great. But, more often than not, companies develop extraordinary goods and services through rigorous research programmes designed to identify customers' constantly changing needs. These goods and services don't design themselves. They are made in the light of the knowledge that market research can bring to our understanding of customers' needs and wants.

We start this chapter with an outline of the origins of market research beginning at the start of the twentieth century. Along with advertising, market research is one of the key sub-disciplines of marketing practice and a fundamental component of the marketing philosophy. In fact, we cannot really implement the marketing concept without it.

Marketing research is particularly affected by the rate of change of technology, which affects how, where, and when we ask questions (see Chapter 18 for more on this feature). We have chosen to call this chapter marketing research rather than market research. The difference is that while market research is conducted with a view to understanding markets—customers, competitors, and industries—marketing research is conducted to determine the impact of marketing strategies and tactics as well as determining information on customers, competitors, and industries. Marketing research subsumes market research (i.e. it includes it). In this chapter, we provide a definition of what marketing research is, before proceeding to outline the research process including how and why it is conducted and commissioned.

We outline how research is both conducted and commissioned with a view to explaining the process for both the practising marketing research manager and the marketing manager who is commissioning research, as well as the student who could end up doing both or either jobs at some point during their careers and perhaps needs an understanding of the research process to guide them in doing their dissertations or theses.

In this chapter, we discuss **marketing information systems**, including a discussion of the development of the field of **competitive intelligence**, where companies obtain information legally on their competitors' trading activities to inform their marketing strategies. We discuss the problems and challenges of conducting international marketing research, a complex field because of the need to ensure that data obtained from one country is comparable to that from another if it is to be used properly in organizational decision making. Finally, we outline the process by which international marketing research should be conducted, to ensure that its results are valid and useful.

The Origins of Marketing Research

It is difficult to determine the genesis of market research but we could probably state that the first systematic data collection exercise began with the census of the Chinese people said to have taken place in AD 2. In Britain, the first serious survey was undertaken by William the Conqueror, who commissioned the Doomsday Book in AD 1085 to discover the extent of land and resources in order to determine suitable tax rates—a preliminary pricing survey, in modern marketing speak. However, this was actually a land survey. The first official census (of people) took place in Britain in 1801 (Anon., 1989).

The techniques of collecting large-scale demographic information informed the techniques that were later used to develop a better understanding of consumer tastes. Quite when the first marketing department was set up is difficult to determine, although one former Procter & Gamble (P&G) executive indicates that an economic research department was established at P&G to 'help anticipate fluctuations in the commodity market'. One of the economists attached to this department, Dr Paul Smelser, then very shortly afterwards established the company's first Market Research Department in 1924 (Stevens, 2003).

But 'serious research into consumer tastes, habits and buying patterns took off in the years following World War I' (Arvidsson, 2004). One of the best-known figures in the development of marketing research was George Gallup (1901–84), the American public opinion analyst who invented the Gallup opinion poll and founded the American Institute for Public Opinion (in 1936) and the British Institute for Public Opinion (in 1937). His work had developed from using statistics to measure reader interest in magazine and newspaper advertisements and features (Anon., 2005). Another pioneer in market research was Arthur Charles Nielson, Sr., who established A. C. Nielson in Chicago in 1923, now a large international company, particularly well known worldwide for its broadcast measurement systems for television audience ratings (A. C. Nielson, 2007).

Definitions of Marketing Research

Marketing research is used to obtain information that provides the management of a company or organization with sufficient insight to make more informed decisions on future activities. It follows the philosophical premiss of marketing that for a business or organization to be successful, an organization must understand the motivations, desires, and behaviour of its customers and consumers. However, there is sometimes confusion between the terms market and marketing research. The ICC/ESOMAR multi-part definition of *marketing* research stresses that:

'Marketing research is a key element within the total field of marketing information. It links the consumer, customer and the public to the marketer through information which is used to identify and define marketing opportunities and

Dyson: What to Do When your Research Sucks!

Growth in the vacuum cleaner market: partly based on the success of the new Dyson machine and other bagless models

iStock

In 2005, in the European Union, there were 90 vacuum cleaners per 100 households, 180 per 100 household in G8 nations generally, in North America 99 vacuum cleaners per 100 households, but only 2 per 100 households in China, excluding Hong Kong, where there are around 90 per 100 households, and 0.1 per 100 households in India. Clearly, in Western markets, the vacuum cleaner is a household accessory. By 2005, the EU market for vacuum cleaners was worth US$3.7 bn and had grown 42% over the period 2000–5.

The growth in the market is at least partly based on the success of the Dyson vacuum cleaner and a new generation of bagless machines. When James Dyson decided to reinvent the vacuum cleaner using a clear bagless bin on the front of his machine, the DC01, market research indicated that customers would not buy it. Seeing the dirt being sucked up the tube put them off buying the cleaner! Despite taking his design around numerous major names in the vacuum cleaner business, no one was interested. But that's fairly common with revolutionary new products and services: they do not always test well with consumers because we are measuring the new product or service against what consumers are currently familiar with rather than how they might behave in the future.

In other words, consumers don't always know what they want, so it's a good job inventors sometimes do. In 1993, James Dyson launched his Dual Cyclone™ vacuum cleaner, and became the UK market leader within two years and market leader in Western Europe shortly after. So much for the negative research then; it's a good job James Dyson ignored it!

Source: Euromonitor (2006).

1 In this case, Dyson was wise to disregard the research. But under what circumstances should you do this?

2 How would you go about researching people's requirements for high-technology products? What questions do you ask when people don't know what they want?

3 Can you think of any products or services which you didn't like at first but changed your mind after using them? How would you go about designing research to determine whether or not other people would be likely to adopt the new product/service?

problems; generate, refine and evaluate marketing actions; improve understanding of marketing as a process and of the ways in which specific marketing activities can be made more effective. Marketing research specifies the information required to address these issues; designs the methods for collecting information; manages and implements the data collection process; analyses the results; and communicates the findings and their implications' (ESOMAR, 1995).

This definition of marketing research has recently been adopted, with modifications, by the American Marketing Association (AMA, 2007). The Market Research Society (MRS), in the UK, defines *market* research as:

'The collection and analysis of data from a sample or census of individuals or organisations relating to their characteristics, behaviour, attitudes, opinions or possessions. It includes all forms of market, opinion and social research such as consumer and industrial surveys, psychological investigations, qualitative interviews and group discussions, observational, ethnographic and **panel studies**' (MRS, 2005).

So, market research is work undertaken to determine either structural characteristics of the industry of concern (demand, market share, market volumes, customer characteristics and segmentation, and so on), while marketing research is work undertaken to understand how to make specific marketing strategy decisions such as for pricing, sales forecasting, product testing, and promotion research (Chisnall, 1992). It could also be argued that marketing research encompasses market research.

Even though marketing research is the foundational element of modern marketing practice, market research is valued by some companies more than others. For example, companies tend to spend between 0.5 and 1 per cent of their revenues on research when they would be better off spending more in order to use the research to fine-tune their advertising and promotion (Kotler, 2005). The difficulty is that it is not always easy to interpret what the research is trying to say. See also Market Insight 4.1 for an example of misleading market research.

Commissioning Marketing Research

Whether or not to conduct your own market research or commission it depends largely on the size of your organization and the type of products/services it handles. Many large companies employ market research agencies to conduct their research for them, although equally very large companies often do much of their own. Those companies that do have their own departments either have a small group in charge of commissioning the research from agencies or a larger department which has the facilities to undertake its own research.

Depending upon the ability and experience of the executives within the department, they may carry out some functions themselves, e.g. writing the questionnaire and/or the report, while leaving the sampling, and the fieldwork, **coding,** and data analysis, to an agency; the latter is called 'field and tab' (short for tabulation) in market research industry jargon. These executives will have the responsibility for selecting the agency and controlling the quality of their work, including keeping the time schedule.

The main advantage of using agencies is that it is relatively cheap compared with undertaking the research in-house and collecting the data independently. The fixed cost of recruiting, training, and maintaining a large panel of interviewers and specialist staff is considerable as is the effort expended. Agencies spread these costs over numerous projects throughout the year. Many agencies also specialize in a particular technique and excel in these niches.

An important difference is the fact that they stand independently from the client's own staff in the research design and reporting and so can be more objective. Sometimes, it is necessary that the client remains anonymous to retain the objectivity of the study. The main disadvantages of using agencies are that the agency sometimes cannot achieve the depth of knowledge of the client's problems nor of the product nor of its market unless it offers a niche specialism in this area. In many syndicated surveys (e.g. **retail audits** and **omnibus surveys**) several rival organizations buy the same data from the agency, so that a cost-effective survey can be carried out.

In order to commission market research, the client must determine whether or not he or she wants to commission an agency, a consultant, a field and tabulation agency, or a data preparation and analysis agency (who unlike field and tab do not undertake the fieldwork). Typically, a consultant might be used for a small job which does not require extensive fieldwork, a field and tab agency when the organization can design its own research but not undertake the data collection, a data preparation and analysis agency when it can both design and collect the data but does not have the expertise to analyse it, and a full-service agency when it does not have the expertise to design the research, and collect or analyse the data. When it is the latter that is needed, an organization can obtain a list of agencies.

Agencies are usually shortlisted according to some criteria and then asked to make a presentation of their services. Visits are made to their premises to check the quality of their staff and facilities, and previous reports may be considered to assess the quality of the organization's work. Permission to interview or obtain references from some of their other clients may also be requested. Each agency would be evaluated on its ability to carry out work of an acceptable quality at an appropriate price. The criteria used to evaluate the agencies' suitability, once they had submitted a proposal, might include the following:

- The agency's reputation;
- The agency's perceived expertise;
- Whether the study offers value for money;
- The time taken to complete the study; and
- The likelihood that the research design will provide insights into the **management problem**.

Shortlisted agencies are given a preliminary outline of the client's needs in a **research brief** and asked to provide proposals on research methodology, timing, and costs. After this, we would then select an agency to do the market research work required. An example of a real market research brief is also provided below.

To take your learning further, you might wish to read this influential paper.

Moorman, C., Zaltmann, G., and Desphandé, R. (1992), 'Relationships between providers and users of market research: the dynamics of trust within and between organisations', *Journal of Marketing Research*, 29, 3, 314–28.

In this highly cited article, the authors investigate the role of trust between market research users and market research providers, developing a theory of user–provider relationships focused on personal trust. The results of their study indicate that trust and perceived quality of interaction between the research user and the research provider contribute most to the findings of the research being implemented. The implications are clear. Use market researchers who you think are highly reputable and work to develop a good working relationship with them and this will ensure the research is more operationalizable.

The Marketing Research Brief

The research brief is a formal document prepared by a client organization submitted to the marketing research agency. When marketing research is conducted in-house, the department manager who requires the research prepares a brief for the marketing research manager. The brief should outline a management problem to be investigated (see Market Insight 4.2 for an example of a market research brief). The typical contents of a research brief might include the following:

- Background summary—providing a brief introduction and details about the company and its products and/or services that the organization offers.
- The management problem—a clear statement of why the research should be undertaken and which business decisions are dependent upon its outcome.
- The marketing research questions—a detailed list of the information necessary in order to make the decisions outlined above.
- The intended scope of the research—the areas to be covered, which industries, type of customer, etc. should be provided. The brief should give an indication of when the information is required and explain why that date is important (e.g. pricing research required for a sales forecast meeting).
- Tendering procedures—the client organization should outline how agencies are to be selected as a result of the tendering process. Specific information may be required such as CVs from agency personnel to be involved in the study, and referee contact addresses. The number of copies of the report required and preferences with regard to layout are usually also outlined.

Evaluating Comprehension Levels for a Public Information Campaign: Example of a Market Research Brief

London Ambulance Service (LAS) has been approached by Independent Television's Channel Four (ITV4) for access to make a 'fly-on-the-wall' documentary on the operation of LAS's 999 emergency service. Following negotiations between LAS and ITV4, agreement was reached that the documentary programme could be made. In return, ITV4 is to allow LAS to broadcast five public information films free of charge.

LAS believes that many lives could be saved, and the extent of injuries minimized, if the general public were better informed as to the simple steps they should take if they find themselves called upon to assist someone suddenly taken seriously ill (e.g. a heart attack) or involved in an accident (e.g. scalded by hot water). Consequently, LAS has made five films that show the public how to deal with the following common events:

- Attending to someone suffering from a suspected heart attack;
- Treating someone who has been scalded by boiling water;
- Giving cardio-pulmonary resuscitation (PBR);
- Assisting someone who is found unconscious; and
- Making an emergency 999 call to the ambulance service.

Each of the films lasts five minutes and they are scheduled for broadcast during prime TV time at 7.55 p.m. for five consecutive week nights (i.e. Monday to Friday). Whilst ITV4 are paying the broadcast costs, LAS is contributing to the production costs. To keep these costs to a minimum, the scripts have been developed by LAS and the 'actors' are all LAS personnel.

LAS sees this as a rare opportunity to reach a large public audience with an important series of messages. At the same time, LAS recognizes it has little experience of TV production and that both its 'actors' and scriptwriters are amateurs. It therefore wishes to carry out a pre-broadcast study to evaluate the likely impact of these films. If the study suggests that one or more of the five films is expected to prove ineffective then broadcast will be delayed and LAS will have the opportunity to rework its material.

There are two broad questions that interest LAS:

1 Did viewers understand the information that LAS is seeking to convey?
2 How much of the most important information did the viewers retain?

Research Objectives. This research has the following specific objectives:

- Assess respondents' knowledge of how to respond to specific situations prior to seeing any of the LAS films.
- Determine which elements of each film proved memorable, and those that did not, for viewers. LAS is seeking advice at to whether a single sample should be drawn up and all respondents asked about all five films or whether sub-samples should be used with each respondent asked about some or only one of the films.
- Determine which points of critically important information viewers understood and those they did not.
- Assess the likely impact of these five films on viewers.
- Recommend any changes to the content and/or style of presentation that are considered essential if the individual films, and the series as a whole, are to prove successful.

Budget. A budget in the range of £8000 – £10,000 (€12,000 – 15,000) has been set for this study, with the research work to be undertaken by a freelance consultant. Given that LAS is reaching the end of its financial year there is no latitude in increasing this budget.

The five films are scheduled for broadcast in six months' time and so this assignment must be completed within 3 – 4 months in order that any changes can be made. Whilst it is possible to reschedule the broadcast dates, both ITV4 and LAS would prefer to abide by the original time schedule that the two parties agreed.

Source: The authors wish to thank Ian Crawford, Visiting Fellow at Cranfield School of Management, for permission to include this material.

1 Do you think this brief has clear research objectives? Why do you say this?

2 Does the research brief indicate or imply that a specific methodology should be used? If so, which method does it imply?

3 Do you think the research objectives are feasible given the budget requirements? Why do you say this?

The Marketing Research Process

There are a number of basic stages in the process that should guide any marketing research project. These are outlined in Figure 4.1. The first, and probably the most crucial, stage of the process involves problem definition, and setting the information needs of the decision makers. The client organization will explain the basis of the problem(s) it faces to the market research agency or consultant

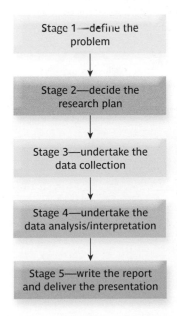

Figure 4.1
Marketing research process

Source: Baines and Chansarkar (2002). © John Wiley & Sons. Reproduced with permission.

Figure 4.2
Example of a
management problem

Management Problem—there has been a decline in sales, possibly due to the emergence of a new competitor

or internal company research department. This might be the need to understand market volumes in a potential new market or the reason for an unexpected, sudden increase in uptake of a product. Problem definition does not always imply threats facing the organization. The initial stage allows the organization to assess its current position, to define its information needs, and to allow it to make informed decisions about its future.

Stage 1. Problem Definition

This process, as outlined earlier, occurs when an organization provides an agency, or consultant, with a marketing research brief defining the management problem. Typically, but not always, the problem is described in vague terms as organizations are not always sure what information they are looking for. An example might be, for example, the Carrefour supermarket chain explaining that sales are down in their flagship store in Paris, France, and wondering whether or not this is due to the emergence of a new competitor supermarket nearby. This problem is shown in Figure 4.2. It is necessary for the marketing researcher to translate the management problem to a marketing research question.

This description of the problem provides the market researcher with relatively little depth of understanding of the situation in which the supermarket finds itself. It becomes important at this stage for the market researcher to discuss the problem with the staff commissioning the study and any other relevant members

A Carrefour
supermarket, France

Carrefour

Marketing Research Question—what are the reasons for the recent decline in sales?

1 Sub-question: has customer disposable income in the area declined over the last six months?

2 Sub-question: is the new competitor, Monoprix, taking away customers?

3 Sub-question: are customers tired/bored of the current product range in the existing supermarket?

4 Sub-question: are customers conducting more of their shopping online?

Figure 4.3
Example of a marketing research question

of staff who can shed further light on the situation. This leads to the development of a marketing research question. This question may include a number of sub-questions that need exploring further. A possible, very general, marketing research question and a number of more specific sub-questions are shown in Figure 4.3.

The marketing research question transforms the management problem into a question while trying to remove any assumptions made by the management of the organization. Sometimes, the management problem is clear. The organization needs a customer profile, an industry profile, an understanding of buyer behaviour, or to test advertising concepts for its next TV advertising campaign or to develop new product range ideas.

The more clearly the commissioning organization defines the management problem, the easier it will be to design the research to solve that problem. Once the agency has discussed the brief with the client, they will provide a detailed outline of how they intend to investigate the problem. This document is called the **research proposal**. Figure 4.4 provides an outline of a typical marketing research proposal.

The basic structure and contents of a typical research proposal should include the following:

- **Executive summary**—a brief summary of the research project including the major outcomes and findings. Rarely more than one page in length. It allows the reader to obtain a summary of the main points of the project without having to read the full report.

- **Background to the research**—an outline of the problem or situation and the issues surrounding this problem. This section demonstrates the researcher's understanding of the management problem.

- **Research objectives**—an outline of the objectives of the research project including the data to be generated and how these will be used to address the management problem.

- **Research design**—a clear non-technical description of the research type adopted and the specific techniques to be used to gather the required information. This will include details on data collection instruments, sampling procedures, and analytical techniques.

- **Personnel specification**—the details of the people involved in the collection and analysis of the data, providing a named liaison person and outlining the company's credibility in undertaking the work.

- **Time schedule**—an outline of the time requirements with dates for the various stages to completion and presentation of results.

- **Costs**—a detailed analysis of the costs involved in the project is usually included for large projects or simply a total cost for the project.

- **References**—typically three references are outlined so that a client can be sure that an agency has the requisite capability to do the job in hand.

Figure 4.4
A marketing research proposal outline

Stage 2. Decide the Research Plan

At this stage, we need to decide whether or not to undertake primary or secondary research or both. Often, we might undertake an initial phase of secondary research to see whether someone has considered the same research question as we now encounter. So, for example, if we had recently bought a new cinema and wanted to know the types of people that lived in the local area, we could consult secondary data sources which could tell us more about the characteristics of people living in the area (e.g. gender, age, population size would be available from census statistics). However, if we wanted to know what types of films they prefer, we might need to resort to a survey of a sample of the population.

Primary versus Secondary Research

Primary research is research conducted for the first time, involving the collection of data for the purpose of a particular project. Secondary data is second-hand data, collected for someone else's purposes. **Secondary research**, sometimes referred to as **desk research**, involves gaining access to the results or outcomes of previous research projects. This is a useful method of research when someone else has carried out a project that provides some of the answers to a client's own management problem since it may be a cheaper and more efficient process of data collection. We can do a large amount of secondary research free-of-charge simply by visiting a business library or by searching the internet. Example sources of secondary data include the following:

- Government sources: these might be export databases, government statistical offices, social trend databases, and other resources.
- The internet: this includes sources identified using search engines, and blogs and discussion groups.
- Company internal records: which may include information housed in a marketing information system (see later) or published reports where they exist. Where no formal marketing information system exists, we would look to identify sales reports, marketing plans, research reports previously commissioned, and so on.
- Professional bodies and trade associations: frequently have databases which can be used for research purposes, often now available online, which may include industry magazine articles, as well as research reports.
- Market research companies: these organizations frequently undertake research into industry sectors or specific product groups and can be highly specialized. Examples include Mintel, Euromonitor, and ICC Keynote.

In practice, most research projects involve a combination of secondary and primary research, with a desk research phase occurring in the beginning so as to ensure that a company is not wasting its money on research which has already been conducted. Once this initial insight has been gleaned we need to determine whether or not to commission a primary data study.

Assuming it is primary research we want to undertake, market researchers usually begin to design their research by considering which type of research to employ. It is important for marketing directors to have some understanding of the different types of study that can be conducted because it has an impact on the type of information that is collected, and hence, the data that they receive to help them solve their management problem. To determine this, we need to decide which type of research we want to conduct.

Types of Research

Generally speaking, most researchers define three categories of research design: (1) exploratory, (2) descriptive, and (3) causal. They specify the procedure adopted for collection and analysis of the data necessary to identify a management problem.

1 **Exploratory research** is used when little is known about a particular management problem and to discover the general nature of the questions that might relate to it. Exploratory designs enable the development of hypotheses. We tend to adopt qualitative methods, e.g. focus groups, in-depth interviews, **projective techniques**, and **observational studies**. Exploratory research also make uses of secondary data, **non-probability** (subjective) **samples**, case analyses, and subjective evaluation of the resultant data.

2 **Descriptive research** focuses on accurately describing the variables being considered. It uses quantitative methods, particularly questionnaire surveys (on- and offline), for example, in consumer profile studies, product usage studies, price surveys, attitude surveys, sales analyses, and media research.

3 **Causal research** is used when there is a need to determine the nature of a relationship between two or more variables. It is used to determine whether one variable causes an effect in another. For example, if we were interesting in determining whether temperature increases cause Coca-Cola sales to increase we might use this method. In fact apparently as temperature increases so too do sales until a certain temperature is reached when consumers then tend to switch to water. Studies into the determination of price elasticity of demand, advertising effectiveness, and sales increase or customer attitude changes are other examples. Causal designs make use of control variables or groups to allow meaningful comparisons between the outcomes of the treatment group and the control group. Slight manipulations of the independent variable, for example, price increases, are undertaken to determine their effect if any on sales, the dependent variable. The problem however is determining whether or not the sales effect was caused by the price increase, or some other unmeasured variable, e.g. an increase in compensation for the salespeople.

Qualitative versus Quantitative Research

At the beginning of a research project, we might consider whether to use qualitative research or quantitative research or some combination of the two. The client, or the in-house marketing research manager, may have specific budget constraints or an idea of which particular approach they wish to adopt. However, the choice really depends on the circumstances of the research project and its objectives. If a lot is known about the management problem either from past research or experience, then it may be more appropriate to use quantitative research to understand the problem further and determine the full extent of the problem. If there is little pre-understanding of the management problem, the researcher may wish to explore the problem further using qualitative research to gather insights.

Quantitative research methods, e.g. the survey questionnaire, are designed to elicit responses to predetermined, standardized questions from a large number of respondents. This involves collecting information from a large number of people, quantifying the responses as frequencies or percentages, and descriptive statistics, and statistically analysing them. Other quantitative research methods include mass observation techniques and experiments.

Qualitative research is different from quantitative research. Qualitative techniques are typically used at the preliminary stages of a research project to identify the basic factors affecting the management problem. The most common forms of qualitative research are focus groups and in-depth interviews. Projective techniques can also be used in both forms. Qualitative research techniques attempt to uncover the underlying motivations behind consumers' opinions, attitudes, perceptions, and behaviour. Consequently, they adopt unstructured methods to elicit information from respondents. We may have a number of basic issues guiding the research but we would not use a structured set of questions for each respondent, as we would with a survey. The two main forms of research are outlined in Figure 4.5, along with the techniques associated with each main form of research. Whereas quantitative research techniques such as surveys emphasize theory testing, qualitative techniques are used to identify meaning and understanding. There are various qualitative research techniques, some of which are shown in Figure 4.5.

In the market research industry, the most familiar qualitative techniques are **in-depth interviews**, **focus groups**, and **consumer juries**. The objective is to uncover feelings, attitudes, memories, and interpretations. They can range in form from an informal conversation to highly structured interviews. They might be used to seek an interviewee's perspective on a new campaign or to develop customer profiles covering a wide range of needs and preferences. Focus groups, or **group discussions** as they are more commonly referred to, have been used extensively in the marketing communications industry for many years (see Market Insight 4.3). They normally consist of a small number of target consumers brought together to discuss elements from the initial concept stage to post-production stage. At the

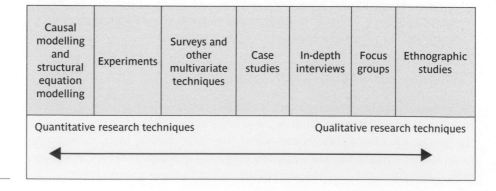

Figure 4.5
A continuum of research techniques

Photodisc

Focus groups: one of the most familiar qualitative techniques in market research

concept stage, the target sample is presented with rough outlines or storyboards (see Chapter 12) giving an idea of the campaign or campaigns under consideration. A professional moderator aims to understand the thoughts, feelings, and attitudes of the group towards a product or service, media, or message. Consumer juries consist, as do focus groups, of a collection of target consumers who are asked to rank in order ideas or concepts put to them and to explain their choices. In addition to these common qualitative techniques there is growing use of more creative qualitative techniques. For example Goulding (2002: 10) describes Semiotic Solutions as a company that 'specializes in cultural qualitative research, drawing upon techniques borrowed from linguistic philosophy, cultural anthropology and the systematic study of signs and codes' (see Chapter 19). The company's research has formed the basis of many national and international television campaigns and brand repositioning exercises for organizations such as British Telecommunications (BT), Tesco, and Coca-Cola. **Ethnographic research** is currently in vogue although it is unlikely that many research agencies submerge themselves in consumer culture as deeply as perhaps they should (See Market Insight 4.4).

Qualitative techniques generally involve a small number of respondents. The emphasis is on obtaining rich, detailed information from a small group of people rather than short, specific answers from a large group of respondents, as with survey questionnaires.

The major characteristics of qualitative and quantitative marketing research techniques are outlined in Table 4.1 on p. 152. Case studies can be both qualitative and quantitative depending on the number of case studies used. One example might be the analysis of a number of different markets to develop product life-cycles, for instance, and to note the impact of advertising. So Colgate-Palmolive

What Is One Thinking? Public Attitudes towards the British Monarchy

In November 1997, shortly after the tragic death of Princess Diana and relatively early into the new Blair government in Britain, Sir Robert Fellowes, Queen Elizabeth II's private secretary, commissioned the market research company MORI (now Ipsos MORI) to conduct focus groups amongst a wide range of British citizens to gather the public's attitudes towards the royal family. Quantitative research, conducted for the monarchy privately by MORI and reported in *The Observer*, was said to indicate that more than 1 in 3 members of the British public felt that the monarchy was 'out of touch'. However, published MORI polls on net satisfaction (i.e. percentage of people reporting that they were satisfied versus dissatisfied when asked 'Are you satisfied or dissatisfied with the way the Queen is doing her job as monarch?) indicated that net satisfaction *had* changed between December 1992 and April 2006, but positively from +58 to +78. In other words, only around 1 in 10 people reported dissatisfaction with the way the Queen was doing her job as monarch in 2006.

MORI have asked the general public many times since December 1981, 'At what age, if at all, should the Queen retire? Should she retire when she reaches 80, when she reaches 85, when she reaches 90 or should she remain Queen as long as she is able?' The proportion of people who think she should remain Queen as long as she is able has only shifted slightly in overall terms between 1981 at 45% and 50% in 2004 but this masks significant shifts in opinion over that period. In 1998, at its height, 67% felt that the Queen should remain in her job as long as she is able; the point at which Prince Charles's popularity was at a relatively low ebb. When the general public were asked 'Do you think that Prince Charles should or should not give up his right to be the next monarch in favour of his eldest son, Prince William?', in August 1998, 32% of the general public felt that he should, although this rose to 43%, during the period of his marriage to Camilla Parker-Bowles, on Saturday, 9 April 2005.

Is the Queen listening to the opinion polls about her?

Corel

So, it seems that the public's attitudes towards the Queen are intimately linked with their attitudes towards her eldest son. But you can be sure of one thing: the Queen would never publicly comment on such a lowly matter as a poll—Mum's the word—but it doesn't mean she isn't listening.

Sources: Hardman (1998); Summerskill (2001); Ipsos MORI (2007).

1 Why did the Queen's private secretary feel it important do you think to take a measure of public opinion?

2 Do you think it is appropriate for the monarchy to be undertaking market research to find out what the public think of the monarchy? Why do you say this?

3 What sort of questions might have been asked in the focus groups?

Guinness Drinking: The Irish Way?

Context-Based Research Group is a specialist research agency, set up in 1999, which focuses on providing clients with insights and meaning from ethnographic research, based in Baltimore in the USA. Its research uses the participant observation methodology, which involves spending time watching people as they go about their lives, observing what they do, in a natural setting. Ethnographic research findings are then delivered in the participants' own words from the perspective of how whatever is being researched fits into their lives (Context, 2007).

The Guinness experience: what are the trends in customer attitudes and behaviour towards the brand in Ireland?

iStock

Context-Based Research Group undertook work for Guinness UDV, the Irish stout producer, by focusing on the Guinness experience in Ireland. Context felt it was fundamental to employ a team of Irish anthropologists who live, work, and study Irish culture in Ireland. Drawing on their proprietary network of professional ethnographers around the world, they assembled a team of Irish ethnographers, who acted as cultural insiders, to conduct a series of participatory research programmes. Working closely with Guinness UDV, Context's anthropologists in the USA directed and led the analysis of the data, while also making field trips to Dublin pubs for additional participant observation with Guinness customers.

The research helped Guinness UDV to understand trends in consumer attitudes and behaviour around the Guinness brand better, and provided numerous recommendations to help Guinness strengthen their long-term relationships with customers within their domestic market. Since the Guinness brand is based on its Irish heritage, getting the experience right for its home customers is a first step to satisfying its international customers. Must have been a tough programme of research to conduct!

Source: Context Research Group (2007).

1 What kind of understanding of Irish Guinness drinking do you think ethnography would provide?

2 How difficult do you think it is to understand the marketing implications of the data that are generated from watching a group of Irish Guinness drinkers?

3 Joking aside, how difficult do you think it would be to watch the subjects interact and behave without affecting their actions?

Table 4.1

Qualitative and
quantitative research
methods compared

Characteristic	Qualitative	Quantitative
Purpose	To identify and understand underlying motivations, memories, attitudes, opinions, perceptions, and behaviours.	To determine the representativeness of the sample to the population, i.e. how similar is the sample to the population?
Size of sample	Involves a small number of respondents, typically less than 30.	Involves a large number of respondents, more than 30.
Type of information generated	Provides detailed information.	Provides narrowly defined descriptive information.
Degree of structuring	Uses an unstructured approach typically using open questions.	Uses a structured questioning process and frequently closed, multiple fixed response questions.
Type of data analysis	Uses a non-statistical word (content-based) analysis, e.g. using the NVivo qualitative analysis software.	Statistical analysis e.g. using SPSS software.
Sampling approach	Uses non-probability sampling methods.	Uses probability sampling techniques.

might well research the product lifecycle of a particular toothpaste brand in Latvia, Romania, Turkey, Germany, France, the USA, and the UK before launching a new brand in India.

Qualitative research is used to uncover underlying motivations for people's behaviour, attitudes, opinions, and perceptions but because the research approach uses small samples, the results derived from this form of research are not generalizable to the wider population of interest and are used to generate insights only. Group discussions are reliant on the skill of the moderator in generating group interaction.

Quantitative research techniques are used to address representativeness of the sample and generalizability because they are based on larger samples of respondents, selected either to match the population or randomly. The researcher establishes the level to which the results will reflect the entire population by choosing the number and type of respondents required. One disadvantage of quantitative research is that because we typically predetermine the answers, there is a chance that the respondents are not allowed fully to express their true opinion but only an opinion which approximates to their views.

Designing the Research Project

When we know what type of research to conduct and if we need secondary data or not to understand the management problem, we should consider the following:

- **Who** to question and how (the sampling plan and procedures to be used)?
- **What** methods to use (e.g. discussion groups or an experiment)?
- **Which** types of questions are required (open questions for qualitative research or closed questions for a survey)?
- **How** should the data be analysed and interpreted (e.g. what approach to data analysis)?

Research methods describe the techniques and procedures we adopt to obtain the necessary information. We could use a survey or a series of in-depth interviews. We might use observation to see how consumers purchase goods online, or how employees greet consumers when they enter a particular shop, i.e. mystery shopping. We could use consumer panels where respondents record their weekly purchases or their TV viewing habits over a specified time period. Fact Finders, an A. C. Nielson company, requests that consumers use specially developed bar code readers (hand-held 'wands') to record their supermarket purchases in return for points which are redeemed for household goods.

Figure 4.6 indicates the key components which we need to consider when designing both qualitative and quantitative research projects. The design of marketing research projects involves determining how each of these components interrelates with the others. The components comprise the following:

- Research objectives;
- The sampling method;
- The research type and methods undertaken;
- The question and questionnaire design;
- Data analysis.

Each of these components impacts upon the others. When designing research projects we must first determine the type of approach to use for a given

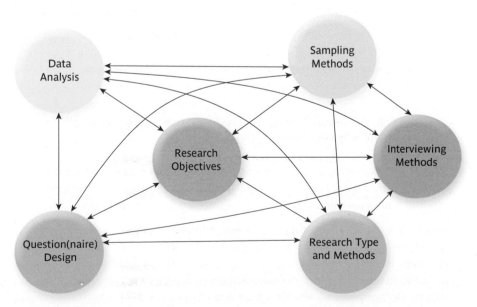

Figure 4.6

The major components of research design

Source: Baines and Chansarkar (2002). © John Wiley & Sons Limited. Reproduced with permission.

management problem (e.g. exploratory, descriptive, or causal). Then we would determine which techniques are most capable of producing the desired data at the least cost and in the minimum time period.

In order to determine whether or not we've got the 'right' data, we measure its value by measuring its validity (i.e. do the data collected correctly describe the phenomenon they are attempting to measure?) and reliability (i.e. would the data be replicated in a future study of the same type if conducted again?). We consider the two concepts again later in this chapter.

Generally, certain types of research (e.g. exploratory, descriptive, causal) use certain methods and techniques. For instance, exploratory research studies use qualitative research methods, non-probability sampling methods, and non-statistical data analysis methods. Descriptive research projects tend to adopt survey interviews using quota or random sampling methods and statistical analysis techniques. Causal researchers use experimental research designs often using convenience or probability sampling methods and statistical data analysis procedures.

Stage 3. Data Collection and Sampling

This stage involves the conduct of the fieldwork and the collection of the required data. At this stage, we send out questionnaires, or run the focus group sessions or conduct telephone surveys, depending on the decisions taken in the first design stage of the fieldwork. The procedures undertaken when conducting the fieldwork might relate to how to ask the questions of the respondents—whether this be using the telephone, mail, or in person, and how to select an appropriate sample, how to **pre-code** the answers to a questionnaire (quantitative research), or how to code the answers arising out of open-ended questions (usually associated more with qualitative research).

The market research manager might be concerned about whether or not to conduct the research in-company or commission a field and tab agency. Other issues concern how to ensure high data quality. When market research companies undertake shopping mall intercept interviews, they usually recontact a proportion of the respondents to check their answers to ensure that the interviews have been conducted properly.

In qualitative research, samples are often selected on a convenience or judgemental basis. In quantitative research, we might use either probability or non-probability methods. Probability methods include:

• **Simple random sampling**, where the population elements are accorded a number and a sample is selected on the basis of a sample of generated random numbers which correspond to those pre-assigned numbers.

• **Systematic random sampling**, where population elements are known and the first sample unit is selected using random number generation but after that each of the succeeding sample units is then selected systematically on the basis of an nth number when n is determined by dividing the population size by the sample size.

- **Stratified random sampling**, where a specific characteristic(s) is used (e.g. gender, age) to design homogeneous subgroups from which a representative sample is then drawn.

Non-random methods include:

- **Quota sampling**, where criteria like gender, ethnicity, or some other customer characteristic are used to restrict the sample, but the selection of the sample unit is left to the judgement of the researcher.
- **Convenience sampling**, where no such restrictions are placed on the selection of the respondents and anybody can be selected.
- **Snowball sampling**, a technique where respondents are from rare populations (e.g. left-handed women over 65). Respondents might initially be selected from responses to newspaper adverts and then further respondents are identified using referrals from the initial respondents and so respondent numbers snowball using this referral method.

Stage 4. Data Analysis and Interpretation

This stage of the market research process comprises data input, analysis, and interpretation. How the data is input usually depends on the type of data collected. Qualitative data, usually alpha-numeric, i.e. words and numbers, is entered into word-processed documents as interview transcripts from audio or video-tape and entered into computer software applications (e.g. NVivo) as text files for content analysis.

Quantitative data analysis makes use of statistical analysis packages (e.g. typically SPSS—Statistical Package for the Social Sciences). In these cases, data is usually numeric and is first entered into spreadsheet packages (e.g. Microsoft Excel) or entered directly into the statistical computer application itself. When computer-assisted methods are used, data input can be direct using a computer programme. This takes much of the pain out of data input and can ensure a higher level of data quality. Modern data collection and analysis methods dramatically reduce the time needed for data input/analysis. If CAPI or CATI methods are used, analysis can occur instantaneously as the interviews are undertaken. Computer-aided interviewing techniques allow the researcher to read the questions from a computer screen and directly enter the responses of the respondents. More recently the advent of the worldwide web has spawned computer-aided web interviewing techniques.

Market research methods are used to aid managerial decision making. Information obtained is required to be valid and reliable as company resources will be deployed on the basis of the information gleaned. **Validity** and **reliability** are important concepts frequently used in conjunction with quantitative market research. They aid researchers in understanding the extent to which the data obtained from the study represent reality and 'truth'.

Qualitative research methods rely on the degree to which the data elicited might be reproduced in a later study (reliability) and the extent to which the data generated is bias free (valid). Validity is defined as 'a criterion for evaluating measurement scales; it represents the extent to which a scale is a true reflection of the underlying variable or construct it is attempting to measure' (Parasuraman, 1991: 441). One way of measuring validity is the use of the researcher's subjective judgement to ascertain whether or not an instrument is measuring what it is supposed to measure (content validity). For instance, a question asked about job satisfaction does not necessarily infer loyalty to the organization. Researchers can also measure the degree to which a variable correlates with other similar or dissimilar variables. When this is done, construct validity is determined.

In qualitative research, concepts of validity and reliability are generally less important, because the data is not used to imply representativeness. Many practitioners believe that qualitative data is highly subjective anyway so there is little need to measure reliability and validity. Qualitative data is more about the generation of ideas and the formulation of hypotheses. Validity may be assured by sending out transcripts to respondents and/or clients for checking, to ensure that what they have said in in-depth interviews or focus groups was properly reproduced for analysis. When the analyst reads the data from a critical perspective to determine whether or not it fits with their expectations, this constitutes what is termed a **face validity** test.

Reliability is defined as 'a criterion for evaluating measurement scales; it represents how consistent or stable the ratings generated by a scale are' (Parasuraman, 1991: 443). Reliability is affected by concepts of time, analytical bias, and questioning error. We can also distinguish between two types of reliability, i.e. internal and external reliability (Bryman, 1989). To determine how reliable the data is, we might conduct the same research over two or more time periods to determine the consistency of the data. This is known as the test-retest method. This measures *external* reliability. Another method used involves dividing the responses into two random sets and testing both sets independently using **t-tests** or **z-tests**. This would illustrate *internal* reliability. The two different sets of results are then correlated. This method is known as split-half reliability testing. These methods are more suited to testing the reliability of rating scales than data generated from qualitative research procedures.

The results of a quantitative marketing research project are reliable if we conduct a similar research project within a short time period and the same or similar results are obtained in the second study. For example, if the marketing department of a travel agency chain interviewed 500 of its customers and discovered that 25 per cent were in favour of a particular resort (e.g. a particular Greek island), then repeated the study the following year and discovered only 10 per cent of the sample were interested in the same resort, then the results of the first study can be said to be unreliable in comparison and the procurement department should not base its purchase of package holidays purely on the previous year's finding.

In qualitative research, reliability is often achieved by checking that similar statements are made by the range of respondents, across and within the interview transcripts. Interviewees' transcripts are checked to assess whether or not the same respondent, or other respondents, have made the discussion point. Such detailed content analysis tends to be conducted using computer applications (e.g. NVivo). In quantitative research, we typically measure the reliability of particular approaches to questioning (e.g. rating scales) using particular statistical techniques.

Stage 5. Report Preparation and Presentation

The final stage of a research project involves reporting the results and the presentation of the findings of the study to the external client or the in-house client. The results should be presented free from bias although clients are increasingly demanding that the results are applied to their existing strategies to make the managerial implications easier for them to infer. Marketing research data has little use unless it can be translated into a format that is meaningful to the manager or client who demanded it at the outset of the project.

Presentations are often attended by senior people within the commissioning organization who may or may not have been involved in commissioning the work in the first place. Usually, agencies and consultants write their reports using a basic pre-written template which corresponds to a 'house style' although the content placed within that template is obviously different for each individual project.

Market Testing

Marketing research is used to reveal attitudes, to a campaign, brand, or some other aspect of the exchange process, whereas market testing, by comparison, measures actual behaviour. There is a difference since attitudes do not always determine action (see Chapter 3). For instance, a consumer may respond very positively to the launch of a new, top of the range TV set in surveys but family circumstances or lack of funds may mean the TV is never purchased. Market testing studies use **test markets** to carry out controlled experiments in specific TV or radio regions, where specific adverts can be shown, before exposing the 'new feature' (product, service, campaign, distribution, etc.) to a full national or even international launch. (See Market Insight 4.5 for test-screening of the film *Final Destination*.) Depending on the feature involved another region or the rest of the market may act as the **control group** against which results can be measured. As an example, films are often test-screened before they are released. Since they represent multi-million-dollar enterprises in their own right, getting them right is an important consideration.

Market Research Online

The internet has had a strong an effect on marketing research, particularly employee type research, and will continue to do so into the future. Many companies have switched their telephone and personal interviewing research approaches towards use of online methods instead. By 2006, online research was the most common method of research used in Australia (25 per cent of all market research expenditure). Strong growth also took place in Japan and the United States, where 21 per cent and 15 per cent of market research expenditure adopted this approach (ESOMAR, 2006).

The *Final Destination* Thrillogy: Testing a Film to Death

Final Destination, the Hollywood movie directed by James Wong and released by New Line Cinema, was a surprise hit in 2000. It was cast with a group of virtual 'nobodies' with a production budget of US$23 m but it went on to gross US$53 m at the US box office alone and US$33 m while in the top ten VHS video rentals listing. Typically, studios earn a further 60% of the rental income when the video drops out of the top 10. The film was so successful that it spawned two sequels in 2003 and 2006. *Final Destination II* took US$46 m at US box office and $9 m while in top ten VHS rentals and *Final Destination III* took US$54 m at US box office and US$45 m for first ten weeks in VHS top ten. In total, gross revenues were well in excess of US$240 m in the USA alone, aside from revenues earned from licensing and distribution around the world. But what was the secret of the film's success?

By test-screening the film prior to release, and questioning audiences on everything from the scenes and characters which they liked, to their general interest in films, they were able to identify alternative scenes to replace those scenes which did not test well with their target audience—teen lovers of the horror genre. In fact, the original ending scene was hated by most test-screeners, who were visibly deflated after seeing it. So, James Wong recast and reshot a spectacular new bloodlust-satisfying ending scene, paving the way for the sequels.

By test-screening the film several times with different audiences, the producers were able to distil the essence of a thrilling horror film—scenes which contain something totally unexpected, but which builds up your anticipation of something genuinely terrifying about to happen.

See a trailer of *Final Destination II* for yourself at: www.deathiscoming.com/.

Sources: IMDB (2007); Rotten Tomatoes (2007); Newline Cinema (2000).

1 Do you think it is always advisable to test-screen a film prior to release?

2 Why do you think some producers never test a film prior to release?

3 Why do you think the film makers only wanted to understand the opinions of horror film lovers? Would it not have been better to have made a horror film for all film-goers? Why do you say this?

There are two types of panel used in online research (Miles, 2004). Access panels provide samples for survey-style information and are made up of targets who have been invited by email to take part with a link to the web survey, an example of which includes the online pollster YouGov (see www.yougov.co.uk). Proprietary Panels are set up or commissioned by a client firm and are usually made up of that company's customers. To encourage participation in these surveys the researchers often use incentives such as the chance to win a prize. But there are pros and cons involved with undertaking online research. These are shown in Table 4.2. (For more on how technology has affected the conduct of marketing research, see Chapter 18.)

To take your learning further, you might wish to read this influential paper.

Ilieva. J., Baron, S., and Healey, N. M. (2002), 'Online surveys in marketing research: pros and cons', *International Journal of Market Research*, 44, 3, 361 – 82.

This article evaluated the use of online research surveys in 2002, as they started to become more widely used, in place of mail and self-completion surveys, and particularly in international marketing research. The authors conclude that online surveys have more pros than cons for this mode of research particularly as the internet evolves, in terms of page download speeds and data transfer rates, and users become more representative of the mainstream population. In particular, they cite very low financial resource implications, short response times, the ability to control the sample, and the fact that data can be loaded directly in analysis software (and so removes the need for data processing) as the benefits of using an online research approach.

Table 4.2
Advantages and disadvantages on online research

The pros of online research	The cons of online research
1 Clients and analysts can see results being compiled in real time	1 Online panels' demographic profile can differ from that of the general population
2 Online surveys save time and money compared with face-to-face interviews	2 If questionnaires take longer than 20 minutes to fill in quality can suffer and they may go uncompleted
3 Consumers welcome surveys they can fill in when they want to and often need no incentive to do so	3 Poor recruitment and badly managed panels can damage the data
4 A more relaxed environment leads to better-quality, honest, and reasoned responses	4 Technical problems, such as browser incompatibility, can mean panellists give up
5 Panellist background data allows immediate access to key target audiences unrestricted by geography	5 Programming costs are higher than for offline questionnaires

Source: Miles (2004: 40). Reproduced with the kind permission of Haymarket Media Group Limited.

Competitive Intelligence and Marketing Information Systems

But it's no good having lots of data unless you know how to use it. Companies are frequently swimming in data but have no means to convert the data into intelligence or no means to store the data and provide it to end users at the appropriate point. One area of research which has become more prevalent in the last ten years is that of competitive intelligence.

Competitive intelligence is defined as 'the organised, professional approach to collection, analysis, and distribution of timely, accurate, and useful information as intelligence products—intelligence that contributes materially to the achievement of strategic and tactical business objectives, as defined by the leadership of an enterprise' (Nolan, 1999). We outline it here because it provides useful information in strategic decision making in addition to standard market research information. There are various techniques used which include:

- Using remote psychological assessment tools to build profiles of business opponents;
- Collecting competitive intelligence at trade shows and conferences;
- Collecting information on rivals from their customers and suppliers using **elicitation techniques**; and
- Collecting intelligence on rivals from third parties using elicitation techniques.

The competitive intelligence industry has particularly developed in the USA since the Economic Espionage and Protection of Proprietary Information Act of 1996 was passed although its professional society, the Society of Competitive Intelligence Professionals, has been in existence since 1986. The Society operates under specific ethical and legal guidelines.

But simply collecting competitive information is not enough. It must also be stored and produced at the right moment. The purpose of using marketing information systems (MkIS) is to provide us with timely information on a continuous basis, to support our decision making. But what kind of information do we actually need as marketers? Typically, we might have the following information needs:

- Aggregated marketing information in quarterly, annual summaries;
- Aggregated marketing information around product/markets (e.g. sales data);
- Analytical information for decision models (e.g. SWOT, segmentation analyses);
- Internally focused marketing information (e.g. sales, costs, marketing performance indicators);
- Externally focused marketing information (e.g. macro and industry trends);
- Historical information (e.g. sales, profitability, market trends);
- Future-oriented marketing information (e.g. environmental scanning information);
- Quantitative marketing information (e.g. costs, profit, market share); and
- Qualitative marketing information (e.g. buyer behaviour, competitor strategy information) (Ashill and Jobber, 2001).

Such information as outlined above could be provided on both a continuous and an ad hoc basis. Continuous information on industry trends can be gleaned from Mintel reports and other secondary data sources. However, the market research manager needs to remember to both buy the reports and input the data into a suitable marketing information system. Other information may be obtained on an ad hoc basis through commissioning specialist market research projects such as for pricing or segmentation research. This also needs to be fed into the MkIS to provide the company with an up-to-date picture of its marketing environment and customer base. The qualitative information related to competitor strategy information might be gleaned from sales reports or reports from overseas agents, for example. The key difficulty for the marketing manager is to obtain and customize the marketing information system to fit their company's specific needs

Mintel reports provide continuous information on industry trends

Mintel

(since the needs will probably change according to their industry), and to ensure that the data is input on a timely and continuous basis. Axelrod (1970) suggests adherence to the following fourteen basis rules for building an MkIS:

1 Get the top management involved;

2 Set the objective for the system carefully;

3 Figure out what decisions your MkIS will influence;

4 Communicate the benefits of the system to users;

5 Hire and motivate the right people;

6 Free the MkIS from accounting domination;

7 Develop the system on a gradual and systematic basis;

8 Run a new MkIS in parallel with existing procedures;

9 Provide results from the system to users quickly after its initiation;

10 Provide information on a fast turnaround basis;

11 Tie the MkIS with existing data collection procedures;

12 Balance the work of the MkIS between development and operations;

13 Feed valid meaningful data into the system not useless information; and

14 Design a security system to ensure different groups get different access to the information.

RESEARCH INSIGHT 4.3

To take your learning further, you might wish to read this influential paper.

Montgomery, D. B., and Weinberg, C. B. (1992), 'Toward strategic intelligence systems', *Journal of Marketing*, 43, 4 (Autumn), 41 – 52.

Although this article was written in the era before computers were really fully utilized in every office, the authors provide insights into the process of setting up a strategic intelligence system, outlining what data should be collected, the procedures to be used to collect the data, and how data are transformed into intelligence. Sources of intelligence include government, competitors, suppliers, customers, professional associations, company personnel, and other sources. The authors argue that the data can be turned into intelligence through any of the following processes: the data can simply be moved from one point outside the organization to another in its existing form within the organization, it can be accumulated, it can be aggregated (with other data), analysed, and mixed into the organization's activities generally in order to provide intelligence.

Marketing Research and Ethics

Many supermarkets and high street retailers have adopted customer loyalty schemes to ensure the loyalty of their customers. In exchange for their continued custom, they provide customers with loyalty points, which may be cashed in for prizes or discounts on future purchases. Nevertheless, the major value of such schemes is the provision of consumption information. Typically, this data is collected at point of sale (e.g. store and supermarket tills) and is analysed by a third party agency and sold back to the retailer to provide them with outlines of patterns and trends in consumption behaviour to inform their procurement, promotion, merchandizing, and further research strategies. (See Market Insight 4.6 for the customer data gathered under the Tesco Clubcard scheme.)

Since marketing research is based on the cooperation of the individuals or organizations that provide the answers or fill in the questionnaires, marketing research should be carried out in an objective, unobtrusive, and honest manner. Researchers have been particularly concerned about the public's increased unwillingness to take part in marketing research and the associated problem of recruiting suitable interviewers. The reasons for this apathy amongst interviewers are not fully clear but it is probably associated with the growing, some might say excessive, amount of research conducted by mail, through newspapers or in response (usually by telephone or email) to radio or television polling, particularly intrusive telephone interviewing, which is increasing, and door-to-door type survey interviewing, which is declining. Another possibility may be the growing consumer literacy of the population who, in return for information, require more and more incentivization.

Marketing research should neither attempt to induce sales of a product or service nor influence consumer attitudes, or intentions of behaviours. Key principles

You Are What You Eat? Tesco's Use of EPOS Data to Profile its Customers

Tesco launched the 'Clubcard' loyalty scheme in 1994, where customers collected points for product items they had bought and Tesco collected customer purchasing information from the electronic point-of-sale (EPOS) data from the product barcodes. Before Clubcard existed, Tesco knew only what people bought, mainly for product replenishment purposes. But it did not know who bought what. That is, until they set up the Clubcard scheme, where customer data was stored against individual purchases.

To manage the analysis of the data, Tesco hired dunnhumby, a specialist customer insight agency. Since the beginning of the relationship, Tesco and dunnhumby have individually and together gone from strength to strength. dunnhumby now processes around 5 billion items of information per week for Tesco or about 156 items of information per week for every household in Britain.

Each customer has a unique profile of past purchase transactions linked to lifestyle data derived from their address details. This information allows Tesco to determine the importance and use of price promotions, the degree of promotional cherry picking (i.e. buying a product only when it is on special offer), the portfolio of products a customer purchases, how much they spend on their groceries, and other issues using a process it calls 'basket analysis'.

In such a situation, data and its use becomes a strategic asset to the firm and allows Tesco to differentiate itself from competitors through highly effective loyalty marketing programmes designed to reward customers for shopping at Tesco stores by providing them with coupons and offers on items of specific interest to them, in addition to a full range of the types of goods that they know the customer likes, in a store format they know the customer appreciates, at a time of their choosing.

Sources: McCawley (2006); Humby (2007).

1 Read the MRS Guidelines on data protection and storage online at www.mrs.org.uk. What are implications for Tesco and dunnhumby?

2 Do you think Tesco really needs all this data to successfully determine what its customers want? Is the investment in customer analytics really worth the cost? Check out Tesco's share price in the last ten years online to see for yourself.

3 What other data might Tesco collect on its customers which will help further understand customer buying patterns, needs, and desires?

of professional market research in the UK are founded on honesty, objectivity, confidentiality, and transparency, derived from the Code of Conduct drawn up by the Market Research Society (MRS). The MRS key principles encompass the following:

- Honesty: Respondents must not be led when asking their cooperation.
- Objectivity: The main purpose of the research should be to collect and analyse information not influence the opinions of the participants.

- Confidentiality: All parties are assured that they will not be identified and the information collected will not be disclosed to anyone else.

- Transparency: Respondents are informed as to the purpose of the research and the time necessary for the collection of the information.

The MRS Code of Conduct—which is itself based on the ESOMAR (European Society for Opinion and Market Research) Code—is binding on all members of the MRS. Research is founded on willing cooperation and depends upon the confidence that it is conducted honestly, objectively, and without unwelcome intrusion or harm to respondents. Its purpose is to collect and analyse information and not to create sales or influence the opinions of anyone participating in it. In this context telephone interviewing is developing a tainted image as it is confused by the respondents with telephone selling.

The general public and other interested parties are entitled to assurances that no information collected in a research survey will be used to identify them, or disclosed to a third party without their consent. Respondents must be informed as to the purpose of the research and the length of time they will be involved in it. Research findings must be reported accurately and not used to mislead, in any way. In conducting any marketing research, researchers have responsibility for themselves, their clients, and the respondents from whom the information is being gathered. The identity of the client for whom the research agency is carrying out the research must always remain confidential. The results of such studies should remain confidential unless agreed by the client and agency and the agency should provide detailed accounts of the methods employed to carry out the research project where this is requested.

International Marketing Research

A great challenge for marketing researchers is to understand how culture operates in international markets and how this impacts upon research design. The complexity of the international business environment ensures that international marketing research is even more complex because of its effect upon the research process and design. More variables need to be considered. The major decision is whether or not to customize international marketing research to each of the separate countries in a study using differing scales, sampling methods, and sizes or try to use one single method for all countries, adopting an international **sampling frame** and where country-specific data would probably no longer be valid in such a situation. In many ways, this debate mirrors the standardization–customization dilemma common in international marketing generally and considered in more detail in Chapter 7 and in the international implications sections of other chapters throughout this text.

The key issue faced by international researchers is to ensure comparable data are collected, despite differences in sampling frames, technological developments, and availability of interviewers. Western approaches to marketing research, data collection, and culture generally might be inappropriate in some research environments because of variations in economic development and consumption patterns. How comparable are the data related to the consumption of McDonald's products collected through personal interviews in Peru, telephone interviews in Canada, and shopping mall intercept questionnaires in the UK? Similarly, we could ask the question is the use of Unilever's Timotei shampoo by consumers in the newly European, former Soviet satellite state Latvia satisfying the same consumer needs as those consumers in the UK?

Ensuring comparability of data in research studies of multiple markets is no simple endeavour. Concepts could be regarded differently, the same products and services could have different functions, language may be used differently—even within a country, products and services might be measured differently, the samples (the people who consume a particular product or service) might be different, and finally the data collection methods adopted may be different because of different country infrastructures. Table 4.3 outlines three types of equivalence: conceptual, functional, and **translation equivalence**. All these types of equivalence impact upon the semantics (i.e. meaning) of words used in different countries, e.g. in developing the wording for questionnaires or in focus groups. Getting the language right is fundamental since it affects how respondents perceive the questions and therefore structure their answers.

Table 4.3 Types of semantic equivalence in international marketing research

Type of equivalence	Explanation	Example
Conceptual equivalence	When interpretation of behaviour, or objects, is similar across countries, conceptual equivalence is said to exist.	Conceptual equivalence needs to be considered when defining the research problem, in wording the questionnaire, and determining the sample unit. There would be less need to investigate 'brand loyalty' in a country in which competition is restricted and choice of products limited.
Functional equivalence	Functional equivalence relates to whether a concept has a similar function in different countries.	Using a bicycle in India where it might be used for transport to and from work, or France where it might be used for shopping, is a different concept from purchasing a bike in the UK, where it might be used for leisure or mountain biking. Functional differences need to be determined before finalizing the research design by ensuring that the constructs used in the research measure what they are supposed to measure, often through focus groups.
Translation equivalence	Translation equivalence is an important aspect of the international research process. Words in some languages have no real equivalent in other languages.	The meaning associated with different words is important in questionnaire design since words can connote a different meaning from that intended when directly translated into another language. To avoid translation errors of these kinds, the researcher can adopt one of the following two methods: 1. Back translation—occurs when a translator fluent in the language in which the questionnaire is to be translated is used and then another translator whose native language was the original language is used to translate back again. Resulting differences in wording can be identified and resolved; 2. Parallel translation—occurs when a questionnaire is translated using a different translator fluent in the language the questionnaire is to be translated into, as well as from, until a final version is agreed upon (Malhotra, 1999: 814).

When designing international research programmes it is important to consider not only how the meaning of words is different but how the data needs to be collected. Different cultures have different ways of measuring concepts. They also live their lives differently which means that it may be necessary to collect the same or similar data in a different way. Table 4.4 outlines how measurement, sampling, and data collection equivalence impacts upon how we conduct international research.

As we can see in Table 4.4, achieving comparability of data when conducting international surveys is very difficult. Generally speaking, the more countries we include in an international study, the more likely it is that error will be introduced and the results and findings will be inaccurate and liable to misinterpretation. International research requires both a local and an international feel and the extent to which one can internationalize certain operations of the research process depends on the objectives of the research.

The International Research Process

With international projects the key task incorporates the decision of how much to centralize and how much to delegate work to local agencies. A multi-country research survey study adopting a survey methodology generally should follow an eleven-stage procedure (Hibbert, 1993). Each stage is outlined in Table 4.5. There is, throughout this process, ample opportunity for misunderstandings, errors, and lack of cultural sensitivity. To proceed as effectively as possible, the central agency should identify a number of trusted local market research providers on a variety of continents. Typically, an international agency will have a network of trusted affiliates who provide such a service and are monitored on a continual basis. As outlined earlier, trying to obtain highly comparable data is difficult and, in such cases, the interpretation of market research reports becomes critical.

RESEARCH INSIGHT 4.4

To take your learning further, you might wish to read this influential paper.

Craig, C. S., and Douglas, S. P (2001), 'Conducting international marketing research in the twenty-first century', *International Marketing Review*, 18, 1, 80–90.

This article outlines how international marketing research practice should change to support firms in the twenty-first century in four key areas. First, international marketing research must focus on market growth opportunities outside the industrialized nations. Second, researchers need to develop the capability to conduct and coordinate research in these diverse research environments. Third, there is a need to develop new creative approaches to probe cultural underpinnings in these countries. Finally, there is a need to incorporate technological changes, including the internet, into the process of conducting and disseminating international research.

Table 4.4

Types of
measurement and
data collection
equivalence

Type of equivalence	Explanation	Example
Measurement equivalence	This concept examines the extent to which measurement scales are comparable across countries.	Surveys are conducted in the USA using imperial systems of measurement, whilst the metric system is used in Europe. Clothing sizes adopt different measurement systems in Europe, North America, or South-East Asia. Multi-item scales present challenges for international researchers as dissatisfaction might not be expressed in the same way in one country compared with another. Some cultures are more open in expressing opinions or describing their behaviour than others.
Sampling equivalence	Determining the appropriate sample to question may provide difficulties when conducting international marketing research projects.	The profile of respondents for the same survey could vary from country to country, e.g. voter research conducted in the UK would question respondents from the age of 18. In South Korea, voting age begins at 21. Different classification systems are in existence for censorship of films shown at the cinema in France compared with Britain, for instance. Where considerable income inequalities exist (e.g. Brazil, Russia, China, Africa), trying to achieve national representativeness could lead to the wrong conclusions where a substantial proportion of the national wealth is concentrated in a small proportion of the population.
Data collection equivalence	When conducting research studies in different countries, it may be appropriate to adopt different data collection strategies.	Typically, data collection methods include mail (or email), personal (or CAPI), or telephone (or CATI). • Mail or email— Used more where literacy or internet access is high and where the mail or email system operates efficiently. Sampling frames are typically compiled from electoral registers, although it is now illegal in some countries to use these lists. European survey respondents can be targeted efficiently and accurately by mail as international sampling frames do exist. • Telephone or CATI (computer-assisted telephone interviewing)—In many countries, telephone penetration may be limited, and computer-assisted telephone interviewing software, using random digit dialling, more limited still. Telephone penetration around 95% in America, although European average figure lower after introduction of new eastern economies. In Germany, use of the telephone for research purposes is illegal. • Personal interviews or CAPI (computer-assisted personal interviewing)—Used most widely in European countries favouring the door-to-door and shopping mall intercept variants. Shopping mall intercept interviews are not appropriate in the Arabic countries where women under sharia law are not to be approached in the street. Here, comparability achieved by using door-to-door interviews. In countries where it is rude to openly disagree with someone, e.g. China, best to use in-depth interviews.

Table 4.5 The international marketing survey research process

Stage	Task	Comments
1	*The project is discussed at length with the client.*	Important to understand client motivations when commissioning the research project. Clients require agency input to determine management problem, whereas more experienced organizations provide an agency with clear problem statements. The research design is determined in draft at this stage with input from the client.
2	*The fieldwork agencies for each country are selected.*	The price of agencies varies greatly in different countries, and they vary on reliability and reputability. Local agencies are often affiliated to larger marketing research organizations, e.g. Wirthlin Europe or Ipsos MORI.
3	*The questionnaire is developed centrally.*	To control research design, and ensure greater fit with strategic objectives, the questionnaire is usually designed centrally to ensure there are no deviations from the original research objectives set.
4	*The questionnaire is translated locally and the translation is checked centrally.*	Although the questionnaire design is undertaken centrally, better to have the questions translated locally so questionnaire is capable of being understood by respondents. People from local agencies are in a better position to know whether or not this is the case.
5	*The questionnaire is piloted locally.*	So that the questionnaire is understood, does not contain errors, and that the research designed for the study is fit for its purpose, the questionnaire should be piloted locally.
6	*The questionnaire is finalized centrally.*	To maintain the client's research objectives, the questionnaire is finalized centrally rather than locally to avoid any misinterpretation.
7	*The interviewers are briefed locally by an executive of the central company.*	A central agency executive should meet local interviewers to ensure that the central company is aware of cultural sensitivities and local difficulties. This allows central staff to monitor how the research project is proceeding at the local level and to maintain quality. The fieldwork is then carried out.
8	*A coding and editing plan is provided for the local agencies.*	This is to ensure that the data corresponds to a set of central standards. Typically, if there are problems with the coding and editing plan, because it does not fit the local understanding, these would be identified before the questionnaires are completed.
9	*The edited and coded questionnaires are returned to the head office.*	Designed to enable the central research agency to cross-tabulate results across countries if necessary and compare data from one country with another, although this is dependent on the extent to which the individual country studies are actually equivalent to one another.
10	*A coding and editing check is carried out centrally.*	This is to ensure that the local agencies have used the appropriate codes and to ensure the validity of the data.
11	*Data processing is carried out centrally.*	To ensure that local offices comply with coding procedures set centrally, the editing and coding checks are carried out centrally. Data processing, including data analysis and interpretation, is also carried out centrally.

Source: Adapted from Hibbert (1993).

Chapter Summary

To consolidate your learning, the key points from this chapter are summarized below.

- Define the terms market research and marketing research.

    Market research originated around the time of the First World War with the first market research department possibly being set up at Procter & Gamble. As a process, market research is intended to provide useful information for the company or organization to design, develop, and implement its decision making in relation to marketing strategy and tactics.

- Explain the role marketing research plays in the decision-making process of a business and the types of research that might be conducted.

    Marketing research plays an important role in the decision-making process of a business and tends to contribute through ad hoc studies as well as continuous data collection, through industry reports and from secondary data sources, as well as through competitive intelligence either commissioned through agencies or conducted internally with data gathered informally through sales forces, customers, and suppliers.

- Explain the importance of competitive intelligence and marketing information systems.

    Competitive intelligence could be regarded as the bastard child of marketing research but has evolved to a distinct sub-discipline which has its own professional society and code of conduct. It comprises information obtained often through informal means from sales force personnel, suppliers, competitors, and customers.

- Recognize the importance of ethics and the adoption of a code of conduct when undertaking marketing research.

    Ethics is an important consideration in marketing research because consumers and customers are providing you with personal information. Their privacy needs to be protected through a professional code of ethics which researchers should adhere to when designing, conducting, and reporting market research programmes.

- Understand the concept of equivalence in relation to obtaining comparable data.

    International market research is complex because of the differences in language, culture, infrastructure, and other factors, which intervene in the data collection process and ensure that obtaining comparable, equivalent data is more difficult.

- Describe the process of coordinating international marketing research.

    International marketing research requires a strong mix of central coordination with local input. It is very important to get the process of international marketing research right, because decisions associated with international markets tend to be more complex and may involve greater investment decisions.

 Visit the **Online Resource Centre** that accompanies this book to read more information relating to marketing research and marketing information systems: www.oxfordtextbooks.co.uk/orc/baines/

❓ Review Questions

1 What are the origins of market research?

2 How do we define market research?

3 What role does marketing research play in the decision-making process of a business?

4 What are the main different types of research that are conducted in marketing?

5 Why is a code of conduct important when conducting marketing research?

6 What is the importance of competitive intelligence and how is it used in a marketing information system?

7 What is the concept of equivalence in relation to obtaining comparable data from different countries?

8 How are the different aspects of the research process affected by differences in equivalence between countries?

9 What is the process of coordinating international marketing research?

❓ Discussion Questions

1 Having read the Case Insight at the beginning of this chapter, how would you advise Bunnyfoot to develop a suitable research proposal? Use the outline proposal in Figure 4.5 to draw up a proposal for a fictional market research agency working with Bunnyfoot to help their financial services client.

2 Orange, the telecommunications company, wants to conduct a market research study aimed particularly at discovering what market segments exist across Europe and how customers and potential customers view the Orange brand. Advise them on the following key components

   (a) Write a market research question and a number of sub-questions for the study.

   (b) How would you go about selecting the particular countries in which to conduct the fieldwork?

   (c) What process would you use when conducting the fieldwork for this multi-country study?

3 What type of research (i.e. causal, descriptive, or exploratory) should be commissioned in the following contexts? Explain why.

   (a) By the management of Bluewater shopping centre in the UK when it wants to determine customer satisfaction with the shopping centre facilities, layout, and store range among the general public.

   (b) By Nintendo when it wants new ideas for new online games for a youth audience.

   (c) By Zara the Spanish fashion retailer when it wants to know what levels of customer service are being offered at its flagship stores.

   (d) By Procter & Gamble, makers of Ariel detergent when it wants to test a new packaging design for six months to see if it is more effective than the existing version. Fifty supermarkets are selected from one key P&G account. In twenty-five of them the new design is used, in the other twenty-five the existing version is used.

4 You've recently set up a new company which has managed to gain 10% of the market for smoothie juice drinks in its first three years. However, in its fourth year, its market share declined due to increased competition in the market. Your key account manager is proposing that you introduce a new vitamin-enhanced organic juice product onto the market. You agree that it sounds like a good idea but want to see what the competitors are doing in this area and how the customers might receive the new product. Suggest a suitable research design for:

(a) Collecting information about what new products the competition is launching.

(b) Deciding whether or not potential customers like the new concept.

In addition, your account manager asks you to:

(c) Outline what secondary data you can find in the area, detailing market shares, market structure, and other industry information, suggesting specific secondary data sources and reports.

5 The following questions are concerned with international marketing research.

(a) How should Colgate Palmolive coordinate international marketing research to determine how to increase sales of its best-selling toothpaste Colgate in different parts of the EMEA (Europe, Middle East, and Africa) market?

(b) Why is it difficult to achieve comparability of data across countries?

📖 References

AMA (2007), 'Marketing Research', Dictionary of Marketing Terms, available at: www.marketingpower.com, accessed 17 June 2007.

Anon. (1989), *The Hutchinson Concise Encyclopedia*, 2nd edn., London: BCA.

——(2005), The Encarta Encyclopedia, http://encarta.msn.com/encyclopedia_761571053/Gallup_George_Horace.html, accessed December 2007.

A. C. Nielson (2007), 'Our History', available at http://acnielsen.com/company/what.shtml, accessed 17 June 2007.

Arvidsson, A. (2004), 'On the "pre-history of the panoptic sort": mobility in market research', *Surveillance and Society*, 4, 1, 456–74.

Ashill, N. J., and Jobber, D. (1999), 'Defining the information needs of senior marketing executives: an exploratory study', *Qualitative Market Research: An International Journal*, 4, 1, 52–60.

Axelrod, J. N. (1970), '14 Rules for building an MIS', *Journal of Advertising Research*, 10, 3, 3–12.

Baines, P., and Chansarkar, B. (2002), *Introducing Marketing Research*, Chichester: John Wiley and Sons.

Bryman, A. (1989), *Research Methods and Organisation Studies*, London: Unwin Hyman.

Chisnall P. M. (1992). *Marketing Research*, 4th edn., Maidenhead: McGraw-Hill.

Context Research Group (2007), 'An ethnography of the Guinness experience across key market segments', available at www.contextresearch.com/context/clients/clients_case_guiness.cfm, accessed 20 June 2007.

Deshpande, R., and Zaltman, G. (1984), 'A comparison of factors affecting researcher and manager perceptions of market research use', *Journal of Marketing Research*, 21, 1, 32–8.

Elle, A. H. (1999), 'From marketing research to competitive intelligence: useful generalisation or loss of focus?', *Management Decision*, 37, 6, 519–25.

ESOMAR (1995), *ICC/ESOMAR International Code of Marketing and Social Research Practice*, 6, available at www.esomar.org, accessed 17 June 2007.

——(2006), Highlights 2006, available at www.esomar.org/uploads/pdf/ESOMAR_Highlights_ 2006.pdf, accessed 14 July 2007.

Euromonitor (2006), Vacuum Cleaner Possession, Retail Sales and Volumes, *Global Market Information Database*, available at www.euromonitor.com, accessed 6 August 2007.

Goulding, C. (2002), *Grounded Theory*, London: Sage Publications.

Hardman, R. (1998), 'Palace focuses on public opinion', *The Telegraph*, Monday, 5 January, available at www.telegraph.co.uk, accessed 19 June 2007.

Hibbert. E. (1993), 'Research international markets: how can we ensure validity of results?', *Marketing and Research Today*, November, 222–8.

Humby, C. (2007), 'R is for relevance: an antidote to CRM hype', Paper presented to the Return on Marketing Investment (ROMI) Club, May, Cranfield: Cranfield University.

IMDB (2007), *DVD Details for Final Destination, I, II, III*, available at www.imdb.com, accessed 17 June 2007.

Ipsos MORI (2007), 'Index of polls on the monarchy', available at http://www.ipsos-mori.com/ polls/monarchy/indexmon.shtml, accessed 20 June 2007.

Kotler, P. (2005), *FAQs on Marketing: Answered by the Guru of Marketing*, London: Cyan Books.

McCawley, I. (2006), 'Analysis: dunnhumby—Department of Tesco', *Marketing Week*, 8 June, 13.

Malhotra, N. K. (1999), *Marketing Research: An Applied Approach*, 3rd edn., Englewood Cliffs, NJ: Prentice-Hall.

Miles, L. (2004), 'Online, on tap', *Marketing*, 16 June, 39–40.

Newline Cinema (2000), 'A look at test screening', in *Final Destination*, DVD edn., New Line Home Cinema.

MRS (2005), 'Research', in *Code of Conduct—September 2005*, London: Market Research Society, available at www.mrs.org.uk, accessed 17 June 2007.

——(2006), BMRA Turnover Summary—Year 2005, www.mrs.org.uk/mrindustry/downloads/ bmra_league_%20tables_2005.pdf, accessed 4 February 2007.

Nolan, J. (1999), *Confidential: Uncover your Competitors' Top Business Secrets Legally and Quickly— and Protect your Own*, New York: HarperBusiness.

Parasuraman, A. (1991), *Marketing Research*, 2nd edn., Wokingham: Addison-Wesley, 280–309.

Penneberg, A. L., and Barry, M. (2000), *Spooked: Espionage in Corporate America*, Cambridge, Mass.: Perseus Publishing.

Pinkerton, R. L. (1969), 'How to develop a marketing intelligence system', *Industrial Marketing*, 5 part series, April–August.

Rotten Tomatoes (2007), *Final Destination (2000), Final Destination II (2003), Final Destination III (2006)*, available at www.rottentomatoes.com, accessed 17 June 2007.

Stevens, R. E. (2003), 'Views from the hills', 'Genesis II: The Second Beginning', www.popsg.org/ views/27oct03.html, accessed 2 December 2007.

Summerskill, B. (2001), 'Queen asks Big Breakfast creator for image makeover', *The Observer*, Sunday, 1 April.

Part 2

Principles of Marketing Management

Part 2 discusses the principles of marketing management. It focuses on marketing strategy, segmentation and positioning, market development, international marketing, and, finally, marketing implementation and control.

Part 1: Marketing Fundamentals

1 Marketing Principles and Society
2 The Marketing Environment
3 Marketing Psychology and Consumer Buying Behaviour
4 Marketing Research and Marketing Information Systems

❯ Part 2: Principles of Marketing Management

5 Marketing Strategy
6 Market Segmentation and Positioning
7 Market Development and International Marketing
8 Marketing implementation and Control

Part 3: The Marketing Mix Principle

9 Products, Services, and Branding Decisions
10 Price Decisions
11 An Introduction to Marketing Communications
12 Marketing Communications: Tools and Techniques
13 Managing Marketing Communications: Strategy, Planning, and Implementation
14 Channel Management and Retailing

Part 4: Principles of Relational Marketing

15 Services Marketing and Non-Profit Marketing
16 Business-to-Business Marketing
17 Relationship Marketing

Part 5: Contemporary Marketing Practice

18 New Technology and Marketing
19 Postmodern Marketing
20 Marketing Ethics

5

Marketing Strategy

Experience is that marvellous thing that enables you to recognize a mistake when you make it again.

Franklin P. Jones

Learning Outcomes

After studying this chapter you should be able to:

✔ Describe the strategic planning process.

✔ Explain the key influences that impact on marketing strategy.

✔ Explain how understanding competitors can assist the development of marketing strategy.

✔ Identify the characteristics of strategic marketing goals and explain the nature of the associated growth strategies.

✔ Describe different approaches and concepts associated with strategic marketing action.

✔ Explain how scenario planning and SWOT analysis can help strategic marketing decision making.

✔ Outline the key elements within a marketing plan.

Innocent Drinks market their smoothies in a highly innovative way. What strategies will they use to market their new water/juice drinks? We speak to Dan Germain, Head of Creative at Innocent, to find out more.

Dan Germain for Innocent Drinks

Innocent Drinks make smoothies, drinks made from pure whole crushed fruit, with no preservatives, colouring, or nasty additives. They're sold in little bottles and big cartons, all of which feature trademark innocent fun and games on the back of the pack. Innocent effectively developed a whole new drinks sector, one that many experts at the start said could not be done. Innocent is now a £100 million business.

In 1999 Innocent's three co-founders had a great product, lots of enthusiasm, but no experience of running a business, no customers, and no turnover. To help get started we made a few smoothies and sold them at a small music festival. We asked our customers to place their empty cups in a 'yes' or 'no' bin to vote whether the three of us should give up our jobs and make smoothies full-time. At the end of the weekend, the 'yes' bin was full and so we quit our jobs the next day, spent several months finding the necessary finance and started a company that is now doubling its profits every year.

> *We asked our customers to place their empty cups in a 'yes' or 'no' bin to vote whether the three of us should give up our jobs and make smoothies full-time*

It has not all been plain sailing, as initially distributors refused to stock our drinks. Innocent's response was to load up a van and take the drinks to delicatessens and health food shops in Notting Hill. As a form of introduction we said, 'we're a local juice company that's just started up, here's four boxes for free, stick them on your shelves and if they sell give us a ring'. Out of the 50 shops reached, 45 wanted more. We then went back to the distributors, told them the story about the delis, and gave them a pallet for free. Now Innocent drinks are sold in over 7,000 outlets—a big change from those early days.

However, with growth and success questions arose about how we should develop the company and the Innocent brand. There are lots of opportunities to move into a number of health-related sectors. The strong ethical and health credentials associated with the brand provide opportunities for development, but these beliefs can constrain and limit the scope of the areas we can move into. For example, one area with great potential is drinks made from fruit juice and spring water.

But there are plenty of these types of products already in the market so could Innocent branded fruit/water juice be successful, and would such a product harm the Innocent brand?

Innocent's range of smoothies

Innocent Drinks

Introduction

Have you ever thought about how organizations organize themselves so that they can make sales, achieve profits, and keep all their stakeholders satisfied? As you can imagine this does not happen accidentally and a great deal of thought, discussion, planning, and action needs to occur. This involves getting answers to questions such as which markets the organization should be operating in, what resources are necessary in order to be successful in these markets, who are the key competitors and what strategies are they using, how can we develop and sustain an advantage over these competitors, and what is happening in the wider world that might affect our organization? These questions refer to issues that represent the strategic context in which organizations operate. These contextual issues can be considered in terms of four main elements, namely: the organization (and its resources, skills, and capabilities), the target customers, a firm's competitors, and the wider environment. These are set out at Figure 5.1.

Motorola's strategic context is shaped by its communications expertise and leading-edge technology skills, customers who expect a stream of added value communication-related products, and Nokia, its main competitor and market leader in the mobile phone handset market. In addition, the wider environment is becoming politically more sensitive to climatic change issues, terrorism anxieties, social change, and surges in technological development. By understanding and managing these four elements it is possible to develop a coherent strategic marketing plan through which products or services have a greater chance of success than if no analysis or planning is undertaken. In order that a marketing strategy be developed successfully, first it is necessary to understand an organization's strategic context and to then fit the marketing strategy so that it matches the strategic context. Many organizations articulate their strategic context and their intended performance in the markets they have targeted, in terms of a framework that defines their vision, mission, values, organizational goals, and organizational strategy.

Figure 5.1
The four elements of
the strategic context

The **vision** sets out an organization's future. A vision is a statement about what an organization wants to become. It should give shape and direction to an organization's future. A vision should stretch an organization in terms of its current position and performance yet at the same time it should help employees feel involved and motivated to want to be part of the organization's future. ASB Bank's vision statement is 'To be the best bank and financial services provider in New Zealand, excelling in customer service'.

The **mission** represents what the organization wishes to achieve in the long term. It should be a broad statement of intention as it sets out an organization's purpose and direction. It should be oriented to particular markets and customers served. A mission applies to all parts of an organization and in that sense serves to bind the many parts of an organization together. However, above all else, the mission should provide a reference point for its managers and employees. The mission should help managers make decisions concerning which opportunities to pursue and which to ignore. It should aid investment and development decision making. See Table 5.1 for examples of different mission statements.

Table 5.1
A selection of mission statements

Organization	Mission statement
Tesco	To create value for customers to earn their lifetime loyalty.
Coca-Cola	Everything we do is inspired by our enduring mission: To refresh the world . . . in body, mind, and spirit. To inspire moments of optimism . . . through our brands and our actions. To create value and make a difference . . . everywhere we engage.
EasyJet	To provide our customers with safe, good-value, point-to-point air services. To effect and to offer a consistent and reliable product and fares appealing to leisure and business markets on a range of European routes. To achieve this we will develop our people and establish lasting relationships with our suppliers.
Oxfam	Oxfam works with others to overcome poverty and suffering.
IBM	At IBM, we strive to lead in the invention, development, and manufacture of the industry's most advanced information technologies, including computer systems, software, storage systems, and microelectronics. We translate these advanced technologies into value for our customers through our professional solutions, services, and consulting businesses worldwide.
JCB	Our mission is to grow our company by providing innovative, strong, and high-performance products and solutions to meet our global customers' needs. We will support our world-class products by providing superior customer care. Our care extends to the environment and the community. We want to help build a better future for our children, where hard work and dedication are given their just reward.

Source: Company websites.

Mission statements are sometimes prepared as a public relations exercise or are so generic that they fail to provide sufficient guidelines or inspiration. Some are just not realistic. For example, to expect an airport such as Adelaide or Hong Kong to become the largest airport is the world is totally infeasible. These are to be avoided. Good mission statements are market not product oriented. For example, the product-oriented approach 'we make and sell lorries and trucks' is too general and runs the risk of becoming outdated and redundant. By focusing on the needs of customers that the organization is seeking to serve, the mission can have a much longer lifespan. So, 'we transport your products quickly and safely to your customers', or 'logistical solutions for your company' provides a market approach to the mission statement. Amazon.com does not sell books, videos, and DVDs (product approach): much better to say that Amazon.com provides a 'friendly, safe and entertaining online buying environment'. Similarly, Haier, the leading Chinese manufacturer, do not make home appliances, 'they make lives more convenient and comfortable through innovative appliances'.

An organization's values must be in line with its vision and mission, if only because they define how people should behave with each other in the organization and help shape how the goals will be achieved. **Organizational values** define the acceptable interpersonal and operating standards of behaviour. They govern and guide the behaviour of individuals within the organization. Organizations that identify and develop a clear, concise, and shared meaning of values and beliefs shape the organizational culture and provide direction so that all participants can understand and contribute.

Organizational values are important because they can help to guide and constrain not only behaviour but also the recruitment and selection decisions. Without them individuals tend to pursue behaviours that are in line with their own individual value systems, which may lead to inappropriate behaviours and a failure to achieve the overall goals.

Organizational goals at the strategic level represent what should be achieved, the outcomes of the organization's various activities. These may be articulated in terms of profit, market share, share value, return on investment, or numbers of customers served. In some cases the long term may not be a viable period and a short-term focus is absolutely essential. For example, should an organization's financial position become precarious then it may be necessary to focus on short-term cash strategies in order to remain solvent and so remove any threat arising from a takeover or administrators being called in prior to bankruptcy.

Organization or corporate strategy is the means by which the resources of the organization are matched with the needs of the environment in which the organization decides to operate. Corporate strategy involves bringing together the human resources, logistics, production, marketing, IT, and financial parts of an organization into a coherent strategic plan that supports, reinforces, and helps accomplish the organizational goals, in the most effective and efficient way. In this chapter we are concerned with the make-up of the marketing strategy that should support and reinforce the corporate strategy.

In some very large organizations the planning process is made complicated and difficult because the organization operates in a number of significantly different markets. In these cases the organization creates **strategic business units** or SBUs. Each SBU assumes the role of a separate company and creates its own strategies and plans in order to achieve its corporate goals and contribution to the overall organization. So, the German company Bosch GmbH also operates through three SBUs, namely Automotive Technologies, Industrial Technologies, and Consumer Goods and Building Technology. Royal Philips Electronics use four SBUs: Domestic Appliances and Personal Care, Lighting, Medical Systems, and Consumer Electronics. All of these represent significantly different markets, each with their own characteristics, customer needs, and competitors.

So, at a broad level the strategic planning process is as follows:

- At the corporate level the organization sets out its overall vision, mission, values.

- These are then converted into measurable (corporate) goals that apply to the whole organization.

- Then, depending upon the size of the organization, the range of businesses (SBUs) and/or products is determined, and then resources are allocated to help and support each one.

- Each business and/or product develops detailed functional and competitive strategies and plans, such as a marketing strategy and plan.

What arises from this is that marketing strategy and planning should support and contribute to the overall company strategy. However, it should also be understood that marketing strategy and planning can occur at the business, product, or market level. In March 2007, Procter & Gamble decided to leave the paper business, and this involved selling off Charmin, its toilet tissue brand, and its market-leading kitchen paper brand Bounty.

Marketing Strategy

There are many areas in which corporate strategy and marketing strategy overlap each other. As a result, many of the techniques that we will now examine can be applied at both a strategic as well as a functional marketing level. However, some of the more important differences can be seen in Figure 5.2. Here it can be seen that there should be positive support, indeed interaction, between the two.

What Are Their Strengths and Weaknesses?

Getting information about a competitor's range of products and their sales volumes and value, their profitability, prices, and discount structures, the nature of their relationships with suppliers and distributors, their communications campaigns and special offers, are all important. In some circumstances, getting information about new products that are either in development or about to be launched can be critical.

In addition to these marketing elements, however, it is important to obtain information about a whole range of other factors, not just their marketing activities. These factors include their production and manufacturing capabilities, their technical, management, and financial resources, and their processes, distribution channels, and relative success in meeting customer and market needs.

As this information accumulates and is updated through time, it is necessary to use the information in order to understand what a competitor's strengths and weaknesses might be and to then use this to either avoid the areas where competitors are strong or exploit the weaknesses. The overall task is to determine what **competitive advantage** a competitor might have and whether this advantage can be sustained, imitated, or undermined. Ideas about competitive advantage are explored in greater detail later in this chapter.

What Are Their Strategic Goals?

Contrary to what is often written in the popular press, profit is not the single, overall strategic goal for most organizations. Firms develop a range of goals, encompassing ambitions such as achieving a certain market share (which is quite common), market leadership, industry recognition for technological prowess or high-quality performance, or market reputation for innovation, environmental concern, or ethical trading.

One way of developing an understanding of a competitor's strategic goals is to build their product portfolio and then project probable goals and intentions. For example, a firm with a recognizable 'star' product will be looking to build this into a 'cash cow' at the earliest opportunity. Firms with products classified as 'dogs' might concentrate on harvesting as much cash as possible.

Developing a full understanding of a competitor's strategic goals is not an easy task and they can usually only be inferred from a competitor's actions. Some firms try to recruit senior executives from their competitors in order to get real insight into their strategic intentions. Although this happens quite frequently it is not an ethical way of operating and organizations can impose severe legal and financial constraints on employees in terms of who they can work for if they leave and the timescale in which they are not allowed to work in the industry.

Which Strategies Are They Following?

Once a competitor's goals are understood it becomes easier to predict what their marketing strategies are likely to be. These strategies can be considered through two main factors, competitive scope and positioning.

Competitive scope refers to the breadth of market addressed. Is the competitor attempting to service the whole of a market, particular segments, or a single niche segment? If they are servicing a niche market one of the key questions to be asked is whether they will want to stay and dominate the niche or are they simply using it as a trial before springboarding into other market segments?

Brands can be positioned in markets according to the particular attributes and benefits a brand offers. Cameras might be positioned according to their technical features, whilst cosmetics are often positioned on style and fashion, frequently with campaigns led by brand ambassadors who are considered to personify the brand values. Once this is understood it is possible to follow the marketing mix elements that are aligned to support the positioning strategy. Some brands are based on price and a low-cost strategy. This approach requires that there is a focus on reducing costs and expenses rather than investing in heavy levels of marketing communications and/or product development. We will consider low-cost strategies in further detail later in this chapter.

How Are They Likely to Respond?

Understanding the strategies of competitors helps inform whether they are intent on outright attack or defence and how they might react to particular strategies initiated by others. For example, a price cut might be met with a similar reduction, a larger reduction, or none at all. Changes in the levels of investment in advertising might produce a similar range of responses.

Some market leaders believe that an aggressive response to a challenger's actions is important otherwise their leadership position might be undermined. There are of course a range of responses that firms may use, reflecting organizational objectives, leadership styles, industry norms, and new strategies born of new owners. (See Market Insight 5.2.)

MARKET INSIGHT 5.2

Challenging and Competitive Games

The games console market is intensely competitive but because of the severe upfront development and launch costs, the launch of a new system is often delayed. This is because of the experience curve effects, namely that as more units are sold and as a market matures a console becomes cheaper to make. Games are expensive to develop but manufacturing costs are very low, which means that successful consoles are extremely profitable, even though hardware is sold at a loss to build market share.

Sony's PlayStation brand has dominated the games console market in recent years. The main competition in the market comes from Microsoft, the market challenger, and the launch of Microsoft's Xbox 360 was an attempt to achieve market leadership. One of the reasons for Sony's success, which has continued with PS3, is that Sony had established the original PlayStation as a brand. This meant that a huge consumer base had been established and one of the key attributes of the PS2 was that it was backwards-compatible with PlayStation games, therefore enabling games developed for the first machine to be used on the PS2. In addition, it was able to play DVDs, unlike the competition, a major point of differentiation.

Sony's PlayStation 3

Sony

Market leaders sometimes like to delay the launch of new products in order to capitalize on the revenue streams and margins associated with established brands. In this case it appears that Sony delayed the launch of its next generation based upon the logistical challenges it faced in producing sufficient stock to have a successful launch. Failing to fulfil market demand might have given the market challenger an opportunity to take share. The key challenger, Microsoft with their Xbox 360, sought to destabilize Sony by introducing new products with new attributes. Part of their strategy was to launch the Xbox 360 simultaneously in all major markets.

Another challenger, Nintendo, launched a radically new games console called Wii in December 2006. The feature of this product was that the conventional key pad was replaced with an innovative motion-sensitive controller. One of the key attributes of the market leader's response, the PS3 launched in the UK in March 2007, was to provide a built-in Blu-ray disc player, as they believe it provides the best next-generation gaming experience, and has the added advantage of being able to play high-definition movies.

Source: Schofield (2005); Andrews (2006); Arthur (2007); www.en.wikipedia.org/wiki/Console_wars.

1 In view of the length of time associated with developing new consoles, to what extent can games consoles compete on attributes?

2 What markets are the console manufacturers in and apart from using product attributes what are the main ways in which they compete?

3 What do you believe are Sony and Microsoft's strategic goals?

4 What advantage do you think Wii thought they would achieve with a radically new product offering?

Suppliers and Distributors

So far, analysis of the performance environment has tended to concentrate on the nature and characteristics of a firm's competitive behaviour. This is of course important, but Porter also realized that suppliers can influence competition and he built this into his Five Forces model. However, since he published his work there have been several significant supply side developments, most notably the development of outsourcing. Outsourcing concerns the transfer of non-core activities to an external organization which specializes in the activity or operation. For example, transport and delivery services are not core activities to most companies although they constitute an important part of the value they offer their customers. In Japan, the Hitachi Transport System, a third-party logistic (3PL) service, is used by companies as an outsourced provider to transport their goods. Many suppliers therefore, have become an integral part of a firm's capabilities. Rather than act aggressively they are more likely to be cooperative and work in support of the firm that has outsourced their work to them.

Similar changes have occurred downstream in terms of a manufacturer's marketing channel. Now it is common to find high levels of integration between a manufacturer and intermediary. Account needs to be taken of the strength of these relationships and consideration needs to be given to how market performance might be strengthened or weakened by the capabilities of the channel intermediairy. Suppliers and distributors have become central to the way in which firms can develop specific competitive advantages. It is important, therefore, that analysis of the performance environment incorporate a review of those organizations that are key suppliers and distributors to the firm under analysis.

Scenario Planning

Environmental scanning, used to monitor the external environment, is about collecting largely historical information concerning the external and performance environments. What is also required is a glimpse into the future but, unfortunately, the past is no predictor of future performance. Market research reports only report on previous trends. They cannot tell us the future. They can outline past trends that may point to future trends but they cannot predict the future with any degree of certainty. In order to cope with this limitation in strategy development, executives developed scenario planning. **Scenario planning** is a technique first developed by Herman Khan and his associates at the Rand Corporation, in the 1950/1960s (Verity, 2003). The scenario planning technique was originally used at Rand Corporation to envisage different scenarios under which nuclear war might break out between the USA and the then Soviet Union. The intention behind scenario planning is to understand how trends might influence the future of an organization and how managers can gain a better understanding of some of the uncertainties an organization faces if it pursues particular strategies (Schoemaker, 1995). The intention behind scenario planning is to create a small number of potential alternative futures using a small, diverse team of managers who meet regularly in workshops for a specified period of time, or on a continuous basis.

RESEARCH INSIGHT 5.2

To take your learning further, you might wish to read this influential paper.

Schoemaker, P. J. H. (1995), 'Scenario planning: a tool for strategic thinking', *Sloan Management Review*, 36, 2 (Winter), 25–40.

A much quoted paper on scenario planning, this outlines the process and why it is necessary for managers to overcome tunnel vision and overconfidence in their strategic decision making by envisaging potential alternative future realities for a company.

In addition, the team should aim to conduct or commission research to support their objectives.

Scenario planning differs from forecasting in that it accepts uncertainty. It is based more on imagination than extrapolation of trends, and so is more likely to cover future situations which arise as a result of discontinuous change rather than incremental change. Scenarios are developed not as predictions or preferred outcomes but as potential and credible stories of what the future might look like for a particular firm. Science fiction really has come to business and government.

Governments and multinational corporations now routinely develop their policy based on long-run scenario planning, sometimes known as strategic foresight. In the USA, the strategic foresight programme is the remit of the Office of Management and Budget, while in the UK this function is performed by the Department for Business, Enterprise and Regulatory Reform, and in the State of Victoria in Australia this function is undertaken within the Department of Premier and Cabinet (Leigh, 2003). (See Market Insight 5.3 for Shell's use of scenario planning.)

SWOT Analysis

Perhaps the most common analytical tool is SWOT analysis. SWOT stands for Strengths, Weaknesses, Opportunities, and Threats. Essentially it is a series of checklists derived from the marketing audit and the PESTLE analysis and is presented as internal strengths and weaknesses, and external opportunities or threats.

Strengths and weaknesses relate to the internal resources and capabilities of the organization, as perceived by customers (Piercy, 2002).

- A strength is something an organization is good at doing or something that gives it particular credibility and market advantage.

- A weakness is something an organization lacks or performs in an inferior way in comparison to others.

Opportunities and threats are externally oriented issues that can potentially influence the performance of an organization or product. Information about these elements is normally generated through the PESTLE analysis.

Shell: What to Do When the Future is Murky

One organization which has wholeheartedly embraced the scenario planning technique is the Anglo-Dutch oil giant Shell. In 1972, Shell produced six future scenarios based on economic growth, oil supply, and oil price options, one of which incorporated a disruption in oil supply, a discontinuous change, which subsequently materialized as the OPEC oil crisis, arising after the Arab oil embargo following the Arab–Israeli Yom Kippur War in 1973. Since then, due to its success, the scenario planning process has been accepted as an appropriate technique to imagine the future and its potential impact.

Shell's latest scenario planning exercise in the early 2000s has imagined the following three worlds facing it in the near future:

- Low Trust Globalization, where governments use market incentives to promote economic efficiency in a strict regulatory and security environment with continual regulatory change, and institutions with overlapping legal authority (e.g. EU, EU members, WTO). The focus of business is to develop superior risk management and public affairs functions.

- Open Doors, where the world develops as a transnational society based on economic incentives (e.g. trade blocs developing into political unions). As a result, regulations are harmonized with increasingly close developments between societies and between businesses. This brings about increased diffusion of knowledge, increasing productivity. The focus of business is to develop enhanced networking, teamworking, and skills in managing diversity.

- Flags, where a reaction occurs against globalization resulting in fragmentation of political, social, and religious groupings, resulting in the rise of the nation state rather than transnational groupings. Governments pass legislation based on populist sentiments, inhibiting international trade. The focus of business is to develop stringent country-by-country risk management strategies.

Source: Cornelius, Van de Putte, and Romani (2005).

1 How useful do you think it really is to imagine a company's futures? Why do you say that?

2 Do you think it matters how broad or how specific the futures that a team come up with are?

3 Why do you think that scenario planners tend to use only 2–3 future scenarios?

- An opportunity is a potential to advance the organization by the development and satisfaction of an unfulfilled market need.

- A threat is something that at some time in the future may destabilize and/or reduce the potential performance of the organization.

SWOT analysis is a tool used to determine an overall view of an organization's strategic position. It highlights the need for a strategy to produce a strong fit between the internal capability (strengths and weaknesses) and the external situation (opportunities and threats). SWOT helps to sort through the information generated in the audit, it serves to identify the key issues, and then prompts thought about converting weaknesses into strengths and threats into opportunities, in other words generating conversion strategies. For example, some companies have developed and run call centres for their own internal use, but saw opportunities to use their strength to run call centres for other companies. It is said that a few years ago, one major computer company only used its call centre during the day and at night the operation was not used. An opportunity was then spotted to run the call centre at night, routing calls for a nationwide pizza company.

SWOT in inexperienced hands often leads to long lists of items. Whilst the SWOT process may lead to the generation of these lists, the analyst should be attempting to identify the *key* strengths and weaknesses and the *key* opportunities and threats. These key elements should impact upon strategy; if they don't then they should not be in the analysis. A strength is not a strength if it does not have strategic implications.

Once the three or four elements of each part of the SWOT matrix have been derived then a number of pertinent questions need to be asked.

1 Does the organization do something far better than its rivals? If it does, this is known as a competitive advantage (distinctive competence, differential advantage) and this can lead to a competitive edge.

2 Which of the organization's weaknesses does strategy need to correct and is it competitively vulnerable?

3 Which opportunities can be pursued and are there the necessary resources and capabilities to exploit them?

4 Which strategies are necessary to defend against the key threats?

Figure 5.4 depicts a SWOT grid for a small digital media agency. The outcome of a successful SWOT analysis is a series of decisions that help develop and formulate strategy and goals.

Note that there are no more than four items against any one category, not a whole list of ten or so items. It is important to prioritize and make a judgement about what is really key rather than just an interesting point. The actions that

Strengths	Weaknesses
Quick to respond to changes in the marketing environment	Too much work from a few clients and at non-premium rates
Flat management encourages fast decision making	Little project-management skills
	High office and finance costs
Use of contractors enables flexibility—lowers employment costs/finance and improves customers' perception of expertise	Low customer base
Opportunities	**Threats**
Emerging markets such as Professional Services (e.g. dentists, lawyers, surveyors)	Larger media houses buying business
New distribution channels	Speed of technological advances
Tax incentives to encourage eCommerce	Contractors have low levels of loyalty

Figure 5.4
A SWOT analysis for a small digital media agency

RESEARCH INSIGHT 5.3

To take your learning further, you might wish to read this influential paper.

Prahalad, C. K., and Hamel, G. (1990), 'The core competence of the organisation', *Harvard Business Review*, 68, 3 (May–June), 79–91.

This paper was incredibly important because it provided a first important insight into the criticality of core competencies as a means of developing superior business performance.

follow the identification of the key issues should be based around matching opportunities with strengths and weaknesses with threats. In this example it may be possible to diversify into professional services, a niche market (an opportunity), using particular contractors who have knowledge and relevant expertise (a strength).

Weaknesses need to be addressed, not avoided. Some can be converted into strengths, others into opportunities. In this example, entering the professional services market would probably increase the number of customers and enable premium rates to be earned.

Threats need to be nullified. For example, by building relationships with key contractors (suppliers) and selected larger media houses, these threats might be dissipated, and even developed into strengths.

Strategic Marketing Goals

The purpose of strategic market analysis is to help managers understand the nature of the industry, the way firms behave competitively within the industry, and how competition is generally undertaken. From this information it becomes easier to determine exactly what the marketing strategy should actually achieve, in other words, what the strategic marketing goals should be.

There are several types of strategic objective but four main ones are considered here. These are niche, hold, harvest, and divest goals and are considered briefly. However, the section that follows considers a further objective, namely growth. Figure 5.5 sets out the content for this section.

Niche objectives are often the most suitable when firms operate in a market dominated by a major competitor and where their financial resources are limited. A niche can either be a small segment or even a small part of a segment. Niche markets often arise because it is not economic for the leading competitors to enter this segment simply because these customers have special needs and the leading firm does not want to devote resources in this way. To be successful in niche markets it is important to have a strongly differentiated product offering, supported by a high level of service. The Australian government identified several niche markets when exploring ways in which it could develop its tourism

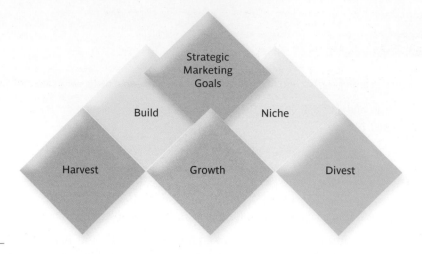

Figure 5.5
Five dimensions of
strategic marketing
goals

business. It identified sports, cycling seniors, culture and the arts, backpackers, health, defence, people with disabilities, caravanning and camping, food, wine, and agritourism as potential niche markets.

Hold objectives are concerned with defence. They are designed to prevent and fend off attack from aggressive competitors. Market leaders are the most likely to adopt a holding strategy as they are prone to attack from new entrants and their closest rivals as they strive for the most market share. Market leadership is important as it generally drives positive cash flows, confers privileges such as strong bargaining positions with suppliers, and enhances image and reputation. Holding strategies can take a number of forms, varying from 'doing nothing' in order to maintain market equilibrium, implementing a counter-offensive defence, to withdrawing from a market completely.

Harvesting objectives are often employed in mature markets as firms/products enter a decline phase. The goal is to maximize short-term profits and stimulate a positive cash flow. By stripping out most of the marketing communications and R&D it becomes possible to generate cash which can be used elsewhere. These funds can be used to generate new products, support 'stars', or to turn 'question marks' into 'dogs' if it is realized that there will not be a long-term profit stream.

Divest objectives are sometimes necessary when products continue to incur losses and generate negative cash flows. Divestment can follow on naturally from a harvesting strategy. Typically low-share products in declining markets are prime candidates to be divested. Divestment may be actioned by selling off the product should a suitable buyer be available, or simply withdrawing from the market. Sunny Delight, a fruit juice brand, achieved phenomenal success when it was launched in the 1990s. However, sales plummeted following poor publicity in particular about its dubious nutritional value, with high sugar levels, a large number of preservatives, and a vast amount of e based artificial colouring. The owners, Procter & Gamble, took the decision to withdraw the brand from the market and sold it to the Sunny Delight Beverages Company who repositioned and relaunched the brand in 2005, this time with 15 per cent real fruit juice, no preservatives or artificial colouring agents.

	Present Products	**New Products**
Present Markets	Market Penetration	Product Development
New Markets	Market Development	Diversification

Figure 5.6
Ansoff matrix
Source: Adapted from Ansoff (1957).

Growth

The vast majority of organizations consider growth to be a primary objective. However, there are different forms of growth and care needs to be taken to ensure that the right growth goals are selected. Growth can be intensive, integrated, or diversified.

- **Intensive** growth refers to concentrating activities on markets and/or products that are familiar. By increasing market share or by introducing new products to an established market growth, growth is achieved by intensifying activities.

- **Integrative** growth occurs where an organization continues to work with the same products and same markets but starts to perform some of the activities in the value chain that were previously undertaken by others. For example, Benetton moved from designing and manufacturing their clothing products into retailing.

- Growth through **diversification** refers to developments outside the current chain of value adding activities. This type of growth brings new value chain activities because the firm is operating with new products and in new markets.

The idea that growth is allied to the product/market relationships is important and Ansoff (1957) proposed that organizations should first consider whether new or established products are to be delivered in new or established markets. His product/market matrix, reproduced at Figure 5.6 above, and otherwise known as Ansoff's matrix, is an important first step in deciding what the marketing strategy should be.

The product/market matrix is examined further in Chapter 7.

Intensive Growth

The product/market matrix helps to focus thoughts on what exactly is to be achieved. Growth through market penetration and both market and product development is regarded as intensive growth. Table 5.2 overleaf sets out the key characteristics of each of the three forms of intensive growth.

A **market penetration** strategy requires continued participation in the same market with the same products. Growth is achieved by capturing a larger share of the market with the same products. As market experience increases it could be said that risk is minimized and the risk of new product development is avoided.

Table 5.2

Characteristics of
intensive growth

Strategic goal	Explanation
Market penetration	To increase the sales of established products in current markets.
Market development	To increase the sales of established products in new markets.
Product development	To increase sales by developing new products for delivery in current markets.
Diversification	To increase sales by developing new products for delivery in new markets.

A **market development strategy** suggests that management are dissatisfied with the potential offered by current markets. However, there are many difficulties associated with this high-risk strategy. For example, there is little market knowledge or understanding about the buyers or the other organizations and products currently competing for the attention of the current customers. This means that a great deal of work needs to be done prior to entry.

A **product development** strategy means that growth is to be achieved through new products generating increased market share. This can be a risky strategy particularly as the success rate of new products is poor. For example, in the confectionery market customers are prone to product switching, brand lifecycles are short and customer loyalty is weak. It is important therefore to make sure that the risk of failure is minimized and that competitor's new products are matched. For example, Cadbury Schweppes, the world's largest confectionery manufacturer, bought Adams, which was then US market leader in chewing gum and related products. In February 2007 they launched four Trident chewing gum brands into the UK market, at a time when there was growing media attention to obesity issues and confectionery sales were falling (Miller, 2007).

Diversified Growth

When an organization adopts a diversification strategy they are essentially moving outside their current, known areas of expertise. Through diversification they begin to work with new products, in new markets, and this brings new risks. Diversified growth can take one of three forms, namely horizontal, concentric, and conglomerate diversification. These are explained in Table 5.3.

Diversification for single-product organizations is an important development for two main reasons. First, risk becomes spread across two or more markets, and secondly, organizational resources such as management, marketing, finance, production, and operations can be used more effectively and efficiently when deployed across more than one product or market. Cadbury's dependency on chocolate-related products has been brought into focus as consumer trends towards healthy eating have resulted in poor chocolate sales. This has helped

Table 5.3

Characteristics of
diversified growth

Strategic goal	Explanation
Horizontal diversification	Horizontal diversification occurs when products that are technologically unrelated to the established product range are introduced to the same target market.
Concentric diversification	Concentric diversification occurs when products that are technologically related to the current portfolio are introduced to new markets.
Conglomerate diversification	Conglomerate diversification occurs when products that are technologically unrelated to the current portfolio are introduced to new markets.

Table 5.4

Characteristics of
integrated growth

Strategic goal	Explanation
Horizontal integration	Growth occurs by acquiring competitors and results in greater market share and/or positioning. For example, Morrison's purchase of Safeway or Procter & Gamble's purchase of Gillette.
Backward integration	Growth occurs by acquiring suppliers of parts, components, or services further up the value chain. The goal is to control quality, regulate supply, and manage the volume of supply. For example, a furniture manufacturer such as Ikea may buy a saw mill or forest in order to control their source of supply.
Forward integration	Growth occurs by acquiring distributors, dealers, and retailers further down the value chain. The goal is to control the distribution process in order to better meet customer needs. For example, soft drinks manufacturers such as Coca-Cola often purchase bottling companies as this enables them to increase their production and distribution efficiency.

prompt diversification into the gum market when the company bought the Trident brand and an Australian brand of healthy sweets (Bowery, 2007).

Integrated Growth

As mentioned earlier, integrated growth concerns ways in which an organization can grow within the same industry as it is currently operating. This means that the organization continues to operate within the same value chain but undertakes new roles and tasks either for reasons of power and control or to improve processes to get improved efficiency and returns. Three main types of integrated growth can be pursued, set out in Table 5.4.

Figure 5.7
Strategic marketing
action

Strategic Market Action

Having analysed the industry and the main competitors, determined suitable strategic marketing goals, and performed a SWOT analysis, the final set of marketing strategy activities concerns the identification of the most appropriate way of achieving the goals. In other words 'how to do it'.

There is no proven formula or tool kit that managers can use simply because of the vast array of internal and external environmental factors. What we can draw upon is experience and a range of strategies that we know are more likely to be successful than others. In the following section we consider ideas about competitive advantage, generic strategies, competitive positioning, strategic intent, and marketing planning (see Figure 5.7).

Competitive Advantage

Competitive advantage is achieved when an organization has an edge over its competitors when attracting buyers. Advantage can also be secured by coping with the competitive forces better than its rivals. Advantage can be developed in many different ways. Some organizations have an advantage simply because they are the best-known organization or brand in the market. Some achieve it by producing the best-quality product or having attributes that other products do not have. For example, some pharmaceutical brands have an advantage whilst patent protection exists. As soon as the patent expires and competitors can produce generic versions of the drug, the advantage is lost. Some organizations have the lowest price whilst others provide the best support and service in the industry. However, whatever the advantage, the superiority has to be sustainable through time.

The conditions necessary for the achievement of sustainable competitive advantage (SCA) are, according to Porter, as follows:

Printing a Competitive Advantage

Some companies achieve competitive advantage through low prices, fast delivery, expert service, or by providing particular product attributes. Kent Art Printers achieve a significant competitive advantage through the use of specialized, environmentally friendly production techniques. By being the first company to use the Kodak Thermal Direct Printing process the Kent Art Printers achieve significant cost savings over those who use the conventional plate-making technology. The Kodak process eliminates the use of water, chemicals, processors, and hazardous waste from the pre-press part of the business. This means it can now make seventeen plates an hour compared to just seven, there are no processors to clean, and there is no production downtime. Print jobs can be turned around much faster, proofing can be undertaken online, thus cutting time and visits, and the company's CO_2 emissions have been cut by 12 per cent, or eight tonnes a year.

Proofs from the presses
at Kent Art Printers

Kent Art Printers Ltd

Source: The Marketer (2007).

1 If the Kent Art Printers company wants to grow which type of growth would you recommend, and why?

2 Look around your home and identify two products with different types of competitive advantage. In your opinion are these advantages sustainable or have they been surpassed already?

3 What other types of competitive advantage might Kent Art Printers develop? What might be the reason why these are not developed?

1 The customer consistently perceives a positive difference between the products and services offered by a company and its competitors.

2 The perceived difference results from the company's relatively greater capability.

3 The perceived difference persists for a reasonable period of time.

SCA is only durable as long as it is not easily imitated. (See Market Insight 5.4 above.)

Generic Strategies

If the importance of achieving a competitive advantage is accepted as a crucial aspect of a successful marketing strategy, then it is necessary to understand how strategies can lead to the development of sustainable competitive advantages. Porter (1985) proposed that there are two essential routes to achieving above average performance. These are to become the lowest-cost producer or to differentiate the product/service to a degree that is of superior value to the customer. These strategies can be implemented in either broad (mass) or narrow (focused) markets. Porter suggested that these give rise to three generic strategies; overall cost leadership, differentiation, and focus strategies.

Cost leadership does not mean a lower price although lower prices are often used to attract customers. By having the lowest cost structure, an organization can offer standard products at acceptable levels of quality, yet still generate above-average profit margins. If attacked by a competitor using lower prices, the low-cost leader has a far bigger cushion than its competitors. It should be appreciated that charging a lower price than its rivals is not the critical point. The competitive advantage is derived from how the organization exploits its cost/price ratio. By reinvesting the profit, for example by improving product quality, investing more in product development, or building extra capacity, long-run superiority is more likely to be achieved.

A **differentiation** strategy requires that all value chain activities are geared to the creation of products that are valued by and which satisfy the needs of particular broad segments. By identifying particular customer groups, where each group has a discrete set of needs, a product can be differentiated from its competitors. Customers are prepared to pay a higher price, a price premium, for products that deliver superior or extra value to them. For example, Callaway Golf developed their very large golf clubs, branded Big Bertha, when they discovered that many people who do not play golf perceived huge difficulties in hitting a little ball with a little golf club. The Big Bertha brand provided a strong point of differentiation and attracted a large number of non-golf players (Kim and Mauborgne, 2005).

Products can be differentiated on a variety of criteria, indeed each element of the marketing mix is capable of providing the means for successful, long-term differentiation. Differentiation can lead to greater levels of brand loyalty. For example, in contrast to low-cost ASDA, Waitrose provide a strongly differentiated supermarket service.

Focus strategies are about organizations seeking gaps in broad market segments or finding gaps in competitors' product ranges. In other words, focus strategies are about seeking out unfulfilled market needs. The focused operator then concentrates all value chain activities on a narrow range of products and services in order that they are generated in an effective way.

Focus strategies can be oriented to being the lowest-cost producer for the particular segment or offering a differentiated product for which the narrow target segment is willing to pay a higher price. This means that there are two options for a company wishing to follow a focus strategy. One is low cost and the other is differentiation, but both occur within a particular, narrow, segment. The difference between a broad differentiator and a focused differentiator is that the former bases its strategy on attributes valued across a number of markets, whereas the latter seeks to meet the needs of particular segments within a market.

Porter argues that, to achieve competitive advantage, organizations must achieve one of these three generic strategies. To fail to be strategically explicit results in organizations' being 'stuck in the middle'. This means that they achieve below-average returns and have no competitive advantage. It has been observed, however, that some organizations have been able to pursue a low-cost and differentiated strategy simultaneously. For example, an organization that develops a large market share through differentiation and by creating very strong brands may well become the cost leader as well. The point is that Porter's contribution is very important yet these generic strategies should not be treated as tablets of stone! It is a useful approach and one that has contributed to our understanding about the way in which markets operate.

Competitive Positioning

Having collected industry information, analysed competitors, and considered our resources, perhaps the single most important aspect of developing marketing strategy is to decide how to compete in the selected target markets. Two key decisions arise: what position do we want in the market, which is considered here, and what will be our strategic intent? This is examined in the following section.

The position that a product adopts in a market is a general reflection of its market share. These positions confer certain roles on the incumbents and these can have a strong influence on the nature and form of the marketing strategies these products are imbued with. Four main positions can be identified; market leader, challenger, follower, and nicher.

Market Leader

By definition there can only be one market leader and this is the product that has the single largest share of the market. The actual size of the leading share varies across different markets according to a variety of criteria, but leadership can be achieved with shares as low as 10 per cent. Market leadership is important as it is these products and brands that can shape the nature of competition in the market, set out standards relating to price, quality, speed of innovation, communications, as well as influencing the key distribution channels. For example, Tesco was an ordinary mid-ranking supermarket in the 1980s but has since grown to become the leading UK supermarket.

Market Challengers

Products that are not market leaders yet aspire to the leadership position are referred to as market challengers. These may be positioned as number two, three, or even four in the market. Their classification as challengers is because they actively seek market share and use aggressive strategies to take share from all of the rivals. For example, Sainsbury's and ASDA are the two main market challengers in the UK supermarket sector.

In addition to the forceful challengers there may be other smaller rival products that have entered the market with the express intent of growing very quickly. These are known as *fast movers* and need to be watched as they can quickly become challengers and pose a threat to the market leader.

Market Followers

These firms have low market shares and are survivors. They do not have the resources to be serious competitors and prefer not to attack anyone. They are sometimes referred to as 'also-rans'. They pose no threat to the market leader or challengers and often adopt me-too strategies when the market leader takes an initiative. If we extend the examples within the supermarket sector then Morrison's might be deemed as a market follower.

Market Nichers

Nichers are specialists. They select small segments within target markets that the larger companies do not want to exploit. They develop specialized marketing mixes designed to meet the needs of their customers. They are threatened by economic downturns when customers either cease buying that type of product or buy more competitively priced products. They are also vulnerable to changes in customer tastes and competitor innovation.

There are two main reasons to understand the competitive positions adopted by companies. The first is to understand the way the various firms are positioned in the market and from that deduce the strategies they are likely to follow and their most probable strategies when attacked by others. The other reason is to understand where the company is currently positioned and to decide where it wants to be positioned at some point in the future. This will shape the nature and

Table 5.5
Prime strategy
characteristics

Competitive position	Prime strategies
Market leader	Attack the market—create new uses, users, or increase frequency of use. Defend the position—regular innovation, larger ranges, price cutting and discounts, increased promotion.
Market challenger	Attack the market leader—use pricing, new product attributes, sharp increase in advertising spend. Attack rivals—special offers and limited editions, offer superior competitive advantages.
Market follower	Maintain 'status quo'. Avoid hostile attacks on rivals. Copy the market leader and provide good-quality products that are well differentiated. Focus on differentiation and profits, not market share.
Market nicher	Provide high level of specialization—geographic, product, service, customer group. Provide tight fit between market needs and the organization's resources.

quantity of the resources to be required and the strategies to be pursed. Some of these strategies are set out in Table 5.5.

More information about positioning can be found in Chapter 6.

Strategic Intent

The previous section provided a general rationale about *why* organizations are positioned the way they are in markets. Consideration is now given to ideas about *how* firms engage strategically within their chosen markets and to assist, two main perspectives are explored. The first considers ideas founded on the principles of warfare. The second considers some contemporary ideas based not on outright competition but on cooperation and collaboration. Here, ideas about strategic relationships are introduced.

Strategic Competition and Warfare

Many early ideas about competitive marketing strategies are based on the military and ideas about warfare and two main approaches can be identified, those based on attack and those on defence.

Many organizations, especially those in the grocery sector, such as Procter & Gamble, Nestlé, Unilever, Kraft, and Heinz, will only contemplate entering or staying in a market if they have a realistic opportunity to become market leader or, at worst, number two. This is because the highest levels of profitability are obtained by being the market leader. The reasons for this were explained earlier in the section on market leadership.

The overall size of many markets is static, therefore individual companies can only really grow by taking market share from their competitors. This can be achieved by developing superior products, using the right distribution channels to reach target markets, implementing effective marketing communications campaigns, and managing pricing astutely. One interpretation of marketing strategy, therefore, is that it is necessary to attack in order to grow market share and, once achieved, it is necessary to defend the share from predators.

Attacking Strategies

Attack-oriented strategies are used mainly to achieve growth objectives and five main strategies have been identified (Kotler and Singh, 1981) as shown in Table 5.6.

Table 5.6
Attacking strategies

Attack Strategies	Explanation
Frontal attack	A head-on assault on a rival, used when there are low levels of customer loyalty, poorly differentiated products, and it when it is easy for customers to switch brands.
Flanking	Involves pressurizing a rival's vulnerable or unguarded areas. This might be a market segment that is not served very well by the existing competitors, a geographic area that is open, weak or unsatisfactory products, or inappropriate distribution channels. The rapid growth of low-cost airlines such as Ryanair and EasyJet have been based upon flanking attacks on the established national carriers, British Airways in particular. BA served broad markets with a differentiated service and ignored the low-cost, niche segment Ryanair spotted the flanking opportunity and have become the market leader in the new market.
Encirclement	Involves attacking a rival on all sides, literally encircling the target rival. The goal is to disrupt the competitor's strategy, causing them to reorganize resources and to create panic as market share is taken from many sides. This can be an effective strategy when the target market is loosely segmented or when market segments are not occupied by firms who have substantial resources.
Bypass	Involves introducing new products or technologies that rewrite the rules of competition in the market and avoid direct conflict with a rival. For example, the introduction of compact disc technology bypassed the established magnetic tape-based technology that previously existed.
Guerrilla	Involves irritating and slowly eroding a rival's market share through a series of unpredictable attacks on their weaker areas. This strategy is useful for small firms who have relatively few resources, in situations when the target is able to defend itself relatively easily from a frontal or flanking attack. Typically, guerrilla attacks involve periods of heavily promoted price discounting, followed by differing lengths of inactivity.

Defensive Strategies

Defence strategies should be in place at all times so that they can be deployed quickly and so save time when faced with frontal or flanking attacks. Six main defensive strategies have been identified: position, flanking, mobile, contraction, pre-emptive, and counter-offensive defences (see Table 5.7 overleaf).

See Market Insight 5.5 for an example of attacking and defensive strategies.

Strategic Cooperation and Relationships

Ideas about strategy have developed from those based on competition to attack and defence strategies. An alternative perspective is to consider ways in which customer value can be increased through cooperation. By working cooperatively with other companies and their brands, relationships evolve. These in turn provide strong opportunities to add value through the differentiation of brands and considerable competitive advantage.

MARKET INSIGHT 5.5

Colgate Fights Back

Colgate has a 51% share in the Indian oral care market and has been a dominant player and market leader for a long time. Dental Cream (CDC) is Colgate's core brand and the largest selling toothpaste brand in the Indian oral care market with a 39% market share. As a core brand and market leader it generates positive cash flows and is highly profitable. However, it is for these reasons that it is constantly under threat from rival brands Pepsodent and Close-Up, both owned by Hindustan Lever.

In order to defend its position Colgate relaunched the Colgate Dental Cream brand in 2001 with a new positioning, and also introduced two new brands, Colgate Herbal, targeted at traditional consumers who prefer natural ingredients, and Colgate Cibaca Top, targeted at the price-sensitive economy segment. This defensive flanking strategy afforded some self-protection, and helped to avoid a frontal battle with Hindustan Lever.

From a challenger's perspective Hindustan Lever faced a huge task trying to dislodge the well-entrenched market leader. In an effort to avoid a frontal attack and all the ensuing costs it repositioned its own brands to attack Colgate's vulnerable flanks. The new positioning saw Close-Up repositioned on freshness, and Pepsodent adopted a health-value proposition, and in so doing challenged Colgate's established claim in this area.

By consolidating its brand strategy with Colgate Dental Cream and developing target flanker brands, Colgate repelled the threat of direct attack. To some extent, therefore, the defensive flanking strategy beat off the attacking flanking strategy of the market challenger.

Source: Ghosh (2005).

1 Using each of the attack strategies suggest ways in which Close-Up might be used to attack CDC.

2 Using each of the defence strategies suggest ways in which CDC might protect its market leader position.

3 Based on the toothpaste market in your own country, identify a market *niche*.

programmes, supported by database management and marketing facilities. Relationships can also be forged through branding. Some consumers develop a strong affinity with a brand to the extent that they want to share their relationship with others and talk openly (word-of-mouth communication) about their positive brand experiences. All of these are explored later in this book.

Relationships with suppliers are important simply because competitive advantages can be developed through both cost reduction and production differentiation. Take for example the case of the detergent manufacturer who asked their supplier to develop a trigger action that delivered 3,000 squirts. Subsequent research found that most people did not use more than 600 squirts. The result was a revised mechanism, lower cost, and increased frequency of consumer purchase (Sclater, 2007).

Marketing strategy should be founded on developing customer value and this can be achieved through a strategy based on building cooperative relationships with suppliers, customers, distributors, and other strategically relevant stakeholders. The centrality of cooperation and relationships within marketing has become an important concept for both organizations and marketing academics. Marketing has evolved from ideas that are based solely around the 4Ps. Now marketers think and act in terms of the different types of relationships that an organization has and tries to find ways of improving the right relationships with the right customers. This is referred to as relationship marketing and is a topic that is explored in depth in Chapter 17.

Marketing Planning

So far in this chapter we have considered the key activities associated with strategic market analysis, goals, and action. In order that organizations are able to develop, implement, and control these activities at product and brand level, a marketing planning process is required, out of which marketing plans are derived. This final section of the chapter considers the marketing planning process, identifies the key characteristics, and considers some of the issues associated with the process. Chapter 8 examines some of the issues associated with the implementation of marketing plans.

Marketing planning is a sequential process involving a series of activities leading to the setting of marketing objectives and the formulation of plans for achieving them (McDonald, 2002: 27). A marketing plan is the key output from the overall marketing planning process. It details a company's or brand's intended marketing activity.

Marketing plans can be developed for periods of one, two to five years, and anything up to twenty-five years. However, too many organizations regard marketing plans as a development of the annual round of setting sales targets that are then extrapolated into quasi marketing plans. This is incorrect as it fails to account for the marketplace, customer needs, and resources. It is important that the strategic appraisal and evaluation phase of the planning process be undertaken first. This should cover a three- to five-year period and provides a strategic insight into the markets, competitors, and the organization's resources that shape the direction and nature of the way the firm has decided to compete. Once agreed, these should then be updated on an annual basis and modified to meet changing internal and external conditions. Only once the strategic marketing plan has been developed should detailed operational or functional marketing plans, covering a one-year period, be developed (McDonald, 2002). This makes marketing planning a continuous process, not something that is undertaken once a year, or worse, just when a product is launched.

A marketing plan designed to support a particular product consists of a series of activities that should be undertaken sequentially. These are presented in Table 5.8.

Activity	Explanation
Executive summary	Brief one-page summary of key points and outcomes.
Overall objectives	Reference should be made to the organization's overall mission and corporate goals, the elements that underpin the strategy.
Product/market background	A short summary of the product and/or market to clarify understanding about target markets, sales history, market trends, main competitors, and the organization's own product portfolio.
Marketing analysis	This provides insight into the market, customers, and the competition. It should consider segment needs, current strategies, and key financial data. The marketing audit and SWOT analysis are used to support this section.
Marketing strategies	This section should be used to state the market(s) to be targeted, the basis on which the firm will compete, the competitive advantages to be used, and the way in which the product is to be positioned in the market.
Marketing goals	Here, the desired outcomes of the strategy should be expressed in terms of the volume of expected sales, the value of sales and market share gains, levels of product awareness, availability, profitability, and customer satisfaction.
Marketing programmes	A marketing mix for each target market segment has to be developed along with a specification of who is responsible for the various activities and actions and the resources that are to be made available.
Implementation	This section sets out the: • way in which the marketing plan is to be controlled and evaluated. • financial scope of the plan. • operational implications in terms of human resources, research and development, and system and process needs.
Supporting documentation	Marketing plans should contain relevant supporting documentation, too bulky to be included in the plan itself but necessary for reference and detail. For example, the full PESTLE and SWOT analyses, marketing research data, and other market reports and information plus key correspondence.

Table 5.8
Key activities within a marketing plan

Many of the corporate level goals and strategies and internal and external environmental analyses that are established within the strategic marketing plan can be replicated within each of the marketing plans written for individual products, product lines, markets, or even SBUs. As a general rule, only detail concerning products, competitors, and related support resources need change prior to the formulation of individual marketing mixes and their implementation, within functional level marketing plans.

Overall Objectives

This opening part provides the objectives that underpin the marketing plan. Therefore, reference should be made to the organization's overall mission and corporate goals. However, marketing objectives such as the volume of desired sales, the vales of sales and market share gains, levels of product awareness, availability, profitability, and customer satisfaction are quite common. What is not so common is the quantification of these objectives in terms of how much is to be achieved and within what timescales. Only by providing this level of detail can the success of the marketing plan be evaluated.

Product/Market Background

The provision of a short summary of the product and/or market is important as it helps clarify understanding for the participants. It also helps those unfamiliar with the operation, for example an outside agency, to understand the plan. Information about target markets, sales history, market trends, main competitors, and the organization's own product portfolio can assist understanding and gets everyone up to speed.

Market Analysis

The market analysis section is crucial as it is from this that insight into the market, customers, and the competition is gained and viable marketing strategies developed. Many of the tools and methods examined earlier in this chapter are deployed here. What also needs to be expressed is the importance that should be attached to the need for accurate financial data about products, markets, and customers. The marketing audit and SWOT analysis discussed earlier as part of the strategic market analysis can be used at this point, refined to meet the needs of the particular target market.

Marketing Strategy and Goals

The marketing strategy identified at this point in the plan should state the market(s) to be targeted, the basis on which the firm will compete, the competitive advantages to be used, and the way in which the product is to be positioned in the market.

In addition, the results expected to be achieved as a consequence of this investment need to be stated. These are usually referred to in terms of sales volume and market shares.

Marketing Programmes

Each target market segment normally requires an explicit, individual marketing mix programme. Based on analysis the detailed marketing mix should specify exactly what needs to be accomplished (goals), why (the analysis and rationale), how (the various to elements of the mix), and when (the timescales).

This part of the plan should also specify who is responsible for the various activities and actions and the resources that are to be made available to them.

Implementation

The implementation of any marketing plan is incomplete without methods to control and evaluate its performance. It is vitally important to monitor the results of the programme as it unfolds, not just when it is completed. Therefore, measures need to be stated in the plan about how the results of the plan will be recorded and disseminated throughout the team. Recording the performance of the marketing plan against targets enables managers to make adjustments should the plan not perform as expected, due possibly to unforeseen market events.

For ease of explanation the marketing planning process has been depicted as a linear, sequential series of management activities. This certainly helps to simplify understanding about how strategy can be developed and it also serves to show how various activities are linked together. However, it should be recognized that strategy development and planning, whether it be at corporate, business, or functional level, is not linear, does not evolve in preset ways, and is not always subject to a regular, predetermined pattern of evolution. Indeed, politics, finance, and inter-personnel conflicts all help shape the nature of an organization's marketing strategy. Further details concerning the implementation and control of marketing plans are available in Chapter 8.

Chapter Summary

To consolidate your learning, the key points from this chapter are summarized below:

- Describe the strategic planning process.

  The strategic planning process commences at corporate level. Here the organization sets out its overall mission, purpose, and values. These are then converted into measurable goals that apply to the whole organization. Then, depending upon the size of the organization, the range of businesses (SBUs) and/or products is determined and resources allocated to help and support each one. Each business and/or product develops detailed functional and competitive strategies and plans, such as a marketing strategy and plan.

- Explain the key influences that impact on marketing strategy.

  There are three key influences on marketing strategy. These are strategic market analysis, which is concerned with developing knowledge and understanding about the marketplace, strategic marketing goals, which are about what the strategy is intended to achieve, and strategic marketing action, which is about how the strategies are to be implemented.

- Explain how understanding competitors can assist the development of marketing strategy.

  An analysis of a firm's competitors involves answers to five key questions. These are Who are our competitors? What are their strengths and weaknesses? What are their strategic goals? Which strategies are they following? How are they likely to respond?

- Identify the characteristics of strategic marketing goals and explain the nature of the associated growth strategies.

  There are several types of strategic objective but the five main ones are niche, hold, harvest, and divest goals and are considered briefly. However, the vast majority of organizations consider growth to be a primary objective. Although there are different forms of growth intensive, integrated, or diversified are generally accepted as the main ones.

- Describe different approaches and concepts associated with strategic marketing action.

  Strategic marketing action is concerned with ways of implementing marketing strategies. Various concepts and frameworks have been proposed and of these we considered ideas about competitive advantage, generic strategies, competitive positioning, and strategic intent.

- Explain how scenario planning and SWOT analysis can help strategic marketing decision making.

  Scenario planning is used to understand how environmental trends might influence the future of an organization and how managers can gain a better understanding of some of the uncertainties an organization faces if it pursues particular strategies. SWOT analysis is a tool used to determine an overall view of the strategic position and highlights the need for a strategy to produce a strong fit between the internal capability (strengths and weaknesses) and the external situation (opportunities and threats). SWOT analysis serves to identify the key issues and then prompts thought about converting weaknesses into strengths and threats into opportunities.

- Outline the key elements within a marketing plan.

  The following represent the key elements associated with the structure of a marketing plan: overall objectives; product/market background; market analysis; marketing strategy and goals: marketing programmes; implementation, evaluation, and control. Although depicted as a linear process many organizations either do not follow this process, do not include all these elements, or undertake many of these elements simultaneously.

 Visit the **Online Resource Centre** that accompanies this book to read more information relating to marketing strategy: www.oxfordtextbooks.co.uk/orc/baines/

Review Questions

1 What is the difference between vision and mission?

2 Draw a diagram that presents the four elements that make up the strategic context.

3 Make brief notes outlining the strategic planning process.

4 How might understanding a firm's competitors help develop marketing strategy?

5 What is scenario planning?

6 Identify the key characteristics of SWOT analysis. What actions should be taken once the SWOT grid is prepared?

7 Describe the difference between intensive and diversified growth.

8 Porter argues that firms can differentiate themselves in one of two main ways. What are they and how do they work?

9 Attack and defence strategies have been derived from the military and warfare. Name and explain three types of attack and three types of defence.

10 List the various parts of a marketing plan.

Discussion Questions

1 Having read the Case Insight at the beginning of this chapter, how would you advise Innocent Drinks to develop their brand?

2 Find three examples of mission statements and associated organizational goals. Then, using these examples, discuss the value of formulating a mission statement and the benefits that are likely to arise from setting organizational-level goals.

3 If the external environment is uncontrollable and markets are changing their shape and characteristics increasingly quickly, there seems little point in developing a strategic marketing plan. Discuss the value of formulating marketing strategies and plans in the light of these comments.

4 After a successful period of twenty years' trading, a bicycle manufacturer noticed that their sales, rather than increasing at a steady rate, were starting to decline. The company, Rapid Cycles, produced a range of bicycles to suit various segments and distributed them mainly through independent cycle shops. In recent years, however, the number of low-cost cycles entering the country had increased, with many distributed through supermarkets and national retail chains. The managing director of Rapid Cycles felt that they could not compete with these low-cost imports and asked you for your opinion about should be done. Discuss the situation facing Rapid Cycles and make recommendations regarding their marketing strategy.

5 Find examples of organizations or products/brands where, in your opinion, they have attacked the market leader or challengers in order to grow quickly.

Are there any common characteristics within these examples?

 References

Andrews, S. (2006), 'Game on: the battle of the superconsoles begins', *Sunday Times*, 5 November, available at http://driving.timesonline.co.uk/tol/life_and_style/driving/article624345.ece, accessed 25 February 2007.

Ansoff, I. H. (1957), 'Strategies for diversification', *Harvard Business Review*, 35, 2, 113–24.

Arthur, C. (2007), 'Retailers suspiciously coy on PlayStation 3 pre-order figures', *The Guardian*, 22 February, available at www.guardian.co.uk/technology/2007/feb/22/sonyplaystation.games.

Bowery, J. (2007), 'Cadbury looks beyond chocolate', *Marketing*, 21 February, 16.

Cornelius, P., Van de Putte, A., and Romani, M. (2005), 'Three decades of scenario planning in Shell', *California Management Review*, 48, 1, 92–109.

Day, G. S., and Wensley, R. (1988), 'Assessing advantage: a framework for diagnosing competitive superiority', *Journal of Marketing*, 52, 2 (April), 1–20.

Eastham, J. (2002), 'This times ahead for Burger King', *Marketing Week*, 1 August, p. 6.

Ghosh, A. (2005), 'The world at war: whose blood is it anyway?', available at www.planmanconsulting.com/the-world-at-war.html, accessed 23 February 2007.

Harbison, J. R., and Pekar, P. (1998), *Smart Alliances: A Practical Guide to Repeatable Success*, San Francisco: Jossey-Bass Publishers.

Kim, W. C. and Mauborgne, R. (2005), *Blue Ocean Strategy: How to Create Uncontested Market Space and Make Competition Irrelevant*, Cambridge, Mass: Harvard University Press.

Kotler, P., and Singh, R. (1981), 'Marketing warfare in the 1980s', *Journal of Business Strategy*, Winter, 30–41.

Leigh, A. (2003), 'Thinking ahead: strategic foresight and government', *Australian Journal of Public Administration*, 62, 2, 3–10.

McDonald, M. (2002), *Marketing Plans and How to Make Them*, 5th edn, Oxford: Butterworth-Heinemann.

Miller, C. (2007), 'The chewing gum war', *The Money Programme*, BBC, available at www.news.bbc.co.uk/2/hi/business/6683389.stm, accessed 27 May 2007.

Mintzberg, H. (1987), 'The strategy concept: five Ps for strategy', *California Management Review*, 30, 1 (Fall), 11–26.

Noble, C. H., Sinha, R. K., and Kumar, A. (2002), 'Market orientation and alternative strategic orientations: a longitudinal assessment of performance implications', *Journal of Marketing*, 66, 4, 25–40.

Piercy, N. (2002), *Market-Led Strategic Change: Transforming the Process of Going to Market*, Oxford: Butterworth-Heinemann.

Porter, M. E. (1985), *The Competitive Advantage: Creating and Sustaining Superior Performance*, New York: Free Press.

Prahalad, C. K., and Hamel, G. (1990), 'The core competence of the organisation', *Harvard Business Review*, 68, 3 (May–June), 79–91.

Schoemaker, P. J. H. (1995), 'Scenario planning: a tool for strategic thinking', *Sloan Management Review*, 36, 2 (Winter), 25–40.

Schofield, J. (2005), 'Console wars: challengers must force the pace to unseat the leader', *The Guardian*, Thursday, 1 December, available at www.guardian.co.uk/technology/2005/dec/01/microsoftbox.games1, accessed December 2007.

Sclater, I. (2007), 'The perfect combination', *The Marketer*, 33 (March), 20–22.

Teague, K. (2007), 'Apple Computer, Inc: Silhouette campaign', *Encyclopedia of Major Marketing Campaigns*, 2, available at www.warc.com, accessed 31 May 2007.

Verity, J. (2003), 'Scenario planning as a strategy technique', *European Business Journal*, 15, 4, 185–95.

6

Market Segmentation and Positioning

Positioning is not what you do to a product; it is what you do to the mind of a prospect.

Ries and Trout (1972)

Learning outcomes

After reading this chapter, you will be able to:

✔ Describe the principles of market segmentation and the STP process.

✔ Explain the characteristics and differences between market segmentation and product differentiation.

✔ Explain how market segmentation can be undertaken in both consumer and business-to-business markets.

✔ Describe different targeting strategies.

✔ Explain the concept of positioning.

✔ Illustrate how the use of perceptual maps can assist the positioning process.

Stagecoach operates bus services across the UK. How does it know who its customers are and where they want to access its services? We speak to Elaine Rosscraig to find out more.

Elaine Rosscraig for Stagecoach

Stagecoach UK Bus is one of the largest bus operators in the UK, operating both express and local bus services across the country. In addition the company operates a comprehensive network of intercity operations under the Megabus Brand. We connect communities in over 100 towns and cities in the UK, operating a fleet of around 7,000 buses. We carry over two million customers every day on our network which stretches from Devon to the north of Inverness. So how do we identify who our customers are and where they may wish to access our services? Well, that's a very interesting and important question.

At Stagecoach we have formulated our segmentation and positioning strategy using primary research. By using the results of the primary research we have identified our key market segments, which have been compiled into three groups, all of which are linked to bus use. These groups may be categorized as: user, lapsed user, and non-user.

> *An important market to target is the non-user segment…[especially those with] a propensity to switch.*

An important target market for Stagecoach is the non-user segment. The customers contained within this segment demonstrate a propensity to switch the mode of transport to bus. We estimate that about 30% of existing non-bus users in the UK have a propensity to switch the mode of transport they are regularly using, given the appropriate incentives. In addition it is essential that Stagecoach address the perceived barriers associated with bus travel amongst this group.

Through geodemographic profiling we have further identified microdemographic segments within each of the local areas which we serve, to whom specific barriers to bus use are an issue. This information has formed the basis of our segmentation strategy and how we subsequently tailor our communication with each of these prospect customer groups.

A major issue to consider is how public transport is currently perceived by these target segments. Public transport in general has a negative reputation in the UK. This is the result historically of limited ongoing customer communication, inadequate staff training, and poor customer relations within the industry.

Customer perception of Stagecoach is linked directly to the journey experience and customer satisfaction. In order of priority the following aspects of service contribute to customer satisfaction with the Stagecoach service: reliability/punctuality, staff attitude, comfort during the journey, cleanliness of the vehicle (interior and exterior), space for bags/pushchairs, and value for money.

Given the primary research findings to date and the market segments identified, what would you recommend Stagecoach do to target and position their brand to the differing market segments to encourage switching in mode of transport and use of Stagecoach's services?

Customer perceptions seem to be entirely driven by the journey experience

Stagecoach

Introduction

Ever wondered why marketers only target certain markets or how these markets are identified? Think about universities for a moment: how do they identify which students to communicate with about degree schemes? What criteria do they use? Do they base it on where you live, your age, your gender, or is it just about your entrance scores? Do they market to postgraduate and undergraduate audiences differently, what about international and domestic student groups—is this difference important for the effective marketing of higher education services to prospective students?

In this chapter, we consider the way organizations determine the markets in which they need to concentrate their commercial efforts. This process is referred to as **market segmentation** and is an integral part of marketing strategy, discussed in Chapter 5. After defining the principles of market segmentation this chapter commences with an exploration of the differences between market segmentation and **product differentiation**, as this helps clarify the underlying principles of segmentation. Consideration is also given to the techniques and issues concerning market segmentation within consumer and business-to-business markets.

The method by which whole markets are subdivided into different segments is referred to as the **STP process**. STP refers to the three activities that should be undertaken, usually sequentially, if segmentation is to be successful. These are segmentation, targeting, and positioning, and this chapter is structured around these key elements.

The STP Process

The growing use of the STP process has occurred as a direct result of the prevalence of mature markets, the greater diversity in customer needs, and the ability to reach specialized or niche segments. As such marketers are increasingly segmenting markets and identifying attractive segments (i.e. who to focus on and why?), in order to identify new product opportunities, develop suitable positioning and communications strategies (i.e. what message to communicate), and effectively allocate resources to key marketing activities (i.e. how much should we spend and where?). Organizations will often commission segmentation research when they want to re-scope their marketing strategy, investigate a declining brand, launch a new product, or restructure their pricing policy. Organizations operating in highly dynamic environments seek to conduct segmentation research at regular intervals, to keep in touch with changes in the marketplace.

STP refers to the three activities segmentation, targeting, and positioning (Figure 6.1).

Key benefits of the STP process include:

- Enhancing a company's competitive position by providing direction and focus for marketing strategies such as targeted advertising, new product development, and brand differentiation. For example, Coca-Cola identified through market

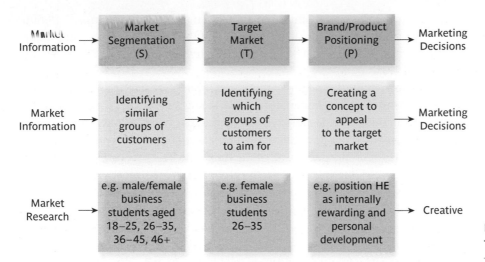

Figure 6.1
The STP process

research that its Diet Coke brand (also marketed as Coca-Cola Lite) was regarded as 'girly' and 'feminine' by male consumers. As a direct result the company developed a new product, branded Coke Zero, which is targeted at the health-conscious male segment of the soft drinks market.

- Examining and identifying growth opportunities in the market through the identification of new customers, growth segments, or new product uses. For example Arm & Hammer was able to attract new customers when existing consumers identified new uses for their baking soda (Christensen, Cook, and Hall, 2005). Lucozade also changed the positioning and targeting from its original marketing strategy positioned for sick children and rebranded to target athletes as an energy drink.

- More effective and efficient matching of company resources to targeted market segments promises the greatest return on marketing investment (ROMI). For example, financial institutions like HSBC and Barclays and large retailing multinationals such as Tesco and ASDA Wal-Mart are utilizing data-informed segmentation strategies to effectively target direct marketing messages and rewards to customers they have classified as offering long-term value to the company, i.e. they are profitable customers.

The Concept of Market Segmentation

Market segmentation is the division of a market into different groups of customers with distinctly similar needs and product/service requirements. Or to put it another way, market segmentation is the division of a mass market into identifiable and distinct groups or segments, each of which have common characteristics and needs and display similar responses to marketing actions.

Market segmentation was first defined as 'a condition of growth when core markets have already been developed on a generalised basis to the point where additional promotional expenditures are yielding diminishing returns' (Smith, 1956). There is now widespread agreement that they form an important foundation for successful marketing strategies and activities (Wind, 1978; Hooley and Saunders, 1993).

The purpose of market segmentation is to leverage scarce resources; in other words, to ensure that the elements of the marketing mix, price, distribution, products and promotion, are designed to meet particular needs of different customer groups. Since companies have finite resources it is not possible to produce all possible products for all the people, all of the time. The best that can be aimed for is to provide selected offerings for selected groups of people, most of the time. This process allows organizations to focus on specific customers' needs, in the most efficient and effective way. As Beane and Ennis (1987) eloquently commented, 'a company with limited resources needs to pick only the best opportunities to pursue'.

The market segmentation concept is related to product differentiation. If you aim at different market segments, you might adapt different variations of your offering to satisfy those segments, and equally if you adapt different versions of your offering, this may appeal to different market segments. Since there is less

The M&S Per Una range: designed to attract the young female shopper

Per Una

competition, your approach is less likely to be copied and so either approach will do.

An example in the area of fashion retailing might be if you adapt your clothing range so that your skirts are more colourful, use lighter fabrics, and a very short hemline, for instance, this styling is more likely to appeal more to younger women. If alternatively, you decide to target older women, then you might need to change the styling of your skirts to suit them by using darker, heavier fabrics, with a longer hemline. This is exactly what Marks and Spencer (M&S) did to attract a younger female shopper into their M&S stores and compete more directly with Next and Debenhams for share of this market. The company launched a range of female clothing called Per Una, and three years on the fashion range has been a huge success reportedly generating annual sales of nearly £230 m—more than 10 per cent of the total womenswear sales at M&S. If you start by adapting new product variants, you are using a product differentiation approach. If you start with the customer's needs, you are using a market segmentation approach. This is illustrated more clearly in Figure 6.2 using offering rather than product to indicate that the same concept may apply to a service.

A relational marketing perspective would replace the marketing mix—the 4Ps —either with the 7Ps (see Chapter 15) or with a discussion of the need to design, develop, and deliver the customer experience (see Chapter 17).

The concept of market segmentation was first proposed as an alternative market development technique in imperfectly competitive markets, that is, in markets where there are relatively few competitors selling an identical product. Where there are lots of competitors selling identical products, market segmentation and product differentiation produce similar results as competitors imitate your strategic approach more quickly and product differentiation approaches meet market segment needs more closely.

With an increasing proliferation of tastes in modern society, consumers have increased disposable incomes. As a result, marketers have sought to design product and service offerings around consumer demand (market segmentation) more than around their own production needs (product differentiation) and they use market research to inform this process (see Market Insight 6.1 and Chapter 4).

A Product Differentiation Approach

A Market Segmentation Approach

Figure 6.2
The difference between market segmentation and product differentiation

A Tale of Two Approaches

Tale 1 is about Amway, a global company that manufactures and distributes over 450 different consumer products and invests heavily in research and development in order to remain competitive and meet customer needs. For example, after several years of research and development, Amway produced a new range of products called Satinique, which used the 'Ceramide Infusion System'. The core attribute is that Satinique contains a moisturizing agent, which can restore the nutrients in hair. Once Amway had developed the product they then undertook market research to determine which group of consumers they should target. Having identified a segment made up of professional women, who always want to look their best and who want professional, salon-quality products and who rely on recommendations from friends when making haircare purchase decisions, they then developed a marketing strategy and implemented a successful marketing plan.

Tale 2 is about NIVEA Sun, the leading sun care brand owned by Beiersdorf. There are three main usage segments in the sun care market: protection (from harmful rays), after sun (for relief and moisturizing after being in the sun), and self-tan (for those who want an all year round 'cosmetic' tan). Beiersdorf have developed their portfolio of NIVEA Sun brands around these usage segments, but unlike Amway have used innovation to develop products to meet customer needs identified through market research and segmentation analysis. For example, market research has shown that awareness of the need for protection from the sun does not necessarily lead to product purchase and usage. It was also found that women enjoy the luxurious nature of sun care products, men prefer convenience, and children don't enjoy the sun cream application process. As a result NIVEA Sun developed and introduced a spray application device, designed specifically to appeal to men and their preference for convenience. They also introduced a coloured formulation for children's sun products in order to make the application process more fun.

1 Which of these two companies use a product differentiation approach and which uses a market segmentation approach? Justify your selection.

2 Choose a beauty, fragrance, or grooming product that you like to use and determine likely segments.

3 Do you believe Amway should change their approach? Justify your decision.

To take your learning further, you might wish to read this influential paper.

Smith, W. R. (1956), 'Product differentiation and market segmentation as alternative marketing strategies', *Journal of Marketing*, July, 3–8.

A seminal article on market segmentation which put forward the idea that because neither supply nor demand sides of marketing were homogeneous (i.e. different groups wanted to produce and consume different things), a product differentiation approach which was concerned with the bending of demand to the will of supply must also be accompanied by an alternative mechanism of the bending of supply to the will of demand. This alternative marketing strategy was termed market segmentation.

The Process of Market Segmentation

The intricacies involved in market segmentation are said to make it an exacting activity. Griffith and Pol (1994) argue this point on the basis of multiple product applications, greater customer variability, and problems associated with the identification of the key differences between groups of customers. However, there have been numerous attempts to define and describe business segmentation, using a variety of variables and ranging from the severely product-based to customer needs-based orientation.

There are two main approaches to segmenting markets. The first adopts the view that the market is considered to consist of customers which are essentially the same, so the task is to identify groups which share particular differences. This is referred to as the **breakdown method**. The second approach considers a market to consist of customers that are all different, so here the task is to find similarities. This is known as the **build-up method**. The breakdown approach is perhaps the most established and well recognized and is the main method used for segmenting consumer markets. The build-up approach seeks to move from the individual level where all customers are different, to a more general level of analysis based on the identification of similarities (Freytag and Clarke, 2001). The build-up method is customer oriented as it seeks to determine common customer needs. The aim of both methods is to identify segments in the market where identifiable differences exist between segments (segment heterogeneity) and similarities exist between members within each segment (member homogeneity). This is displayed in Figure 6.3.

Other segmentation researchers have distinguished between **a priori** or **post hoc** segmentation methods (Green, 1979). In the former, segments are predetermined using the judgement of the researchers beforehand (i.e. a priori). This approach typically progresses along seven stages encompassing the following steps (Wind, 1978) including:

1 Selection of the base (a priori) for segmentation (e.g. **demographics**, socio-economics).

2 Selection of segment descriptors (including hypotheses on the possible link between these descriptors and the basis for segmentation).

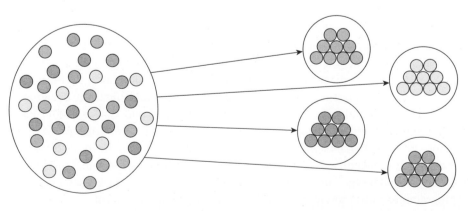

Figure 6.3
Segment heterogeneity and member homogeneity

3 Sample design—mostly using stratified sampling approaches and occasionally a quota sample (see Chapter 4).

4 Data collection.

5 Formation of the segments based on a sorting of respondents into categories.

6 Establishment of the profile of the segments using multivariate statistical methods (e.g. multiple discriminate analysis, multiple regression analysis).

7 Translation of the findings about the segments' estimated size and profile into specific marketing strategies, including the selection of target segments and the design or modification of specific marketing strategy.

With the post hoc approach, the segments are deduced from the research and instead pursue the following process:

1 Sample design—mostly using quota or random sampling approaches (see Chapter 4).

2 Identification of suitable statistical methods of analysis.

3 Data collection.

4 Data analysis—formation of distinct segments using multivariate statistical methods (e.g. cluster analysis, CHAID).

5 Establishment of the profile of the segments using multivariate statistical methods (e.g. factor analysis) and selection of segment descriptors (based on the key aspects of the profile for each segment).

6 Translation of the findings about the segments' estimated size and profile into specific marketing strategies, including the selection of target segments and the design or modification of specific marketing strategy.

Segmentation in business markets should reflect the relationship needs of the parties involved and should not be based solely on the traditional consumer market approach, which is primarily the breakdown method. Through use of both the breakdown and the build-up approaches, a more accurate, in-depth, and potentially more profitable view of industrial markets can be achieved (Crittenden, Crittenden, and Muzyka, 2002). However, problems remain concerning the practical application and implementation of B2B segmentation. Managers report that the analysis processes are reasonably clear, but it is not clear how they should 'choose and evaluate between the market segments' which have been determined (Naudé and Cheng, 2003).

Much segmentation theory has been developed during the period when transactional marketing was the principal approach to marketing, rather than the more relational approaches adopted in today's service-dominated environment. Under these circumstances, the allocation of resources to achieve the designated marketing mix goals was of key importance. Freytag and Clarke (2001) have quite rightly identified that market segmentation is not a static concept. In other words, those customers who make up the various segments have needs which may change, and consequently, those customers may no longer remain members of the particular segment to which they originally belonged. Market segmentation programmes must therefore use customer data which are current.

The segmentation process will therefore vary according to the prevailing conditions in the marketplace and the changing needs of the parties involved, not simply the needs of the selling organization.

Market Segmentation in Consumer Markets

To segment consumer goods and service markets, we use market information we have collected based on certain key customer-, product-, or situation-related criteria (variables). These are classified as segmentation bases and include profile (e.g. who are my market and where are they?); behavioural (e.g. where, when, and how does my market behave?); and psychological criteria (e.g. why does my market behave that way?). These differing types of segmentation bases are depicted in Figure 6.4. A fourth segmentation criterion that can be added is contact data, a customer's name and full contact details beyond just their postcode (e.g. postal address, email, mobile and home telephone number). The data are useful for tactical-level marketing activities such as addressable direct marketing (see Chapter 12).

Table 6.1 illustrates the key characteristics associated with each of the main approaches to consumer market segmentation.

An important consideration when selecting the differing bases for segmentation is the trade-off between ease and cost of measurement or data acquisition and the degree to which the criteria for which data has been acquired can provide an accurate snapshot of current and future customer behaviour, especially its predictability of customer choice behaviour.

As is depicted in Figure 6.5 demographics and **geodemographics** are relatively easy to measure or the data to obtain; however, these bases suffer from low

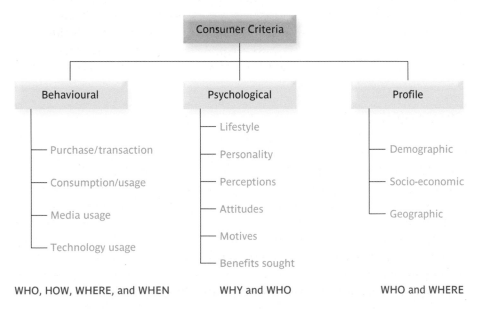

Figure 6.4
Segmentation criteria for consumer markets

Table 6.1

Segmenting criteria for goods and services markets

Base type	Segmentation criteria	Explanation
Profile	Demographic	Key variables concern age, sex, occupation, level of education, religion, social class, and income characteristics, many of which determine a potential buyer's ability to purchase a product or service.
	Lifestage	Lifestage analysis is based on the principle that people need different products and services at different stages in their lives (e.g. childhood, adulthood, young couples, retired).
	Geographic	In many situations the needs of potential customers in one geographic area are different from those in another area. This may be due to climate, custom, or tradition.
	Geodemographic	This approach to segmentation presumes that there is a relationship between the type of housing and location that people live in and their purchasing behaviours.
Psychological	Psychographic (lifestyles)	Analysing consumers' activities, interests, and opinions, we can understand individual lifestyles and patterns of behaviour, which in turn affect their buying behaviour and decision-making processes. On this basis, we can also identify similar product and/or media usage patterns.
	Benefits sought	By understanding the motivations customers derive from their purchases it is possible to have an insight into the benefits they seek from product use.
Behavioural	Purchase/ transaction	Data about customer purchases and transactions provides scope for analysing who buys what, when, how often, how much they spend, and through what transactional channel they purchase. This provides very rich data for identifying 'profitable' customer segments.
	Product usage	Segments are derived from analysing markets on the basis of their usage of the product offering, brand, or product category. This may be in the form of usage frequency, time of usage, and usage situations.
	Media usage	Data on what media channels are used, by whom, when, where, and for how long provides useful insight into the reach potential for certain market segments through differing media channels, and also insight into their media lifestyle.

levels of accurate predictability of a customer's future behaviour. In contrast, behavioural data, what a customer does, their **product usage**, purchase history, and media usage, although more difficult and costly to acquire (although with changes in technology this cost/accessibility is changing), provides a more accurate predictability of future behaviour. This is founded on the notion that humans are creatures of habit and behavioural trends. Therefore the brand of toothpaste you purchased on the last three occasions is more than likely going to be the brand of toothpaste you purchase next time. However, this is also influenced by a

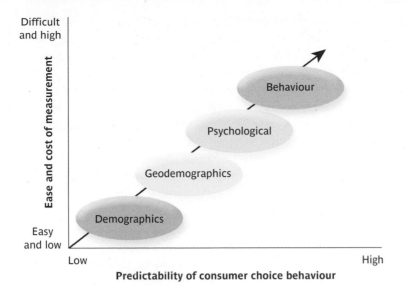

Axis label (y): Ease and cost of measurement
- Difficult and high
- Easy and low

Bubbles (bottom to top): Demographics, Geodemographics, Psychological, Behaviour

Axis label (x): Predictability of consumer choice behaviour
- Low
- High

Figure 6.5

Considerations for segmentation criteria accessibility and use

Source: Integrated Marketing Communications in Advertising and Promotion (AISE; 7th edn. by SHIMP, 2007). Reprinted with permission of South-Western, a division of Thomson Learning.

customer's susceptibility to marketing communications such as sales promotions (**media usage** and response behaviour) and market environment.

Profile Criteria

A core customer-related method of segmenting consumer goods and service markets is using criteria to profile who the market is and where they are. This is called profile segmentation criteria and includes using demographic methods (e.g. age, gender, race), socio-economics (e.g. determined by social class, or income levels) and **geographic** location (often using sophisticated postal or zip code systems). For example, a utility company might segment households based on geographical area to assess brand penetration in certain regions; or a financial investment fund might segment the market based on age, employment, income, and asset net worth to identify attractive market segments for a new investment portfolio. All these are examples of segmentation based on profile criteria.

Demographic

Demographic variables relate to age, gender, family size and lifecycle, generation (such as baby boomers, Generation X, etc.), income, occupation, education, ethnicity, nationality, religion, and social class. These relate to the profile of a consumer and are particularly useful in assisting marketing communications and media planning, simply because media selection criteria have been developed around these variables.

Age is a common way of segmenting markets and is the first way in which a market is delineated. Children are targeted with confectionery, clothes, music, toys, and food simply because their needs and tastes are radically different from older people. For example, Yoplait Dairy Crest (YDC) has launched Petits Filous Plus probiotic yogurt drinks to extend the brand and increase its appeal among 4 to 9 year olds and inform parents that 'one Petits Filous Plus yogurt drink consumed every day as part of a balanced diet can help maintain kids' wellbeing'. In the drinks market we often see the use of age. For example, the popular chocolate drink Milo is targeted to children and teenagers as an after school chocolate energy drink. In contrast Red Bull is positioned as an energy drink for young adults. In the travel industry we see organized tours and holidays for the 18–35s, with the differing needs of senior citizens met by brands such as Saga Holidays which are exclusively targeted at the over 50s. Stena Stair Lifts provide products to meet the needs of physically disadvantaged older consumers.

Gender differences have also spawned a raft of products targeted at women such as beauty products and fragrances (e.g. Clinique, Bobby Brown, Chanel); magazines (e.g. *New Woman*, *Cleo*, *Cosmopolitan*); hairdressing (e.g. Pantene, Clairol); and clothes (e.g. New Look, Sussan, Zara). Products targeted at men include magazines (e.g. *Ralph*, *Nuts*); grooming products (e.g. hair gel and styling mousse); and beverages (e.g. beers like Heineken, Carlsberg). Some brands develop products targeted at both men and women, for example fragrances (e.g. Calvin Klein) and watches (e.g. Tag). Increasingly marketers are also recognizing the importance of segments that have not traditionally been targeted by certain product categories, such as insurance products designed for women (e.g. First For Women Insurance—FFW in South Africa and Sheila's Wheels in the UK) and beauty products for men (e.g. Clinique men's range).

An example of a product designed according to the combination of age and gender is Dove's new Dove ProAge product range. These products reflect the unique needs of women in their later years, continuing Dove's campaign for Real Beauty by launching a new series of products with television and print advertisements targeted to women in their fifties.

Income or socio-economic status is another important demographic variable because it determines whether a consumer will be able to afford a product. As discussed in Chapter 3, this comprises information about consumer personal income, household income, employment status, disposable income, and asset net worth. Many companies target affluent consumers (e.g. Chanel, DKNY, Bentley,

The Dove ProAge product range aimed at women in their fifties

Dove ProAge

and Ferrari) offering high-end exclusive product offerings. Targeting low-income earners can also be profitable. Discount stores such as Dollar Dazzlers, Crazy Clarks, and Pound Stretcher make a considerable impact on the retail market by developing an offer for low-income market segments. The socio-economic distinction in marketing strategies is also increasingly apparent in the development of differing retail brand labels of large multinational retailers like Tesco, ASDA Wal-Mart, and Coles Myer. For example, Tesco Finest is developed for markets with more disposable income in contrast to Tesco Value, which is marketed to the more price-conscious and low-income market segment.

Lifecycle

The lifestage approach to segmenting markets is based on the premise that people at different stages in the lifecycle need different products and services. Adolescents need different products from a single 26-year-old person, who in turn needs different products from a 26 year old who is married with young children. For example, Tesco, ASDA Wal-Mart, and Sainsbury's have all invested in the development of product lines targeted at singles with high disposable incomes and busy lifestyles with their 'meal for one' ranges. This is in contrast with the 'family value' and 'multi-packs' targeted at families. However, as families grow and children leave home so the needs of the parents change and their disposable income increases. Holidays (e.g. Butlins and Disneyland) and automobiles (e.g. people carriers) are key product categories that are influenced by the lifestage of the market.

Historically the family lifecycle consisted of five categories through which individuals and households would progress: single bachelor, newly married, married with children, empty nester, and solitary survivor. However, since this classification was developed, society has changed and continues to change in values, beliefs, and family lifecycle. A more modern lifecycle classification was developed with support from the British Market Research Bureau (BMRB) called the Target Group Index (TGI) or BMRB-TGI Lifestage Segmentation Product which classifies 12–13 lifestage groups based on age, marital status, household composition, and children (e.g. if they have children and the child's age). These groups are presented in Table 6.2. (See Market Insight 6.2.)

Geographics

This approach is useful when there are clear locational differences in tastes, consumption, and preferences. For example, what do you put on your toast in the morning: Vegemite, Marmite, jam, or jelly? Or perhaps you don't east toast at all and prefer cold meats or noodles for your morning meal. These consumption patterns provide an indication of preferences according to differing geographic regions. Markets can be considered by country or region, by size of city or town, postcode, or by population density such as urban, suburban, or rural. For example, it is often said that American beer drinkers prefer lighter beers, compared with their UK counterparts and particularly compared with German beer drinkers, who prefer a much stronger drink. In contrast Australians prefer colder more carbonated beer than the UK or the USA. In the UK there are generalizations which state that Scottish beer drinkers prefer heavy bitters, northerners in

products such as a car or house (Belk, Bahn, and Mayer, 1982; Solomon, 1983). For example, Greenpeace launched a television campaign targeting owners of four-wheel drive cars or 'Gas Guzzlers', highlighting the environmental social stigma of this car purchase.

- Experiential consumption perspective investigates emotional and sensory experiences as a result of usage, especially consumer experience such as satisfaction, and 'fantasies, feelings and fun', the hedonic consumption of products (Holbrook and Hirschman, 1982). For example, the Oxo gravy campaign concentrates on the usage of Oxo as bringing families together, emotionally appealing to consumers and expressing family values like love, sharing, time together.

- Functional utilization perspective examines the functional usage of products and their attributes in different situations (McAlister and Pessemier, 1982; Srivastava, Shocker, and Day, 1978). For example, when the product is used, how often, and in what contexts.

Service providers may segment the market on the basis of the purchase behaviour of their customers. This might involve segmentation on the basis of loyalty to the service provider, or length of relationship, or some other mechanism. Usage of soft drinks can be considered in terms of purchase patterns (two bottles per week), usage situations (parties, picnics, or as an alcohol substitute), or purchase location (supermarket, convenience store, or wine merchant). **Lifestage** analysis is based on the principle that people have varying amounts of disposable income and different needs at different stages in their lives. Their priorities for spending change at different trigger points and these points or lifestages do not occur at the same time.

One method of segmenting service customers defines four segments based on propensity to switch suppliers: definitely will not switch, probably will not switch, might switch, and definitely will switch (Payne and Frow, 1999). The services literature points out that customers often stay with a service provider even when they are dissatisfied (Bitner, Booms, and Tetreault, 1990; Kelley, Hoffman, and Davis, 1993) and this is particularly true in retail banking for current accounts, for example, where customers seldom can see the point in shifting their funds from one account to another for very limited gains. Customers only shift suppliers when they perceive the service to be poorly priced, when inconvenienced by the service provider, when there is a core service failure (e.g. a hotel room is inadequately cleaned), when service encounters fail (e.g. arriving at a hotel with a pre-booked room and finding no room is available), when there is a poor response to service failures (e.g. in a hotel when complaining about the poor cleaning), competition (a rival hotel chain offers better rates), ethical problems, and when they have to (for example, the hotel customer is forced to move to another city and a Marriot Hotel is not available, for example, but a Hilton is).

Transaction and Purchase

The development of electronic technologies has facilitated the rapid growth in the collection of consumer purchase and transactional data, providing an additional consumer characteristic upon which to base market segmentation. The collection of purchase data has been enabled through the installation of electronic-point-of-sale (EPOS) computing systems, coupled with standardized universal product codes (UPC) in the USA or European article numbers (EAN) in Europe and the growth of integrated purchasing systems (e.g. web, in-store, telephone). These have enabled retailers to track more accurately who buys what, when, for how much, in what quantities, and with what incentives (e.g. sales promotions). This provides companies with the ability to monitor purchase patterns in differing geographic regions, times, or seasons of the year, for differing product lines, and increasingly for differing market segments.

Transactional and purchase information is very useful for marketers to assess who their most profitable customers are. This is through an analytical formula called the **RFM analysis**. RFM analysis is based on the principle postulated in 1897 by an Italian economist, Vilfredo Pareto. Pareto's Principle ascertains that '80% of a company's profits are usually delivered by just 20% of their customers'. As such there is a significant need to segment markets and create precisely targeted marketing programmes for those most profitable to the company. RFM analysis is a method by which marketers can identify market segments comprising customers that are most profitable. RFM stands for recency, frequency, and monetary value. Thus, those customers who purchased from you most recently, purchase from you frequently, and spend a high unit value per purchase (or the life of their relationship with you) would be classified as profitable customers. The acquisition of purchase data per customer through electronic technologies either in-store or online provides increased effectiveness of profitable segment identification.

However, one thing to note is that transactional data is just behaviour and although it might provide some insight into useful purchase trends, it will not be able to shed deeper insight into why those trends in purchase and consumption are occurring. With the rise in loyalty card schemes such as the famous Tesco Clubcard or customer reward programmes such as the many airline frequent flyer clubs (e.g. Star Alliance, KLM Flying Blue), and the precision of ACORN and MOSAIC geodemographic databases, we are seeing the merging of transactional and purchase data with customer profile and psychological data. This provides the bases for more effective targeting of marketing strategies to specific and defined market segments.

Media Usage

The understanding and profiling of audience media usage is central to the process of communications planning. From the 1950s television viewing information was collected by organizations such as Arbitron in the USA and AGB Ltd in the UK, providing a basis for classic studies of television viewing. Similar developments occurred with radio and print, which made possible formal studies of listening and readership. In more recent years, web usage data has been collected by market researchers such as Media Metrix, A. C. Nielsen, and NetRatings, to help profile web users. See Table 6.5 for an example of web user segmentation based on usage characteristics.

The logic of segmenting on the basis of frequency of readership, viewership, or patronage of media vehicles can be found in media research conducted in

is paramount: how can the defined group be reached with suitable communications? What is the media consumption pattern of the target audience? Where can they get access to our product and purchase it?

Targeting Approaches

Once identified, the organization needs to select its approach to target marketing it is going to adopt. Four differing approaches can be considered. These include undifferentiated, differentiated, concentrated or focused, and customized target marketing approaches (see Figure 6.9).

In an **undifferentiated approach** there is no delineation between market segments, and instead the market is viewed as one mass market with one marketing strategy for the entire market. Although very expensive, this targeting approach is often selected in markets where there is limited segment differentiation. For example, the Olympics is marketed at a world market, or certain government services. The UK postal service uses an undifferentiated marketing strategy, targeting everyone, although the Post Offices do differentiate between other products and services.

A **differentiated targeting approach** recognizes that there are several market segments to target, each being attractive to the marketing organization. As such, to exploit market segments, a marketing strategy is developed for each segment. For example, Hewlett Packard has developed its product range and marketing strategy to target the following user segments of computing equipment: home officer users; small and medium businesses; large businesses; and health, education, and government departments. The clothing brand Levi's uses multiple marketing strategies to target the trendy/casual, the price shopper, the traditionalist, the utilitarian, and the mainstream clothing shopper. A disadvantage of this approach is the loss of economies of scale due to the resources required to meet the needs of many market segments.

A **concentrated** or **niche-marketing strategy** recognizes that there are segments in the market, but implements a concentrated strategy by focusing on just a few market segments. This is often adopted by firms that either have limited resources by which to fund their marketing strategy, or are adopting a very exclusive

Figure 6.9
Target marketing approaches

strategy in the market. Jordan's the cereal company originally used this approach to target just consumers interested in organic food products. This approach is also used a lot by small to medium and micro-sized organizations, given their limited resources: the local electrician, for example, focusing on the residential market or the cement manufacturer who targets the building market.

The final approach is a **customized targeting strategy** in which a marketing strategy is developed for each customer as opposed to each market segment. This approach is more predominant in B2B markets (e.g. marketing research or advertising services) or consumer markets with high-value highly customized products (e.g. purchase of a custom-made car). For example, a manufacturer of industrial electronics for assembly lines might target and customize its product differently from Nissan, Unilever, and Levi's, given the differing requirements in assembly line processes for the manufacture of automobiles, foodstuffs, and clothing.

Jordan's

Jordan's used a concentrated strategy to market its organic food range

strategies. The main considerations are the degree of risk and adjustment an organization is willing to take and the identification of potential opportunities within certain markets. For some organizations an international strategy is deeply ingrained into their marketing strategy and domestic operations are considered of minor importance. For example, Foster's concentrates its marketing efforts more on international markets than in the Australian market. Some organizations take an ad hoc approach, only responding to customer export enquiries when they occur, whereas others proactively seek to develop an international marketing strategy (e.g. McDonald's). This can depend on the resources available, the industry, and the type of product. For example, some products such as information technologies, electronics, and cars are international by nature. The high degree of investment in research and product development in these industries necessitates the move into international markets as domestic markets often do not provide enough sales. Irrespective of the motivation, we are seeing today a growing rise in international and global marketing activities.

Perlmutter (1969) was one of the first to discuss the various attitudes or orientations that can be taken in international market development with the EPRG classification (see Figure 7.2). This highlights four approaches. An **ethnocentric approach** views the domestic market (home market) as the most important, extending local market perceptions over foreign markets and overseas markets and foreign imports not seen as representing a serious threat. With a **polycentric approach**, each overseas market is seen as a separate domestic market, each country seen as a separate entity, and the firm seeks to be seen as a local firm within that country. In some instances, each market has its own manufacturing and marketing facilities, with only a limited overlap. These two approaches take a more localized approach than regional and geocentric approaches.

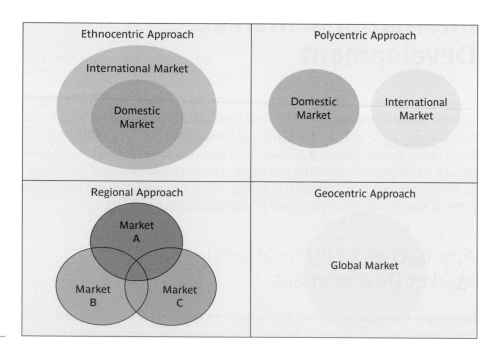

Figure 7.2
EPRG classification

A **regional approach** groups countries together, usually on a geographical basis (e.g. Europe), and provides for the specific needs of consumers within those countries. In this instance, national boundaries are respected, but do not have the same importance as cultural differences. A **geocentric approach** sees the world as a single market—global, with the organization looking for global segments (e.g. ageing market) and global opportunities to rationalize communications, production, and product development.

In a study conducted of European organizations, Lynch (1994) proposed five broad categories of organizations that differ in their approach towards international marketing. These categories differ not only according to the organization attitudes, but also the scale of the operations in markets being developed, be it local, national, regional, European, or world-scale market development.

Local-scale organizations: These organizations operate within national and local boundaries and have little opportunity or desire to trade internationally or there might be little to gain from transferring skills and placing focus on new markets further abroad. For example, the local convenience store, the car repair garage.

National-scale organizations: These organizations focus mainly on their domestic market, but might find a number of opportunities emerging from a more integrated Europe as well as responding to more ad hoc customer enquiries.

Regional-scale organizations: These benefit from growth by focusing on specific regions within Europe as opposed to operating throughout Europe (e.g. Eastern or Western Europe, Scandinavian countries) and gain experience of operating abroad on a smaller scale, and are thus subject to less risk. In the UK, for example, Irish and Welsh companies have a long tradition of trade relations with the wider UK as a first experience of cross-national trade.

European-scale organizations: This is where there has been considerable growth since Lynch (1994) first proposed these five categories for European internationalization. With increasing changes to the European Union in both trade relations and regulations, and the rise in the number of member states, many companies have turned their attentions to marketing throughout Europe, strengthening their European base. Some might argue that Europe is in fact one geographic market with a number of segments that transcend national boundaries. Although some of the risks of international trade have been reduced or eliminated (e.g. currency), some will forever remain (e.g. language, culture, infrastructure), requiring differing investment in communications, product compositions, and distribution for effective market entry.

World-scale organizations: These organizations have a strong European base, but now operate in a range of different world markets, either through direct investment, joint venture, or on an **exporting** basis. For example, Unilever, BP, GlaxoSmithKline, Nestlé derive a significant portion of sales from outside Europe. Europe is increasingly being seen as one geographic market comprising segments that transcend national boundaries, with competition from the Far East and US companies. One example is that of Hennes & Mauritz (H&M), a leading Swedish clothing retailer which is currently striving for world-scale operations and brand image appeal through its market expansions into Asia (see Market Insight 7.1).

H&M Heads East

Hennes & Mauritz (H&M) was established in Sweden in 1947. Today H&M operates in 28 countries and has more than 60,000 employees all working to the same philosophy: to bring you fashion and quality at the best price. H&M has expanded substantially in recent years and today they have around 1,400 stores spread across 28 countries. Germany is the biggest market, followed by the UK and Sweden. H&M have great potential for continued expansion and growth, launching a franchise operation in the Middle East, in Dubai and Kuwait, during Autumn 2006 and expanding in China throughout 2007.

On 12 April 2007, H&M landed in China with a splash, a particularly bright, turquoise splash of images for the brand's new summery Kylie Minogue collection and the 'H&M loves Kylie' campaign.

The campaign and store opening was promoted on thousands of billboards around this city leading up to the 12 April launch of the fast-fashion retailer's first store in mainland China. Following the first store, within 2007, H&M will have four Hong Kong stores and two in Shanghai with a big Asian expansion: Japan in 2008, and Taiwan.

H&M was relatively late to arrive in the Far East because the retailer was preoccupied with expansion in other markets, and because of its perception of when Asia would be ready for the brand. Starting with Hong Kong and mainland China the business was built on the back of thirty years of manufacturing experience here: H&M sources about 30 per cent of its production from China. Last year, it opened a greater Asia office in Hong Kong with 20 to 25 staff members.

H&M offers stylish clothing for women

H&M

Source: Movius (2007); http://www.hm.com.

1 Using the EPRG classification, how would you classify H&M's approach to international marketing?

2 Using Lynch's (1994) study of European organizations, how would you classify H&M?

3 Why was H&M 'late' to arrive in the Far East? Discuss.

RESEARCH INSIGHT 7.1

To take your learning further, you might wish to read this influential paper.

Lewis, K. S., Lim, F. A., and Rusetski, A. (2006), 'Development of archetypes of international marketing strategy', *Journal of International Business Studies*, 37, 4, 499–524.

This article provides a discussion of three separate characterizations of international marketing strategy: standardization–adaptation, concentration–dispersion, and integration–independence. With an aim towards creating a classification scheme, this paper presents evidence of three distinct international marketing strategy archetypes obtained through an exploratory case coding/clustering study. These include: 'standardized', 'concentrated', and 'integrated'.

International Competitive Strategy

In the analysis of the rise of global competition Hout, Porter, and Rudden (1982) suggest that from a strategic point of view, a firm can adopt either a local/global approach, a multi-domestic approach, or a global competitive approach to their international marketing strategy (see Figure 7.3). The key decision is do we standardize or adapt our marketing strategy when entering international markets?

This brings to the forefront of this discussion the debate about international orientation by the degree of adaptation or standardization in our marketing strategy (Herbig, 1998).

Globalization refers to increasing global connectivity, integration, and interdependence in the economic, social, technological, cultural, political, and

Figure 7.3
The spectrum of competitive strategies.

ecological spheres. It can be seen as the 'process by which the experience of everyday life is becoming standardized around the world' or the free flow of four major components: goods and services, people, capital, and information (Sirgy *et al.* 2007). The origins of the preoccupation with global marketing may be traced back to Levitt (1983), who emphasized the importance of global trade when he stated that 'only global companies will achieve long-term success by concentrating on what everyone wants rather than worrying about the details of what everyone thinks they might like'.

This view is accelerated by the new industrialized countries' (NICs) desire for modernity (e.g. Eastern European countries like Poland and Slovenia and Asian countries like China and Taiwan). Countries and companies that have appreciated this trend enjoy enormous economies of scale in production, distribution, and marketing, and by using price as a competitive weapon are able to devastate the competition. Furthermore there is increasing consolidation in many industries in world markets (e.g. pharmaceutical, financial services, and telecommunication industries).

However, there have been detractors from this argument, those who disagreed with what he said, and who argued that while it was appropriate to operate a global approach to business, the key to success was to customize the offering (Quelch and Hoff, 1986). In the twenty-first century, there still seems to be no true consensus on whether or not to offer standardized or customized products and services.

Multi-domestic Competitive Strategy

In a **multi-domestic competitive strategy**, an organization pursues a separate marketing strategy in each of its foreign markets. It also views the competitive challenge independently from market to market. In a pure **adaptation orientation**, a firm believes that each country should be approached separately as a different market, buying or conducting market research into the particular country and developing a specific market strategy for that particular market.

The adaptation approach looks to accommodate cultural, legal, language, communication, and geographical differences in markets. For example, Marks and Spencer's formal businessmen's shirts suffered poor sales in the northern European market. Quality and design were identical to those sold in the UK market. However, research revealed that the M&S shirts lacked a key feature: breast pockets for items such as pens and cigarettes. Redesign resulted in an increase in sales. (See also Market Insight 7.2 about global versus local beer tastes.)

When adopting an adaptation orientation, operations in each overseas market are strategically independent, with essentially autonomous operations. The multinational headquarters will coordinate financial controls and marketing (including brand name) policies worldwide and may centralize some research and development activities, but strategy and operations are decentralized. As such each subsidiary is a profit centre and expected to contribute earnings and

Global Beer: What's on Tap?

At some point globalization turns from a game of cross-border competition for market share among individual companies into a contest about the key elements of the industry in which they compete—brands, relationships, and technology. For such industries as computers and soft drinks, this new form of globalization has already struck. The top four players in soft drinks, for example, share almost 80% of the market, and Coca-Cola alone commands nearly 50%. It might be reasonable to think that the beer industry would tell a similar story. Reasonable, perhaps, but wrong.

In fact, beer is surprisingly local. Until the middle of the last century, the short shelf life and difficulty of transporting beer meant that it could be sold only locally. Things have changed, but history has left its legacy. Research suggests that consumers may be getting somewhat more adventurous, but even where imports are readily available, most consumers in most countries continue to buy local brands produced by local brewers and sold through local stores, pubs, and restaurants at prices that vary widely in localities around the globe. As a result, the beer industry is a collection of tiny players. The top four command just a 20% share of the world market, and the largest, the US brewer Anheuser-Busch, makes more than 85% of its sales in its home market. Although no brewer comes close to dominating the world, in most countries, the top two or three brewers share more than 80% of the market. Two prominent exceptions, Germany and China, are themselves highly concentrated, but at the city or provincial rather than the national level.

Heineken now has the single best prospect of ranking among the global giants of the future. It has a global brand; a widespread presence, both in its own right and through alliances; and strong skills in such areas as marketing and production. Guinness is another international marketing success with 10 million glasses of Guinness drunk in over 150 countries every day. Aside from Ireland, Guinness is brewed in fifty other markets, and while the UK, and Ireland in particular, seem to be falling out of love with stout, ale, and therefore Guinness, the rest of the world can't get enough of it. Anheuser-Busch too is in good shape; Belgium's Interbrew and South African Breweries are not far behind; and Carlsberg shows signs of regaining its position in the global running. Yet all of these companies, Heineken included, are years away from replicating the global success of Coke or Nike.

Heineken

Heineken beer is
marketed globally

Source: Benson-Armer, Leibowitz, and Ramachandran (1999); Anon. (2005); Ward (2006).

1 Why do you think some beer brands are so grounded in local appeal and struggle to find a 'global voice'?

2 What market factors contribute to such individual tastes when it comes to beer?

3 What could Heineken, Guinness, and Carlsberg learn from Coke or Nike in terms of pursuing an international marketing strategy?

growth consistent with market opportunity, and competition is on a market-by-market basis (Hout, Porter, and Rudden, 1982).

Global Competitive Strategy

In a pure **standardization orientation**, a firm operates as if the world were one large market (global market), ignoring regional and national differences, selling the same products and services the same way throughout the world. The standardization approach operates on the belief that global culture is converging, or that the cultural differences are superficial. This is supported by various studies (see Wind and Perlmutter, 1973; Levitt, 1983; Douglas and Douglas, 1987). The standardization approach has many immediate benefits including cost reductions, improved efficiency, enhanced customer preference, and increased competitive leverage (Herbig, 1998).

The problem with this approach is that cultural, legal, and national differences can inhibit trade—if the firm was wrong in assuming the differences were superficial. Communication is one of the biggest barriers when doing business internationally and can be heightened when using the standardization approach. Advertising messages may be misrepresented or misunderstood. Some famous communication blunders are reported in Table 7.6. Despite attempts to standardize world trade the world still comprises a large number of independent countries of vastly differing sizes, economic philosophy, and stage of economic development, not to mention societal and cultural values and aspirations.

To qualify as pursuing a global competitive strategy, a company needs to be able to demonstrate two things: (1) that it can contest any market it chooses to compete in and (2) that it can bring its entire worldwide resources to bear on any competitive situation it finds it in, regardless of where that might be. Two basic concepts are contained with this definition: **selective contestability** and **global capability**.

The concept of selective contestability is central to successful marketing practice with its core principle of segmentation, targeting, and positioning. Irrespective of whether the company is competing in a regional, national, or global market, the ability to divide generic markets into meaningful sub-markets or segments, select those most attractive, and position the product offering appropriately is at the very heart of devising a competitive strategy. Global capability is the willingness and capability of operating anywhere in the world with a direct result in global

Table 7.3
Five key attributes of
global strategy

Attribute	Description
Possessing a standard product (or core) that is marketed uniformly across the world	Both the product and service offering is marketed using the same marketing mix in differing national markets, representing what most regard as a global strategy.
Sourcing all assets, not just production, on an optimal basis	If one were to pursue this to its ultimate level, one might find that nationalistic factors might well result in one finishing up with an essentially multi-domestic operation due to local requirements in capital ownership, employment, and so on.
Achieving market access in line with the break-even volume of the needed infrastructure	Global competitor must be of sufficient size and generate sufficient volume/revenue in each of the markets in which it competes to justify the marketing investment needed to compete effectively.
The ability to contest assets as much as products when circumstances require	This reflects the firm's ability to match its principal competitors in gaining access to and control over assets critical to its success, for example technology.
Providing all functions (or competencies) with a global orientation, even they are primarily local in scope	This is the most difficult to achieve and to measure as it reflects the 'mental set' of those responsible for devising a strategy as well as those responsible for its execution.

Source: Table adapted from Vijay (1997).

brand recognition. The idea of a global brand goes far beyond the firm's physical presence in a number of differing national markets and reflects the existence of a global image. It is this universal recognition which enables one to distinguish the firm pursuing a focused strategy in numerous national markets from a global player like Ford, McDonald's, Coca-Cola, and Levi's.

Vijay (1997) indicates that to distinguish between multi-domestic and global competitive strategies, one should assess a company in terms of five key attributes. These are presented in Table 7.3.

Anti-Globalization Movement

In contrast to the perspective presented above about the growth of international trade relations and globalization movements, there also exists an anti-globalization movement. **Anti-globalization** is a term most commonly used to refer to the political stance of people and groups who oppose certain aspects of globalization in its current form. Anti-globalization is considered by many to be a social movement, while others consider it to be an umbrella term that encompasses a number of separate social movements. In either case, participants are united in opposition to the political power of large corporations, as exercised

in trade agreements and elsewhere, which they say undermines democracy, the environment, labour rights, national sovereignty, the third world, and other concerns. The groups and individuals that would come to be known as the anti-globalization movement developed in the late twentieth century to combat the globalization of corporate economic activity and the free trade with developing nations that might result from such activity.

Protesters believe that the global financial institutions and agreements undermine local decision-making methods with many governments and free trade institutions seen as acting for the good of multinational corporations (e.g. Microsoft, McDonald's). These corporations are seen as having privileges that most human persons do not have: moving freely across borders, extracting desired natural resources, and utilizing a diversity of human resources. They are perceived to be able to move on after doing permanent damage to the natural capital and biodiversity of a nation, in a manner impossible for that nation's citizens.

Activists also claim that corporations impose a kind of global monoculture. Some of the movement's common goals are, therefore, an end to the legal status of so-called 'corporate personhood' and the dissolution or dramatic reform of the World Bank, IMF, and WTO.

Two documentaries *The Corporation* (2003) and *Life and Debt* (2001) present a very chilling and raw view of the impact on local economies, society, and our civil liberties of growing international trade relations and the multinational corporation (see Marketing Insight 7.3).

(opposite) **Marketing materials for *The Corporation* film**

The Corporation

The Multinational on Show

The Corporation (2003) is a Canadian documentary film critical of the modern-day corporation, considering it as a class of person and evaluating its behaviour towards society and the world at large as a psychologist might evaluate an ordinary person. The film gives insight into the inner workings of large and powerful corporations, what the anti-global activists call a devilish instrument of environmental destruction, class oppression, and imperial conquest, and how these affect our society.

The film charts the development of the corporation as a legal entity entitled to some of the legal rights of a 'person'. One central theme of the documentary is an attempt to assess the 'personality' of the corporate 'person', comparing the modern, profit-driven corporation to that of a clinically diagnosed psychopath. The film focuses mostly on the corporation in North America, especially in the United States.

Life and Debt (2001) is a feature-length documentary which addresses the impact of the International Monetary Fund, the World Bank, the Inter-American Development Bank, and current globalization policies on a developing country such as Jamaica.

Jamaica—land of sea, sand, and sun—is a prime example of the impact economic globalization can have on a developing country. Using conventional and unconventional documentary techniques, this searing film dissects the 'mechanism of debt' that is destroying local agriculture and industry while substituting sweatshops and cheap imports. With a voice-over narration written by Jamaica Kincaid, adapted from her book *A Small*

A still from
The Corporation

The Corporation

If you come to Jamaica as a tourist,
This is what you will see...

LIFE AND DEBT
A film by STEPHANIE BLACK

⚠ **About the Film**
⚠ **Film Credits**
⚠ **Related Info**

Marketing materials for
the *Life and Debt* film

Life and Debt

Place, Life and Debt is an unapologetic look at the 'new world order', from the point of view of Jamaican workers, farmers, government, and policy officials who see the reality of globalization from the ground up.

Source: Anon. (2004).

1 *The Corporation* follows the 'personality' of the corporate 'person'. What do you think the producers and directors were trying to achieve with this film?

2 What is the core message of *Life and Debt*?

3 What impact do you think these documentaries have on public perceptions of globalization and international trade?

To take your learning further, you might wish to read this influential paper.

Levitt, T. (1983), 'Globalisation of markets', *Harvard Business Review*, May–June, 9–11.

This article provides a thought-provoking essay about the movement from an emphasis on customizing items to offering globally standardized products that are advanced, functional, reliable—and low priced. The authors assert that only global companies will achieve long-term success by concentrating on what everyone wants rather than worrying about the details of what everyone thinks they might like and should focus on the world as one market, ignoring national and regional differences.

The Drive for International Market Development

Many factors motivate a company to develop markets on foreign shores. The drive to international marketing and globalization is driven by a number of key marketplace forces, such as those presented in Figure 7.4.

Some of the most common motivations for organizations investing in international market development include the following:

Excess stock: Some organizations need to get rid of some excess stock and, with limited opportunity for sales in domestic markets, seek overseas markets by which to offload some of this stock. This is an activity called **dumping** and is an international marketing version of 'clearance pricing'. Excess stock of a particular product is cleared onto another country's market at very low prices in order to liquidate capital. There is no long-term entry strategy, just a hit and run exercise.

Historical accident: Being in the right place at the right time. This was the reason behind the growth of Coca-Cola's international marketing operations. In 1928 Coca-Cola was the first ever sponsor of the Olympic Games and in the 1940s US forces took the drink with them when they went into the Second World War. These historical events provided opportunities for Coca-Cola to build upon with an aggressive distribution policy resulting in the red and white livery as one of the most internationally recognizable brands (see Market Insight 7.4).

Limited growth in domestic markets: If there is limited growth in the domestic market the organization is therefore motivated to enter international markets to avoid the intensity of domestic competition. An example is UK Cadbury's purchase of Adams, a chewing gum business, from Pfizer in 2002. This purchase was motivated to open up new distribution opportunities in the US market as Cadbury were operating in a very competitive but stagnant market in the UK.

Comparative advantage: Companies are also increasingly not only selling products overseas, but certain regions and countries have developed core competencies to produce certain products, provide raw resources, or provide a core

Figure 7.4
Motivations for international market development

Coca-Cola and International Market Opportunity

The Coca-Cola Company has long been a worldwide business. The first soda fountain sales to Canada and Mexico were recorded in 1897 with the first international bottler established in Panama in 1906. Coca-Cola entered China in 1927 and the 100th country, Sierra Leone, in 1957. Today, the Coca-Cola Company is the largest beverage company with the most extensive distribution system in the world.

In the first two decades of the twentieth century, the international growth of Coca-Cola had been rather haphazard. It began in 1900, when Charles Howard Candler, eldest son of Asa Candler, took a jug of syrup with him on vacation to England. A modest order for five gallons of syrup was mailed back to Atlanta. The same year, Coca-Cola travelled to Cuba and Puerto Rico, and it wasn't long before the international distribution of syrup began. Through the early 1900s, bottling operations were built in Cuba, Panama, Canada, Puerto Rico, the Philippines, and Guam (western Pacific island). In 1920, a bottling company began operating in France as the first bottler of Coca-Cola on the European continent.

In 1926, Robert W. Woodruff, chief executive officer and chairman of the board, committed the company to organized international expansion by establishing the Foreign Department, which in 1930 became a subsidiary known as the Coca-Cola Export Corporation. By that time, the number of countries with bottling operations had almost quadrupled, and the company had initiated a partnership with the Olympic Games that transcended cultural boundaries. Coca-Cola and the Olympic Games began their association in the summer of 1928, when an American freighter arrived in Amsterdam carrying the United States Olympic team and 1,000 cases of Coca-Cola. Forty thousand spectators filled the stadium to witness two firsts: the first lighting of the

Olympic flame and the first sale of Coke at an Olympiad. Dressed in caps and coats bearing the Coca-Cola trademark, vendors satisfied the fans' thirst, while outside the stadium, refreshment stands, cafés, restaurants, and small shops called 'winkles' served Coke in bottles and from soda fountains.

The company began a major push to establish bottling operations outside the USA. Plants were opened in France, Guatemala, Honduras, Mexico, Belgium, Italy, and South Africa. By the time the Second World War began, Coca-Cola was being bottled in forty-four countries, including those on both sides of the conflict. Far from devastating the business, the war simply presented a new set of challenges and opportunities for the entire Coca-Cola system. The entry of the United States into the war brought an order from Robert Woodruff in 1941 'to see that every man in uniform gets a bottle of Coca-Cola for 5 cents, wherever he is and whatever it costs the Company.' This effort to supply the armed forces with Coke was being launched when an urgent cablegram arrived from General Dwight Eisenhower's Allied Headquarters in North Africa. Dated 29 June 1943, it requested shipment of materials and equipment for ten bottling plants. Prefaced by the directive that the shipments were not to replace other military cargo, the cablegram also requested shipment of 3 million filled bottles of Coca-Cola, along with supplies for producing the same quantity twice monthly.

Within six months, a company engineer had flown to Algiers and opened the first plant, the forerunner of sixty-four bottling plants shipped abroad during the Second World War. The plants were set up as close as possible to combat areas in Europe and the Pacific. More than 5 billion bottles of Coke were consumed by military service personnel during the war, in addition to countless servings through dispensers and mobile, self-contained units in battle areas. But the presence of Coca-Cola did more than just lift the morale of the troops. In many areas, it gave local people their first taste of Coca-Cola. When peace returned, the Coca-Cola system was poised for unprecedented worldwide growth. From the mid-1940s until 1960, the number of countries with bottling operations nearly doubled. As the world emerged from a time of conflict, Coca-Cola emerged as a worldwide symbol of friendship and refreshment.

The Coca-Cola Company is now operating in more than 200 countries and producing nearly 400 brands; the Coca-Cola system has successfully applied a simple formula on a global scale: provide a moment of refreshment for a very small amount of money—a billion times a day. The Coca-Cola Company and its network of bottlers comprise the most sophisticated and pervasive production and distribution system in the world. From Boston to Beijing, from Montreal to Moscow, Coca-Cola, more than any other consumer product, has brought pleasure to thirsty consumers around the globe.

1 What key market forces were the drive for internationalization for Coca-Cola?

2 What marketing elements were imperative for the successful international market strategy for Coca-Cola?

3 Was Coca-Cola in the right place at the right time or was this a planned international marketing strategy? Discuss.

skill competency. This presents a comparative advantage for the manufacture and production of goods in certain regions. For example, with respect to olive oil, over 750 million olive trees are cultivated worldwide, with about 95 per cent in the Mediterranean region. About three-quarters of global olive oil production comes from European Union member states with 77 per cent from Spain, Italy, and Greece.

With respect to skill competencies, certain countries have developed core advantages offering differential labour costs and skills when compared to domestic markets; for example, China and textile manufacturing or India and the provision of business process outsourcing (BPOs) such as customer call centre service provision. This presents an advantage not only in labour and possible operating costs, but for some industries savings in transport and import costs in manufacturing dependent on country geographic proximity and government incentives for inward investment.

Economies of scale: Some companies enter foreign markets to achieve economies of scale. For some products the cost of development and production is high and thus requires mass production runs for effective return on investment and thus to function effectively factories need to serve large world markets. Examples include consumer electronic goods and the automotive industry. A high degree of standardization is evident in the manufacture of certain car parts, the chassis and engines, with superficial changes tailored for local markets (e.g. air conditioning). Therefore, car manufacturers are able to achieve economies of scale in certain parts, but not other elements (Pitcher, 1999).

Trade liberalization: With the creation of trading blocs such as the European Union and the reduction of barriers to trade worldwide as a result of the WTO, the notion of free trade has received increased impetus in recent years. As such increasingly we are seeing many firms engage in global competition with international firms in domestic markets and domestic firms moving abroad to compete overseas and markets opening up.

International product lifecycle: This is when a product reaches a differing stage of the product lifecycle in differing countries, such as a product reaching maturity in country A, while it is in growth in country B. For example the original Volkswagen Beetle ceased production in Germany in 1978, but commenced production and sales in South America.

Technological changes: Advances in electronic communications and innovations in air travel and international air freight have enabled increased ability to trade across and within international borders. One such technology that has had a dramatic impact is the internet. Online channels are increasingly being used to sell into new markets, taking advantage of low costs for international market entry. This is a good way for SMEs to increase exports at a low cost. However, changes in the technological infrastructure worldwide are providing many new opportunities for firms to internationalize.

Customer relationships: As customers move further abroad, and internationalize, so too must suppliers and intermediaries consider the prospect by which to maintain or strengthen customer–supplier relations and remain competitive. For example, as Ford expands into foreign markets, its demands and needs with respect to product components will change. Suppliers will need to follow suit, providing components that match the requirements of Ford's manufacturing and assembly production process that have been designed to meet the needs of the new foreign markets. The impact on international marketing activities can be felt throughout the supply chain, from end consumer to supplier of product components.

This is also true for service-based industries. However, the difference lies in that there will be an increasing need to locate an organization's services even closer to the customer, either through branch offices or subsidiaries strategically placed throughout a number of foreign markets. For example, in the market research industry, with the increasing need to be more knowledgeable about foreign markets comes the need for companies to be based in and have sound market knowledge of these new markets. A. C. Nielsen, the world's leading marketing information company, has research operations that span more than 100 countries. Headquartered in New York, the company's major regional business centres are located in Schaumburg, Illinois; Wavre, Belgium; Hong Kong; Sydney, Australia; Buenos Aires, Argentina; and Nicosia, Cyprus.

Transnational market segments: A growing factor in globalization is the existence of groups of customers with similar needs who inhabit different countries. These are called transnational market segments. This occurs because of migration (e.g. Malaysians working in Australia); because of similarities in demographics (e.g. baby boomers); or because of similarities in lifestyle (e.g. working women). From a conceptual perspective, a truly global company should be dividing market segments up based on similar characteristics across national borders, and not country of residence. Country of residence is becoming less and less relevant as migration increases and national borders diminish.

Organizational sustainability: A very basic reason for international marketing is that of sustainability. The broader the range of markets served, the less likely that market failure in one market will result in corporate decline. Different markets are always at different stages of development and competitive intensity. Therefore an effectively positioning international market portfolio will provide an organization with the ability to move and share resources to counter any market difficulties in any one market. Many markets in the Far East offer growth opportunities, whereas many Western markets are considered to be in maturity.

However, whatever the motivation for international market development, a planned approach considerably increases the chances for success. Irrespective of the reasons or motives for market entry, once entry has been decided as an organizational growth strategy, certain decisions have to be made. These include determining:

- Which markets to pursue: international market selection;
- The best method for entering new markets; and
- Which strategy to adopt in new markets, such as how much adaptation/ standardization of the product offering is necessary to appeal to desired needs of the foreign markets.

International Market Selection

Assessing market attractiveness is very important when considering international market development. Once the marketing environment is understood (see later in this chapter), the organization needs to match opportunities and threats in the markets that are attractive with the organization's own strengths, weaknesses, assets, skills, and aspirations. The quality of this assessment will have a big impact on the success or failure of the international marketing strategy (Anderson and Strandskov, 1998). Markets may be chosen according to the following criteria, with the criteria of marketing accessibility and size regarded as the two most important criteria for assessing international market attractiveness.

Market size and growth rate: Market size refers to the number of customers and/or prospects within a market and given a large market is more likely to redeem increased amount/volume of sales than a small market, market size is regarded as a very important criterion for assessing international market attractiveness. International market segments are often attractive to international marketers because of the number of customers involved and thus the potential opportunity to benefit from economies of scale. Certain areas in the world grow in attractiveness while others decline. Ohmae (1985, 1992) was one of the first marketing writers to point to the domination of world markets by what he called the Triad—the three major world players of Europe, America, and Japan. However this is susceptible to turbulent change.

The rapidly developing countries of the Pacific Rim (i.e. China, Singapore, South Korea, and Taiwan), are going through a period of unparalleled economic growth. Income in their countries is sill unevenly distributed in these populations; however, increasing prosperity has created markets hungry for Western luxury brands to reflect their rising personal wealth. Names like Burberry, Ralph Lauren, and new developing technologies appear prominently. As industrial sectors have grown in these areas, agriculture has decreased in importance, altering the mix of goods and service required for business markets and creating opportunities for information technologies, business services, and construction. For insight on China, see Market Insight 7.5.

Furthermore, high growth rates are seen as considerably attractive due to lower perceived competition in these contexts than stable and declining markets. Whitelock (1994) reports in fact that growth rate is a far more important consideration than market size.

Market access: Accessibility means that customers can be reached with marketing communications and distribution. Local industry structure, infrastructure, and local cultural norms can limit market access. These can include government restrictions on imports or local competition rules. For example, in Japan, the monolithic structure of the industry with the giant Sogo Sosha general trading companies (GTC) controlling everything means that there are few openings for foreign companies, despite no legal problems with importing. The six largest are Mitsubishi Corporation, Mitsui & Co., ITOCHU, Sumitomo Corporation, Marubeni, and Sojitz. In contrast some countries have high tariffs on products in order to protect local produce and industry.

Market segmentation frequently identifies consumers with similar needs and aspirations across a number of national boundaries. For example, working women in Beijing, China, may have similar needs and aspirations to working women in Paris or Madrid, but differ increasingly from women in rural China. However, the use of media to reach these women may differ considerably given differing media coverage between countries.

Geographic proximity: closeness of the market in physical terms to the domestic market. For example, trading between Australia and the UK requires larger resources than trade between the UK and other European countries such as France.

Psychological proximity: Perceived cultural and societal similarities between countries. For example cultural similarity is perceived by some as greater between the USA and the UK than the UK and France, given perceived similarities in language and cultural values; thus some firms perceive the USA as more attractive to

Transforming China

Napoleon Bonaparte predicted, 'When China awakens, it will astonish the world.'

Photodisc

In the nineteenth century, Napoleon Bonaparte predicted, 'When China awakens, it will astonish the world.' China's recent stirring from its centuries-old slumber has far-reaching implications for international business and politics, as well as for science and technology development.

With rapid industrial development and a market of more than 1.3 billion increasingly prosperous consumers, the expected rewards of doing business in China are now widely viewed as outweighing the risk of investing capital there. The economy of the People's Republic of China is the fourth largest in the world when measured by nominal GDP. Its economic output for 2006 was US$2.68 trillion. Its per capita GDP in 2006 was approximately US$2,000 (US$7,600 with PPP), still low by world standards (110th of 183 nations in 2005), but rising rapidly.

The overall growth of the Chinese economy has been accompanied by significant evolutions and perhaps transformation in the focus of its business activities. It is already the world's biggest market for many commodities, including cement and steel, and consumer goods, including mobile phones and soft drinks. China is also fast becoming the world's factory, dominating many labour-intensive industries such as low-end electronics, toys, and most clothing items. Little companies drive China's economic growth with China's industries composed of hundreds of thousands of tiny factories and farms, plus traders, brokers, hauliers, and agents, all of whom take control of the goods and materials. China's economic development is increasingly being complemented by activities based on knowledge and mental labour including software development and e-commerce.

China wants to be a technology powerhouse. Progress is evident in products based on IT (such as mobile phones and PCs); IT-based exports have grown at annual rates of 40–60% over the past decade reaching US$160 million in 2004. However, manufacturing export-quality goods depends on imported technology and foreign capital. China still faces the huge challenge of moving beyond technology transfer and contract manufacturing toward being a technology innovator and global leader in brands and products.

Source: Martinsons (2005); Haft (2007); Parker (2007).

1 What implications do you think the above market insight has for companies thinking of doing business in China?

2 What are key factors influencing market growth in China?

3 What impact do you think market growth in China will have on the balance of power and trade with other leading trading regions (e.g. Europe, USA)?

firms in the UK for possible trade relations. Psychological proximity is often based on language—the UK close to Australia, Canada, and even India given cultural, language, and historical similarities.

Level and quality of competition already in the market: Intense market competition is unlikely to respond favourably to foreign market entrants, thus assessing marketing competition is increasingly important. Furthermore, market positioning in a foreign market upon entry may differ from that held within the domestic market.

Cost of entering the market: This can vary greatly between markets and between entry strategy (exporting, sales office, distribution, etc.). For example, physical distribution costs can be extremely high in a country such as the USA or Australia where distances are large. In other countries distribution channels and supply chains can be long and complex resulting in increased cost due to supply chain complexity. Some countries may lack the infrastructure to support operations considered essential or cheaper in domestic markets. For example the telecommunications infrastructure in various African countries differs greatly from more established Western European countries such as Germany and France.

Profit potential: This is a factor of the number of potential customers and the profit margin the product might produce. A country with a large potential market might be attractive even though per unit profit margins would be small. For example, India and China might offer large future profit potential. Powerful buying groups, low per capita income, and strong competition are all factors which tend to reduce profit margins; in contrast, high incomes, inefficient competition, and good positioning could yield high profit margins.

Market selection therefore requires careful consideration. There is a need for sound market intelligence and information about the market environment and market opportunities. Screening of potential markets will reveal markets with unfavourable market forces. Desk research can show markets with low potential, leaving a much smaller number of markets for a more detailed investigation. In reality, market screening can be random, driven by customer enquiries or market demand for a product offering or knowledge gained through media or social networks. Visits to the potential markets will also be required for further insights and first-hand market knowledge and to aid the development of networks and relationships from within the system. Questions that might be considered are detailed in Table 7.4.

RESEARCH INSIGHT 7.3

To take your learning further, you might wish to read this influential paper.

Young, R. B., and Javalgi, R. G. (2007), 'International marketing research: A global project management perspective', *Business Horizons*, 50, 2, 113–22.

This article provides a useful insight into the importance and role of marketing research as the primary mechanism through which companies understand their current, as well as potential, customers in international markets. The authors discuss the context for international market research and provide a framework for conducting international market research projects.

Table 7.4
International market
screening questions

Factor	Questions to consider
Market	• What stage is it in growth cycle? Early development, growth, maturity, decline? • Is there sufficient future demand or potential? • Are there established distribution channels? • How sophisticated is the infrastructure?
Product fit	• Is there opportunity in the market for this product? • Is there demand or interest in this type of product? • Would the product need to be adapted or changed in any way?
Competition	• Who are the existing competitors in this market—national and international? • How intense or aggressive is the competitive environment? • What degree of controls or influence do existing competitors have in the marketplace? • What are some of the competitive barriers to entry? • What is likely to be the competitive response to our market entry?
Market entry	• What entry methods are feasible for this market and the organization? • How much would market entry cost us? • Do we have any contacts or relationships in the market that could assist us? • How similar are the culture, values, attitudes of this market to our own domestic market? • How well do we understand the differences in this market?
Resources	• What do we need to invest to enter this market? • Are we going to have employ staff locally or relocate staff to enter this market? • What training and/or education do we require to enter this market—culture, languages, exporting, etc.? • Do we need to invest in the establishment of new or differing distribution channels for market entry or can we rely on existing distribution channels?
Trade barriers	• What legal or regulatory factors will influence market entry or operations in the market? • Are the advertising and/or marketing research activities similar to our national market? • Will import tariffs or quotas apply to us? • Will we be able to take profits earned out of the country? • Are there any constraints on foreign companies operating in this market? • Do we have to manufacture or produce our product to differing quality and/or health and safety standards?

International Marketing Environment

Once the decision has been made to pursue an international market development strategy, the organization has to choose which markets to enter. Understanding the marketing environments of the countries of interest can form the foundation of a detailed market assessment and market selection process. Because of the complexity and unfamiliarity of the international marketing environment, successful international marketing requires vigilant attention to environmental factors. The analysis of environmental forces can help to identify which countries (e.g. Australia, France, Brazil) or regions (e.g. Western Europe, South America) should be given priority and which market entry strategy would be best suited.

As introduced in Chapter 2 marketing responds to a number of variables in the external environment, such as socio-cultural, technological, political and legal, economic factors. These elements also present the company with possible threats and opportunities in entering foreign markets. Young (2001) argues that international marketers pay too little attention to the potential impact that global economic, legal/institutional, and political/social developments could have on their ability to trade. There is a need for sound market intelligence and information.

Socio-Cultural

It is imperative marketers pay attention to socio-cultural factors in international marketing. Differences might exist in terms of culture, language, social structures, gender roles, effect of religion, as well as values, perceptions, and attitudes. Social factors can affect what is and what is not acceptable in terms of business conduct, marketing communications, product offering characteristics, and market suitability.

The changing social structure is an important consideration. The role of women, the role of the elderly, or the positioning of the family within society can have an impact on product positioning and advertising. Consider the changing family structures and household compositions throughout the Western world as divorce and non-children families rise. Also increasingly we are seeing more mothers returning to work placing more reliance on grandparents for child-care responsibilities in regions like the UK, America, and Australia—changing the retirement age and lifestyle patterns of the greying consumer in these markets. This contrasts with the long-held tradition in other markets of cross-generation households (e.g. China and Japan), where grandparents are considered a central part of the family unit and reside in the family household. Japan is also beginning to loosen its immigration and employment policies in response to concerns about an ageing workforce. An awareness of changes and differences in social structure is therefore imperative.

Culture is a set of learned behaviours that unite a group of people, often along national lines. Language, education, religion, lifestyle, taboos, norms, and values are some of the areas that culture embraces. Culture also affects the way people define their wants and needs through consumption. For example, DeBeers control 80 per cent of the £32.5 billion world market in gem diamonds. The company markets them to differing countries according to the cultural norms. In the UK a diamond ring is synonymous with getting engaged; in Spain it is bought after the birth of a child; in Saudi Arabia diamonds are an important wedding gift. Saudi brides not only receive rings, but necklaces, earrings, and tiaras are also usually included (IPA, 1997).

Culture also influences the way we interact, relate, and work and do business together. For example, following the movement of many call centre jobs to India, some have had to be transferred back to the UK. In 2005, for instance, Norwich Union relocated the job of taking a customer's first call back to the UK to make an insurance claim, following misunderstandings arising from cultural differences. For instance, customers with flooding from immersion heaters struggled to get their message across to staff in India who didn't have such heaters (Warren, 2007). Clearly for firms which are serious about international marketing, cultural sensitivity is paramount as this could affect not only the way the product is marketed, but also the way in which business is negotiated and how employees work together between national markets. For example, difficulties often arise due to the problem of people from differing cultures working together. English managers tend to be pragmatic and informal whereas the French are trained to be far more analytical in the way they approach problems and justify their solutions with argument and evidence. Table 7.5 outlines some behavioural factors that have been known to influence business conduct in international environments.

Population movements through the expansions of multinationals and immigration are also influencing social factors through the migration of values and culture. Take Canada for example: immigration now accounts for 70 per cent of Canada's population growth. The fastest-growing groups, South Asians and Chinese, are typically young, educated, and wealthy. By 2017, roughly half of all visible minorities in Canada will be South Asian or Chinese, with the population of each community estimated at 1.8 million, according to Statistics Canada (Harris, 2007). This presents opportunities and threats for foreign companies considering entering the Canadian market. Mughan (1993) suggests that companies adapt best to cultural difference by:

- Self-analysis—recognizing the situation from the customer's point of view and adapting behaviour accordingly;
- Cultural training—particularly for personnel working with counterparts from other countries or dealing direct with distributors or customers (see Market Insight 7.6);
- Recruitment—the shortest route to widening the culture of an organization is through direct recruitment in the international labour market. As we have noted, one of the characteristics of most international companies is the presence of a range of nationalities in senior management.

Table 7.5

Business conduct in international markets

Factor	Description
Time	• Attitudes towards punctuality • Sanctity of deadlines • Acquaintance time • Discussion time
Business cards	• When to offer them • Whether to translate them • Who gives them first • How to attend to them
Gifts	• Should they be given • Size/value • Should they be opened in front of the giver
Dress	• Dress codes • Formality
Entertainment	• Type/formality of social occasions • Table manners and etiquette • Cuisine • Cultural and religious taboos • Venues (e.g. restaurant, private home)
Space	• Office size and location • Selection, quality, and arrangement of furniture
Body language	• Greeting conventions (e.g. kiss, handshake, bow) • Facial and hand gestures and their meaning • Physical proximity • Touching and posture
Material possessions	• Is it appropriate to comment and admire?

Source: Mead (1990). © John Wiley & Sons Limited, Reproduced with permission.

UK Cultural Training in Aviva's Call Centres

Globalization means employers want staff to learn about other cultures. Interest in cross-cultural training has sharply increased in the past five years as more and more European enterprises have become involved in Asia. Aviva Global Services' (AGS) workforce sounds like an HR professional's dream: highly educated and hungry for success. But they need the right cultural training to connect with their customers in the UK. If you ask customer care executives in call centres in India what they remember about training on UK culture, it's clear that Scotland had a big impact: *'Kilts and bagpipes and we watched* Braveheart.' Employees also learn about the Houses of Parliament and the national anthem, they know the UK has motorways (not national ways or highways), and can tell you about the finer points of the English language—thanks in part to Eliza Doolittle.

Cultural training is taken very seriously by Aviva. After all, for many of the workforce in Pune, a city some 170 kilometres from Mumbai, the chances of visiting the UK are slim.

The company therefore has got to spend a fair amount of time familiarizing everyone with UK culture because they are so far removed from their customers physically and because Indian ways of doing things are so different from the UK way. 'We take them through everything from sports and weather to dress, car models and homes. We also take them through the nuances of language: what the British say and what they mean, and what we say and what we mean,' says V. J. Rao, HR director at Aviva Global Services (AGS).

Aviva's overseas employees are trained in the ways of UK culture

Aviva

Source: McLuhan (2004); Steinborn (2007); Warren (2007).

1 Why do you think cultural training is important for the employees in Aviva's call centres in India?

2 Why impact do you think knowing about sports, the weather, dress, car models, and homes would have on an Indian employee's interaction with customers in UK?

3 What other initiatives could Aviva do to culturally educate and train its staff effectively?

Attitudes and Values

Values and attitudes can affect perceptions of a product, customer reactions to it, or perceptions of the product's origins. For example, following the BSE crisis in the UK, the British beef industry had to invest in marketing to convince foreign markets that its beef was safe. A reliable strategy is to first enter international markets that have similar attitudes and values and are regarded as culturally similar to their own; for example, Irish companies exporting to UK, Swedish companies to other Scandinavian companies, New Zealand to Australia. Through these lower-risk strategies companies can develop knowledge and learning before entering markets regarded as very different in terms of attitudes, values, and culture.

Monitoring trends and the context of the value systems and attitudes of the buying country is increasingly important in international market development. For example, mainland China had long been an unfriendly market for mid-range fashion, since consumer tastes tend to split into the extremes of mass and luxury. However, in recent years, a swelling demographic of young, white-collar, lower-middle-class women has created a demand for mid-price fashion, as evidenced by the success of Zara's launch and H&M. The shift in consumer taste in China, however, is further reported as representative of a global trend, and not just unique to the China market. 'Fashion is not a matter of price. People tend to mix high- and low-priced items. It is a shift in customer attitude that is happening all over, including here' (Movius, 2007).

Some cultures are more resistant to foreign imports than others. Even within Europe there are differing attitudes towards the origins of differing imports. Germans are more traditionalist, where as France and Italy are more open to foreign products (Paitra, 1993). Country of origin of foreign imports is also an important criterion to consider. Some companies trade very effectively based on their country of origin: for example, Foster's on the laid-back Australian attitude, Ikea on its Swedishness and clean Scandinavian design, McDonald's and Coca-Cola on the American dream, and increasingly Japan for precision and electronics.

Language is critical for an international marketer. Increasingly it is becoming an expectation that a company deals with its customer in their own language. However we still see many UK executives assume that all foreigners can speak and negotiate in English (Kelly, 2002). In fact in the UK only about one-third of business executives have a foreign language, comparing very poorly to European organizations that very often conduct business in a minimum of two languages. It was further identified that in countries such as Denmark, Finland, and Poland over 80 per cent of executives operate in at least one foreign language.

Language further has implications for marketing communications, be it brand names, company slogans and advertising taglines, or product packaging. In French-speaking Quebec, Canada, KFC is known as PFK (Poulet Frit Kentucky); this is one of the few instances in which the KFC initialism is changed for the local language (even in France itself, it is called KFC). In several Spanish-speaking areas of the United States, KFC is known as PFK (Pollo Frito Kentucky). All forms of marketing communications have to be translated and back translated to ensure correct interpretation and meaning. Things to consider include do all the words, phrases, sayings, and metaphors translate directly to the target language? Would it be wise to translate the phrase 'every man for himself' in text describing a company or product if this is going to be read by a highly collectivist culture? Does the content use humour and if so will the target culture appreciate or even understand it?

When translating into another language carefully consider the variants. If it is to be in Arabic then is it aimed at Tunisians or Iraqis, Egyptians or Yemenis? You must also analyse the style of the language and the target audience. If the audience is foreign business personnel, the vocabulary, grammar, and punctuation must reflect this. If the audience is informal or youth oriented then a more relaxed language must used. Should we be using 'posh' English or 'street' English if in the UK, or in other cultures, as they too will have the same perceptions of language? Using the wrong language for the wrong audience can be devastating, and incorrect or less than adequate translations can result in customer frustration and a negative impact on the organization's brand image. See Table 7.6 for some examples.

Technological Factors

The market's stage of technological development is imperative as it can have many implications for marketing communications, new product development, and the overall success of market entry. In many international markets, new technology is increasingly changing the way that companies go to market through moves towards more email and web-based marketing and greater efficiency in direct and database marketing techniques (Sclater, 2005). However, in developing markets, radio still remains the main channel for marketing communications, with limited television diffusion. This highlights the importance of profiling the penetration of electronic technologies in potential new markets.

Penetration rates of electronic technologies can reflect country population and/or region size, and can also be indicators of certain important market trends. The world's population is estimated at 6.6 billion and growing at over 80 million annually. However, in terms of numbers of people who can and do access electronic technologies, only around 16.6 per cent of the world's population has access to the internet, and two-thirds of the world's population does not subscribe to a mobile phone. More specifically, not all demographic groups have participated in the information revolution that has occurred since the 1980s: those who are poorer, less educated, from rural areas, and females consistently have been slower to use both computers and the internet (Bikson and Panis, 1997; Tapscott, 1998). Thus, although certain electronic technologies are becoming everyday conveniences for some market segments, some clusters are being left out—at both the consumer and business level. These factors have implications for not only marketing communications, but also product manufacture of products such audio-visual entertainment.

Many customer needs and wants are further bound up with the technological infrastructure within which they reside. For example, the type of fuel used for cooking will depend on the country's use of natural resources and competitive infrastructure for utilities (gas, electric, etc.); the type of telephone used will

Measures invoked by governments in order to protect their domestic industries include the following:

- **Quotas** to limit the number of goods allowed in;
- Duties, like a special tax on imports (which then makes them non-competitive on price); and
- **Non-tariff barriers** such as product legislation which means that expensive adaptation needs to be made before the item is legally saleable in the **host country**.

Governments are also under pressure to assist in alleviating unemployment and stimulating economic activity. As such, many countries encourage foreign investment by providing tax concessions and support of various kinds to persuade international companies to site their manufacturing units in depressed areas. This is true for not only production industries but also service industries.

Some countries are more politically stable than others. Political conditions can also cause severe difficulties for international marketers, even to the point of withdrawing from a market (e.g. Coca-Cola from India) or writing off an entire operation (e.g. Chrysler in post-revolutionary Iran). Some industries, like natural resources, do not however have this option. A change in government can further make little difference to commercial life, but in other countries (e.g. Iraq) the change can be dramatic. Certain governments can restrict foreign investment and ownership and thus a company might be required to enter the market through a joint venture with a local company, with the local company holding the larger percentage of ownership. However, companies need to look at more than just ownership restrictions: other examples of political and legal factors include employment law, health and safety regulations, financial law, patent protection, data protection, and electronic transactions legislation.

Knowledge of pricing law and legislation and regulation for direct marketing, advertising, and marketing research activities also differ cross-country. For example, vending machines are an important delivery mechanism for Coca-Cola's

RESEARCH INSIGHT 7.4

To take your learning further, you might wish to read this influential paper.

Robertson, K. R., and Wood, V. R. (2001), 'The relative importance of types of information in the foreign market selection process', *International Business Review*, 10, 363–79.

This article provides a useful study designed to investigate export decision making. It specifically examines the relative importance of foreign market information used by international managers when choosing export markets. Finding information related to market potential (i.e. foreign buyers' ability to pay for imported products, and the nature of competition in export markets) and legal environment (i.e. non-tariff and tariff barriers) was rated most important when selecting export markets, with the cultural environment rated as least important.

distribution strategy. However vending machines are practically impossible to place legally in Russia. A mass of by-laws for food and drink retailing, real estate, and taxation—which require all sales to be conducted with a cash register—means that vending machines only appear with the assistance of 'security firms'.

Market Entry Approach

Once it has been decided which markets to enter, an organization must consider how to enter these markets. This decision is complicated due to the differing objectives of management, the product offering itself, and the market for which entry has been selected. For example, some product offerings are more suited to international franchising (e.g. fast food restaurants, coffee houses), some to offshore manufacturing (e.g. textiles, car components), and others to exporting (e.g. regional products such as wine, cheese, chocolate, and luxury food items). Certain criteria should be considered to help select which market entry mode is most appropriate.

Selection Criteria

To aid in the decision for market entry method, Paliwoda (1993) proposes six main factors that should be taken into consideration. These are displayed in Figure 7.5. The importance of each of these is dependent on the organization's international marketing objectives: for example, how quickly they want to enter a market, how much they are prepared to invest, how much risk they are prepared to take, how flexible they want their marketing activities in the foreign market to be, and the company's long-term objectives.

1 **Speed and Timing:** Some market entry methods take longer than others and as such some take months to enter into a foreign market, while others can be put into action immediately. The organization needs to review how quickly they wish to enter the market selected.

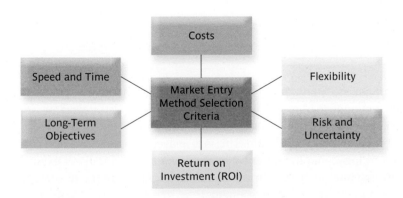

Figure 7.5
Market entry method selection criteria

2 **Costs:** Differing methods also require differing levels of investment. As such the benefits and costs of each method need to be considered. How much is it going to cost to use a certain method and what are the direct and indirect benefits of each method considered?

3 **Flexibility:** Some market entry methods provide the organization with differing levels of flexibility over their activities in the new market, and future development opportunities. For example, some might require long-term contractual agreements or financial commitments. As such organizations need to consider the degree of flexibility they want (or that is available to them) in the new market they are entering.

4 **Risk and uncertainty:** There are numerous risk factors involved with entry into new and foreign markets, from financial risks, risk emerging from political forces, and legal restrictions. Some entry methods assist in the reduction or management of risk and uncertainty. For example, joint ventures or direct foreign investment in the foreign market can be seen as favourable politically in some markets, and thus can act to reduce tariff barriers and import quotas. However these methods also require a larger degree of financial investment than indirect exporting or licensing.

5 **Return on investment (ROI):** Every organization has a different motivation for entering new foreign markets. This criterion coincides with the first and second criteria, speed, timing, and costs. Some organizations want a fast ROI through their market entry strategies and thus the speed and timing of market entry and commencement of operations are crucial to ensure quick return on foreign investment. For example, it may take years to build a factory in a foreign market, and thus it's more suitable to develop a partnership with an existing manufacturer in the local market who can provide the resources for product manufacture, increasing the speed for ROI. However, given the cost of certain methods, ROI might be greater or lower for alternative options. Thus organizations need to consider their needs and expectations in terms of ROI from their market entry strategy.

6 **Long-term objectives:** The market entry strategy is just the first step in a long-term strategy for foreign and international marketing. As such the organization needs to review what it wants to achieve in the long term from its entry into the new foreign market as certain market entry methods will provide more flexibility for long-term opportunities than others.

Market Entry Method

Organizations might use a number of methods or strategies by which to engage with their international markets. In classifying the differing strategies or approaches available, they vary according to the level of commitment, level of risks, and the level of rewards a firm can obtain. This is displayed in Figure 7.6. For example a low-risk and low-commitment entry method would be an indirect exporting strategy through intermediaries. In contrast, a high-risk commitment strategy is joint ventures and direct foreign investment.

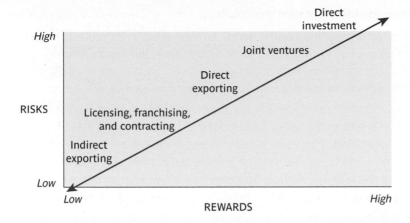

Figure 7.6
Market entry methods

Some firms may move from one end to the other as the importance of their international activities increases. However other firms may jump from indirect exporting to direct investment. For example, Nissan established a UK manufacturing base in the 1980s despite a relatively small share of the UK market, because of the advent of an important change in the political climate—the coming of the Single European Market. Companies can also move back along the spectrum.

Some of the most successful international marketing operations are franchise based, with the level of the commitment of the parent firm being low-risk strategy as part of the business operation it runs in its domestic market. The higher the risk, the higher the likely rate of return. The options depend on the firm's ability to commit resources, managerial, financial, and operational.

The kind of product offering or good and service involved, whether operating in a consumer or industrial sector, and the level and nature of the competition are all factors considered for the best market entry strategy. Especially for start-up companies, it's the balance between support needs of the customer and the resources the company has available that determines the international market entry strategies (Burgel and Murray, 2000).

Indirect Exporting

Indirect exporting takes place where production and manufacture of the product offering occurs in the domestic market and involves the services of other companies (intermediaries) to sell the product in the foreign market. This is in contrast to direct exporting, where the foreign firm deals directly with its customers in foreign markets. Companies in the Australian wine industry increasingly rely on indirect exporting to reach foreign markets, and with great success: 54.4 million litres of wine were exported from Australia in 1990–1 which nearly doubled to 100 million litres in 1992–3. A growth of 41.8 per cent was experienced 1998–2000 and a 21.1 per cent increase in 2003–5. In November 2006 exported wines reached 68.9 million litres and were valued at $251.2 million. The exporting of Australian wine has achieved rapid growth over the last fifteen years through indirect exportation of its product offering.

Two examples of indirect exporting include:

1 When a buying organization from another country sources its product for sale in the foreign market as companies try to benefit from the price differences present in various markets. Import music shops are a good example of this type of activity for products not released in the domestic market on a large scale.

2 Use of the services of an export management company or agent. An export agent acts on behalf of the seller, undertaking to sell on a commission basis in a particular market. The agent handles export arrangement for a number of clients, like a functional distribution intermediary. They manage several accounts and the range of services and expertise offered varies company to company. Services could include: purchasing, shipping, financing, and negotiation of foreign orders.

Whether agent or merchant, an exporting manufacturer benefits from intermediaries' knowledge, their contact and business networks, and their experience in the market which the foreign organization is entering. Given this reliance on the expertise of intermediaries, indirect exporting carries little risk and commitment as there is no direct investment in market development. This is suitable strategy for market testing due to market entry uncertainty, product suitability, small organization with limited resources for allocation to foreign markets, and/or when dealing with small volumes of product offering for distribution.

Licensing, Franchising, and Contracting

In addition to the transfer of goods and services from a domestic to foreign market, sometimes entering foreign markets involves the transfer of ideas, concepts, and processes, so that goods and services can be manufactured abroad. This involves the market entry method of licensing, franchising, and/or contracting.

Licensing is an agreement under which an organization (the licensor) grants another organization (the licensee) the right to manufacturer goods, use patents, use particular processes, or exploit trade marks in a defined market. It is a frequent method for entry into the drinks market. For example, Budweiser is made in the UK under licence from the US brewing company Anheuser-Busch, and is positioned in the UK as a premium drink, despite domestic positioning in US markets as a working man's drink.

Licensing is a low-risk and cheap method of accessing income from foreign markets by avoiding high import tariffs and high costs of direct investment. However this method offers little control, with risks of the licensee damaging the reputation and image of the licensor's name due to poor product quality and ineffective marketing. It can also create future problems as the licensee can develop the expertise and knowledge for product manufacture and start to compete directly, offering dangerous competition. Licensors (granters of licences) have to keep devising innovations that increase dependence on the relationship.

Franchising is a contractual vertical marketing system in which a franchisor licenses a franchisee to produce or market goods or services to certain criteria laid down by the franchisor in return for fees and/or royalties. Franchising is both a distribution method though which market coverage can be extended and a system through which enterprises can launch and grow. Some large franchises include KFC, Subway, and McDonald's (see Table 14.1 in Chapter 14). Kentucky Fried Chicken (KFC) has some 11,000-plus KFC restaurants in over 80 countries, with more than 1,400 KFC restaurants in more than 200 cities in China alone.

McDonald's is one of the largest franchises in the world and the leading franchise in Europe, with over 30,000 outlets in 121 countries. However, as presented in Market Insight 7.7, it's Goody's, not McDonald's, who dominate the fast food market in Greece.

There are two main benefits of franchising: managerial and financial. Financially, rapid growth in coverage of the market and penetration can be achieved for the franchisor with the franchisee bearing the risk through the provision of investment in both capital assets (e.g. equipment, premises), working capital, and other operating costs. The franchisee also provides a committed managerial resource and benefits of economies of scale in marketing, purchasing, and corporate image. However the effectiveness of this form of market entry method is reliant on the franchisor–franchisee relationship, the commitment of the franchisee, and the resources and support provided by the franchisor.

Contracting is where a manufacturer contracts an organization in a foreign market to manufacture or assemble to the product in the foreign market, thus avoiding the cost involved in physical distribution and logistics of the product offering abroad and providing benefits of contractor control over marketing, unlike licensing. This method also provides a more flexible approach to entering the foreign market, avoiding the problems of currency fluctuations, import barriers, and high costs, and knowledge required for international distribution.

MARKET INSIGHT 7.7

It's All Goody's in Greece

Greece is the one country where McDonald's does not dominate the fast food market. The Greek fast food restaurant Goody's enjoys overwhelming support from the Greek consumer and especially the kids who eat in these places. Goody's not only dominates the fast food market in Greece but this hamburger chain, originally from northern Greece, also introduced franchising to the country in the late 1970s. The current Deputy Minister for Economy and Finance in Greece is one of the pioneer entrepreneurs who developed the Goody's 'concept' and launched the Thessaloniki restaurant as a franchise throughout Greece in 1975.

In contrast, McDonald's opened its first restaurant in Greece in 1991. Today there are 48 McDonald's restaurants employing 1,500 individuals throughout Greece. In contrast, there are over 185 Goody's restaurants in Greece, Cyprus, and Bulgaria. Goody's restaurants dominate the fast food market in Greece, leaving multinational titans such as McDonald's and KFC restaurants way behind.

1 Why do you think Goody's dominates the fast food market in Greece?

2 What do you recommend McDonald's do to build market share and consumer support in Greece?

Direct Exporting

Direct exporting involves the manufacturing firm itself distributing its product offering to foreign markets, direct to customers. The organization produces the product in its domestic/national market and sells it direct to a foreign customer, with the firm treating its foreign customers like its domestic customers. The organization takes responsibility for finding and selecting customers, agents, and distributors and directly supports their efforts. This approach to market entry is very time consuming and expensive, and involves some considerable investment. It can also represent a big step, especially for the smaller firm. However, it gives the manufacturer more control and profits than relying on intermediaries. Further advantages include direct access to market intelligence and also the building of a clear presence in the market. This strategy very much suits business-to-business marketing due to the high capital costs often required.

Joint Ventures and Acquisition

A **joint venture** is when two organizations come together to create a jointly owned third company. This is an example of cooperative as opposed to competitive operations in international marketing. A foreign company and a domestic company join forces either by buying into each other, or by establishing a third jointly owned enterprise. The partners might feel that separately they do not have the resources to develop or enter the foreign market. One might have cash, the other know-how and experience. The complementary strengths facilitate success and sometimes a joint venture is the only way a firm can enter or gain a foothold in a foreign market.

Joint ventures tend to have a limited lifespan as the need for the joint venture changes over time as each party's needs alter and develop. They further work best in sectors where there is a high degree of local adaptation to the market. Figure 7.7 shows a list of factors that can contribute to a successful joint venture partnership.

RESEARCH INSIGHT 7.5

To take your learning further, you might wish to read this influential paper.

Rundh, B. (2007), 'International marketing behaviour amongst exporting firms', *European Journal of Marketing*, 41, 1/2, 181–98.

This article provides a useful insight into factors affecting market entry through exporting to international markets for small and large organizations. Success factors relate to geographic proximity with the need for local representation and service and management commitment. The authors discuss the main obstacles of administration, technical, and fierce competition in local markets.

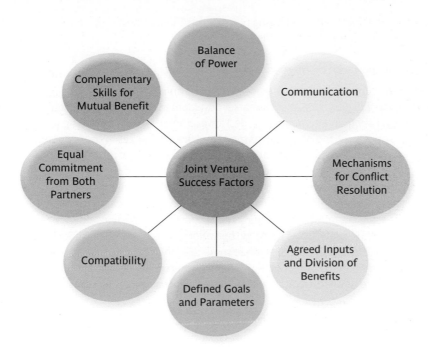

Figure 7.7
Factors contributing to the success of joint ventures

Direct Investment

Direct investment or foreign manufacture, thus some form of manufacture or production in the foreign or host country, is sometimes necessary. Advantages include a commitment to the local market, speedy availability of parts, market detection of changes in local environment—thus market intelligence, providing a sense of competitive advantage. The extent of direct investment can range from superficial assembly of product offering from parts to research and development-led innovation. Another means of market entry through direct investment is company acquisition or takeover in the foreign market. For example India's home textiles exporters are moving up the value chain and aiming at the lucrative US and Western markets.

Chapter Summary

To consolidate your learning, the key points from this chapter are summarized below:

• Define and discuss 'market development' as a key growth strategy.

Marketing strategy is about matching market opportunities to the organization's resources (what it can do) and objectives (what management wants to do). Successful strategies begin with identification of an attractive market opportunity. One such strategy is a marketing development strategy. A market development strategy involves increasing sales by selling existing or 'old' products in new markets, either by targeting new audiences domestically or entering new markets internationally. So, you're trying to sell more of the same things to different people.

- **Discuss the importance of international market entry.**

  Typically, opportunities that are far removed from the current experiences of a company involve higher risks. As such market development in domestic markets is seen as less risky than international trade. However international marketing is growing in importance and necessity for marketers due to changes in the economic, social, and political landscape. International marketing as a market development opportunity is therefore receiving enormous growth in both scale and complexity. The main considerations are the degree of risk and adjustment an organization is willing to take and the identification of potential opportunities within certain markets. For some organizations an international strategy is deeply ingrained into their marketing strategy and domestic operations are considered of minor importance (e.g. Foster's in Australia), while some take an ad hoc approach responding to customer export enquiries, whereas others fall in between and proactively seek to develop an international marketing strategy (e.g. McDonald's).

- **Compare and contrast internationalization and globalization.**

  Irrespective of the motivation, we are seeing today a growing rise in international and global marketing activities. Perlmutter (1969) was one of the first of many to discuss the various attitudes or orientations that can be taken in international market development in the EPRG classification. An organization taking an ethnocentric approach views the domestic market (home market) as the most important, and overseas markets as inferior, with foreign imports not seen as representing a serious threat. With a polycentric approach, each overseas market is seen as a separate domestic market, each country seen as a separate entity, and the firm seeks to be seen as a local firm within that country. In some instances, each market has its own manufacturing and marketing facilities, with only a limited overlap. These two approaches take a more localized approach than regional and geocentric approaches. A regional approach groups countries together, usually on a geographical basis (e.g. Europe), and provides for the specific needs of consumers within those countries. In this instance, national boundaries are respected, but do not have the same importance as cultural differences. The final classification, the geocentric approach, sees the world as a single market—global, with the organization looking for global segments (e.g. ageing market) and global opportunities to rationalize communications, production, and product development. Here globalization refers to increasing global connectivity, integration, and interdependence in the economic, social, technological, cultural, political, and ecological spheres.

- **Discuss the growing importance of international marketing and key drivers.**

  In light of increasing internationalization of world markets, increased foreign trade, and international travel, international marketing is becoming a necessity for the survival of many organizations. Today it is almost impossible to avoid the trend shift to internationalization and globalization. Even companies that only compete in domestic markets are affected, as they compete increasingly with foreign companies in their home markets. Home or domestic markets are further changing due to increase in foreign travel, changes in technology, and mass immigration, and increasing customer knowledge of product choices. An understanding of international business, marketing, and globalization is thus essential for marketers. Many factors motivate a company to develop markets on foreign shores. These include: historical accident (e.g. Coca-Cola), need to move excess stock (e.g. dumping), limited growth in domestic markets, comparative advantages, economies of scale, trade liberalization, international PLC, technological changes (e.g. internet), customer relationships, the development of transnational market segments through immigration, and organization sustainability.

- Discuss the various criteria used for international market identification and selection and the methods used for assessing market attractiveness.

  Assessing market attractiveness is very important when considering international market development given differing markets have very differing levels of attractiveness. Once the marketing environment is understood the organization needs to match opportunities and threats in the markets that are attractive with the organization's own strengths, weaknesses, assets, skills, and aspirations. Markets may be chosen according to the following criteria, with the criteria of marketing accessibility and market size regarded as the two most important criteria for assessing international market attractiveness. Other criteria include: geographic proximity; psychological proximity; level and quality of competition already in the market; cost of entering the market; and a market's profit potential.

- Consider the various methods for international market entry.

  To aid in the decision for market entry method, Paliwoda (1993) proposes six main factors that should be taken into consideration when selecting a market entry method. These include: speed and timing; costs and levels of investment required; flexibility with some market entry methods providing the organization with differing levels of flexibility over their activities; risk and uncertainty; expected return on investment (ROI); and long-term objectives. Once reviewed the organization can select from a number of differing strategies to enter foreign markets. These differ according to risks and returns: indirect exporting; licensing, franchising, and contracting; direct exporting; joint ventures; and direct investment.

- Understand the role of culture and other key elements in the success of international marketing strategies.

  Once the decision has been made to pursue an international market development strategy, the organization has to choose which markets to enter. Understanding the marketing environments of the countries of interest can form the foundation of a detailed market assessment and market selection process. Because of the complexity and unfamiliarity of the international marketing environment, successful international marketing requires vigilant attention to environmental factors. The analysis of environmental forces can help to identify which countries (e.g. Australia, France, Brazil) or regions (e.g. Western Europe, South America) should be given priority and which market entry strategy would be best suited. As introduced in Chapter 2 marketing responds to a number of variables in the external environment, such as socio-cultural, technological, political and legal, economic factors. These elements also present the company with possible threats and opportunities in entering foreign markets. Young (2001) argues that international marketers pay too little attention to the potential impact that global economic, legal/institutional, and political/social developments could have on their ability to trade.

 Visit the **Online Resource Centre** that accompanies this book to read more information relating to market development and international marketing: www.oxfordtextbooks.co.uk/orc/baines/

? Review Questions

1 What factors are increasing the trend towards international and global marketing?

2 What are the key differences between a multi-domestic and global competitive strategy?

3 What is the anti-globalization movement and why is it of increasing importance?

4 What should a company consider when deciding on which international markets to enter?

5 What are the pros and cons of the differing methods for entering foreign markets?

6 What factors should be considered when selecting an international market entry method?

7 What are key differences between indirect and direct exporting?

8 What are the benefits of franchises in international market?

9 What are the key success factors for international joint ventures?

10 Outline the main environment factors in the international marketing environment?

? Discussion Questions

1 Having read the Case Insight at the beginning of this chapter, how would you advise Oxford Instruments to measure the market potential of the Russian market for its products? What market entry method should Oxford Instruments use to further penetrate the market?

2 What advice would you give to a SME thinking about entering a new international market? What would be the main criteria they should consider in their decision?

3 Which of these would have the greatest impact on a textile manufacturer's appraisal of a foreign market's attractiveness: political-legal, social-cultural, or technological? Why?

4 What cultural issues have McDonald's had to consider when expanding into new geographical markets?

5 The international wine industry is based on indirect exporting of wine products throughout the world. Marketed heavily on their country-of-origin brand image, what impact do you think joint ventures with domestic vineyards or direct investment would have on brands entering a foreign market?

6 Visit your local grocery or department store. Spend 15 minutes browsing the store, taking note of the goods and their country of manufacture, assembly, and origin. What countries and regions are represented? What impact do you think the political and legal environment has on their importation?

📖 References

Anderson, P., and Strandskov, J. (1998), 'International market selection: a cognitive mapping perspective', *Journal of Global Marketing*, 11, 3, 65–84.

Anon. (2004), 'A rising tide', *Economist*, 372, (17 July), 54.

—— (2005), 'Guinness: the trials of the black stuff', *Brand Strategy*, 20 (7 February).

Ansoff, H. I. (1957), 'Strategies of diversification', *Harvard Business Review*, 25, 5, 113–25.

Benson-Armer, R., Leibowitz, J., and Ramachandran, D. (1999), 'Global beer: what's on tap?', *McKinsey Quarterly*, 1, 110–22.

Bikson, T., and Panis, C. (1997), 'Computers and connectivity: current trends', in S. Kiesler (ed.), *Culture of the Internet*, Mahwah, NJ: Lawrence Erlbaum, 407–30.

Burgel, O., and Murray, G. (2000), 'The international market entry choices of start-up companies in high-technology industries', *Journal of International Marketing*, 8, 2, 33–62.

Douglas, S., and Douglas, Y. W. (1987), 'The myth of globalisation', *Columbia Journal of World Business*, Winter, 19–29.

Haft, J. (2007), 'The China syndrome', *Wall Street Journal* (Eastern edition), 16 July, A.12.

Harris, R. (2007), 'Skin deep', *Marketing Magazine*, 112, 29 January.

Herbig, P. A. (1998), *Handbook of Cross-Cultural Marketing*, New York: Halworth Press, Inc.

—— and Day, K. (1993), 'Managerial implications of the North American Free Trade Agreement', *International Marketing Review*, 10, 4, 15–35.

Hout, T., Porter, M. E., and Rudden, E. (1982), 'How global companies win out!', *Harvard Business Review*, September–October.

IPA (1997), *International*, Institute of Practitioners in Advertising (IPA).

Kelly, J. (2002), 'Executives fail the business language test', *Financial Times*, 16 February, 4.

Lawrence, P. (1993), 'Developments in European business in the 1990s: the Single European Market in context', *Journal of Marketing Management*, 9, 3–9.

Levitt, T. (1983), 'The globalization of markets', *Harvard Business Review*, May–June, 2–11.

Lewis, K. S., Lim, F. A., and Rusetski, A. (2006), 'Development of archetypes of international marketing strategy', *Journal of International Business Studies*, 37, 4, 499–524.

Lynch, R. (1994), *European Business Strategies: The European and Global Strategies of Europe's Top Companies*, London: Kogan Page.

McLuhan, R. (2004), 'Calling India', *Marketing*, 18 March, 23.

Martinsons, M. G. (2005), 'Transforming China', *Communications of the ACM*, 48, 44–8.

Mead, R. (1990), *Cross-Cultural Management Communication*, New York: John Wiley & Sons.

Movius, L. (2007), 'H&M heads east with first unit in Shanghai', *WWD: Women's Wear Daily*, 17 April, 193.

Mughan, T. (1993), 'Culture as an asset in international business'. In J. Preston (ed.), *International Business: Texts & Cases*, London: Pitman, 78–86.

Ohmae, K. (1985), *Triad Power*, London: Macmillan.

—— (1992), *The Borderless World: Power and Strategy in the Interlinked Economy*, London: Fontana.

Paitra, J. (1993), 'The euro-consumer: myth or reality?', in C. Halliburton and R. Hunerberg (eds.), *European Marketing: Readings and Cases*, Boston: Addison-Wesley.

Paliwoda, S. (1993), *International Marketing*, 2nd edn., London: Butterworth-Heinemann.

Parker, E. (2007), 'Made in China', *Wall Street Journal* (Eastern edition), 12 July, A.15.

Perlmutter, H. V. (1969), 'The tortuous evolution of the multinational corporation', *Columbia Journal of World Business*, January–February, 9–18.

Pitcher, G. (1999), 'Ford takes pole position in the battle for world wide domination', *Marketing Week*, 4 February, 25.

Quelch, J. A., and Hoff, E. J. (1986), 'Customising global marketing', *Harvard Business Review*, May–June, 59–68.

Rienstra, D., and Hulm, P. (2004), 'New EU countries expand market horizons', *International Trade Forum*, 1, 29–30.

Robertson, K. R., and Wood, V. R. (2001), 'The relative importance of types of information in the foreign market selection process', *International Business Review*, 10, 363–79.

Rugman, A. (2000), *The End of Globalisation*, London: Random House Business Books.

Sclater, I. (2005), 'The digital dimension', *The Marketer*, May, 22–3.

Sirgy, M., Lee, D.-J., Miller, C., Littlefield, J., and Atay, E. (2007), 'The impact of imports and exports on a country's quality of life', *Social Indicators Research*, 83, 2, 245–81.

Steinborn, D. (2007), 'Cross-cultural training gains', *Wall Street Journal* (Eastern edition), 4 April.

Tapscott, D. (1998), *Growing Up Digital: The Rise of the Net Generation*, New York: McGraw-Hill.

Vijay, J. (1997), 'Global strategies in the 1990's', in *Mastering Management*, London: Financial Times, 572–7.

Ward, A. (2006), 'US brewers left to cry into their beers: competition from imports and local speciality brews are hitting home', *Financial Times*, 31 July, 23.

Warren, C. (2007), 'Stars of India', *People Management*, 22 February, 13.

Whitelock, J., and Jobber, D. (1994), *The Impact of Competitor Environment on Initial Market Entry in a New Non-Domestic Market*, paper presented at the Proceedings of the Marketing Education Group Conference, Coleraine.

Wind Y., and Perlmutter, H. V. (1973), 'Guidelines for developing international marketing strategies', *Journal of Marketing*, 37 (April), 14–23.

Young, S. (2001), 'What do researchers know about the global business environment?', *International Marketing Review*, 18, 2, 120–9.

Introduction

How do we organize a marketing department within a company? Who should report to whom? Why do brilliant strategies sometimes fail to work as we have intended? How do we measure the effectiveness of a particular strategy? How much should we spend on marketing activities? How do we control the marketing function to get the most out of it? These and other questions are considered in more detail in this chapter.

Marketing implementation is a fundamental process in marketing because it is the actioning phase of the marketing process. While many of the concepts in this text help us to design marketing programmes, the implementation phase is about actually doing it. In reality, then, it is the most exciting part of marketing because it is the least predictable.

We begin by discussing how marketing implementation fits into the strategic marketing planning process. We consider how **marketing metrics** can be used to control and measure the effectiveness of marketing implementation. We discuss planning mechanisms and the reality of marketing implementation. We also consider how to structure the marketing function within an organization, recognizing that in practice there are multiple forms of marketing organization from firm to firm within any particular industry sector. We explore how in some organizations no formal marketing function exists. Because teamworking is such an important concept in marketing, either as teams of co-workers within a company, or teams involving external consultants (e.g. advertising account planners, or outsourced customer service representatives), we consider how to form successful teams.

Because strategy implementation involves persuading, and sometimes failing to persuade, employees to adopt and implement new marketing strategies, we consider how employees resist marketing implementation initiatives. To determine how well a particular company or organization is implementing its chosen strategy, we consider how to measure the effectiveness of marketing implementation initiatives in order to control them. We consider the rapidly developing field of marketing metrics, including the celebrated balanced scorecard concept, developed by Kaplan and Norton (1992). Many marketers now think that the measurement of revenue will become as important as the measurement of costs. Finally, because marketing strategists use them to determine how well a particular marketing initiative did, we briefly consider how to calculate market potential and the importance of sales forecasting and sales variance analysis.

The Strategic Marketing Planning Process

The process of strategic marketing planning follows a number of steps, although these steps may differ slightly from one type of industry to another. Morgan (1991) identifies eight separate steps in the strategic marketing planning process (see Figure 8.1), components of which we have discussed earlier in Chapters 2 and 5.

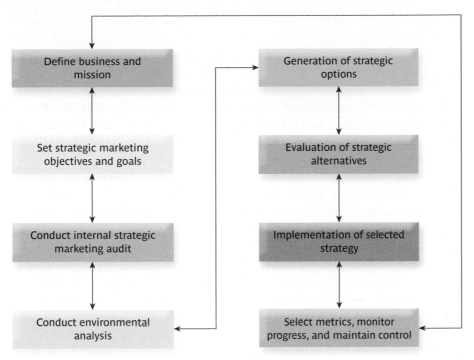

Figure 8.1
The strategic marketing planning process

Source: Adapted from Morgan (1991). © Elsevier (1991).

Authors have often stressed the difficulty of using models of strategic marketing planning that ignore the practical realities of the business environment. In other words, it's very easy to plan but quite another thing to put the plan into action.

In this chapter, we focus on the implementation of selected strategy and control components of the strategic marketing planning process, highlighted in the dotted boxes in Figure 8.1. It is important to recognize that implementation of a selected strategy is dependent on how we evaluated the various strategic directions we identified in the previous stage for the business, which are themselves based on the options generated (see Chapter 5) from scanning the marketing environment and conducting the internal marketing audit (see Chapter 2), and the marketing objectives set based on the organization's business and mission (see Chapter 5).

Once the implementation plan has been developed, considering who will do what by when, we need to measure the success of the plan. However, before the organization or company can measure its success, it needs to determine first how to measure success. This might be in terms of increase in market share, or improvements in customer loyalty, for example. We use marketing metrics to measure our progress towards achieving our marketing objectives. However, it is important to determine what we measure, since we use this to control the business and determine future business and mission.

The Marketing Organization

How we organize ourselves to undertake the task of marketing has an impact upon how effective we actually are and can be. In addition, the way we organize the marketing function has an impact on how our colleagues in other professional disciplines view us and our effectiveness. For example, in a survey undertaken in the UK by the Marketing Forum/Consumers' Association (see Mitchell, 2001), only 38 per cent of executives rated their marketing colleagues as good or excellent. According to a recent Chartered Institute of Marketing survey, only 14 per cent of the UK's largest companies (the FTSE-100 share index of publicly quoted, leading companies) had a marketing practitioner on their board of directors, although a further 15 per cent did have a marketing professional on their senior management team. Marketing professionals are also much less likely to become CEOs (17 per cent) when compared with their finance (34 per cent), operations (29 per cent), and general management colleagues (19 per cent) (Anon., 2006b). As a consequence, marketing is often delegated to middle managers (Ambler, 2000).

So, it seems that marketing professionals are either less effective than their professional colleagues or they are underrated. The question is how do marketers organize a more effective function with their organization?

A further problem is that marketers do not always control all the elements of the marketing mix which are assumed to be under their control. For example, marketers seldom control pricing, distribution, product development, and even promotion (since this is often outsourced to agencies) (O'Malley and Patterson, 1998), although they may exercise influence over all these activities and more. In addition, marketing may not necessarily be organized as a separate department but the ethos and influence of marketing philosophy may still be apparent and impact upon an organization's decision making (Harris and Ogbonna, 2003).

Marketing is present in all aspects of an organization, since all departments have some role to play with respect to creating, delivering, and satisfying customers. For example, employees in the R&D department designing new products to meet poorly met existing customer needs are performing a marketing role. Similarly, members of the procurement department buying components for a new product or service must purchase components of specific quality and at a certain cost which will meet customer needs. In fact, we can go through all departments of a company, and find that in each department, there is a marketing role to be played to some extent. In other words, marketing is distributed throughout the organization, and all employees might be considered as part-time marketers (Gummesson, 1990). (See Market Insight 8.1 below.)

MARKET INSIGHT 8.1

Pret À Manger: Marketing with a Smile

Pret À Manger was founded in 1986 by two university friends, Julian Metcalfe and Sinclair Beecham, in London. Offering sandwiches, soups, sushi boxes, and salads, the brand name literally means ready to eat in French. The two friends wanted to create a sophisticated sandwich chain which dispensed with the preservatives and chemicals found in competitors' offerings, and provided good, clean, 'honest', but exciting, food at reasonable prices. Sandwich offerings include crayfish and avocado, brie, tomato, and basil, and pastrami wraps, as well as staples like tuna mayo and ham, cheese, and pickle. Soups such as carrot, ginger, and coriander, and pea, smoked, bacon and mint, add to the appeal.

Pret À Manger has enjoyed rapid success

Pret À Manger

The mechanism for delivery of the customer proposition involves making up the sandwiches in the morning every day before the shop opens, using fresh ingredients delivered and immediately refrigerated very early that morning. The sandwiches are served ready to eat in chilled display cabinets. Competitors tend to make the food in advance in central 'factories', using preservatives and plastic packaging, so their sandwiches can be stored for several days.

Pret À Manger has enjoyed rapid success. In 2001, it sold a 33 per cent non-controlling stake to the fast food burger chain McDonald's for £25 m principally to obtain the funding, and the know-how, necessary to develop the Pret concept around the world. By 2007, Pret had 180 outlets, 158 in the UK, 11 in New York, and 11 in Hong Kong, making pre-tax profits of £17.8 m from a turnover of nearly £200 m. The company was worth somewhere between £150 m and £280 m.

But what is remarkable about Pret, apart from its obvious success, is that it has no formal marketing, advertising, or public relations departments. It does centralize customer service and recruitment but incredibly Pret does no formal customer service training. Instead, it relies on the shop employees to sell the company's enthusiasm for its food.

So, it's the shop employees who, as future co-workers, carefully select new recruits on the basis of their friendliness and ability to do the job well after the applicant has spent a day in a Pret outlet. Staff are encouraged to be nice to customers through the offer of a wage bonus, on top of a generous hourly pay rate, based on the results of extensive mystery shopping research.

So, with a business model like that, and fantastic tasting products, who needs full-time marketers?

Sources: Clark (2001); Anon. (2007); Skapinker (2007).

1 Do you think the Pret À Manger business is held back because it does not employ marketing centrally? If yes, how is it held back?

2 Why do you think the Pret À Manger chain has been so successful until now? Will the fact that McDonald's owns a proportion of the chain and an option to buy more affect Pret's business in the future?

3 Are you aware of any other companies, either in this sector or another one, where a central marketing department is not employed?

To take your learning further, you might wish to read this influential paper.

Gummesson, E. (1990), 'Marketing orientation revisited: the crucial role of the part-time marketer', *European Journal of Marketing*, 25, 2, 60 – 75.

In this article, European relationship marketing expert Evert Gummesson illustrates how marketing operates not only within the marketing department but within all departments within the company to contribute to improved customer relations and customer satisfaction. Gummesson indicated how companies become market oriented through internal marketing processes, and the need to see all employees as part-time marketers, by providing the necessary training and development.

Types of Marketing Organization

Marketers have not always been able to highlight easily the performance of their departments against the return on investment made in paying marketing salaries and budgets by senior management. As a result, organizations have developed different ways of organizing their sales and marketing functions (see Figure 8.2).

In Figure 8.2a marketing and sales are separate departments reporting to the manager in charge of a particular **strategic business unit** (SBU). In this situation, it is the job of the manager to coordinate the different departmental inputs into a coherent and complementary set of strategies. In Figure 8.2b each sales and marketing department reports to an SBU manager who will then report to a corporate headquarters. Corporate headquarters also has a corporate marketing group, which will tend to handle the marketing for the group as a whole (e.g. corporate identity, group market research). In Figure 8.2c, the marketing department still reports to a SBU manager, but the sales force is centralized and sells the products for other SBUs as well. In Figure 8.2d, sales and marketing operate for each individual SBU, but **research and development** (R&D) and manufacturing are undertaken centrally across the SBUs. Finally, in Figure 8.2e, manufacturing and R&D operate for each individual SBU, but sales and marketing are corporate functions.

Marketing organizations have changed in recent years. There is now an increased emphasis on key account management (see Chapter 16), where senior marketing personnel serve important accounts or customer segments, sometimes through cross-functional teams involving sales, marketing, and supply chain management personnel, particularly in sales and operation planning (S&OP) meetings, where detailed supply and demand plans are considered and reconciled (e.g. at AstraZeneca, the pharmaceutical giant). Where firms are operating in more than one country, the role of the country manager has been reduced. As companies have globalized (e.g. Nike), and their efforts spread across countries, senior managers now tend to operate across whole continental regions (e.g. Europe, Middle East, and Africa). In addition, product managers have lost their role as the primary marketing coordinator of sales, marketing, R&D, manufacturing, and other

(a) Marketing and Sales in a Functionally Organized
Autonomous Business Unit

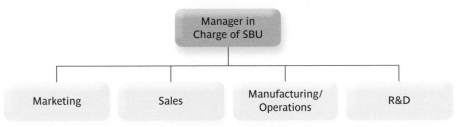

(b) Marketing and Sales in a Functionally Organized
Business Unit with a Corporate Marketing Group

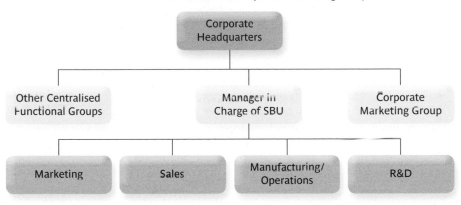

(c) Marketing in a Business Unit that Shares a Sales Force
with Other Business Units

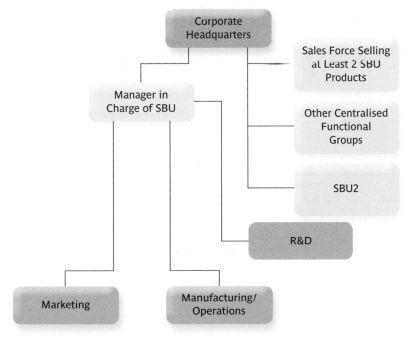

Figure 8.2

Typology of intra-
organizational
marketing relationships

Note: Support groups such
as finance, human resources
(HR), and legal are not shown
here. R&D = research and
development.

Source: Reproduced with kind
permission from the *Journal
of Marketing* (American
Marketing Association),
Workman, Homburg, and
Gruner (1998).

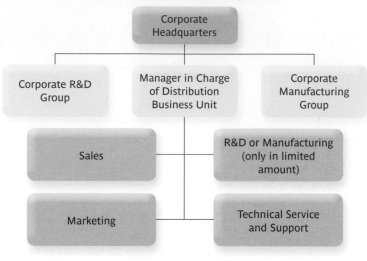

(d) Marketing and Sales in a 'Distribution Business Unit' with Few R&D or Production Capabilities

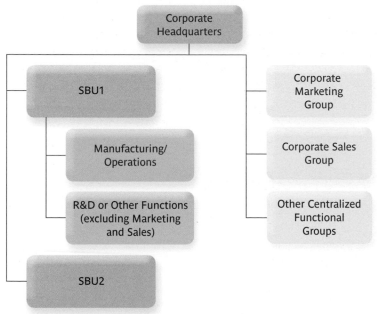

(e) Marketing and Sales in Corporate Groups Shared By Multiple Business Units

Figure 8.2 (*cont'd*)

functions. This role has shifted to key account managers or category managers (e.g. Procter & Gamble), who oversee whole brand categories rather than individual products: see Chapter 14.

In addition, there has been an increasing shift towards outsourcing aspects of the marketing organization. For example, while advertising and market research have traditionally been outsourced to agencies by large multinational and many medium-sized firms, e.g. Ogilvy and Mather and Saatchi and Saatchi in advertising, or Research International and Millward Brown International in market research, there is an increasing shift towards outsourcing data warehousing, e.g. General Motors, customer relationship tracking, e.g. Ericsson, and customer data

Tesco's Outsourcing of Customer Analytics: As Appetizing as it Looks?

In 1994, Tesco decided to develop its own, now famous, 'Clubcard' loyalty scheme, where customers collected points for product items they had bought and Tesco collected customer purchasing information. At the heart of the scheme was the idea that customers would be more loyal to a supermarket if they were offered discounts and deals on items that they were particularly interested in purchasing, which Tesco could determine from the customer data. But Tesco didn't have the operational set-up or the specialist know-how to undertake the type of customer analytics it needed at the time.

So Tesco hired husband and wife team Edina Dunn and Clive Humby of dunnhumby and Tesco, an already strong British retailer at the time, went from strength to strength on the back of its customer insight, which matched point-of-sale data at the till with household address and lifestyle data derived from the customer's postcode details. Amazingly, dunnhumby processes around 5 billion items of information every week for Tesco, which now owns an 84 per cent stake in the firm.

The customer information has also been put to good use not only in enticing customers with appetizing food and non-food propositions but to help it thwart competitive efforts to steal its customers. For example, after Wal-Mart bought ASDA, Tesco singled out shoppers in its database who buy the cheapest item available, figuring that these customers were probably the most likely to be tempted by ASDA's promotional efforts. Tesco then identified 300 product items that these shoppers bought regularly and lowered the price of these items so that shoppers didn't defect to ASDA. As a measure of the appeal of its product ranges to its customers, Tesco's sales have increased 16 per cent in the year ending 25 February 2006 to £43 billion.

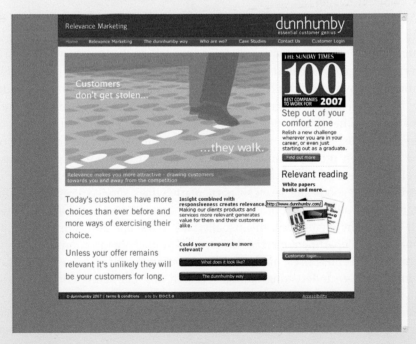

Tesco hired dunnhumby to undertake its customer analytics

dunnhumby

But owning a large stake in dunnhumby may also cause a stomach ache for Tesco; dunnhumby has been working for several years with Kroger, a grocery retailer in the United States, which operates a chain of convenience stores under different brand names. Recently Tesco has also announced its intention to open a chain of rival stores in California. So, with Tesco already strong in the UK, Kroger developing in the USA, and Tesco keen to penetrate the US market, what are the implications for the Tesco/dunnhumby relationship?

Sources: McCawley (2006); Rohwedder (2006); Anon. (2006a).

1 What other marketing functions could Tesco outsource if it wanted to?

2 What would be the relationship implications if dunnhumby wanted to work for both Tesco and Kroger in the USA?

3 What other marketing functions are you aware of that companies have tended to outsource over the course of the late 1990s and early 2000s, particularly to Bangalore, in India?

analytics, e.g. Tesco and American Express (McGovern and Quelch, 2005). (See Market Insight 8.2.)

Marketing Organization as a Team Effort

Whether customer service or marketing communications initiatives are outsourced or not, marketers have to be strong team players (see Chapter 1), especially as more and more departments take over functions which were once most closely associated with marketing, e.g. pricing and product development (Bristow and Frankwick, 2001).

Marketers are typically organizers of other people's efforts. For example, they may liaise with an in-house market research manager to determine the research plan for the year ahead for a particular product, or they might work with the advertising agency account planner and her team to formulate an integrated marketing communications campaign. If they are involved in pricing and budgeting, it is frequently as a result of discussions with an executive from the finance department rather than undertaking the detailed costing work in their own capacity. Marketing personnel may have conversations with sales personnel over how to support the sales functions' objectives, but they do not get personally involved in selling. Similarly, marketing personnel should have an input into distribution of goods and services, particularly where service design might form a competitive advantage, but they would not actually undertake a service redesign exercise by themselves; this usually falls to the operations or supply chain management department instead. In less well-funded organizations, e.g. small to medium-sized enterprises, marketing executives may pick up some of these tasks themselves, e.g. undertaking market research and marketing communications activities in-house more, to offset costs.

Marketing is an activity aimed at generating customer value. It concerns many and often all departments of an organization. Yet despite the recognized central importance of the customer (Levitt, 1960), marketers are often still organized into silos as a line function—a department—rather than as a cross-departmental staff function, e.g. like human resources or information technology (Sheth and Sisodia, 2006). This is still the case despite the fact that 'there is now increasing recognition that cross-functional working relationships have a key role to play in the successful implementation of marketing decisions' (Chimhanzi, 2002). In order to develop marketing's influence in a team setting, organizations must:

- Develop joint reward systems, which work across departments and reduce interdepartmental conflict (Chimhanzi, 2002). Successful marketing teams are appropriately rewarded. So, it is important that salespeople are evaluated and compensated not only for achieving sales volume targets but also for their contribution to the implementation of marketing programmes more generally, which may have wider objectives than short-term sales revenue increases (Strahle, Spiro, and Acito, 1996).

- Communicate the value of the marketing department to other teams—for example, firms that are market oriented tend to show greater profitability (Wong and Saunders, 1993).

- Through their senior managers, encourage informal integration of departments and greater interfunctional coordination (Day, 1994).

Implementing Marketing Strategy

The problems identified in implementing marketing strategy are not particularly well researched. It seems likely that some companies are better at implementing marketing strategies than others. According to Piercy (1998), this may be because a company's marketing implementation capabilities are time specific, culture specific, partial, latent, internally consistent, strategy specific, and person specific, as outlined in Table 8.1.

Internal Politics and Negotiation

Part of the task of introducing a new marketing strategy into an organization is the process of persuading colleagues that the marketing strategy is the right strategy to adopt and implement. Sometimes marketing colleagues resist efforts to implement strategy. However, there has been a movement away from forms of organization which stress central coordination and multi-level hierarchies toward more flexible organizational forms where numerous organizations are tied together in cooperative supply chains (Achrol and Kotler, 1999).

Whether we are operating in networks of organizations or as part of a central marketing department within a company, it is important to overcome resistance to strategy implementation. Resistance to marketing implementation is known as **counter-implementation**. It is defined as encompassing 'a variety of different resistant behaviours that are motivated by anxiety on behalf of those tasked with or involved in the implementation process. Such behaviour may be motivated intentionally or unintentionally, but all may reduce the effectiveness of strategic

Table 8.3 Itemized marketing budget expenditure in the UK

	Advertising	Public relations	Sponsorship	Direct mail	Email	Promotions	Telephone marketing	Lead generation	CRM	Branding	Internal marketing
UK average	12.9	10.1	7.4	11.2	7.1	8.5	5.6	9.0	8.4	9.5	6.4
Sector											
Food, beverages, and tobacco	20.0	8.8	7.1	4.4	5.0	11.4	7.9	5.0	7.9	15.7	10.7
Consumer durables	7.5	10.0	0.0	2.5	2.5	7.5	2.5	10.0	17.5	15.0	5.0
Retail/ wholesale	14.4	8.9	6.5	17.5	8.5	9.4	6.1	6.5	9.4	7.5	5
Consumer services	10.0	12.0	6.0	7.0	4.0	13.0	4.0	17.0	6.0	9.0	8.0
Technology	8.9	8.9	3.4	11.3	6.8	5.5	7.4	10.8	6.9	10.5	6.6
Financial services	13.5	9.0	13.5	16.4	6.5	7.0	9.5	9.5	11.0	12.0	7.5
Property	8.3	13.0	4.0	10.0	5.0	7.0	6.7	20.0	12.5	12.5	7.0
Business services	5.2	10.2	6.0	14.2	8.0	3.3	11.4	10.3	6.8	7.9	5.9
Utilities	15.0	15.0	5.0	0	5.0	15.0	0.0	15.0	15.0	15.0	15.0
Public sector	13.2	10.5	5.9	9.5	12.5	5.5	4.1	4.0	5.9	7.3	5.5
Turnover											
Below £1 m	9.0	7.6	4.6	11.7	12.3	4.2	11.3	13.0	7.2	8.5	5.3
£1–10 m	10.7	10.0	4.7	12.6	6.5	7.8	6.2	7.0	7.0	8.6	5.7
£15–50 m	13.3	10.3	7.2	10.2	3.9	8.5	5.0	6.7	7.8	7.6	4.7
£55–100 m	12.1	7.9	3.3	7.5	5.8	12.9	2.9	9.2	7.9	6.7	5.0
Over £100 m	14.2	11.0	12.1	14.0	6.7	7.4	6.4	9.4	8.7	12.6	7.6

Note: Average proportion of total marketing budget spent on the different activities this sales year (figures may not sum due to rounding).

To take your learning further, you might wish to read this influential paper.

Kaplan, R. S., and Norton, D. P. (1992), 'The balanced scorecard: measures that drive performance', *Harvard Business Review*, January – February, 71 – 9.

This seminal much-quoted article outlined how companies should move beyond financial measures of performance to measures of performance incorporating financial, internal, innovation, and learning, and customer perspectives, seeking to answer questions such as: how do we look to shareholders? What must we excel at? Can we continue to improve and create value? And how do customers see us? The paper sparked a revolution in company performance measurement practice.

profitability, some measure of efficiency (e.g. number of employees as a proportion of revenue or in retailing, net profit per square foot of retail space), or in terms of market share or some other strategic measure. But in the past, these measures have been focused towards financial or human resource measures. More recently, there has been a considerable shift in thinking towards the need for customer-based measurements (Kaplan and Norton, 1992). There has been a move towards setting key performance indicators, which companies set and measure their progress towards in order to determine whether or not they have improved or maintained their performance over a given period of time.

Recent research indicates that British companies are now using a variety of marketing metrics as key performance indicators in marketing. In a telephone study of 200 UK marketing and finance senior executives, nearly 7 in 10 respondents claimed to use the 10 metrics identified in Table 8.4 (see Ambler, Kokkinaki, and Puntoni, 2004).

We discuss the benefits and limitations of using each of these key marketing performance metrics—as outlined in Figure 8.3—in the next section.

Table 8.4
Top ten marketing performance metrics

Rank	Metric	% Claiming to use measure	% Firms rating as very important
1	Profit/profitability	92	80
2	Sales, value, and/or volume	91	71
3	Gross margin	81	66
4	Awareness	78	28
5	Market share (volume or value)	78	37
6	Number of new products	73	18
7	Relative price	70	36
8	No. of consumer complaints or relative dissatisfaction	69	45
9	Consumer satisfaction	68	48
10	Distribution/availability	66	18

Source: Adapted from Ambler, Kokkinaki, and Puntoni (2004). With the kind permission of Westborn Publishers.

Figure 8.3
Key marketing
performance metrics

Profit/Profitability

Unsurprisingly, profit and profitability was the main key performance measure, where profit is broadly how much cash there is left in the business when all expenses are subtracted from all revenues generated. The benefit of this approach is that it indicates the 'bottom line'. It represents what is left over either for distribution to the shareholders of the business, whether that be a private or public business, or for reinvestment in the business.

However, the problem with profit/profitability as a marketing metric is that its link with marketing activity is not always clear. The process required to determine the link requires considerable input from the finance department to measure the contributions individual products/services make towards the overall profit levels of a business. So, it can be difficult to determine whether or not the marketing activity itself has led to improved levels of profitability or whether some other factor led to it, e.g. the collapse of a competitor. Finally, we might have a very profitable business operating in the short term, e.g. with customers buying more of a low-value overpriced product, but in the long term, customers would defect and leave the business.

Sales

Sales value or volume is a key performance measure, where sales value is determined by measuring how many units of a product or service are sold multiplied by the average unit price and sales volume is calculated by determining how many units of a product or service have been sold. The benefit of using this metric is that sales value and volume can be measured directly against individual product or services. Sales values and volumes are easier to determine and require limited input from the finance department, unlike in the determination of profit/profitability. Sales values and volumes may be linked to geographic sales territories and so when sales fall in a particular territory, and efforts have been made to increase sales, it is relatively easy to determine whether those efforts have been successful.

The use of sales volumes as a marketing metric is more problematic because with high-volume turnover products, particularly in brokerages where companies sell other companies' products and services, the profit may actually be disproportionately low. In such a situation, it would be wiser to measure profit/profitability, where the data are available. However, sales values may also hide the fact that a product or service is being sold at unprofitable levels. Rewarding a sales force for selling large quantities of product or service at unprofitable levels is a recipe for disaster, a recipe for the long-term decline and death of a company.

Gross Margin

Frequently, companies measure their performance based on the gross profit margins they can achieve in a particular industry. For example, the gross profit margin for supermarkets in the UK is around 5–8 per cent, whereas in the USA, gross profit margins are considerably lower at around 2–5 per cent. However, supermarkets generally operate on very high-volume sales. Therefore, they can afford to operate on low gross profit margins.

Some restaurants may operate a 200–300 per cent gross margin or 'mark-up', as it is known in the trade (see Chapter 10), on their wine, for example. When gross margins for one company are compared with those of other companies in the industry, where the data are available, e.g. for publicly quoted companies, companies can determine whether or not they need to reduce their costs, or perhaps increase their prices.

The problem with using gross margins as a marketing metric is that they do not always provide an indication of how much the customer is actually willing to pay. For example, smoothie manufacturers (e.g. Innocent, P&J Smoothies) generally operate higher gross margins (because they charge higher prices) than manufacturers in the fruit juice category (e.g. Del Monte, Minute Maid), but if they had set their initial prices based on typical fruit juice margins, they would never have been as successful as they have, especially when we consider that the Innocent Drinks for example, has achieved sales revenue of around £100 m in less than ten years.

Awareness

Nearly eight in ten respondents mentioned (brand) awareness as an important marketing metric. However, although a customer may be aware of a brand, it does not mean they will buy that brand. Correspondingly, (brand) awareness is not a particularly good measure for determining the effectiveness of marketing activity, particularly in the short term, since it may take time for the increased awareness to lead to an increase in sales, if it does at all.

However, (brand) awareness is a very useful metric for determining whether your marketing communications activity is entering your customers' consciousness more generally (see Chapter 3). The more a target market recognizes a brand, the more likely they are to become purchasers of it. Nevertheless, building awareness may not necessarily build sales. As consumers we can become well aware of a brand, but not particularly like it, and therefore, not buy it. Brands can be marketed heavily but not achieve success; examples include the Ford Edsel in the USA and the British retailer Marks and Spencer (M&S) in Far Eastern markets in the 1990 and early 2000s.

Market Share

One of the principal measures of market performance, the measurement of market share, is enshrined in many marketing strategy models such as the Boston Consulting Group's growth-share matrix (see Chapter 2). Measuring market share is particularly useful in determining a company's performance within the marketplace, particularly when measured relative to the market leader, because it gives an indication of how competitive a company is. Cadbury's, the confectionery company, use this metric, in conjunction with other marketing metrics such as brand awareness and advertising spend (Ambler, 2000).

A company A's market share is determined by measuring the company's sales revenues, incorporating the sales of all companies within the industry including company A, as a proportion of total industry sales revenues as follows:

$$\text{Market share}_{(\text{company A, \%})} = (\text{Sales Revenue}_{(\text{company A, £})}/\text{Total Industry Sales Revenue}_{(£)}) \times 100$$

Relative market share is determined by measuring the market share of company A against the market share of the market leader, or the nearest competitor (if company A is market leader), as follows:

$$\text{Relative Market Share}_{(\text{company A, units})} = \text{Market Share}_{(\text{company A, \%})}/\text{Market Share}_{(\text{market leader, \%})}$$

Where company A is market leader, relative market share is a value greater than 1 unit (see Chapter 2).

RESEARCH INSIGHT 8.4

To take your learning further, you might wish to read this influential paper.

Buzzell, R. D., Gale, B. T., and Sultan, R. G. M. (1975), 'Market share: a key to profitability', *Harvard Business Review*, January–February, 97–106.

This seminal article, outlining the profit impact of marketing strategies (PIMS), revealed a link between the return on investment made in individual businesses and market share. The Buzzell *et al.* article definitively indicated how as market share improves, profit margin rises considerably, marketing costs fall, and higher prices can be charged. Companies have been chasing market share ever since.

Nevertheless, a company's market share, as determined by the value of the sales, does not necessarily point to a profitable company. Many a company has started a price war (see Chapter 10) in order to try to steal market share from a competitor, only to find prices fall generally in the industry, which inevitably leads to a decline in their own profitability.

Number of New Products

Most companies pride themselves on their capacity to innovate. However, in many industries, innovating new products and services is vital for the prosperity of the industry. For example, pharmaceutical companies must manage a pipeline of new drug compounds at various stages in the process of new product development. When they do finally develop a drug, they quickly patent it to protect their multi-billion-dollar investments and to ensure that they can reap the financial rewards from the drug's development.

In 2006, pipeline problems occurred for global pharmaceutical manufacturers AstraZeneca and GlaxoSmithKline, when various high-profile compounds failed at the clinical trial stage, sending their share prices lower as a result (Griffiths, 2006).

3M (formerly the Minnesota Manufacturing and Mining Corporation), the company behind the Post-it note, among other innovations, uses the proportion of sales attributable to new products as one of its marketing metrics (Ambler, 2000).

Nevertheless, simply developing new products/services without measuring or predicting their impact on the sales of existing products can be problematic since the new product/service can take away sales from the existing sales without adding any new business (so-called cannibalization). In addition, this strategy may cause customer confusion as customers try to determine what they want from a variety of offers.

Mobile telephone companies quickly learned in the late 1990s and early 2000s that many consumers wanted a monthly charge service offering a limited range of telephone call packages which included text message bundles and set levels of call time or a pay-as-you-go plan with more limited options. What they didn't want was lots of different-priced telephone handset offers with many different call packages, offering different call charges for different times and so on. Consumers wanted price transparency.

Relative Price

The price of a company's products/services can be indicative of how much they are valued in the marketplace. **Relative price** is determined by measuring the price of company A's product/service against the price of the market leading company, or the nearest competitor (if company A is the market leader) as follows:

Relative Price$_{\text{(company A's offering, units)}}$

$= \text{Price}_{\text{(company A's offering, £)}}/\text{Price}_{\text{(market leader's offering/nearest competitor, £)}}$

Where company A is the market leader, relative price is a value greater than 1 unit.

There is increasing recognition that a company that can charge a price premium, vis-à-vis its competitors, has a competitive advantage over them. One approach to measuring brand equity actually uses relative price premiums (Ailawadi, Lehmann, and Neslin, 2003). (See Chapter 10 for further discussion.)

The problem with measuring marketing effectiveness using relative price only is that a company may only obtain a proportion of the total revenue possible in a marketplace if the price it charges is too high. In other words, a higher relative price may lead to a smaller market share if customers do not value your offering more than the competitors' offerings.

Customer Satisfaction

Many companies operate on the principle of satisfying their customers. Companies in the travel and leisure industry, e.g. TUI, Lunn Poly, Saga, work hard to satisfy their customers and to ensure an enjoyable experience. In the past, this meant measuring service quality levels (see Chapter 15) to determine whether companies were providing the level of quality of service that customers expected. In some industries, customer satisfaction is notoriously low but customers perceive the costs of switching their business to other providers to be too high. Retail banking services are a good example here since customers are reluctant to switch banks even when they are dissatisfied (Keaveney, 1995). Mobile phone companies (e.g. Orange, T-Mobile) measure the proportion of customers who fail to renew user contracts against the proportion of new customers acquired, termed 'churn rate' in the industry. Churn rate is a measure of disaffected customers as a proportion of new customers.

Some companies have gone beyond the concept of simply satisfying customers, e.g. the car maintenance company Kwik Fit operated the principle of '100% customer delight'. This is a principle which helped Scottish founder Sir Tom Farmer build a £1 bn business empire before he eventually sold the business to Ford in 1999 (Bain, 2003).

Nevertheless, businesses may be spending too much serving those customers who are not necessarily either the most profitable or offer the most profit potential in the future. Generating very high levels of customer satisfaction or delight may ultimately reduce shareholder value in the longer term because the costs to generate such high levels of satisfaction produce lower levels of profitability. In other words, the cost of improving customer satisfaction from 95 per cent to 99.5 per cent of customers may not actually be worth the extra costs.

Distribution/Availability

The extent to which a product or service is distributed within the marketplace can also be an important marketing metric. For example, a Hollywood blockbuster film studio will want to ensure maximum take-up of its motion pictures through as many cinemas as possible since the more cinemas the film is shown in, the higher the box office takings are likely to be. In other businesses, it is not necessarily the quantity of locations within which a product is sold, but the quality of those locations. For example, Nokia sells its premium mobile phone brand, Vertu, through specialist retail outlets only like Selfridges and Harrods in London, Paragon in Singapore, Brusco Gioielli in Rome, and Vertu branded shops in such countries as Russia and Lebanon.

Cosmetics companies (e.g. French cosmetics giant L'Oréal) frequently distribute their new products initially through speciality cosmetics outlets and prestigious department stores before stocking the products in supermarkets and other department stores later in the campaign.

Unilever, the world's biggest ice cream manufacturer, recognized the importance of providing confectioners, tobacconists, and newsagents (CTNs) with branded freezers to store its heartbrand ice cream products within the many overseas markets in which it operates, i.e. as Walls in the UK, Ola in the Netherlands, Algida in Hungary. Providing the freezers meant that CTNs could stock more of its ice cream products as opposed to those of their competitors, until an EU ruling in a case brought by Mars forced Unilever to allow CTNs to stock a small proportion of competing brands in the Unilever freezers.

In a wide range of diverse product and service industry sectors, distribution is critical so that customers can readily purchase a company's product/services. For this reason, companies often set up sophisticated systems designed to link their customers purchasing needs with their own purchasing and distribution needs. Airline yield management systems, for example, reconcile customer pricing information with live seat availability, taking into account customers' **price elasticities** (see Chapter 10), in order to maximize total sales revenues. Measures of distribution and product/service availability are critical in this and many other industries.

Managing and Controlling Marketing Programmes

There is increasing debate in marketing about how we measure the performance of marketing programmes so that we can control them better. Most of the time, companies are not excellent at all marketing activities, e.g. the American crisp producer Frito-Lay has refined the functions of selling and distribution, whereas Gillette's Personal Care Division has mastered the power of advertising, but few companies master more than one or two specialist marketing functions excellently (Bonoma, 1984).

Companies often try to maximize marketing effectiveness, e.g. measured by market share growth, revenue growth, and market position, and marketing efficiency, e.g. measured by sales and marketing expenses as a proportion of gross revenue. However, there is some evidence that companies that succeed on one dimension, i.e. either marketing efficiency or effectiveness, succeed less on the other dimension (Vorhies and Morgan, 2003). But this makes sense because, to be effective at marketing, we have to spend more on marketing activity (which

Figure 8.4

The marketing strategy/
implementation matrix

Note: KPI denotes key
performance indicators
(or marketing metric
benchmarks); efficiency =
sales and marketing expenses
as a proportion of gross
revenue; effectiveness =
market share growth, or
revenue growth, or market
position.

Sources: Adapted from
Bonoma (1984) and
McDonald (1985).
Reproduced with the kind
permission of Harvard
Business School Publishing
and Westburn Publishers.

makes us marketing inefficient!). Nevertheless, this is an important finding. Firms that can be both marketing effective and marketing efficient probably do so by changing the 'rules of the game'. They do not spend on high-cost activities like advertising to achieve effectiveness, instead they consider new and innovative approaches which make customers pay more attention. (See Market Insight 8.4.)

One problem that arises is that marketers often consider strategy formulation to be problematic, but not strategy implementation. Managers frequently assume that implementation follows strategy as a sequential process. In fact, the two processes are often interlinked and run in parallel (Piercy, 1998). In other words, marketing strategy may be, and often is, formulated on the basis of implementation considerations in the same way implementation decisions are based on strategy formulation decisions.

In Figure 8.4, we can measure how effective and efficient our strategy has been, by using the metrics for efficiency and effectiveness outlined above. Where we consider that our marketing implementation has been efficient, but our marketing strategy has not been effective, we should reformulate our strategy since key performance indicators have not been met, otherwise we are likely to reduce shareholder value in the longer term. This situation means that we have spent marketing resources well in achieving what we set out as our strategy, but we employed the wrong strategy for what we really wanted to do. The control imperative is to intervene quickly to reformulate our marketing strategy.

The dream situation is that we operate an efficient implementation plan and an effective marketing strategy. In this situation, we prosper. There is no control imperative except to maintain a watching brief to see how competition might react, since this may force us to rethink our strategy.

Where we operate inefficient marketing implementation for an ineffective marketing strategy plan, we are likely to face rapid ruin! We are spending scarce resources badly on doing the wrong things. The control imperative requires a fundamental rethink of what we are doing and how we are doing it.

The Blair Witch Project: Frighteningly Good Marketing Effectiveness

Made with a paltry production budget of $30,000 in 1999 by two first-time film-makers and a cast of unknown actors, and released by Artisan Films, *The Blair Witch Project* was designed to look like footage shot by three film students who go missing when travelling to the woods in western Maryland in 1994 to investigate the legend of the Blair Witch, a mysterious murderer in the local area.

The film is cleverly set up as a (mock) documentary, and was even marketed as such, with the film's official website designed around the idea that the film was real footage. The jittery cinematography and the dull dialogue add a realistic 'look and feel' which enhances the fear factor when viewing the film. But it wasn't just the frightening nature of the film which was spectacular. So was its success at the box office. Film revenues totalled $248 m worldwide, based on a prints and advertising budget of $6.5 m, a sales and marketing/revenue ratio of only 2.6%.

With the internet still a relatively new phenomenon in 1999, the film-makers made impressive use of the opportunities it offered. The official website had 13 million hits alone before the film was actually released. The cyberhype the film created by pretending it was based on real events (a pseudo-'snuff' movie; is it or isn't real?) ensured discussions were created around the world in online discussions groups and teenagers' conversations. There is some contention as to whether the internet campaign created the buzz on its own or whether a series of creative movie trailers, saturation press coverage, or a one-hour documentary special made by the producers for the Sci-Fi Channel were the cause of the film's success. Whatever the answer, the film's marketing impact was extraordinary given its limited budget.

Sources: Nash Information Services (2007); O'Reilly (1999); Walker (2000).

1   Did the marketers of the film cheat by planting fake stories in online discussion groups of the film's supposedly real documentary credentials or, if they did, was this simply good marketing?

2   What do you think would have been most effective at the time: the internet campaign or the publicity campaign?

3   Can you think of another low-budget film which has been so successful? What marketing activity surrounded its success?

British Airways: Flying High Again

When two terrorist-controlled planes slammed into the World Trade Centre (WTC) complex in New York and a third airliner into the Pentagon American military compound on 11 September 2001, causing more than 3,000 deaths, consumer confidence dropped in world airline travel and a subsequent general downturn in airline travel resulted. Passenger volumes dropped sharply as travellers worried about future terrorist attacks. Total passenger volumes declined within Europe by over 10%, by 35% from Europe to the USA, and by 17% from Europe to Asia, in September and October 2001. In the UK, British Airways—the national carrier—anticipated the likely downturn in airline travel by announcing, shortly after the attacks, a package of 7,000 job losses and the withdrawal of 20 aircraft from the fleet in the wake of an anticipated 10% cut in demand. As a result of the drop in consumer confidence, and the cut-throat competition from low-cost airlines such as EasyJet and Ryanair, BA posted a pre-tax loss of £200 m, against a profit of £150 m the previous year, in 2001 although it returned to profitability in 2003, when it posted a pre-tax profit of £230 m. By 2005/6, pre-tax profits had reached £620 m, principally as a result of a 'Future Size and Shape' review, which saw the airline reduce its workforce further, slash commissions to travel agents, enhance its online service, simplify its fleet by cutting the number and types of planes, and reduce its operations at London Gatwick.

To ensure that BA stays on track, it measures its performance in three key areas: traffic and capacity, financial, and operations which include, but are not limited to, the key performance indicators outlined in Table 8.5.

Table 8.5 BA key performance indicators

Area	KPI	Units	2006	2005	2004	2003	2002
Traffic and capacity	Revenue passenger km (RPK)	m	111,859	107,892	103,092	100,112	106,270
	Available seat km (ASK)	m	147,934	144,189	141,273	139,172	151,046
	Passenger load factor	%	75.6	74.8	73.0	71.9	70.4
	Passengers carried	000	35,634	35,717	36,103	38,019	40,004
	Tonnes of cargo carried	000	795	877	796	764	755
Financial	Passenger revenue per RPK		6.10	6.02	6.30	6.58	6.67
	Passenger revenue per ASK		4.61	4.51	4.59	4.74	4.69
	Average fuel price	US cents per US gallon	188.22	136.44	94.49	86.01	81.29
Operations	Average manpower equivalent (MPE)		47,012	47,472	49,072	53,440	60,468
	Aircraft utilization	Average hours/ aircraft/day	10.14	9.83	9.21	8.91	8.32
	Punctuality—within 15 minutes	%	75	76	81	76	81

Source: http://www.britishairways.com/travel/bapress/public/en_gb. With the kind permission of British Airways.

Sources: Anon. (2001); BA (2001a); BA (2002–6).

1 How do you think British Airways managed to estimate that passenger volumes would drop by at least 10% after 9/11?

2 What other areas of key performance besides traffic and capacity, financial and operations, might BA measure? Why?

3 Can you think of another example of an organization which responded rapidly to a change in market conditions? How did it manage, or how do you think it managed, to measure its progress?

Finally, where we are operating an effective marketing strategy, but implementing it inefficiently, the control imperative is to reconsider how we implement marketing programmes. While this situation may not be disastrous in the short term, where competition is adopting a more efficient approach, it could lead to mergers, sales, or takeovers in highly competitive industry sectors.

Sales Forecasting and Sales Variance Analysis

The sales forecasting process and its output provides us with a benchmark for where we think our company should be in a selected time period (see Chapter 5 for an earlier consideration from an environmental analysis perspective). Future performance can then be measured against this benchmark so that we can determine whether or not we need to make changes to the strategy. (See Market Insight 8.5.) When we conduct sales forecast exercises for marketing decision making, we might typically ask ourselves the following questions:

- What market metrics do we need to forecast (e.g. sales, markets share, marketing costs)?
- What situation are we in (e.g. stage in the product lifecycle, state of the economy)?
- What timeframe do we need to use (e.g. short, medium, or long term)?
- What data do we need, what do we have, and what is available from elsewhere?
- How often do we need to prepare our forecasts (e.g. monthly, quarterly)?
- Who will prepare the forecasts and how?
- Who will use the forecast and how?
- What process should we use when presenting the forecast?
- When do we need the forecasts for?
- What provision do we make for error and uncertainty (Armstrong, Brodie, and McIntyre, 1987)?

When we make market forecasts, we should frequently update our current sales estimates and other market data, and regularly update our marketing information system (see Chapter 3), if we wish to improve the accuracy of our forecasts (Armstrong, Brodie, and McIntyre, 1987).

To determine a company's yearly sales forecast, we forecast total industry sales revenues and multiply this measure by forecast market share, although it is possible to determine forecast company sales directly, through opinion studies of sales personnel. Increasingly, market intelligence reports like those offered by Mintel and Euromonitor offered detailed forecasts for how particular markets will develop over a set period of time.

Twenty years ago, firms did not prepare alternative sales forecasts for different strategies, environments, and capabilities, and firms tended to use different

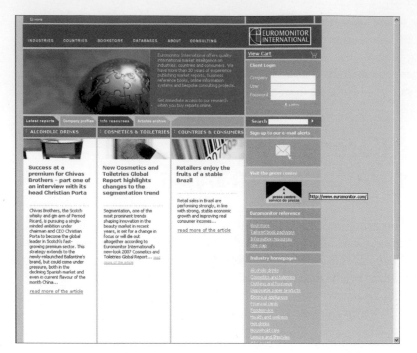

Euromonitor

sales forecasting techniques depending on the size of the firm, time horizon adopted, and type of product (Dalrymple, 1987). Today, there is greater use of these techniques. Increasingly, companies use multiple scenarios as an input into forecasting despite the fact that this does not tend to improve the accuracy of sales forecasts. What it does do, however, is allow sales forecasters to feel more confident about the predictions they make than if they didn't have such data (Schnaars and Topol, 1987).

Once we have calculated the sales forecast for our company's revenues from the different product and service offerings, we must determine whether or not our actual sales meet the sales forecasts for a given period. (See Market Insight 8.6.) Typically, we do this by measuring the **sales variance**—the difference between

MARKET INSIGHT 8.6

Luxottica Eyes the Chinese Market

Spectacles in their modern form were probably invented in thirteenth-century Italy and are most closely associated with Alessandro di Spina of Florence. Nero is said to have used an emerald and its refractive properties to correct his poor eyesight, and to allow him to view the gladiatorial competitions he set up in imperial Rome. So, it's no surprise that an Italian company, Luxottica Group, is the world's leading designer, manufacturer, and distributor of prescription frames and sunglasses in modern times. Focusing particularly in the premium and luxury segments, Luxottica's distribution network covers the world's key wholesale and retail markets, with approximately 5,500 sunglasses and optical stores worldwide.

Italian company, Luxottica Group, is the world's leading designer, manufacturer and distributor of prescription sunglasses

Photodisc

The Group targets the North American market through LensCrafters, Pearle Vision, and Sunglass Hut, Australia and New Zealand through OPSM, Laubman & Pank, and Sunglass Hut. With an enviable brand portfolio including a total of twenty-six brands (eight house brands and eighteen licence brands), Luxottica Group's house brands include Ray-Ban, the world's most well known prescription and sunglass brand, as well as Vogue, Persol, Arnette, and Revo. Licensed brands include Bulgari, Chanel, Dolce & Gabbana, Donna Karan, Prada, Versace, as well as Burberry and Polo Ralph Lauren.

But Luxottica Group is also the leader in premium and luxury optical retail in China and Hong Kong, with over 276 stores, having decided to enter the market in the 1990s through a series of takeovers including Beijing Xueliang Glasses Co. Ltd, Minglang Optical Co. Ltd in Gaungdong, and a Shanghai producer. Luxottica also makes a sizeable proportion, about 25%, of its glasses there, although it is considering reducing this because of high-end consumer prejudice.

But what really interests Luxottica's chief executive, Andrea Guerra, is that about 90% of the Chinese nation's 1.3bn population is myopic! So while the market potential is enormous, do the Chinese really want to buy high-end Italian glasses, and can they afford them?

Sources: Britannica (2007); Pliny the Elder (1962); Luxottica (2007); Anon. (2005).

1 How would you go about determining how much the Chinese people would be prepared to pay for a pair of Luxottica branded sun- and prescription glasses?

2 How would you go about developing the sales forecast for Luxottica branded spectacles in China?

3 Some eyeware companies that invested in China have started to come home. What problems do you think they had in marketing spectacles that they could not overcome?

Table 8.6

Fictional sales
forecast
(for month 8)

Sales by product/service	YTD sales (€000)	F'Cast (€000)	Variance (%)
At month 8	2008/9	2008/9	2008/9
Product A	24	41	−41%
Product B	216	270	−20%
Product C	280	135	+107%
Totals	520	446	+17%

Notes: YTD = year to date revenues (for month 8), F'cast = forecasted sales revenues (for month 8). Variance = difference between forecast sales and actual sales as a proportion of the forecast sales expressed as a percentage.

forecast sales and actual sales as a proportion of the forecast sales expressed as a percentage. This is expressed graphically below:

Sales variance = ((actual sales − sales forecast)/sales forecast) × 100

A sales variance analysis might include the forecast revenues for a variety of product and service areas (see Table 8.6). In the example, we can see the sales for month 8 in the first column, with sales forecast figures in the middle column. The variance, expressed as a percentage, is outlined in the far right-hand column. In the example, we can clearly see how the overall company position looks positive (sales up on the forecast for the month by 17 per cent). But in fact, this overall figure hides the need to reconsider the marketing strategies for products A and B, both of which have significant negative sales variances.

Chapter Summary

To consolidate your learning, the key points from this chapter are summarized below:

- Describe how marketing implementation fits into the strategic marketing planning process.

  Implementation of a selected marketing strategy depends on how we evaluated the various strategic directions we identified in the previous stage for the business, which are based on the options generated from the audit of the marketing environment and the internal marketing audit, and the marketing objectives set, as a result of the organization's business and mission. Once the marketing implementation plan has been developed, there is a need to measure the success of the initiative. Before the organization or company can measure its success, it first needs to determine how it will measure its own success or effectiveness. We use marketing metrics to measure our progress towards achieving our marketing objectives.

- Recognize the different forms of marketing organization.

  There are five key marketing organizational forms outlined in this chapter. In the first, marketing and sales can be separate departments reporting to the manager in charge of a particular strategic business unit (SBU). In the second, the sales and marketing departments report to an SBU manager who reports to a corporate headquarters.

Corporate headquarters also has a corporate marketing group, which handles the marketing for the group as a whole (e.g. corporate identity, group market research). In the third, the marketing department still reports to a SBU manager, but the sales force is centralized and sells the products for other SBUs as well. In the fourth, sales and marketing operate for each individual SBU, but research and development (R&D) and manufacturing are undertaken centrally across the SBUs. Finally, in the fifth, manufacturing and R&D operate for each individual SBU, but sales and marketing are corporate functions. It is also possible for a company to be market oriented but have no central marketing department. In these circumstances, marketing as a function is distributed through many other departments including, for example, customer service. There has been a marked shift towards key account management and the outsourcing of components of the marketing organization.

- Explain the key features of successful marketing teams.

  Marketers frequently operate within teams both within their own organizations, for example, in interdepartmental teams, and in networks externally, with employees from other organizations (e.g. with advertising agency staff and other outsourced functions). As a result, it is important that marketers work well in teams. Marketers tend to work best in teams when they work in teams which have joint reward systems across departments and organizations; when top management communicate the value of the marketing department to other teams; and when senior managers encourage informal integration of departments and greater interfunctional coordination and information sharing.

- Understand employees' motivations for resisting marketing implementation tasks.

  These may be either passive or intentional. Either way, they must be negotiated because otherwise they might derail a good marketing strategic plan. Passive reasons for implementation failure include the following: managers may simply fail to implement strategy to maintain the status quo; poor-quality administration hinders implementation; insufficient information is provided to implement the strategy properly; senior management have unclear expectations; or inappropriate timeframes are provided. Intentional reasons for implementation failure include the desire to resist power balance changes; fear of uncertainty and failure; lack of trust in the ability of top management or implementation group; and possibly even a genuine desire to betray a manager or sabotage the company's plans.

- Understand the importance and use of marketing metrics.

  There is increasing recognition of the importance of using marketing metrics in the control mechanism of the implementation phase of a marketing programme. Many companies now use some variant of the balanced scorecard (Kaplan and Norton, 1992). Recent research has highlighted widespread use of marketing metrics in firms including metrics in the following areas: profit/profitability; sales, value, and volume; gross margin; awareness; market share; number of new products; relative price; number of customer complaints; consumer satisfaction; distribution/availability; total number of customers; marketing spend; perceived quality/esteem; loyalty/retention; and relative perceived quality (Ambler, Kokkinaki, and Puntoni, 2004).

- Understand the principles of sales forecasting and sales variance analysis.

  The sales forecasting process provides the marketer with an indication of what a company's sales should be over a selected time period. This allows us to measure our current performance against this benchmark anticipated performance. To determine a company's yearly sales forecast, we forecast total industry sales revenues and multiply this measure by forecast market share. We can also determine sales forecasts directly, through opinion studies of sales personnel, or using market intelligence reports. Sales variance analysis allows us to determine whether we are meeting our target sales forecasts by measuring how much our actual sales revenues differ from those forecast.

 Visit the **Online Resource Centre** that accompanies this book to read more information relating to marketing implementation and control: www.oxfordtextbooks.co.uk/orc/baines/

? Review Questions

1 How does marketing implementation fit into the strategic marketing planning process?

2 How many different forms of marketing organization do we outline in this chapter?

3 What are the key features of successful marketing teams?

4 What are the principal reasons that employees resist marketing implementation tasks?

5 What are marketing metrics used for?

6 What are the key measurement areas in Kaplan and Norton's balanced scorecard?

7 Which marketing metrics are used most in British companies?

8 How do we calculate sales forecasts?

? Discussion Questions

1 Having read the Case Insight at the beginning of this chapter, how would you advise Molly Maid to develop a national campaign aimed at getting people who had never used the maid service before to trial the service? What role would the franchise owners play in this initiative?

2 Explain which marketing metric(s) might be used in the following circumstances:

   (a) A newly themed Irish pub with a marketing objective to give customers the best pub experience in the immediate area in the first year of its operation.

   (b) A large health and fitness organization wanting to expand its chain of gymnasiums to other countries across Europe within a five-year timescale.

   (c) The manufacturers of a designer cosmetic, such as the Gucci Pour Homme II, wishing to determine how well distributed their product is.

   (d) A pharmaceutical company wanting to understand whether its new asthma product will be better received in the marketplace in the next twelve months compared with competing brands and if it can hold its price premium.

3 Have a look at the job section for marketers of some key companies that you are familiar with on the internet. See if you can identify how they organize their

marketing functions based on the job descriptions and the company information. It may be easier to find these kinds of jobs in public sector organizations, or organizations with products and services funded through public funding (e.g. universities). If possible, try to find an organizational chart. What are your findings? How do the organizational structures compare with the five main organizational approaches outlined in this chapter?

📖 References

Achrol, R. S., and Kotler, P. (1999), 'Marketing in the network economy', *Journal of Marketing*, 63, 146–63.

Ailawadi, K., Lehmann, D. R., and Neslin, S. A. (2003), 'Revenue premium as an outcome measure of brand equity', *Journal of Marketing*, 67 (October), 1–17.

Ambler, T. (2000), 'Marketing metrics', *Business Strategy Review*, 11, 2, 59–66.

—— Kokkinaki, F., and Puntoni, S. (2004), 'Assessing marketing performance: reasons for metrics selection', *Journal of Marketing Management*, 20, 475–98.

Anderson, E. W., Fornell, C., and Lehmann, D. R. (1994), 'Customer satisfaction, market share and profitability: findings from Sweden', *Journal of Marketing*, 58 (July), 53–65.

Anon. (2001), 'Airlines: the unpalatable truth', *The Economist*, 24 November, 361, 8249, 75–6.

—— (2005), 'Business: looking east; designer glasses', *The Economist*, 8 October, 377, 8447, 79.

—— (2006a), 'dunnhumby data link with major rival to Tesco in US', *Marketing Week*, 16 February, 5.

—— (2006b), 'Marketing directors frozen out of the boardroom', *Marketing Week*, 7 September, 8.

—— (2007), 'Pret pair could have their cake and eat it', *Daily Mail*, 25 April, 73.

Armstrong, J. S., Brodie, R. J., and McIntyre, S. H. (1987), 'Forecasting methods for marketing', *International Journal of Forecasting*, 3, 355–76.

BA (2001a), 'Series of measures announced', Company press release, 20 September, available at www.britishairways.com/travel/bapress/public/en_gb, accessed 6 May 2007.

—— (2001b), 'Year end results 2001–02', available at www.britishairways.com/travel/bapress/public/en_gb, accessed 6 May 2007.

—— (2002–6), 'Year end results 2002–03, 2003–04, 2004–05, 2005–06', available at www.britishairways.com/travel/bapress/public/en_gb, accessed 6 May 2007.

Bain, S. (2003), 'Sir Tom Farmer: as if growing a £1bn business wasn't enough, he's nurturing the entrepreneurial spirit in others', *The Herald*, 20 December, 17.

Bonoma, T. V. (1984), 'Making your marketing strategy work', *Harvard Business Review*, March–April, 69–76.

Bristow, D. N., and Frankwick, G. L. (2001), 'Product managers influence tactics in marketing strategy development and implementation', *Journal of Strategic Marketing*, 2, 211–27.

Britannica (2007), 'Eyeglasses', available at www.britannica.com, accessed 7 May, 2007.

Buzzell, R. D., Gale, B. T., and Sultan, R. G. M. (1975), 'Market share: a key to profitability', *Harvard Business Review*, January–February, 97–106.

Chimhanzi, J. (2002), 'The impact of marketing/HR interactions on marketing strategy implementation', *European Journal of Marketing*, 38, 1–2, 73–98.

CIM (2001), *A Report on Marketing Effectiveness*, November, available at www.cim.co.uk/mediastore/pdfs_services/marketing_effectiveness_(4th_draft).pdf, accesed 28 May 2007.

—— (2005), 'Marketing trends survey: spring 2005', available at www.cim.co.uk/mediastore/MTS/CIM_MTS_Report_Spring_2005.pdf, accessed 28 May 2007.

—— (2006), 'Marketing trends survey: spring 2006', available at www.cim.co.uk/mediastore/MTS/Key_Findings_-_MTS_April_2006_(2).pdf, accessed 28 May 2007.

Clark, A. (2001), 'Mine's a McLatte', *The Guardian*, 1 February.

Clydesdale (2007), *Press Releases and Annual Reports*, available at www.cbonline.co.uk, accessed 8 May 2007.

Dalrymple, D. J. (1987), 'Sales forecasting practices: results from a United States survey', *International Journal of Forecasting*, 3, 379–91.

Day, G. S. (1994), 'The capabilities of market-driven organisations', *Journal of Marketing*, 58, 3, 37–52.

Fraser, I. (2005), 'The tricky art of corporate makeover', *Sunday Herald*, 6 March, 7.

Griffiths, K. (2006), 'Pharmaceuticals: UK drug giants hit by pipeline problems', *The Daily Telegraph*, 27 October, 3.

Gummesson, E. (1990), 'Marketing orientation revisited: the crucial role of the part-time marketer', *European Journal of Marketing*, 25, 2, 60–75.

Harris, L. C., and Ogbonna, E. (2003), 'The organisation of marketing: a study of decentralised, devolved and dispersed marketing activity', *Journal of Management Studies*, 40, 2, 483–512.

Homburg, C., Workman, J. P., Jr., and Jensen, O. (2000), 'Fundamental changes in marketing organisation: the movement toward a customer-focused organisational structure', *Journal of the Academy of Marketing Science*, 28, 4, 459–78.

Humby, C. (2007), 'It's time to tear up the rule book and develop some new metrics of customer investments', *Presentation to the Return on Marketing Investment Club 1-Day Conference,* 9 May, Cranfield: Cranfield University.

Jamieson, B. (2005), 'Analysis: uncertainty hangs over "jaded" brand', *The Scotsman*, 31 March, 3.

Kaplan, R. S., and Norton, D. P. (1992), 'The balanced scorecard: measures that drive performance', *Harvard Business Review*, January–February, 71–9.

Keaveney, S. M. (1995), 'Customer switching behavior in service industries: an exploratory study', *Journal of Marketing*, 59 (April), 71–82.

Kelvin, Lord (1889), 'Electrical units of measurement', Popular Lectures and Addresses, vol. i, in Elizabeth Knowles (ed.), *The Concise Oxford Dictionary of Quotations*, Oxford: Oxford University Press, 2003.

Levitt, T. (1960), 'Marketing myopia', *Harvard Business Review*, July–August.

Luxottica (2007), www.luxottica.com, accessed December 2007.

McCawley, I. (2006), 'Analysis: dunnhumby—Department of Tesco', *Marketing Week*, 8 June, 13.

McDonald, M. H. B. (1985), 'Marketing planning and Britain's disoriented directors', *Journal of Marketing Management*, 1, 21–5.

McGovern, G., and Quelch, J. (2005), 'Outsourcing marketing', *Harvard Business Review*, March, 1–2.

Mitchell, A. (2001), 'Have marketers missed the point?', *Marketing Week*, 27 September, 32.

Morgan, N. A. (1991), *Professional Services Marketing*, Oxford: Butterworth Heinneman, 75–86.

Nash Information Services (2007), 'The Blair Witch Project', available at www.the-numbers.com/movies/1999/BLAIR.php, accessed 6 May 2007.

O'Malley, L., and Patterson, M. (1998), 'Vanishing point: the mix management paradigm reviewed', *Journal of Marketing Management*, 14, 8, 829–51.

O'Reilly, J. (1999), 'The Blair Witch Project: Casting a Powerful Spell', VNU Business Publications, available at www.vnunet.com/articles/print/2129626, accessed 6 May 2007.

Piercy, N. F. (1987), 'The marketing budgeting process: marketing management implications', *Journal of Marketing*, 51 (October), 45–59.

—— (1998), 'Marketing implementation: the implications of marketing paradigm weakness for the strategy execution process', *Journal of the Academy of Marketing Science*, 26, 3, 222–36.

Pliny the Elder (1962), *The Natural History*, trans. D. E. Eichholz, book XXXVII, Chapter 16, Cambridge, Mass.: Loeb Classical Library.

Rohwedder, C. (2006), 'Stores of knowledge: No.1 retailer in Britain uses "Clubcard" to thwart Wal-Mart; data from loyalty program help Tesco tailor products as it resists U.S. invader', *Wall Street Journal* (Eastern edition), 6 June, A1.

Schnaars, S. P., and Topol, M. T. (1987), 'The use of multiple scenarios in sales forecasting', *International Journal of Forecasting*, 3, 405–19.

Sheth, S. N., and Sisodia, R. S. (2006), *Does Marketing Need Reform? Fresh Perspectives on the Future*, New York: M. E. Sharpe.

Skapinker, M. (2007), 'Interview: thinking outside the sandwich box', *Financial Times*, 19/20 May, Life and Arts Supplement, 3.

Strahle, W. M., Spiro, R. L., and Acito, F. (1996), 'Marketing and sales: strategic alignment and functional implementation', *Journal of Personal Selling and Sales Management*, 16, 1 (Winter), 1–20.

Thomas, L. C. (2002), 'The nature and dynamic of counter-implementation in strategic marketing: a propositional inventory', *Journal of Strategic Marketing*, 10, 189–204.

Vorhies, D. W., and Morgan, N. A. (2003), 'A configuration theory assessment of marketing organisation fit with business strategy and its relationship with marketing performance', *Journal of Marketing*, 67 (January), 100–15.

Walker, R. (2000), 'The real secret of the Blair witch', www.cnnmoney.com, 18 September, accessed 8 May 2007.

Wong, V., and Saunders, J. (1993), 'Business orientations and corporate success', *Journal of Strategic Marketing*, 1, 20–40.

Workman, J. P., Jr., Homburg, C., and Gruner, K. (1998), 'Marketing organisation: an integrative framework of dimensions and determinants', *Journal of Marketing*, 62 (July), 21–41.

Part 3

The Marketing Mix Principle

Part 3 focuses on the marketing mix principle. It explores pricing decisions, the different aspects of marketing communications, and then looks at retailing management.

Part 1: Marketing Fundamentals

1 Marketing Principles and Society
2 The Marketing Environment
3 Marketing Psychology and Consumer Buying Behaviour
4 Marketing Research and Marketing Information Systems

Part 2: Principles of Marketing Management

5 Marketing Strategy
6 Market Segmentation and Positioning
7 Market Development and International Marketing
8 Marketing implementation and Control

❯ **Part 3: The Marketing Mix Principle**

9 Products, Services, and Branding Decisions
10 Price Decisions
11 An Introduction to Marketing Communications
12 Marketing Communications: Tools and Techniques
13 Managing Marketing Communications: Strategy, Planning, and Implementation
14 Channel Management and Retailing

Part 4: Principles of Relational Marketing

15 Services Marketing and Non-Profit Marketing
16 Business-to-Business Marketing
17 Relationship Marketing

Part 5: Contemporary Marketing Practice

18 New Technology and Marketing
19 Postmodern Marketing
20 Marketing Ethics

9

Products, Services, and Branding Decisions

I think we're having fun. I think our customers really like our products. And we're always trying to do better.

Steve Jobs (1955 –)
US computer engineer and industrialist and founder of Apple Inc.

Learning Outcomes

After studying this chapter you should be able to:

✔ Explain the nature and characteristics of products and describe the product/service spectrum.

✔ Identify and describe the various types of products and explain particular concepts relating to the management of products.

✔ Understand how the management of products changes over the different stages of the lifecycle and explain the process by which new products are developed and adopted by markets.

✔ Describe the principles of branding and explain the different types of brand.

✔ Explain the benefits that branding offers both customers and organizations.

✔ Understand why the value of a brand is important and explain some of the issues associated with measuring brand equity.

✔ Explain how packaging and labelling can contribute to a brand's success.

Royal Philips Electronics of the Netherlands delivers healthcare, lifestyle, and technology-based products, services, and solutions through the brand promise of 'sense and simplicity'. We speak to the Global Marketing Management team to find out more.

Philips Logo

Our aim is to improve the quality of people's lives through meaningful technological innovations. Our brand promise is 'sense and simplicity' which encapsulates our commitment to delivering products and solutions that are advanced, easy to use, and designed to meet the needs of all our users, wherever in the world they may be.

Ease of use is a social trend—the lives of western consumers are becoming more complicated at the same time as technology is becoming more indispensable. No matter how sophisticated it may be, consumers want the technology to be accessible and simple to use. At the same time it must not be primitive or offer reduced functionality.

In order to fulfil our aim we need to bring to market a stream of new products and services that strike a balance between our technological development and research-led activities and the changing needs of the marketplace. For example, Senseo, which we launched in 2001, revolutionized the flat and completely saturated coffee market. This particular success was built on the consumer insight that the coffee/coffee appliance market was based on an innovation which was over twenty years old with the result that way people drank coffee at home hadn't changed. However, key elements of consumers' lifestyles had changed. Consumers

were living in smaller households, the economy was developing towards a 24-hour cycle, more women were working, and time was becoming scarcer. With rising prosperity, people were willing to make these scarce moments more quality moments. This meant that the characteristics of typical coffee consumption were changing. For example, there were fewer group or 'jug' moments, taste and variety was much more individualized, the out-of-home coffee market was growing, coffee-to-go solutions and coffee shops were growing fast, whilst out-of-home coffee preferences had changed rapidly from pure 'black coffee' to all kind of coffee varieties, from 'real Espresso' to 'high-indulgence' lattés and cappucinos. So, whilst the out-of-home coffee market had changed the in-home consumption had not, because the traditional domestic drip-filter preparation had not been updated.

> *coffee preferences had changed rapidly from pure 'black coffee' to all kinds of coffee varieties*

This understanding that consumers were looking for more individualized, better tasting, and more convenient coffee solutions at home led us to join forces with Douwe Egberts to develop the revolutionary Senseo coffee pod system. We worked on the principle that people want to drink the best coffee they can get by first pressing a single button. This means the device has to be as simple as possible to use. Senseo, if not the market leader, is now a leading brand in each of the twelve countries into which it has been launched.

Despite the outstanding success of Senseo we knew we had to establish a more systemized approach to new product development.

The question therefore was: how should Royal Philips Electronics approach the development of new technological products to meet changing customer needs? How do you think they should do this?

Philips' range of domestic appliances

Philips Electronics BV

Introduction

A Samsung HD television, a train journey from Budapest to Berlin, a cappuccino at Costa Coffee, the *Guardian* newspaper, a copy of *Vogue* magazine, a haircut, and a manicure all have one thing in common. They are all **products**.

Now this might seem a bit strange but the term product includes the tangible and intangible attributes related not just to physical goods but also to services, ideas, people, places, experiences, and even a mix of these various elements. Anything that can be offered for use and consumption, in exchange for money or some other form of value, is referred to as a product.

Tangibility refers to an item's ability to be touched and whether it is capable of being stored. For example, a bar of soap, a Rimmel lipstick, or a Vega factory conveyor belt are all tangible products and are capable of being touched and stored. A ferry trip from Sabah to Labuan in Malaysia, or a visit to Toni and Guy the hairdresser, cannot be touched and are not capable of being stored. These are intangible products and are referred to as services.

Soap is a purely tangible good whereas a financial services product, such as a pension or ISA savings account, is a pure service. They lie at opposite ends of a spectrum, which is set out at Figure 9.1. In between the pure good and the pure service lie a host of goods/services combinations. Indeed, many organizations have developed the service aspect of their market offering in order to help differentiate themselves in the market.

However, this strategy of developing the service element in order to provide a point of differentiation has not always been successful as strong competition can cause prices to fall and in turn this can lead to offerings becoming commoditized. Faced with this situation organizations have developed fresh strategies to achieve their marketing goals. One of these is based on the approach adopted by theme and leisure parks, most notable of which is Disney (see Market Insight 9.1). This third category is called customer experiences. These are neither tangible nor intangible, but refer to the memories individuals retain as a result of their interaction with an offering. Memories of experiences related to events, visits, or activities are internalized, unlike products and services which are generally external to each person.

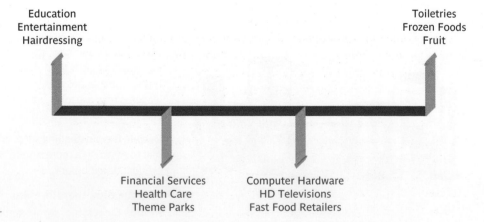

Figure 9.1
A spectrum of product combinations

Education
Entertainment
Hairdressing

Toiletries
Frozen Foods
Fruit

Financial Services
Health Care
Theme Parks

Computer Hardware
HD Televisions
Fast Food Retailers

Customer Experiences at Disney

Disney World is widely recognized as the master of managing customer experiences. At peak times the queues of people waiting for rides can be long, boring, and can distract from the overall experience at a theme park. One early solution was to reconstruct the physical queue into a 'snake' so that people felt they were moving forward, and it started at a point where visitors could see the ride or attraction. In addition to this Disney worked out the length of time people are prepared to wait before they need to be distracted. Now queues are entertained by videos, peripatetic characters, and mirrors, all carefully choreographed to commence at predetermined intervals.

Destination Disney, the name for Disney's customer experience strategy, uses technology to help personalize the park experience. Through the use of global positioning satellites, wireless technology, smart sensors, and mobile devices, Disney tries to enhance the customer experience, influence visitor behaviour, and ease crowding throughout the parks.

One of the innovations is Pal Mickey, a 10.5-inch-tall stuffed doll. Visitors carry Pal Mickey into the park, and sensors receive data wirelessly from one of the 500 infrared beacons. These are concealed in park lamp posts, rooftops, and bushes, and transmit information from a Disney data centre. The doll giggles and vibrates when it receives a new piece of information from a nearby beacon. Information about a parade, rides that have short queues, or just trivia about the area of the park you're walking through is provided, keeping guests informed, up to date, and involved with the experience.

1 In what other ways could digital technology be used to help improve the customer experience at a hotel, airline, and hospital?

2 What do you think guests expect to take away from their visit to a theme park?

3 Identify three other items that Disney could offer guests to make their visit more tangible.

Product Levels

When people buy products they are not just buying the simple functional aspect a product offers, there are other complexities involved in the purchase. For example, the taste of coffee granules is an important benefit arising from the purchase of a jar of instant coffee. However, in addition to this core benefit, people are also attracted to the **packaging**, the price, the strength of the coffee, and also some of the psychosocial associations that we have learned about a brand. The Cafédirect brand, for instance, seeks to help people understand its ties with the Fairtrade movement.

In order to understand these different elements and benefits we refer to three different product levels: the core, the embodied, and the augmented product levels. These are depicted in Figure 9.2.

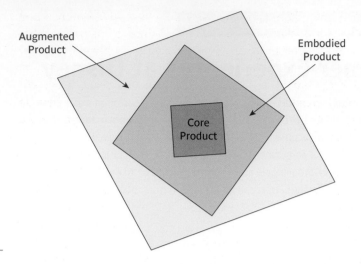

Figure 9.2
The three levels of a product

These levels are:

- The core product—consists of the real core benefit or service. This may be a functional benefit in terms of what the product will enable you to do, or it may be an emotional benefit in terms of how the product or service will make you feel. Cars provide transportation and a means of self-expression. Cameras make memories by recording a scene, person, or object through the use of film or digital processes.

- The embodied product—consists of the physical good or delivered service that provides the expected benefit. It consists of many factors, for example the features and capabilities, the durability, design, packaging, and brand name. Cars are supplied with different styles, engines, seats, colours, boot space, whilst digital cameras are offered with a variety of picture qualities, screen sizes, pixels, zoom and telephoto features, editing, and relay facilities.

- The augmented product—consists of the embodied product plus all those other factors that are necessary to support the purchase and any post-purchase activities. For example, credit and finance, training, delivery, installation, guarantees, and the overall perception of customer service.

When these levels are brought together it is hoped that they will provide customers with a reason to buy and to keep buying. Each individual combination or bundle of benefits constitutes added value and serves to differentiate one sports car from another sports car, one disposable camera from another. Marketing strategies need to be designed around the actual and the augmented products as it is through these that competition occurs and people are able to understand how one disposable camera differs from another.

Understanding a brand and what it means to its core customers and their experience of a brand is vitally important. Pepsi's battle with Coca-Cola during the 1960s and 1970s saw it gradually reduce Coke's dominant market share. The battle culminated in 1985 when Coke abandoned its original recipe and introduced New Coke, a sweeter formulation designed to attract Pepsi's young market. Coke's customers boycotted New Coke, there was public outrage, and Pepsi became market leader, but only temporarily. New Coke was soon dropped and the original brought back and relaunched as Classic Cola, re-establishing its credentials with its customers and retrieving number one spot in a couple of months. The problem was that Coke had not appreciated the value that the product as a whole represented to its core customers. The sum of the core, embodied, and augmented product, encapsulated as the brand Coca-Cola, drew passion from its customers and was overlooked by the market researchers when searching for a means to arrest Pepsi's progress.

The development of the internet and digital technologies has impacted on the nature of the product and the benefits accruing from product usage. This has opened opportunities for organizations to redefine their core and actual products, often by supplementing them with 'information' about the product or service, for example providing white papers or games designed to engage site visitors with the brand. Another approach has been to transform current products into digital products, for example Napster and music downloads. A further approach is to change the bundle of products offered, sometimes achieved by presenting an online catalogue that offers a wider array than the offline catalogue.

Chaffey *et al.* (2006) refer to Ghosh (1998) and his early identification of the number of ways in which 'digital value' can help augment products. For example, many companies provide evidence of the awards their products have won, while

Napster LLC

Napster offers music downloads

others parade testimonials, endorsements, and customer comments. These are designed to provide credibility, reduce risk, and enable people to engage with or purchase a brand. The key contribution of the internet, in this context, is that it offers digital value to customers sometimes as a supplement and sometimes as a complete alternative to the conventional, established core product offering.

Classifying Products

Now that we understand that products may be tangible goods, intangible services, or even experiences, and that they consist of several layers, the next step is to classify or categorize products. This is important because only through understanding how customers think and feel about products, how they use products, and how their purchasing behaviours vary can marketing mixes and new products be developed that meet customer needs.

There are two main classifications, consumer products and business-to-business products. Consumer products are bought to satisfy personal and family needs and industrial and business products are bought either as a part of the business's operations or in order to make other products for resale. Although there are some products such as light bulbs and toilet paper that are bought by both consumers and businesses, it is helpful to use this grouping simply because there are considerable differences in the way these two types of customers buy products and services. If you are unsure about buying behaviour issues we suggest you read Chapter 3.

Consumer Products

The first way of classifying consumer products is to consider them in terms of their durability. **Durable goods** such as bicycles, music players, and refrigerators can be used repeatedly and provide benefits each time they are used. **Non-durable goods**, such as yoghurt, newspapers, and plastic packaging, have a limited duration, often only capable of being used once. Services are intangible products and cannot be stored.

Durable goods reflect a purchaser's high level of involvement in the purchase decision. There is high perceived risk in these decisions so consumers spend a great deal of time, care, and energy searching, formulating, and making the final decision. As a result marketers need to understand these patterns of behaviour, provide, and make accessible sufficient amounts of appropriate information, and ensure there is the right type of service and support necessary to meet the needs of the target market.

Non-durable goods, typically food and grocery items, usually reflect low levels of involvement and buyers are not concerned which particular product they buy. Risk is perceived to be low and so there is little or no need (or time usually) to shop around for the best possible price. Buyers may buy on availability, price, habit, or brand experience.

One of the key characteristics of services is that they are intangible and another is that they are perishable. This means that they cannot be touched and because they are perishable they are not capable of being stored. Their use and consumption therefore has to be based on an 'on-demand' basis. Levels of involvement may be high or low and marketing mixes need to set up and deliver customer expectations. Due to their complexity Chapter 15 is devoted to the marketing services.

A deeper and more meaningful way of classifying consumer products is to consider how and where consumers buy products. In Chapter 3 we considered different ways in which consumers make purchases. In particular, we looked at **extensive problem solving**, **limited problem solving**, and routinized response behaviour.

Classifying products according to the behaviour consumers demonstrate when buying them enables marketing managers to develop more suitable and appropriate marketing strategies. Four main behavioural categories have been established; **convenience products, shopping products, speciality products**, and unsought products.

Convenience products are non-durable goods or services and as the name suggests are bought because the consumer does not want to put very much effort, if any, into the buying decision. **Routinized response behaviour** corresponds most closely to convenience products as they are bought frequently and are inexpensive. Most decisions in this category are made through habit, and if a usual brand is not available an alternative brand will be selected or none at all as it would be too inconvenient to go and visit another store.

Convenience products may be subdivided into three further categories. These are staples, impulse, and emergency products and are explained in Table 9.1.

Type of convenience product	Explanation
Staple products	Characteristically, staples are available almost everywhere. They include groceries such as bread, milk, soft drinks, and breakfast cereals but they also include petrol. They are bought frequently and form the basis of our daily pattern of behaviour. In France the daily purchase of a fresh French stick of bread or baguette constitutes an important part of social behaviour.
Impulse products	These are products that consumers had not planned to buy but are persuaded at the very last minute to pick up and put in their trolley or basket. Typically these items are located very near to the tills in supermarkets (the point of sale) so that whilst customers are waiting to pay for their planned or considered purchases they become attracted to these impulse items. Chewing gum, chocolate bars, and magazines are typical impulse purchases, unlike a bottle of milk or petrol which are planned.
Emergency products	Bought when a very special need arises; buyers are more intent on buying a solution than buying the right quality or image-related product. So, the purchase of a bandage when someone is cut or injured, a plumber when a pipe starts leaking in the middle of the night, or even umbrellas in the middle of summer when an unexpected downpour occurs all constitute emergency products.

Table 9.1

Categories of convenience products

All of these types of convenience products indicate that slightly different marketing strategies are required to make each of them work. However, one element common to them all is distribution. If the product is not available when an emergency arises, or when a consumer is waiting to pay or walking towards the milk racks, then a sale will not be made. Pricing is important as customers know the expected price of convenience items and they may well switch brands if price exceeds that of the competition.

Shopping products are not bought as frequently as convenience products and as a result consumers do not always have sufficient up-to-date information to make a buying decision. The purchase of shopping products such as furniture, electrical appliances, jewellery, and mobile phones requires some search for information, if only to find out about the latest features. Consumers give time and effort to planning these purchases if only because the level of risk is more substantial than that associated with convenience products. They will visit several stores and use the internet and word-of-mouth communications for price comparisons, product information, and the experience of other customers. Not surprisingly levels of brand loyalty are quite low as consumers are quite happy to switch brands in order to get the level of functionality and overall value they need.

The marketing strategies followed by manufacturers, and to some extent retailers, need to accommodate the characteristics of limited problem solving. Shopping products do not require the mass distribution strategies associated with convenience products. Here a selective distribution strategy is required as consumers often want the specialist advice offered by knowledgeable, expert retailers. The volume of purchases is lower, so although margins are higher, marketing communications have two important roles to play. The first is to establish a strong brand name so that when consumers are ready to start the purchase process they are able to associate a brand with the product category. The second is that manufacturers must use advertising, public relations, personal selling, and sales promotions to support retailers. This is necessary because between the manufacturer and the retailer they must provide customers with the information they need when and how they need it, the confidence to proceed, and an overall sense of value in the purchase.

Speciality products represent high risk, are very expensive, and are bought infrequently, often only once, and correspond to extended problem solving. People plan these purchases, search intensively for information about the object, are only concerned with a particular brand and in finding a way of gaining access to an outlet which can supply them. It is possible to find speciality products in many areas, for example, limited edition sports equipment (Big Bertha golf clubs), rare paintings and artwork (Picasso's), custom cars (see Marketing Insight 9.2), watches (Rolex), haute couture (Stella McCartney), and certain restaurants and holidays. All of them have unique characteristics, which to buyers means that there are no substitute products available or worth considering.

Marketing strategies to support speciality products focus heavily on a very limited number of distribution outlets and advertising which seeks to establish brand name and values. The few retailers appointed to carry the item require detailed training and support so that the buyer experiences high levels of customers service and associated prestige throughout the entire purchase process.

Very Special Cars

Several speciality products can be observed in the car market. The waiting list to buy a specialist hand-built car, such as a Morgan, can be years. When the Morgan Car Company announced their intention in 2006 to build 100 AeroMax coupés, deposits for 50 of them were paid within eight weeks, even though production would not start until January 2008.

Another speciality area concerns customized cars. These are normal production cars that have had their engines changed, their wheels enlarged, and body work transformed so that the car becomes unique and sought after. For example, a car which was bought as a wreck and rebuilt by Ian Walker now has celebrity status and can be hired for weddings and other events.

The BMW M1 pictured below was painted by pop artist Andy Warhol. He is quoted, 'I tried to portray speed pictorially. If a car is moving really quickly, all the lines and colours are blurred.' It was claimed that he spent 23 minutes painting the car and he used his fingers to sweep through the paint in order to provide a personal touch. This and other cars command exceedingly high prices because of their rarity and, in the case of the BMW, because of the fame of the artist.

The BMW M1: painted by pop artist Andy Warhol

1 Who do you think might be interested in buying the BMW M1 and who might want to own a custom car?

2 What risks might buyers of speciality products experience?

3 Identify three other speciality products in different markets and industries.

Unsought products refers to a group of products which people do not normally anticipate buying or indeed want to buy. Consumers have little knowledge or awareness of the brands in the marketplace and are only motivated to find out about them when a specific need arises. So, a windscreen cracks or a water pipe bursts necessitating repairs and unsought products. In a similar way life insurance was once sold through heavy pressurized selling as people did not see the need. That has changed through changes in legislation, but double glazing and timeshare holiday salespeople still have a reputation for getting people to buy their products and services who would not normally have bought them.

Business Products

Unlike some consumer products that are bought for personal and psychological rewards, business products are generally bought on a rational basis to meet organizational goals. These products are used to either enable the organization to function smoothly or they form an integral part of the products, processes, and services supplied by the organization for resale.

In the same way as consumer products are classified according to how customers use them, so business products are classified according to how organizational customers use them. Six main categories can be identified: equipment goods, raw materials, semi-finished goods, maintenance repair and operating goods, component parts, and business services.

Equipment goods cover two main areas and both concern the everyday operations of the organization: **capital equipment goods** and **accessory equipment goods**. Capital equipment goods refer to buildings, heavy plant, and factory equipment necessary to build or assemble products. They might also refer to major government schemes to build hospitals, motorways, and bridges. Whatever their nature, they all require substantial investment, are subject to long planning processes, are often one-off purchases designed to remain for a considerable amount of time, and require the involvement of a number of different people and groups in the purchase process. Accessory equipment goods should support the key operational processes and activities of the organization. Typically they are photocopiers, computers, stationery, and office furniture. These items cost less than capital equipment goods, are not expected to last as long as capital equipment goods, and are often portable rather than fixed. Whereas a poor capital equipment purchase may put the entire organization at risk, a poor accessory purchase will at worst be frustrating and slow down activities but is unlikely to threaten the existence of the organization.

Raw materials are the basic materials that are used in order to produce finished goods. Minerals, chemicals, timber, and food staples such as grain, vegetables, fruit, meat, and fish are extracted, grown, or farmed as necessary and transported to organizations who process the raw materials into finished or semi-finished products. Bought in large quantities, buyers often negotiate heavily on price as there is little to differentiate raw materials. However, these buying decisions can be influenced by non-product factors such as length of relationship, service quality, and credit facilities.

Semi-finished goods are raw materials that have been converted into a temporary state. Iron ore is converted into sheets that can be used by car and aircraft manufacturers, washing machines, and building contractors.

Maintenance, repair, and operating (MRO) are products, other than raw materials, that are necessary to ensure that the organization is able to continue functioning. Maintenance and repair goods such as nuts and bolts, light bulbs, and cleaning supplies are used to maintain the capital and accessory equipment goods. Operating supplies are not directly involved in the production of the finished goods nor are they a constituent part, but oil for lubricating machinery, paper, pens, and flash drives are all necessary to keep the overall organization functioning.

Component parts are finished, complete parts bought from other organizations. These components are then incorporated directly into the finished product. So, for example, Ford will buy in finished headlight assemblies and mount them directly into their Ford Fusion, Focus, or Transit models as appropriate.

Business services are intangible services used to enhance the operational aspects of the organizations. Most commonly these concern management consultancy, finance, and accounting, including auditing, legal, marketing research, IT, and marketing communications.

Product Range, Line, and Mix

In order to meet the needs of a number of different target markets, most organizations offer a variety of products and services. Although some offer an assortment based on an individual core product it is rare that an organization offers just a single product. Consumer organizations such as Gillette offer a range of shaving products for men, industrial organizations such as Oliver Valves offer a range of valves for the offshore and onshore petrochemical, gas, and power generation industries.

In order to make sense of and understand the relationships that one set of products have with another a variety of terms have emerged. Table 9.2 sets out these different terms.

Product Lifecycles

Underpinning the product lifecycle (PLC) concept is the belief that products move through a sequential, predetermined pattern of development similar to the biological path that life forms follow. This pathway, known as the **product lifecycle**, consists of five distinct stages, namely development, introduction, growth, maturity, and decline. Sales and profits rise and fall across the various lifestages of the product, as shown in Figure 9.3.

Products move through an overall cycle that consists of different stages. Speed of movement through the stages will vary but each product has a limited lifespan. Although the life of a product can be extended in many ways, such as introducing new ways of using the product, finding new users, developing new attributes,

Table 9.2

Product range
terminology

Product term	Explanation
Product mix	The total group of products offered by an organization: at Nokia this would mean all the phones and all the accessories they offer.
Product line	A group of closely related products—related through technical, marketing, or user considerations. For example all the flip phones offered by Nokia constitute a product line.
Product item	A distinct product within a product line. Nokia's N73 is a product item (see Nokia ad).
Product line length	The number of products available in a product line: the 9 products available within the 'NSeries'.
Product line depth	The number of variations available within a product line: the 15 types of flip phone.
Product mix width	The number of product lines within a product mix: 13 different forms of functionality offered by Nokia.

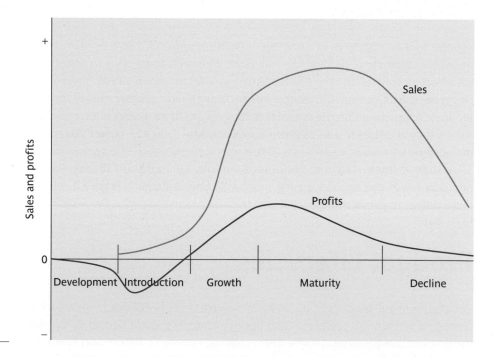

Figure 9.3

The five stages of the product lifecycle

the majority of products have a finite period during which management need to maximize their returns on the investment made in each of their products.

Just as the nature and expectations of customer groups differ at each stage so do the competitive conditions. This means that different marketing strategies, relating to the product and its distribution, pricing, and promotion, need to be deployed at particular times so as to maximize the financial return on a product's entire life.

The product lifecycle does not apply to all products in the same way. For example, some products reach the end of the introduction stage and then die as it becomes clear that there is no market to sustain the product. Some products follow the path into decline and then hang around sustained by heavy advertising and sales promotions or they get recycled back into the growth stage by repositioning activities. Some products grow really quickly and then fade away rapidly. When Pot Noodle products were first introduced demand grew quickly but then died off steeply at the end of the growth stage. The reason for this was that people did not like the taste of these early products and so there was no repeat buying; everybody tried it once, and that was enough!

When discussing the PLC care must be taken to clarify what exactly is being described. The PLC concept can apply to a **product class** (computers), a product form (a laptop), or a brand (Sony). The shape of the curve varies, with product classes having the longest cycle as the mature stage is often extended. Product forms tend to comply most closely with the traditional cycle shape while brand cycles tend to be the shortest. This is because they are subject to competitive forces and sudden change. So, while hatchback cars (product form) enjoy a long period of success, brands such as the Ford Escort have shorter cycles and have been replaced by cars that have more contemporary designs and features, in this case, the Ford Focus.

Fads and Fashions

One final aspect of the PLC concept concerns fads and fashions. Rather like the Pot Noodle example described earlier, fashions and fads concern products whose sales grow very quickly, peak, and then fall way, equally quickly. The overall cycle time can be very short and only involve a well-defined small group of customers. Toys, such as Rubik's Cube, are often subject to fad status as, of course, are particular styles of dress, clothing, or furniture. Timing and entry into these markets is crucial and there is no scope for late entrants, simply because the cycle length is so short.

Usefulness of the PLC Concept

The PLC is a well-known and popular concept and is a useful means of explaining the path a product or brand has taken. It also clearly sets out that no product, service, or brand lasts forever. In principle the PLC concept allows marketing managers to adapt strategies and tactics to meet the needs of evolving conditions and product circumstances. In this sense it is clear, simple, and predictable. However, in practice the PLC is not of great use. For example, one problem concerns understanding about which stage a product has reached in the cycle. Historical sales data does not help managers identify when a product moves from one stage to another. This means that it is difficult to forecast sales, and hence determine the future shape of the PLC curve.

China Mobile Rings Lots of Bells

Mobile phone technology is approaching the end of the growth stage of the PLC as saturation point is reached in terms of the number of customers who have mobile phones. Competition, especially in Western economies, for mobile phone handsets is becoming intense. However, growth in the mobile phone market is still possible in China, where the market leader, China Mobile, registers an additional 4 million customers a month. At the time of writing, the brand, which only commenced operations in 2000, has over 260 million customers and provides roaming services stretching across 271 operators in 206 countries and regions in the world.

In order to consolidate their position, retain customers, and extend the growth period, China Mobile uses various marketing strategies. These involve segmentation, product development, and a range of value added services such as data, IP telephone, and multimedia. China Mobile operates consumer brands such as 'GoTone', 'Shenzhouxing', and 'M-Zone'. 'GoTone' has been hugely popular among its wealthier customers, mainly because of the high perceived value of its services. Innovative brands like 'M-Zone' are targeted at youth groups.

Source: Ritson (2006).

Adapted from www.chinamobile.com/ENGLISH/index.html.

1 If you were the marketing manager for China Mobile what strategies would you use when the brand moves into the mature stage?

2 Use a major search engine to search and find the leading mobile phone company in Australia, Canada, and another country of your choice. What do they all have in common?

3 Make brief notes about the needs customers have for mobile phones. How might this change over the next five years?

The model worked reasonably well when the environment was relatively stable and not subject to dynamic swings or short-lived customer preferences. However, contemporary marketing managers are not concerned where their brand is within the product lifecycle: there are many other more meaningful ways and metrics to understand the competitive strength and development of a brand, for example, benchmarking. Some brands do not follow the classical S-shaped curve, but rise steeply and then fall away immediately sales reach a crest. These shapes reflect a consumer fad, a craze for a particular piece of merchandise, typified by fashion clothing, skateboards, and toys.

It was mentioned earlier that the PLC could be used to develop strategy. Again, few marketing managers would develop strategy based on a detailed analysis of the PLC, if only because strategy might evolve either because of the PLC or in spite of it. Wood (1990) refers to this as the self-fulfilling prophecy and argues that a manager may identify that a product is in a particular stage, implements strategies pertinent to the next stage, and then sees that the product is behaving as if it is in the next stage, whether it was appropriate or not. So, great care is required when using the PLC, as its role in commerce and when developing strategy is weak but as a way of explaining how brands develop generally, it is helpful. (See Market Insight 9.3.)

RESEARCH INSIGHT 9.1

To take your learning further, you might wish to read this influential paper.

Wood, L. (1990), 'The end of the product life cycle? Education says goodbye to an old friend', *Journal of Marketing Management*, 6, 2, 145–55.

This paper has been highlighted because it challenges the conventional wisdom about how useful the product lifecycle is. It identifies some of the problems associated with this popular concept and suggests that the concept is good for marketing education but not so good for marketing practitioners.

New Product Development

One of the key facts that the product lifecycle concept tells us is that products do not last forever: their usefulness starts to diminish at some point and eventually they all come to an end, and they die. There are many reasons for this cycle: technology is changing quickly so products are developed and adopted faster, lifecycles are becoming shorter, and so new products are required faster than before. In addition to this, global competition means that if an organization is to compete successfully and survive it will need to constantly offer superior value to its customers. One of management's tasks, therefore, is to be able to control the organization's range or portfolio of products and to anticipate when one product will become relatively tired and when new ones are necessary in order to sustain the organization and help it to grow.

The term new products can be slightly misleading as there can be a range of newness, both to the organization and to customers. Some new products might be totally new to both the organization and the market, for example the Dyson floor cleaner revolutionized the market previously dominated by suction-based 'hoovers'. However, some products might only be minor product adaptions that have no real impact on a market other than offering an interesting new feature. For example, features such as new colours, flavours, pack sizes, and electronic facilities on CD players, digital cameras, and mobile personal players.

Unfortunately these 'new' products do not appear at the click of a pair of fingers. They have to be considered, planned, developed, and introduced carefully to the market. In order that there is a stream of new products organizations have three main options.

- Buy in finished products from other suppliers, perhaps from other parts of the world, or license the use of other products for specific periods of time.

- Develop products through collaboration with suppliers or even competitors.

- Develop new products internally, often through research and development departments (R&D) or through adapting current products through minor design and engineering changes.

Whatever the preferred route they all necessitate a procedure or development pattern through which they are brought to the market. It would be wrong to suggest that there should be a uniform process (Ozer, 2003) as not only are there many approaches to new product development but also the procedures adopted by an organization reflect its attitude to risk, its culture, strategy, the product and market, and, above all else, its approach to customer relationships.

The success rate of new products is consistently poor. No more than 1 in 10 new products succeed and there are three main reasons for this, according to Drucker (1985):

1 There is no market for the product.

2 There is a market need but the product does not meet customer requirements.

3 The product's ability to meet the market need although satisfactory is not adequately communicated to the target market.

Successful new products are developed partly by understanding the market and partly by developing technology to meet the identified needs. Energizer batteries demonstrate this orientation with their 15-minute charger. The charger was designed to meet the needs of people who want batteries to cope with the demands of high-draining products such as digital cameras and who also want to reduce the recharge time. Advances in technology enabled Energizer to make their batteries last four times as long as alkaline batteries, and they reduced the recharge time from 8 hours to just 15 minutes (Tiltman, 2006).

The development of new products is complex and high risk so organizations usually adopt a procedural approach. The procedure consists of several phases that enable progress to be monitored, test trials to be conducted, and the results analysed before there is any commitment to the market. The most common general new product development process (NPDP) is set out in Figure 9.4.

The NPDP presented here should be considered as a generalization, and it should be understood that the various phases or episodes do not always occur in the linear sequence shown here. Actions can overlap or even occur completely out of sequence, depending on the speed, complexity, and number of people or organizations involved in the NPDP. Apart from some minor issues, the process is essentially the same when developing new products for both consumer and business markets.

Idea Generation

Ideas for new products generally come from customers and external and internal sources.

The first and best source is customers who can bring to attention specific problems, but this is not always feasible, as customers do not always know what they want. The second source refers to ideas generated by competitors, website,

Energizer Group Ltd

Advances in technology enabled Energizer to make their batteries last four times as long as alkaline batteries

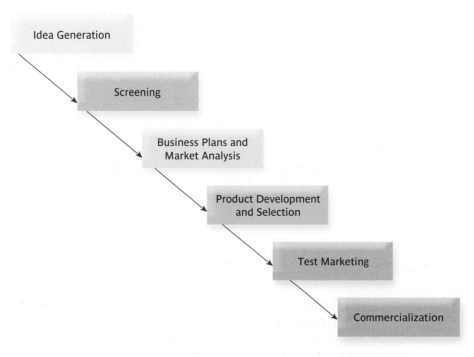

Idea Generation

Screening

Business Plans and Market Analysis

Product Development and Selection

Test Marketing

Commercialization

Figure 9.4
The new product development process

and sales literature analysis. In addition, market research data often bought as a report, commissioned or undertaken by external organizations, can be the source of ideas for products.

The third source refers to ideas that are generated internally to the organization. For example, research and development departments, customer service employees, the sales force, project development teams, and secondary data sources such as sales records can all generate ideas or products. What this means is that organizations should foster a corporate culture that encourages creativity and supports people when they bring forward new ideas for product enhancements and other improvements.

Screening

All ideas need to be assessed so that only those that meet predetermined criteria are taken forward. One key criterion concerns the fit between the proposed new product idea and the overall corporate strategy and objectives. It is not a good idea for a manufacturer to invest in and develop a new carburettor for a petrol engine if the strategy is to develop new fuel technologies.

Another criterion concerns the views of customers. This can be undertaken by using concept testing. This approach requires a small representative sample of customers to review the idea as early as possible. This can reveal their attitudes and intentions towards the idea before any substantial investment is made. Other approaches consider how the market will react to the idea and what effort the organization will need to make if the product is to be brought to the market successfully.

Whatever approaches are used, screening must be a separate activity to the idea generation stage. If it is not then creativity might be impaired.

Business Planning and Market Analysis

The development of a business plan is crucial, simply because it will indicate the potential and relative profitability of the product. In order to prepare the plan important information about the size, shape, and dynamics of the market need to be determined. The resultant profitability forecasts will be significant in determining how and when the product will be developed, if at all. Various indicators, for example weak profit forecasts, problematic manufacturing requirements, inadequate distribution, market need already being met by stronger competitive products, or the market is just not strong enough, indicate that the product proposal should be dropped.

Product Development and Selection

In many organizations several product ideas are considered simultaneously. It is management's task to select those that have commercial potential and are in the best interests of the organization and its longer-term strategy, goals, and use of resources. There is a trade-off between the need to test and reduce risk and the need to go to market and drive income and get a return on the investment committed to the new product.

This phase is expensive so only a limited number of projects are allowed to proceed into development. Those projects that are selected for further development have prototypes and test versions developed. These are then subjected to functional performance tests, design revisions, manufacturing requirements analysis, distribution analysis, and a multitude of other testing procedures. The objective is to work out the technical issues involved in producing the product and to determine whether the costs are acceptable. (See Market Insight 9.4 for a product which was deemed unprofitable but went on to become a huge success.)

Test Marketing

Before committing a new product to a market, most organizations decide to test market the finished product. By piloting and testing the product under controlled, real market conditions many of the genuine issues as perceived by customers can be raised and resolved whilst minimizing any damage or risk to the organization and the brand.

Test marketing can be undertaken using a particular geographical region or specific number of customer locations. The intention is to evaluate the product and the whole marketing programme under real working conditions. Test marketing, or field trials, enables the product and marketing plan to be refined or adapted in the light of market reaction, yet before release to the whole market. See Chapter 4 for more information about test marketing.

Commercialization

The launch of a fully finished product into a target market represents the culmination of the preceding tests, analysis, and development work. To commercialize a new product organizations normally require the preparation of a launch plan. This considers the needs of distributors, end user customers, marketing communication agencies, and other relevant stakeholders. The objective is to schedule all those activities that are required to make the launch successful.

In addition to communications such as the preparation of articles and features to appear in trade and technical journals, customers and/or dealers need to be advised. First, they need to be informed and educated in terms of product capabilities. Next, they need to be trained to use the product. In addition to the obvious need to train and instruct the sales force, internal customer support services, such as finance, distribution, order processing, and the communications team, should be included in the launch plan. The purpose is to enable them to provide product support based on appropriate knowledge and training so that they understand how customers are expected to use the product and what to do to enable them to derive its full benefits.

Developing Viagra: Determining Size

Pfizer was once a medium-sized pharmaceutical manufacturer. Now it is the world's leading player in a highly competitive sector. The reason for this considerable uplift in sales and profits was Viagra, the first drug to provide a cure for impotence. The development and launch of Viagra took thirteen years, involved screening in excess of 1,500 compounds, and it is estimated that the research and development costs exceeded £600 million.

Originally, Pfizer had invested in a research programme designed to find a treatment for angina. However, the angina trials proved unsuccessful but some patients reported that they experienced penile erections as a side effect. Although this was noted by Pfizer, they were reluctant to develop further research using the 'angina' compounds, simply because formal research showed that only 1 in 20 million men suffered from erectile dysfunction, that it was commonly accepted to be a psychological problem. Furthermore, who was going to allow themselves to be part of the testing procedure during the trials?

Despite these reservations and associated business risk, Pfizer agreed to proceed. Plenty of people volunteered for the clinical trials between 1993 and 1996 which were an overwhelming success. This was followed by the issue of a full licence in 1998. In view of the 2.9 million prescriptions made in the first three months alone (Pfizer.com), sales of $1.2 billion in 2004, and the entry of two similar drugs into the market, it might be concluded that the original research failed to reflect the true size of the market.

Not only has Viagra helped millions of people it has been a major new product success story. Despite the poor business case for the product during development, the inaccuracy of the market research was subsequently revealed by the demand for the drug.

Source: Adapted from Trott (2007).

1 The Viagra case highlights the problems associated with developing a business case. What other problems might occur with the development of medicines?

2 To what extent is the business case and market analysis case stage useful?

3 Find examples of other recently launched new products. Where and how were they launched?

To take your learning further, you might wish to read this influential paper.

Wind, J., and Mahajan, V. (1997), 'Issues and opportunities in new product development: an introduction to the special issue', *Journal of Marketing Research*, 34, 1, 1–12.

This paper introduces a special issue on new product development (NPD). So, although not a complete paper in its own right it is useful because it comments upon a range of NPD issues, written about in depth in the academic papers included in that issue, current to the 1990s.

The Process of Adoption

The process through which individuals accept and use new products is referred to as the **process of adoption** (Rogers, 1983). The different stages in the adoption process are sequential and are characterized by the different factors that are involved at each stage (e.g. the media used by each individual). The process starts with people gaining awareness of a product and moves through various stages of adaption before a purchase is eventually made. Figure 9.5 below sets out the various stages in the process of adoption.

In the **knowledge stage** consumers become aware of the new product. They have little information and have yet to develop any particular attitudes towards the product. Indeed, at this stage consumers are not interested in finding out any more information.

The **persuasion stage** is characterized by consumers becoming aware that the innovation may be of use in solving a potential problem. Consumers become sufficiently motivated to find out more about the product's characteristics, including its features, price, and availability.

In the **decision stage** individuals develop an attitude toward the product or service and they reach a decision about whether the innovation will meet their needs. If this is positive they will go on to try the innovation.

During the **implementation stage** the innovation is tried for the first time. Sales promotions are often used as the use of samples enables individuals to test the product without any undue risk. Individuals accept or reject an innovation on the basis of their experience of the trial. Note the way supermarkets use sampling to encourage people to try new food and drink products.

The final **confirmation stage** is signalled when an individual successfully adopts the product on a regular purchase basis without the help of sales promotion or other incentives.

This model assumes that the adoption stages occur in a predictable sequence, but this cannot always be assumed to be the case. Rejection of the innovation can occur at any point, even during implementation and the very early phases

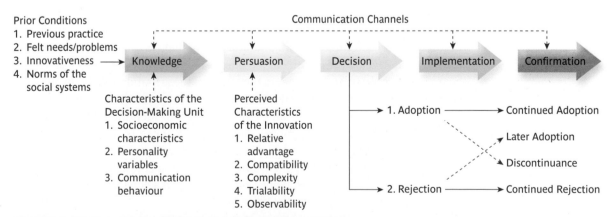

Figure 9.5 Stages in the innovation decision process of adoption

Source: Reprinted from Rogers (1983) with the permission of the Free Press. © 1962, 1971, 1983 by the Free Press.

of the confirmation stage. Generally, mass communications are going to be more effective in the earlier phases of the adoption process for products that buyers are actively interested in, and more interpersonal forms are more appropriate at the later stages, especially implementation and confirmation.

Branding

Branding is a method through which manufacturers and retailers help customers to differentiate between the various offerings in a market. It enables them to make associations with certain attributes or feelings with a particular brand. If this differentiation can be achieved and sustained, then a brand is considered to have a competitive advantage. It is not necessary for people to buy brands in order to enjoy and understand them. Successful brands create strong, positive, and lasting impressions through their communications and associated psychological feelings and emotions, not just their functionality through use.

Brand names provide information about content, taste, durability, quality, price, and performance, without requiring the buyer to undertake time-consuming comparison tests with similar offerings or other risk reduction approaches to purchase decisions. In some categories brands can be developed through the use of messages that are entirely emotional or image based. Many of the 'products' in fast-moving consumer goods (FMCG) sectors, where there is low involvement, use communications based largely on imagery. Other sectors, such as cars or pharmaceuticals where involvement tends to be high, require rational information-based messages supported by image-based messages (Boehringer, 1996). In other words, a blend of messages may well be required to achieve the objectives and goals of the campaign.

What is a Brand?

Brands are products and services that have added value. This value has been deliberately designed and presented by marketing managers in an attempt to augment their products with values and associations that are recognized by and are meaningful to their customers. Although marketing managers have to create, sustain, protect, and develop the identity of the brands for which they are responsible, it is customer perception and the images they form of these brands and their value that is important. Both managers and customers are involved in the branding process.

Although Chernatony and Dall'Olmo Riley (1998) identified twelve types of brand definition, one of the more common approaches is that offered by the American Marketing Association, cited by Kotler and Keller. This considers a brand to be 'a name, term, sign, symbol or design or a combination, intended to identify the goods, or services of one seller or group of sellers, and to differentiate them from those of competitors' (2006: 274).

However, brands consist of much more than these various elements. Brands have character, even personalities, and in order to develop character it is important to understand that brands are constructed of two main types of attributes:

RESEARCH INSIGHT 9.3

To take your learning further, you might wish to read this influential paper.

Doyle, P. (1993), 'Building successful brands; the strategic options', *Journal of Consumer Marketing*, 7, 2, 5–20.

This paper demonstrates that having a strong brand is not enough. Doyle shows that successful brands deliver against four criteria: a strong consumer proposition, integrated with other assets, being positioned within an attractive market, and being managed in order to realize the value of the brand's long-term cash flow.

intrinsic and extrinsic. Intrinsic attributes refer to the functional characteristics of a product such as its shape, performance, and physical capacity. If any of these intrinsic attributes were changed, it would directly alter the product. Extrinsic attributes refer to those elements that are not intrinsic and if changed do not alter the material functioning and performance of the product itself: devices such as the brand name, marketing communications, packaging, price, and mechanisms that enable consumers to form associations that give meaning to the brand. Buyers often use the extrinsic attributes to help them distinguish one brand from another because in certain categories it is difficult for them to make decisions based on the intrinsic attributes alone.

Why Brand?

Brands represent opportunities for both consumers and organizations (manufacturers and retailers) to buy and to sell products easily, more efficiently, and relatively quickly. The benefits are now considered from each perspective.

Consumers like brands for the following reasons. They:

- Assist people to identify their preferred products.
- Reduce levels of perceived risk and in doing so improve the quality of the shopping experience.
- Help people to gauge the level of product quality.
- Reduce the amount of time spent making product-based decisions and in turn decrease the time spent shopping.
- Provide psychological reassurance or reward, especially for products bought on an occasional basis.
- Inform consumers about the source of a product (country or company).

Branding helps customers identify the products and services they prefer to use in order to satisfy their needs and wants. Equally, branding helps them to avoid the brands that they dislike as a result of previous use or because of other image, associations, or other psychological reasoning.

Consumers experience a range of perceived risks when buying different products. These might be financial risks (can I afford this?), social risks (what will other people think about me wearing this dress or going to this bar?) or functional risks (will this MP3 player work?). Branding helps to reduce these risks so that buyers can proceed with a purchase without fear or uncertainty. Strong brands encapsulate a range of values that communicate safety and purchase security.

In markets which are unknown to a buyer or where there is technical complexity (e.g. computing, financial services) consumers use branding to make judgements about the quality of a product. This in turn helps consumers save shopping time and again helps reduce the amount of risk they experience.

Perhaps above all other factors, branding helps consumers develop relationships based upon trust. Strong brands are normally well trusted and annual surveys often announce that Nokia, Google, and British Airways are some of the most trusted brands. Similarly, these surveys declare those brands that are least trusted by consumers and very often these coincide with falling sales and reducing market share. Creating trust is important as it enables consumers to buy with confidence.

Many brands are deliberately imbued with human characteristics to the point that they are identified as having particular personalities. These brand personalities might be based around being seen as friendly, approachable, distant, aloof, calculating, honest, fun, or even robust or caring. Marketing communications play an important role in communicating the essence of a brand's personality. By developing positive emotional links with a brand, consumers can find reassurance through their brand purchases.

Manufacturers and retailers enjoy brands for the following reasons. They:

- Enable premium pricing.
- Help differentiate the product from competitive offerings.
- Encourage cross-selling to other brands owned by the manufacturer.
- Develop customer loyalty/retention and repeat-purchase buyer behaviour.
- Assist the development and use of integrated marketing communications.
- Contribute to corporate identity programmes.
- Provide some legal protection.

Branding is an important way for manufacturers to differentiate their brands in crowded marketplaces. This in turn enables buyers to recognize the brand quickly and make fast, unhindered purchase decisions. One of the brand owner's goals is to create strong brand loyalty to the extent that customers always seek out the brand, and become better prepared to accept cross-product promotions and **brand extensions**.

Perhaps one of the strongest motivations for branding is that it can allow manufacturers to set premium prices. Brands such as Andrex, Stella Artois, and L'Oréal charge a premium price, often around 20 per cent higher than the average price in their respective product categories. Premium prices allow brand managers to reinvest in brand development, and in competitive markets this is important in order to remain competitive.

The greater the number of product-based brands the greater the motivation for an organization to want to develop a corporate brand. Using this umbrella branding approach organizations only need to invest heavily in one brand, rather than each and every product-based brand. This approach is not applicable to all sectors, although in business-to-business markets where there is product complexity, corporate branding is an effective way of communicating and focusing on a few core brand values.

Types of Brands

There are three main types of brands; manufacturer, distributor, and **generic brands**.

Manufacturer Brands

In many markets, and especially the FMCG sector, retailers are able to influence the way in which a product is displayed and presented to customers. As a result manufacturers try to create brand recognition and name recall through their direct marketing communications activities with end users. The goal is to help customers identify the producer of a particular brand at the point of purchase. For example, Persil, Heinz, Cadbury's, and Coca-Cola are strong manufacturers' brands, they are promoted heavily, and customers develop preferences based on performance, experience, communications, and availability. So, when customers are shopping they use the images they have of various manufacturers, combined with their own experiences, to seek out their preferred brands. Retailers who choose not to stock certain major **manufacturer brands** run the risk of losing customers.

Distributor (or Own-Label) Brands

The various organizations that make up the marketing channel often choose to create a distinct identity for themselves. The term distributor or own-label brand refers to the identities and images developed by the wholesalers, distributors, dealers, and retailers who make up the marketing channel. Wholesalers, such as Nurdin & Peacock, and retailers, such as Argos, Harvey Nichols, Sainsbury's, Next, and HMV, have all created strong brands.

This brand strategy offers many advantages to both the manufacturer, who can use excess capacity, and retailers, who can earn a higher margin than they can with manufacturers' branded goods and at the same time develop strong store images. Retailers have the additional cost of promotional initiatives, necessary in the absence of a manufacturer's support. Some manufacturers, such as Kellogg's, refuse to make products for distributors to brand, although others (Cereal Partners) are happy to supply a variety of competitors. Occasionally conflict emerges, especially when a **distributor brand** displays characteristics that are very similar to the manufacturer's market leader brand. Coca-Cola defended their brand when it was alleged that the packaging of Sainsbury's new cola drink was too similar to their own established design.

Generic Brands

These are brands that are sold without any promotional materials or any means of identifying the company, whilst the packaging only displays information required by law. The only form of identification is the relevant product category, for example, plain flour. Without having to pay for promotional support these brands are sold at prices that are substantially below the price of normal brands. However, although briefly successful in the 1990s their popularity has declined and manufacturers see no reason to produce these 'white carton' products. Only firms in the pharmaceutical sector use this type of brand.

Brand Strategies

Brands constitute a critical part of an organization's competitive strategy so the development of strategies in order to manage and sustain them is really important. However, the original idea that brands provide a point of differentiation has been supplemented, not replaced, by an understanding of the relational dimension. Brands provide a way through which organizations can create and maintain relationships with customers. Therefore, brand strategies need to encompass relationship issues and to ensure that the way a customer relates to a brand is both appropriate and offers opportunities for cross-selling customers into other products and services in an organization's portfolio.

Brand Name

Choosing a name for a brand is a critical foundation stone because ideally, it should enable all of the following to be accomplished:

- Be easily recalled, spelled, and spoken;
- Be strategically consistent with the organization's branding policies;
- Be indicative of the product's major benefits and characteristics;
- Be distinctive;
- Be meaningful to the customer;
- Be capable of registration and protection.

Brand names need to transfer easily across markets and to do so successfully it helps if customers can not only pronounce the name but can also recall the name unaided. One of the reasons high-profile grocery brands are advertised so frequently is to create brand name awareness so that when a customer thinks of cat food they think of Felix or Whiskas. Names that are difficult to spell or are difficult to pronounce are unlikely to be accepted by customers. Short names such as Lego, Mars, Sony, Flash, or Shell have this strength.

Brand names should have some internal strategic consistency and be compatible with the organization's overall positioning. The Ford Transit, Virgin Atlantic, and Cadbury's Dairy Milk are names that reflect their parent company's policies that the company name prefixes their product brand names. Some brand names incorporate a combination of words, numbers, or initials. The portable 'sat nav' brand Tom Tom GO 910 and Canon's Pixma MP600 photo printer use names that do not inform about the functionality yet use a combination of words and numbers to reflect the parent company, product line to which they belong, and hint of their technological content.

A brand's functional benefit can also be incorporated within a name as this helps to convey its distinctive qualities. Deodorant brands such as Sure and Right Guard use this approach although Lynx relies on fragrance and dryness. Although the scope of the content has moved on, the *Radio Times* magazine has very high name awareness and recognition that its distinctiveness is a brand strength.

Most brands do not have sufficient financial resources to be advertised on television or in any mainstream media. Therefore, it is not possible to convey brand values through imagery and brand advertising. For these brands it is important that the name of the brand reflects the functionality of the product itself. So, the super adhesive brand 'No More Nails', Cling Film, and 'Snap-on-Tools' all convey precisely what they do through their names. For these brands packaging and merchandising is important in order to communicate with customers in store.

Finally, brands can represent considerable value to their owners and therefore names need to be registered and protected for two main reasons. First, brand name protection helps organizations prevent others from copying and counterfeiting the brand. Although copying products is now commonplace, preventing the use of the brand name helps protect the brand owners and enables them to maintain aspects of their brand positioning. The second reason for name registration is that the searches required when registering a name mean that the organization will not infringe the rights of others who already own the name. This can avoid costly legal arguments and delays in establishing a brand.

Brand Policies

Once a decision has been taken to brand an organization's products, an overall branding policy is required. There are three main strategies, individual, family, and corporate branding, and within these there are a number of brand combinations and variations in the way brands can be developed.

Individual Branding

Once referred to as a multi-brand policy, individual branding requires that each product offered by an organization is branded independently of all the others. Grocery brands offered by Unilever (e.g. Knorr, Cif, and Dove) and Procter & Gamble (e.g. Fairy, Crest, and Head & Shoulders) typify this approach.

One of the advantages of this approach is that it is easy to target specific segments and to enter new markets with separate names. If a brand fails or becomes subject to negative media attention, the other brands are not likely to be damaged. However, there is a heavy financial cost as each brand needs to have its own promotional programme and associated support.

Family Branding

Once referred to as a multi-product brand policy, family branding requires that all the products use the organization's name, either entirely or in part. Microsoft, Heinz, and Kellogg's all incorporate the company name as it is hoped that customer trust will develop across all brands. Therefore, promotional investment need not be as high as there will always be a halo effect across all the brands when one is communicated.

Line family branding is a derivative policy whereby a family branding policy is followed for all products within a single line. Bosch is a technology company operating in the automotive, industry, and home markets. Many of its products are branded Bosch but they use line branding for their Blaupunkt and Qualcast brands in their car entertainment and garden products divisions.

Corporate Brands

Many retail brands adopt a single umbrella brand, based on the name of the organization. This name is then used at all locations and is a way of identifying the brand and providing a form of consistent differentiation, whether on the high street or online. Major supermarkets such as Tesco in the UK, Carrefour in France, and ASDA Wal-Mart worldwide use this branding strategy to attract and help retain customers.

Corporate branding strategies are also used extensively in business markets, such as IBM, Cisco, and Caterpillar, and in consumer markets where there is technical complexity, such as financial services. Companies such as HSBC, Prudential, and FirstDirect adopt a single name strategy. One of the advantages of this approach is that promotional investments are limited to one brand. However, the risk is similar to family branding where damage to one product or operational area can cause problems across the organization. For example, organizations such as Hitachi Corporation, Dell, Apple, Toshiba, Lenovo, and Fujitsu all recalled Sony batteries during the summer of 2006 on advice by Sony themselves. Sony announced that they were recalling certain batteries in laptops because they could fuse, as pieces of metal were left in their cells during the manufacturing process in Japan (Allison, 2006). The recall was said to cost up to $265 m and involved approximately 6 million batteries worldwide. The immediate impact on Sony's reputation was that they had to revise both income and profit forecasts.

Brand extensions are a way of capitalizing on the recognition, goodwill, and any positive associations of an established brand (Hem, Chernatony, and Iversen, 2003), and using the name to lever itself into a new market. Mars successfully leveraged their confectionery bar into the ice cream market and in doing so deseaonalized their sales by providing income in the summer when chocolate sales are normally at their lowest. (See Market Insight 9.5.)

The attractiveness of brand extension is that time and money does not need to be spent building awareness or brand values. The key role for marketing communications is to position the new extended brand in the new market and give potential customers a reason to try it.

Successful brands are usually associated with a set of enduring brand values, often co-created by the brand and its loyal customers. These values provide the means through which brand extensions become possible but understanding these values can be critical. For example, Harley-Davidson's (HD) values are essentially rugged and masculine, born out of the power and rumble associated with the motorbike. This had contributed to the development of the HD brand but was not understood or recognized when the chain of HD shops began selling wine coolers, baby clothes, and fragrances. This alienated its very loyal customers and

Elastic Brands?

To get an insight into how some companies stretch their brands across new categories, consider the following two case studies as examples.

The organic chocolate bar Green and Black's is a Fairtrade brand, one that has been successfully extended into several related areas. Using organic chocolate as their platform, Green and Black's have moved into biscuits, gift packs, and even ice cream.

One of the Range Rover ads for its sports utility vehicles

Cogent Elliott/Alister Thorpe

A six-month waiting list developed when Range Rover extended their established brand into the sports utility vehicle sector. Using advertising and direct marketing to launch their sports model, the campaign included a direct mailer that contained a bottle of Tabasco designed to demonstrate the new brand's extra power.

Source: Gray (2006).

1 Make a list of four brands in different markets and think about how they might be extended.

2 How do you think the brand Green and Black's got its name? For the answer visit the Green and Black's website www.greenandblacks.com/uk/.

3 Why do you think it is so difficult to extend a brand?

the inappropriate products were withdrawn. Harley-Davidson had developed a strong brand by sticking consistently to making big, classic, US motorbikes and being proud about it. By moving away from this core activity and associating itself, through brand extensions, with categories that did not reflect the strong, masculine values, the brand alienated its customers and threatened the strength of the brand itself (Anon., 2006).

Licensing the trademark of an established brand and using it to develop another brand is proving to be another popular way of using brands. In return for a fee, one company permits another to use its trademark to promote other products over a defined period of time, in a defined area. Companies such as Disney use licensing because it provides revenue at virtually no cost and constitutes a form of marketing communications which takes the brand to new customers and markets. On the downside, brand licensing can proliferate the brand to the extent that the market is swamped with brand messages that fail to position the brand properly. In addition, problems with manufacturing or contractual compliance can lead to costly legal redress.

Licensing was for a long time a marketing activity that was the preserve of child-related toys, characters, and clothing. Now licensing is used increasingly with adult brands such as Gucci, Armani, Coca-Cola, and sports teams such as Manchester United, Formula One, and the national Australian cricket team.

Co-branding occurs when two established brands work together, either on one product or service. The principle behind co-branding is that the combined power of the two brands generates increased consumer appeal and attraction. It also enables brands to move into markets and segments where they would normally have great difficulty in establishing themselves. Another reason for co-branding is that it enables organizations to share resources based on their different strengths. The co-branding arrangement between Microsoft and the UK charity NSPCC (National Society for the Prevention of Cruelty to Children) gives the charity access to the financial resources of Microsoft for marketing communications to reach new donors and raise awareness of their cause. Microsoft benefit from their association with a softer brand, one that helps reposition Microsoft as a brand that cares.

Brand Equity

Brand equity is a measure of the value of a brand. It is an assessment of a brand's wealth, sometimes referred to as goodwill. Financially, brands consist of their physical assets plus a sum that represents their reputation or goodwill, with the latter far exceeding the former. So, when Premier Foods, who own Branston sauces and Ambrosia Creamed Rice, paid £1.2 billion to buy Rank Hovis McDougall (RHM), who own Oxo, Hovis, and Mr Kipling cakes, in 2006, they bought the physical assets and the reputation of RHM brands, whose sales amount to £1.6 billion annually (OFT, 2007).

Brand equity is considered important because of the increasing interest in trying to measure the return on promotional investments and pressure by various stakeholders to value brands for balance sheet purposes. A brand with a strong equity is more likely to be able to preserve its customer loyalty and so fend off competitor attacks.

There are two main views about how brand equity should be valued, namely a financial and a marketing perspective (Lasser, Mittal, and Sharma, 1995). The financial view is founded on a consideration of a brand's asset value that is based upon the net value of all the cash the brand is expected to generate over its lifetime. The marketing perspective is grounded in the images, beliefs, and core associations consumers have about particular brands, and the degree of loyalty or retention a brand is able to sustain. Measures of market penetration,

To take your learning further, you might wish to read this influential paper.

Chernatony, L. de, Harris, F., and Dall'Olmo Riley, F. (2000), 'Added value: its nature, roles and sustainability', *European Journal of Marketing*, 34, 1–2, 39–56.

This paper explores the meaning of added value, a key concept in branding. Based on research involving 'brand experts' the paper examines what the term means and how it is interpreted by both academics and those who practise branding for a living.

involvement, attitudes, and purchase intervals (frequency) are typical. In an attempt to overcome these two approaches Feldwick (1996) suggests that there are three parts associated with brand equity:

- **brand value**, based on a financial and accounting base;
- **brand strength**, measuring the strength of a consumer's attachment to a brand; and
- **brand description**, represented by the specific attitudes customers have towards a brand.

Brand equity is strongly related to marketing and brand strategy because this type of measurement can help focus management on brand development. However, there is little agreement about what is to be measured and how and when it is measured. Ambler and Vakratsas (1998) argue that organizations should not seek a single set of measures simply because of the varying circumstances and contextual factors that impinge on brand performance. In reality the measures used by most forms share many common elements.

Packaging

In an age when climate and environmental issues are becoming increasingly prominent, there is societal and political pressure to ensure that the design of packaging and the materials used are appropriate and capable of being recycled. Packaging, also examined in Chapter 2, is therefore an important aspect of product and branding strategy and one that can reflect strongly on the reputation and credentials of the brand and its parent organization.

There are two main roles that packaging has to perform, functional and communicative. The functional role refers to the need to protect products during transit, and while they remain in store or on a shelf prior to purchase and consumption. The contents need to be preserved and that means protecting them in order prevent damage, tampering, or deterioration. A further functional aspect of packaging is the convenience it should provide customers. Packaging which relates to the target market's preferred serving sizes, ease of opening, convenience of storage, and transportation can all contribute to a product's perceived added value.

The second role is to help customers, particularly in consumer markets, to make brand choice decisions by communicating elements of a package's content. At its simplistic level packaging should convey clear messages about the contents of the product, its features, uses, and any dangers that may arise from its use. Indeed the packaging itself can be a danger and statutory warnings are to be found on plastic bags. At a more complex level packaging should also convey messages that seek to add value and which try to develop positive attitudes, stand out among competitive products, particularly those on a shelf, and persuade buyers to pick up the item.

Sometimes the packaging is designed to complement the physical attributes of the product itself and can be a strong form of persuasion. For example, the Scotch whisky brand Famous Grouse redesigned its bottle with a more angular neck and decluttered the label. While these minor design changes might go unnoticed some believe that such subtle packaging changes can have a significant impact on customer perception and sales. In the year after the design changed UK sales volumes for Famous Grouse rose 6 per cent, in a market that fell 2 per cent (Dowdy, 2006).

Packaging can also be used as a means of brand identification and reassurance, as a cue by which buyers recognize and differentiate a brand. The unique shape of the Coca-Cola contour bottle gives it immense power to provoke brand recognition at the point of purchase and elsewhere.

Packaging has also been found to be strongly associated with the positioning of a brand, discussed previously in Chapter 5. Ampuero and Vila (2006) found that four elements of packaging, namely colour, typography, form, and illustration, can be configured in different ways so that they mean something particular to the target audience. Positioning strategy should encompass a product's packaging design.

Labelling

Labels are important because they can deliver information about product usage, help promote a brand, and enable the brand owners to comply with various regulations and statutory requirements.

All packages have to carry information concerning the ingredients, nutritional values, and safety requirements, including sell-by and use-by dates. In addition, labels should describe the source of a product, its main features, how to use, care, and store the product. Non-food packages must also attempt to be sales agents and provide all the information that a prospective buyer might need.

Labels are a primary means through which manufacturers try to make their brands stand out among the competition. This is important because the brand needs to be recognized quickly and then convey messages that reflect the key attributes and positioning of the brand. Labels also offer opportunities to manufacturers to harmonize the in-store presentation of their products in such a way that buyers from different countries can still identify the brand and remain brand loyal. For example, Buckley (1993) suggests that Unilever decided not to change their different brands of washing powder in favour of a pan-European brand. They decided instead to retain the existing names, which at the time consisted

Redesigning Sunny D

Sunny D was once a highly successful fruit juice brand. Apart from being given lots of shelf space in supermarkets, it achieved high media coverage because of its dubious nutritional content. It was said to have a very high sugar content, too many preservatives and a vast amount of 'e'-based artificial colouring. It was also notoriously low in fruit content and vitamins. After an initial few years of spectacular success under the ownership of Procter & Gamble, the brand faded and was sold to the Sunny Delight Beverages Company (SDBC) in 2004.

Sunny Delight
Beverages Company

Reinventing Sunny D

Part of SDBC's task was to revitalize the brand and to re-establish it in the market for all the right reasons, not the wrong ones. The product was reformulated with a new recipe that included more fruit juice, the removal of the artificial colourings, and a reduction in sugar. To help reposition the brand and to communicate everything that was new about Sunny D, new packaging and labelling information was required. Using a Parents Advisory Panel, the Sunny D brand now provides copious and explicit information about the nutritional content, even to the point of including a guideline daily amount (GDA), thought to be the first for a soft drink.

Source: Adapted from material at www.sunny-d.co.uk/home.php/.

1 Why do you think this brand was so successful, despite the poor quality of the original contents?

2 Visit the Sunny D website at www.sunny-d.co.uk and look at the information the brand provides through its labels.

3 Look at the new label and identify how it reflects the positive attributes of the new brand.

of Omo, Skip, Via, Persil, and All, and to package them in a similar way, using similar visual devices, typography, and colours. This not only allows customers to remain loyal but also presents opportunities to save on advertising and design costs and gain access to satellite and other cross-border media.

The third main task of labelling is to ensure compliance with the various regulations and statutory requirements. Cigarette cartons are required by law to display the notice that 'Smoking Kills' and food products must contain particular nutritional information. Whether this information is read or of use is debatable but the law requires that it be made available. Finally, many labels contain a barcode, the universal product code (UPC). This consists of a series of thick and thin black lines which is read by scanners at the till, or point of sale, to identify and update relevant stock and pricing information. (See also Market Insight 9.6.)

Chapter Summary

To consolidate your learning, the key points from this chapter are summarized below:

- Explain the nature and characteristics of products and describe the product/service spectrum.

  A product encompasses all the tangible and intangible attributes related not just to physical goods but also to services, ideas, people, places, experiences, and even a mix of these various elements. Anything that can be offered for use and consumption, in exchange for money or some other form of value, is referred to as a product. The product/service spectrum recognizes that many products combine physical goods with a service element.

- Identify and describe the various types of products and explain particular concepts relating to the management of products.

  Consumer and business products are classified in different ways but both classifications are related to the way customers use them. Consumer products are bought to satisfy personal and family needs and industrial and business products are bought either as a part of the business's operations or in order to make other products for resale. In order to meet the needs of different target markets, most organizations offer a range of products and services, which are grouped together in terms of **product lines** and **product mix**.

- Understand how the management of products changes over the different stages of the lifecycle and explain the process by which new products are developed and adopted by markets.

  Products move through a sequential pattern of development, referred to as the product lifecycle. It consists of five distinct stages, namely development, birth, growth, maturity, and decline. Each stage of the cycle represents a different set of market circumstances and customer expectations that need to be met with different strategies.

- Describe the principles of branding and explain the different types of brand.

  Brands are products and services that have added value. Brands help customers to differentiate between the various offerings and to make associations with certain attributes or feelings with a particular brand. There are three main types of brands: manufacturer, distributor, and generic brands.

- Explain the benefits that branding offers both customers and organizations.

  Brands reduce risk and uncertainty in the buying process. They provide a snapshot of the quality and positioning helping customers understand how one brand relates to another. As a result branding helps consumers and organizations to buy and to sell products easily, more efficiently, and relatively quickly.

- Understand why the value of a brand is important and explain some of the issues associated with measuring brand equity.

  Brand equity is a measure of the value of a brand. It is an assessment of a brand's wealth, sometimes referred to as goodwill. Financially, brands consist of their physical assets plus a sum that represents their reputation or goodwill, with the latter far exceeding the former. There are two main views about how brand equity should be valued, namely a financial and a marketing perspective.

- Explain how packaging and labelling can contribute to a brand's success.

  Packaging has a functional role to protect and preserve products during transit, and while they remain in store or on a shelf prior to purchase and consumption. Another role is to communicate elements of a package's content to help customers, particularly in consumer markets, to make brand choice decisions. Labels are important because they can deliver information about product usage, they can promote the brand, and third, they enable the brand owners to comply with various regulations and statutory requirements.

 Visit the **Online Resource Centre** that accompanies this book to read more information relating to products, services, and branding decisions: www.oxfordtextbooks.co.uk/orc/baines/

? Review Questions

1 Draw the spectrum of product/service combinations and briefly explain its main characteristics.

2 Identify the three levels that make up a product.

3 Describe the three types of convenience good and find examples to illustrate each of them.

4 Explain the difference between a durable and a non-durable consumer good.

5 Write brief notes that explain each of the six types of business products.

6 Explain the product lifecycle and identify the key characteristics that make up each of the stages.

7 What are the main stages associated with the new product development process?

8 Why should marketers know about the process of adoption?

9 Why is branding important to consumers and to organizations?

10 Write brief notes explaining the two main views about brand equity.

❓ Discussion Questions

1 Having the read the Case Insight at the beginning of this chapter, how would you advise Philips Electronics to develop a new product development programme? How would you suggest they balance their technological competences with market needs? What approach do you suggest they take in order to develop new products?

2 Consider the different types of consumer product and discuss how this knowledge can assist those responsible for marketing these products.

3 As a marketing assistant assigned to a major grocery brand (of your choice), you have noticed that your main brand competitors are pursuing marketing strategies that are significantly different from those of your brand. You have mentioned this to your manager who has asked you to prepare a briefing note explaining why this might be. As part of your note you have decided to refer to the role and impact of the product lifecycle on the strategies assigned to grocery brands. Your task therefore is to prepare a brief report in which you explain the nature of the product lifecycle and discuss how it might be used to improve your brand's marketing activities.

4 Discuss the view that it is not worth the huge investment that is necessary to develop new products, when it is just as easy to copy the market leader's products.

5 The celebrity chef Gordon Ramsay owns and runs a series of high-profile restaurants. He is opening restaurants abroad, stars in his own ground-breaking chef/food-based television programmes, and has a number of books and other business interests. Discuss the view that celebrities cannot be brands as they do not meet the common brand criteria.

📖 References

Allison, K. (2006), 'Apple recall deepens Sony battery crisis', *Financial Times*, 24 August, available at www.ft.com/cms/s/c2eab782-3394-11db-981f-0000779e2340,_i_rssPage=6700d4e4-6714-11da-a650-0000779e2340.html, accessed December 2007.

Ambler, T., and Vakratsas, D. (1998), 'Why not let the agency decide the advertising', *Market Leader*, 1 (Spring), 32–7.

Ampuero, O., and Vila, N. (2006), 'Consumer perceptions of product packaging', *Journal of Consumer Marketing*, 23, 2, 100–12.

Anon. (2006), http://brandfailures.blogspot.com/2006/11/extension-brand-failures-harley.html, accessed December 2007.

Boehringer, C. (1996), 'How can you build a better brand?', *Pharmaceutical Marketing*, July, 35–6.

Buckley, N. (1993), 'More than just a pretty picture', *Financial Times*, 13 October, 23.

Byrnes, J. (2005), http://hbswk.hbs.edu/archive/4569.html, accessed December 2007.

Chaffey, D., Mayer, R., Johnston, K., and Ellis-Chadwick, F. (2006), *Internet Marketing*, 3rd edn., Harlow: FT/Prentice Hall.

Chernatony, L. de, and Dall'Olmo Riley, F. (1998), 'Defining a brand: beyond the literature with experts' interpretations', *Journal of Marketing Management*, 14, 417–43.

——Harris, F., and Dall'Olmo Riley, F. (2000), 'Added value: its nature, roles and sustainability', *European Journal of Marketing*, 34, 1/2, 39–56.

D'Agostino, D. (2003), 'Walt Disney World resorts and CRM strategy: a better mousetrap?', 1 December, available at www.eweek.com/article2/0,1895,1604980,00.asp, accessed December 2007.

Dowdy, C. (2006), 'The radicals versus the tweakers', *FT*, 4 December, available at www.search.ft.com/, accessed 5 December 2007.

Doyle, P. (1993), 'Building successful brands: the strategic options', *Journal of Consumer Marketing*, 7, 2, 5–20.

Drucker, P. F. (1985), 'The discipline of innovation', *Harvard Business Review*, 63, May–June, 67–72.

Feldwick, P. (1996), 'What is brand equity anyway, and how do you measure it?', *Journal of Market Research*, 38, 2, 85–104.

Ghosh, S. (1998), 'Making business sense of the internet', *Harvard Business Review*, March–April, 127–35.

Gray, R. (2006), 'Grounded in reality', *Marketing*, 14 June, 33–4.

Hem, L., Chernatony, L. de, and Iversen, M. (2003), 'Factors influencing successful brand extensions', *Journal of Marketing Management*, 19, 7–8, 781–806.

Kotler, P., and Keller, K. (2006), *Marketing Management*, 12th edn., Upper Saddle River, NJ: Pearson.

Lasser, W., Mittal, B., and Sharma, A. (1995), 'Measuring customer based brand equity', *Journal of Consumer Marketing*, 12, 4, 11–19.

OFT (2007), www.oft.gov.uk/shared_oft/mergers_eaoz/361227/premier.pdf, accessed 2 December 2007.

Ozer, M. (2003), 'Process implications of the use of the internet in new product development: a conceptual analysis', *Industrial Marketing Management*, 32, 6 (August), 517–30.

Ritson, M. (2006), 'Strength in numbers', *Marketing*, 5 April, 16.

Rogers, E. M. (1983), *Diffusion of Innovations*, 3rd edn., New York: Free Press.

Tiltman, D. (2006), 'In with the new', *Marketing*, 1 February, 37–8.

Trott, P. (2007), 'The long and difficult 13 year journey to the markeplace: a case study of Pfizer's Viagra', unpublished, Internal Working Case Study, January.

Wind, J., and Mahajan, V. (1997), 'Issues and opportunities in new product development: an introduction to the special issue', *Journal of Marketing Research*, 34, 1, 1–12.

Wood, L. (1990), 'The end of the product life cycle? Education says goodbye to an old friend', *Journal of Marketing Management*, 6, 2, 145–55.

10

Price Decisions

Quality is remembered long after the price is forgotten.

Gucci family slogan

Learning Outcomes

After reading this chapter, you will be able to:

✔ Define price, and understand its relationship with costs, quality, and value.

✔ Explain the concept of price elasticity of demand.

✔ Describe how consumers and customers perceive price.

✔ Recognize which pricing policies are most appropriate for which situations.

✔ Understand how to price new products and services.

✔ Understand the conditions under which a price war is more or less likely to ignite.

P&O Ferries now operates in competition with low-cost airlines as well as low-cost ferry operators. How does it make its pricing decisions? We speak to Simon Johnson to find out more.

*Simon Johnson
for P&O Ferries*

P&O Ferries was part of the Peninsular and Oriental Steam Navigation Company. The company was taken over after 169 years of independence by Dubai Ports World (DPW), a large Middle Eastern ports operator, in 2006 for £3.92 bn, at a 15% premium above the offer from Singapore's ports operator, PSA. P&O is probably best known in the UK for its operation of ferries between the UK, Belgium, France, the Netherlands, and Spain, but it also operated container terminals and logistics operations in over 100 ports, offering its new owner the opportunity to expand its global reach.

However, the ferry division's outlook had not been so rosy a couple of years earlier. By the end of 2004, the challenge facing our marketing team was substantial. Ferry travel was in long-term decline as a result of the competition from low-cost airlines and the reduction of duty-free incentives, which had driven the 'booze cruise' day-tripper market—people who travelled from Dover in the UK to Calais in France for cheaper wine, beers, and spirits. In addition, the popularity of France as a holiday destination for the British was in decline. Ferry travel was

P&O Pride of Canterbury ship

P&O Ferries

starting to look outmoded. Annual passenger volumes for P&O on the Dover–Calais route dropped from around 10 m in 2003 to just over 7 m by 2005.

> *Rising crude oil prices, a declining advertising share of voice…and an ageing ferry fleet added to our woes*

But this wasn't all. Within the ferry market itself, we faced stiff competition on key routes from a new breed of low-cost ferry operators such as Speedferries and Norfolk Line, which had resulted in significant over-capacity in the market. Rising crude oil prices, a declining advertising share of voice (as low-cost airlines spent more and more on advertising), and an ageing ferry fleet added to our woes.

The company research we carried out among existing and lapsed passengers indicated that the low-cost airline model—of flexible, demand-based pricing and online ticket buying—had become widely understood by, and acceptable to, customers. To survive, we felt that P&O needed to do something similar with its own pricing approach. Research identified two key customer groups: the ferry *loyalists* who had stuck with the company despite intense competition and the *convertibles*, who could be persuaded to shift back to ferry travel having lapsed. We made the decision to develop a campaign with the key objective of delivering more customers, more cost effectively, online. Advertising messages which seemed to resonate were that travelling by ferry was more relaxing and less hassle than travelling by air, and customers wanted a simplified pricing structure, demonstrating greater value for money.

If you were developing the ticket pricing policy, how would you design it to clearly demonstrate value for money?

Introduction

Do you remember the last time you bought something which you thought was seriously expensive? Have you ever wondered whether others might have thought it expensive too? Just when is a price expensive and when is it not? How do companies actually set prices? What procedures do they use? Why do companies get involved in price wars? These are just some of the questions that we set out to consider in this chapter.

The chapter considers various approaches to pricing strategy used in business today. Our understanding of pricing, and costing, has been developed through accounting. The discipline of economics contributes to our understanding of pricing through models of supply and demand, which operate at an aggregate level (i.e. across all customers in an industry). The field of psychology has also contributed greatly to our understanding of customers' perceptions of prices. Marketing as a field integrates all these components to provide us with a better understanding of how the firm can manipulate price to achieve higher profits and maintain a satisfied customer base.

In this chapter, we provide an insight into how customers respond to price changes, a concept that economists call **price elasticity** of demand. We consider pricing decisions in relation to developing differentiated or low-cost approaches and the pricing of services. As a topic, pricing is perhaps the most difficult component of the marketing mix to understand because the price of a good is linked to the cost of all the many and various elements which come together to make a particular product or service. The marketing manager seldom controls costs and prices of a particular product, and usually refers to the accounting department, or marketing controller, to set prices for particular goods and services.

We also provide an indication of how to set prices for new products and services, and how to change prices to existing products and services. Since making price changes for products and services often invokes a response from competitors, who may also drop their prices, we include a section on how to avoid competitive price wars. In some markets, a company does not control its own price setting, and so we also consider in this chapter some of the markets where prices are regulated by government. Finally, we consider briefly how the internet is affecting pricing, particularly in the newly formed consumer-to-consumer market.

The Concept of Pricing and Product Costs

Pricing

Pricing is a very complex component of the marketing mix. The term **price** has come to encompass any and all of the following meanings: 'the amount of money expected, required, or given in payment for something; something expended or endured in order to achieve an objective; the odds in betting and also archaic value; or worth' (Concise Oxford English Dictionary, 2006). In marketing terms, we consider price as the amount the customer has to pay or exchange to receive a good or service. For example, when purchasing a McDonald's hamburger meal, the price exchanged for the meal might be $4.49, £3.49, 150 rupees, or 100 yuan depending on where you live. The $4.49 element is the price, the assigned numerical monetary worth of the hamburger. However, this notion of pricing a good or service is often confused with a number of other key concepts used in marketing when discussing how and why we set pricing levels, particularly cost and value.

Product Costs

In order to price a product properly we must also have some idea of what the product costs us to make or buy. Cost represents the total money, time, and resources sacrificed to produce or acquire a good or service. For example, the costs incurred to produce the McDonald's hamburger meal discussed above will include the cost of heat and light in the restaurant, advertising and sales promotion costs, costs of rent or of the mortgage interest accrued from owning the restaurant, management and staffing costs, and the franchise fees paid to McDonald's central headquarters to cover training, management, and marketing. Furthermore, there are costs associated with the distribution of the product components to, and from, farms and other catering suppliers to the restaurants. There are the costs of computer systems and purchasing systems. There are the costs of the packaging, bags, and extras like gifts and toys.

Typically a firm will first determine what their **fixed costs** are, and what their **variable costs** are in relation to each product or service. These items vary for individual industries but Table 10.1 provides some indication of what these are in general. Fixed costs are the costs which do not vary according to the number of units of goods made or services sold, so are independent of sales volume. In a McDonald's restaurant this could include the cost of heating and lighting, rent, and staffing costs. In contrast, variable costs vary according to the number of units of goods made or services sold. For example, with the production of McDonald's hamburger meals, when sales and demand decrease, fewer raw goods such as hamburger ingredients, product packaging, and novelty items such as toys are required, so less spending on raw materials occurs. However, when sales increase, more raw materials are used and spending rises.

The Relationship between Pricing and Product Costs

The relationship between price and costs is an important one. Costs for example are likely to be substantially less than the price assigned to a good or service, otherwise the firm would not make a long-term profit.

Table 10.1

Examples of fixed and variable costs

Fixed costs	Variable costs
Manufacturing plant and equipment (in a business selling product)	Equipment servicing costs
Office buildings	Energy costs
Cars and other vehicles	Mileage allowances
Salaries	Overtime and bonus payments
Professional service fees (e.g. legal)	Professional services fees (e.g. legal) in a business with a strong regulatory regime (e.g. pharmaceuticals)

Total Revenue = Volume Sold × Unit Price

Profit = Total Revenue − Total Costs

The price at which a good or service is set is an important strategic decision because increases in price typically have a disproportionately positive effect on profits and decreases in price typically have a disproportionately negative effect on profits. For example, in one study it was identified that a:

- 1 per cent improvement in price brings an 11.1 per cent improvement in operating profit;

- 1 per cent improvement in variable costs only brings a 7.8 per cent improvement in operating profit;

- 1 per cent improvement in volume sales brings a 3.3 per cent improvement in operating profit; and

- 1 per cent improvement in fixed costs brings only a 2.3 per cent improvement in operating profits (Marn and Rosiello, 1992).

Put another way, a 1 per cent profit increase, where the normal profit on sales is 10 per cent, is equivalent to 10 per cent gain on return on investment, and a 1 per cent profit increase where the normal profit on sales is 5 per cent represents a 20 per cent improvement on return on investment (Walker, 1967). Looked at from this perspective, price setting is a strategic concern and, where we can, we should be looking to increase prices every time.

However, deciding on exactly how to price a good or a service is not a simple task. Take the example presented earlier for McDonald's. A firm like McDonald's might well have 100 products on any one restaurant menu (including meals, individual burgers, ice creams, drinks, salads, etc.) in any one country. If we bear in mind that different countries have slightly different menus to incorporate food products for local tastes (for example, the Chicken Maharaja Mac™ in India where beef and pork are not eaten, and the McArabia™ Grilled Kofta available in Jordan), then we can imagine that, worldwide, McDonald's must have an enormous menu of products, despite the appearance of standardization. But how do we go about costing and pricing each individual product?

In any one restaurant how do we go about allocating fixed costs such as heat and light, rent and tax, amongst each of the individual products that we sell? And once we've allocated the fixed costs, how do we determine the true variable costs for each product? Once we've allocated fixed costs and determined the variable costs associated with a product, we need to set the initial price of a product. But costs of components, such as heat and light, and other costs are constantly changing over time. How do we go about determining whether or not we need to change our prices on any one item after we set them initially because of the changes in component costs? After all, we can't keep changing prices every single time a component cost changes. So, at what point do we decide to change a product price?

As you can see from this short example, determining a product's cost is not simple. In fact, determining the accuracy of a product cost is a complex exercise. Because of the cost of information, in order to increase the accuracy of the cost data, we also need to spend more time collecting and analysing the data. Therefore, determining costs is an exercise where we have to trade off the accuracy and the benefits and costs of data collection, storage, and processing (Babad and Balachandran, 1993). Determining costs and prices is made even more difficult when organizations are divided into separate profit centres, selling on to other divisions within the same company, especially when these adopt inefficient **transfer pricing** mechanisms (Ward, 1993). For example, Airbus, the airline company owned by parent EADS (European Aeronautic Defence and Space Company), assembles its planes using parts made in several European countries. When these parts are made by the respective divisions, they are sold on to the main holding company which assembles the plane from its component parts. The pricing mechanism it uses is known as transfer pricing.

But it's not just costs that matter; we might well observe changes in demand for our products, as customers' desires shift across our own product ranges and those of our competitors. In setting pricing levels, we must therefore consider our customers' price perceptions of our product offering.

Customer Perceptions of Pricing, Quality, and Value

Psychologists are particularly interested in how we react as individuals to the way products are priced. They ask the question how do we perceive prices and why do we perceive them as we do? Here we take into account individual perceptions of product quality and value and their relationship to customer response to the pricing levels assigned to a product offering.

Product Quality

Product quality is a very important concept when considering product pricing levels. Quality is defined as 'the standard of something as measured against other things of a similar kind; general excellence and/or archaic high social standing'

(Concise Oxford English Dictionary, 2006). The International Organization for Standardization has defined quality as the 'degree to which a set of inherent characteristic fulfils requirements' (ISO 9000). In this context, quality of goods and services relates to standards to which that product or service performs as a need-satisfier. For example a very high-quality car will more than satisfy both our aesthetic needs for aerodynamic beauty and our ego and functional needs for high performance road handling, speed, and power. But quality is not a single standard in a product or service. It encompasses many standards since there are many levels at which our needs might or might not be satisfied.

Goods and service quality is multifaceted (i.e. different functional and non-functional needs) and multi-layered (i.e. differing levels or intensities of satisfaction). The American Society for Quality defines quality as a subjective term, suggesting that each person has his or her own definition of quality. So, we prefer to talk of 'perceived quality'. We find consumers have differing views of the quality of the product offering they have purchased, e.g. some might be very dissatisfied, and some highly satisfied, with exactly the same product offering.

The Relationship between Product Quality and Pricing Levels

The relationship between price and quality (perceived quality) is complex. There is an assumption that as price increases so too does quality, and that in general price reflects quality. But this is not always the case. For example, 'snob' consumers in the fashion clothing and perfume sectors (see Amaldoss and Jain, 2005; Yeoman and McMahon-Beattie, 2006) assume higher prices reflect higher-quality garments and fragrances. The general idea that price indicates quality (**perceived quality**) assumes that the prices of goods are objectively determined by the interaction of supply and demand in competitive markets (Sjolander, 1992).

In truth, people within firms set prices, often in a less than dispassionate manner, so as to try to obtain the maximum profit possible. Various studies conducted to determine whether or not price bears a relation to quality have found that a general price–perceived quality relationship does not in fact exist (Zeithaml, 1988; Sjolander, 1992), except perhaps for wine and perfume (Zeithaml, 1988).

The Relationship between Perceived Value, Product Quality, and Pricing Levels

Value is defined as 'the regard that something is held to deserve; importance or worth; material or monetary worth; the worth of something compared to its price: at £12.50 the book is good value' (Concise Oxford English Dictionary, 2006). In marketing terms, perceived value refers to what we get for what we pay. It is often expressed as the equation:

$$\text{Value} = \frac{\text{quality}}{\text{price}}$$

This approach to value indicates that to increase a customer's perception of the value of a product offering, we must either lower the price, or increase the quality. In some ways, this is a simplistic concept of value. There are other intervening effects on the value we perceive a product or item to hold. Sometimes our initial

RESEARCH INSIGHT 10.1

To take your learning further, you might wish to read this influential paper.

Zeithaml, V. A. (1988), 'Consumer perceptions of price, quality and value: a means–end model and synthesis of evidence', *Journal of Marketing*, 52 (July), 2–22.

The above article was the first study to provide evidence, based on previous research and a literature review, in an exploratory investigation into how pricing relates to costs, quality, and value from a customer perspective. The authors suggest that marketers should understand quality from a customer perspective, determining how customers measure quality, recognizing that these evaluations change over time and that customers consider value as a function of both monetary and non-monetary terms, indicating that there are multiple means of increasing value to the customer.

assessment is faulty, or needs to be reconsidered. Sometimes as customers, we are not sufficiently skilled to recognize or evaluate the quality. The average wine drinker, for example, would not regard themselves as knowledgeable about wine and so might find it hard to work out the product quality without any hints from a wine expert.

Measuring Customer Price Perceptions

One way of ascertaining how customers perceive prices is by asking them. In an online consumer survey conducted at Bentley College and Emory University in the USA, American consumers were asked to provide their perceptions of price (i.e. positive, negative, or neutral) across a range of product and service categories (see Figure 10.1). The graph indicates that the American consumer has

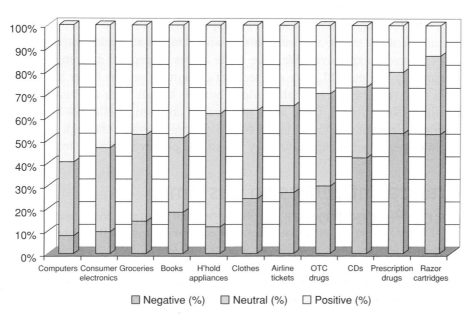

Figure 10.1

US consumer perceptions of price in different product categories

Source: Data taken from Sheth, Sisodia, and Barbulescu (2006). Reproduced with the kind permission of M. E. Sharpe, Inc.

the consumers' own minds, brought about through prior experience with those products and services or through word-of-mouth discussions with others. They depend on brand choice, purchase quantity, purchase timing (e.g. products bought at Christmas time in Western European markets tend to be more expensive than at other times), price history, promotion history, the shop visit history, whether or not the visit was planned, the store choice, whether or not the price was well advertised, whether or not the product is frequently purchased, whether there are different components of the product or service which make it easy to understand the pricing structure, and customer characteristics such as price sensitivity, brand loyalty, and so on. Reference prices do vary across consumers and so there is a clear opportunity to segment and target consumers on the basis of reference price (Mazumdar, Raj, and Sinha, 2005).

Think about it yourself. How much would you be prepared to pay for a haircut? In the UK, a male cut-and-blow-dry haircut would cost between £6 and £40 dependent on whether or not you went to a barber's or a hair stylist. A woman's cut-and-blow-dry haircut might cost between £20 and £60. So a salon charging £3.50 for a woman's haircut and another charging £350 would catch her eye. She probably would not trust the first place with a price of £3.50. She might well think that they would damage her hair or make a poor job of it. Equally, the £350 haircut, a haircut at a celebrity price, would have to be pretty special. So, the woman's reference price band for a haircut in the UK is around £20–60 or so and a man's is around £6–40.

But in addition to deciding whether or not a price is fair (how products and services ought to be priced), or what they expect to pay (expectation-based pricing) or what significant others would pay (so-called aspirational pricing), we also need to know whether or not customers are actually conscious of prices in a particular category or not.

Interestingly enough, people do not have as good a knowledge of prices as you might think. Think of your mum and dad or a friend or a relative significantly older than you. Do they know the price of a pop concert ticket? Do you know the price of a good-quality dining table? As an industrial buyer, how much should you pay for the installation and servicing of a new HR computer system, say Peoplesoft, designed to keep records for about 5,000 staff? How much should you pay as a supermarket buyer for 60 pallets (around 216 two-litre bottles) of Diet Coke from the wholesaler? We use these examples to indicate that our experience of prices contributes to what we know about reference prices but also to explain that our experience, by its very nature, is limited to what we have done in the past.

There is an American TV gameshow, *The Price is Right*, hosted by Bob Barker, where contestants have to guess prices of common household items, which has been shown on the CBS channel since 1972 and is probably America's best-known TV gameshow. The format of the show is so successful that it has been exported around the world. What is clear from the show is that people very often do not know the prices of many common household items (Anderson and Simester, 2003).

In a research study conducted in the 1960s for the *Progressive Grocer*, using seven commodity items (i.e. items people buy on a regular basis), only 51 per cent of respondents knew the correct price, 28 per cent guessed incorrectly and the other 21 per cent did not guess at all (Shapiro, 1968). In fact, there are certain groups of grocery items that supermarket shoppers are more likely to know, and it is these items that supermarkets frequently discount, and advertise, to attract shoppers, not the other lesser known items, where prices may even be raised. Examples include everyday items such as bread, milk, and tins of baked beans. Shoppers assume that because these items are discounted, all other items must be similarly so discounted. So, if people do not know the prices of goods and services, how can they possibly determine whether or not those prices are fair or reasonable?

To be fair to grocery shoppers, estimating reference prices is subject to seasonality for items such as flowers, fruit, and vegetables (particularly the more exotic varieties from around the world), quality and sizes of items are not universal across companies' offerings, product designs vary over time, and customers may not purchase some goods frequently (Anderson and Simester, 2003). Instead, when customers assess prices, they estimate value using **pricing cues**, because they do not always know the true cost and price of the item that they are purchasing.

Sale Signs

Sale signs act in this way, as cues, usually indicating to a potential customer that there is a bargain to be had, consequently this entices the customer to purchase, because it also suggests to the buyer that the item is desirable and so may be bought by another customer if we are not quick enough to buy it. The sale sign uses one of the most persuasive devices known in marketing, the notion of scarcity. The more scarce we perceive a product or service to be, the more we are likely to want it (Cialdini, 1993), often regardless of whether we even need it.

Odd-Number Pricing

Another pricing cue is the use of odd-number endings, prices that end in 9. Have you ever wondered why the Sony PlayStation you bought was say $199, or £149, or 749 (Polish) zloty? Why not simply round it up to $200, £150, or 750 zloty? According to Anderson and Simester (2003), raising the price of a woman's dress in a national mail order catalogue from $34 to $39 increased demand by 33 per cent but demand remained unchanged when the price was raised to $44! The question is why did the increase in demand take place when there was an increase in price? It is unlikely that there would have been such an increase, if the item had been priced at $38. The reason for this is that we perceive the first price as relative to a reference price of £30 (which is £33 rounded down to the nearest unit of ten) and more expensive while the second price of $39 we perceive as cheaper than a reference price of $40 (which we rounded up to the nearest ten). (See Market Insight 10.2.)

Purchase Context in Pricing

Another important element in pricing is the purchase context. In some cases, the purchase context can be used a frame of reference by the customer in determining prices. EasyJet when it was first set up in 1995 used this technique to its advantage when it advertised its flights as cheaper than a pair of jeans at £29

found that a $700 rebate for its Ranger Super Cab encouraged more than half of those customers considering the less expensive base model Ranger to upgrade to the higher-priced model. The lost revenues from purchases of the Ranger model were more than offset by the purchases of the higher-priced Ranger Super Cab, even after the rebate (Cross and Dixit, 2005). Similarly, credit card companies often offer cashback schemes on money spent on their credit cards, typically as a proportion of the total amount spent. Banks are increasingly offering mortgage deals for homebuyers using this approach, since homebuyers can then use the cash to purchase furniture or some other household necessity or save it.

Pricing Objectives

How a company prices its products depends on what its pricing objectives are. Typically, these can be financial with offerings priced to maximize profit or sales or to achieve a satisfactory level of profits or sales, or a particular return on investment. Companies may price by offering discounts for quick payment (see discount pricing). A firm's pricing objectives could be marketing based, e.g. pricing to achieve a particular market share (so-called market penetration pricing), or to position the brand so that it is perceived to be of a certain quality.

Sometimes companies price their products and services simply to survive. Examples might include pricing to discourage new competitors from entering the market (perhaps pricing products and services at a lower rate) or lowering prices to maintain sales volumes when competitors lower their prices (although this can be dangerous as we discuss later). Alternatively, a company might price to avoid price wars, maintaining prices at levels similar to its competitors (so-called competitor-oriented pricing). Finally, a company may price to achieve certain social goals. There are many ways in which a company can price its products and services.

The important consideration is whether or not the pricing objective is reasonable and measurable. Often companies pursue more than one pricing objective simultaneously and some pricing objectives may be incompatible with each other. For example, pricing to increase cash flow by offering quick payment discounts is not compatible with maximizing profitability. It is, however, compatible with

Photodisc

obtaining a satisfactory profitability, so long as the discounts offered are not greater than the cost of goods sold.

Pricing Approaches

The setting of prices depends on a number of factors including how price affects demand, how sales revenue is linked to price, how cost is linked to price, and how investment costs are linked to price (Doyle, 2000). Price setting also depends on how sales revenue relates to price. Raising prices tends to increase revenue up to a point, but then further increases in unit price produce declining increases in revenue. The relationship between price and sales revenue corresponds to the bell curve shape (see Figure 10.3a).

Third, investment costs, including both **working capital** and **fixed capital** (cost of plant and machinery etc.), also affect prices, with lower prices tending to require higher sales volume targets to be set, with correspondingly higher levels of investment. Investments tend to be made at fixed intervals (e.g. on a six-monthly cycle), with investment costs dropping compared to price increases (and sales volumes decreases) and so the relationship between investment and price looks something like a downward staircase (see Figure 10.3c).

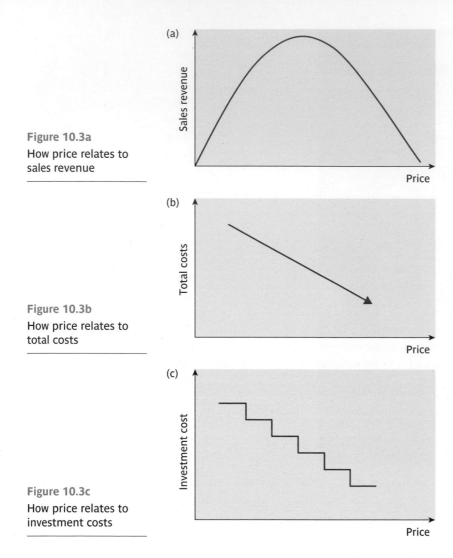

Figure 10.3a

How price relates to
sales revenue

Figure 10.3b

How price relates to
total costs

Figure 10.3c

How price relates to
investment costs

Broadly, there are four types of pricing approaches, each of which is described in the following sections:

1 the cost-oriented approach (where prices are set based on costs);

2 the demand-oriented approach (where prices are based on price sensitivity and levels of demand);

3 the competitor-oriented approach (where prices are set based on what competitors are charging); and

4 the value-oriented approach (where prices are set based on what customers believe to offer value).

The Cost-Oriented Approach

This approach to pricing has traditionally been the one best described in textbooks on pricing, and was considered to be the original theory of pricing. At the heart of the approach is the notion that the most important determinant of pricing is the cost of the scarce component resources that combine to make up the product.

The marketer sells output at the highest price possible, regardless of the firm's own preference or costs. If that price is high enough compared with costs, the firm stays in business. If not, either the firm find a way of increasing the price or lowering costs or both, or they go out of business (Lockley, 1949). The cost-oriented approach takes into account the total costs of a product or service in the pricing equation but does not take into account non-cost factors, e.g. brand image, degree of prestige in ownership, or effort expended.

The cost-oriented approach works on the basis that the most important element in pricing our offering is the cost of producing that offering. If we can make a set amount above what our product costs are, we can earn a profit. One approach to determining price is using mark-up pricing, a process used particularly in the retail sector.

This method operates on the base of a set percentage mark-up. When used, the cost-oriented method leads to the use of list prices (see later in this chapter), with single prices set for all customers. We simply add a mark-up to the cost of X per cent and this constitutes the price. In British supermarket retailing the mark-up is around 6–8 per cent, but in American supermarket retailing is often even less at around 4 per cent or less. Mark-ups on wine served in restaurants are typically between 200 per cent and 300 per cent. The cost-oriented approach requires us first to determine the price we set that just covers our costs. This is known as break-even pricing. It represents the point at which our total costs and our total revenues are exactly equal.

To exemplify the concept of mark-up pricing further, we can use the example of a computer company selling high-quality laptop computers, at a cost of £1,000 per unit to make. Suppose the computer company uses the mark-up pricing method and adds 40 per cent (or 0.4 when expressed as a decimal figure between 0 and 1). The final price set would be given by the equation below:

$$\text{Price} = \frac{\text{unit item cost}}{(1 - \text{mark-up})} = \frac{£1000}{(1 - 0.4)} = £1{,}667.$$

If we consider that in a supply chain there is typically more than one customer interaction, as we move along the supply chain, each partner takes their share, adding to the costs and the final selling price. So a toy, say a teddy bear, bought by a UK importer from a Chinese toy manufacturer based in Hong Kong, typically free on board (which means all costs after placing onto the ship are borne by the importer), brought to Britain, warehoused, stored, financed, and eventually sold at £5.90 (in cases of 12), may well have cost around £4.50 to that importer. The eventual retail price would probably be around the £10 retail price point, i.e. £9.99. The mark-up here for the retailer is 69 per cent = (£9.99 − £5.90)/£5.90. The mark-up for the importer is much lower at 31 per cent = (£5.90 − £4.50)/(£4.50). However, the importer may well buy a container of the teddy bears, comprising say 4,800 individual teddy bears (400 boxes, each containing 12 units), and sell these over three months between August until October for the Christmas retail season. The retailer, by contrast, may sell only 6 boxes of 12 during the period October until December so the retailer has to make a higher profit on a smaller volume with a wider range of items to give the customer some choice.

The cost-oriented approach does not always mean that we use a mark-up pricing approach. In some industries, prices are set based on fixed formulae, which are set with a supplier's costs in mind. For example, in the ethical prescription pharmaceutical industry, in France, Italy, and Spain, government-fixed formulae dictate prices with limited scope for pharmaceutical manufacturers to negotiate, while in the UK and Germany, the tradition has been for the country's national health authorities not to fix individual product prices but to set an overall level of profitability with which the pharmaceutical manufacturer must agree, based on a submission of their costs (Attridge, 2003).

The Demand-Oriented Approach

The demand approach to pricing works on the basis that the firm sets prices according to how much customers are prepared to pay. One of the best-known types of companies to operate this approach to pricing is the airline industry, where different groups of customers pay different amounts for airline seats with varying levels of service attached. Most airline companies operate three types of service. Malaysia Airlines, for instance, offers First Class, Golden Club Class, and Economy with the following core benefits:

- First Class—offers complimentary limousine transfer service to and from airports, substantial legroom between seats, individual stand-alone seating arrangements, luxury seating transforming into a comfortable bed, an enhanced in-flight entertainment service, gourmet cuisine served on fine china, personalized and individual attention from cabin crew, premier lanes allowing customers through immigration checks more quickly at selected airports, and free entry into the Golden Lounge executive club at selected airports.

- Business Class—offers complimentary limousine transfer service to and from airports, enhanced legroom between seats (but less than first class), double and triple seating arrangements, luxury seating transforming into a comfortable bed (but less recline than first class), an enhanced in-flight entertainment service (but with fewer options than first class), gourmet cuisine served on fine china (but with less luxurious options than first class), individual attention from cabin crew, premier lanes allowing customers through immigration checks more quickly at selected airports, and free entry into the Golden Lounge executive club at selected airports.

- Economy Class—comfortable seating with seating arrangements in banks of 3–5 seats, reclining seating, an in-flight entertainment service, and a selection of cuisine from two hot dishes.

By contrast the low-cost carriers in Europe such as Ryanair and EasyJet operate fairly sophisticated yield management systems which try to set prices to ensure planes operate at full capacity but which price tickets at substantially less than the national airline carriers such as British Airways, Lufthansa, Air France, and so on. The result is a low-margin, yield-based pricing policy.

Companies operating a demand pricing policy should be wary of overcharging their customers, particularly where customers urgently need a particular product or service. Examples include emergency purchases such as funeral services, or prescription pharmaceutical products for life-threatening diseases. When companies do set charges which are perceived to be unfair, they are liable to the claim that they are **price gouging**. In the pharmaceutical industry, allegations of so-called price gouging are frequent (Hartley, 1993; Spinello, 1992), because, unlike most industries, there are few or no alternative brands available. It is for this reason that governments regulate prices of pharmaceutical products around the world, to ensure that those products reach all patients, not only those who can personally afford to pay for them privately.

The Competitor-Oriented Approach

In this approach, companies set their prices based on the prices of their competitors, the so-called 'going rate'. This is also called 'me-too' pricing. The advantage of this approach is that when your prices are lower than your competitors, customers are more likely to purchase from you, providing that they know that your prices are lower, which is not always the case. (See Market Insight 10.3.)

Esso, the global oil company and petrol retailer, has for many years offered a scheme that it called Price Promise where it would provide a refund of the difference between the price of a litre of petrol at its garage forecourt and the price at a competitor's garage forecourt, within a specified distance, but only where that competitor charged a lower price.

Price guarantee schemes like the one outlined above are aimed at providing customers with the peace of mind of knowing that the company they are purchasing from is competitive in price. In reality, such schemes are often expensive to operate since they require continuous monitoring of the full range of competitors' prices, and a strong focus on cost control to maintain those competitive prices in the first place. Adopting a competitor-oriented pricing strategy can, and often does, also lead to price wars. But supermarket retailing is highly competitive in most major markets around the world, since there are frequently relatively few players in the market. In Australia, supermarket retailing is dominated by Coles and Woolworths/Safeway. When Coles introduced everyday low pricing, Woolworths introduced its 'price roll back' scheme, particularly in relation to milk and petrol prices (Sankey, 2003).

Price wars occur when competitors' pricing policies are almost exclusively focused on competitors rather than customers, when price is pushed downwards, and when pricing results in interactions between competitors which lead to unsustainable prices. In a review of more than 1,000 price wars, researchers found that price wars could usually be averted if companies responded to market-based, firm-based, product-based, and consumer-based early warning signals. In other words, some firms under certain circumstances within certain industries were more susceptible to price wars than others (see Market Insight 10.4; Table 10.3).

Calculating and anticipating competitors' responses is important when setting prices and responding to competitors' price cuts. But we do not always have to respond with a price cut in this situation. Instead, we might respond with improvements in service quality, to offer the customer greater value for money as a defensive strategy to offset the competitor's price reductions (Rust, Danaher,

Tesco's Value Pricing Approach

The leading British supermarket Tesco now retails grocery products around the world (e.g. in Japan and in Thailand with a local partner, as Tesco Lotus). In Britain, it has by far the largest market share of the retail grocery market with around 25% of market by value in 2005, against its nearest competitors' shares of 11% (ASDA Wal-Mart), 10.5% (Sainsbury's), and 8% (Morrison's). In order to remain competitive, Tesco conducts mystery shopping exercises, where market researchers pose as shoppers recording product, store, and service information, to check the prices of over 10,000 items against the prices charged by its key competitors (i.e. ASDA Wal-Mart, Morrison's, and Sainsbury's) on a weekly basis. Tesco call the scheme Tesco Price Check and make the results of the whole exercise available to its customers online, with an indexing facility allowing customers to search the website for the cheapest store on any one particular item.

Tesco's Price Check service is available online

Tesco

In order to defend its low-price image and reputation, Tesco has even resorted to taking ASDA Wal-Mart, its main supermarket rival, to the Advertising Standards Authority (ASA), over ASDA's claim to be 'officially Britain's lowest-priced supermarket' based on a survey by *The Grocer*, an industry magazine, of 33 product lines in late 2004. Tesco claimed the independent A. C. Nielson 500 survey found it to be around 1% cheaper across all lines in June and July of the same year.

Sources: Barnes (2004); Euromonitor (2006).

1 Do you think the cost of collecting all this competitor data on prices is justified commercially? Why?

2 How might Tesco use this price data in determining their own prices? What is the difference between promotional pricing and everyday low pricing and when might you use each one?

3 What other data do Tesco need to determine how customers perceive competing prices from different supermarkets?

Circumstances under which price wars are more likely to occur:	Table 10.3
	Circumstances under which price wars are more or less likely to occur

Circumstances under which price wars are more likely to occur:

1 As market entry occurs and an entrant gains or is expected to gain a sizeable market position
2 When an industry possesses excess production capacity; this will also stimulate the intensity of the price war
3 When markets had marginal or negative growth prospects
4 Where market power within an industry is highly concentrated
5 Where barriers to exit are greater (meaning it's more difficult to leave an industry, e.g. because of high investment costs)
6 Where financial conditions of at least one firm in the industry worsen or as a firm approaches bankruptcy
7 Where the product concerned is of strategic importance to the company
8 When a product is more like a commodity and so does not command a price premium
9 When firms introduce very similar products to one another
10 When there is little brand loyalty in evidence from customers, and
11 When customers are more highly price sensitive; this also increases the intensity of the price war

Circumstances under which price wars are less likely to occur:

1 One or more firms have established a reputation for strong and tough responses to past price wars
2 Where markets have intermediate levels of market power concentration (in other words, neither suppliers nor buyers are dominant in a market)

and Varki, 2000). Equally, we might also introduce another low-cost brand particularly aimed at the competitors' market segment, as the major airline manufacturers did when Ryanair and EasyJet opened low-cost airlines in the European market by setting up Buzz (KLM, the Netherlands) and Go! (British Airways), both of which have since been sold (to the low-cost airlines themselves!).

The Value-Oriented Approach

Even in the consumer durables category (e.g. furniture, white goods—washing machines and refrigerators—carpets), where we might expect customers to be

RESEARCH INSIGHT 10.3

To take your learning further, you might wish to read this influential paper.

Heil, O. P., and Helsen, K. (2001), 'Toward an understanding of price wars: their nature and how they erupt', *International Journal of Research in Marketing*, 18, 83–98.

The above article is unique in covering a very important topic of considerable interest to practitioners, which has received surprisingly little attention in the academic marketing literature. Price wars are defined with an insight into how they are likely to be characterized, as well as what early warning signals to look out for so that we can avoid cut-throat price competition in our pricing management efforts.

Vertu—Pricey or Priceless?

A more extreme example of the value-oriented approach in pricing is that adopted by Vertu, the exclusive mobile phone brand owned by Finnish industrial giant Nokia. Vertu offers diamond-encrusted mobile phones, available in the most prestigious high street and luxury shopping malls around the world with prices ranging between £4 k and 15 k when they were first launched in 2002. Vertu typifies the luxury brand. Nokia would have found it much harder to launch a luxury diamond-encrusted Nokia mobile phone.

The Vertu luxury brand of mobile phone

Vertu

In luxury markets, where prices can often seem extreme to the average person in the street, the key is to extend the price range and positioning of the brand to such an extent that it drives the aspirations of some of the wealthiest people in the world. Pricing in these situations may be decided based on a form of reverse-demand curve, especially as some groups of people (i.e. the risk averse and the prestige conscious) view price as an indicator of quality. In other words, for some goods, people are prepared to pay more for them the more expensive they are, simply for 'snob' value, for the sake of their own expensiveness, or because of their uniqueness. The challenge with the value-oriented approach to pricing is ensuring that you do not price a product or service so high that customers feel 'ripped off' rather than recognizing the true value of the product.

Sources: Wakefield (2002); Yeoman and McMahon-Beattie (2006); Zeithaml (1988); Shapiro (1968); Amaldoss and Jain (2005).

1 When a product is very valuable, do you think it is harder or easier to set its price? Why?

2 Do you think Nokia made the right decision in developing Vertu as a separate brand?

3 What other examples of luxurious products can you think of which are priced at very high levels? Why do some people continue to buy them, do you think?

when they are sold, acquired, or merged, and so it is likely that companies will increasingly focus on trying to generate price premiums for goods and services in a wide variety of markets in the future, particularly as a population's wealth increases.

Pricing Policies

In reality, in setting prices, the company has to trade off the factors associated with competition (i.e. how much competitors are charging for similar products/services), factors associated with cost (i.e. how much the individual components that make up our product/service cost), factors associated with demand (i.e. how much of this product or service will we sell at what price?), and factors associated with value (i.e. what components of the product/service does the customer value and how much are they prepared to pay for them?). Most pricing decisions are trade-offs between these and other factors. (See Market Insight 10.6.) So, while there are four main pricing approaches outlined in this chapter, there are in fact many different possible pricing policies which could be used and include the following:

- *List pricing*: this is an unsophisticated approach to pricing, where a single price is set for a product or service. Hotels frequently try to charge what they call 'rack rates' for hotel conferencing facilities, which combine residential accommodation for a set number of delegates with daytime accommodation for a seminar/workshop/conference, refreshments, and lunch.

- *Loss-leader pricing*: where the price of a product or service is set at a level lower than the actual cost to produce it. This pricing tactic is often used in supermarkets on popular, price-sensitive items (e.g. baked beans, milk) to entice customers into the store. The loss incurred on these items is made up by increasing the prices of other less price-sensitive items or absorbed as a short-term promotional cost on the basis that it brings in more customers.

- *Promotional pricing*: this occurs when companies temporarily reduce their prices below the standard price for a period of time to raise awareness of the product or service, encourage trial, and raise brand awareness in the short term. Such pricing approaches incorporate the use of loss-leaders, sales discounts, cash rebates, low-interest financing (e.g. some car manufacturers, such as Peugeot UK, typically offer low or 0 per cent interest-free financing deals), and other price-based promotional incentives.

- *Segmentation pricing*: where varying prices are set for different groups of customers. For example, Unilever's ice cream is offered as various different ice cream products at differing levels of quality and price ranging from their superpremium (e.g. Ben & Jerry's ice cream available in video shops, cinemas, and elsewhere) to economy offerings (e.g. standard low-priced vanilla ice cream available in supermarkets). Economists refer to this approach as **price discrimination** (see Chapter 11).

- *Customer-centric pricing*: Cross and Dixit (2005) suggest that companies can take advantage of customer segments by carefully measuring their value perceptions, measuring the value created, and designing a unique bundle of products and services to cater to the value requirements of each segment, and continually assess the impact this has on company profitability, taking advantage of up-selling (e.g. offering a customer a more expensive product or service in the same category) and cross-selling (e.g. selling other, different products and services to the same customer).

Pricing for New Products and Services

When launching new products and services, we adopt one of two particular pricing strategies. With the first, we charge a higher price initially and then reduce the price, recouping the cost of the research and development investment over time from sales to the group of customers that is prepared to pay the higher price (hence 'skimming' the market). In the second approach, we charge a lower price with the hopes of generating a large volume of sales and recoup our research and development investment that way (hence market penetration).

Figure 10.4 shows both market penetration and market skimming price strategies and their hypothetical impact on quantity demanded, Q1 and Q2 respectively. For any given demand curve, the market skimming price offers a higher unit price than the market penetration price. The actual amount sold at each of these unit prices depends on the price elasticity of demand and a more inelastic product demand curve would give greater revenue from a market skimming price than a market penetration price since the quantity sold would not be so different between the two prices. On average the market skimming price is likely to yield a lower quantity of goods/services sold than the market penetration price.

The skim pricing approach is a fairly standard approach for high-technology goods and services or those products and services that require substantial research and development cost input initially e.g. prescription pharmaceuticals. The UK pharmaceutical giant Glaxo priced its new anti-ulcer drug Zantac in 1981 at a

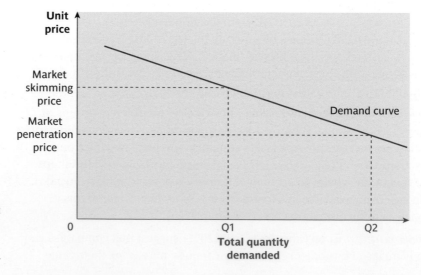

Figure 10.4
New product/service pricing strategies

Source: Adapted from Burnett (2002). Reproduced with the kind permission of the author, John Burnett.

English Higher Education: How Much for a Degree?

The pricing approach for undergraduate degrees has a significant impact on students

Photodisc

After the British government passed the Higher Education Bill, universities in England were able to offer variable tuition fees of up to £3,000 (€4,500) for undergraduate degrees for home students (from the UK and EU) from autumn 2006. Previously, home students were required to pay an upfront fee of £1,175 (€1,760), regardless of the type of course they were on, whether this was an engineering, science, humanities, or business and management degree. In reality, only a handful of university courses charged less than the £3,000 when the law allowed them to do so.

But what was different about this pricing approach was that from 2006, the students paid nothing upfront. Or rather, their parents paid nothing upfront as they were usually the ones who paid the fees. Instead, the government paid the £3,000 tuition fee to the university, and the student pays it back once they graduate, and as long as they earn over a set income. Since most undergraduate degrees in the UK are three years in length, the first students under the new system will begin to pay back their fees, in the form of loans which attract a set rate of interest at levels of inflation (around 3%), from autumn 2009. For international students (from outside the EU), fees remain uncapped which means that they can be up to two or three times higher than the rate for home students, particularly for postgraduate degrees and MBAs.

The rate remains capped for the home student tuition rate until 2010 and a change in the rate would require a parliamentary vote in the Houses of Parliament. But despite the increase in tuition fees some universities, notably Oxford University, have argued that the fee is still not high enough and does not reflect the true cost of teaching an undergraduate course, which is at least £6,000 (€9,000) higher (Halpin, 2005). There is also an argument that it costs a lot more to run a course in physics or chemistry (with the need for sophisticated equipment and laboratories) than it does to run a course in the humanities.

In addition, universities were expected to provide bursaries to support home students from poorer backgrounds, which is policed by a new official body called the Office For Fair Access (OFFA). Although the increase in prices caused a dip in applications for 2005/6, the Universities and Colleges Admissions Service (UCAS) reported that applications across the UK were up by 6.4% in 2006/7. So, it seems that many would-be home students think a degree is still good value, after all.

Source: Baker (2007).

1 What pricing policy has been adopted by most universities in England after the introduction of so-called 'top-up' fees?

2 Do you think it is fair that universities charge home (UK and EU) students a different price for undergraduate degrees compared with international students? Why do you say this?

3 If there was no government regulation on how universities might charge for undergraduate degrees, what are the main approaches that you could use to work out the price of a degree?

significant premium price compared to the market leader in major markets (UK, Italy, France, Germany, USA, and Japan), SmithKlineBeecham's billion-dollar blockbuster drug Tagamet. It did this despite the fact that there was little obvious improvement in performance of the drug, although it arguably had fewer side effects. The decision to price higher than the market leader ran counter to what the market research advice was recommending (which was to price at 10 per cent below the market leader to penetrate the market), and was taken by the then Glaxo CEO, Sir Paul Girolami. Sir Paul felt that Glaxo's previous major blockbuster drug, Ventolin, had been launched at a competitive price despite being better (in terms of performance) than existing competitors but had failed to reach its true market potential as a result. He decided to price Zantac differently, at what he felt the customer would be prepared to pay for a drug which Glaxo marketed as safer and which had no side effects, particularly on patients' sex lives (Angelmar and Pinson, 1992). The skim pricing approach is particularly appropriate under certain conditions (Dean, 1950; Doyle, 2000). These conditions are shown in Table 10.4.

The market penetration pricing approach is often used for fast-moving consumer goods and consumer durables items, where the new product introduced is not a demonstrably different product from existing formulations available. So, if a car manufacturer introduced a new coupé, which was relatively similar to its previous model, and had no new features, and was not significantly better than competing models, it would probably be priced using the market penetration pricing approach. Similarly, items aimed at capturing price-sensitive customers might well adopt this approach. New entrants to the multiple retail grocery market have tended to adopt penetration pricing, for example, the discount grocery stores Aldi, Netto, and Lidl, with limited success. The approach should be used under certain conditions when it is more likely to be most effective (Dean, 1950; Doyle, 2000), as outlined in Table 10.5.

Table 10.4
Conditions for effective skim pricing

1 When companies need to recover their research and development investment quickly
2 When demand is likely to be price inelastic
3 Where there is an unknown elasticity of demand since it is safer to offer a higher price and then lower it, than offer a lower price and try to increase it
4 Where there are high barriers to entry within the market
5 Where there are few economies of scale or experience
6 Where product lifecycles are expected to be short

Table 10.5
Conditions for effective market penetration pricing

1 Where there is a strong threat of competition
2 When our product/service is likely to exhibit a high price elasticity of demand in the short term
3 Where there are substantial savings to be made from volume production
4 Where there are low barriers to entry
5 Where product lifecycles are expected to be long
6 Where there are economies of scale and experience to take advantage of

RESEARCH INSIGHT 10.4

To take your learning further, you might wish to read this influential paper.

Dean, J. (1950), 'Pricing policies for new products', *Harvard Business Review*, November, 45–53 (reprinted with retrospective commentary in *HBR*, November–December, 1978).

A very early seminal article introducing the reader to the concepts of price skimming and penetration pricing as pricing policies for pioneer product marketers. The author indicates that the new product should be priced through the customers' eyes, by consideration of the rate of return of a customer's investment. Reprinted twice since its original publication in *Harvard Business Review*, this article remains a classic, as true today as it was when it was first written.

Pricing in the Business-to-Business Setting

Business-to-business markets exist on the basis that firms sell products and services to one another rather than to end users. The demand for their products and services comes from the demand for the finished goods and services required by the end user. The role of business-to-business marketers is to manufacture, assemble, store, wholesale, import or export, finance, research and develop, or commercialize market offerings (or some combination of these activities) or to offer commercial services or products to firms who are involved in doing these activities.

Business markets are different in the sense that buyers are usually professionally trained purchasing executives, often professionally accredited (e.g. the Chartered Institute of Purchasing and Supply in the UK), and have frequently attended training programmes to familiarize themselves with the products and services bought within their own organizations. Their function within the company as organizational buyers is a highly technical one, even for an apparently simple product. For example, German buyers of stationery based in Frankfurt would typically need to know for a simple pen set in blister packaging what the market prices are for various types of stationery products and the components that make them up. For instance, the pens themselves may be bought in Italy, packaging and printing from China, refills from Germany, and the final product assembled in Bulgaria. They would typically make their purchases either at a trade fair, at their own premises having been visited by various sales representatives, at the showrooms and offices of the various companies from which they buy, or online using an extranet website or an e-procurement portal. Because the buying function is technical, the relationship between the buyer and the supply is even more important.

The buyer–seller dyadic (i.e. two-way) relationship is the fundamental component of the business-to-business marketing interaction. Pricing has an important function in this relationship. If a buyer thinks he or she is being overcharged, he or she will quickly look elsewhere. Equally, if a seller is forced to make a sale too cheaply and is reprimanded for this by his or her superiors, he or she will not wish to sell at that lower price in future, and the relationship may be equally damaged. Under such circumstances, the seller may then seek to sell elsewhere.

In the business-to-business context, the discussion of price takes place between the buyer and the seller in an atmosphere where both are trying to make the best commercial decision for their organizations. The seller wants to sell at a high price to make the maximum profit, and the buyer wants to buy at a low price to lower his or her own costs and maximize profits. Their task is to resolve their mutual needs in a win-win situation (otherwise if one side is taken advantage of, the relationship is less likely to last in the longer term).

From the business-to-business seller's perspective, there are numerous approaches to pricing products and services including the following:

- *Geographical pricing*: prices are determined on the basis of where customers are located (e.g. pharmaceutical companies often sell their prescription drugs at varying prices in different countries at levels set by the governments themselves rather than the pharmaceutical companies). This might include FOB (free on board) factory prices where the price represents the cost of the goods and the buyer must pay for all transport costs incurred. FOB destination pricing is where the manufacturer agrees to cover the cost of shipping to the destination but not transport costs incurred on arrival at the port (air or sea).

- *Negotiated pricing*: prices are set according to specific agreements between a company and its clients or customers (e.g. professional services such as architectural or structural engineering practices or IT installation and servicing). This approach typically occurs where a sale is complex and consultative, but sales and marketing representatives should beware of conceding on price too quickly before properly understanding a client's needs for the product or service (Rackham, 2001).

- *Discount pricing*: companies reduce the price of a good or service on the basis that a customer is prepared to commit either to buying a large volume of that good or service now or in the future or paying for it within a specified time period. Large retailers work on the discount principle when buying goods for their stores. Their mighty procurement budgets and long experience ensure that they buy at cheaper prices from their manufacturer suppliers and so lower their costs. Consequently, they can set their own cheaper prices to their retail customers. Sometimes discount pricing works on the basis of payment terms. For example in the British toy and gift market, where retail buyers are used to buying their goods on credit, suppliers frequently offer their retail buyers discounts for quicker payment (e.g. 5 per cent discount for payment within 7 days, 2.5 per cent 14 days). However, each time a product or service price is reduced, we disproportionately reduce the operating profit (Marn and Rosiello, 1992).

- *Value-in-use pricing*: this approach focuses our attention upon customer perceptions of product attributes and away from cost-oriented approaches. It uses an approach which prices products and services according to what the customer is prepared to pay for individual benefits received from that product or service so the company must first ascertain what benefit components the customer perceives to be important, then quantify those benefit values, then determine the price equivalence of value, then rate competitive and alternative products to provide a benchmark for price determination, then quantify the value in use (i.e. the value in using our product vis-à-vis our competitors), and only then do we actually fix the price (see Christopher, 1982, for a more detailed discussion). The approach is a particularly useful one for industrial products and services, although the actual process of price determination is complex.

- *Relationship pricing*: this approach to pricing is based on understanding a customer's needs and pricing the product or service according to these needs in order to generate a long-term relationship. This could mean offering good financial terms, perhaps credit or more lenient time periods for payment, or discounts on the basis of product/service volumes predicted into the future. The difficulty with this approach is that it relies on a greater degree of trust and commitment between the two companies particularly on the part of the seller in relation to the buyer. Where this trust is misplaced, the seller incurs an **opportunity cost**.

- *Transfer pricing*: this occurs in very large organizations where there is considerable internal dealing between different divisions of the company and across national boundaries. Prices may be set at commercial rates, on the basis of negotiated prices between divisions, or using a cost-based approach. It entirely depends on whether each division is a cost- or profit-centre. The danger is that such internal dealings can sometimes mean that the final product or service is priced at too high a level for the customer. A good example of a company which adopts this approach is Airbus Industries, the European aircraft manufacturer, owned by parent company EADS (European Aeronautic Defence and Space Company), which constructs its planes built from components made in several different countries.

- *Economic value to the customer (EVC) pricing*: this approach works on the basis that a company prices an industrial good or service according to its value to the purchasing organization typically through a comparison with a reference or market-leading product or service, taking into consideration not only the actual purchase price of the product or service, but start-up and post-purchase costs as well to give an overall indication of how much better your pricing structure is, compared with that of a competitor.

Tendering and Bidding

In business-to-business markets, companies bid for the right to provide products and services for a fixed period of time to a successful bidder through a competitive bidding process. In other words, a company sets up a form of competition (the tender process) where they either ask a number of selected companies (their 'preferred suppliers') or they set an open competition where they ask any number of companies to put together a proposal for a set of services or the supply of products and services (known as a bid), which has to be submitted by a set deadline. Where a company does not have a pool of preferred suppliers, or wants to widen its pool of potential suppliers, this phase is sometimes preceded by an initial phase where the company invites 'expressions of interest' from interested potential suppliers. The submissions are then screened by the company, which removes those companies that it does not want to deal with, and the rest are advanced to the next phase of the competition.

The company goes on to consider the individual full bids in some form of ranking process, often requiring the bid submitters to make a presentation and discuss the detail of their bids individually. On the basis of those bids and the presentation, either the company will make a choice of who they want to supply their company, or they will take the process to a second round or third round of bidding, and so on. Eventually, they will decide to which company they want to award the temporary contract. The tendering process is a set requirement for the provision of public services and goods in the European Union above certain financial values of contract with strict rules on how the contracts must be promoted and awarded.

Private companies dealing with private companies tend to adopt the same forms of bidding and tendering, but without the same level of strict regulation. Generally, the formal tendering and bidding process takes a considerable period of time, effort, and expense.

Bidding processes like that described are common in industrial markets, and are used around the world as a means to introduce competition, particularly to the provision of public sector services, such as in telecommunications, public utilities (such as gas, electricity, and water), transport (e.g. train, underground, monorail, maglev), oil and gas exploration, defence contracting, and so on.

The difficulty in designing, writing, and submitting a suitable contract is that the details of competitors' bids usually remain highly confidential. When trying to second guess competitors' bid prices it is important to use the sales force as a source of intelligence (since they often pick up information from talks with friendly companies that they supply and even colleagues in other companies at industry events). The manager should know his or her own profitability when determining the price and aim to discover the winning bidder's name and price on lost jobs, although this is not always possible (Walker, 1967). Ross (1984) argues that it is often better not to ask 'what price will it take to win this order?' but 'Do we want this order, given the price our competitors are likely to quote?' There is the notion of the **winner's curse**, where the winning bidder obtains an unprofitable contract which she or he is duty bound to deliver because their bid price was set so low so that they won the contract.

Sometimes, companies and governments have apparently breached laws to obtain confidential commercial intelligence on pricing. For instance, controversy still surrounds the $40 billion Al Yamamah 'Oil for Arms' deal negotiated by the British Ministry of Defence officials and BAE Systems executives with the Kingdom of Saudi Arabia, in 1985, against French government competition, apparently because Britain's secret services allegedly learned France's rival bid details about which Saudi officials they intended to bribe and the size of their commissions (Urban, 1996).

Ten years later, the American defence contractor Raytheon allegedly walked away with a $1.4 billion Brazilian contract for a satellite surveillance system due to go to the French company Thomson CSF, after the CIA (US secret service, Central Intelligence Agency) discovered that bribes had been paid to Brazilian officials and intervened in negotiations (Smith, 1996).

Chapter Summary

To consolidate your learning, the key points from this chapter are summarized below:

- Define price, and understand its relationship with costs, quality, and value.

    Price, costs, quality, and value are all interrelated. Price is what a product or service is sold for and cost is what it is bought for. When value is added to a good or service the price that can be obtained for that good exceeds the cost. The two are often confused and assumed even by major international dictionaries to be the same thing. They are not. Quality is a measure of how well a product or service satisfies the need it is designed to cater for. Value is a function of the quality of a good or service as a proportion of the price paid.

- Explain the concept of price elasticity of demand.

    Price elasticity of demand is an important concept in marketing. It allows us to determine how the quantity of a good or service relates to the price at which it is offered. Inelastic goods and services are defined as such because increases (decreases) in price produce relatively smaller decreases (increases) in sales volumes, where elastic goods have larger similar effects. We need to understand this concept in order to understand demand-oriented pricing mechanisms.

- Describe how customers and consumers perceive price.

    Understanding how customers and consumers perceive pricing is important when setting prices. Customers tend to have an idea of reference prices based on either what they ought to pay for a good or service, what others would pay, or what they would like to pay. Their knowledge of actual prices is actually limited to well-known and frequently bought and advertised goods and services. Consequently, customers tend to rely on price cues such as odd-number pricing, sale signs, the purchase context, and price bundles to determine whether or not value exists in a particular offering.

- Recognize which pricing policies are most appropriate for which situations.

    There are a variety of different pricing policies in operation which can be used dependent on whether you are pricing for a consumer or industrial product or service. They tend to be either cost oriented (based on what you paid for it and what mark-up you intend to add), competitor oriented (the so-called 'going rate' or based on what price competitors sell a product or service at), demand oriented (based on how much of a good or service can be sold at what price), or value oriented (what attributes of the product or service are of benefit to your customer and what will they pay for them?).

- Understand how to price new products and services.

    The two dominant approaches to pricing new products and services are the market skimming pricing method and the market penetration pricing method. The former is favoured when a company needs to recover its R&D investment quickly, when customers are price insensitive or of unknown price sensitivity, when product lifecycles are short, and barriers to entry to competitors are high. The latter is favoured when these conditions are not in existence.

- Understand the conditions under which a price war is more or less likely to ignite.

  Price wars can devastate companies within industries. Research indicates that it is usually better to avoid price wars by recognizing the early warning signals. Eleven signals are outlined which indicate when price wars are more likely including factors related to the industry (e.g. low growth rates), the firm itself (e.g. where the product is of strategic importance to the company), the product category (e.g. where it is a commodity), and the nature of the customers (e.g. where they are price sensitive), and two factors which reduce the incidence of price wars, including when competitors have a reputation for swift retaliatory pricing actions and when there are intermediate levels of market power.

 Visit the **Online Resource Centre** that accompanies this book to read more information relating to price decisions: www.oxfordtextbooks.co.uk/orc/baines/

? Review Questions

1 Define price, cost, quality, and value in your own words.

2 Explain the concept of price elasticity of demand, naming examples of products which are both price elastic and price inelastic.

3 What are pricing cues?

4 What pricing policies are most appropriate for which situations?

5 What are the main business-to-business pricing policies?

6 What are the main two approaches to pricing for new products and services?

7 When should you use price skimming as a pricing approach?

8 When should you use market penetration as a pricing approach?

9 Describe in your own words the economic value to the customer pricing approach.

? Discussion Questions

1 Having read the Case Insight at the beginning of this chapter, what approach to ticket pricing would you advise P&O Ferries to adopt? Why do you think this approach would be more effective than the alternative possibilities?

2 A range of scenarios are presented below in which you are given some information on the price context. What pricing policy would you use when setting the price in the following situation (state the assumptions under which you are working when you decide on which one)?

   (a) The owner of a newly refurbished themed Irish pub in a central city location (e.g. Paris) wants to set the prices for his range of beers with the objective of attracting a new customer base.

(b) Explain which pricing policies the product manager at Italian car maker Alfa Romeo might have used when they set the price that they did for the 2006 launch of the Alfa Brera 2+2 seater coupé at prices starting from £22,800 on the road in the UK.

(c) You are the manager at a large well-known consulting services organization (e.g. Boston Consulting Group) in Germany, and your client, from a €15 m turnover medium-sized import/export company, commissions a study from you on how they can improve their marketing operations. What further information would you require in order to price such a study and what pricing approach would you adopt and why?

3 How would you go about determining the price sensitivity of your customers if you were a cinema marketing manager and you wanted your cinema to operate at full capacity throughout the week, including the weekday matinee slots (between 9 a.m. and 5 p.m.) not just at weekends and in the evenings?

4 Identify a shop owner or an entrepreneur with which you are familiar. Ask them how they set the prices for the product or services that they sell? What pricing policies do they use?

5 Research and examine the prices of ten different items in three different supermarkets (finding similar or identical products and pack sizes in each where possible to allow easier comparison). What are the average prices for each of the items and how does each supermarket compare with the average?

📖 References

Ailawadi, K., Lehmann, D. R., and Neslin, S. A. (2003), 'Revenue premium as a outcome measure of brand equity', *Journal of Marketing*, 67 (October), 1–17.

Amaldoss, W., and Jain, S. (2005), 'Pricing of conspicuous goods: a competitive analysis of social effects', *Journal of Marketing Research*, 42 (February), 30–42.

Anderson, E., and Simester, D. (2003), 'Mind your pricing cues', *Harvard Business Review*, September, 96–103.

Angelmar, R., and Pinson, C. (1992), 'Zantac A', *Case Study* 592-045-1, Fontainbleau, France: INSEAD.

Attridge, J. (2003), 'A single European market for pharmaceuticals: could less regulation and more negotiation be the answer?', *European Business Journal*, 15, 3, 122–43.

Avert (2001), 'Number of people living with HIV/AIDS reaches 40 million', *Global HIV and AIDS News*, available at www.avert.org.uk/news.htm, accessed 28 December 2007.

Babad, Y. M., and Balachandran, B. V. (1993), 'Cost driver optimisation in activity-based costing', *Accounting Review*, 68, 3, 563–75.

Baker, M. (2007), 'What price a university degree?', BBC News 24, 17 February, available at http://news.bbc.co.uk/1/hi/education/4749575.stm, accessed 15 June 2007.

Barnes, R. (2004), 'Tesco complains to ASA over Asda low-price ads', *Marketing*, 8 November.

Bhaskaran, S., Rajakumari, D., Kumar, K., and Dilipan, A. (2005), 'HLL vs P&G: price wars—an effective business strategy', *Case Study* 505-122-1, Chennai, India: ICFAI Business School.

Bijmolt, T. H. A., van Heerde, H. J., and Pieters, R. G. M. (2005), 'New empirical generalisations on the determinants of price elasticity', *Journal of Marketing Research*, 42 (May), 141–56.

Brennan, R., and Baines, P. (2006), 'Is there a morally right price for anti-retroviral drugs in the developing world?', *Business Ethics: European Review*, 15, 1, 29–43.

Burnett, J. (2002), *Core Concepts in Marketing*, London: John Wiley and Sons.

Christopher, M. (1982), 'Value-in-use pricing', *European Journal of Marketing*, 16, 5, 35–46.

Cialdini, R. B. (1993), *Influence: The Psychology of Persuasion*, New York: Quill William Morrow.

Concise Oxford English Dictionary (2006), 'Price', 'Value', 'Quality', available at www.oxfordreference.com, accessed 8 October 2006.

Cross, R. G., and Dixit, A. (2005), 'Customer-centric pricing: the surprising secret for profitability', *Business Horizons*, 48, 483–91.

Dean, J. (1950), 'Pricing policies for new products', *Harvard Business Review*, November, 45–53.

Dolan, R. J., and Simon, H. (1997), *Power Pricing: How Managing Price Transforms the Bottom Line*, New York: Free Press.

Doyle, P. (2000), *Value-Based Marketing: Marketing Strategies for Corporate Growth and Shareholder Value*, Chichester: John Wiley and Sons.

Euromonitor (2006), *Retailing—United Kingdom*, 5 December, Euromonitor International: Global Market Information Database, available at www.gmid.euromonitor.com, accessed December 2007.

Foxall, G. (1972), 'A descriptive theory of pricing for marketing', *European Journal of Marketing*, 6, 3, 190–4.

Gourville, J., and Soman, D. (2002), 'Pricing and the psychology of consumption', *Harvard Business Review*, September, 90–6.

Halpin, T. (2005), 'Oxford may cut undergraduates to save £200m', *The Times*, 21 September, 2.

Hartley, R. F. (1993), *Business Ethics: Violations of the Public Trust*, New York: John Wiley and Sons.

Heil, O. P., and Helsen, K. (2001), 'Toward an understanding of price wars: their nature and how they erupt', *International Journal of Research in Marketing*, 18, 83–98.

ING Barings (1999), 'The demographic impact of AIDS on the South African economy', *Company Report*, December, Johannesburg.

Lockley, L. C. (1949), 'Theories of pricing in marketing', *Journal of Marketing*, 13, 3, 364–7.

Marn, M. V., and Rosiello, R. L. (1992), 'Managing price, gaining profit', *Harvard Business Review*, September–October, 84–94.

Mazumdar, T., Raj, S. P., and Sinha, I. (2005), 'Reference price research: review and propositions', *Journal of Marketing*, 69 (October), 84–102.

Mintel (2005), *Food Retailing—UK: November 2005*, London: Mintel, available at www.mintel.com, accessed December 2007.

Nunes, J. C., and Boatwright, P. (2001), 'Pricey encounters', *Harvard Business Review*, July–August, 18–19.

Parkin, M. (1990), *Microeconomics*, 1st edn., Wokingham: Addison-Wesley.

Rackham, N. (2001), 'Winning the price war', *Sales and Marketing Management*, 253, 11 (November), 26.

Rice, M. (2001), 'An introduction to brand/perceptual mapping', available at www.yorku.ca/faculty/academic/mrice/index/docs/brandmap.htm, accessed December 2007.

Ross, E. B. (1984), 'Making money with proactive pricing', *Harvard Business Review*, November–December, 145–55.

Rust, R. T., Danaher, P. J., and Varki, S. (2000), 'Using service quality data for competitive marketing decisions', *International Journal of Service Industry Management*, 11, 5, 438–69.

Sankey, J. (2003), 'Retail wars just boomerang back', *Precision Marketing*, 29 August, 3.

Shapiro, B. P. (1968), 'The psychology of pricing', *Harvard Business Review*, July–August, 14–25, 160.

Sheth, J. N., Sisodia, R. S., and Barbulescu, A. (2006), 'The image of marketing', in J. N. Sheth and R. S. Sisodia (eds.), *Does Marketing Need Reform*, New York: M. E. Sharpe, Inc., 26–36.

Sjolander, R. (1992), 'Cross-cultural effects of price on perceived product quality', *European Journal of Marketing*, 26, 7, 34–44.

Smith, G. E., and Nagle, T. T. (1995), 'Frames of reference and buyer's perceptions of value', *California Management Review*, 38, 1, 98–116.

Smith, M. (1996), *New Cloak, Old Dagger: How Britain's Spies Came in from the Cold*, London: Victor Gollancz.

Spinello, R. A. (1992), 'Ethics, pricing and the pharmaceutical industry', *Journal of Business Ethics*, 11, 617–26.

Urban, M. (1996), *UK Eyes Alpha: The Inside Story of British Intelligence*, London: Faber and Faber.

Vachani, S., and Smith, N. C. (2004), 'Socially responsible pricing: lessons from the pricing of AIDS drugs in developing countries', *California Management Review*, 47, 1, 117–44.

Wakefield, J. (2002), 'When a phone call is a luxury', *BBC News Online*, available at http://news.bbc.co.uk/1/hi/sci/tech/1775496.stm, accessed 30 September 2006.

Walker, A. W. (1967), 'How to price industrial products', *Harvard Business Review*, September–October, 125–32.

Ward, K. (1993), 'Gaining a marketing advantage through the strategic use of transfer pricing', *Journal of Marketing Management*, 9, 245–53.

Yeoman, I., and McMahon-Beattie, U. (2006), 'Luxury markets and premium pricing', *Journal of Revenue and Pricing Management*, 4, 4, 319–28.

Zeithaml, V. A. (1988), 'Consumer perceptions of price, quality and value: a means–end model and synthesis of evidence', *Journal of Marketing*, 52 (July), 2–22.

11

An Introduction to Marketing Communications

Think like a wise man but communicate in the language of the people.

William Butler Yeats

Learning Outcomes

After studying this chapter you should be able to:

✔ Explain three models of communication and describe how personal influences can enhance the effectiveness of marketing communication activities.

✔ Describe the nature, purpose, and scope of marketing communications.

✔ Understand the role and various tasks of marketing communications.

✔ Explain the key characteristics associated with developing promotional messages.

✔ Understand the models used to explain how advertising and marketing communication is considered to work.

✔ Describe what culture is and explain how it can impact on the use of marketing communications in international environments.

The British Airways London Eye uses marketing communications in a number of interesting ways and has become the UK's most popular visitor attraction. We speak to Helen Bull to find out more.

Helen Bull for the London Eye

The British Airways London Eye is the world's tallest observation wheel at 135 m high and since opening at the turn of the century has become an iconic landmark, with a status that can be compared with Tower Bridge, Big Ben, Eros, and the Tower of London. The London Eye has become the most popular paid-for UK visitor attraction, visited by over 3.5 million people a year; that is an average of 10,000 a day.

The BA London Eye: the world's tallest observation wheel

The London Eye

At the London Eye we use marketing communications in a number of interesting ways. During the construction phase for example, public relations was used to build high pre-opening interest and awareness and to challenge any negative perceptions associated with ferris wheels or thrill rides. We gave the media access to key individuals and organizations throughout this period in order to win public favour by involving them in the entire process and giving them ownership of what will become a global icon. For the same reason, the media was given access to the construction site at regular key stages of the build, the biggest day being the raising of the wheel from barges on the River Thames. The London Eye project was watched by millions of people on a daily basis and we used regular, consistent media exposure to keep the public interested and instill a sense of pride in Londoners. By the time the London Eye was due to open, hundreds of thousands of people had already pre-booked their tickets.

> *advertising is used as part of our marketing communications to drive awareness and footfall*

Advertising is used as part of our marketing communications to drive both awareness and footfall. Building awareness with target audiences ensures that the London Eye as a global icon is at the forefront of everyone's mind. Through advertising, the London Eye targets audiences in London and the South-East as well as visitors to London once they arrive in the capital.

Other marketing activity includes seasonal campaigns, sales promotions, and the tactical distribution of leaflets. Seasonal campaigns centre around key periods such as Easter, Christmas, and Halloween where we target Londoners and the South-East market. The latter makes it ideal to focus on local London media, such as the *Evening Standard*, all the free London papers, and marketing emails.

Sales promotions are used to drive incremental off-peak revenue and visitors. These kinds of campaigns are normally used tactically to encourage guests to trial additional products and also to extend brand communication. Leaflets are distributed via British Tourist Authority offices worldwide, trade clients, and Tourist Information Centres throughout the UK. In addition, 'word of mouth' plays a key role to encourage visits to the London Eye. More than 30% of London Eye guests visit as the result of a recommendation from family or friends. There is a definite consumer trend towards trusting word of mouth and personal recommendations above any form of advertising.

It is extremely important for us to build relationships with industry representative organizations such as Visit London and Visit Britain who actively go out to other territories around the world to promote London and Britain as a destination. Through working with these organizations, the London Eye is able to target audiences in desired countries and areas as well as specific demographics. At the London Eye we also undertake a number of sales missions to different countries where key sales people will meet with travel agents and organizers in a small group or individual basis in order to communicate and educate buyers on the London Eye portfolio of products. In the world of corporate events as well as journalist familiarization trips, personal communications make a much bigger impact.

As March 2007 approached we knew our 25 millionth visitor would be arriving and two important questions emerged. How should we celebrate the occasion and how should we use marketing communications to mark it?

Introduction

Have you ever wondered how organizations manage to communicate with so many different people and organizations? Well, this is the first of three chapters that explain how this can be accomplished through the use of marketing communications. This one introduces and explains what marketing communications is. The next chapter considers each of the communication tools and **media**, whilst the third one examines issues concerning the management and integration of marketing communications.

The overall purpose of this chapter is to introduce some of the fundamental ideas and concepts associated with marketing communications. In order to achieve this the chapter commences with a consideration of communication theory. This is important because it provides a basis upon which it is easier to appreciate the different ways in which marketing communication is used.

Following a definition we explain the role and tasks of marketing communications. Again this is important as it specifies the scope of the subject and provides a framework within which to appreciate the various communication activities undertaken by organizations. The tools and media used by marketing communications are an important aspect of this topic. Although the next chapter is devoted to a fuller examination of each of them, a brief overview is presented here.

Marketing communication is about shared meaning and that means developing messages that can be understood and acted on by target audiences. We present some principles by which marketing messages are communicated and then consider how marketing communications might work. This chapter concludes with an overview of what **culture** is and how it can impact on marketing communications before we briefly consider some of the issues that relate to the use of marketing communications in an international environment.

Introducing Marketing Communications

Marketing communications, or **promotion** as it was originally called, is one of the 4Ps of the marketing mix. It is used to communicate elements of an organization's offering to a target audience. This offer might refer to a product, a service, or the organization itself as it tries to build its reputation. However, this is a broad view of marketing communication and we need understand the various issues, dimensions, and elements that make up this important communication activity. For example, there are the communications experienced by audiences relating to both their use of products (how good is this hairdryer?) and the consumption of associated services (just how good was the service when I was in Argos?). There are communications arising from unplanned or unintended experiences (empty stock shelves or accidents) and there are planned marketing communications (Grönroos, 2004), which is the main focus of this and the following two chapters. These are all represented in Figure 11.1 (Hughes and Fill, 2007), which is the point at which we start our exploration of marketing communications.

Figure 11.1 depicts not just the breadth but also the complexity of managing marketing communications. However, this framework fails to provide any detailed understanding, particularly of the planned marketing communications element. This element is really important because it has the potential not only to present

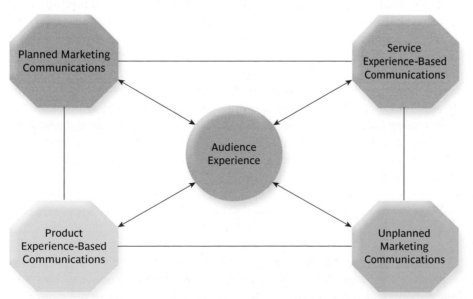

Figure 11.1
A macro perspective of the marketing communications mix

Source: Hughes and Fill (2007). Adapted with the kind permission of Emerald Group Publishing Limited and Westburn Publishers.

Heineken, Not Shaken and Not Stirred

Heineken used the actual set of the *Casino Royale* James Bond film for a global marketing communications campaign. The ad uses Eva Green who plays Vespa Lynd, Bond's leading lady in the film, and many of the *Casino Royale* make-up artists, stylists, and members of the costume department and production team, to try to capture the authenticity of the world of James Bond in the ad.

The story line follows the trail of a bottle of Heineken being taken by a waiter to Bond's hotel room. With the traditional Bond music playing in the background the ad finishes with Green walking into Bond's room with the bottle of Heineken, having knocked out the waiter. Bond is heard to shout from the bathroom: 'Have you seen room service? I ordered you a Heineken.'

The idea is to associate the humour, storyline, and values of the Bond film with the Heineken brand. The ad campaign was used not only for TV around the world, but also for cinema and the internet. In addition to this 'Waiter', as the campaign is known, was also used in magazines and outdoor advertising. Public relations were used to get coverage and exposure and interest in the Waiter campaign whilst sales promotions in the form of consumer competitions to win James Bond prizes were used to provoke involvement with the brand.

Source: Woods (2006) and Heineken International Press Release (at www.biz.yahoo.com/iw/061030/0177874.html).

1 Go to www.casinoroyale.heineken.com/index.html and play the ad. Why do you think Heineken decided to associate themselves and their audiences with James Bond?

2 What other brands do you believe might be successfully associated with the Bond theme?

3 Think of five other ways in which Heineken might communicate with their target audiences?

products and services in the best possible way but also to influence people's expectations about both product and service experiences.

Organizations plan, design, implement, and evaluate their marketing communication activities. Often referred to as campaigns, these activities involve the delivery of messages either to or with target audiences, through various communication tools and media.

This chapter is intended to help you understand some of the fundamental ideas associated with planned marketing communications. It sets out the broad scope of the subject and enables readers to appreciate the complexity and diversity of this fascinating subject. See Market Insight 11.1 above for an example of marketing communications drawing on a well-known brand.

Communication Theory

We start with a consideration of communication theory. This is important as it helps explain how and why certain marketing communication activities take place. Communication is the process by which individuals share meaning. It is necessary, therefore, that participants are able to interpret the meanings embedded in the messages they receive, and then, as far as the sender is concerned, able to respond coherently. The act of responding is important as it completes an episode in the communication process. Communication that travels only from the sender to the receiver is essentially a one-way process and the full communication process remains incomplete. This form of communication is shown at Figure 11.2. When Cadbury's present their Dairy Milk chocolate bar on a poster in the London underground, the person standing on the platform can read it, understand it, and may even enjoy being entertained by it. They do not, however, have any immediate opportunity to respond to the ad in such a way that Cadbury's can hear, understand, and act on the person's comments and feelings. When that same ad is presented on a website or a sales promotion representative offers that same person a chunk of Cadbury's Dairy Milk when they are shopping in a supermarket, there are opportunities to hear, record, and even respond to the comments that person makes. This form of communication travels from a sender (Cadbury's) to a receiver (the person in the supermarket) and back again to Cadbury's and is referred to as a two-way communication and represents a complete communication episode. This type of communication is depicted in Figure 11.3.

These basic models form the basis of this introduction to communication theory. For those involved in managing and delivering marketing communications it is important that these processes and associated complexities are understood. Through knowledge and understanding of the communications process they are more likely to achieve their objective of sharing meaning with each member of their target audiences. This not only helps create opportunities to interact with their audiences but it also encourages some people to develop a **dialogue**, the richest and most meaningful form of communication.

Understanding the way communication works therefore provides a foundation upon which we can better understand the way marketing communications not only works, but also how it can be used effectively by organizations. Three main models or interpretations of how communication works are considered here. These are the linear model, the two-way model, and the interactive model of communication.

Communication theory is an important consideration for marketing Cadbury's chocolate bars

Cadbury

The Linear Model of Communication

The linear model of communication is regarded as the basic model of mass communications. First developed by Wilbur Schramm (1955), the key components of the linear model of communication are set out in Figure 11.2.

The model can be broken down into a number of phases, each of which has distinct characteristics. The linear model emphasizes that each phase occurs in a particular sequence, a linear progression, which, according to Theodorson and Theodorson (1969), enables the 'transmission of information, ideas, attitudes, or emotion from one person or group to another (or others), primarily through symbols'. The model and its components are straightforward, but it is the quality of the linkages between the various elements in the process that determines whether the communication will be successful.

The source is an individual or organization which identifies a problem that requires the need to transmit a message. The source of a message is an important factor in the communication process. First, the source must identify the right problem, and second, a **receiver** who perceives a source which lacks conviction, authority, trust, or expertise is likely not to believe the messages sent by that source.

Encoding is the process whereby the source selects a combination of appropiate words, pictures, symbols, and music to represent the message to be transmitted.

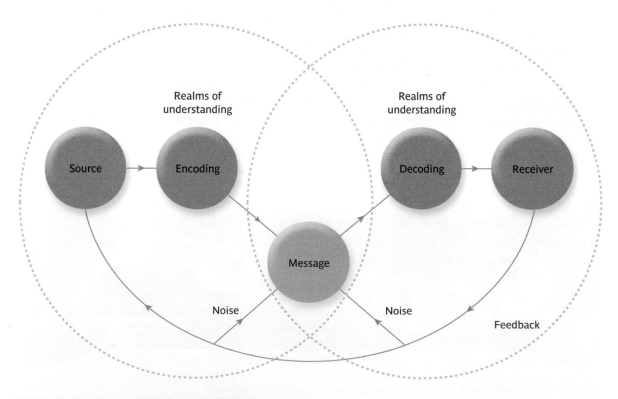

Figure 11.2 A linear model of communications

Source: Based on Schramm (1955) and Shannon and Weaver (1962).

The various bits are 'packed' in such a way that they can be unpacked and understood. The goal is to create a message that is capable of being comprehended easily by the receiver.

Once encoded, the message must be put into a form that is capable of transmission. It may be oral or written, verbal or non-verbal, in a symbolic form or in a sign. The channel is the means by which the message is transmitted from the source to the receiver. These channels may be personal or non-personal. The former involves face-to-face contact and **word-of-mouth** communications, which can be extremely influential. Non-personal channels are characterized by mass media advertising, which can reach large audiences. Whatever the format chosen, the source must be sure that what is being put into the message is what they want to be decoded by the receiver.

Once the receiver, an individual or organization, has seen, heard, smelt, or read the message they decode it. In effect they are 'unpacking' the various components of the message, starting to make sense of it and give it meaning. The more clearly the message is encoded the easier it is to 'unpack' and comprehend what the source intended to convey when they constructed the message. **Decoding**, therefore, is that part of the communication process where receivers give meaning to a message.

Once understood receivers provide a set of reactions referred to as a response. These reactions may vary from an emotional response based on a set of feelings and thoughts about the message to a behavioural or action response.

Feedback is another part of the response process. It is important to know not just that the message has been received but also that it has been correctly decoded and the right meaning attributed. However, although feedback is an essential aspect of a successful communication event, feedback through mass media channels is generally difficult to obtain, mainly because of the inherent time delay involved in the feedback process. Feedback through **personal selling** however can be instantaneous, through explicit means such as questioning, raising objections, or signing an order form. For the mass media advertiser, the process can be vague and prone to misinterpretation. If a suitable feedback system is not in place then the source will be unaware that the communication has been unsuccessful and is liable to continue wasting resources. This represents inefficient and ineffective marketing communications.

Noise is concerned with influences that distort information and which in turn make it difficult for the receiver to correctly decode and interpret the message as intended by the source. So, if a telephone rings, or someone rustles sweet papers during a sensitive part of a film screened in a cinema, the receiver is distracted from the message.

The final component in the linear model concerns the 'realm of understanding'. This is an important element in the communication process because it recognizes that successful communications are more likely to be achieved if the source and the receiver understand each other. This understanding concerns attitudes, perceptions, behaviour, and experience: the values of both parties to the communication process. Effective communication is more likely when there is some common ground, a realm of understanding between the source and receiver. See Market Insight 11.2 for an insight into one of the ways in which organizations developed their realm of understanding.

Bottled, Iced, and Refreshed

Magner's innovative 2006 ad campaign

Magner's Irish Cider

The campaign used by Magner's during the summer of 2006 to roll out their brand of cider across the UK was based primarily on observational consumer research. The basis for the campaign was to position the drink as 'naturally refreshing' by showing it poured over ice, in an apple orchard and in a pint bottle.

However, the ideas for the innovative campaign evolved from C&C's experience with the Bulmer's brand which they distribute in Ireland. Their first task with Bulmer's in the early 1990s was to elevate cider out of the 'embarrassed-to-be-seen-drinking' category and to do this they repositioned Bulmer's closer to beer by adding long-neck bottles and cans to its on tap offering. C&C then observed 40- and 50-something golfers choosing Bulmer's to quench their thirst. This led to campaigns that helped to encourage drinkers to consider cider as a refreshing drink. Magner's has a high natural apple juice content and a lower alcohol content than other ciders so it is much easier to make refreshment the key point of differentiation. These elements were critical when positioning Magner's as a quality, refreshing drink rather than a cheap intoxicant, which was how cider was largely viewed in the UK.

In 1997 C&C noticed consumers were adding ice to Bulmer's draught to cool it down. This use of ice was then adopted in Magner's campaigns. By showing consumers how to serve and drink the product it helped to create a clear point of difference for the brand. It was the first cider brand to do this and its success has led to competitive responses such as Sirrus from Scottish & Newcastle, especially formulated to be poured over ice.

'You observe human behavior, recognize an opportunity and use your instinct—that is what we did,' says Maurice Pratt, the CEO of C&C.

Source: Baker (2006).

1 Explain how the Magner's case illustrates the realm of understanding.

2 Find ads for two other beer or cider brands. How do they provide for audience feedback?

3 Watch commercial TV and a make a note of three ads in which viewers are shown how to use the brand. What is common to the way these ads are presented?

One of the problems associated with the linear model of communication is that it ignores the impact that other people can have on the communication process. However, people are not passive, they actively use information and the views and actions of other people can impact on the way information is sent, received, processed, and given meaning. One of the other difficulties with the linear model is that it is based on communication through mass media. Developed at a time when first radio and then television, with a just a few channels, were the only media available, it can be seen why the model was developed. Today there are hundreds of television channels, audiences now use the internet, mobile phones, and an increasing array of digital equipment to manage their work, leisure, and entertainment. Increasing numbers of people now engage with interactive-based communications, and in some circumstances organizations and individuals can be involved in real dialogue, such as online gaming. The linear model therefore is no longer entirely appropriate.

The Two-Step Model of Communication

One interpretation of the linear model is that it is a one-step explanation. Information is directed and shot at prospective audiences, rather like a bullet is propelled from a gun. However, we know that people can have a significant impact on the communication process and the **two-step model** goes some way to reflecting their influence.

The two-step model compensates for the linear or one-step model because it recognizes the importance of personal influences when informing and persuading audiences to think or behave in particular ways. This model depicts information flowing via various media channels, to particular types of people to whom other members of the audience refer for information and guidance. There are two main types of influencer. The first is referred to as an **opinion leader** and the other is an **opinion former**. The first is just an ordinary person who has a heightened

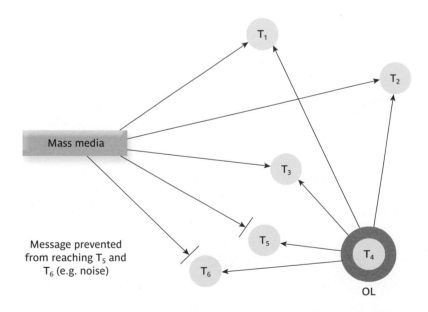

Figure 11.3
The two-step model of communications

Note: OL = opinion leader.

Source: *Marketing Communications*, 4th edn., Fill, C., Pearson Education Limited (2006). Reproduced with the kind permission of Pearson Education Limited.

interest in a particular topic. The second is involved professionally in the topic of interest. These are discussed in more detail later in this chapter, but they both have enormous potential to influence audiences. This may be because messages from personal influencers provide reinforcement and message credibility or it might be because this is the only way of reaching the end user audience.

The Interaction Model of Communications

This model is similar to the two-step model but it contains one important difference. In this interpretation the parties are seen to interact among themselves and communication flows among all the members in what is regarded as a communication network (Figure 11.4). Mass media is not the only source of the communication.

Unlike the linear model where messages flow from the source to the receiver, through a channel, the **interaction model** recognizes that messages can flow through various channels and that people can influence the direction and impact of a message. It is not necessarily one-way but interactive communication that typifies much of contemporary communications.

Interaction is an integral part of the communication process. Think of a conversation with a friend: the face-to-face oral- and visual-based communication enables both of you to consider what each of you is saying, and to react in whatever way is appropriate. Mass communication does not facilitate this interactional element and so the linear model might therefore be regarded as an incomplete form of the pure communication process.

Interaction is about actions that lead to a response and much attention is now given to the interaction that occurs between people. However, care needs to be taken because the content associated with an interactional event might be

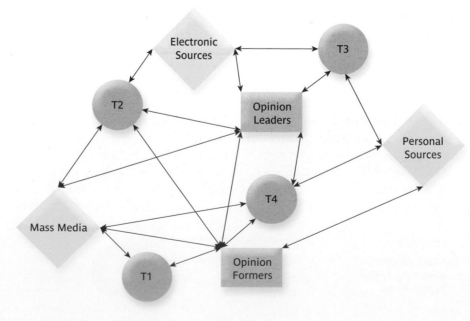

Figure 11.4
An interaction model

based on an argument, a statement of opinion, or a mere casual social encounter. What is important here is interaction that leads to mutual understanding. This type of interaction concerns 'relationship specific knowledge' (Ballantyne, 2004). That is, the interaction is about information that is relevant to both parties. Once this is established increased levels of trust develop between the participants so that eventually a dialogue emerges between communication partners. Interactivity, therefore, is a prelude to dialogue, the highest or purest form of communication.

Dialogue occurs through reasoning which requires both listening and adaptation skills. Dialogue is concerned with the development of knowledge that is specific to the parties involved and is referred to as 'learning together' (Ballantyne, 2004: 119). The development of digital technologies has been instrumental in enabling organizations to provide increased interaction opportunities with their customers and other audiences. Think of the number of times when watching television that you are prompted to press the red button to get more information. For example, many news programmes now encourage viewers to phone or send in their emails and pictures about particular issues. This is an attempt to get audiences to express their views about a subject and in doing so promote access to and interaction with the programme. Whereas interaction at one time only really occurred through personal selling, it is now possible to interact, and so build mutual understanding with consumers, through the internet and other digital technologies. Indeed, Hoffman and Novak (1996) claim that interactivity between people is now supplemented by interactivity between machines. This means that the interaction, or indeed dialogue, that previously occurred *through* machines can now occur *with* the equipment facilitating the communication.

Personal Influencers

As mentioned earlier two main types of personal influencer can be recognized: opinion leaders and opinion formers. These are now discussed in turn.

Opinion Leaders

Studies by Katz and Lazarsfeld (1955) into American voting and purchase behaviour led them to conclude that some individuals were more predisposed to receiving information and then reprocessing it to influence others. They found that these individuals had the capacity to be more persuasive than information received directly from the mass media. They called these people opinion leaders and one of their defining characteristics is that they belong to the same peer group as the people they influence, they are not distant or removed.

It has been reported in subsequent research that opinion leaders have a greater exposure to relevant media and as a result have more knowledge/familiarity and involvement with a product category than others. Non-leaders, or **opinion followers**, turn to opinion leaders for advice and information about products and services they are interested in. Opinion leaders are also more gregarious and more self-confident than non-leaders and are more confident of their role as an influencer (Chan and Misra, 1990). It is not surprising, therefore, that many marketing communication strategies are targeted at influencing opinion leaders as they will in turn influence others. This approach has been used to convey particular information and help educate large target audiences through television and radio programmes. For example, television programmes such as *Coronation Street*, *Eastenders*, and *Emmerdale* and radio programmes such as *The Archers* (soaps), have been used as opinion leadership vehicles to bring to attention and open up debates about many controversial social issues, such as contraception, abortion, drug use and abuse, and serious illness and mental health concerns.

Opinion Formers

The other main form of independent personal influencer is opinion formers. They are not part of the same peer group as the people they influence. Their defining characteristic is that they exert personal influence because of their profession, authority, education, or status associated with the object of the communication process. They provide information and advice as part of the formal expertise they are perceived to hold. For example, shop assistants in music equipment shops are often experienced musicians in their own right. Aspiring musicians seeking to buy their first proper guitar will often consult these perceived 'experts' about guitar brands, styles, models, and associated equipment such as amplifiers. In the same way doctors carry such conviction that they can influence the rate at which medicines are consumed.

Drug manufacturers such as GlaxoSmithKline and Pfizer often launch new drugs by enlisting the support of eminent professors, consultants, or doctors who are recognized by others in the profession as experts. These opinion formers are invited to lead symposia and associated events and in doing so build credibility and activity around the new product. (See Market Insight 11.3.)

Organizations target their marketing communications at opinion leaders and formers in order to penetrate the market more quickly than relying on communicating directly with the target audience. However, in addition to these forms of influence reference needs to be made to spokespersons. There are some potential problems that advertisers need to be aware of when considering the use of celebrities. First, does the celebrity fit the image of the brand and will the celebrity be acceptable to the target audience, now and in the long run? So, should the lifestyle of the celebrity change, what impact will the change have on the target audience and their attitude towards the brand? For example, the well-publicized allegations about the behaviour of the supermodel Kate Moss led to several sponsorship and brand endorsement contracts being lost (e.g. H&M and Burberry), although it is alleged that her overall income actually increased as a result of the publicity, and sales through her new Topshop brand have soared. The second problem concerns the impact that the celebrity makes relative to the brand. There is a danger that the receiver remembers the celebrity but not the message or the brand. The *celebrity* becomes the hero, rather than the product being advertised.

All of the models of communication discussed have a role to play in marketing communications. Mass media communication in the form of broadcast television

Opinionated Ice Creamers

One common approach when launching new brands such as cigarettes and both alcoholic and soft drinks is to encourage staff at nightclubs and other venues appropriate to the target market to be seen drinking/using the product. The use of these people is deliberate because they are of the same age and peer group as the clubs' guests. They are therefore perceived as opinion leaders, and, when seen consuming the brand in the right context, can provide the necessary credibility for a new brand. This not only helps to inform clubbers of its availability and that it is cool to be seen drinking it but it can also motivate subsequent purchase. It is quite common for free samples to be available as this encourages people to experience the brand at little or no risk.

When Häagen-Dazs first launched into the UK market they distributed free samples to guests at society events such as the Henley Regatta, Wimbledon, Polo at Cowdray Park, and Windsor. This enabled key opinion leaders to create a word-of-mouth campaign around the super premium ice cream and gave the brand both mystery and legitimacy. This was picked up by the media who wrote stories about the brand, simply because it was newsworthy. Only later was the famous mass media television ad campaign released.

1   Using a product or brand with which you are familiar, think about three ways in which opinion leadership might be used to develop the brand.

2   Think of a hobby or pastime that you might enjoy. Now, out of all your friends and social networks and contacts, who would you ask for advice about taking up the pastime? Why did you choose them?

To take your learning further, you might wish to read this influential paper.

Kitchen, P. (1993), 'Marketing communications renaissance', *International Journal of Advertising*, 12, 4, 367–86.

This paper provides a helpful review of the literature in relation to developments in marketing communications in the early 1990s, at a time when initial ideas about integrated marketing communications were emerging. It signals changes in **public relations** and shows how advertising, **sales promotion**, and personal selling were adapting to a changing environment.

and radio is still used by organizations to reach large audiences. Two-way and interaction forms of communication are used to reach smaller, specific target audiences and to enable a range of people to contribute to the process. Interaction and dialogue are higher levels of communication and are used increasingly to generate personal communication with individual customers. The skill for marketing practitioners is to know when to move from one-way, to two-way, to interactive, and then dialogue-based marketing communications.

The Role of Marketing Communications

Now that ideas about how communication works have been established it is time to examine what marketing communications is and the tasks it undertakes. Marketing communications is a relatively new term for what was previously referred to as promotion. As you know from your previous reading (Chapter 1) promotion is one of the 4Ps and is responsible for the communication of the marketing offer to the target market. While recognizing that there is implicit and important communication through the other elements of the marketing mix (for example, a high price is symbolic of high quality), it is the task of a planned and integrated set of activities to communicate effectively with each of an organization's **stakeholder** groups.

Fundamentally, marketing communications comprises three elements; a set of tools, the media, and messages. The five common tools are advertising, sales promotion, personal selling, direct marketing, and public relations. In addition there are a range of media, such as television, radio, press, and the internet, which are used to convey messages to target audiences.

These various tools have been developed in response to changing market and environmental conditions. For example, public relations are now seen by some to have both a product and a corporate dimension. Direct marketing is now recognized as an important way of developing closer relationships with buyers, both consumer and organizational, while new and innovative forms of communication through sponsorship, floor advertising, video screens on supermarket trolleys and checkout coupon dispensers, and the internet and associated technologies, mean that effective communication requires the selection and integration of an increasing variety of communication tools and media. Communication is no longer restricted to promoting and persuading audiences as the tasks are now much broader and strategic. Today the term marketing communications is a more appropriate and established term used to reflect an organization's communication activities.

Marketing communications is used to achieve one of two principal goals. The first concerns the development of brand values. Advertising, and to some extent public relations, have for a long time concentrated on establishing a set of feelings, emotions, and beliefs about a brand or organization. Brand communication seeks to make us think positively about a brand, helps us to remember and develop positive brand attitudes in the hope that when we are ready to buy that type of product again, we will buy brand x because we feel positively about it.

The alternative and more contemporary goal is to use communications to make us behave in particular ways. Rather than spend lots of money developing worthy and positive attitudes towards brands, the view of many today is that we should use this money to encourage people to behave differently. This might be through buying the product, or driving them to a website, requesting a brochure, or making a telephone call. This is called behaviour change and is driven by using messages that provide audiences with a reason to act or what is referred to as a 'call-to-action'.

So, on the one hand communications can be used to develop brand feelings and on the other to change or manage the behaviour of the target audience. These are not mutually exclusive, for example, many television advertisements are referred to as direct-response ads because not only do they attempt to create brand values but they also carry a website address, telephone number, or details of a special offer (sales promotion). In other words, the two goals are mixed into a hybrid approach.

The success of marketing communication depends upon the extent to which messages engage their audiences. (See Market Insight 11.4.) These audiences can be seen to fall into three main groups.

- Customers—these may be consumers or they may be end user organizations.
- Channel members—each organization is part of a network of other organizations such as suppliers, retailers, wholesalers, value added resellers,

Engaging with Urban Youth Audiences

Identifying, finding, and reaching audiences is never easy, but engaging with them is always a challenge, and urban youth markets are extremely challenging.

A campaign by Sony to launch the PlayStation Portable in the USA used street artists to spray-paint buildings with graffiti-style images of kids using the handset. However, the campaign backfired as many images were vandalized with enraged messages such as 'Stop hawking corporate products and big business on our neighbourhood walls' and 'Corporate vandals not welcome'.

Critics claimed Sony tried to commercialize the credibility of street art and ended up patronizing the very market they wanted to reach. Adidas, however, appeared to get it right. They used graffiti art to launch the adicolor trainer range. Their classic white adicolor line of shoes is accompanied by a set of colouring pens. This allows people to customize the design of their trainers.

First devised in 1983 the line was revived in 2006 and was supported by a promotional campaign that reflected the inherent creativity of the shoes. Just as Sony used graffiti so did Adidas but this time the approach was designed to incorporate the audience. Branded with the Adidas logo, blank white posters provided a canvas for street artists. Fresh posters were placed over the graffiti, some days later, but this time with the shape of the adicolor shoe cut out to reveal the graffiti underneath. This allowed the street art to be incorporated, creating a customized shoe on the poster that simply and effectively demonstrated the idea behind the product.

Source: Curtis (2006), www.brandrepublic.com/bulletins/br/article/599163/youth-marketing-whats-hood/.

1 What do you think about the approach by Adidas to reach their target market?

2 Identify two other products that might be best associated with urban youth markets. Find out the main media used to reach these audiences and look for similarities.

3 Visit the websites of three brands of trainers and make a judgement about the overall message they convey to you.

distributors, and other retailers, who join together, often freely, to make the product or service available to end users.

- General stakeholders—organizations and people who either influence or are influenced by the organization. These may be shareholders, the financial community, trade unions, employees, local community, and others.

Marketing communications therefore involves not just customers but also a range of other stakeholders. Marketing communications can be used to reach consumers as well as business audiences.

As explained earlier in Chapter 1, the concept of exchange is central to our understanding of marketing. For an exchange to take place there must be two or more parties, each of whom can offer something of value to the other and who are prepared to enter freely into the exchange process, a transaction. There are of course many types of exchange but two are of particular importance: **transactional exchanges** and **collaborative exchanges**.

- *Transactional exchanges* (Bagozzi, 1978; Houston and Gassenheimer, 1987) are transactions that occur independently of any previous or subsequent exchanges. They have a short-term orientation and are primarily motivated by self-interest. So, when a consumer buys a MP3 player, a brand that they have not bought before, then a transactional exchange can be identified.

- *Collaborative exchanges* (Dwyer, Schurr, and Oh, 1987) have a longer-term orientation and develop between parties who wish to build long-term supportive relationships. So, when a consumer buys their third product from the same brand as the MP3 player, perhaps from the same dealer, collaborative exchanges are considered to be taking place.

These two types of exchange transactions represent the extremes of a spectrum. In mature industrial societies transactional exchanges have tended to dominate commercial transactions although recently there has been a substantial movement towards collaborative exchanges. Each organization has a mix of audiences so it should not be surprising that they use a range of communication tools and media to suit different exchange preferences of customers, suppliers, and other stakeholder audiences.

The impact on marketing communications is essentially about the choice of tools, media, and messages. Audiences who prefer transactional exchanges might be better engaged with advertising and mass media-based communications, with messages that are impersonal and largely rational and product focused. Audiences that prefer more collaborative exchanges should be engaged through personal, informal, and interactive communications, with messages that are generally emotional and relationship oriented.

Shoes can be purchased from a range of different retail outlets and the store they are purchased from is often insignificant, especially as price can be an important purchasing factor. The approach adopted by Clarks, the shoe company, recognizes the importance of building a long-term relationship with their customers. The First Shoes campaign run by Clarks demonstrates good marketing communications and is based on the significance of a child's first pair of shoes and what they can mean to the parents. These tiny shoes are often kept for years and years as a memento. Clarks now provide a souvenir of the occasion in the form of a free, framed Polaroid photograph of a child's very first shop visit and fitting. A simple campaign that engages audiences with an important event but it also enables both the parents and Clarks to remember the event through longer-term memories. What might have been a transactional exchange is transformed into one that is more collaborative and relationship oriented.

What is Marketing Communications?

Quite naturally definitions of marketing communication have evolved as the topic and our understanding have developed. Original views assumed that these types of communication were used to persuade people to buy products and services. The focus was on products, one-way communications, persuasion, and there was a short-term perspective. In short, an organization's products and services were *promoted* to audiences.

However, this perspective has given way to the term marketing communications. This was partly a result of an increase in the tasks that the communications departments were expected to undertake and a widening of the tools and media that could be used. At the same time there has been a shift from mass to personal communications and a greater focus on integration activities. The following represents a contemporary definition of marketing communications.

'Marketing communications is a management process through which an organisation attempts to engage with its various audiences. By understanding an audience's communications environment, organisations seek to develop and present messages for its identified stakeholder groups, before evaluating and acting upon the responses. By conveying messages that are of significant value, audiences are encouraged to offer attitudinal and behavioural responses' (Fill, 2005).

There are three main aspects associated with this definition: engagement, audiences, and responses.

- Engagement—What are the audiences' communications needs and is it possible to engage with them on their terms using one-way, two-way, or dialogic communications?

- Audiences—Which specific audience(s) do we need to communicate with and what are their various behaviour and information-processing needs?

- Responses—What are the desired outcomes of the communication process? Are they based on changes in perception, values, and beliefs or are changes in behaviour required?

Marketing communications can therefore be considered from a number of perspectives. Whilst it is a complex activity and used by organizations with varying degrees of sophistication, it is undoubtedly concerned with the way in which audiences are encouraged to perceive an organization and/or its offerings. It should therefore be regarded as an audience-centred activity.

The Tasks of Marketing Communications

However, promotion (essentially persuasion) alone is insufficient as marketing communications undertakes other tasks in the name of engaging audiences. So, what is it that marketing communications does and why do organizations use it in varying ways? Well, fundamentally marketing communications can be used to engage audiences by undertaking one of four main tasks, referred by Fill as the DRIP model (2002). In no particular order, communications can be used to *differentiate* brands and organizations, to *reinforce* brand memories and expectations, to *inform*, that is make aware and educate audiences, and finally to *persuade* them to do things or to behave in particular ways. See Table 11.1 for an explanation of each of these tasks.

These tasks are not mutually exclusive, indeed campaigns might be designed to achieve two or three of them. For example, the launch of a new brand will require that audiences be informed, made aware, of its existence and enabled to understand how it is different from competitor brands. A brand that is well established might try to reach lapsed customers by reminding them of the key features and benefits and offering them an incentive (persuasion) to buy again. The RAC

Table 11.1

The key DRIP tasks for marketing communications

Marketing communication tasks	Explanation
To differentiate	In many markets there is little to separate brands (e.g. mineral water, coffee, printers). In these cases it is the images created by marketing communications that help differentiate one brand from another and position them so that consumers develop positive attitudes and make purchasing decisions.
To reinforce	Communications may be used to *remind* people of a need they might have or of the benefits of past transactions with a view to convincing them that they should enter into a similar exchange. In addition, it is possible to provide *reassurance* or comfort either immediately prior to an exchange or, more commonly, post purchase. This is important as it helps to retain current customers and improve profitability. This approach to business is much more cost effective than constantly striving to lure new customers.
To inform	One of the most common uses of marketing communications is to *inform* and make potential customers aware of the features and benefits of an organization's offering. In addition, marketing communications can be used to educate audiences, to show them how to use a product or what to do in particular circumstances.
To persuade	Communication may attempt to *persuade* current and potential customers of the desirability of entering into an exchange relationship.

launched a customer magazine in 2007 partly to keep in contact with customers whose only contact with the brand is at renewal time or when their car breaks down. By communicating through the magazine three times a year, the whole range of RAC services is presented in a positive atmosphere (Britt, 2007).

Marketing Communication Messages

The importance of sending the right message was established earlier when considering communication theory. From a receiver's perspective, the process of decoding and giving meaning to messages is affected by the volume and quality of information received and the judgement they make about the methods and how well the message was communicated. What we also know is that in order for a message to be processed successfully messages should reflect a balance between the need for information and the need for pleasure or enjoyment in consuming the message. Messages can be categorized as either product oriented and rational or customer oriented and based upon feelings and emotions.

As a general guideline, when audiences experience high involvement, the emphasis of the message should be on the information content with the key attributes and the associated benefits emphasized. This style is often factual and product oriented. If audiences experience low involvement then messages should attempt to gain an emotional response. There are, of course, many situations where both rational and emotional messages are needed by buyers in order to make purchasing decisions. Nokia, the Finnish mobile phone manufacturer, announced early in 2007 that it was reviewing its global advertising and that it was intending to put emotional engagement at the centre of its brand strategy and communications (Kemp, 2007).

The presentation of messages should reflect the degree to which factual information or emotional content is required for the message to command attention and then be processed. There are numerous presentational or executional techniques, but Table 11.2 outlines some of the more commonly used appeals.

The Marketing Communications Mix

We learned earlier that marketing communications activities concern the use of three main elements; tools, media, and messages. These are considered here briefly although a fuller exposition of the tools and media can be found in Chapter 12.

The traditional marketing communications mix consists of a set of five primary tools. These are advertising, sales promotion, direct marketing, public relations, and personal selling. Additionally these tools, and in particular advertising, use media in order to reach their audiences. Tools and media are not the same as they have different characteristics and are used for different purposes.

Table 11.2

Information and
emotional appeals

Information-based messages	
Factual	Messages provide rational, logical information, and are presented in a straightforward, no-frills manner.
Slice of life	Uses people who are similar to the target audience and presented in scenes to which the target audience can readily associate and understand. For example, washing powder brands are often presented by stereotypical 'housewives', who are seen discussing the brand in a kitchen.
Demonstration	Brands are presented in a problem-solving context. So, people with headaches are seen to be in pain, but then take brand x which resolves the problem.
Comparative	In this approach, brand x is compared favourably, on two or three main attributes, with a leading competitor.
Emotion-based messages	
Fear	Products are shown either to relieve danger or ill health through usage (e.g. toothpaste) or they can dispel the fear of social rejection (anti-dandruff shampoos).
Humour	The use of humour can draw attention, stimulate interest, and place audiences in a positive mood.
Animation	Used to reach children and as a way of communicating potentially boring and uninteresting products (gas, insurance) to adults.
Sex	Excellent for getting the attention of the target audience, but unless the product is related (e.g. perfume, clothing) these ads generally do not work.
Music	Good for getting attention and differentiating between brands.
Fantasy and surrealism	Used increasingly to provide a point of differentiation and brand intrigue (e.g. mobile phone networks).

The five primary tools of marketing communications are used in various combinations and with different degrees of intensity in order to achieve different communication goals with target audiences.

Media enable messages to be delivered to target audiences. Some media are owned by organizations (a building or delivery van can constitute media) but in most cases media to reach large audiences are owned by third-party organizations. As a result clients have to pay media owners for the right to send their messages through their media vehicles.

For a long time the range of available media was fairly limited but since the early 1990s the array of media has been growing rapidly and changing the media landscape. Now there is a huge choice of media so that media selection has become crucial when trying to reach increasingly smaller audiences. The cost of some media can be immense although in many cases fees are related to the number of people reached through a media vehicle. Space (or time) within traditional media is limited and costs rise as demand for the limited space/time and audience size increases. As a generalization, space within digital media is unlimited and so contact costs fall as audience size increases.

For a consideration of each of the tools and key media readers are advised to read Chapter 12.

Word of Mouth

Planned marketing communications have traditionally used paid-for media to convey messages to target audiences. However, as mentioned previously in respect of opinion formers and leaders, some messages are best relayed through personal communications. This type of communication does not involve any payment for media because communication is freely given through word-of-mouth conversation.

Word-of-mouth communication is 'interpersonal communication regarding products or services where the receiver regards the communicator as impartial' (Stokes and Lomax, 2002).

Personal influence within the communication process is important. This is because customers perceive word-of-mouth recommendations as objective and unbiased. In comparison to advertising messages, word-of-mouth communications are more robust (Berkman and Gilson, 1986). Word-of-mouth messages are used either as information inputs prior to purchase or as a support and reinforcement of their own purchasing decisions.

People like to talk about their product (service) experiences. The main stimulus for behaviour is that the product or service in question either gave them particular pleasure or displeasure. These motivations to discuss products and their associative experiences vary between individuals and with the intensity of the motivation at any one particular moment. One hotel gave away teddy bears to guests on the basis that the guests would be happy to talk about their stay at the hotel, with the teddy bear acting as a prompt to provoke or induce conversation.

For every single positive comment there are ten negative comments. For this reason word-of-mouth communication was once seen as negative, unplanned, and as having a corrosive effect on a brand's overall communications. Today organizations actively manage word-of-mouth communications in order to generate positive comments and as a way of differentiating themselves in the market. e-viral marketing or word-of-mouse communication is an electronic version of the spoken endorsement of a product or service. Often using humorous messages, games, video clips, and screen savers, information can be targeted at key individuals who then voluntarily pass the message to friends and colleagues and in doing so bestow, endorse, and provide the message with much valued credibility.

For organizations it is important to target messages at those individuals who are predisposed to such discussion, as it is likely that they will propel word-of-mouth recommendations. The target, therefore, is not necessarily the target market, but opinion leaders within target markets, individuals who are most likely to volunteer their positive opinions about the offering and who, potentially, have some influence over people in their peer group.

Integrated Marketing Communications

So far in this chapter we have looked briefly at the five main tools, the media, and ideas about how messages should be developed. However, in order that these work most effectively and most efficiently, it makes sense to bring them together so that they work together as a unit. In doing so they will have a greater overall impact and hence bring benefits for organizations as well as audiences. This bringing together is referred to as integrated marketing communications, or **IMC**.

Integrated marketing communications has become a popular approach with both clients and communication agencies. Ideas about IMC originated in the early 1990s and IMC was regarded as a means of orchestrating the tools of the marketing communications mix, so that audiences perceive a single, consistent, unified message whenever they have contact with a brand. Duncan and Everett (1993) referred to this new, largely media-oriented approach as *orchestration*, *whole egg*, and *seamless* communication. Since this time many authors have explored ideas concerning IMC and more recently Duncan (2002), Grönroos (2004), and Kitchen *et al.* (2004) have provided various definitions and valuable insights into IMC. For our purposes the following definition is used:

'IMC is a strategic approach to the planned management of an organisation's communications. IMC requires that organisations coordinate their various strategies, resources and messages in order that it engage coherently and meaningfully with target audiences. The main purpose is to develop relationships with audiences that are of mutual value' (Fill, 2005).

Embedded within this definition are links with both busines-level and marketing strategies plus confirmation of the importance regarding the coherent use of resources and messages. What should also be evident is that IMC can be used to support the development and maintenance of effective relationships, a point made first by Duncan and Moriarty (1998) and then by Grönroos (2004) and Ballantyne (2004).

One quite common use of an integrated approach can be seen in the use of the tools. For example, rather than use advertising, public relations, sales promotions, personal selling, and direct marketing separately, better to use them in a coordinated manner. So, organizations often use advertising or sales promotion to create awareness, then involve public relations to provoke media comment, and then reinforce these messages through direct marketing or personal selling. The internet can also be incorporated to encourage comment, interest, and involvement in a brand yet still convey the same message in a consistent way. Mobile communications are used to reach audiences to reinforce messages and persuade audiences to behave in particular ways, wherever they are.

IMC has emerged for many reasons but two main ones concern customers and costs. First, organizations began to realize that their customers are more likely to understand a single message, delivered through various sources, rather than try to understand a series of different messages transmitted through different tools and a variety of media. IMC, therefore, is concerned with harmonizing the messages conveyed through each of the promotional tools, so that audiences perceive a consistent set of meanings within the messages they receive. The second reason concerns costs. As organizations seek to lower their costs, it became clear that it is far more cost effective to send a single message, using a limited number of agencies and other resources, rather than develop several messages through a number of agencies.

At first glance IMC might appear to be a practical and logical development, one that should benefit all concerned with an organization's marketing communications. However, there are issues concerning the concept, including what should be integrated, over and above the tools, media, and messages. For example, what about the impact of employees on a brand, the other elements of the marketing mix as well as the structure, systems, processes, and procedures necessary to deliver IMC consistently through time? There is some debate about the nature and contribution IMC can make to an organization, if only because there is a no main theory to underpin the topic.

Although IMC has yet to become an established marketing theory, the original ideas inherent in the overall approach are intuitively appealing and appear to be of value. However, what is integration to one person may be coordination and good practice to another, and until there is a theoretical base upon which to build IMC the phrase will continue to be misused, misunderstood, and used in a haphazard and inconsistent way.

How Marketing Communications Works

Ideas about how advertising, and then promotion, works have been a constant source of investigation, endeavour, and conceptual speculation. To suggest a firm conclusion has been reached would be misleading and untrue. However,

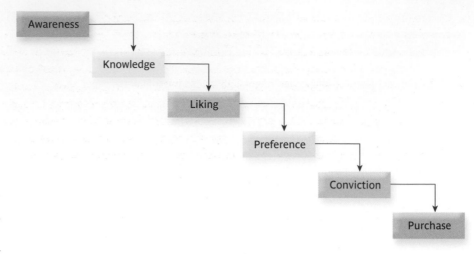

Figure 11.5
Stages in a hierarchy of
effects model

particular ideas have stood out and have played a more influential role in shaping our ideas about this fascinating topic. Some of these are presented here.

The first important idea about how advertising works was based on how the personal selling process works. Developed by Strong (1925), the **AIDA** model has become extremely well known and used by many practitioners. AIDA refers to the need to first create *awareness*, secondly generate *interest*, then drive *desire*, from which *action* (a sale) emerges. As a broad interpretation of the sales process this is generally correct but it fails to provide insight into the depths of how advertising works. Thirty-six years later Lavidge and Steiner (1961) presented a model based on what is referred to as the **hierarchy of effects** approach. Similar in nature to AIDA, it assumes that there are a series of steps a prospect must pass through in order that a purchase is made. It is assumed, correctly, that advertising cannot generate an immediate sale because there are a series of thought processes that need to be fulfilled prior to action. These steps are represented in Figure 11.5.

These models have become known as hierarchy of effects (HoE) models, simply because the effects (on audiences) are thought to occur in a top-down sequence. Some of the attractions of these HoE models and frameworks are that they are straightforward, simple, easy to understand, and, if creating advertising materials, provide a helpful broad template on which to develop and evaluate campaigns.

However, although attractive, this sequential approach has several drawbacks. People do not always process information nor do they always purchase products following a series of sequential steps. This logical progression is not reflected in reality when, for example, an impulse purchase is followed by an emotional feeling toward a brand. There are also questions about what actually constitutes adequate levels of awareness, comprehension, and conviction, how can it be known which stage the majority of the target audience has reached at any one point in time, and is this purchase sequence applicable to all consumers for all purchases?

Most of the frameworks presented so far have their roots in advertising. If we are to establish a model that explains how marketing communications works a different perspective is required, one that draws on the key parts of all the models.

Only Starting Point

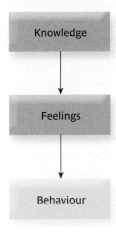

Figure 11.6
Attitude construct—
linear

This is possible as the three key components of the attitude construct lie within these different models. Attitudes have been regarded as an important aspect of promotional activity, and advertising is thought to be capable of influencing the development of positive attitudes towards brands.

The three stages of attitude formation are that we learn something (cognitive or learning component), feel something (an affective or emotional component), and then we act on our attitudes (behavioural or the conative component). So, in many situations we learn something, feel something towards a brand, and then proceed to buy or not buy. These stages are set out in Figure 11.6.

The hierarchy of effects models and the strong theory contain this sequential approach of learn, feel, do. However, we do not always pass through this particular sequence and the weak theory (see Chapter 12 for more on this), puts greater emphasis on familiarity and reminding (awareness) than the other components.

So, if we look at Figure 11.7 we can see that these components have been worked into a circular format. This means that when using marketing communications it is not necessary to slavishly follow each component in turn. The focus can be on what the audience requires and this might be on the learning, feeling, or doing components, as determined by the audience. In other words, for marketing communications to be audience centred we should develop campaigns based on the overriding need of the audience at any one point in time, based around either the need to learn, to feel, or to behave in particular ways.

- Learn

Where learning is the priority the overall goal should be to inform or educate the target audience. If the product is new it will be important to make the target audience aware of the product's existence and to inform them of the brand's key attributes and benefits. This is a common use for advertising as it has the capacity to reach both large and targeted audiences. Other than making them aware of the product's existence other tasks include showing the target audience how a brand is superior to competitive offerings, perhaps demonstrating how a product works and educating the audience about when and in what circumstances the brand should be used.

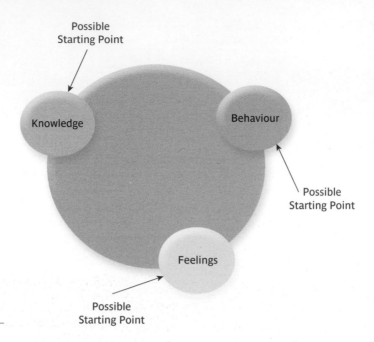

Figure 11.7
Attitude construct—circular

- Feel

Once the audience is aware of a brand and knows something about how it might be useful to them, it is important that they develop a positive attitude towards the brand. This can be achieved by presenting the brand with a set of emotional values that is thought will appeal and be of interest to the audience. These values need to be repeated in subsequent communications in order to reinforce the brand attitudes.

Marketing communications should be used to involve and immerse people in a brand. So, for example, advertising or product placement within films and music videos will help show how a brand fits in with a desirable set of values and lifestyles. Use of suitable music, characters that reflect the values of either the current target audience or an aspirational group, a tone of voice, colours, and images all help to create a particular emotional disposition and understanding about what the brand represents or stands for. For some people, advertising only works at an emotional level and the cognitive approach is irrelevant.

- Do

For a long time advertising was used by many organizations as their primary marketing communications tool. At a time when competition was not as intense as it is today, when product lifecycles were longer and innovation slower, generating and sustaining a set of brand values was often sufficient for many brands to survive. Times have changed and now most organizations find that to be successful they need to use a much broader set of tools, many of which are used to change the behaviour of the target audience. This behavioural change may be about getting people to buy the brand but it may often be about motivating them to visit a website, call for a brochure, fill in an application form, or just encouraging them to visit a shop and sample the brand free of money and any other risk. This behavioural change is also referred to as a 'call-to-action'. (See Market Insight 11.5.)

Call-to-Action against the Government

Most organizations in the UK airline industry were hit when the UK government raised air passenger duty (APD) on 1 February 2007. The rise, as much as £40 on long-haul journeys, was an attempt by the government to respond to climate warming and the carbon emissions of the airline industry.

First Choice Holidays reacted by organizing a petition requesting their customers to send a postcard of complaint to the then Chancellor, Gordon Brown. The call-to-action was founded on the postcards, all of which were pre-printed and provided free of charge by First Choice. The cards were distributed in three main ways. One, they were emailed in a letter to all their customers, from their database. Two, they were distributed in person in First Choice stores, and three, they could be downloaded from their website.

Dear Mr Brown

I believe in looking after the environment

I do, however, disagree with you putting up my holiday price and not putting the money to good use on environmental projects.

Please re-consider the introduction of this stealth tax on families.

Name ....

Address ....

....

....

Your name and address will **not** be added to any mailing lists or used for any other purpose than to forward your opposition to Gordon Brown.

Rt Hon Gordon Brown MP
Chancellor of the Exchequer
HM Treasury
1 Horse Guards Road
LONDON
SW1A 2HQ

Stealth tax on family holidays

Gordon Brown will benefit from £900 million of extra taxes every year. Tax you will have to pay unless you help us take action now.

☀ First Choice

The First Choice Holidays call to customers to complain to then Chancellor, Gordon Brown

First Choice

Although it was unlikely that a solitary event of this nature would change the government's position it did offer some interesting opportunities. For example, the imposition of the new tax rate drew complaint from many people, not because of the reasoning but because of the retrospective nature by which the tax was applied. What it did was provide companies such as First Choice with an excuse to communicate with their customers, provide a means for customer empathy, and motivate them into action and in doing so reinforce relationships.

Source: Bokaie (2007).

1 Which part of the attitude construct were First Choice trying to influence?

2 How might First Choice have used word-of-mouth communications?

RESEARCH INSIGHT 11.3

To take your learning further, you might wish to read this influential paper.

Grönroos, C. (2004), 'The relationship marketing process: communication, interaction, dialogue, value', *Journal of Business and Industrial Marketing*, 19, 2, 99–113.

Professor Grönroos is a leading researcher within the services marketing sector. In this paper he suggests that if the interaction and marketing communications processes are geared towards customers' value processes, then a relationship dialogue may develop.

When the accent is on using marketing communications to drive behaviour and action, **direct-response advertising** can be effective. It is said that 40 per cent of television ads have a telephone number or website address. However, sales promotion, direct marketing, and personal selling are particularly effective at influencing behaviour and calling the audience to act.

Cultural Aspects of Marketing Communications

Marketing communications has the potential to influence more than just customers Indeed it can be used by a wide range of other stakeholders, such as suppliers, employees, religious and faith groups, trade unions, and local communities.

The tools, media, and messages used by organizations influence and are influenced by the culture and environment in which they operate. Culture and related belief systems are significant factors in the way organizations choose to communicate in the different areas and regions in which they operate. At a broad level, for example, cases of the strong theory of advertising are observed more frequently in North America whereas examples of the weak theory are quite prevalent in Europe. (See Chapter 12 for more on strong and weak theories of advertising.)

In this final part of the chapter consideration is given to some of the cultural issues associated with marketing communication. Following a brief review of some of the key cultural elements attention is given to international marketing communications and the interesting area of signs and symbols commonly referred to as semiotics.

Culture

Operating in international markets requires a number of complex skills simply because the cultural context can be radically different from the known domestic market. International markets can be difficult to understand, if only because of

Table 11.3
Characteristics of culture

Cultural characteristic	Explanation
Learned	Culture is not innate or instinctual otherwise everyone would behave in the same way. Human beings across the world do not behave uniformly or predictably and they learn values and behaviours that are shared with common groups. Therefore, different cultures exist and there are boundaries within cultures, framing behaviours, and lifestyles.
Interrelated	There are deep connections between different elements within a culture. Therefore, family, religion, business/work, and social status are interlinked.
Shared	Cultural values are passed through family, religion, education, and the media. This progression of values enables culture to be passed from generation to generation. This is important as it provides consistency, stability, and direction for social behaviour and beliefs.

Source: Adapted from Hollensen (2005).

the depth and variety of the cultural elements, and in some regions the cultural diversity can impose restrictions on the way marketing communications is used.

Culture refers to the values, beliefs, ideas, customs, actions, and symbols that are learned by members of particular societies. Culture is important because it provides individuals within a society with a sense of identity and an understanding of what is deemed to be acceptable behaviour. According to Hollensen (2005) it is commonly agreed that culture has three key characteristics: that culture is learned, interrelated, and shared. See Table 11.3 for a fuller account of these variables.

These boundaries between cultures are not fixed or rigid, as this would suggest that cultures are static. Instead they evolve and change as members of a society adjust to new technologies, government policies, changing values, and demographic changes, to mention but a few dynamic variables. Unsurprisingly, therefore, brands and symbols used to represent brands have different meanings as they are interpreted in the light of the prevailing culture.

Before examining the different aspects of culture and their influence on marketing communications it is useful to consider the idea that culture consists of various layers. Hollensen (2005) refers to a nest of cultures, with one inside another, a structure that is similar to a 'Russian doll' (Figure 11.8).

Here it can be imagined that the buyer in one country and a seller in another are faced with several layers of culture, all interrelated and all influencing an individual's behaviour.

- **National culture**—sets out the cultural concepts and the legislative framework governing the way business is undertaken.
- **Industry/business culture**—particular business sectors adopt a way of doing business within a competitive framework. The shipping business, for example, will have its own way of conducting itself based on its own heritage. As a result all participants know what is expected and understand the rules of the game.

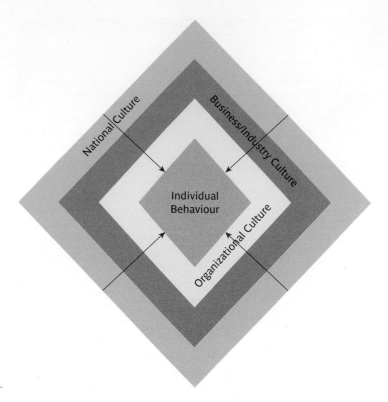

Figure 11.8
Layers of culture

Source: Global Marketing, 3rd edn., Hollensen, S., Pearson Education Limited (2005). Used with permission.

- **Organizational culture**—not only does an organization have an overall culture but the various subcultures also have a system of shared values, beliefs, meanings, and behaviours.

- **Individual behaviour**—each individual is affected by and learns from the various cultural levels.

Marketing communications, at both a formal and informal level, needs to assimilate these different levels to ensure that an individual's behaviour is understood and the decision-making processes and procedures within which they operate are appreciated. In many markets there is little to separate brands (e.g. mineral water, coffee, printers). In these cases it is the images created by marketing communications that help differentiate one brand from another and position them so that consumers develop positive attitudes and make purchasing decisions. The way in which different societies perceive these same brands is a reflection of the cultural drivers that frame people's perceptions.

Elements of Culture

Culture consists of multiple elements. These vary from language, customs, and social institutions through to education, religion, and technology to name a few. Those that are of direct relevance to marketing communications are the values and beliefs associated with symbols, such as language and aesthetics, institutions

Culturally Driven Flaxseed

Northern Edge International is a relatively small organization that markets and distributes Canadian-produced milled flaxseed. The flaxseed is highly nutritious and is used to supplement foods by sprinkling onto ice cream, breakfast cereals, and into drinks such as fruit juices and smoothies. Once successfully established in the UK the company faced some interesting and challenging marketing questions as it considered developing internationally.

The company recognized that replicating their UK success in international markets would require an understanding of different cultures and dietary habits. It is one thing for the British to accept the idea of sprinkling a food supplement on their breakfast cereal, but a different product format and marketing strategy would be needed in southern Europe, where breakfast might consist of a pastry and coffee grabbed on the way to work.

A combination of area agents, who provide local knowledge and linguistic expertise 'on the ground', and multilingual websites, with relevant information translated for key target markets, were used to anchor their international strategy. In addition, they translated the usage instructions on the packaging, and engaged professional linguists to assist with sales follow-up queries. To date, French, Lithuanian, Russian, and Thai languages have been accommodated.

Source: www.chamberonline.co.uk/YRWbQvk.html.

1 Find two other consumer goods that have been taken to new countries. Identify how they were launched in these countries noting the marketing communications tasks they were expected to accomplish.

2 What sort of marketing communication problems might a Chinese car manufacturer experience when marketing their cars in Western Europe and South America?

3 Choose a product that is manufactured or produced in your own country and consider the problems that might arise when trying to export it to Alaska.

and groups, such as those embracing the family, work, education, media, and religion, and finally technology. These are now considered in turn.

Symbols

Language is a powerful cultural element and consists of both verbal language (the spoken word) and non-verbal language such as body language, social distance, and silences. Language is important because it enables interaction between members of a society, which in turn should help shared meaning. From a marketing communications perspective it is also important to use the local language because it provides a point of access to a market, helps the collection of market information, and enables communication with local customers, distributors, and employees on terms that they easily understand and identify. (See Market Insight 11.6.)

Non-verbal language includes elements such as the distance between people when talking. Some societies prefer closeness whereas others prefer space between the participants. Being on time is important for some but punctuality is of minor importance to other societies.

Aesthetics, that is the form of design, style, and colour, can be a significant factor when attributing meaning to symbols and artistic forms. It is an integral part of packaging, sales promotions, and advertising. For example, the use of colour and brand names can be an extremely sensitive matter in some parts of the world.

Those involved in personal selling must be aware of the symbolic impact of formal and informal dress codes and the impact that overall personal appearances and gestures, for example, when greeting or leaving people, may have on people in different cultures. Advertisers need to take care that they do not infringe a culture's aesthetic codes when designing visuals or when translating copy into the local language.

Institutions and groups

Social institutions such as businesses, political parties, or families help form the fabric of most societies. In particular cultures, social institutions provide a means by which culture is communicated and perpetuated through time. These groups provide the mechanisms by which the process of socialization occurs simply because these institutions influence people's behaviour and the different ways people interrelate. Of these groups, the family plays a major role. The form of the family is evolving in some Western cultures, such that the traditional family unit is declining and the number of single-parent families is increasing. In many developing economies the extended family, with several generations living together, continues to be a central, stable part of society. Marketing communication messages need to reflect these characteristics. The impact and importance of various decision makers need to be recognized and the central creative idea needs to be up to date and sensitive to the family unit.

Education serves not only to transmit the established culture but it is also capable of changing culture. One direct outcome of education within a society is the level of literacy that is achieved. Literacy affects the ability of target audiences to understand marketing communication messages. This means that the balance between visual and non-visual components in messages and the relative complexity of messages should be considered in the light of the education levels that different countries and regions have reached.

In some countries religion is a major cultural determinant and has usually played an important part in shaping the values and attitudes of most societies. Links between religion and authority are understood and known to play important roles in family networks, in forming gender decision-making roles, and nurturing the child-rearing process. The consumption of particular foods, the role of alcohol, and role of women in some societies is governed strictly by religious beliefs. Marketing managers should take care to base their marketing communications on researched and well-informed data so as not offend their audiences. (See Market Insight 11.7.)

Technology

The way in which a society organizes its economic activity is reflected in its technological ability and development. One of the key technologies is the media, which is of course, directly related to the effectiveness of marketing communications. Media availability is far from uniform, and the range and types of media vary considerably across countries. However, media development does not occur in isolation and is normally associated with major structural and regulatory change. In many countries and regions, governments have deregulated their control over the media and as a result new trading relationships have developed.

A result of this is the emergence of cross-ownership of the media whereby one large organization owns television, newspapers, magazines, cable, satellite, film, publishing, advertising, cinema, retailing, and recorded music interests. This is referred to as media convergence and is about communications companies

MARKET INSIGHT 11.7

Promoting Brands at Ramadan

For Muslims, Ramadan is a holy period during which individuals reflect upon spiritual matters and spend the month fasting during daylight hours. For advertisers it is a bonanza month simply because at night everyone is at home with family and friends, eating, digesting, and watching television.

The media house MindShare estimate that 23% of the total television ad spend in the Middle East is invested during Ramadan. It is reported that one client puts 80% of their entire year's budget into this period. Not surprisingly heavy emphasis is given to awareness campaigns for mass audiences.

TV stations hold back some of their more popular shows, such as talk shows, soap operas, and game shows, for Ramadan because the audiences are large and they watch into the early hours of the morning whilst food is being digested. The result is that ratings are high and the cost of advertising spots can be increased, even doubled.

The messages used by advertisers in the period become more culturally sensitive in order to reflect the feeling of goodwill. For example, Pepsico see themselves as adding a bit of enjoyment and fun. Food brands start to advertise ahead of Ramadan and their messages are often geared to identifying with the festival.

As Ramadan draws to a close advertising begins to move away from food and into home furnishing, kitchen appliances, and bed and bath products. Many Muslim couples get married after the Eid Al Fitr holiday and so it is no surprise that nearly 60% of sales of 'white and brown' goods happen during and right after Ramadan.

Source: Bayte (2005); Pfanner (2005).

1 Do you think it is morally right for advertisers to take advantage of these captive audiences in this way or do they provide added value and entertainment?

2 Think about other religious events or national festivals, perhaps in your country, and consider whether the quantity of advertising increases at this time.

making their various media properties work together. Convergence arises because of three activities. The first is corporate concentration, whereby a few large organizations own more and more media properties. The second concerns digitization, whereby media content is adapted for use in any medium. The third concerns government deregulation. This means that the few media conglomerates are allowed to own different kinds of media (e.g. television and radio stations and newspapers) in the same markets. This has led to organizations that deliver content (e.g. Virgin Media) to organizations that make or produce content (e.g. speciality TV channels). This has created opportunities for client advertisers to have to go to only one media provider, who will then provide access to a raft of media content across the globe. This means that these few media conglomerates can use the same media content across many different media outlets.

International Marketing Communications

From a brief consideration of culture it is a short step to consider international marketing communications. Each of the tools of the marketing communications mix discussed earlier has a role to play in international marketing communications. The way in which the tools are used will, of course, vary and care needs to be given to ensure that the right balance and levels of integration are achieved.

However, one of the overriding issues concerns the decision about whether to use the same marketing communications approach across all operational countries or to adapt the approach to suit the needs of local customers. This standardization/adaptation debate has been very prominent since Levitt (1983) wrote a seminal paper on the topic (see Chapter 7).

The argument in favour of using the same message is based on the premise that customers in many product categories have a number of similar characteristics. As brand images are capable of universal meaning, there is little reason to develop countless brand messages. The expansion of media, technology, and international travel opportunities have affected increasing numbers of people, making it increasingly possible for strong brand images to be developed. Central managerial control helps the development and implementation of standardized campaigns. Theoretically, this should free local managers to concentrate on managing the campaign and removes from them the responsibility of generating creative ideas and associated issues with local agencies. This also means that there are cost savings, opportunities to improve the consistency of messages, communication effectiveness, and other internally related efficiencies such as staff morale, cohesion, and organizational identity.

In practice, however, there are very few brands that are truly global. Some, such as McDonald's, Coca-Cola and Levi's, are able to capitalize upon the identification and inherent brand value that they have been able to establish across cultures. The majority of brands lack this depth of personality, and because individual needs vary across cultures so enterprises need to retune their messages in order that their reception is as clear and distinct as possible.

RESEARCH INSIGHT 11.4

To take your learning further, you might wish to read this influential paper.

Harris, G., and Attour, S. (2003), 'The international advertising practices of multinational companies: a content analysis', *European Journal of Marketing*, 37, 1, 154–68.

This research demonstrates the flexible way in which the 'standardization of advertising' strategy is interpreted by different companies. The results suggest that organizations adapt their standardization policy to meet the needs of different circumstances and differing market conditions. The debate therefore should not be about total adaptation or total standardization but on the the form of standardization.

The arguments in favour of adapting marketing communications to meet the needs of particular local and/or regional needs are based around the belief that customer needs are different and vary in intensity. It is unlikely that buyers across international borders share similar experiences, abilities, and potential either to process information in a standardized way or to ascribe similar sets of meanings to the messages they perceive. Ideas and message concepts generated centrally may be inappropriate for local markets.

There are considerable variations in educational levels, the available infrastructure necessary to support the conveyance of standardized messages, and the ways in which the industry is controlled.

While a few organizations do operate at either end of the standardization/adaptation spectrum, the majority operate a middle approach, sometimes referred to as 'glocalization'. This means that there is some standardization, where, for example, creative themes, standard messages, ideas, and campaign planning are driven centrally and other campaign elements such as language, scenes, models, and media are adapted by the local country areas to meet local cultural needs.

Chapter Summary

To consolidate your learning, the key points from this chapter are summarized below:

- Explain three models of communication and describe how personal influences can enhance the effectiveness of marketing communication activities.

  The linear or one-way model of communication is the traditional mass media interpretation of how communication works. The two-way model incorporates the influence of other people in the communication process whilst the interactional model explains how communication flows not just between sender and receiver but throughout a network of people. Interaction is about actions that lead to a response and, most importantly in an age of interactive communication, interactivity is a prelude to dialogue, the highest or purest form of communication.

- Describe the nature, purpose, and scope of marketing communications.

  Marketing communications, or promotion as it was originally called, is one of the Ps of the marketing mix. It is used to communicate an organization's offer relating to products, services, or the overall organization. In broad terms the management activity consists of several components. There are the communications experienced by audiences relating to both their use of products and the consumption of associated services. There are communications arising from unplanned or unintended experiences and there are planned marketing communications.

- Understand the role and various tasks of marketing communications.

  The role of marketing communications is to engage audiences and there are four main tasks that it can be used to complete. These tasks are summarized as DRIP, that is, to differentiate, reinforce, inform, or persuade audiences to behave in particular ways. Several of these tasks can be undertaken simultaneously within a campaign.

- Explain the key characteristics associated with developing promotional messages.

  The main issues associated with message development concern the balance between providing sufficient product/service-related information and emotional content. When the customer experiences high involvement, the informational content should dominate. When audiences experience low involvement the emotional aspects should be emphasized.

- Understand the models used to explain how marketing communication is considered to work.

  These models have evolved from sequential approaches such as AIDA and the hierarchy of effects models. A circular model of the attitude construct helps understanding of the tasks of marketing communication, namely to inform audiences, to create feelings and a value associated with products and services, and to drive behaviour.

- Describe what culture is and explain how it can impact on the use of marketing communications in international environments.

  Culture refers to the values, beliefs, ideas, customs, actions, and symbols that are learned by members of particular societies. Culture is important because it provides individuals, within a society, with a sense of identity and an understanding of what is deemed to be acceptable behaviour. Culture is learned, the elements are interrelated, and culture is shared amongst members of a society or group.

  Organizations that practise marketing communications in international environments have to be fully aware of the cultural dimensions associated with each of their markets. In addition they need to consider whether it is better to use a standardized approach and use the same unmodified campaigns across all markets, or adapt campaigns to meet the needs of local markets.

 Visit the **Online Resource Centre** that accompanies this book to read more information relating to marketing communications: www.oxfordtextbooks.co.uk/orc/baines/

? Review Questions

1 Draw the linear model of communication and briefly explain each of the main elements.

2 Make brief notes outlining the meaning of interaction and how dialogue can develop.

3 Describe the main differences between opinion leaders and opinion formers.

4 Explain the key role of marketing communications and find examples to illustrate the meaning of each element in the DRIP framework.

5 What constitutes the marketing communications mix?

6 What is a hierarchy of effects model?

7 Using examples, explain the difference between informational and emotional messages.

8 Why is the circular interpretation of the attitude construct better than the linear form?

9 Hollensen (2005) argues that culture is made up of three elements and four layers. Name them.

10 Write brief notes explaining why glocalization is a better approach to international marketing communications than either standardization or adaptation alone.

? Discussion Questions

1 Having the read the Case Insight at the beginning of this chapter, how would you advise the marketing team at the London Eye to celebrate the 25 millionth visitor and how would you recommend they use marketing communications to mark the occasion?

2 Consider the key market exchange characteristics that will favour the use of linear or one-way communication and then repeat the exercise with respect to interactional communication. Discuss the differences and find examples to illustrate these conditions.

3 Jupiter Fashions provide a range of low-cost fashion clothing for young people aged 18 to 35. These are distributed though independent high street retailers. As a marketing assistant you have just returned from a conference at which the role of personal influencers was highlighted. You now wish to convey your new knowledge to your manager. Prepare a brief report in which you explain the nature of opinion leaders and formers and discuss how they might be used by Jupiter Fashions to improve their marketing communications. Using at least three examples, make it clear who you think would make good opinion formers for Jupiter.

4 Discuss the extent to which marketing communications should be used by organizations just to persuade audiences to buy products and services.

5 To what extent should organizations operating a standardization policy consider the culture of the countries they are operating in?

# References

Bagozzi, R. (1978), 'Marketing as exchange: a theory of transactions in the market place', *American Behavioural Science*, 21, 4, 257–61.

Baker, A. (2006), 'Cider brand rules', *Brand Republic*, 9 August, available at www.brandrepublic.com/news/search/article/576158/cider-brand-rules/, accessed December 2007.

Ballantyne, D. (2004), 'Dialogue and its role in the development of relationship specific knowledge', *Journal of Business & Industrial Marketing*, 19, 2, 114–23.

Bayte, A. (2005), 'What a difference a month makes', *Communicate*, available at www.communicate.ae/article_advertising.php?cle=28, accessed 5 October 2006.

Berkman, H., and Gilson, C. (1986), *Consumer Behavior: Concepts and Strategies*, Boston: Kent Publishing Co.

Bokaie, J. (2007), 'First Choice in customer call to arms on air duty', *Marketing*, 24 January, 4.

Britt, B. (2007), 'RAC readies roll-out of customer magazine', *Marketing*, 24 January, 6.

Chan, Kenny K., and Misra, Shekhar (1990), 'Characteristics of the opinion leader: a new dimension', *Journal of Advertising*, 19, 3, 53–60.

Curtis, J. (2006), 'Youth marketing: What's under the hood?', *Marketing*, 18 October, available at www.brandrepublic.com/bulletins/br/article/599163/youth-marketing-whats-hood/, accessed 31 October 2006.

Duncan, T. (2002), *IMC: Using Advertising and Promotion to Build Brand*, international edn., New York: McGraw Hill.

—— and Everett, S. (1993), 'Client perceptions of integrated marketing communications', *Journal of Advertising Research*, 3, 3, 30–9.

—— and Moriarty, S. (1998), 'A communication-based marketing model for managing relationships', *Journal of Marketing*, 62 (April), 1–13.

Dwyer, R., Schurr, P., and Oh, S. (1987), 'Developing buyer–seller relationships', *Journal of Marketing*, 51 (April), 11–27.

Fill, C. (2002), *Marketing Communications: Contexts, Strategies and Applications*, 3rd edn., Harlow: FT/Prentice Hall.

—— (2005), *Marketing Communications: Engagement, Strategy and Practice*, 4th edn., Harlow: FT/Prentice Hall.

Grönroos, C. (2004), 'The relationship marketing process: communication, interaction, dialogue, value', *Journal of Business and Industrial Marketing*, 19, 2, 99–113.

Harris, G., and Attour, S. (2003), 'The international advertising practices of multinational companies: a content analysis', *European Journal of Marketing*, 37, 1, 154–68.

Hoffman, D. L., and Novak, P. T. (1996), 'Marketing in hyper computer-mediated environments: conceptual foundations', *Journal of Marketing*, 60 (July), 50–68.

Hollensen, S. (2005), *Global Marketing*, 3rd edn., Harlow: FT/Prentice Hall.

Houston, F., and Gassenheimer, J. (1987), 'Marketing and exchange', *Journal of Marketing*, 51 (October), 3–18.

Hughes, G., and Fill, C. (2007), 'Redefining the nature and format of the marketing communications mix', *Marketing Review*, 7, 1 (March), 45–57.

Katz, E., and Lazarsfeld, P. F. (1955), *Personal Influence: The Part Played by People in the Flow of Mass Communication*, Glencoe, Ill.: Free Press.

Kemp, E. (2007), 'Nokia strategy rethink spurs global as review', *Marketing*, 24 January, 2.

Kitchen, P. (1993), 'Marketing communications renaissance', *International Journal of Advertising*, 12, 4, 367–86.

—— Brignell, J., Li, T., and Spickett Jones, G. (2004), 'The emergence of IMC: a theoretical perspective', *Journal of Advertising Research*, 44 (March), 19–30.

Lavidge, R. J., and Steiner, G. A. (1961), 'A model for predictive measurements of advertising effectiveness', *Journal of Marketing*, 25, 6 (October), 59–62.

Levitt, T. (1983), 'The globalization of markets', *Harvard Business Review*, 61 (May–June), 92–102.

Pfanner, E. (2005), 'On advertising: ad agencies see revenue in Ramadan', *International Herald Tribune*, Sunday, 2 October, available at www.iht.com/articles/2005/10/02/business/ad03.php, accessed 4 October 2006.

Schramm, W. (1955), 'How communication works', in W. Schramm (ed.), *The Process and Effects of Mass Communications*, Urbana, Ill.: University of Illinois Press, 3–26.

Shannon, C., and Weaver, W. (1962), *The Mathematical Theory of Communication*, Urbana, Ill.: University of Illinois Press.

Stokes, D., and Lomax, W. (2002), 'Taking control of word of mouth marketing: the case of an entrepreneurial hotelier', *Journal of Small Business and Enterprise Development*, 9, 4, 349–57.

Strong, E. K. (1925), *The Psychology of Selling*, New York: McGraw-Hill.

Theodorson, S. A., and Theodorson, G. R. (1969), *A Modern Dictionary of Sociology*, New York: Cromwell.

Woods, S. (2006), 'Heineken launches *Casino Royale*-themed ad campaign', *Brand Republic*, 30 October, available at www.brandrepublic.com/bulletins/br/article/601475/heineken-launches-casino-royalethemed-ad-campaign/, accessed 29 January, 2007.

12

Marketing Communications: Tools and Techniques

The medium is the message.

Marshall McLuhan

Learning Outcomes

After studying this chapter you should be able to:

✔ Describe the configuration and role of the marketing communications mix.

✔ Explain the role and characteristics of each of the primary tools of the communication mix.

✔ Understand and set out the criteria that should be used to select the right communication mix.

✔ Explain the characteristics of the different media and how they are categorized.

✔ Discuss some of the changes that are happening in the media and communication landscape.

London Zoo, located in The Regent's Park in the centre of London, has recently changed its name to ZSL London Zoo. Why? We speak to James Bailey to find out more.

James Bailey
for ZSL London Zoo

Following a segmentation exercise it was revealed that 18% of the UK population are what we call 'open conservationists'. These people would be more likely to visit zoos if they were aware of the conservation work that zoos did. This presented us with an opportunity, an opportunity to increase the potential audience within 90 minutes' drive time by 1.4 m people. We believe that if we could make London Zoo more synonymous with conservation it would give these people permission to visit the Zoo.

So, we changed the name to ZSL to reflect the conservation work of the Zoological Society of London, a charity that operates London Zoo and the sister Zoo, Whipsnade. ZSL carries out conservation work in 30 countries around the world but there is very little awareness about ZSL. By using ZSL as a master brand we hope to accelerate the awareness of ZSL and prompt people to ask the question who is ZSL and what do they do? Once people become more aware of ZSL and its work they will associate the two zoos with conservation.

To attract visitors ZSL use a range of marketing communications tools and media. Public relations is very important as it allows us to convey the wider message of ZSL's conservation work whilst personal selling has become more important recently as we strive to develop relationships with key customers in the travel trade industry so that they sell more tickets to their own clients through various distribution outlets. Direct marketing is used to target specific consumer and trade groups, using a mixture of direct mail and email communications. Advertising is a key tool and is used to sell tickets. Sales promotion is not a key tool as ZSL need to maintain high levels of per capita income although we did discount heavily to get people back to the zoo following the bombs in London in 2005.

> *the use of the various [marketing] tools and media is very important… we use a media agency to help advise on the mix*

The main visitor season commences during the spring each year and runs through to the end of September. In order to maximize the number of visitors in this period the use of the various tools and media is very important. The objectives that we set ourselves also determine the mix. Budget constraints play a key part in determining the media used. We use a media agency to help and advise on the mix and to do this we provide the agency with information such as the demographics of the target market, which they then run against TGI data. This analysis produces a whole range of different tactics that are appropriate for our target market. We then use our knowledge of the market to make the final decision.

When we launched 'Gorilla Kingdom' recently we needed to promote the exhibit as a key attraction. Once the product was named, the brand developed, and the creative direction established, the crucial question was which tools and which media we should we use.

Which tools and media would you use to attract visitors to see Gorilla Kingdom?

ZSL
LONDON
ZOO

GORILLA KINGDOM
NEW UP-CLOSE EXPERIENCE

Opens 30th March 2007

ZSL
LIVING CONSERVATION

The Zoological Society of London (ZSL) is a charity devoted
to the worldwide conservation of animals and their habitats.
Registered Charity in England & Wales: no 208728

enjoyEngland
Awards for:
Excellence 2006
GOLD WINNER

SAVE 10%
at zsl.org

GORILLA
KINGDOM

CAMDEN TOWN

MAYOR OF LONDON

Introduction

What are the 'touchpoints' that you have with your mobile phone provider? Email, telephone, direct mail items, and snail mail for personal **communications**? What about television ads, web pages, articles and ads in magazines, posters, and perhaps news items that generate general brand awareness? Organizations use a variety of tools and **media** to engage their audiences. Collectively these are referred to as the **marketing communications mix**, a set of five tools that can be used in various combinations, and different degrees of intensity, in order to communicate with target audiences. The five principal marketing communications tools are: **advertising**, **sales promotion**, **public relations**, **direct marketing**, and **personal selling**, and are set out at Figure 12.1.

In addition to this mix of tools there is the media, used primarily, but not exclusively, to deliver advertising messages to target audiences. Although the term media refers to any mechanism or device that can carry a message, we refer to paid-for media, processes and systems that are owned by third parties, such as the News Corporation (they own the *Sun* and the *Sunday Times* newspapers plus the BSkyB television platform), Condé Nast (who own *Tatler*, *Vanity Fair*, and *Vogue* magazines, amongst others), Singapore Press Holdings (who own the *Business Times* in Singapore), and Time Warner Inc., a 'leading media and entertainment company, whose businesses include interactive services, cable systems, filmed entertainment, television networks and publishing'. These organizations rent out time and space to client organizations so that they can send their messages and make content available to various audiences. The list of available paid-for media is expanding all the time but it is possible to identify six key classes of media. These are broadcast, print, outdoor, in-store, digital, and other (which includes both cinema and ambient media). All of these are explored in this chapter.

When we refer to the marketing communications mix, we do not include the media as they have different characteristics and are used in different ways to achieve different goals. On completing this chapter readers should understand that each of the tools and each of the media possesses various characteristics.

(opposite)

An advert for the rebranded ZSL London Zoo

ZSL London Zoo

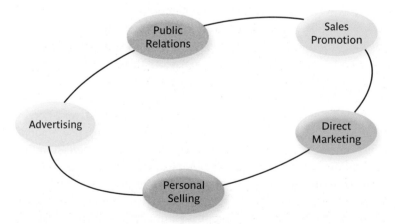

Figure 12.1

Tools of the communication mix

This means that it is possible to configure different mixes of tools and media and that these can be shaped to achieve different goals.

The next section considers the role of marketing communications, before examining each of the tools of the mix. This is followed by a consideration of the main types of media, the principles of media planning and an examination of the way in which the nature and role of the media has changed.

The Role and Purpose of the Marketing Communications Mix

Up until the mid-1980s organizations were able to use a fairly predictable and stable range of tools and media. Advertising was used to build awareness and brand values, sales promotions were used to stimulate demand, public relations conveyed goodwill messages about organizations, and personal selling was seen as a means of getting orders, particularly in the business-to-business market. However, there have been some major changes in the environment and in the way organizations communicate with their target audiences. New technology has given rise to a raft of different media and opportunities for advertisers to reach their audiences. We now have access to hundreds of commercial television and radio channels, not just a few. Cinemas show multiple films at multiplex sites, and the internet has transformed the way in which we communicate, educate, inform, and entertain ourselves. This expansion of the media is referred to as **media fragmentation**. At the same time people have developed a whole host of new ways to spend their leisure time; they are no longer locked in and restricted to a few media. This expansion of media choice is referred to as **audience fragmentation**. So, whilst the range and type of media has expanded, the size of audiences that each medium commands has generally shrunk.

For organizations, one of the key challenges is to find the right mix of tools and media that allow them to reach their target audiences economically. To do this they have had to revise and develop their marketing communication mixes in order to reach their audiences. For example, in the 1990s there was a dramatic rise in the use of direct-response media as direct marketing emerged as a new tool to be added to the mix. Now the internet and digital technologies have enabled new interactive forms of communication, where the receiver has greater responsibility for their part in the communication process and is now encouraged to interact with the sender. As a result of these changes many organizations are reducing their investment in traditional media and putting it into digital media.

The role of the mix has changed from one based on persuading customers in the short term to buy products and services, to a longer-term perspective, whereby the mix is intended to facilitate communication with a wide range of stakeholders, and on a broader range of issues. New goals such as developing understanding and preference, reminding and reassuring customers, have now become accepted as important aspects of marketing communications. The pursuit of integrated marketing communications has become a popular activity and some organizations are trying to use the mix to help develop relationships with not just key customers, but key suppliers and other important stakeholders. Today, therefore, an increasing number of organizations are using the mix to develop relationships with key suppliers and customers, as customer retention, not acquisition, becomes a strategic marketing goal.

Each of the tools of the marketing communications mix has developed in an off-line environment. However, the development of the internet has presented new opportunities for each of the tools to be delivered through online media. Many organizations have found that the principles through which particular tools work offline do not apply in an online environment. New approaches and ideas have been sought and there is no established way of operating in an online context. (See Chapter 18 for more information about the way the tools work online, but read this chapter first, to establish the principles.)

The marketing communications mix is a vital part of the process that conveys added value to stakeholders. It is expected that marketing communications, and the mix of tools and media it uses, needs to embrace a wider remit, to move beyond the product information model and become an integral part of an organization's overall communications and relationship management strategy. Above all else, the marketing communications mix should be utilized as an audience-centred activity. (See Market Insight 12.1 for the marketing communications mix used by Virgin Media.)

Advertising

Many people confuse advertising with marketing: they believe that they are the same, that marketing is advertising. However, as readers of this book realize, advertising is just a part of the much broader marketing remit, albeit a very visible element.

Advertising is a non-personal form of communication, where a clearly identifiable sponsor pays for a message to be transmitted through media. Advertising is one of several tools used to communicate an organization's marketing offer. One of the distinctive qualities that advertising brings to the mix is that it reaches large, often mass audiences in an impersonal way.

Advertising, together with the other tools of the communications mix, is a means of managing demand. At a general level, advertising can be used in one of two main ways. First, it can be used to influence demand for products (and services) or, second, it can be used to manage perceptions and understanding about the organization as a whole. Such organizational (or institutional) advertising seeks to influence the opinions, attitudes, and perception of different stakeholders towards the organization. However, the role of advertising is to engage audiences and this engagement is dependent upon the context in which the communication occurs.

Virgin Media Announce Themselves

In 2007 the Virgin Media brand was launched following the merger and integration of cable operators NTL and Telewest, with broadband provider Virgin.net and mobile provider Virgin Mobile. The result was the creation of a media company designed to meet all consumer media and entertainment needs, through the provision of digital TV, broadband, mobile, and fixed line phone services. The rebranding and launch of this major new media company was critical in order for it to establish itself in the market and to retain its current customers.

The heavyweight campaign used a variety of media, led by email messages and a direct mail pack sent to the established 7.5 m customers informing them of the change and the benefits Virgin Media were to provide. This was followed by a £20 m TV campaign, launched on Valentine's Day, designed to create awareness of the new media provider. This campaign was led by Hollywood film star Uma Thurman, who recently starred as lead actor in *Kill Bill*. Newspaper advertising and the free *Metro* newspaper that was wrapped in Virgin Media promotional materials were used to support the launch and convey information about the various package costs and the £30 deal for customers who bought into all the services. Inevitably there was substantial press coverage of the launch, partly stimulated by press releases on the Virgin Media website with comment to be found in all the leading newspapers, online, and television.

Although the Virgin Media campaign was fairly conventional, there were some interesting and contemporary associated developments. Major competitor Sky pre-empted the campaign with a series of ads, on TV and in magazines and outdoor, that attempted to disrupt the Virgin Media launch. They undercut Virgin on price. Their message was that Virgin Media would not be screening key programmes such as *Lost*, *24*, and *The Simpsons*; only Sky could deliver these. The other interesting development concerned the amount of word-of-mouth communication. In addition to comment about the launch and possibly the slightly provocative script of the TV ad itself, various blogs proclaimed the disenchantment of some customers who had bought into the new £30 package only to experience broadband set-up difficulties and questionable levels of customer service.

Sources: Virginmedia.com; Goodman (2007); Sweney (2007); White (2007).

1 Why did Virgin Media use direct mail before TV advertising and which tools and media were not used?

2 In addition to creating awareness, what else might the TV campaign have set out to achieve?

3 Why was Uma Thurman used? Who would you have used to front the campaign, and why?

The Strong and the Weak Theories of Advertising

In Chapter 11 we saw how understanding about the way marketing communications works drew on earlier ideas principally concerning **hierarchy of effects** models. However, these sequential approaches have not proved to be universally applicable to all buying situations. So, if advertising cannot be assumed to work in just one particular way what other explanations are there? Of the various models put forward two in particular stand out. These are the strong (Jones, 1991) and the weak (Ehrenberg, 1974) theories of advertising.

The Strong Theory of Advertising

According to Jones (1991) advertising is capable of persuading people to buy a product that they have not previously purchased. Advertising can also generate long-run purchase behaviour. Under the strong theory, advertising is believed to be capable of increasing sales for a brand and for the product class. These upward shifts are achieved through the use of manipulative and psychological techniques, which are deployed against largely passive consumers, who, possibly due to apathy, are either generally incapable of processing information intelligently or have little or no motivation to become involved.

This interpretation is a persuasion view and corresponds very well with the hierarchy of effects models referred to earlier. Persuasion occurs by moving buyers towards a purchase by easing them through a series of steps, prompted by timely and suitable promotional messages. It seems that this approach correlates closely with new products where new buying behaviours are required.

The strong theory has close affiliation with an advertising style that is product oriented, where features and benefits are outlined clearly for audiences, and where pack shots are considered important.

The Weak Theory of Advertising

Contrary to the strong perspective is the view that a consumer's brand choices are driven by purchasing habit rather than by exposure to promotional messages. One of the more prominent researchers in this area is Ehrenberg (1997), who believes that advertising represents a weak force and that consumers are active information processors.

Ehrenberg proposes that the **ATR** framework (awareness–trial–reinforcement) is a more appropriate interpretation of how advertising works. Both Jones and Ehrenberg agree that awareness is required before any purchase can be made, although the elapsed time between awareness and action may be very short or very long. Out of the mass of people exposed to a message a few will be sufficiently intrigued to want to try a product (trial), the next phase. Reinforcement follows to maintain awareness and provide reassurance to help customers repeat the pattern of thinking and behaviour. Advertising's role is to breed brand familiarity and identification (Ehrenberg, 1997).

According to the weak theory, advertising is employed as a defence, to retain customers and to increase product or brand usage. Advertising is used to reinforce existing attitudes, not necessarily to drastically change them. This means that when people say that they 'are not influenced by advertising' they are in the main correct.

Both the strong and the weak theories of advertising are important because they are equally right and they are equally wrong. The answer to the question

RESEARCH INSIGHT 12.1

To take your learning further, you might wish to read this influential paper.

Vakratsas, D., and Ambler, T. (1999), 'How advertising works: what do we really know?', *Journal of Marketing*, 63 (January), 26–43.

In an attempt to understand the interaction between consumers and advertising the authors review more than 250 journal articles and books. They conclude that there is no support for any particular hierarchical model that explains how advertising works. They propose that advertising should be considered in terms of affect, cognition, and experience (see the general model proposed in Chapter 11) and that understanding the context is absolutely imperative (e.g. goals, product category, competition, other aspects of mix, stage of product lifecycle, and target market).

'How does advertising work?' lies somewhere between the two and is dependent upon the context. For advertising to work involvement is likely to be high and so here the strong theory is the most applicable. However, the vast majority of product purchase decisions generate low involvement, and so decision making is likely to be driven by habit. Here advertising's role is to maintain a brand's awareness with the purchase cycle.

Sales Promotion

For a long time sales promotion was regarded by many as a rather grubby and squalid occupation. However, its prestige grew as organizations began to realize the opportunities sales promotions offered to snatch customers from rival brands and stimulate short-term sales results. This resulted in funds being switched out of advertising into sales promotion activities. Now, in the UK, the sales promotion business is worth over £7 billion per annum (ISP, 2007) and has become an established, professional, and effective part of the marketing communications mix.

Sales promotions are used extensively in consumer markets, especially when launching new brands, and in markets that are mature, where market growth is limited and where price and sales promotion work are the only ways of inducing brand-switching behaviour and improving performance. However, sales promotions should not be used in isolation from the other tools in the mix, indeed they work more effectively when supported by advertising and personal selling.

Although there are many sales promotion techniques, the one thing they have in common is that they all offer a direct inducement or an incentive to encourage customers to buy a product/service. These inducements can be targeted at consumers, distributors, agents, and members of the sales force.

Sales promotions are concerned with offering customers additional value, in order to induce an immediate sale. These sales might well have taken place without the presence of an incentive, it is simply that the inducement brings the time of the sale forward. It is said that the sales promotions work by 'accelerating' sales. Imagine a consumer who is brand loyal to Gold Blend, Café Noir, or Tesco own-brand coffee. They buy the favourite brand of coffee regularly every three weeks. However, in week two of the cycle they notice a bonus pack offer on their preferred brand. By buying early not only are they locked into that brand for a further six weeks they have also excluded all competitor brands from getting their business for at least the same period.

There are a variety of sales promotion methods or techniques and the main ones are set out in Table 12.1. These methods vary in their characteristics but they are essentially incentives, designed to reward buyers behaving in particular ways.

Retailers use sales promotions to generate 'store traffic' and to increase the number of people who become store (brand) loyal. These promotions are therefore targeted at store switchers and non-store users. They are also used to simply

Table 12.1

Sales promotions: targets, goals, and methods

Audience	Method	Explanation
Targeted at retailers	Stock allowances	Goal = to incentivize stores to trial a new product. Method = Resellers are entitled to a refund or allowance of x per cent off the regular case or carton price, in return for specific orders between certain dates.
	Performance allowances	Goal = to reward stores for good sales performance. Method = Provides a reward (allowance) for product sold into a store during a specified period of time.
	Advertising allowances	Goal = to incentivize stores to keep selling a product. Method = Either prices are discounted for purchases made during a particular campaign or a contribution is made to the reseller's advertising campaign.
Targeted at customers	Sampling	Goal = to incentivize customers to trial a new product. Method = Free miniature versions of the actual product can be used to win new customers and to protect a customer base. Samples can take the form of demonstrations, trial size packs that have to be purchased, or free use for a certain period of time.
	Coupons	Goal = to incentivize customers to trial a new product. Method = A certificate valid for a set period of time is presented when buying the product entitling the customer to a price discount.
	Deals	Goal = to incentivize customers to keep buying a product. Method = Price-offs, bonus packs, and refunds and rebates all designed to encourage trial or repeat purchase.
	Premiums	Goal = to incentivize customers to increase their consumption. Method = Items of merchandise offered free or at a low cost in return for purchase of one or many products or services.
	Contests and sweepstakes	Goal = to incentivize customers to increase their consumption. Method = A contest occurs when customers compete for prizes or money on the basis of skills or ability. Entry requires a proof of purchase and winners are judged against a set of predetermined criteria. A sweepstake is a sales promotion technique where the winners are determined by chance and proof of purchase is not required.

move stock (and associated costs) from the retailers' shelves to the cupboards, freezers, and refrigerators of their customers.

Manufacturers also use sales promotions to incentivize their dealers' sales force teams. Contests and sales meetings are used a great deal, and if organized and planned properly can be very effective in raising the performance. By appealing to their competitive nature, contests can bring about effective new product introductions, revive falling sales, offset a rival's competitive moves, and build a strong customer base. Sales meetings provide an opportunity for management to supply fresh information to the sales force about performance, stock positions, competitor activities, price deals, consumer or reseller promotions, and new products.

Public Relations

Public relations is an important tool within the marketing communication mix because, unlike the other tools in the mix, its primary purpose is to influence the way an organization is perceived by various groups of stakeholders. An early view held that public relations should influence levels of interest and goodwill towards an organization. A more contemporary view is that public relations is concerned with the management of relationships between organizations and their publics (Bruning and Ledingham, 2000). Public relations should be used by management as a means of understanding issues from a stakeholder perspective. Good relationships are developed by appreciating the views held by others and by 'putting oneself in their shoes'.

Kent and Taylor (2002) emphasize the point that communication is a means of managing relationships. In order to realize the full potential within relationships it is argued that organizations need to develop communications that are based on dialogue rather than a simple exchange of information. In order to make this happen it is necessary at a practical level to place email, web addresses, 0800 telephone numbers, contact names, and organizational addresses prominently in all forms of external communication, most notably advertisements and websites, as these enable interaction and dialogue.

Our definition of public relations builds on these relationship dimensions. 'Public relations is a management activity that attempts to shape the attitudes and opinions held by an organization's stakeholders. It attempts to identify its own policies with the interests of its stakeholders and formulates and executes a programme of action to develop mutual goodwill and understanding. Through this process relationships are developed which are in the long-run interests of all parties.'

The Role of Public Relations

There are three main roles that public relations plays within an organization's marketing communications. These are the development and maintenance of corporate goodwill, the continuity necessary for good product support, and through these the development and maintenance of suitable relationships.

The first role involves the creation of goodwill and interest between the organization and its various key stakeholders. The role is to provide a series of cues by which the stakeholders can recognize, understand, and position the organization in such a way that the organization builds a strong reputation.

The second role is to support the marketing of the organization's products and services, with a view to integrating the other elements of the communication mix. For example, the complementary role of public relations and advertising is important when launching a new product. Normally, this type of campaign would commence with public relations informing editors and news broadcasters that a new product is about to be launched. This news material can be used within the trade and consumer press before advertising is used to build customer awareness.

The third role is to help build relationships. Public relations is used to encourage interaction and dialogue and to provide the means through which information exchange and discussion can occur. This is a complex role, as the communication process needs to enable messages to be conveyed, listened to, considered, and acted upon.

There are a range of public relations methods available to organizations and different organizations use different permutations in order that they can communicate effectively with their various stakeholder audiences. For the purposes of simplicity a short summary of each approach is provided within Table 12.2.

Characteristics of Public Relations

One of the key characteristics that differentiate public relations from the other tools is that it does not require the purchase of airtime or space in media vehicles, such as television or magazines. The decision about whether an organization's intended public relations messages are transmitted, or not, rests with those charged with managing the media resource, not the client organization. The outcome is that these messages usually carry greater perceived credibility than those messages transmitted through paid media, such as advertising. The people who make these decisions are often journalists and editors. In many ways they represent opinion formers, people who through their professional expertise can influence the decisions made by others.

This leads to the next key characteristic, namely that messages received through public relations are deemed to be highly credible. As a result these messages are regarded as more trustworthy and hence a greater degree of confidence can be placed in their content. Against these positive aspects is the low level of control that management can exert on a message, as it is the editor who decides whether a message will be conveyed. For example, a press release may have been carefully prepared in-house, but as soon as it is passed to the editor of a magazine or newspaper, a possible opinion former, all control is lost. The release may be destroyed (highly probable), printed as it stands (highly unlikely), or changed to fit the available space in the **media vehicle** (almost certain, if it is decided to use the material). This means that any changes to the message may not have been agreed with management, so the context and style of the original message may be lost or corrupted.

Table 12.2
Public relations:
methods and
techniques

Form of public relations	Explanation
Media relations	Consists of a range of activities (press releases, interviews, press kits, and press conferences) designed to provide media journalists and editors with information. Information received is then conveyed through the media, for consumption by the target audiences.
Publicity and events	There are three main event activities: product events (focused upon increasing sales), corporate events (providing entertainment leading to interest and goodwill), and community events (these contribute to the life of the local community and in doing so develop goodwill and awareness in the community).
Lobbying	Used by organizations when legislation or regulations are being prepared. The goal is to ensure that the views of the organization are heard in order that legislation can be shaped appropriately, limiting any potential damage that new legislation might bring. Used a great deal by the pharmaceutical and tobacco industries.
Sponsorship	Sponsorship allows one organization to reach the audience of another in order to develop new or established product and service-based associations.
Crisis management	Crises may happen due to uncontrollable events (e.g. climate change) or events which are potentially controllable but due to mismanagement an organization suffers a temporary or even permanent failure. Crisis communications aim to avert or diminish the impact of both offline and online threats.
Public affairs	A means by which organizations seek to influence public policy and use lobbying and the media to influence opinion.
Industry relations	Maintaining and enhancing relationships with suppliers, trade associations, and other industry-related stakeholders is necessary in order to influence the direction and public voice of the trade.
Issues management	The success of an organization can be affected by the way in which public policies allow the organization to operate. Issues management is about addressing public policy and reputation issues that can affect the way in which an organization operates, in the long term.

The costs associated with public relations also make this an important tool in the communication mix. The absolute costs are minimal, except for those organizations that retain an agency, but even then their costs are low compared with those associated with advertising. The relative costs (the proportional costs associated with reaching each member of the target audience) are also very low. The main costs associated with public relations are the time and opportunity costs associated with the preparation of press releases, associated literature, and events.

A further characteristic of this tool is that it can be used to reach specific audiences, in a way that paid media cannot. With increasing media fragmentation and finer segmentation (customization) of markets, public relations activities represent a cost-effective way of reaching such markets and audiences.

Digital technology has transformed the development and practice of public relations (Gregory, 2004). With regard to the use of the internet by public relations practitioners Gregory identifies two main schools. One refers to those who use the internet as an extension to traditional or pre-internet forms of communication. The second see opportunities through the internet to develop two-way, enhanced communication.

Market Insight 12.2 explores the PR campaign used by Australian Airline Qantas.

MARKET INSIGHT 12.2

PR Taking Off

The Qantas advertising campaign with its 'pilot', actor John Travolta

Qantas

The Australian airline Qantas worked with the Hollywood actor and fully qualified pilot John Travolta in a programme called *Spirit of Friendship*. The aim of the programme was to use Travolta as a brand ambassador, to encourage people to cross borders, rekindle friendships and make new friends, and, of course, fly Qantas.

In order to attract media other than aviation and business publications, the public relations exercise focused on the relationship between Travolta and Qantas as a 'unique global initiative' with intrinsic newsworthiness. This leverage was used to attract the entertainment and international press in addition to wire services and major market newspapers.

The PR campaign featured major conferences in Los Angeles and New York. BWR, the agency appointed to run the programme, sent media invitations for the Los Angeles press conference using only Travolta's name and the hint of a 'unique global initiative', leaving the press to speculate what the fuss was all about. The agency then pursued key media, both national and international, to attend both press conferences in Los Angeles and New York, often using the promise of exclusives to guarantee position in critical media. They also transformed the abandoned Imperial Terminal at Los Angeles International Airport so that it replicated the Qantas Airways First-Class Lounge in Sydney, Australia. In addition to this they created extensive b-roll footage and photography that was later distributed to media to remind and support the programme. Finally, the agency created a brand/project-specific press package to highlight the tour and showcase John Travolta in a classic 1964 pilot uniform as well as managing the media on site.

The results of the *Spirit of Friendship* campaign serve to demonstrate the effectiveness of a well-run and creatively excellent public relations campaign. The following information is taken directly from the Ogilvy PR website.

- Qantas key markets had numerous international hits from the Los Angeles and New York press conferences. The global public relations value exceeded $42 million.

- More than 300 local and national television breaks highlighted the Qantas *Spirit of Friendship* Global Tour including segments on *Entertainment Tonight*, *Access Hollywood*, *Live with Regis and Kelly*, and *CNN Headline News*.

- The Los Angeles and New York press conferences garnered more than 450 print articles with items ranging from *Time* to *People*; extensive coverage in many of the major market newspapers throughout the country including *Los Angeles Times* and *Chicago Tribune*.

- Total audience reached: 50 million+ in the United States alone.

- More than 900 television breaks worldwide highlighted the Qantas *Spirit of Friendship* Global Tour including segments on *HBO Asia* in Hong Kong, *BBC News* in London, and *RAI 1* in Rome.

- More than 2,000 print articles worldwide featured the Qantas *Spirit of Friendship* Global Tour with items ranging from the *Sunday Telegraph* in Australia to the *Sunday Times* in London; extensive print coverage in all US markets for every stop of the tour.

Source: www.ogilvypr.com/case-studies/qantas.cfm. Used with permission.

1 What is the role of the press release and how were these used in the *Spirit of Friendship* campaign?

2 To what extent was the *Spirit of Friendship* a credible campaign?

3 Identity the key stakeholders you believe Qantas tried to reach with the Travolta-inspired campaign.

Direct Marketing

Direct marketing is concerned with the management of customer behaviour and refers to all media-based activities that generate a series of communications and responses directly with an existing or potential customer. Direct marketing is often used to complement the strengths and weaknesses of the other communication tools as all the elements of the mix can be used, with direct marketing, to support and build meaningful relationships with both consumers and business customers.

Direct marketing is used to create and sustain a personal and intermediary-free communication with customers, potential customers, and other significant stakeholders. In most cases this is a media-based activity and offers great scope for the collection and utilization of pertinent and measurable data (Fill, 2005). This definition highlights the point that direct marketing should be a measurable activity, that is, any response(s) must be associated with a particular individual, a particular media activity, and a particular outcome, such as a sale or enquiry for further information. A further point concerns the rewards that direct marketing can bring. Recipients of direct marketing benefit from shopping convenience, time utility, and the satisfaction and trust associated with the personal attention that direct marketing can provide.

For organizations, one of the key benefits of direct marketing is that there is limited communication wastage. The precision associated with target marketing means that messages are sent to, received, processed, and responded to by members of the target audience, and no others. This is unlike advertising where messages often reach some people who are not targets and are unlikely to be involved with the brand.

The direct marketer also derives benefits by interacting with established customers and not having to always find new customers. Yes, direct marketing is used to acquire new customers but the opportunity to cross-sell related products to customers who have knowledge and a certain level of trust and confidence in you is very attractive.

The Role of Direct Marketing

The primary role of both advertising and public relations is to provide information and to develop brand values. However, the primary role of sales promotion, direct marketing, and personal selling is to drive a response and shape the behaviour of the target audience.

The key role of direct marketing is to reach target audiences with personalized and customized messages that aim to provoke a change in the audience's behaviour. These direct communications often carry a behavioural or what is referred to as a **call-to-action** message. In order to reach audiences with call-to-action messages, direct marketing uses a variety of media. These include the telephone, internet, direct mail, email, press, and posters.

A secondary role of direct marketing is to collect customer information, vast quantities of information in many cases, in order to feed future strategies and campaigns. This role has been made easier with the development of Information Systems and Technology (IST). In particular, developments within database technologies have enabled the introduction of a range of other, primarily electronic media, to carry direct messages and provide detailed information about a customer's product likes and dislikes, brand preferences, purchase frequencies, and even data about birthdays and pastimes. For example, British Gas used email and

Direct Contacts at the Airport

The role of contact centres within direct marketing has become increasingly critical. For example, the BAA (the British Airports Authority) which operates seven of Britain's largest airports, including Heathrow, has expanded its business, partly by using an outsourced multichannel contact centre. Inbound enquiries from travellers about car parking and those seeking to complain about services and facilities represented an opportunity to cross-sell a range of other services. Enquiries totalling 500,000 each year, routed through email, web, and telephone channels, are now redirected to the MMTelepresence contact centre network. The operators handle orders and process payments, advise people not only about car parking but also offer foreign currency, travel insurance, and hotel rooms.

BAA have developed a database around the information generated from their 250,000 active customers. This data is used to inform further marketing communications with the goal of generating responses and purchase activity at all stages in the customer lifecycle. The contact centre operation now generates £10 m in revenue which is important but they also help to raise the profile of BAA, add value, and in the long run influence its reputation.

Source: McLuhan (2006).

1 Why do BAA use a contact centre when a well-developed website with a Frequently Asked Question (FAQ) section could save them millions of pounds?

2 How might the database be used to inform marketing communications?

direct mail to offer clock-calculators as an incentive to their Home Care Service customers to switch to direct debit payments. Likewise, Market Insight 12.3 looks at BAA's use of direct marketing to build a customer database.

Direct-Response Media

The main reason for using direct-response media is that direct contact is made with prospects and customers. This should lead to a direct response or interaction that can lead to a dialogue. Direct mail, telemarketing, and door-to-door activities are the main direct-response media, as they allow more personal, direct, and evaluative means of reaching precisely targeted customers. However, in reality any type of media can be used, simply by attaching a telephone number, website address, mailing address, or response card. Table 12.3 sets out the main media used within direct-response marketing.

Originally direct mail and telemarketing were the dominant direct-response media. The growth in consumer-based direct mail activities has outstripped that of the business-to-business sector. Organizations in the financial services sectors

Table 12.3

Direct response
media

Types of DR media	Explanation
Direct mail	Direct mail refers to personally addressed advertising that is delivered through the postal system. It can be personalized and targeted with great accuracy, and its results are capable of precise measurement. Direct mail can be expensive, at anything between £250 and £500 per 1,000 items dispatched. It should, therefore, be used selectively and for purposes other than creating awareness.
Telemarketing	The telephone provides interaction, flexibility, immediate feedback, and the opportunity to overcome objections, all within the same communication event. Telemarketing also allows organizations to undertake separate marketing research which is both highly measurable and accountable in that the effectiveness can be verified continuously and call rates, contacts reached, and the number and quality of positive and negative responses are easily recorded and monitored.
Carelines	Carelines and contact centres enable customers to complain about a product performance and related experiences seek product-related advice, make suggestions regarding product or packaging development, and comment about an action or development concerning the brand as a whole.
Inserts	Inserts are media materials that are placed inside magazines or direct mail letters. These provide factual information about the product or service and enable the recipient to respond to the request of the direct marketer. This request might be to place an order, visit a website, or post back a card for more information, such as a brochure. Inserts are popular because they are good at generating leads, even though their cost is substantially higher than a four-colour advertisement in the magazine in which the insert is carried.
Print	There are two main forms of direct-response advertising through the printed media: first, catalogues, and secondly, magazines and newspapers. Consumer direct print ads sometimes offer an incentive, and are designed explicitly to drive customers to a website, where transactions can be completed without reference to retailers, dealers, or other intermediaries.
Door to door	Although the content and quality can be controlled in the same way, door-to-door response rates are lower than direct mail because of the lack of a personal address mechanism. Door to door can be much cheaper than direct mail as there are no postage charges to be accounted for.
Radio and television	Television has much greater potential than radio as a direct-response mechanism because it can provide a visual dimension. Originally pricing restrictions limited the use of television in this context, but now following deregulation, nearly half of all television ads carry a response mechanism.
Digital media	The recent development of digital technologies, and the impact on digital television, internet, email, viral marketing, blogging, and social networking sites, now represents a major new form of interactive and direct marketing opportunities. Driven initially by developments in home shopping and banking facilities that were attractive to particular target groups, these facilities have now become fully interactive. As a result these services are now accessible by a much wider audience and encompass leisure and entertainment opportunities.

Online customer
questions can be
routed to a call centre
for a response

iStock

are prolific users of direct mail. The costs of telemarketing, however, are high. For example, it costs approximately £15 to reach a decision maker in an organization. When this is compared with £5 for a piece of direct mail or £250 for a personal sales call to the same individual, it is the effectiveness of the call and the return on the investment that determines whether the costs are really high. Changes have occurred as new media have evolved, especially digital media. For example, the development of telemarketing in the business-to-business sector has been largely at the expense of personal selling. Here the goals have been to reduce costs and to utilize the expensive sales force and their skills to build on the openings and leads created by telemarketing and other lead generation activities. Now the use of websites and the internet has replaced some of the activities undertaken by telemarketing, especially inbound calls searching for product information.

The use of 'carelines' has grown partly because they are essentially a post-purchase support mechanism that facilitates market feedback and intelligence gathering. In addition, they can warn of imminent problems (product defects), provide ideas for new products or variants, and of course provide a valuable method to reassure customers and improve customer retention levels. Call operators, or agents, have to handle calls from a variety of new sources—web, email, interactive TV, and mobile devices. Instant messaging channels enable online shoppers to ask questions that are routed to a call centre for response. Sales

RESEARCH   INSIGHT 12.2

To take your learning further, you might wish to read this influential paper.

Sharma, A., and Mehrotra, A. (2007), 'Choosing an optimal channel mix in multichannel environments', *Industrial Marketing Management*, 36, 1, 21 – 8.

Multichannel strategies enable organizations to reach their business customers in multiple ways, and in doing so increase the firms' reach. This recent paper is useful because the researchers develop and test a framework designed to allow firms to develop optimal channel mixes in these multichannel environments.

conversion ratios can be up by 40–50 per cent and costs are about £1 to answer an inbound question, compared with £3.50 by phone (Murphy, 2000). Food manufacturers can provide cooking and recipe advice while cosmetic and toiletries companies can provide healthcare advice and application guidelines.

Personal Selling

Personal selling is an activity undertaken by an individual representing an organization. It can also be considered as a group activity in the form of a sales force. Personal selling is a highly potent form of communication simply because messages can be adapted to meet the requirements of both parties, who meet face to face, as the communication develops. Objections can be overcome, information provided in the context of the buyer's environment, and the conviction and power of demonstration can be brought to the buyer when requested.

Personal selling is different from the other forms of communication as the messages represent dyadic communications. This means that there are two persons involved in the communication process. Feedback and evaluation of transmitted messages are possible, more or less instantaneously, so that personal selling messages can be tailored and made much more personal than any of the other methods of communication.

The amount of control that can be exercised over the messages delivered through personal selling depends upon a number of factors. Essentially, the level of control must be regarded as low, because each salesperson has the freedom to adapt messages to meet changing circumstances as negotiations proceed. In practice, however, the professionalism and training that many members of the sales force receive and the increasing accent on measuring levels of customer satisfaction mean that the degree of control over the message can be regarded, in most circumstances, as very good, although it can never, for example, be as high as that of advertising.

Sales personnel provide a source of information for buyers so that they can make the right purchase decisions. In that sense they provide a good level of credibility, but they are also perceived, understandably, as biased. The degree of expertise held by a salesperson may be high, but the degree of perceived trustworthiness will vary, especially during the formative period of a relationship, unless other transactions with the selling organization have been satisfactory. Once a number of transactions have been completed and product quality established, trustworthiness may improve.

The Role of Personal Selling

Personal selling concerns interpersonal communication and its role can encompass the whole spectrum of the attitude construct (see Chapter 11). This means providing information, developing positive feelings, and stimulating behaviour. In many cases those involved in personal selling undertake all these roles although management's astute use of the marketing communication mix can relieve the sales force of the information and awareness component and allow the sales team to concentrate on the other sales activities.

Many authors consider the development, organization, and completion of a sale to be the key role of personal selling. However, this is a very narrow interpretation and not one that embraces the full contribution that personal selling can make to marketing communications. A more contemporary interpretation suggests that the role of personal selling is largely one of representation. Sales personnel operate at the boundary of the organization and they provide a vital link between the needs of their own organization and the needs of their customers. This linkage, or boundary spanning role, is absolutely vital if a meaningful relationship between the two organizations is to be developed and maintained. Without personal selling, communication with other organizations would occur through electronic or print media and would foster discrete closed systems. Representation in this sense therefore refers to face-to-face encounters between people from different organizations.

Account Management

One of the major issues that has concerned organizations for a long time is how best to look after and nurture their more important customers. Most companies have a small number of customers, often just 20 per cent, who either generate 80 per cent of their profits or who are essential for their survival. **Key account management**, an extension of personal selling, has emerged as a way of managing these critical customers and ensuring that the potential within the accounts is realized.

These particular customers have been referred to as national accounts, house accounts, major accounts, and **key accounts**. Although Ojasalo (2001) sees little difference in the terminology KAM, national account marketing (NAM), and strategic account management (SAM), Millman and Wilson (1995) argue that key account is the only one that is not sales oriented and is really appropriate.

Key accounts are strategically important customers, not just the ones that provide volume sales. Key accounts are customers that are willing to enter into collaborative exchanges and which are of strategic importance. The key account is strategically important because it might offer opportunities for entry to new markets, represent access to other key organizations or resources, or provide symbolic value in terms of influence, power, and stature. See Chapter 16 for more information about key account management.

A natural extension of KAM involves the management of customers who have a global presence, that is they are multinationals who look to suppliers to provide a consistent and coordinated supply of products and services at all of their worldwide locations. **Global account management** (GAM) is concerned with the collaborative and centralized processes necessary to coordinate the worldwide buying and selling activities between global customers and global suppliers.

RESEARCH INSIGHT 12.3

To take your learning further, you might wish to read this influential paper.

Hui, L. S., Zou, S., and Cavusgil, S. T. (2004), 'A conceptual framework of global account management capabilities and firm performance', *International Business Review*, 13, 5 (October), 539–53.

This paper provides background information about the development and issues associated with global account management before proposing a conceptual framework that reflects the need for suppliers and buyers to establish collaborative processes in order to achieve competitive advantage.

Selecting the Right Mix of Tools

So far, we have considered the tools of the marketing communications mix as individual elements. However, a truly effective mix works when the tools are used to complement each other and to work as an interacting unit. This is sometimes referred to as integrated marketing communications, a topic considered in the previous chapter. Each of the tools has some key capabilities and one of the challenges facing marketing communication managers is to extract the full potential from the tools selected. Only by appreciating their characteristics is it really possible to get an insight into how to select the right mix of tools for each communication task.

Our overview of each of the tools has highlighted a number of characteristics that are shared among all of the tools. These are the degree to which a tool and the message conveyed is controllable, the credibility of the message conveyed, the costs of using a tool, the degree to which a target audience is dispersed, and the DRIP task that marketing communications is required to accomplish. These five elements can serve as a starting point when selecting the right marketing communications mix and each is considered in turn.

Table 12.4 provides a summary of the relative strengths of each of the tools of the communications mix. However, although depicted individually the elements of the mix should be regarded as a set of complementary instruments, each potentially stronger when it draws on the potential of the others. The tools are, to a limited extent, partially interchangeable and in different circumstances different tools should be used to meet different objectives. For example, in a business context personal selling will be the predominant tool whereas in a consumer market context, advertising has traditionally reigned supreme.

What is clear is that the nature, configuration, and use of what was once called the promotional mix is changing. No longer can the traditional grouping of promotional tools be assumed to be the most effective forms of communication. The role of the media in the communication process is now much more significant than it has ever been. The arrival and development of digital media expands

Social Networking Media

The rapidly increasing interest in social networking sites such as MySpace, Second Life, and YouTube has led brands to question how they might benefit from involvement with these or by founding their own sites. These brands are not just those aimed at young adults; people in all ages, sectors, and with different backgrounds and interests are targeted. Miller Homes, for example, the UK's biggest privately owned house builder, announced the launch of its own social networking site in April 2007. The site was partly developed as a response to the government's desire that we create communities that are largely sustainable. By providing residents on Miller Homes developments with information about their area, forums, and message boards, the intention is to create a community with the purpose of encouraging residents to get to know each other. The site is also intended to allow users to measure their carbon footprint, water use, and recycling activities.

The Miller Homes customer website

Miller Homes

In contrast, the car brand Skoda announced in the same week as Miller Homes that they are relaunching their website as a social network. Their intentions are partly competitive as it is alleged that they want to use the web as a form of competitive weapon to be used against key rivals, Vauxhall and Honda in particular. The site is intended to attract not only potential customers but also general car enthusiasts.

Other developments include Sony's 'Home'. Home is a virtual world associated with their PS3 platform. Players can furnish their own living areas with virtual accessories, accolades, and videos. Microsoft is intending to launch a networking portal targeted at the finance industry, where connections and fast information exchange are crucial.

But it is not guaranteed that creating a social network will automatically lead to success. For example, Joga.com, launched by Google and Nike in the lead-up to the 2006 football World Cup, has not achieved the success expected. Joga.com was designed for football fans to discuss the game, create games and clubs, view video clips and photos uploaded by users, and view exclusive content on Nike-sponsored stars. Well intentioned but there has been little interest outside Brazil.

Sources: Jones (2007); Yin (2007); Hagel (2007).

1 Why should brands want to be involved with social networking sites? What are the dangers of close involvement?

2 What reasons can you suggest for the Joga.com failure?

3 Visit a social networking site with which you are familiar and make a list of the primary characteristics of the site and the way it is designed to enable users to contact others.

These provide clients with opportunities to communicate with their audiences in radically different ways from those previously available through non-digital media. Generally, most traditional media provide one-way communications, where information passes from a source to a receiver but there is little opportunity for feedback, let alone interaction. Digital media enables two-way, interactive communication. Information can flow back to the source and again to the receiver, as each participant adapts their message to meet the requirements of their audience. For example, banner ads can provoke a click, this takes the receiver to a new website where the source presents new information and the receiver makes choices, responds to questions (e.g. registers at the site), and the source again provides fresh information. Indeed, the identity of the source and receiver in this type of communication becomes less clear.

These interactions are conducted at high speed, low cost, and usually with great clarity. People drive these interactions at a speed that is convenient to them; they are not driven by others. Space (or time) within traditional media is limited so costs rise as demand for the limited space/time increases. To generalize, as space is unlimited on the internet, so costs per contact fall as more visitors are received. A further point of interest concerns the client's message. Digital media are superior at providing rational, product-based messages whereas traditional media are much better at conveying emotional brand values. However, there are signs that some clients believe there are greater opportunities to use digital media for branding purposes.

Other Media

This class is intended to cover the variety of media not covered by the previous five. Two main media can be identified, cinema and ambient. Cinema advertising has all the advantages of television-based messages such as the high-quality audio and visual dimensions, which combine to provide high impact. As cinema audiences are usually more attentive because the main film has yet to be shown and as there are fewer distractions or noise in the communication system, this

Table 12.6

A comparison of traditional and digital media

Traditional media	Digital media
One to many	One-to-one and many-to-many
Greater monologue	Greater dialogue
Active provision	Passive provision
Mass marketing	Individualized
General need	Personalized
Branding	Information
Segmentation	Communities

Source: *Marketing Communications*, 4th edn., Fill, C., Pearson Education Limited (2006). Reproduced with the kind permission of Pearson Education Limited.

means that cinema advertising has potentially greater power than television advertisements to communicate with the target audience. When the relatively low production and transmission costs are considered cinema becomes an attractive media vehicle. However, the vast majority of cinema visitors are people aged 18 to 35 so if an advertiser wishes to reach different age group segments, or perhaps a national audience, not only will cinema be inappropriate but also the costs will be much higher than those for television.

Ambient media are regarded as out-of-home media that fail to fit any of the established outdoor categories. Ambient media can be classified according to a variety of factors. These include posters (typically found in washrooms), distribution (for example, ads on tickets and carrier bags), digital media (in the form of video and LCD screens), **sponsorships** (as in golf holes and petrol pump nozzles), and aerials (in the form of balloons, blimps, towed banners).

Table 12.6 provides a comparison of traditional and digital media. The development of digital media has had a profound impact on the way client organizations communicate with their audiences. Generally there has been a trend to reduce the amount of traditional media used and an increase in the amount of digital and online media used. Reports that television and print advertising is dead have been proved to be premature but it is clear that the mix of media used by organizations is in transition and new ways of delivering messages are evolving.

The Changing Role of the Media

For a long time commercial media have been used to convey messages designed to develop consumers' attitudes and feelings towards brands. Today, many of the messages are designed to provoke audiences into responding, either physically or mentally. The former is referred to as an attitudinal response, the latter a behavioural response. It follows that attitude- and behavioural-oriented communications require different media.

Direct-response media are characterized by the provision of a telephone number or web address. This is the mechanism through which receivers can respond to a message. Response can be interpreted as interaction. Direct-response media also allow clients the opportunity to measure the volume, frequency, and value of audience responses. This enables them to determine which direct-response media work best and so helps them become more efficient as well as effective. Estimates vary, but somewhere between 30 per cent and 40 per cent of all television advertisements are now direct response. Direct-response television (DRTV) is attractive to service providers such as those in financial services, charities, and tourism but increasingly grocery brands such as Tango and Peperami have used this media format.

One aspect that is crucial to the success of a direct-response campaign is not the number of responses but the conversion of leads into sales. This means that the infrastructure to support these activities must be thought through and implemented, otherwise the work and resources put into the visible level will be wasted if customers are unable to get the information they require, when they respond.

Another key area of change within the media concerns content. Traditionally content is provided by a client organization which uses the media to interrupt and transfer their message of persuasion to their target audience, usually a mass audience. Digital media and changes in consumer behaviour now enable audiences to not only generate their own content but also discuss and consider the opinions and attitudes of others. This means that advertisers no longer have complete control over what is said about their brands, who says it, and when. The rise of online communities and social networking sites such as MySpace (see Marketing Insight 12.5), blogging, wikis, and RSS feeds enable users to create content and become more involved with a brand. Such brand participation presents clients such as Procter & Gamble with opportunities to enable and encourage their customers to become involved in a brand's development (see Silverman, 2006). In January 2007 Cadbury extended their long-running campaign 'how do you eat yours?', suggesting that their customers create videos of themselves eating Crème Eggs and that they share them on its 'Gootube' site (Simms, 2007). By creating websites and facilities that foster discussion, idea generation, and involvement in product development, at times when people want to participate, these new forms of digital media are reshaping the way in which content and marketing communications are developed and used.

RESEARCH INSIGHT 12.4

To take your learning further, you might wish to read this influential paper.

Kent, M. L., Taylor, M., and White, W. J. (2003), 'The relationship between web site design and organisational responsiveness to stakeholders', *Public Relations Review*, 29, 1 (March), 63–77.

As the title indicates, this paper examines the relationship between website design and organizational responsiveness to stakeholder information needs. Written at a time when there was little or no empirical evidence about the extent to which new technologies can assist organizations to develop relationships, this paper provides an interesting and readable first insight.

Introduction

Have you ever seen an ad for cigarettes in the doctor's waiting room or an ad for the latest £3,000 LCD TV on the student union notice boards? The quotation at the top of this chapter suggests that placing ads in the right place, at the right time, for the right audience is important. Indeed it is, and this chapter examines the issues that need to be considered when managing marketing communications activities in order to get the right messages in the right place, at the right time, for the right audience. These 'issues' embrace a range of activities such as developing strategy in the light of both audience and brand characteristics, agreeing **communication objectives**, and then formulating, implementing, and evaluating marketing communication strategies and plans, many of which need to be integrated, an important topic itself in contemporary marketing communications. Further issues that demand management attention include the creation of the right message, the designation of the right marketing communication mix, the specification of the right media (mix), the allocation of financial and human resources, the coordination and control of related activities, and the management of various relationships. These relationships are not just those with internal colleagues, critical as these are, but they also encompass those external stakeholders who work with the organization in order to deliver particular elements of a marketing communications plan. For example, they might provide research information, they might be agencies that design the message (or creative as it is referred to in the trade), or those who plan and buy media in order that the message is conveyed to the target audience. All of these issues are referred to in this chapter.

Marketing Communications: Strategy

Marketing communications is an activity that supports the marketing strategy and associated plan. It therefore needs to be coordinated with the aims and objectives of the marketing plan and needs to complement a range of predetermined activities.

As noted previously in Chapter 5, on corporate and marketing strategy, it is important at the outset to develop an understanding of the environment in which the marketing communications activity is to be undertaken. This means analysing and understanding the context in which communications are to occur, essentially the environment experienced by the target audience. This leads to the first important statement about strategy and marketing communications, namely that it is an activity to be guided by the nature, characteristics, and communication needs of the audience, not the communication tools or media. There are three types of audience and hence three types of strategy. These audiences are target customers, channel intermediaries (such as wholesalers and added value resellers), and an organization's stakeholder network.

The 3Ps of Marketing Communications Strategy

The traditional approach to marketing communications strategy has been to identify a mix of the marketing communication tools used to support a particular campaign, and to label this as 'the strategy'. However, this is an inward-looking perspective and is essentially production oriented or resource driven. Another incorrect approach has been to refer to strategy in terms of the objectives to be achieved. So, comments such as 'the strategy was to raise awareness', 'to gain market share', or 'to gain more customers' are misleading because these are goals not strategies. However, as a generalization, strategy is about matching environmental conditions with organizational resources. In achieving this match there needs to be a balance between a market orientation, that is the needs of the audience, and the resource capability of the organization, in terms of the various messages, media, and disciplines necessary to accomplish the strategy.

Marketing communications is a complex activity if only because different audiences have different characteristics and this means that different messages and media mixes are required to reach them. This means that we can identify three core marketing communication strategies, each based on broad target audiences. These are pull, push, and profile strategies and are set out in Table 13.1.

- **Pull strategies:** These are used to communicate with end user customers. These may be consumers but they might also be other organizations within a business-to-business context.

- **Push strategies:** These are used to communicate with channel intermediaries, such as dealers, distributors, and retailers, otherwise referred to as the 'trade' or channel buyers.

- **Profile strategies:** These are used to communicate with a range of stakeholders, such as the local community, trade unions, suppliers, local and national government.

Push and pull communication strategies relate to the direction of the communication with respect to the marketing channel. Push strategies refer to communications that are 'pressed' or forced through the marketing channel in order to

Strategy	Target audience	Message focus	Communication goal
Pull	Consumers End user B2B customers	Product/service Product/service	Purchase Purchase
Push	Channel intermediaries	Product/service	Developing relationships and distribution network
Profile	All relevant stakeholders	The organization	Building reputation

Source: Marketing Communications, 4th edn., Fill, C., Pearson Education Limited (2006). Reproduced with the kind permission of Pearson Education Limited.

Table 13.1
Marketing communications strategies

reach the intermediaries. Pull strategies refer to communications that pull or attract consumers/buyers into the market channel via retailers. Profile strategies refer to the ways an organization prefers to present itself. The identity of an organization is 'profiled' to various other target stakeholder audiences, which may well include consumers, trade buyers, business-to-business customers, and a range of other influential stakeholders. Normally, profile strategies do not contain or make reference to specific products or services that the organization offers. Table 13.1 depicts these strategies and sets out the focus of the messages and ultimate communications goals.

This three-way demarcation may be blurred where the name of a company is the name of its primary (only) product, or, as is the case with many financial service brands, where the range of the products is broad and the offering is technically complex. For example, messages about mobile phones or fashion brands are very often designed to convey meaning about the positioning, values, and what a brand stands for. There is little or no scope to detail individual products yet the intention is to create awareness about the brand and the types, benefits, and quality of the overall services it offers.

In order that these strategies are implemented, it is normal procedure to develop a marketing communications plan. The degree to which these plans are developed varies across organizations and many rely on their agencies to undertake this work for them. However, there can be major benefits as a result of developing these plans in-house, for example by involving and discussing issues internally and developing a sense of ownership.

A Pull Strategy

Messages directed at targeted end user customers are often intended to generate increased levels of awareness, change and/or reinforce attitudes, reduce risk, encourage involvement, develop an emotional attachment, and ultimately influence customer behaviour. The ultimate goal is to stimulate action so that the target audience can expect the offering to be available to them when they decide to enquire, go shopping, test a product, or make a first or repeat purchase. This approach is known as a *pull* strategy and is aimed at encouraging customers to demand access to a product. In doing so they 'pull' products through the distribution channel. See Figure 13.1 for a visual interpretation of this sequence of activities. This usually means that consumers go into shops or to a website to enquire about a particular product and/or buy it. (See Market Insight 13.1.) B2B customers are encouraged to buy from dealers and distributors while both groups of consumers and B2B customers have opportunities to buy through direct marketing channels where there is no intermediary and to engage in an exchange direct with the manufacturer through direct mail, telemarketing, or the internet.

The conventional pull-based strategy used to be heavily based on network television in order to reach mass audiences. This, as we have seen, is no longer possible due to media and audience fragmentation. There has been greater use of direct marketing in non-FMCG sectors and use of the internet presents huge opportunities to reach audiences in new ways and so reduce any reliance on the old formulaic approach to pull-based strategies. As a result organizations are finding new ways to deliver pull strategies. However, it should not be inferred

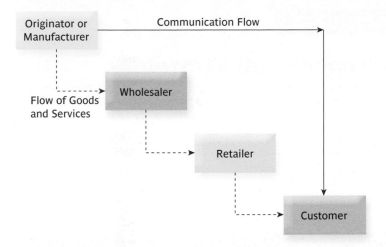

Figure 13.1
Direction of communication in a pull strategy

Source: *Marketing Communications*, 4th edn., Fill, C., Pearson Education Limited (2006). Reproduced with the kind permission of Pearson Education Limited.

that television advertising is a thing of the past as far as pull-based strategies are concerned, far from it. Procter & Gamble, for example, reduced their spend on network television ads in the USA by nearly 23 per cent in 2005, but redirected much of this to cable and local television ads. They have also increased their spend on magazines (Silverman, 2006).

Outside the grocery market, marketing communications are just as important to reach consumers. The development of the iPod, for example, demonstrates how pull strategies need be oriented to the needs of the audience. When the iPod was first launched in 2001, Teague (2007) recalls how Apple used ads that focused on the technology and were computer-centric and in effect demonstrated to audiences 'this is how it works', a functional approach. Then Apple used ads showing people singing out loud in tune with their iPod, 'this is what it will do for you', an emotional approach.

As more people get broadband connections and with mobile phone ownership at saturation point so mobile-based media strategies are set to develop rapidly. The sheer ubiquity of mobile communications suggests that as technology develops so will the range of marketing communication opportunities. For example, current mobile facilities based around calls, text messaging, and camera pictures are likely to be supplemented with transactional facilities, barcode capture, video, radio, and blogging (Saunders, 2006). Pull strategies will need to incorporate these digital technologies in order reach particular target audiences.

A Push Strategy

Push strategies are directed at organizations in the marketing channel. These organizations do not consume the products and services bought from the producer or manufacturer, because their role is to add value to the product before moving it on to others in the demand chain. Pull strategies are targeted at customers who make purchase decisions related largely to their personal (or organizational) consumption of products and services. *Push* strategies are targeted at organizations who buy products and services, perform some added value activity, and move the product through the distribution channel.

Supermarkets' Use of Pull Strategies

ASDA Wal-Mart has used a pull-based communication strategy to good effect, helping to take the supermarket to the No. 2 position in the UK. Its strong market share is mainly a result of a marketing strategy designed to deliver quality products at low prices. Price competition in the form of everyday low pricing (EDLP) has been central to their communications. This is reflected in a marketing communication strategy that consistently delivers messages about low prices (pull/price). Morrison's, the No. 4 ranked supermarket, also run an everyday low pricing or value approach but use sales promotions as a form of complementary positioning (pull/price/promotions). Tesco, the market leader, use 'every little helps' to emphasize their low price claim.

The Sainsbury's branding campaign with celeb chef Jamie Oliver

Sainsbury's

The remaining big four supermarket, Sainsbury's, has used classical pull strategies to try to regain market share from ASDA. Based around a brand ambassador, the celebrity chef Jamie Oliver, Sainsbury's branding campaign makes heavy use of television, and positions the brand around a quality and value proposition of its product range. It also differentiates itself by using the strapline 'try something new today'. This refers to recipes, product selection, and also attempts to stimulate brand (store) switching behaviour (pull/quality/repositioning). Sainsbury's know that the day after a Jamie Oliver television advert the sales of the ingredients used in the ad will soar. It was estimated that the £41 m spent by Sainsbury's on the campaign generated more than £1.12 bn in extra sales during its two-year lifespan. The 'Take one Celebrity Chef' ads used in the 2005 campaign are said to have quadrupled sales of the products featured such as nutmeg, while sales of other featured products such as sausages and apples 'had enjoyed their strongest sales on record' according to the chief executive.

Sources: Adams and Finch (2003); Sheppard (2005).

1 Choose an industry of your choice (e.g. airlines, mobile phones, or perhaps perfumes and cosmetics), select three major brands, visit their websites, and decide how they have differentiated themselves.

2 Choose a brand and work out which promotional tools and media they could use to reach consumers.

3 Using a retail brand of your choice, nominate a celebrity spokesperson to front the brand in the same way as Jamie Oliver. Justify your selection.

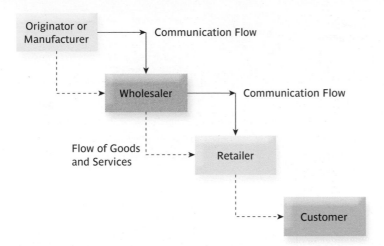

Figure 13.2

Direction of communication in a push strategy

Source: *Marketing Communications*, 4th edn., Fill, C., Pearson Education Limited (2006). Reproduced with the kind permission of Pearson Education Limited.

The distribution or marketing channel consists of a chain of organizations running from the manufacturer through dealers, wholesalers, distributors, and retailers. The final link in this channel involves end user customers who purchase the product for consumption. A push communication strategy mirrors this channel and involves targeting communications at each member of the marketing channel. See Figure 13.2. for a visual interpretation of this approach.

Push communication strategies are about influencing trade channel organizations in several ways. One area of influence is about encouraging distributors to take stock and to allocate resources to support the manufacturer's brand. A second is to help channel members become fully aware of the key attributes and benefits associated with each product line so that they can add the appropriate value. A third area of influence concerns the maintenance and development of the relationship between the two organizations. A fourth area of influence, linked to the relationship dimension, concerns the way in which the intermediary represents the manufacturer and their brands. Communications that are up to date, accurate, and which make promises that are subsequently fulfilled are likely to gain a high level of respect and result in positive word-of-mouth communications.

Personal selling is one of the key marketing communications tools used to reach people involved in organizational buying decisions. Trade advertising, trade sales promotions, and public relations all have important, yet secondary roles. Direct marketing has become increasingly important and the development of the internet has had a profound impact on b2b communications and inter-organizational relationships. However, personal selling has traditionally been the most significant part of the marketing communications mix where a push strategy has been instigated.

A Profile Strategy

In addition to communication strategies that are used to target customers (pull) and trade channel intermediaries (push) there is a third type of communication aimed at influencing an organization's stakeholders, in varying ways depending

Figure 13.3

Direction of communication in a profile-based strategy

Source: Marketing Communications, 4th edn., Fill, C., Pearson Education Limited (2006). Reproduced with the kind permission of Pearson Education Limited.

upon the nature of the message to be communicated. These are referred to as *profile* strategies and concern information about the organization and its values, policies, and position on issues, rather than its products and services (see Market Insight 13.2). Target audiences for profile strategies are set out in Figure 13.3 and include financial analysts, trade unions, government bodies, employees, and the local community. These different stakeholder groups have the potential to influence the organization in different ways and, in doing so, need to receive (and respond to) different types of messages. So, the financial analysts need to know about financial and trading performance and expectations, and the local community may be interested in employment and the impact of the organization on the local environment, whereas the government may be interested in the way the organization applies health and safety regulations and pays corporation, VAT, and other taxes. It should also be remembered that consumers and business-to-business customers may also be more interested in the organization itself and so help initiate an umbrella branding strategy.

Traditionally these types of communication have been referred to as corporate communications, as they deal more or less exclusively with the corporate entity or organization. Products, services, and other offerings are not normally the focus of these communications. It is the organization and its role in the context of the particular stakeholders' activities that is the crucial aspect of this type of strategy.

The awareness, perception, and attitudes held by stakeholders towards an organization need to be understood, shaped, and acted upon. This can be accomplished though continual dialogue, which will normally lead to the development of trust and commitment and enable relationships to grow. This is necessary in order that stakeholders act favourably towards an organization and enable strategies to flourish and objectives to be achieved.

A profile strategy is one that focuses an organization's communications upon the development of corporate image and reputation, whether that is just internally, externally, or both. To accomplish and deliver a profile strategy public relations, including sponsorship and corporate advertising, becomes the pivotal tool of the marketing communications mix. Personal selling may remain a vital element delivering both product/service and corporate messages.

Finally, the 3Ps are not independent strategies and should be used as a mix, a combination. In most organizations it is possible to identify an element of each strategy at any one time. In reality, most organizations are structured in such a way that those responsible for communications with each of these three main audiences do so without reference to or coordination with each other. This is an example of how **integrated marketing communications**, which is examined in Chapter 11, needs to have one senior person responsible for all organizational

Profile Strategies at Shell

Major energy companies such as Exxon, Shell, and BP have had to work hard at maintaining a positive reputation in the face of pressure from a variety of sources and stakeholders. For example, scientists and environmentalists have had to respond to concerns about climate change and sometimes the public, in the light of oil spillage disasters and other perceived anti-society misdemeanours. Maintaining their corporate reputation is therefore an extremely important activity and they use profile strategies on a fairly regular basis.

In March 2007 Royal Dutch Shell announced a £55 million advertising campaign designed to demonstrate its environmental credentials. The global campaign uses a series of long-format dramatized films. Films for the cinema, online, and interactive audiences were nine minutes in length but these were shortened to 90-second versions for television. Twenty-second television 'teasers' ads were used to direct viewers to its website, where they were able to watch the film and play interactive games. Print media focused on attention-getting ads. These highlighted specific projects that demonstrated the Shell culture of innovation and the inventiveness of Shell employees. DVDs of the campaign material were also distributed as inserts through print media.

The campaign seeks to present Shell as an environmentally responsible energy organization and uses drama to tell real-life stories. For example, the first film, entitled *Eureka*, tells the real-life story of a Shell engineer who found inspiration in daily life to develop the 'snake wells' technology now used in offshore fields in Brunei. Shell decided to use realistic storytelling, based on what their people do and how they think. It was thought that their messages would stand out from conventional corporate messages, especially those in the energy sector.

Sources: www.shell.com/; Payne (2007); Hawkes (2007).

1   Go to the Shell website at www.shell.com/home/. Follow the links and play the film *Eureka*. How does the exeprience of watching the film influence your opinion of Shell?

2   Do you believe Shell made the film to change the opinions of particular audiences? If so which ones and why?

3   Make brief notes listing the advantages and disadvantages of using employees in promotional communications, especially ads.

communications. Only through a single point of reference is it realistically possible to develop and communicate an integrated set of brand values that are consistent and credible.

The role of each element of the marketing communications mix is important in promotional strategy. Each tool has different strengths and should be used accordingly. For example, direct marketing and sales promotion are more likely to be effective in persuading consumer audiences, while personal selling is likely to be more effective in B2B situations. A profile strategy designed to change perception and understanding of the organization is more likely to utilize public relations and corporate advertising.

Marketing Communications: Planning

Marketing communication planning is a systematic process that involves a series of procedures and activities that lead to the setting of marketing communication objectives and the formulation of plans for achieving them. The strategy development activity discussed earlier should have been used to identify particular broad types of audience, based around the 3Ps. The aim of the planning process is to formulate and convey messages to particular target audiences that encourage them to think, emote, behave, or respond in particular ways. It is the skill and responsibility of those in charge of marketing communications planning to ensure that there is the right blend of communication tools, that they create memorable messages and convey them through a suitable media mix.

In order to better understand what a marketing communications plan should achieve it is helpful to appreciate the principal tasks facing marketing communications managers. These are to decide:

• Who should receive the messages;

• What the messages should say;

• What image of the organization/brand receivers are expected to retain;

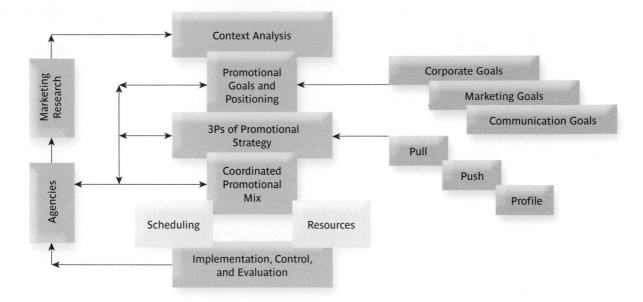

Figure 13.4 The marketing communications planning framework

Source: *Marketing Communications*, 4th edn., Fill, C., Pearson Education Limited (2006). Reproduced with the kind permission of Pearson Education Limited.

- How much is to be spent establishing this new image;
- How the messages are to be delivered;
- What actions the receivers should take;
- How to control the whole process once implemented; and
- What was achieved.

For many reasons, planning is an essential management activity, and if marketing communications are to be developed in an orderly and efficient way, planning should be developed around a suitable framework. A framework for integrated marketing communications plans is presented in Figure 13.4.

The **marketing communications planning framework** (MCPF) provides a visual guide to what needs to be achieved and brings together the various elements into a logical sequence of activities. As with all hierarchical planning models each level of decision making is built upon information generated at a previous level in the model. Another advantage of using the MCPF is that it provides a suitable checklist of activities that need to be considered.

The MCPF represents a sequence of decisions that marketing managers undertake when preparing, implementing, and evaluating communication strategies and plans. This framework reflects a deliberate or planned approach to strategic marketing communications. However, marketing communications planning is not always developed as a linear process in practice, as depicted in this framework. Indeed, many marketing communications decisions are made outside any recognizable framework as some organizations approach the process as an integrative and sometimes spontaneous activity. However, the MCPF approach presented here is intended to highlight the tasks to be achieved, the way in which they relate to one another, and the order in which they should be accomplished.

Elements of the MCPF

A marketing communications plan should be developed for each level of communication activity, from strategy to individual aspects of a campaign. The difference between them is the level of detail that is included.

Context Analysis

The marketing plan is the bedrock of the **context analysis** (CA). This will already have been prepared and contains important information about the target segment, the business and marketing goals, competitors, and the timescales in which the goals are to be achieved. The CA needs to elaborate and build upon this information so as to provide the detail in order that the plan can be developed and justified.

The first and vital step in the planning process is to analyse the context in which marketing communication activities are to occur. Unlike a situation analysis used in general planning processes, the context analysis should be communication oriented and use the marketing plan as a foundation. There are four main components to the communication context analysis: the customer, business, internal, and external environmental contexts.

Understanding the **customer context** requires information and market research data about the target audiences specified in the marketing plan. Here detailed information about their needs, perception, motivation, attitudes, and decision-making characteristics relative to the product category (or issue) is necessary. In addition, information about the media and the people they use for information about the product category needs to be determined.

Understanding about the **business or marketing context**, and the marketing communications environment in particular, is also important as these influence what has to be achieved. If the marketing strategy specifies growth through market penetration then not only will messages need to reflect this goal but it will be important to understand how competitors are communicating with the target audience and which media they are using to do this.

Analysis of the **internal context** is undertaken to determine the resource capability with respect to supporting marketing communications. Three principal areas need to be reviewed:

- People resources (are people, including agencies, with suitable marketing communications skills available?);
- Financial resources (how much is available to invest in marketing communications?); and
- Technological resources (are the right systems and processes available to support marketing communications?).

The final area to be reviewed is the wider **external context**. Similar to the areas considered during the strategic analysis, emphasis is given to the political, economic, societal, ecological, and technological conditions. However, stress needs to be given to the impact on marketing communications. For example, if economic conditions get tough then people have lower levels of disposable income. Sales promotions, promotional offers, and extended credit terms become more attractive in this context.

The context analysis provides the rationale for the rest of the plan. It is from the CA that the marketing objectives (from the marketing plan) and the marketing communications objectives are derived. The type, form, and style of the message are rooted in the characteristics of the target audience, and the media selected to convey messages should be based upon the nature of the tasks, the media preferences and habits of the audience, and the resources available.

Marketing Communication Objectives

Many organizations assume that their marketing communications goals are the same as their sales targets. This is incorrect because there are so many elements that contribute to sales, such as competitor pricing, product attributes, and distributor policies, that making marketing communications solely responsible for sales is naive and unrealistic. Ideally, marketing communication objectives should consist of three main elements, corporate, marketing, and communication objectives.

- **Corporate objectives** are derived from the business or marketing plan. They refer to the mission and the business area that the organization believes it should be in.

- **Marketing objectives** are derived from the marketing plan and are sales oriented. These might be market share, sales revenues, volumes, ROI (return on investment), and other profitability indicators.

- **Communication objectives** are derived from the context analysis and refer to levels of awareness, perception, comprehension/knowledge, attitudes, and overall degree of preference for a brand. The choice of communication goal depends upon the tasks that need to be accomplished.

These three elements constitute the overall set of marketing communication objectives. They should be set out in **SMART** terminology, that is, each should be specific, measurable, achievable, realistic, and timed (see Chapter 6 for information about the SMART approach). However, many brands need to refine the way they are perceived by customers, commonly referred to as a brand's position. Positioning is not applicable to all communication plans: for example, government-sponsored information campaigns do not have a positioning goal. However, most commercial and brand-oriented communication programmes need to be seen to occupy a clear position in the market. So, at this point in the planning process, the brand's positioning intentions are developed and these should be related to the market, the customers, or a product dimension. The justification for this will have been identified in the context analysis.

Marketing Communication Strategy

The marketing communication strategy is derived from the objectives and context analysis. As mentioned earlier all of the 3Ps provide the strategic foundation but the 3Ps alone provide insufficient information to inform about the strategic direction and thrust. The DRIP roles of marketing communications, established in Chapter 11, can be used to elaborate the strategy to be pursued. For example, if a new brand is being launched, the first task will be to inform and differentiate the brand for members of the trade before using a pull strategy to inform and differentiate the brand for the target end user customers. For example, when Diageo launched its Johnny Walker Whisky brand into the Greek market it first informed and then educated its key distributors and business partners about how each brand should be presented and served. This was achieved by the slightly unusual approach of acting out the style and image of each brand through a theatrical performance. Naturally, this was followed by a tasting session to familiarize the distributors with each brand's attributes (Anon., 2006). An organization wishing to signal a change of strategy and/or a change of name following a merger or acquisition may choose to use a profile strategy and the primary task will be to inform of the name change. An organization experiencing declining sales may choose to remind customers of a need or it may choose to improve sales through persuasion.

A traditional pull strategy in the grocery sector used to be based on delivering mass media advertising supported by below-the-line communications, most notably sales promotions delivered in-store and through direct mail and email to registered customers (e.g. Tesco Clubcard customers). The decision to use a pull strategy should be supported by a core message that will try to differentiate (position), remind or reassure, inform, or persuade the audience to think, feel, or behave in a particular way. This approach can be interpreted as a pull/remind or pull/position communication strategy, as this describes the audience and direction of the strategy and also clarifies what the strategy seeks to achieve.

A push strategy should be treated in a similar way. The need to consider the core message is paramount as it conveys information about the essence of the strategy. Push/inform, push/position, or push/key accounts/discount might be examples of possible terminology.

Although these three strategies are represented here as individual entities, they are often used as a 'cluster'. For example, the launch of a new toothpaste brand will involve a push strategy to get the product on the shelves of the key supermarkets and independent retailers. The strategy would be to gain retailer acceptance of the new brand and to position it for them as a profitable new brand. The goal is to get the toothpaste on the retailers' shelves. To achieve this, personal selling supported by trade sales promotions will be the main marketing communications tools. A push strategy alone would be insufficient to persuade a retailer to stock a new brand. The promise of a pull strategy aimed to create brand awareness and customer excitement needs to be created, accompanied by appropriate public relations activities and any initial sales promotions necessary to motivate consumers to change their brand of toothpaste. The next step is to create particular brand associations and thereby position the brand in the minds of the target consumer audience. Messages may be primarily informational or emotional but will endeavour to convey a brand promise. (See Market Insight 13.3.) This may be accompanied or followed by the use of incentives to encourage consumers to trial the product. To support the brand, carelines and a website will need to be put in place to provide credibility, as well as a buyer reference point.

Communication Methods

This part of the plan is relatively complex as a number of activities need to be accomplished. For each specified target audience in the strategy, a creative or

Competitive Drinking in Asia

The global competition between Coca-Cola and Pepsi-Cola has been raging for several decades and takes different forms in different parts of the world. For example, the battle to increase their market shares in Asia is reflected in their support for their key brands, Sprite and Mirinda respectively.

The market leader in the flavoured soft drink segment in Asia is Fanta, and competition is intense as consumers switch to alternatives such as green tea, fruit juices, cereal and corn milk. Both Pepsi and Coca-Cola have developed global campaigns for their brands and have had them adapted to meet the tastes and needs of local markets.

Coca-Cola launched a global campaign 'Freedom from thirst' to support Sprite, and was adapted to reach 20- to 29-year-old Thais. The campaign was developed by Coca-Cola's lead agency Ogilvy & Mather Hong Kong, with local agency Lowe Thailand, adapting the concept and creating the Sprite integrated marketing communication plan and ad materials specifically for the target market in Thailand.

The 30-second Thai television commercial shows a group of hot and tired boys on a basketball court. One of them quenches his thirst with Sprite, and this motivates one of the others to enter the 'Sprite world of liquid freedom'. He plunges headfirst onto the concrete floor which immediately converts into a swimming pool. All the others follow suit and enjoy the freedom 'only Sprite can offer'.

Pepsi, in an attempt to strengthen their brand image and re-emphasize the 'Intense taste, intense fun' positioning for its Mirinda brand, launched their 'Batman begins' campaign jointly with Motorola as their main partner. The Mirinda campaign featured a 15-second television commercial, developed locally by BBDO Thailand, and showed Batman involved with redemptions, discounts, and lucky draws. The campaign used TV, cinema, POP, billboards, and transit (railway) media supported by in-store promotional activities and roadshows to highlight and attract attention to the campaign.

Source: Prasad (2007).

1 Which type of communication strategy has been demonstrated by these two cola campaigns?

2 Using the campaign messages to guide you, what do you believe might have been the objectives of each of the campaigns?

3 What are the advantages of using a local agency to adapt a central campaign idea?

message needs to be developed. This should be based on the positioning requirements and will often be developed by an outside communications agency.

Simultaneously, it is necessary to formulate the right mix of communication tools to reach each particular audience. In addition, the right media mix needs to be determined, both on- and offline. Again this task will most probably be undertaken by media experts. Here, integration is regarded as an important feature of the communication mix. For example, when LG Electronics launched its global campaign in May 2007 for its premium 'Full HD' 1080p flat-panel high-definition televisions (HDTVs) they used both offline and online advertising formats. These featured broadcast, print, outdoor, and online in three creative concepts that all feature an LG Red Couch, their symbol of the consumers' all-encompassing high-definition viewing experience. The LG campaign also incorporated LG's corporate sponsorship of the Cannes Film Festival and also targeted public relations activities highlighting the Full HD technology and flat-panel designs. The selected media reflected the product's key purpose.

The Schedule

The next step is to schedule the way in which the campaign is to be delivered. Events and activities should be scheduled according to the goals and the strategic thrust. So, if it is necessary to communicate with the trade prior to a public launch, those activities tied into the push strategy should be scheduled prior to those calculated to support the pull strategy. Similarly, if awareness is a goal then, funds permitting, it may be best to first use television and poster ads offline plus banners and search engine ads online, before using sales promotions (unless sampling is used), direct marketing, point of purchase, and personal selling.

Resources

The resources necessary to support the plan need to be determined. These refer not only to the financial issues but also to the quality of available marketing expertise. This means that internally the right sort of marketing knowledge may not be present and may have to be recruited. For example, if launching a customer relationship management system (CRM) initiative, then it will be important to have people with knowledge and skills related to running CRM programmes. With regard to external skills, it is necessary that the current communications agencies are capable of delivering the creative and media plan.

This is an important part of the plan, one that is often avoided or forgotten about. Software project planning tools, simple spreadsheets, or Gantt charts can be used not only to schedule the campaign but to also chart the resources relating to the actual and budgeted costs of using the selected tools and media.

Control and Evaluation

Campaigns, once launched, should be monitored. This is to ensure that should there be any major deviance from plan, opportunities exist to get back on track as soon as possible. In addition, all marketing communications plans need to be evaluated. There are numerous methods to evaluate the individual performance of the tools and the media used, but perhaps the most important measures concern the achievement of the communication objectives.

Feedback

The marketing communication planning process is completed when feedback is provided. Not only should information regarding the overall outcome of a campaign be considered but so should individual aspects of the activity. For example, the performance of the individual tools used within the campaign, whether sufficient resources were invested, the appropriateness of the strategy in the first place, whether any problems had been encountered during implementation, and the relative ease with which the objectives were accomplished are aspects that need to be fed back to all internal and external parties associated with the planning process.

This feedback is vitally important because it provides information for the context analysis that anchors the next campaign. Information fed back in a formal and systematic manner constitutes an opportunity for organizations to learn from their previous campaign activities, a point often overlooked and neglected.

Integrated Planning

The development and establishment of an integrated approach to marketing communications (IMC), as discussed previously in Chapter 11, needs to be implemented as a management activity, some of it within the planning process. However, this task is easier said than done, simply because of the question, what is it that should be integrated? When IMC was first proposed, the focus was on harmonizing the tools of the marketing communications mix, in order to generate a consistent message. Since then ideas concerning the integration of messages, media, employees (especially in service-based environments), communication planning processes, client–agency relationships and operations, and systems have all been proposed as key elements to be integrated. Although the integration idea is conceptually interesting, defining what integration actually means and what should be integrated has not been agreed, especially as there is an absence of any empirical evidence or definitive research in the area (Cornelissen, 2003). A further criticism of IMC is that there is no universally agreed IMC evaluation system so that the claims made, especially by communication agencies, that IMC delivers superior returns have yet to be validated (Swain, 2004). To date there is no real agreement about what IMC is and how the process of integration should work.

Integrated planning requires clients to provide a coordinated structure and their communication agencies to be able to provide an integrated portfolio of services. Both of these requirements are hard to establish as clients have difficulty establishing internal systems and processes that encourage integration and often specify the media to be used in their briefing documents. Agencies on the other hand struggle to bring traditional and digital media together so that there is a single point of contact and each discipline tries to keep a client's business within public relations, advertising, or sales promotion. One result of this imbalance is compromise and less than optimum outcomes. Agencies have experimented with various approaches in the name of integration. For example, both JWT and Mind-Share have worked successfully with cross-agency teams on behalf of their clients Vodafone, Unilever, and HSBC, respectively (Murphy, 2006).

The development and establishment of IMC by organizations has not been as widespread as the amount of discussion around the subject might suggest. Recent technological advances and the benefits of the internet and related technologies have meant that organizations have had a reason to reconsider their marketing communications and have re-evaluated their approach. Whatever route taken,

JWT

JWT

the development of IMC requires change, a change in thinking, actions, and expectations. The changes required to achieve IMC are large and the barriers are strong. What can be observed in practice are formative approaches to IMC, organizational experiments undertaken within their resource and cultural contexts. (See Market Insight 13.4 below.)

MARKET INSIGHT 13.4

Getting it All Together

Many agencies proclaim their ability to provide clients with services that deliver integrated marketing communications. However, some clients question whether agencies can plan campaigns in conjunction with sister agencies and avoid media channel bias.

In 2006 Unilever announced that it was to strengthen its in-house communications planning facilities. The aim was to control campaigns that include a variety of communications tools and media. One of the common reasons cited for this type of move is that clients perceive a gap between creative thinking and media management, often due to internal agency structural barriers. Getting group-based agencies to work together can be difficult because they each have independent profit centres, and as a result want to retain each client's work to reflect their own success.

Where integration can be seen to work is within media selection, rather than an overall campaign. A campaign by BA designed to encourage customers to use its online check-in service was planned on the basis that digital was to be the key medium. The campaign included television and press, used to drive visits to the BA website, plus ATMs, outdoor LCD transvision screens, digital escalator panels, and online advertising. Each ad used the tagline 'Have you clicked yet?', designed to provide consistency. The campaign also tapped into specific lifestyle situations where the core message would resonate more strongly. For example, the frustration experienced by people when queuing at railway stations was used to push the message that BA's online check-in service could cut out queueing. To do this transvision screens were used to allow people to download information to their mobiles via Bluetooth.

Source: Murphy (2006); www.brandrepublic.com/InDepth/Features/560323/Revolution-Masterclass-cross-media-planning/.

1 What effects might Unilever's decision to take planning in-house have on its communications agencies?

2 To what extent was BA's planning a central aspect of their campaign success?

3 With so many different organizations involved in marketing communications, is truly integrated planning possible?

To take your learning further, you might wish to read this influential paper.

Cornelissen, J. P. (2001), 'Integrated marketing communications and the language of marketing development', *International Journal of Advertising*, 20, 4, 483–98.

Cornelissen has written many papers about IMC and associated communication management and planning issues. His view of the subject provides a useful counterbalance to the whole-hearted support expressed by most other IMC authors and that alone is good reason to read this paper.

The restraints that prevent the development of IMC need to be overcome. Indeed, many organizations that have made significant progress in developing IMC have done so by instigating approaches and measures that aim to reduce or negate the impact of the barriers that people put up to prevent change. IMC at the practitioner level still appears to be oriented to coordinating the tools, media, and messages. Academics and researchers appear to be concerned with a wider and deeper set of integrative issues that have yet to be adopted by those who produce work in the name of IMC.

Managing the Communication Mix and Budgets

Over the past five years there have been some sizeable changes to the way the marketing communication industry is structured, not just in the UK but across the globe. One of the most important of these has been the emergence of a number of powerful and dominant industry groups, such as WPP and the News Corporation, whose business interests span cross-media ownership, content development, and delivery. The battle in 2007 between Virgin Media and BSkyB over fees to deliver Sky content through Virgin Media reflects the criticality of some of these issues. The changing industry structure is partly a response to several variables, namely developments in technology, the configuration of the communication mix and media used by organizations, and the way in which client-side managers are expected to operate.

It has already been established that technology has had a dramatic impact on the communications industry as a result of which the way organizations use the communication mix has changed considerably. Traditionally, clients working in consumer markets preferred to place the majority of their media advertising into offline, mass media vehicles. Similarly, the sales force was the dominant tool of the mix used by organizations operating in business markets. Today, the use of sponsorship, direct and event marketing, and online, digitally driven interactive communications is growing at the expense of offline mass media advertising and sales promotions in consumer markets. Many organizations in the business-to-business market have slashed the size of their sales forces, partly to cut costs but also to use technology more efficiently.

The reasons for these shifts in behaviour are indicative of the increasing attention and accountability that management is attaching to the communication spend. Increasingly, marketing managers are being asked to justify the amounts they spend on their budgets, including advertising and sales promotion. Senior managers now want to know the return they are getting on their marketing communication investments. This is because there is pressure to use their scarce resources more effectively and efficiently so that they can meet their corporate and business-level objectives.

The amount of investment in marketing communications that some organizations make each year is huge. Procter & Gamble spent over £179 m on media alone in the UK in 2006 while retailers such as Boots and B&Q spent £42.5 m and £38.7 m and Orange and Vodafone spent £74 m and £62 m (Nielsen Media Research, cited by Marketing, 2007). These figures do not take account of the direct and indirect costs of employment, the production costs, or the costs associated with the other tools of the mix. It is not surprising, therefore, that managing marketing communications budgets is a critical activity.

Determining the Budget: Marketing Communications

Part of the management process involves determining how much should be allocated to a budget. Another part considers how that sum is managed when it is disbursed. Here we are concerned with the first question, how much is to be spent, and there are two broad spend decisions that need to be addressed. First, how much of the available financial resources (or relevant part) should be allocated to marketing communications and second, how much of this total should be allocated to each of the individual tools of the mix?

The allocation of scarce resources across a budget presents not only financial but also political difficulties, especially where the returns are difficult to identify. The development and significance of technology within marketing can lead to disputes concerning ownership and the control of resources. For example, in many companies management and responsibility for the website rests with the IT department, which understandably take a technological view of issues. Those in marketing, however, see the use of the website from a marketing perspective and need a budget to manage it. Tension between the two can result in different types of website design and effectiveness that can lead to considerable differences of customer perception and support.

Marginal analysis is the main theoretical approach to setting optimal budgets. This determines the point at which maximum returns are achieved based on an extra unit of investment in promotional activities. The main problem with this

Table 13.2

Practical approaches
to setting promotional
budgets

Budget-setting methodology	Explanation
Arbitrary	This approach is based on a guess made by the chairman or CEO. Very often the budget is decided on the hoof, and as each demand for communication resources arrives so decisions are made in isolation from any overall strategy. Not recommended.
Inertia	This approach directs that the same amount as last time is spent. Here all elements of the environment and the costs associated with the tasks facing the organization are ignored. Not recommended.
Media multiplier	Here, last year's spend is increased by the rate at which media costs have increased. Not recommended.
Percentage of sales	This requires a budget to be set at a level equal to a predetermined percentage of past or expected sales. Although more market oriented, organizations invariably select a percentage that is traditional to the organization, such as 'we always aim to spend 5.0% of our sales on advertising'. Not recommended.
Affordable	This requires that each unit of output is allocated a proportion of all the input costs and all the costs associated with the value-adding activities in production and manufacturing, together with all the other costs in distributing the output. After making an allowance for profit, what is left is to be spent on advertising and communication. In other words, what is left is what we can afford to spend. Not recommended.
Objective and task	This approach attempts to determine the resources required to achieve each marketing communication objective. For example, the costs associated with buying a DM list, for the creative, envelope, and mailing, for the telemarketing follow up, plus costs for sales promotion and public relations and campaign analysis are aggregated into an overall budget. Recommended.

Source: *Simply Marketing Communications*, Fill, C., Pearson Education Limited (2006). Reproduced with the kind permission of Pearson Education Limited.

approach is that it has little practical application because the data to run the analysis are either non-existent in many organizations or insufficient to withstand the analysis. Not surprisingly, therefore, other more practical approaches have been developed. These are set out in Table 13.2.

These approaches to budget setting have their strengths and weaknesses but of them all, only the objective and task method is recommended. This approach is market oriented, factual, and accurate and allows for adjustments to be made according to the campaign goals. So, if the objective is to build awareness but the resultant budget requirement is too high, then either the level of required awareness is reduced or a different mix is developed and costed in order to achieve the required awareness figure.

RESEARCH INSIGHT 13.3

To take your learning further, you might wish to read this influential paper.

Jones, J. P. (1990), 'Ad spending: maintaining market share', *Harvard Business Review*, January – February, 38 – 42.

This paper provided a first and important link between advertising strategy and budgeting. The paper is built upon the research findings emanating from a very large sample of brands. It draws some interesting conclusions about the level of advertising investment relative to market share.

The Marketing Communications Industry

Over the last twenty years the size of the marketing communications industry has changed in many ways. First it has increased in size, partly as a response to the growth in the number of activities undertaken in the name of marketing communications. Also, the real value of the activities such as advertising, sales promotion, public relations, and direct marketing has increased substantially. The rate of growth among these tools has been variable with only direct marketing showing consistent levels of real growth. It is inevitable that when this level of growth occurs so the structure and nature of the constituent organizations also change.

The marketing communications industry consists of a number of different types of organizations whose purpose is to enable clients to communicate effectively and efficiently with their target audiences. In most countries the marketing communications industry consists of four main types of organization. These are shown in Figure 13.5.

Clients underpin the communication process by financing various activities and tasks. Agencies act on behalf of clients and either directly or indirectly undertake to design and implement their clients' campaign activities. Production houses produce campaign materials, for example, film, video, soundtrack, mailers, or leaflets. Media owners sell time and space in the media vehicles so that the client's message can be conveyed to target audiences.

Client organizations can choose to run their campaigns rather than outsource to industry experts. This is referred to as the in-house approach but this is both costly, inefficient, and might suffer from a lack of objectivity that outsiders can bring to a campaign. As a result most organizations appoint agencies to manage their external communication requirements. Of the four main groups, production and media houses require that the clients and agencies agree and specify campaigns in order that they are able to contribute. So, it can be argued that agencies and clients are the lead players in this industry. It is within this industry context

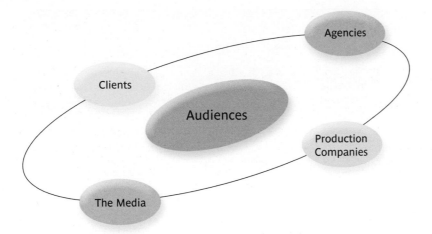

Figure 13.5
The main organizations
in the communication
industry

that managers have to manage their organization's marketing communications activities.

As mentioned earlier organizations have the opportunity to do their own marketing communications in-house, a DIY approach. Whilst this offers some attraction, most substantial organizations use agencies, simply because they can provide objectivity, access to expertise, and specialist technologies, whilst allowing the client to concentrate on their core business activities. Outsourcing is popular because it permits organizations the opportunity to use specialist services and experts as and when required. However, although this flexibility and access to experts is attractive, there are several managerial decisions that need to be made. For example, which type(s) of agency should be used, how are they to be selected, what can we expect them to do, how will they be managed, and how shall we pay for their services?

Types of Agency

Originally agents acted on behalf of media owners who wanted to sell media time and space. This was essentially a production and selling role but agents learned to work more closely with their clients and in doing so became more customer oriented. Their two main roles, designing messages and planning and buying media, became central to what were referred to as **full-service agencies**. Today the media component has been spun off to specialist media agencies (media houses) in what might be regarded as a 360-degree revolution to become a direct function of the media owners once again. Unsurprisingly, a number of different types of agency have emerged as the industry evolves. Table 13.3 presents some of the more common types of communication agency, most based on an advertising background. This table does not include some of the more specialist types of agency, for example those that fulfil public relations, direct marketing, field marketing, sales promotion, or merchandising roles.

Many advertising agencies have changed their identity so that they are now referred to as communication agencies. This enables them to operate in other

Table 13.3

Types of agency

Type of agency	Nature and role
Full service	Offers a full range of services that a client requires in order to advertise its products and services. These services include strategic planning, research, creative development, production, and media planning. Some of these activities may be subcontracted, but overall responsibility rests with the full-service agency.
Creative hotshops	'Hotshops' provide specialist creative design services for clients who wish to use particular styles and approaches for their creative work. Often founded by creative personnel (teams) who leave full-service agencies to set up their own business.
Media independents	Provide specialist media services for planning, buying, and monitoring the purchase of a client's media requirements. There are two main forms: media independents, where the organization is owned and run free of the direction and policy requirements of a full-service agency, and media dependents, where the organization is a subsidiary of a creative or full-service organization.
À la carte	Managed by the client this approach allows clients to use the services of a range of different organizations. So, the planning skills of a full-service agency, the creative talent of a particular hotshop, and the critical mass of a media-buying independent provide an *à la carte* approach.
New media	Developed out of the growth in the number of online brands and the desire of established offline brands to reach their customers electronically.
Media house	Developed from full-service agencies or by media owners, these agencies plan, buy, and monitor media for clients.

areas of marketing communications and some make claims to providing integrated marketing communication services.

Working with Agencies

The management of marketing communications normally requires that campaigns be developed by outsourced specialist agencies. This means there are a range of tasks that need to be accomplished, or managed, to ensure a successful outcome. Time and space do not permit a review of all the management issues, but some of the key ones, agency selection, interacting with agency personnel, and paying the agency for their work, are considered in this last part of the chapter. (See also Market Insight 13.5 and 13.6 for the impact digital technology has had on agencies.)

Agency Selection

The process of selecting an agency is theoretically straightforward. A list of potential agencies is established, and they are filtered using various criteria until a small number remain. The remaining few are 'interviewed' and the best agency is contracted. Unfortunately this seemingly rational approach is rarely adhered to due to a variety of organizational, political, and economic reasons.

The selection process commences with a *search* activity. The task at this stage is to formulate a list of potential candidates and this is accomplished by referring to publications such as Campaign Portfolio and the Advertising Agency Roster, viewing samples of agency work available such as DigiReels, together with personal recommendations. The latter is perhaps the most potent and influential of these sources. As many as ten or twelve agencies might be listed, although it is normal for six or seven to be identified.

The stage is referred to as a **credentials presentation**. This involves the client visiting each of the shortlisted candidates in an attempt to determine whether the agency is likely to 'fit' with the client's expectations and requirements. Information about the agency's experience and quality of work, the ability of the agency people, its image and reputation, its geographic coverage, and relationships with existing clients are sought.

Agencies that are deemed to provide a good level of potential fit are then invited to **pitch** for the business. The pitch is a presentation, made by competing agencies, to the client. The pitch is based on a **brief** that documents information about the client, its markets, and the communication task. The presentation is about how the agency would approach the strategic and creative issues and the account is awarded to whichever agency produces the most suitable proposal and demonstrates insight and expertise. Suitability is a relative term, and a whole range of objective and subjective factors need to be considered when selecting an organization to be responsible for a large part of a brand's visibility. Objective factors include the quality of work, ability to meet deadlines, and costs. One of the subjective factors is 'chemistry' and this refers to how well the client believes they will be able to work with the agency, the interpersonal factor.

In Indonesia the owners of the leading biscuit brand, Tango, decided to appoint a new agency as their requirements had changed. With a marketing strategy geared to increasing brand consumption they needed an agency that would provide marketing consultancy and advice on brand positioning and new product development as well as advertising strategy. Three agencies were invited to pitch for the business: Grey, Ogilvy & Mather, and incumbent agency JWT (Anon., 2007).

The selection process represents a bringing together of two organizations whose expectations may be different but whose cooperative behaviour is essential for their respective goals to be met. For example, agencies must have access to comprehensive and often commercially confidential data about products and markets if they are to operate efficiently. Otherwise, they cannot provide the service that is expected. However, it should be noted that pitches are not mandatory, and as Jones (2004) reports, nearly a third of clients move their accounts without involving pitches.

The suitability of this selection process has been questioned. Jones reports that a single pitch can cost an agency as much as £50,000 and the high cost of pitching has led to a reluctance by some agencies to get involved. Some clients are not prepared to wait for up to three months for an agency to be appointed, especially in the digital era. The pitching process also fails to give sufficient insight into the potential working relationships and is very often led by senior managers who will not be involved in the day-to-day operations.

All Change at the Agency

The interest and rapid development of digital media has spawned a range of changes, not just for clients and their mix of media but for agencies as well. In 2006 there were a raft of agency restructures all aimed at trying to realize the potential arising from the growth of digital technology.

For example, in 2006 the Starcom agency axed several senior staff positions in traditional media buying departments in order to boost its digital resources together with its data management capacity. Walker Media also launched its own digital division, Walker-I, after winning the £70 m Barclays media planning and buying account. Carat created a series of 'multidisciplinary' teams to deal with individual clients' business and to offer a fully integrated set of services. Another media agency, OMD, appointed Sheryl Norman, the former head of integrated marketing services at Coca-Cola Great Britain, as its new director of digital, responsible for UK operations.

In addition to these strategic decisions MindShare, formerly identified as a media agency, repositioned itself in 2007 as a communications agency. The transformation process was assisted by an organizational restructure. This involved the creation of a central strategy department, so that strategists could work alongside account handlers on all of the agency's accounts and all media channels.

Sources: Quinn (2007); Long (2007).

1 Why have agencies made these expensive strategic changes when it would be just as easy to outsource a client's digital work to specialists, on a need-to-do basis?

2 Select any two major agencies, visit their websites, and make a judgement about their respective digital service offering.

3 Which two items within the agency selection criteria mentioned earlier do you feel are the most important, and which are the two least important. Why?

Agency Personnel

The key roles within agencies are the **account manager**, **account planner**, the **creative team**, and the **media team**.

A full-service agency consists of several departments, all of which contribute to the development of a client's campaign. Most communications agencies are generally organized according to job function and its hierarchical position relative to campaign development and customer satisfaction. Recognizing the need for human resources and finance the main departments are designated for planning campaigns, creating messages, planning and buying media, plus departments which manage the production of communication pieces such as art work, videos, roughs, or mailers. This is sometimes referred to as traffic management.

The Account Manager (or Executive)

The account manager, often referred to as account handler or executive, is responsible for representing the interests of the client within the agency and for ensuring that all those working on the client's account are fully informed, working to deadline, and to budget. They have a key representational role in the client–agency relationship. They act as gatekeeper and control the flow of communications between the client and the agency so that it is both timely and accurate. The account manager has to perform several roles, from internal coordinator and negotiator to presenter (of the agency's work), conflict manager, and information gatherer. Very often account managers experience tension as they seek to achieve their clients' needs while trying to balance the needs of their employer and colleagues.

The Account Planner

In addition to the account manager is the role undertaken by account planners (or creative planners). The role of the account planner has been the subject of much discussion (Grant, Gilmore, and Crosier, 2003; Hackley, 2003; Collin, 2003; Zambarino and Goodfellow, 2003) as it seems that a new role is emerging in response to integrated marketing communication and media-neutral planning initiatives. The traditional role of the account planner was research oriented. It was their task to understand the client's target consumers, now referred to as consumer insight, and to develop strategies to guide the work of the creative and media departments. With the development of integrated perspectives and the move towards a broader view of a client's communication needs there is now an expectation that the planning role will evolve into a strategic role. The role will be to work with a broader range of marketing tools and media. Planners have an important role because their work grounds a campaign and should impact directly on the creative strategy. As Hackley (2003) puts it, one of their tasks is to provide the consumer insight and to then ensure that the creative execution reflects the client's marketing goals.

Creative Teams

Creative teams consist of two people, an art director and a copywriter, supported by a service team. This team is responsible for translating the proposal into an advertisement and they work mainly from the **creative brief**, although there is a balance between the formality of a written document and the inspiration and imagination necessary to communicate ideas about products and services in ways which are memorable and which have meaning for the target audience. The majority of ideas the creatives generate are rejected but eventually an idea emerges which can be shaped into an ad that can be communicated through particular media, for example TV, press, magazines, radio, web, or outdoor.

Media Teams

Media teams perform two main functions, media planning and media buying. The former is concerned with planning the best fit between the available media and the target audience. The latter buy the media schedule that has been determined by the media planners. Planners research the target audience to understand their media usage. They then build a media mix that will deliver the message to the target audience, the required number of times, within the client's budget and timescale.

The task of media buyers is to purchase the media that the planner has set out in the plan (or schedule) and which best reflects the client's strategy. Buyers negotiate with the sales houses appointed by media owners, to purchase the necessary time and space at the best price, so that their client's messages reach their target audience.

Agency Relationships

The structure of any communications agency will need to reflect the tasks that need to be accomplished. However, one of the key issues associated with structure and operating personnel is the prevailing organizational culture. Here it is crucial that the principal purpose is to ensure that an agency's clients are understood, catered for, handled promptly, efficiently, and, above all else, oriented to ensuring that their commercial needs and expectations are satisfied and exceeded respectively.

What this means is that the relationship between a client and the agency should be as strong as it can be. A failure in the client–agency relationship is one of the most cited reasons for an agency to be dropped and another appointed.

The agency–client relationship is based on a series of interactions (West and Paliwoda, 1996) through which trust and commitment can be developed. The more an agency produces work that meets a client's needs and expectations, the longer the relationship is likely to last. It is through a series of continued interactions and the accomplishment of the agreed tasks that the quality of the agency–client relationship can be measured. All relationships are a function of trust, which is developed through successful interaction. Commitment is derived from a belief that the relationship is worth continuing and that effort is needed to maintain it (Morgan and Hunt, 1994). Poor client–agency relationships are likely to result from a lack of trust and falling commitment. As communication is an important element in the development of relationships, both parties should be advised to use their range of marketing communication facilities to their fullest extent.

RESEARCH INSIGHT 13.4

To take your learning further, you might wish to read this influential paper.

Crosier, K., Grant, I., and Gilmore, C. (2003), 'Account planning in Scottish advertising agencies: a discipline in transition', *Journal of Marketing Communications*, 9, 1–15.

Although this paper is developed out of a research programme based on a relatively small sample of agencies, it is useful because it provides a coherent review of the various roles an account planner undertakes.

Briefing

In order that agencies fulfil their contractual obligations with their clients a number of operational processes and procedures have evolved. One of these processes is referred to as the briefing process, and is used extensively across the communication industry. A brief is a written document that serves to exchange information between parties involved with the development and implementation of a campaign. Three main types of brief can be identified. **Client briefs** are used to inform the agency of the client's organization, work, and operations and give an insight to the task or communication problem. Creative briefs are used to help agency personnel develop ads, and **media briefs** help those who buy media on the client's behalf. These are all examined in greater detail later in this chapter.

The briefing process has a number of advantages, one of which is that it leads to better use of resources. A clearly written brief increases the chances of developing a campaign that works at the first attempt. This is preferable to having to rework creative ideas, strategy, or positioning statements further down the line. Briefing promotes efficiency that in turn leads to improved effectiveness, client satisfaction, and ultimately stronger relationships.

So, briefing serves to link together different people, activities, and functions, both internally and externally. Briefing acts as a conduit through which rich information can be communicated to the various agency departments charged with the development and implementation of campaigns. Briefing is a process that is common across all client–agency relationships in the communication industry. Regardless of whether working in direct marketing, sales promotion, advertising, public relations, media planning and buying, or other specialist areas, the brief has a special importance in making the process work and the outcomes significant.

The Client Brief

Briefs prompt action and provide the information necessary for the designated people to do their jobs. The client brief is perhaps the key document as it provides the main platform upon which a campaign is developed. Without it, both the creative and media teams have little idea upon how to build a campaign. The client brief is developed by the client to provide their appointed agencies with key information about their markets, goals, strategies, resources, and contacts.

Once an account has been signed a client brief is prepared that provides information about the client organization. It sets out the nature of the industry it operates in together with data about trends, market share, customers, competitors, and the problem that the agency is required to address. This is used to inform agency personnel. In particular, the account planner will undertake research to determine market, media, and audience characteristics and make proposals to the rest of the account team as to how the client problem is to be resolved.

The Creative Brief

The creative brief provides information to those responsible for the creation of the actual message (the creative) that is to be communicated. The creative brief is important because it serves to link not only people but also the key processes involved in the development of communications material. For example, it links research and communication strategy, it translates all background information into actual materials, helps ensure that the outcomes will address the needs of the client as well as the needs of their target audiences. It may be that the creative team responsible for the client's work are external to the lead agency but this should not distract from the point that these documents should state quite clearly the campaign objectives, the characteristics of the target audience, and any consumer insight research that has been undertaken.

The creative brief is used to inform the creative team about background information and the overall shape, style, and tone of the desired communications. The goal of the brief is to provide a clear idea of what the communication should accomplish.

The Media Brief

The media brief serves to guide the media team with regard to their selection and subsequent purchase of the right media mix. This means the brief should refer to

CREATIVE BRIEF

DATE: April 5, 2007
CLIENT: Univar USA
JOB TITLE: CHEMCENTRAL Acquisition Announcement Ad
JOB NUMBER: 3500-006

ASSIGNMENT What, succinctly, are you asking us to do?
Develop and produce a full-page magazine ad to announce to customers, suppliers, and employees the acquisition of CHEMCENTRAL by UnivarUSA and what it means to each of those audiences.

AUDIENCE Who is this effort aimed at? What are they like?
Primary audience: Purchasing, engineering, and management of manufacturing companies who use industrial chemicals and are likely customers of Univar, CHEMCENTRAL or both. They may have already read or heard about this acquisition and may have doubts or questions about how this will affect them.

Secondary audience: Chemical producers, employees of CHEMCENTRAL and Univar, as well as employees of other chemical distribution companies.

OBJECTIVE What specific results are we after, when must they be achieved?   What do we want the audience to do?
While there's no measurable objective for this ad, the goal is to help stakeholders realize that this acquisition is a positive move, and will yield benefits for customers, employees, and suppliers.

SITUATION What's the current environment—especially with respect to competitors?
The chemical industry—like most segments of business—has been going through consolidation over the past several years. Accordingly, no one will be shocked to hear about this acquisition. There may, however, be some skepticism on the part of customers who may fear they're losing some price leverage by taking a major competitor out of the equation. Employees of both companies—but especially CHEMCENTRAL —might have reason to wonder if they'll lose their jobs as a result of the duplication this acquisition may bring.

ATTITUDES What does the audience think now? What do we want them to think?
Now: I had heard that Univar had bought CHEMCENTRAL, but I wonder if that's a good thing for me or not.

Future: I know that the deal between Univar and CHEMCENTRAL went through, and it sounds like it's actually going to be a good deal for us—and all concerned.

300 Aurora Avenue North
Suite 103
Seattle, WA 98109

T 206-930-3417
M 206-930-3417
F 206-930-3417

STRATEGY/TAKE-AWAY "You should (action) (product) because (reason with NO conjunctions)."
You should look at the acquisition of CHEMCENTRAL by Univar as a positive move for customers, as it's going to create more of an efficient, complete source for chemicals, while giving their employees opportunities to grow in their careers.

Specific advantages by audience:
Customers – broader, more complete line of products and services; improved geographical coverage; adds new producer to product offerings of both companies; stronger delivery of technical support

Suppliers – more access to more markets; opportunity to optimize supply chain activities; no plans to consolidate producers

Employees – opportunity—especially for CHEMCENTRAL employees—to be part of a larger, global organization with prospects for growth and career advancement

COPY POINTS/CAUTIONS/TONALITY Other things that should or could be mentioned.
- Style should be serious, positive, and friendly
- Typically, ads announcing mergers and acquisitions tend to be overly rosy and don't have a great deal of credibility—we need to consider approaches that will be believed by the readers
- Consider staying with graphic style of existing Univar ads that have run in these pubs
- Ad should include both the Univar and CHEMCENTRAL logos
- Target date for close of the deal is April 20. Ad should run as soon thereafter as possible.
- Include url: www.univarusa.com

DEADLINES
CREATIVE BRIEF APPROVAL: 4/6	PRESENT ROUGH CONCEPTS: 4/18
CONCEPT APPROVAL 4/23	FIRST COPY DRAFT: 4/25
APPROVED COPY: 4/30	FIRST PROOF (LAYOUT WITH COPY): 5/3
PROOF COMMENTS: 5/4	FINAL APPROVAL: 5/7
PREPARE MAT'LS FOR PUBS: 5/10	FIRST EXTENDED MATERIALS CLOSE: 5/14

ISSUE DATES: **Chemical Week, 5/23/07; ICIS 5/21/07, Purchasing/Chemicals 6/14/07**

CLIENT APPROVAL _____ DATE _____

Example of a creative brief

Creative Media

the objectives of the campaign and especially the communication goals, the target audience and their media preferences, the available budget, timescales, and the history of previous campaigns plus the scope of the other tools being used in the campaign.

The vast majority of media planning work is now undertaken by specialist media agencies and media independents, and the media agency will be briefed directly by the client, with some support from those responsible for the creative.

On the agency side there are decisions to be made about how to incorporate digital within their organizations. Many specialist yet small digital agencies have been created but the larger traditional agencies have to decide how best to provide their clients with straightforward digital facilities, such as online advertising and video. One approach adopted by Bartle Bogle Hegerty (BBH), a leading London-based advertising agency, has been to buy a stake in a smaller digital-based organization (Dare) and become involved with their online work. Having learned from this arrangement BBH began to set up their own internal digital facilities and experts and in January 2007 won a digital-only brief for the Lynx/Axe brand. This dual structural approach enables BBH to meet the needs of clients who want specialist digital work and those who want digital as an extension to their offline advertising work, BBH's core business.

Sources: Silverman (2006); Tiltman (2007).

1 Go to Dare's website at www.Dare.co.uk and look at their work. Can you identify any similarities among their clients?

2 How would you advise a client organization to select a digital media agency?

3 In your opinion, is the media or creative brief the most important? Why?

4 Evaluate the digital capability of the Lynx/Axe brand website. www.thelynxeffect.com.

Agency Remuneration

If there is one thing that will cause disruption, tension, and even a 'falling out' between a client and an agency, it is the amount an agency is paid, or remunerated, for the work they undertake. There are three main ways in which agencies are paid. These are commission, fees, and payment by results. A fourth way, a mixture or combination of these methods, can also be supported.

The **commission** system works on the basis that an advertising agency buys media for their clients, from media owners. So, media owners reward the agency with 15 per cent of the cost of the media purchased. The more media bought the higher an agency is rewarded. The 15 per cent figure has been renegotiated in many cases and figures of 6 or 7 per cent are now quite common. The main problem with commission is that agencies suffer disproportionately when the economy enters recession and clients stop using advertising.

Fees have been around for a long time, either in the form of retainers or on a project-by-project basis. Indeed, many agencies charge a fee for services over and above any commission earned from media owners. The big question is about the basis for calculation of fees (and this extends to all areas of marketing communications, not just advertising), and protracted, complicated negotiations can damage client–agency relationships.

As managers have become increasingly accountable for their advertising spend so a **payment-by-results** (PBR) system has evolved. This approach has become increasingly popular as it overcomes some of the difficulties posed by the commission system. It should be recognized, however, that the agency does not have any real influence over their client's other marketing activities and final decisions about how much is spent and which creative ideas should be used remain the client's.

With over 30 per cent of business now remunerated via payment by results (Lace, 2000) it seems likely that the reliance on the commission as the only form of remuneration to the agency has passed and that a combination of all three methods appears to be the accepted way of remunerating agencies.

Evaluating and Measuring Marketing Communications Activities

It might be safely assumed that the final aspect of a manager's responsibilities concerns the measurement of their marketing communications activities. This is partly correct but measurement and evaluation should be an ongoing activity, used throughout the development and implementation of a campaign. The importance of evaluating marketing communications activities should not be underestimated. The process can provide a potentially rich source of material for the next campaign and the ongoing communications that all organizations operate. Unfortunately, many organizations choose to either ignore or not to devote too many resources or significance to this aspect of their work. However, in an age of increasing accountability, measuring and determining just how well a campaign ran and what was accomplished is an essential part of marketing communications.

There are three main perspectives for the evaluation of marketing communications The first perspective concerns the degree to which a marketing communications campaign achieved the goals it was created to achieve. The second perspective concerns the contribution made by each activity within a campaign, most notably each communication tool, medium, and message. Again, this can be determined from a holistic perspective or it can be explored by using a variety of individual techniques and methodologies. Those techniques most applicable to measuring the use of the marketing communication tools are set out in Table 13.4.

The third perspective concerns the systems and processes associated with the marketing communications planning process. It is relatively easy for parts of the planning process to be deteriorate and in doing so affect the overall efficiency of the planning process.

Should an organization have suitable resources it is helpful to test effectiveness before, during, and after exposure to each campaign activity, in order that the degree and speed of change can be determined. While pre- and post-testing is normally an advertising-related approach, the principle can be applied across all the tools of the mix.

Only by attempting to measure effectiveness and efficiency of a marketing communications campaign can managers improve their understanding of what does and does not work. Some organizations adopt sales-based measures but, as mentioned earlier, sales result from a variety of factors. Marketing communications managers should avoid this approach, despite its low cost and speed of administration, and focus their attention on the communication impact of their work and the achievement of the communication objectives.

Table 13.4
Evaluation
methods: marketing
communications tools

Marketing communication tool	Method of testing
Advertising	Pretesting—*unfinished* ads—concept testing, focus groups, consumer juries Pretesting—*finished* ads—dummy vehicles, readability test, theatre tests Physiological—pupil dilation, eye tracking, galvanic skin response, tachistoscopes, electrocephalographs Post-testing—enquiry tests, recall tests, recognition tests, sales-tracking studies, financial analysis, likeability
Sales promotion	Trial, sales, stock turn, redemption levels
Public relations	Press cuttings, content analysis, media evaluation, tracking studies, recruitment levels
Direct marketing	Response rates, sales, opening/reading ratios, trial
Personal selling	Activities, costs, knowledge and skills, sales, performance ratios, territory analysis, team outputs, customer satisfaction

Chapter Summary

To consolidate your learning, the key points from this chapter are summarized below:

- Understand the nature and characteristics of marketing communications strategy.

  The development of marketing communications strategy is a management activity that should be guided, primarily, by the nature, characteristics, and communication needs of the audience, rather than the communication tools or media at the disposal of the organization. There are three types of audience and hence three types of strategy. These audiences are target customers (a pull strategy), channel intermediaries such as wholesalers and added value resellers (a push strategy), and an organization's stakeholder network (a profile strategy).

- Explain how marketing communication activities are planned and implemented.

  Marketing communication planning is a systematic process that involves a series of procedures and activities that lead to the setting of marketing communication objectives and the formulation of plans for achieving them. The marketing communications planning framework (MCPF) provides a structure and checklist though which the sequence of decisions that marketing managers undertake when preparing, implementing, and evaluating communication strategies and plans can be designed. The framework reflects a deliberate or planned approach to strategic marketing communications, one which may not always occur in practice.

- Explain the different activities associated with managing marketing communications.

  There is a large range of tasks associated with managing marketing communications. At one level, there are decisions to be made about the overall strategy and direction of the marketing communications, and issues associated with the process and, of course, the content of marketing communications plans. At another level, decisions need to be made about the right mix of tools and media necessary to engage with target audiences, and to decide about what is to be said in the message and how it is to be presented. Behind all of these activities are issues associated with the management of resources, both human and financial, and the agency relationships necessary to generate the communication materials. Once implemented, management are still involved through the control, monitoring, evaluation, and feedback processes.

- Describe the ways organizations determine their marketing communication budgets.

  There are a number of ways organizations determine their marketing communications budgets. These range from the largely inaccurate and inappropriate methods such as inertia, arbitrary, affordable, and media multiplier approaches to the more commonly used percentage of sales and the most reliable objective and task methods.

  In addition to these methods, some companies relate their advertising investment decisions to: how much their competitors are spending (competitive parity), how much is invested in advertising by the industry as a whole (advertising to sales ratio) and the relationship between the amount each brand invests in advertising as a percentage of the total amount invested in advertising (share of voice).

- Comprehend the processes, procedures, and operations used to manage client–agency operations and relationships.

  Clients select agencies to produce and distribute communication materials. There is an established procedure concerning the selection of the 'right' agency. This involves the search, credentials presentation, pitching, and contracting phases. Once selected the client–agency relationship is normally managed through the 'briefing' process. This system is based on the provision of written documents that provide information to help others perform their part of the marketing communication process effectively and efficiently. Agencies designate different tasks to different roles, so account planners, managers, creative teams, and media planners are connected internally, and externally to their client, through the briefing process.

  There are three main types of brief, namely, client, creative, and media briefs. Originally, these briefs were handwritten but, of course, new technology has helped transform the speed, accuracy, and dissemination of these important operational documents. There are three main ways by which agencies are rewarded financially for their work. These are the traditional commission system, which is giving way to a combination of payment-by-results and fee-based methods.

- Explain the principles associated with the measurement and evaluation of marketing communication activities.

  The measurement and evaluation of marketing communications activities is indisputably an important aspect of the managerial task. There are three main perspectives for the evaluation of marketing communications. The first perspective concerns the degree to which a marketing communications campaign achieved the goals it was created to achieve. The second perspective concerns the contribution made by each activity within a campaign, most notably each communication tool, medium, and message. The third perspective concerns the systems and processes associated with the marketing communications planning process.

Evaluating the effectiveness of marketing communications should take place before, during, and after exposure to each campaign activity.

 Visit the **Online Resource Centre** that accompanies this book to read more information about managing marketing communications: www.oxfordtextbooks.co.uk/orc/baines/

❓ Review Questions

1. Make brief notes outlining the characteristics and dimensions of each of the 3Ps of communication strategy.

2. List the principal tasks facing marketing communications managers.

3. Draw the marketing communications planning framework. Try this first without referring to the diagram. If stuck refer to the diagram.

4. Explain how the context analysis should underpin a marketing communication plan and identify three linkages between the context analysis and other parts of the planning framework.

5. Make a list of the elements that should be integrated when developing integrated marketing communications.

6. Describe four ways in which a marketing communications budget can be worked out.

7. Find two examples of each of the main types of organization that make up the marketing communication industry.

8. Describe the process by which an organization selects an agency to undertake its marketing communications. Identify two problems with this process.

9. Explain the briefing process and identify three types of brief.

10. Describe the three main ways in which an agency can be paid for the work it does.

❓ Discussion Questions

1. Having the read the Case Insight at the beginning of this chapter, how would you advise the management of Pergo to develop their marketing communication strategies?

2. Discuss the view that if marketing communications strategy is about being audience centred then there is little need to prepare a context analysis.

3. Select an organization in the consumer technology industry or one which you would like to work for. Visit their website and see their ad archive and then read the

press releases. Try to determine their approach to marketing communications. Now visit the website for their main competitor and again, determine their marketing communications. Discuss the similarities and differences.

4 Bendy Foods had worked with its advertising agency, ClearVision, for over fifteen years and had established a good working relationship. However, the arrival of Andrew Dear, Bendy Foods' new marketing manager, threatened the stability of the client–agency relationship. At his previous company, Andrew had been involved with the development of an integrated marketing communications strategy and he has indicated that he wants to do the same at Bendy Foods. However, ClearVision does not have experience of IMC and has started to become concerned that it may lose the Bendy Foods account. Discuss the situation facing Bendy Foods and suggest ways in which they might acquire the expertise they need. Then discuss ways in which ClearVision might acquire an IMC capability.

5 Consider the soft drinks and water markets and find examples of drinks producers and identify their distributors. What is the nature of their marketing communications and do you think it is likely to be effective?

📖 References

Adams, R., and Finch, J. (2003), 'Take one celebrity chef', *The Guardian*, Wednesday, 1 January, available at www.business.guardian.co.uk/story/, accessed 29 March 2007.

Anon. (2006), Diageo (Greece) Theatrical Staff Seminar, available at www.warc.com, accessed 28 March 2007.

—— (2007), 'Three vie for Tango biscuit accountThree vie for Tango biscuit account', Media Asia 21 March, available at www.brandrepublic.com/News/645029/Three-vie-Tango-biscuit-accountThree-vie-Tango-biscuit-account, accessed 24 March 2007.

Collin, W. (2003), 'The interface between account planning and media planning: a practitioner perspective', *Marketing Intelligence and Planning*, 21, 7, 440–5.

Cornelissen, J. P. (2003), 'Change, continuity and progress: the concept of integrated marketing communications and marketing communications practice', *Journal of Strategic Marketing*, 11 (December), 217–34.

Crosier, K., Grant, I., and Gilmore, C. (2003), 'Account planning in Scottish advertising agencies: a discipline in transition', *Journal of Marketing Communications*, 9, 1–15.

Fill, C. (2002), *Marketing Communications: Contexts, Strategies and Applications*, 3rd edn., Harlow: FT/Prentice Hall.

—— (2005), *Marketing Communications: Engagements, Strategies and Practice*, 4th edn., Harlow: FT/Prentice Hall.

—— (2006), *Simply Marketing Communications*, Harlow: FT/Prentice Hall.

Grant, I., Gilmore, C., and Crosier, K. (2003), 'Account planning: whose role is it anyway?', *Marketing Intelligence and Planning*, 21, 7, 462–72.

Hackley, C. E. (2003), 'Account planning: current agency perspectives on an advertising enigma', *Journal of Advertising Research*, 43, 235–45.

Hawkes, S. (2007), 'Short film is central to $100m campaign', *The Times*, 2 March, available at www.business.timesonline.co.uk/tol/business/industry_sectors/natural_resources/, accessed 8 March 2007.

Jones, J. P. (1990), 'Ad spending: maintaining market share', *Harvard Business Review*, January–February, 38–42.

Jones, M. (2004), '10 things agencies need to know about clients', *Admap*, 39, 5 (May), 21–3.

Lace, J. M. (2000), 'Payment-by-results: is there a pot of gold at the end of the rainbow?', *International Journal of Advertising*, 19, 167–83.

Long, D. (2007), 'MindShare revamps business model', *Campaign*, 23 March, available at www.brandrepublic.com/News/645312/MindShare-revamps-business-model, accessed 26 March 2007.

Melewar, T. C. (2003), 'Determinants of the corporate identity construct: a review of the literature', *Journal of Marketing Communications*, 9, 4, 195–220.

Morgan, R. M., and Hunt, S. D. (1994), 'The commitment–trust theory of relationship marketing', *Journal of Marketing*, 58 (July), 20–38.

Murphy, C. (2006), 'Integration incomplete', *Marketing*, 22 March, 15.

Payne, J. (2007), 'Shell rolls out environmentally conscious ad campaign', *Brand Republic*, available at www.brandrepublic.com/News/636287/Shell-rolls-environmentally-conscious-ad-campaign/, accessed 9 March 2007.

Prasad, G. (2007), 'Mirinda declares war in face-off with Sprite', Media Asia, 15 July, available at www.brandrepublic.com/News/484722/Mirinda-declares-war-face-off-Sprite/, accessed 30 May 2007.

Quinn, I. (2007), 'Digital integration will be key in 2007', *Media Week*, 9 January, available at www.brandrepublic.com/News/625244/Digital-integration-will-key-2007/, accessed 26 March 2007.

Saunders, J. (2006), 'Growing up digitally: change drivers in marketing', *Market Leader*, 33, Summer, available at www.warc.com, accessed 28 March 2007.

Sheppard, F. (2005), 'Oliver helps supermarket cook up sales rise', *The Scotsman*, Saturday, 8 October, available at www.thescotsman.com/, accessed 28 March 2007.

Silverman, G. (2006), 'How can I help you?', *FT Magazine*, 4–5 February, 16–21.

Swain, W. N. (2004), 'Perceptions of IMC after a decade of development: who's at the wheel, and how can we measure success?', *Journal of Advertising Research*, 44, 1 (March), 46–65.

Teague, K. (2007), 'Apple Computer, Inc: Silhoutte campaign', *Encyclopedia of Major Marketing Campaigns*, 2, available at www.warc.com, accessed 31 May 2007.

Tiltman, D. (2007), 'Advertising leagues', *Marketing*, 14 March, 14–16.

West, D. C., and Paliwoda, S. J. (1996), 'Advertising client–agency relationships', *European Journal of Marketing*, 30, 8, 22–39.

Zambarino, A., and Goodfellow, J. (2003), 'Account planning in the new marketing and communications environment (has the Stephen King challenge been met?)', *Marketing Intelligence and Planning*, 21, 7, 424–34.

14

Channel Management and Retailing

Whoever said money can't buy happiness simply didn't know where to go shopping.

Bo Derek

Learning Outcomes

After studying this chapter you should be able to:

✔ Define what a channel of distribution is and key considerations in channel strategy and decision making.

✔ Define and discuss the differing types of intermediaries and their roles in the distribution channel.

✔ Differentiate between differing distribution channel structures and selection criteria.

✔ Discuss the factors influencing channel design, structure, and strategy.

✔ Distinguish between the logistical functions, identifying key considerations for effective management.

✔ Define the role, function, and importance of retailers in the distribution channel.

✔ Compare and contrast the differing types of retailers.

✔ Discuss the key strategic and operational considerations in retailing strategies.

Established in 1995, Ekinoks is a Turkish-based firm that provides technical services and spare parts support to the plastics and machinery industry. How does it manage its relationships with suppliers? We speak to Alper Behar to find out.

Alper Behar for Ekinoks

We represent leading manufacturers all over the world, providing them with manufacturing facilities, efficiency improvement equipment, OEM systems, and appraisal and investment services. Our vision is to provide innovative solutions through long-term cooperation with our customers with the core aim of sustaining long-term stakeholder relationships.

However, in order to provide high-value quality services and support to our customers, Ekinoks are dependent on managing effective relationships with members of our supply chain and in particular cultivating good sustainable relationships with our suppliers. This is grounded on effective communication between and with our suppliers.

To help cultivate sustainable relationships between suppliers in our supply chain we organize yearly supplier meetings, bringing our suppliers together in Istanbul so that they can share information and experiences. These meetings are coupled with social events such as banquets and sightseeing tours which are successful in

Ekinoks aims to provide innovative solutions through long-term cooporation with its customers

Ekinoks

developing deeper social bonds amongst our suppliers and with Ekinoks.

To help build sustainable relationships between Ekinoks employees and our suppliers we believe in old-fashioned human contact as an essential element, relying on telephone, fax, and more recently email contact with our suppliers at all tiers: management, sales, and service levels. Given the importance of communication in supplier management, one growing trend we have experienced some difficulties with in recent years, however, is the growth in the use of email communications.

> *email could be far more cost effective than telephone and face to face interactions [but] we have started to question its effectiveness in terms of cultivating sustainable relationships*

Ekinoks saw that email could be far more cost effective than telephone and face-to-face interactions, especially when our suppliers are based all over the world. It is also more time efficient. However, we have started to question its effectiveness in terms of cultivating sustainable relationships. Most of our problems with suppliers have occurred due to poor communication and as a result of relying mainly on email and faxes as the main modes of communication as opposed to discussions.

For example, once we had a supplier who felt that Ekinoks was not providing an appropriate level of service to a certain customer when representing the supplier. The supplier felt their reputation was being negatively influenced as a result. Over a three-week period we exchanged emails with the supplier about the situation. However, rather than easing the situation, the emails became heated and personal to the extent that some very unprofessional exchanges of words resulted.

It was at this point that Ekinoks picked up the telephone and started talking to the supplier. It became clear that there had been a misunderstanding about the role of the customer. In an attempt to avoid paying for service calls and spare parts provided by Ekinoks, the customer complained about Ekinoks to the supplier. This created an atmosphere of unease and concern for the supplier that was misinterpreted by Ekinoks during email communications. In fact, both Ekinoks and the supplier had the same intentions but the customer was not fulfilling their side of the service-level agreement. The supplier addressed this directly and as a result this supplier has since evolved into our second biggest supplier today.

As you can see, effective communication is essential for managing supplier relationships, and especially when conditions of channel conflict arise. The mode of communication also has a direct impact on its effectiveness.

If you were Ekinoks, what would you do now to ensure that the effective management of supplier relationships and communication with Ekinoks continues?

Introduction

Where do you do your banking or buy your groceries? How do you purchase tickets for a concert, a football match, or air travel? At what time of the day do you pay your electricity and phone bills? For many people, the time and place they deal with these things have changed. We can get cash 24 hours a day, 365 days per year, from automatic teller machines (ATMs); bills can be paid and banking completed any time at home or at work, on the phone or through the internet; and drink and snack dispensing machines now appear on railway station platforms, airline terminals, in shopping malls, and hospital waiting rooms. These examples demonstrate that in the last two decades **place** (or **distribution**) has undergone substantial change.

Many organizations still believe that it plays a relatively small part in their marketing activities, seeing 'place' as only the tangible activities involved in transporting goods physically from where they are manufactured, via intermediaries, to the customer. However, as competition increases, and margins are reduced, the focus on distribution efficiency and effectiveness continues to dramatically increase. If goods do not arrive in the proper place, or in the proper condition, no sale can be made (Douglas, James, and Ellram, 1998).

This chapter demonstrates that place embraces a broader concept than just the delivery of goods. It includes understanding the strategic importance of distribution channels, member roles in the channel, and the rising importance of customer service. This chapter introduces you to the fundamental principle of 'place' in the marketing mix and to management decisions concerning distribution channels, channel members, and logistics management. A detailed discussion of retailing and wholesaling is also included.

Place

'Place' or distribution is about how you can place the optimum amount of goods and/or services before the maximum number of your target market at the times and locations they want. The way distribution occurs can be physical, like supplying MS Office software through a computing retailer; a service, such as a training service for the use of MS Office; or electronic, such as downloading MS Office updates through the internet. Irrespective of the mode used, distribution activities have a direct effect on other marketing strategy elements. For example, Hershey Co. had to raise the wholesale prices of its confectionery line by 4–5 per cent, because of its rising costs in the distribution process. Here we can see that distribution activities had a direct effect on Hershey Co.'s pricing strategy.

Distribution activities are a vital element in creating customer value. A product will provide customer value and satisfaction only if it is available to the customer when and where it is needed, and in the appropriate quantity (Douglas, James, and Ellram, 1998). It goes without saying that customers must have access to the product. For example, in India and China, Motorola took their products to rural customers who couldn't get to the retail outlets by setting up 'Moto-vehicles', jeeps, motorcycles, vans, and other vehicles that transformed into Motorola showrooms on the side of the road. Variables that influence customer perceptions of distribution quality include:

- Dependability—consistency of service;
- Time in transit;
- Market coverage;
- The ability to provide door-to-door service;
- Flexibility—handling and meeting the special needs of shippers;
- Loss and damage performance; and
- The ability to provide more than basic product delivery service.

As product delivery has a direct effect on customer evaluations of service quality and satisfaction we need to understand 'what do customers or end consumers want from our distribution activities?' Do they want speedy delivery, a reliable supply of products, a good range of choice or product assortment, increased availability, convenience, service and support, a good price, or after-sales service? Insight to these questions helps inform effective distribution and channel management strategies, but these too are dependent on the buyer type and type of product being delivered. For more information on Motorola plans to reach the rural customer in India, see Market Insight 14.1.

Distribution Channel Management

Distribution ranges from production and manufacturing to logistics, warehousing, and the final delivery of goods to the customer (Handfield and Nichols, 1999). Very few organizations are able to deliver products to all possible customers and

Motorola Reaches out in India

Twenty-first-century India is a highly attractive marketplace for Western companies looking to expand their global sales. The nation's $785 billion economy is growing at around 9% annually and per capita income has risen to about $3,400 a year. However, the country's population of 1.1 billion is still largely rural, and the Asian Development Bank has reported that about 35% of Indians currently live on less than $1 a day. Companies looking to expand sales in India are therefore likely to encounter a number of significant people, process, infrastructure, and technology challenges. This, however, hasn't deterred Motorola, the second largest mobile phone maker in the world, with global market share rising from 14% in 2003 to 22% in 2006, from being innovative about its distribution strategy to reach the rural Indian consumer.

In terms of mobile phone technologies, India has the largest subscriber base after China and the USA with 160 million subscribers, and growth at 6 million per month, making it a very attractive market. However, this represents less than 15% of the population owning a mobile phone. The main issue for companies like Motorola is that 72% of the people in India live in rural villages that lack mobile networks, and the infrastructure of supplying mobile phone handsets and associated services. According to a nationwide survey conducted by consultants McKinsey and Co. of 593 rural districts, 248 are 'deprived' and lack basic infrastructure like all-weather roads. Adil Zainulbhai, managing director, McKinsey and Co., says: 'Almost half of India's rural population does not have access to good roads and decent infrastructure.' Given these market conditions, how does a company like Motorola get its product to the rural Indian consumer?

To reach India's rural consumer, Motorola has forged alliances with rural retailers like ITC's eChoupal, DCM group's Hariyali Kisaan Bazaar, and Godrej's Aadhaar outlets for sales and distribution of handsets, acquiring unparalleled penetration for its handsets sales in India. The alliance is a perfect match of expertise in rural retail, and an initiative aimed at connecting India's mass market consumers in rural/semi-urban areas.

The alliance will offer consumers direct, over-the-counter access to a wide range of handsets across categories and price bands. Consumers will also benefit from the assurance of a first ever direct channel for the purchase of new handsets. This is a boon for a segment which has traditionally suffered from grey market imports and/or refurbished units. In keeping with its focus on service, sale of all handsets will be covered by Motorola's robust after-sales support. Just as communication technology has improved the quality of life in urban areas, these partnerships will offer similar benefits to the rural population, helping them enhance their productivity levels. Addressing rural/semi-urban consumers is a strategic imperative in Motorola's efforts to empower existing and potential customers in largely neglected parts of the country. The alliance approach is ground breaking and pivotal in Motorola's efforts to connect the next billion people.

Sources: Srinivasan (2005); Anon. (2006a, 2006b); Ibison and Taylor (2007); Lath *et al.* (2007); Thomas (2007).

1 What are the challenges in distributing to the Indian consumer?

2 What has Motorola done to overcome these challenges?

3 What benefits do these types of alliances offer the Indian consumer?

thus rely on other parties, such as distributors, for assistance. These organisations form what we call a **distribution channel**, an organized network of agencies and organizations which perform all the activities required to link producers and manufacturers with purchasers and consumers (Bennet, 1988). The aim is the orderly flow of material, personnel, and information throughout the distribution channel to ensure product delivery (Russell, 2000). Distributors thus perform an important intermediary role in matching supply with demand through their interactions with suppliers, manufacturers, and end customers.

Management of distribution channels concerns two key elements: (1) managing the design of the channel and its activities and (2) managing the relationship of members in the channel. First, we need to design an appropriate channel structure, channel length, and select the members of the channel and their roles. This helps us to determine what is the most effective and efficient way to get the product to the customer. How can we reach the optimum number of customers? And what organizations do we need to help us achieve this? Next we turn our attention to managing the social, political, and economic relationships of channel members (Gandhi, 1979). A good understanding of the relationships in the channel will help to improve the effectiveness and efficiency of product delivery.

Channel decisions are also one of the most important decisions that a manager faces. An organization's pricing strategies will depend on whether the product is distributed through mass retailers or high-quality speciality stores. Likewise, sales force and advertising decisions will depend on how much persuasion, training, motivation, and support dealers in the channel need. If an organization does not pay sufficient attention to the distribution channel, it will be detrimental to its marketing efforts. Some organizations have actually created an industry in improved distribution. FedEx Express for example is the world's largest cargo airline using a fleet of over 670 aircraft and 40,000 local delivery trucks to move packages, guaranteeing delivery of goods.

Key Considerations

When managing distribution channels we need to consider a number of factors to make sure the channel best suits the organization's objectives. This includes balancing the three elements of economics, coverage, and control.

- Economics requires us to recognize where costs are being spent and profits being made, or should be made, in a channel to maximize our return on investment;

- **Coverage** is about maximizing the amount of contact and benefits for the customer in terms of making the product available. This satisfies the marketer's desire to have the product available to the largest number of customers, in as many locations as possible, at the widest range of times.

- **Control** refers to achieving the optimum distribution costs without losing decision-making authority over the product and the way it is marketed and supported in the delivery channel. This includes decisions about the product, its pricing, promotion, and delivery in the distribution channel.

Sometimes by covering a wide range of delivery times and locations through the use of intermediaries the organization sacrifices some control in decision making. Intermediaries start changing the price, image, display, and so on as they seek to maximize sales of a whole range of products, including the products of competitors. Think about the position of Nokia, Sony Ericsson, or Motorola. In order to get the maximum number of customers using their mobile phone handsets they need to have the maximum number of retailers and mobile phone networks promoting and selling their phones. But the same networks and retailers also sell the handsets of their competitors. As the retailers and networks compete to sign up customers, they push for lower prices, or they demand advertising subsidies to help them sell the phones. So Nokia, Sony Ericsson, or Motorola may discover that their phones are being sold at very low prices, and their brand image compromised, by retailers and networks who are desperately seeking to maximize their own sales. What happens if Motorola reduce the number of retailers or networks they deal with in order to increase control over their marketing mix? The danger of course is that their competitors will gain market share by continuing to deal with these retailers and networks. They face a trade-off between economics, coverage, and control.

Intermediaries

As we saw in the example above for Nokia, Sony Ericsson, and Motorola, organizations often rely on **intermediaries**. Intermediaries are independent organizations that provide a link between producers and end consumers, assisting the physical movement of the product and the transfer of legal title to the end consumer. Various functions they perform include managing inventory, physical delivery, and financial services, enabling firms to offer just about everything a buyer wants, from availability, speed of delivery, reliable supply, range of choice in product assortment, and so on. Figure 14.1 displays a number of the benefits offered by intermediaries.

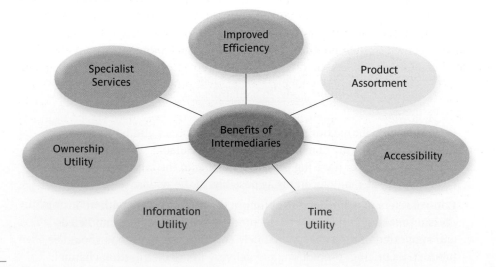

Figure 14.1
Benefits of intermediaries

The benefits of intermediaries include some or all of the following:

- **Improved efficiency:** Producers usually manufacture a small range of products in large quantities whereas consumers consume a wide range of products in small quantities. An intermediary such as a wholesaler improves efficiency in the delivery channel by breaking large deliveries from producers into single units and assorting them into a range of goods available for retailers (i.e. **product assortment efficiency**).

- **Accessibility:** Usually the location where production occurs is miles from the point of usage or consumption. Think about the clothes you purchase on a UK high street; these can be manufactured as far afield as China or India. Intermediaries assist by bringing the product to a more convenient location for purchase, providing place utility.

- **Time utility:** Manufacturing, purchase, and consumption can also occur at differing points in time. The product might be manufactured during the day but purchased and consumed at the weekend. Intermediaries such as retailers provide time utility.

- **Ownership utility:** Through intermediaries like retailers, products are available immediately from the intermediaries' stocks, enabling ownership to pass to the consumer within a limited amount of time.

- **Specialist services:** Intermediaries might also provide specialist services such as after-sales, maintenance, installation, or even training services to increase the effective use of the product. These services are best offered and performed by those closest to the purchaser or user of the product.

- **Information utility:** Sometimes intermediaries also provide information about the product to aid sales and product usage. The internet has further led to the development of a new type of intermediary, an information intermediary whose key role is to manage information to improve the efficiency and effectiveness of the distribution channel.

These benefits are offset by certain disadvantages. With an increasing number of intermediaries, and certain types in a distribution channel, a lack of control over the product can result. Manufacturers are often at the mercy of intermediaries in terms of where their product is placed in-store and how much it is finally priced for. Furthermore, intermediaries might be susceptable to competitor inducement such as trade promotions which pre-empt rival products from shelf space. For many manufacturers and producers intermediaries often become a market in their own right, requiring considerable time, money, and personnel to support and develop a relationship with them. Sony provides a good example of the effect a supplier's brand can have on the activities and behaviour of intermediaries such as retailers in the electronics sector. Despite product similarity, Sony remains a premium electronics brand, and any electrical retailer without the Sony brand in stock will suffer in terms of store traffic as shoppers will expect to see it. Sony thus has supplier power in this way and can negotiate high margins and better shelf positioning for its products than its rivals (combining both pull and push strategies).

Red Bull Grows Wings

If the mantra for retailers is 'location, location, location', the rallying cry for small beverage companies is 'distribution, distribution, distribution'. However, with Coca-Cola and Pepsi owning the widest and most powerful distributor networks, especially in the United States, penetrating these networks can prove very difficult, especially for a small beverage manufacturer like Red Bull GmbH.

Red Bull GmbH, founded in Austria in 1984, was credited with creating the energy drinks category. The company built its market share by securing unusual distribution outlets and piggybacking on established distributors. As the drink caught on, the company began taking a narrow approach to distribution. The company built a network of student sales representatives each with contacts with small distributors, insisting that they sell only Red Bull, then set up warehouses and hired students to load up delivery vans and deliver the product. These start-up distributors focused their entire energies on getting Red Bull fully stocked in stores with prominent shelf placement.

The sales team visited key on-premise accounts such as new or hot clubs and trendy bars. When owners began buying a few cases, they would receive a Red Bull branded cooler and other POP items. The company adopted on-premise accounts (vs. retailers) first, giving the product lots of visibility and providing fertile ground for new drink trends. These young emerging distributors also found it faster to deal with individual accounts, not big chains and their authorization process. These tactics soon developed into more than a guerrilla strategy building buzz at clubs. Sales teams started to open off-premise accounts at convenience stores near colleges, gyms, health-food stores, and supermarkets. The mission was to find out where the target market (men and women aged 16–29) hung out and what interested them, and then to get the message out to the right clubs and at the right events.

The success of this early distribution strategy is evident today with more than 3 billion cans of Red Bull sold in over 130 countries, generating 2.6 billion euros in turnover. However, soon Red Bull outgrew these tactics. They were fine for a growing small business but weren't really capable of growing with a Red Bull business that is now using aggressive marketing. Today Red Bull's distribution strategy is very different with its logistics and distribution plan fitting its enormous expansion strategy. The company has today created a supply chain strategy that blends logistics and transportation with the need for flexibility and expansion. The effort included new approaches toward transportation and to warehousing and to how those two wings of logistics fit in together.

Sources: Hein (2001, 2004); Page (2005); http://www.redbull.com/.

1 How does Red Bull balance economics, coverage, and control in its early distribution strategy?

2 What specific benefits does this 'student sales rep' approach offer Red Bull?

3 Why do you think the early on-premise distribution strategy was attractive to Red Bull?

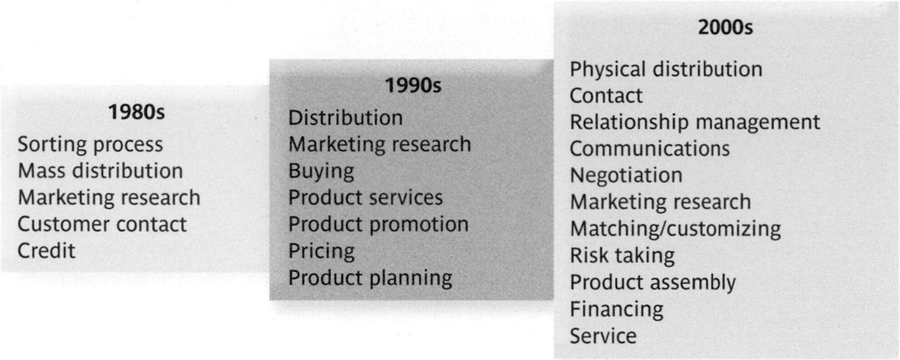

1980s	1990s	2000s
Sorting process	Distribution	Physical distribution
Mass distribution	Marketing research	Contact
Marketing research	Buying	Relationship management
Customer contact	Product services	Communications
Credit	Product promotion	Negotiation
	Pricing	Marketing research
	Product planning	Matching/customizing
		Risk taking
		Product assembly
		Financing
		Service

Figure 14.2
Evolution of the channel member functions

Member Channel Functions

Channel members perform a number of functions within the distribution channel. As shown in Figure 14.2, these functions have evolved since the 1980s from as few as five key functions to as many as eleven. There is a saying in marketing that 'you can eliminate the intermediaries but you cannot eliminate their functions' (Michman, 1990).

Managing the distribution functions involves managing the sourcing of organizational resources upstream from manufacturers and suppliers and distributing resources downstream to customers. The aim is to provide a reliable and responsive service to meet customer orders with a guaranteed delivery date, of the right amount, with the expected level of quality. To achieve this, there is often a trade-off between the customer objectives of time, quality, and accessibility and the cost to the supplier or distributor. The main strategy is to offer maximum flexibility in meeting customer requirements for a range of products, in any quantity, without incurring significant costs. See Market Insight 14.2 for an example of how Red Bull used a unique distribution strategy to penetrate the market and create a new drinks category, energy drinks.

Distribution Channel Strategy

When devising a distribution channel strategy, several key decisions need to be made in order to serve customers and establish and maintain buyer–seller relationships. These are summarized in Figure 14.3. The first decision is selecting how the channel will be structured. If the channel requires intermediaries, we need to consider the type of market coverage we want, the number and type of intermediaries to use, and how we should manage the relationships between members in the channel. These choices are important as they can affect the benefits provided to customers.

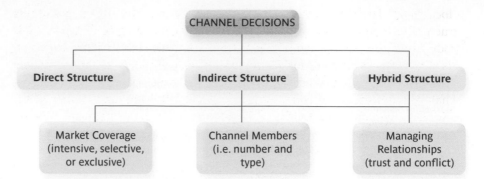

Figure 14.3
Distribution channel
strategy decisions

Channel Structure

Distribution channels can be structured in a number of ways. Three examples
of how relationships between producers, intermediaries, and customers can be
structured include either a 'direct', 'indirect', or a 'hybrid' channel structure. A
direct structure involves selling directly to customers with minimal involvement
from other organizations; an indirect structure uses intermediaries; and a hybrid
structure combines both. These are displayed in Figure 14.4. The degree of
efficiency that an intermediary can introduce to the performance of a distribution
channel is what ultimately determines what form a channel structure will take.

We will now consider the advantages and disadvantages of each of the three
types of channel structure.

Direct Distribution Channel Structure

In direct channels, the producer uses strategies to reach end customers directly
rather than dealing via an intermediary like an agent, broker, retailer, or wholesaler (see Figure 14.4). Have you ever been to a farmers' market and purchased
produce directly from a farmer, or downloaded music from the MySpace site of

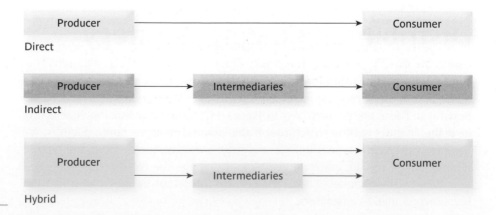

Figure 14.4
Distribution channel
structure

a local band? These are examples of direct distribution. The advantages of this structure include the producer or manufacturer maintaining control over their product and profitability, and building strong customer relationships. However, this structure is not suitable for all products. It is ideally suited to those products which require significant customization, technical expertise, or commitment on behalf of the producer to complete a sale (Parker, Bridson, and Evans, 2006). However electronic technologies like the internet are enabling more and differing product manufactures to reach customers directly. Efficiency of the **direct channel structure** is being improved in the following ways:

- **Processing orders and distributing the product electronically directly to customers**—RKS Software is a small manufacturer of computing software such as PC facsimile software called 'Mighty Fax'. To increase the efficiency of order processing and delivery of this product to customers, the organization employs a direct structure via email, telephone, and fax, providing direct customer support.

- **Supporting the physical distribution of the product offering directly to customers**—One of the most well-known examples of this is Dell Computer Corp's system. Dell sells computer equipment through the company website, using telesales for product ordering, database technology for order processing, tracking, and inventory and delivery management. The organization further physically distributes its product offering though company-employed delivery and installation staff.

The disadvantages of a direct channel structure typically include the amount of capital and resources required to reach customers directly, resulting in the potential loss of economies of scale. Manufacturers might also suffer from offering a low variety of products which is not consistent with the needs of the buyer. This is especially apparent in B2C markets, such as fast-moving consumer goods (FMCGs). Imagine having to shop for bread, milk, and your favourite soft drink at three differing retail outlets owned by each product manufacturer. Few consumers today would purchase their products from individual manufacturers due to the inconvenience and time costs involved. Retailers there fulfil the needs of end consumers for product variety, something a direct channel of distribution would not necessarily fulfil.

Indirect Distribution Channel Structure

In an **indirect channel structure**, the producer concentrates on the skills and processes involved in producing the product and relies on the skills and infrastructure of one or more intermediaries for distribution. An example here is Procter & Gamble who focus their resources and expertise on developing new types of FMCGs and Sainsbury's who alternatively focus on making these new products available to end consumers. An intermediary must add some value that the producing organization cannot offer. Equally, the producing organization must add some value for the intermediary.

Using intermediaries often involves a trade-off between the benefits gained and the costs incurred, both financial and strategic. The benefits include reaching

Table 14.1

Top European franchises by rank

Franchise	Origin country	Industry	Rank
McDonald's	USA	Food: Restaurants	1
Tecnocasa	Italy	Real Estate	2
Fornetti	Hungary	Food: Distribution	3
Burger King	USA	Food: Restaurants	4
Jean Louis David	France	Health and Beauty: Hairstyling and Cosmetics	5
Point S	France	Automotive: Exhaust, Tyre, and Windscreen Repair	6
Foto Quelle	Germany	Photo, Frame, Art	7
Remax	USA	Real Estate	8
Pro et Cie	France	Retail: Appliances	9
Glassinter	Spain	Automotive: Exhaust, Tyre, and Windscreen Repair	10
Punto SMA	Italy	Food: Other	11
Vival (Casino)	France	Food: Convenience Stores	12
Dia (Carrefour)	Spain	Food: Supermarkets	13
Chemex International	UK	Commercial Hygiene	14
Otto Shop	Germany	Retail: Clothing and Footwear	15
Novus	USA	Automotive: Exhaust, Tyre, and Windscreen Repair	16
Pirelli RE Franchising	Italy	Real Estate	17
Cruji Coques	Spain	Food: Restaurants	18
Sylvan (Schuelerhilfe)	USA	Education: Children	19
Pegastar	Germany	Education: Children	20
Paellador	Spain	Food: Restaurants	21
5àSec	France	Dry Cleaning, Laundry	22
Yves Rocher	France	Health and Beauty: Other	23
Kamps	Germany	Food: Baked Goods, Doughnuts, and Pastry	24
Pizza Hut	USA	Food: Restaurants	25

Note: Franchise Europe has identified the Top 500 biggest franchise opportunities operating across Europe. This year's list is based on the number of units the franchise currently operates in Europe.

Source: Franchise Europe, 2005. Reproduced with the kind permission of Franchise Europe (www.franchiseeurope.com), a leading portal for the franchise industry worldwide.

Makro: a wholesaler in the UK

Makro Self Service Wholesalers Ltd

BigBarn Keeps it Local

Increasingly we are seeing changing national and international trends in how we buy and consume foods stuffs. Consumers are demanding more organic, healthy, and convenient food choices. However there is another trend growing in impact, the purchase of local products. Locavora is a term used to describe consumers that simply opt out of buying big national brands and shift to purchasing locally owned, supplied, or produced goods. Not only does local produce support the local economy, it is also seen as very environmentally friendly. Bill McKibben's book *Deep Economy: The Wealth of Communities and the Durable Future* acknowledges that 'the average American meal travels 1,500 miles before it lands on the dinner plate'. This trend is seeing the growth in farmers' markets and farm shops across the UK, Europe, and America as consumer demand to seek out more local grown, supplied, and produced products increases. However the biggest difficulty for consumers is sourcing local produce. Where do you find farmers' markets, how do you know which farmers sell goods locally or have a farm shop?

What about an infomediary? Would they help? An informediary is an internet-based business whose sole purpose is to bring buyers and sellers together through information, leveraging their knowledge of the marketplace. For example, they might provide a search facility of possible vendors; functions to help evaluate these vendors across criteria (e.g. price, location); and even provide value-added services like buyer–seller match making. All this is based on marketplace, buyer, and seller information. A famous example in the car industry is Autobytel.com Inc., an infomediary bringing buyers and sellers of cars into a virtual marketplace. However the new internet business model is also seeing an impact on the consumer trend in the purchase of local products.

BigBarn is the UK's no. 1 local food website. The company helps people to find good, safe, accountable food from local sources. The BigBarn website is the leading local produce website in the UK. It has 6,500 local producers listed on its postcode-specific maps and receives around 74,000 unique visitors every month, generating in excess of 140,000 page impressions. With the increasing interest in local food, those numbers are rising all the time.

BigBarn: The UK's number 1 local food website

BigBarn

RESEARCH INSIGHT 14.1

To take your learning further, you might wish to read this influential paper.

Mills, J. F., and Camek, V. (2004), 'The risks, threats and opportunities of disintermediation: A distributor's view', *International Journal of Physical Distribution and Logistics Management*, 34, 9, 714–27.

This paper discusses the trend in disintermediation observed in many industries. Where many recent papers see disintermediation as a phenomenon related to online transactions, this paper defines it more broadly as the removal or a weakening of an intermediary within a supply chain. The paper attempts to explain why disintermediation of distributors/import agents often occurs at the growth phase of a product's lifecycle, highlighting possible opportunities and outcomes for distributors threatened by disintermediation.

or at least they would not need so many of them. Imagine that a music publisher like Sony could reach and sell to every potential customer directly through its website (www.sony.com). Given the state of technology such as PC sound systems, CD burners, or MP3 players, customers could purchase their music directly from Sony and it could be 'distributed' electronically straight to their PC. In such a scenario, Sony would no longer need to deal with music stores like Virgin and HMV—leading to the disintermediation of the distribution channel. Or would it in fact result in the growth in electronic intermedaries such as iTunes for music distribution?

The technical possibility of reducing the number of intermediaries does not just affect 'bricks-and-mortar' intermediaries but also electronic intermediaries. In Amazon's case, for example, more consumers could skip the intermediary and buy books online directly from publishers. Even publishers and printers might be disintermediated if authors were to sell 'e-books' directly to the consumer, as mystery writer Stephen King has attempted to do (Kane, 2000). The evidence to date is that where disintermediation does occur, it is very much dependent on the nature of the products being distributed. Whilst there are significant numbers of customers who like buying certain products directly, many customers value and prefer the role of traditional intermediaries like bricks-and-mortar retailers for the purchase of certain goods. In fact, such is the value of some intermediaries to both customers and producers that there has been a trend towards **reintermediation**, the introduction of additional intermediaries into the distribution channel.

Managing Relationships in the Channel

An important aspect in any channel strategy is managing relationships throughout the distribution channel. However, by their very nature there is often a continuous struggle between channel members. Trust and channel conflict are

Table 14.3
Channel conflict

Types	Occurs between	Causes of conflict
Horizontal conflict	• Intermediaries on the same level of the same type (e.g. large grocery retailers like Tesco, Sainsbury's, and ASDA Wal-Mart) • Different types of intermediaries on the same level (e.g. a high street fashion retailer such as Miss Selfridge, a large department store like Marks and Spencer, or a multi-retailer like Tesco Extra)	Channel members impinge on the market territory of other intermediaries at the same level
Vertical conflict	Most frequently occurs between producer and wholesaler or producer and retailer (e.g. Unilever and Sainsbury's)	• Intense price competition • Disagreement about promotion activities • Cost of services rendered • Differing expectations as to channel or intermediary performance • Attempts to bypass intermediary and distribute direct • Tough economic times • Differing policies • Allocation of slotting allowances for premium shelf space
Hybrid channel conflict	Producers compete with retailers by selling through their producer-owned stores (e.g. Esprit and Levi-Strauss stores compete with department stores who also carry their stock)	• Grey marketing

the key issues here. **Channel conflict** is where one channel member perceives another channel member to be acting in a way that prevents the first member from achieving its distribution activities. Conflict in channels of distribution may involve intermediaries on the same level (tier), such as between retailers (**horizontal conflict**) or between members on different levels (tiers), thus between the producer, wholesaler, and the retailer (**vertical conflict**). These types of channel conflict are presented in Table 14.3.

Member Incentives

Channel conflict can be reduced if manufacturers provide incentives to channel members and if the risks, costs, and rewards of doing business are distributed fairly across the channel. Misaligned incentives are often the cause of channel conflict and also excess inventory, stock-outs, incorrect forecasts, inadequate sales efforts, and even poor customer service (Narayanan and Raman, 2004). A historical example is that of Campbell Soup. In the late 1980s, Campbell Soup offered distributors discounts several times every year, hoping that the savings would be passed on to retailers. However, distributors bought more units than

To take your learning further, your might wish to read this influential paper.

Webb, K. L., and Hogan, J. E. (2002), 'Hybrid channel conflict: causes and effects on channel performance', *Journal of Business and Industrial Marketing*, 17, 5, 338–57.

This paper discusses the role of **hybrid channel conflict** in not only reducing channel performance but also serving as a mechanism for forcing internal channel coalitions to work harder and smarter to serve their market. The findings indicate that hybrid channel conflict is an important determinant of both channel performance and satisfaction. Furthermore the authors support the view that the frequency of conflict, but not its intensity, has a negative effect on channel system performance.

they sold to retailers, so Campbell's sales fluctuated wildly. The company sold 40 per cent of its chicken noodle soup each year during the six-week promotional periods. This put a lot of pressure on the company's distribution channel. Campbell invested in a system to not just track purchases of distributors, but also their sales, and with this system provided distributors with discounts on sales as opposed to purchases. This helped to improve the performance of the distribution channel.

Grey Marketing

Another area of channel conflict is **grey marketing**, the unauthorized sale of new, branded products diverted from authorized distribution channels or imported into a country for sale without the consent or knowledge of the manufacturer. What occurs is that the prices of authorized dealers in a market are undercut through unauthorized sales. This activity is not necessarily illegal, but could fall foul of licensing agreements or trade regulations (Myers and Griffith, 1999).

Logistics Management

Organizations must decide on the best way to store, handle, and move their product so that it is available to customers in the right quantity, at the right time, and in the right place. Logistics includes the activities that relate to the flow of products from the manufacturer to the customer or end consumer. Whilst these are not traditionally marketing decisions or activities, they require marketing insight. The production schedule may mean that customers are asked to wait too long for products to arrive: this will affect product promotion. Inventory management might mean that there isn't enough stock to meet urgent customer needs or unforeseen peaks in demand: this will affect customer satisfaction. So while these areas are typically managed outside the marketing function (although this too is evolving), the need for everyone in the organization to share data and information about how a product is delivered is very important.

Importance of Logistics

Logistics management is the coordination of activities of the entire distribution channel. It addresses not just activities of moving products from the factory to customers (outbound distribution), but also moving products and materials from suppliers to the factory (inbound distribution). An example of an efficient inbound logistics system is provided by ASDA Wal-Mart, who use computerized scanning to inform manufacturers very quickly which products need delivery and in what quantities. More recent developments in electronic technologies, such as radio frequency identification (RFID) tags, are further improving the efficiency and effectiveness with which the logistical activities are managed and implemented.

A core motivation for the growth in the management of logistics is an attempt to lower costs given about 15 per cent of an average product's price is accounted for in shipping and transport costs alone. Ikea can sell its furniture 20 per cent cheaper than competitors as it buys furniture ready for assembly, thereby saving on transport and inventory costs. The Benetton distribution centre in Italy is run largely by robots, delivering numerous goods to 120 countries within 12 days. Benetton also uses just-in-time (JIT) manufacturing with some garments manufactured in neutral colours and then dyed to order, with very fast turnaround to suit customer requirements. However, beyond lowering costs, many organizations are increasing their focus on managing logistical activities due to demands for improved customer service, the explosion in product variety, and improvements in information and communication technologies. Logistical functions or activities include order processing, inventory control, warehousing, and transportation.

Logistical Functions

Logistical activities or functions include order processing, inventory control, warehousing, and transportation. See Figure 14.6.

Order Processing

Accuracy and speed of billing and invoicing customers is vitally important, especially for customer relationships. Increasingly we are seeing the use of information technology to help manage order-processing activities. Think about when you last purchased something online: perhaps it was music from iTunes, or a book from Amazon, or a train ticket. Did you receive an automated email about your purchase or order? How quickly did you receive it? What did it say?

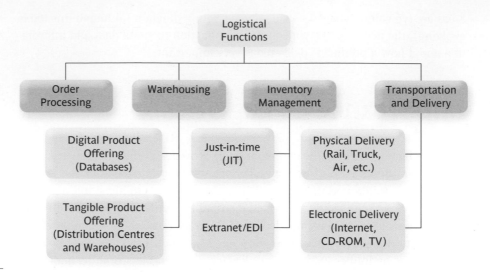

Figure 14.6
Key logistics functions

In the retailing sector, order-processing technologies provide quick-response programmes to help manage a retailer's inventory replenishment of products from suppliers. Kmart uses this kind of system, with EDI/extranets to transmit daily records of product sales to suppliers, who analyse the information, create an order, and send it back to Kmart. Once in Kmart's system, the order is treated as though Kmart created it itself. Many technologies also speed up the billing cycle. For example, General Electric operates a computer-based system that, on receipt of a customer order, checks the customer's credit rating as well as whether and where the items are in stock. The computer then issues an order to ship, bills the customer, updates the inventory records, sends a production order for new stock, and sends a message back to the salesperson that the customer's order is on the way—all in less than 15 seconds. The hospitality industry also uses order-processing technology to improve service delivery efficiency. Fast food outlets like McDonald's and KFC have for years recorded food orders through telecommunications systems, transmitting them to food preparation areas, with orders fulfilled within a matter of minutes, improving customer satisfaction in service delivery.

Warehousing and Materials Handling

Many organizations exchange tangible goods that require storage while they are waiting to be sold, largely due to the mismatch between when the product is produced and when it is sold and consumed. Books, for example, dry goods such as sugar and canned goods, and even clothing require some degree of storage between the time they leave the manufacturer and when they need delivery to customers. An organization must decide on how many and what types of 'warehouses' it needs, and where they should be located. The type of warehouse is dependent on the type of product: tangible or digital, perishable or not.

Warehousing Tangible Goods

For the storage of tangible goods, such as FMCGs, an organization can use either **storage warehouses** or **distribution centres**. Storage warehouses store goods for moderate to long periods (they have a long shelf life), whereas distribution centres are designed to move goods, rather than just store them. For products that are highly perishable with a short shelf life such as fruit and vegetables, distribution centres are more appropriate. Grocery chains like Woolworths in Australia and Tesco in the UK use large cold-store distribution centres to move perishable items such as fruit and vegetables to their various retail outlets. For products with a long shelf life or that might require stockpiling to meet seasonal demands, storage centres are more appropriate.

Warehousing Digital 'Products'

Electronic warehousing systems, or database systems, are being used more and more for the storage of products (or product components) that can be digitized. These systems can be searched or browsed electronically, providing the user with immediate electronic delivery options. For example, emerald-library.com, ABI-Inform, or ScienceDirect are electronic databases accessible through the web that store a vast array of documents electronically in order to facilitate customers' search for information. In addition, many organizations use data warehousing facilities where product information or even actual products are stored in digital form awaiting distribution. Apple iTunes features more than 5 million songs, 100,000 free podcasts, 27,000 audiobooks, 350 TV shows, and now, movies and iPod games. Customers can find, download, play, and sync in a fraction of the time it takes to drive to any store.

ScienceDirect: an electronic database facilitating customer searches for information

ScienceDirect/Elsevier BV

Inventory Management

Inventory management is an issue that arises from trying to balance responsiveness to customer needs with the resources required to store inventory. Zero-inventory or just-in-time (JIT) production is an ideal for many organizations as it minimizes the use of resources that are often tied up in stock that doesn't sell. This must be balanced against the risk of not having the products available when customers want them.

Do we store the product so that it is available when customers needed it or do we produce the product when it is ordered or stock is low? A balance must be maintained between carrying too little inventory and carrying too much, as carrying larger than needed inventories can be expensive. Imagine the cost of storing all the books Amazon has listed for sale, or the storage of fashion items in the spring ready for Summer demand. With just-in-time systems, producers and retailers carry only small inventories of merchandise, often only enough for a few days' operations. New stock arrives exactly when it is needed, rather than being stored. ASDA Wal-Mart and even Burger King use these systems to track sales to service their outlets worldwide, automatically replenishing their ingredients according to product sales.

Transportation and Delivery

Transportation is considered to be the most important activity in logistics. Transportation is the physical movement of the product using truck, rail, air, pipeline, shipping, and so on. Often transportation is just seen as concern for suppling tangible goods, but it is just as relevant to many service organizations and delivery of electronic (or digital) products. Consultants, IT companies, and health organizations have to move staff around, incurring transport and accommodation costs. Management of transport usually involves making decisions between usage of one or more transportation methods and ensuring vehicle capacity. Transportation methods include physical transport modes such as rail, truck, water, pipeline, and air; and electronic delivery modes such as electronic vending machines, the telephone, the internet, or EDI.

Physical Delivery

ICT have improved physical product delivery. For example, where freight moves, the size of typical shipments and the time periods within which goods must be delivered has changed with significant economic benefits to all transportation activities. The top of the list of 'must have' systems for transportation are in-vehicle navigation and route guidance solutions to help manage transport fleets, track shipments, and optimize transportation (Dreier, 2003). FedEx's tracking system assigns a tracking number and, using proprietary software, provides information to customers in real time about where the package or shipment is located, thereby managing customer satisfaction.

Electronic Delivery

As early as the introduction of the television, radio, or even the telephone, electronic technologies have been used to deliver products electronically. Producers of music, games, video, or software are typically unconstrained by the needs of physical distribution due to product digitization; this has been increased with the development of the internet. For example, Wall Street seemed at first to smirk at the E*Trade group's invitation to investors to make their own trades on the internet. Then the Charles Schwab Corporation jumped at the challenge, and by the late 1990s other brokerages, such as Merrill Lynch and Quick and Reilly (now called Bank of America Investment Services Inc.), were scrambling to catch up. Organizations like travel agents, banks, and insurance companies that traditionally relied on customers coming to a branch or agency have quickly moved to using telecommunications, ATMs, and the internet to reach more customers. The internet has clearly added to the capacity of these electronic distribution channels. In developed economies around the world large numbers of customers now bank, trade stocks, arrange insurance and travel, investigate and book accommodation, and so on online.

We will now look more closely at one type of intermediary used in B2C markets, that of the retailer and the activity of retailing.

Retailing

Retailing is all the activities directly related to the sale of products to the ultimate end consumer for personal and non-business use. These differ from wholesalers, who distribute the product to businesses, not end consumers. For every successful large retailer like ASDA Wal-Mart, Marks and Spencer, or Tesco plc, there are thousands of small retailers, with all of them having two key features in common: they link producers and end consumers and they perform an invaluable service for both.

Customer Value

In order to purchase a product, consumers must have access to it. The purpose of a retailer is to provide this access. As such it is very important to find out what consumers actually want from a retailer in order to deliver value. Convenience is the primary concern for most consumers, with people increasingly being 'leisure time poor' and keen to trade off shopping time for leisure time (Seiders, Berry, and Gresham, 2000). Consequently, convenience has driven just about every innovation in retailing such as supermarkets, department stores, shopping malls, the web, and self-scanning kiosks in pursuit of providing customer convenience. As noted by Seiders, Berry, and Gresham (2000), from a customer's perspective convenience means speed and ease in acquiring a product and consists of the following four key elements listed overleaf:

RESEARCH   INSIGHT 14.3

To take your learning further, your might wish to read this influential paper.

Seiders, K., Berry, L. L., and Gresham, L. G. (2000), 'Attention retailers! How convenient is your convenience strategy?', *Sloan Management Review*, Spring, 79–89.

In this paper the authors discuss the key value and benefits consumers derived from retailing. The authors particularly discuss the key benefit of convenience in retailing strategy from a customer's perspective. From this perspective convenience means speed and ease, and consists of four key elements—access, search, possession, and transaction.

- **Access**—being easy to reach;
- **Search**—enabling customers to be easily able to identify what they want;
- **Possession**—ease of obtaining products; and
- **Transaction**—ease of purchase and return of products.

These are outlined in more detail in Table 14.4.

Retailer Types

There are numerous types of retailers. These can be classified according to the marketing strategy employed (i.e. product, price, and service) and the store presence (i.e. store or non-store retailing).

Marketing Strategy

Major types of retailers can be classified according to the marketing strategies employed, paying particular attention to three specific elements:

- Product assortment;
- Price level; and
- Customer service.

Table 14.5, although not exhaustive, provides a useful summary of these elements across the differing types of retailing channels.

These retailing establishments can be further distinguished as follows:

Department Stores: These are large-scale retailing institution that offer a very broad and deep assortment of products (both hard and soft goods), and provide a wide array of customer service facilities for store customers. Debenhams has a wide array of products including home furnishings, foods, cosmetics, clothing,

Element	Description
Access convenience	• Accessibility factors include location, availability, hours of operation, parking, proximity to other outlets, as well as telephone, mail, and internet. • Convenience does not exist without access. • Increasingly customers want access to products and services to be as fast and direct as possible with very little hassle. • Global trend, e.g. rise of convenience stores in Japan. • Direct shopping driven by time and place utility.
Search convenience	• Identifying and selecting the products you want is connected to product focus, intelligence outlet design and layout (servicescape), knowledgeable staff, interactive systems, product displays, package and signage, etc. • Solutions can be provided in the form of in-store kiosks, clearly posted prices, and mobile phones for sales staff linked to knowledge centres. • One example of good practice is German discount chain Adler Mode Market GmbH which uses colour-coded tags to help customers quickly spot the sizes.
Possession convenience	• Is about having merchandise in stock and available on a timely basis. For example, Nordstrom clothing store guarantees that advertised products will be in stock. • However possession convenience has its limitations for certain channels. • The internet scores highly for search convenience, yet is generally low in terms of possession convenience, unless digital products.
Transaction convenience	• The speed and ease with which consumers can effect and amend transaction before and after the purchase. • A number of innovations in transactions —self-scanning in ASDA Wal-Mart, Tesco, and Waitrose. Well-designed service systems can mitigate the peaks and troughs in store traffic as with the use of in-store traffic counters as in Sainsbury's to monitor store traffic. • Even queue design, single queues in post offices and banks differ from supermarkets due to space and servicescape design. • Transaction convenience is a significant issue on the internet, with pure internet retailers having problems with returns and customers not prepared to pay for shipping and handling costs.

Source: Developed from Seiders, Berry, and Gresham (2000). © 2007 by Massachusetts Insitute of Technology. All rights reserved. Distributed by Tribune Media Services. Reproduced with the kind permission of MIT Sloan Management Review.

books, and furniture and further provides variety within each product category (e.g. brand, feature variety). Debenhams, like many department stores, further provides a wide array of customer service facilities to rationalize higher prices and minimize price competition. Value added services include wedding registries, clothing alterations, shoe repairs, lay-by facilities, home delivery, and installation.

Discount Retailers: This type of retailer is positioned based on low prices combined with the reduced costs of doing business. The key characteristics here

Table 14.5 Marketing strategy and retail store classification

Retail store	Product assortment	Pricing	Customer service	Example
Department	Very broad, deep, with layout and presentation of products critical	Minimize price competition	Wide array and good quality	David Jones; Debenhams; Harrods
Discount	Broad and shallow	Low price positioning	Few customer service options	Pound Stretcher; Dollar Dazzlers
Convenience	Narrow and shallow	High prices	Avoids price competition	Co-op; 7-Eleven
Limited line	Narrow and deep	Traditional = avoids price competition; new kinds = low prices	Vary by type	bicycle stores; sports stores; ladies fashion
Speciality	Very narrow and deep	Avoids price competition	Standard; extensive in some	running shops; bridal boutiques
Category killer	Narrow, very deep	Low prices	Few to moderate	Staples and Office Works; Ikea
Supermarket	Broad and deep	Some = low price; other avoid price disadvantages	Few and self-service	Tesco plc; Woolworths; Sainsbury's
Superstores	Very broad and very deep	Low prices	Few and self-service	Tesco Extra ASDA Wal-Mart

involve a broad but shallow assortment of products, low prices, and very few customer services. Matalan in the UK for example, Kmart in Australia, and Target in the USA all carry a broad array of soft goods (e.g. apparel) combined with hard goods such as appliances and home furnishings. To keep prices down, the retailers negotiate extensively with suppliers to ensure low merchandise costs.

Limited Line Retailers: This type of retailer has a narrow but deep product assortment and customer services that vary from store to store. Clothing retailers, butchers, baked goods, furniture stores that specialize in a small number but related product categories are all examples. The breadth of product variety differs across limited line stores, and a store may choose to concentrate on: several related product lines (e.g. shoes and clothing accessories), a single product line (e.g. shoes), or a specific part of one product line (e.g. sports shoes). Examples include bookstores, jewellers, athletic footwear stores, dress shops, newsagents, etc.

Category Killer Stores: As the name suggests these retailers design to kill off the competition and are characterized by narrow but very deep assortment of products, low prices, and few to moderate customer services. Successful examples include Ikea in home furnishings, Staples in office supplies, and B&Q in hardware.

Supermarkets were founded in the 1930s and are large self-service retailing environments defined as large-scale department retailing organizations that offer a wide variety of differing merchandise to a large consumer base. Tesco Extra in the UK stocks products from clothing, hardware, music, groceries, and dairy products to soft furnishings. Operating largely on a self-service basis with minimum customer service and centralized register and transactional terminals, supermarkets provide the benefits of a wide product assortment in a single location, offering convenience and variety. Today supermarkets are the dominant institution for food retailing.

Convenience Stores or corner shops offer a range of grocery and household items that cater for convenience and last-minute purchase needs of consumers. Key characteristics include: long opening times (e.g. 24/7), being family run, and belonging to a trading group. The 7-Eleven, Spar, and Co-op are all examples. Increasingly we are seeing smaller convenience stores threatened by large supermarket chains such as ASDA Wal-Mart and Tesco, especially as laws for longer open times for larger stores are being relaxed (e.g. Sunday trading hours in the UK).

Store Presence

We can further categorize retailers according to their presence, store or non-store retailing. Most retailing occurs through fixed stores, with existing operators having 'sunk' investments in physical building. The physical location of a store is seen as a source of competitive advantage, providing crucial entry barriers to competitors. Several characteristics make store retailing unique from the customer viewpoint. The retail environment provides the sensation of touch, feel, and smell, which is very important for many product categories, such as clothing, books, or perfumes. Furthermore, the customer might interact with in-store staff, who provide purchase advice. Once the product is selected and the purchase decision made, the customer can walk out of the store with the merchandise in hand.

In contrast, retailing can also involve **non-store retailers**, retailing activities resulting in transactions that occur away from a fixed store location. Examples include automatic vending machines, direct selling, and the rise of internet retailing (Bennett, 1988). **Direct selling** is one of the oldest forms of retailing methods and is the personal contact between a salesperson and a consumer away from the retailing environment. Activities such as door-to-door canvassing and party plans where a sales presentation is made within the home to a party of guests are examples. Examples include cosmetics companies like Avon, Nutri-Metics skin care, and Amway household products. **Telemarketing** or telesales is another form of non-store retailing when purchase occurs over the telephone. During the 1990s this form of non-store retailing grew extensively due to rapid developments in computer-assisted and television shopping networks.

A more recent development of non-store retailing is the **electronic kiosk** which is being placed in shopping malls to assist the retailing experience. These computer-based retailing environments offer increased self-service opportunities, a wide array of products, and a large amount of data and information to help

Tuning into iTunes

According to new research by uSwitch, online shopping is set to account for nearly 40% of all UK retail sales by 2020, with online sales forecast to reach £40 billion in 2007 and set to quadruple to £162 billion by 2020. According to uSwitch, eight million UK households spend, on average, two hours a day shopping online. The most popular online purchases are holidays, films, and music.

This rise in online retailing is having a significant impact on the preferred channel of choice for music lovers, moving from units shipped to digital downloads. According to the Recording Industry Association of America, the value of recorded music shipped to US retailers plunged 16% from their $14.5 billion peak in 1999 to $12.2 billion at the end of 2005. In contrast, sales of digital downloads have continued to rise, but at a slower rate than in previous years. One company playing a key role in the facilitation of this growth of digital sales is Apples iTunes Music Store (iTMS).

The iTunes Store is an online business run by Apple Inc. which sells media files that are accessed through its iTunes application. Opened as the iTunes Music Store on 28 April 2003, it proved the viability of online music sales. The virtual record shop sells music videos, TV shows, movies, and video games in addition to music. iTunes now has several personalization options, and one of them is Just For You, an early version of a feature that suggests songs and albums one might enjoy, basing its recommendations on past purchases at the iTMS. Apple thoroughly dominates the market, with more than 90% of online song sales in the USA, and as of January 2007, the store had sold more than 80% of the worldwide online digital music sales.

iTunes was the first online music retailer to gain widespread media attention. Apple's store allows the users to purchase songs and transfer them easily to the iPod through iTunes. The store began after Apple signed deals with the five major record labels at the time, EMI, Universal, Warner Bros., Sony Music Entertainment, and BMG (the latter two would later merge to form Sony BMG). Music by more than 600 independent label artists was added later, the first being Moby on 29 July 2003. The store now has more than 5,000,000 songs, including exclusive tracks from numerous popular artists.

New songs are added to the iTunes catalogue every day, while the iTunes Store is updated each Tuesday. Apple also releases a 'Single of the Week' and usually a 'Discovery Download' on Tuesdays, which are available free for one week. To buy files through the store, a user must pay with an iTunes gift card or a credit card with a billing address in Australia, Austria, Belgium, Canada, Denmark, Finland, France, Germany, Greece, Republic of Ireland, Italy, Japan, Luxembourg, the Netherlands, New Zealand, Norway, Portugal, Spain, Sweden, Switzerland, the United Kingdom, or the United States. Residents in other countries can only download free podcasts and previews.

On 9 April 2007 Apple announced that the iTunes Store had sold more than 2.5 billion songs, and soon after on 11 April 2007 Apple announced that the iTunes Music Store had sold more than two million movies, making it the world's most popular online movie store. In the words of Apple's CEO, Steve Jobs, 'In 1984 we introduced the Macintosh. It didn't just change Apple, it changed the whole computer industry. In 2001, we introduced the first iPod and it didn't just change the way we all listen to music, it changed the entire music industry' (Allison and Palmer, 2007).

Sources: Anon. (2007); Pinkerfield (2007); Wingfield and Smith (2007); Breen (2007); Apple (2007); Benson (2007).

1 Why do you think the offline retail sale of music is declining?

2 Why do you think iTunes has been such a success as an online music retailer?

3 Consider your own recent purchases of music. What retail channel did you use to purchase the music and why?

RESEARCH INSIGHT 14.4

To take your learning further, you might wish to read this influential paper.

O'Cass, A., and French, T. (2003), 'Web retailing adoption: exploring the nature of internet users' web retailing behaviour', *Journal of Retailing and Consumer Services*, 10, 81–94.

In this paper the authors provide a discussion of the nature of internet retailing, its growth and importance. The authors further discuss the key elements that influence web retailing adoption and profile online users' web retailing behaviour.

decision making. Somewhat different from the electronic kiosk is the **automatic vending machine**, providing product access 24 hours a day, 7 days a week. From cigarettes, soft drinks, hot beverages, to newspapers and magazines, products distributed through vending machines are typical of low-priced products and convenience products. However we also see the wide adoption of automatic teller machines (ATMs) to facilitate the delivery of financial retailing services. Another form of non-store retailing is online or internet retailing. The year 2006 shows some remarkable e-commerce statistics with some 100 million European online shoppers spending an average of €1,000 each, driving online retailing past the €100 billion mark. It is further estimated that online retail sales in Europe will more than double in the next five years, to €263 billion in 2011 (Forrester, 2006). The winning purchase categories on the internet are travel, clothes, groceries, and consumer electronics, all above the €10 billion per year mark. Market Insight 14.5 provides a specific snapshot of the impact the leading online music retailer, iTunes, is having on the retail purchase of music.

Chapter Summary

To consolidate your learning, the key points from this chapter are summarized below:

- Define what a channel of distribution is and key considerations in channel strategy and decision making.

  Distribution channels can be defined as an organized network of agencies and organizations which, in combination, perform all the activities required to link producers and manufacturers with consumers, purchasers, and users. Distribution channel decisions are about managing which channel best suits the organization's objectives. The key consideration which reveals itself here is the importance of optimizing the balance between the three elements of economics, coverage, and control.

- Define and discuss the differing types of intermediaries and their roles in the distribution channel.

  An intermediary is an independent business concern that operates as a link between producers and ultimate consumers or end-industrial users. If using an indirect or hybrid channel structure, the next strategic decision is what type of intermediaries to use. The key difference between the various types is that not all intermediaries take legal title of the product offering or physical possession of it. There are several different types of intermediaries; these include: agents, merchants, distributors, franchise, wholesalers, and retailers.

- Differentiate between differing distribution channel structures and selection criteria.

  The relationship between producers, intermediaries, and customers will form either a 'direct', 'indirect', or 'hybrid' channel structure. A direct structure involves selling directly to customers; an indirect structure involves using intermediaries; and a hybrid structure will involve both. The degree of efficiency that an intermediary can introduce to the performance of distribution tasks determines what form a channel structure will take. At the simplest level, direct channels offer maximum control but sometimes at the expense of reaching your target market. Indirect channels can maximize coverage but often at the expense of control as the intermediaries start 'playing' with the marketing mix strategies and demand a share of the profits in return for their involvement. Hybrid strategies often result in greater channel conflict as the intermediaries feel the organization that is supplying them is also the competitor.

- Discuss the factors influencing channel design, structure, and strategy.

  In setting down a distribution channel strategy, most organizations make key decisions in order to serve their customers and establish and maintain buyer–seller relationships. The first decision is the selection of the structure of the channel. If it is decided that intermediaries will be required, management then need to consider the type of market coverage that will be required; the number and type of intermediaries to use; and how to manage the relationships between channel members. These choices are important as they can affect the value that is ultimately provided to customers.

- Distinguish between the logistical functions, identifying key considerations for effective management.

  Logistics management concerns all the activities that, when added together, relate to the flow of products from the organization to the customer or end consumer. It includes decision areas such as production scheduling, plant location, and purchasing, which are traditionally the domain of production management. It also covers decision areas that are the province of physical distribution management such as transportation, inventory management, and order processing. Whilst these are not traditionally marketing management decisions, it is important to understand that they require a marketing focus and marketing insight.

- Define the role, function, and importance of retailers in the distribution channel.

  Distributing consumer products begins with the producer and ends with the end consumer. However, between the two there is usually an intermediary called a retailer. Retailing is all the activities directly related to the sale of goods and services to the ultimate end consumer for personal and non-business use. This is also called the retail trade. A retailer or retail store is a business enterprise whose primary function is to sell to ultimate consumers for non-business use. However, they all have in common two key features: they link producers and end consumers and they perform an invaluable service for both.

- Compare and contrast the differing types of retailers.

  Types of retailing establishments can be classified as differentiated by two key characteristics: marketing strategy employed (i.e. product, price, and service) and the store presence (i.e. store or non-store retailing). Examples include: department stores, discount stores, convenience stores, limited line retailers, speciality retailers, category killer stores, supermarkets, and superstores. In addition to the underlying marketing strategy, retailing establishments can be further characterized according to store or non-store presence.

- Discuss the key strategic and operational considerations in retailing strategies.

  Most retailing occurs through fixed stores, with existing operators having 'sunk' investments in physical fabric. The physical location of a store is seen as a source of competitive advantage, providing crucial entry barriers to competitors, and is in most cases an expensive asset. There are several characteristics that make store retailing unique from the customer viewpoint. First and foremost, the retail environment provides the sensation of touch, feel, and smell. For many product categories, such as clothing, books, and perfumes, this aspect provides the customer with valuable data points before the purchase decision can be made. Furthermore, the customer might interact with in-store staff, who might give professional suggestions to assist the customer in the purchase process. However, the use of these access points and their commercial value may require major reassessment with the rise in non-store retailing.

 Visit the **Online Resource Centre** that accompanies this book to read more information relating to channel management and retailing: www.oxfordtextbooks.co.uk/orc/baines/

? Review Questions

1 Define distribution channel management.

2 What are the differing benefits of using intermediaries?

3 Why are economics, coverage, and control important when making distribution channel decisions?

4 What are the key elements of a distribution channel strategy?

5 What are the advantages and disadvantages of the three differing channel structures?

6 What are the benefits of an exclusive distribution strategy over an intensive strategy?

7 Why is logistics management of increasing importance to marketers?

8 What are some of the reasons for channel conflict?

9 What are the differing types of retailers?

10 What do we mean by non-store retailing and what are the main types?

? Discussion Questions

1 Having read the Case Insight at the beginning of this chapter, how would you advise Ekinoks about how to manage its relationships between suppliers in its supply chain and effective communication between the company and its suppliers? What factors would you take into consideration?

2 Discuss the importance of intermediaries. In your discussion outline the benefits and limitations of the following types of intermediaries:

(a) Avon sales representative;

(b) Electrical wholesaler;

(c) Airline;

(d) Advertising agency;

(e) Grocery retailer;

(f) Bank.

3 From your reading and experience, identify the types of product that use the following channels to distribute direct to customers. Discuss the benefits of this channel strategy.

(a) Telephone;

(b) Internet;

(c) Mobile technology;

(d) Catalogues;

(e) Interactive digital and/or satellite TV;

(f) Automated teller machines;

(g) Electronic kiosks.

4 Convenience has come to the fore as one of the key elements on which to base distribution channel decisions. Assess the arguments for and against focusing on convenience from a customer's perspective.

5 What sort of marketing or distribution channels would you imagine might be most relevant in the following markets in the year 2015? List what you think would be the three most relevant distribution channels for each product offering, and why.

(a) Music and video;

(b) Home entertainment software (e.g. video games);

(c) Business application software;

(d) Engineering consulting advice (say on mining or construction applications);

(e) Financial services;

(f) Shampoo;

(g) Personal services (e.g. hairdressing, beauty therapies).

6 Some claim that electronic technologies in the distribution channel are creating what is called 'infomediaries'. Discuss what we mean by infomediaries and the changed roles of intermediaries in the channel strategy.

📖 References

Allison, K., and Palmer, M. (2007), 'Into the pack: Apple takes risks in its bid to shake up the mobile market', *Financial Times* (London), 26 June, 11.

Anon. (2006a), 'India's supply chain conundrum', *Supply and Demand Chain Executive*, October.

—— (2006b), 'Motorola and Hariyali Kisaan Bazaar announce major alliance for handset distribution', press release, available at www.motorola.com/content.jsp?globalObjectId=7170, accessed May 2007.

—— (2007), 'The third act—Apple: Apple', *The Economist*, 383 (9 June), 81.

Apple (2007), 'iTunes store tops two billion songs', press release, available at Apple.com, accessed 11 January.

Atkinson, R. D. (2001), 'The revenge of the disintermediated: how the middleman is fighting e-commerce and hurting consumers', available at www.ppionline.org/ppi_ci.cfm?contentid= 2941andknlgAreaID=140andsubsecid=900055, accessed December 2007.

Bennet, P. D. (1988), *Dictionary of Marketing Terms*, Chicago: Amercian Marketing Association.

Benson, C. (2007), 'Retail recovery', *Billboard*, 9 June, 119.

Boulden, J. (2007), 'Rent-a-farmer', *Fast Company*, July–August, 56.

Breen, C. (2007), 'Hints of change', *Macworld*, 24, 1.

Douglas, M. L., James, R. S., and Ellram, L. M. (1998), *Fundamentals of Logistics Management*, New York: Irwin/McGraw-Hill.

Dreier, G. (2003), 'Technology that drives transportation', *Transport Technology Today*, July, 9.

Evans, J. R., and Bermans, B. (1982), *Marketing Management*, New York: Mcmillan.

Ferdows, K., Lewis, M. A., and Machuca, J. A. D. (2004), 'Rapid-fire fulfillment', *Harvard Business Review*, 82, 11 (November), 104–10.

Forrester (2006), 'European net retail crosses the €100 billion mark—and keeps growing', *Forrester Research European eCommerce Forecast: 2006 to 2011*, 4 July, accessed 11 January 2007.

Franchise Europe (2005), 'Top 500 franchises', available at www.franchiseeurope.com/index.php, accessed February 2007.

Frazier, M. (2007), 'Farmstands vs. big brands', *Advertising Age*, 78 (4 June), 16.

Gandhi (1979), 'Marketing channels', *American Journal of Small Business*, 3, 3 (January), 50–3.

Hamilton, A. (2007), 'Fast fashion, the remix', *Time*, (11 June), 54.

Handfield, R. B., and Nichols, E. L. (1999), *Introduction to Supply Chain Management*, Upper Saddle River, NJ: Prentice-Hall.

Hein, K. (2001), 'A bull's market: the marketing of Red Bull energy drink', *Brandweek*, 28 May.

—— (2004), 'Odds against the little guys', *Brandweek* 23–30 August, 20–5.

Ibison, D., and Taylor, P. (2007), 'A market where margins shrink as fast as handsets: the competition between Nokia and Motorola for worldwide sales is being won by the Finnish group', *Financial Times*, 23.

Kane, M. (2000), 'Stephen King rewrites e-book biz', available at http://zdnet.com.com/ 2100-11-519243.html?legacy=zdnn, accessed December 2007.

King, J. (1999), 'Infomediary', *Computerworld*, 33 (1 November), 58.

Lath, S., Sachitanand, R., Sharma, E. K., Srivastava, P., and Varadarajan, N. (2007), 'Salvation in a sachet: rural marketing sounds great, but some 320 million Indians reside in villages that most marketers find impossible and unviable to penetrate. Now, a clutch of brands is attempting to go where none has gone before', *Business Today*, 11 February, 98.

Michman, R. D. (1990), 'Managing structural changes in marketing channels', *Journal of Business and Industrial Marketing*, Summer/Fall, 5–14.

Mills, J. F., and Camek, V. (2004), 'The risks, threats and opportunities of disintermediation: a distributor's view', *International Journal of Physical Distribution and Logistics Management*, 34, 9, 714–27.

Myers, M. B., and Griffith, D. A. (1999), 'Strategies for combating grey market activity', *Business Horizons*, 42, 6, 71–5.

Narayanan, V. G., and Raman, A. (2004), 'Aligning incentives in supply chains', *Harvard Business Review*, 82, 11 (November), 94–102.

Page, P. (2005), 'Finding the energy for logistics flexibility', *Traffic World*, 1.

Park, S. Y., and Keh, H. T. (2003), 'Modelling hybrid distribution channels: a game theory analysis', *Journal of Retailing and Consumer Services*, 10, 155–67.

Parker, M., Bridson, K., and Evans, J. (2006), 'Motivations for developing direct trade relationships', *International Journal of Retail and Distribution Management*, 34, 2, 121–34.

Pinkerfield, H. (2007), 'Broadband fuelling online shopping boom', *Revolution*, May, 27.

Russell, S. W. (2000), *Marketing Management*, Englewood Cliffs, NJ: Prentice Hall.

Seiders, K., Berry, L. L., and Gresham, L. G. (2000), 'Attention retailers! How convenient is your convenience strategy?', *Sloan Management Review*, Spring, 79–89.

Son, J.-Y. K., Sung, S., and Riggins, F. J. (2006), 'Consumer adoption of net-enabled infomediaries: theoretical explanations and an empirical test', *Journal of the Association for Information Systems*, 7, 7, 473–508.

Srinivasan, P. (2005), 'We'd like to be number one in everything we do', *Business Today*, 88.

Thomas, D. (2007), 'Ericsson aims deeper inside India, China: biofuel help, easier financing are part of pitch for more mobile business', *Wall Street Journal* (Eastern edition), 14 June, B.3.

Wingfield, N., and Smith, E. (2007), 'Jobs's new tune raises pressure on music firms: Apple chief now favors making downloads of songs freely tradable', *Wall Street Journal* (Eastern edition), A.1.

Part 4

Principles of Relational Marketing

Part 4 explores the principles of relational marketing. It looks at services and non-profit marketing, business-to-business marketing, and relationship marketing.

Part 1: Marketing Fundamentals

 1 Marketing Principles and Society
 2 The Marketing Environment
 3 Marketing Psychology and Consumer Buying Behaviour
 4 Marketing Research and Marketing Information Systems

Part 2: Principles of Marketing Management

 5 Marketing Strategy
 6 Market Segmentation and Positioning
 7 Market Development and International Marketing
 8 Marketing implementation and Control

Part 3: The Marketing Mix Principle

 9 Products, Services, and Branding Decisions
 10 Price Decisions
 11 An Introduction to Marketing Communications
 12 Marketing Communications: Tools and Techniques
 13 Managing Marketing Communications: Strategy, Planning, and Implementation
 14 Channel Management and Retailing

❯ Part 4: Principles of Relational Marketing

 15 Services Marketing and Non-Profit Marketing
 16 Business-to-Business Marketing
 17 Relationship Marketing

Part 5: Contemporary Marketing Practice

 18 New Technology and Marketing
 19 Postmodern Marketing
 20 Marketing Ethics

15

Services Marketing and Non-Profit Marketing

Quality in a service or product is not what you put into it. It is what the client or customer gets out of it.

Peter Drucker

Learning Outcomes

After studying this chapter you should be able to:

✔ Explain what a service is and describe the relationship between products and services.

✔ Explain the main characteristics of a service.

✔ Understand the different service processes and outline each element of the services marketing mix.

✔ Explain the term service encounters and describe how service management should seek to maintain service performance.

✔ Explain the principles associated with measuring service quality.

✔ Understand the principles of non-profit marketing.

Radisson SAS is an internationally recognized hotel brand. Though the group has expanded dramatically from its Scandinavian roots, it still believes in the absolute importance of delivering first-class customer service. We speak to John Kennedy to find out more.

John Kennedy for Radisson SAS

Our philosophy of delivering first-class customer service applies to all our guests, each and every time they encounter our brand, at each of our hotels around the world. Indeed, our brand promises are all about the stay experience, a celebration of individuality, and developing continuously to stay ahead of our competitors.

The Radisson SAS brand experience is driven by the quality of customer touch points; that is, how our staff interact with guests. The only way you can truly deliver on the brand promise and achieve customer satisfaction is through staff living the brand values in their everyday working lives. To achieve this all staff undergo 'Yes I Can!' training (YIC!). This is designed to provide suitable service attitudes, which are translated into treating each and every guest as an individual. This training strategy has become a part of our everyday culture, one that embodies our spirit of customer service. Staff who complete the training are presented with a YIC! Pin and wear this at all times. We retrain our staff on a monthly basis with what we call 'Yes I Can! Activities'. This aims to keep the spirit and culture alive. In cases where our service is not quite up to guest expectations, we make it right. Service recovery (making it right) is a fundamental part of the 'Yes I Can!' approach, enabling and empowering all of our staff to satisfy an unhappy client immediately.

- *For our company the biggest possible*
- *asset is a happy customer*

For our company the biggest possible asset is a happy customer, one who will come back to the same hotel and choose other properties from the chain for their next trip. This we ensure by providing the 'Yes I Can!' service at all points of customer contact. Only a happy guest is a good ambassador and will tell their colleagues and friends about the service and product experience they receive from staying at one of our hotels.

Hospitality is all about welcoming your guests and making them feel at home or comfortable within an environment that allows them to get on with what they want to do. To help achieve this many of our service concepts are based on feedback received from guests. For example, we provide satellite reception areas (individual desks to check in, i.e. no barrier between the guest and staff), free high speed internet access (Radisson SAS is still the only chain to offer this service across Europe, the Middle East, and Africa), our one touch service (one call connects you directly to our team of problem solvers), individual room styles, and 100% guest satisfaction guarantee; these all have been developed as a result of acting on customer feedback.

We are aware that service recovery is really important when customer expectations are not met. We know that if service failures are handled properly, a potentially negative situation can be turned into something positive, with guests informing their friends of the brilliant way they were treated by Radisson SAS. Although we plan to get it right first time, we need to consider ways in which our service recovery programmes, making it right, can be further improved.

How would you further improve Radisson SAS's service recovery programmes?

Radisson's Frankfurt hotel
SAS Radisson

Introduction

Have you ever been frustrated trying to get through to customer **services** to sort out a mobile phone issue, or to the administrators at a university or college to get answers to important questions about your course or exam results? Well, if you have then you understand just how much better it would be if the provider delivered a better service. Services are important because they impact immediately on people and their perception of an organization. It is important, therefore, to understand how marketing activities can enhance the performance of service providers.

In this chapter we consider the nature, characteristics, and issues associated with the marketing of services and non-profit organizations. Time is spent first considering the distinguishing characteristics and then how the service marketing mix needs to reflect and deliver realistic marketing activities.

One of the critical aspects of services is the **service encounter**, the point at which a service is provided and simultaneously consumed. Getting the service performance right, and getting it right each time the service is delivered, that is each time you phone customer services at your mobile phone operator, is probably one of the most difficult aspects of service marketing management. Therefore, consideration is given to branding, **internal marketing**, and how to measure **service quality**, as these are key dimensions of services marketing.

The chapter closes with a review of the non-profit sector and the different types of organizations that make up this part of the economy. The implications for marketing in this sector, in particular **cause-related marketing**, are considered.

What is a Service?

Services are different from products. One of the distinguishing dimensions of products is that they have a physical presence. Services do not have a physical presence and they cannot be touched. This is because their distinguishing characteristic is that they are an act or a performance (Berry, 1980). A service cannot be put in a bag, taken home, stored in a cupboard, and used at a later date. A service is consumed at the point where it is produced. For example, watching a play at a theatre, learning maths at school, or taking a holiday all involve the simultaneous production and consumption of the play, new knowledge, and leisure and relaxation. (See Market Insight 15.1.)

The service industry sector forms a substantial part of most developed economies. Not surprisingly, the range of services is enormous and we consume services in nearly all areas of our work, business, home, and leisure activities. Table 15.1 indicates the variety of sectors and some of the areas in which we consume different types of services.

The sheer number of services that are available has grown, partly because it is not always easy to differentiate products just on features, benefits, quality, or price. Competition can be very intense and most product innovations or developments are copied quickly. Services provide an opportunity to add value yet not be

Table 15.1
Sector services

Sector	Examples
Business	Financial, airlines, hotels, solicitors, and lawyers
Manufacturing	Finance and accountants, computer operators, administrators, trainers
Retail	Sales personnel, cashiers, customer support advisers
Institutions	Hospitals, education, museums, charities, churches
Government	Legal system, prisons, military, customs and excise, police

copied as each service is a unique experience. Most products contain an element of service: there is a product/service combination designed to provide a means of adding value, differentiation, and earning a higher return. The extent to which a service envelops a product varies according to a number of factors. These concern the level of tangibility associated with the type of product, the way in which the service is delivered, variations in supply and demand, the level of customization, the type of relationship between service providers and customers, and the degree of involvement people experience in the service (Lovelock, Vandermerwe, and Lewis, 1999).

The product/service spectrum, explored at the beginning of Chapter 9, identifies that there are some products that have very few services and some services that have little product tangibility. Many grocery products have few supporting services, just shelf stocking and checkout operators. The purchase of new fitted bedroom furniture involves the cupboards, dressers, and wardrobes plus the professional installation service necessary to make the furniture usable. At the other end of the spectrum a visit to the dentist or an evening class entails little physical product-based support as the personal service is delivered by the service deliverer in the form of the dentist or tutor.

The Nature of Services

In view of these comments about the range and variety of services and before moving on, it is necessary to define what a service is. As with any topic there is no firm agreement but for our purposes the following definition, derived from a number of authors, will be used.

A service is any act or performance offered by one party to another that is essentially intangible. Consumption of the service does not result in any transfer of ownership even though the service process may be attached to a physical product.

Much of this definition is derived from the work of Grönroos (1990) who considered a range of definitions and interpretations. What this definition provides is an indication of the various characteristics and properties that set services apart from products. The two sections that follow examine the key characteristics of services and the way in which the service mix, as opposed to the product mix, is configured.

Nearly Pure Products and Services

Rexam are one of the world's leading consumer packaging groups supporting the beverage, beauty, pharmaceuticals, and food markets. They claim to 'help shape the experiences consumers have with their customers' brands . . . helping to create the packaging that people want today and to evolve solutions to meet their future needs'. Their products are very tangible and apart from packaging design and advice facilities to help meet their business customers needs, there are few additional services that they can offer.

Alternatively, PwC are one of the world's largest management consulting organizations. Owned by IBM, PwC offer a huge range of services across many industries and sectors. Their approach to work is stated to be through 'connectedthinking'. They do not make or sell any products, they provide knowledge and skills, pure services.

Source: www.rexam.com/ and www.pwc.com/.

1 Using the comments made by the Rexam representative, identify ways in which packaging might shape consumer experiences.

2 Think about the role of a marketing consultant and make a list of the different types of knowledge that might constitute 'connectedthinking'.

3 Draw the product/service spectrum and place on it various product/service combinations.

To take your learning further, you might wish to read this influential paper.

Shostack, G. L. (1977), 'Breaking free from product marketing', *Journal of Marketing*, 41 (April), 73–80.

This passionately written paper seeks to draw a clear and distinct line between the requirements for marketing products and services. Shostack states that a marketing mix that is appropriate for products is not suitable for services. A key thrust of the paper draws on the need for an understanding of the difference between image (for products) and evidence (for services).

Distinguishing Characteristics

Services are characterized by five distinct characteristics depicted in Figure 15.1. These are **intangibility**, **perishability**, **variability**, **inseparability**, and a lack of ownership. These are important aspects that shape the way in which marketers design, deliver, and evaluate the marketing of services.

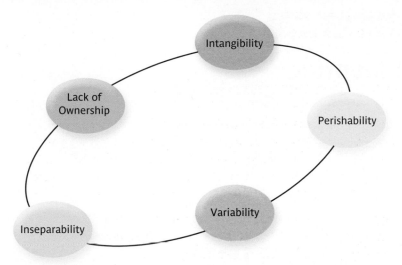

Figure 15.1
The five distinguishing characteristics of a service

Intangibility

The purchase of products involves the use of most of our senses. We can touch, see, smell, hear, or even taste products before we buy them let alone use them. Think of a trip to buy an MP3 player. You can see the physical product and its various attributes such as size and colour, you can feel the weight and touch it. These are important purchasing decision cues and even if the equipment fails to work properly it is possible to take it back for a replacement. However, if you decide to buy additional insurance/support, you will walk away from the store with the insurance itemized on the receipt but you cannot touch, taste, see, hear, or smell the insurance you have bought. Services are intangible and they are only delivered and experienced post-purchase.

Intangibility does not mean that customers buy services without using their senses. What it does mean is that they use substitute cues to help make these purchasing decisions and to reduce the uncertainty because they cannot touch, see, smell, or hear the service. People make judgements based on a range of quality-related cues. These cues serve to make tangible the intangible service. These cues might involve an assessment about the people delivering the service, the location, equipment used, the messages and tone of the communications and associated branding devices, and, of course, price. Carbone and Haeckel (1994) refer to this process of 'tangibilizing the intangible' as 'customer service engineering'. This requires that the service organization first decides on what the customer experience should be like, in other words designs a service blueprint, and then designs a set of facilities and cues that lead customers to the required experience. So, a five-star hotel will determine what constitutes a five-star hotel experience and then provide a series of context cues to be delivered by people (humanics) and things (mechanics). These will include appropriate communication devices such as brochures and a website designed to position the hotel as five-star brand and as a desirable place to stay. Staff will be trained and reservation systems installed

The Hilton Blueprint

The welcoming reception area at a Hilton Hotel

Hilton Hotels

Hotel group Hilton International focus on the need to deliver exceptional service. Their vice president of marketing comments, 'Delivering the brand experience is the principal marketing tool we have, and is the beginning and end of what we do.'

Hilton have specified the ideal guest experience (established the service blueprint) and strive to deliver it consistently at all their hotels. It is the Hilton marketing department who set out the requirements for their recruitment, training, and development. They also monitor and evaluate the extent to which the desired service level is achieved and take action to correct service delivery when standards are not met.

Source: Adapted from McLuhan (2006).

1 Consider a service offered by a hotel and make a judgement about what you perceive to be the level of customer participation required for the service to be considered excellent.

2 Write notes explaining your interpretation of the phrase 'delivering the brand experience'.

3 Identify three different hotels and list three main service differences.

such that the humanics and mechanics of customer handling are seamless and consistently high. The next step is to decorate and furnish the premises to a standard that reflects the desired positioning before finally providing additional services. At all stages there should be a consistent level of service performance standards, all of which are designed to shape a customer's experiences to meet the original blueprint. (See Market Insight 15.2.)

Perishability

A bottle of shampoo on a supermarket shelf attracts a number of opportunities to be sold and consumed. When the store closes and opens again the following day, the bottle is still available to be sold and it remains available until purchased or the expiry date is reached. This is not the case with services. Once a train pulls out of a station, or an aeroplane takes off or a film starts, those seats are lost and can never be sold. This is referred to as perishability and is an important aspect of services marketing. Services are manufactured and consumed simultaneously; they cannot be stored either prior to or after the service encounter.

The reason why these seats remain empty reflects variations in demand. This may be due to changes in the wider environment and may follow easily predictable patterns of behaviour, for example family holiday travel. One of the tasks of service marketers is to ensure the number of empty seats and lost forever revenue is minimized. In cases of predictable demand, service managers can vary the level of service capacity; a longer train, a bigger aircraft, or extra screenings of a film (multiplex facilities). However, demand may vary unpredictably in which case service managers are challenged to provide varying levels of service capacity at short notice.

One of the main ways in which demand patterns can be influenced is through differential pricing. By lowering prices to attract custom during quieter times and raising prices when demand is at its highest, demand can be levelled and marginal revenues increased. Hotel and transport reservation systems have become very sophisticated, making it easier to manage demand and improve efficiency and of course customer service. Some football clubs categorize matches according to the prestige or ranking of the opposition, and adjust prices in order to fill the stadium. In addition to differential pricing, extra services can be introduced to divert demand. Hotels offer specialist weekend breaks such as golfing or fishing and mini vacations to attract retired people outside the holiday season. Leisure parks offer family discounts and bundle free rides into prices to stimulate demand.

Variability

As already stated an important characteristic of services is that they are produced and consumed by people, simultaneously, as a single event. One of the outcomes of this unique process is that it is exceedingly difficult to standardize the delivery of services around the blueprint model mentioned earlier. It is also difficult to deliver services so that they always meet the brand promise, especially as these promises often serve to frame customer service expectations. If demand increases unexpectedly and there is insufficient capacity to deal with the excess number of customers, service breakdown may occur. A flood of customers at a restaurant may extend the arrival of meals for customers already seated and who have ordered their meals. Too many train passengers may mean that there are not enough seats. In both these cases it is not possible to provide a service level that can be consistently reproduced. (See Market Insight 15.3.)

A different way of looking at this is to consider a theatre. The show may be doing well and the lead actors performing to critical acclaim. However, the actual performance that each actor delivers each night will be slightly different. This change may be subtle, such as a change in the tone of voice or an inflexion, and will pass by relatively unnoticed. At the other extreme some actors go out of their way to make their performance very different. It is alleged that the actor Jane Horrocks once remarked that during the performance of a certain theatre play she deliberately changed each evening's show in order to relieve the boredom.

There has been substantial criticism of some organizations that, in an effort to lower costs, have relocated some or all of their call centre operations offshore. These strategies sometimes fail as the new provider has insufficient training, local or product knowledge, or in some cases simply cannot be understood. This type of service experience will vary amongst customers and by each customer. The resulting fall in customer satisfaction can lead to increased numbers of customers defecting to competitors.

The variability of services does not mean that planning is a worthless activity. By anticipating situations when service breakdown might occur service managers can provide facilities, for example entertainment for queues at cinemas or theme parks, in order to change the perception of the length of the time it takes to experience the service (film or ride).

Inseparability

As established previously, products can be built, distributed, stored, and eventually consumed at a time specified by the ultimate end user customer. Services on the other hand are consumed at the point they are produced. In other words, service delivery cannot be separated or split out of service provision or service consumption.

This event where delivery coincides with consumption means that not only do customers come into contact with the service providers but also there must be interaction between the two parties. This interaction is of particular importance, not just to the quality of service production but also to the experience enjoyed by the customer. So, following the earlier example of a theatre play, the show itself may provide suitable entertainment but the experience may be considerably enhanced if the leading lady, Jane Horrocks, Judi Dench, or Scarlett Johansson, actually performs rather than have a night off because they are unwell. Alternatively, private doctors may develop a strong reputation and should there be an increase in demand beyond manageable levels, pricing can be used to reduce or reschedule demand for their services.

The service experiences described in the preceding paragraph highlight service delivery as a mass service experience (the play) and as a solo experience (the doctor). The differences impact on the nature of the interaction process. In the mass service experience the other members of the audience have the

Variable Recovery Services

Service quality can vary because people get tired, their workload might become too heavy, they might be stressed, lack sufficient experience, or have a poor attitude due to inadequate recruitment, selection, or training.

Companies such as Cisco, Dell, and IBM provide IT service and maintenance contracts each of which may contain a range of service packages. These might be 'the regular package' which guarantees a response in 6–8 hours, a 'gold service' which brings response in 4–6 hours, or a 'platinum service' which provides immediate, on-call support.

Car recovery and breakdown organizations such as the RAC, AA, and Green Flag do not offer different response times but offer a range of types of services. Typically these are roadside, recovery, at home, and European. These help to shape customer expectations about the type of service they can expect to receive.

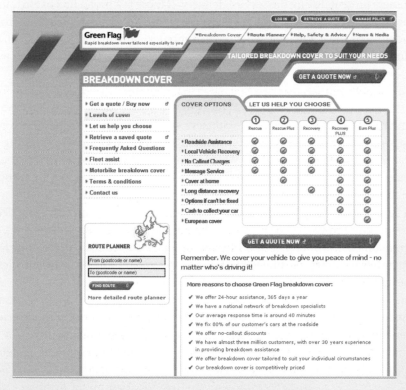

Green Flag's customer website

Green Flag

Whether the service is IT- or car-related, customer concern about service consistency can be addressed by providing positive third-party referrals, word-of-mouth and written testimonials, and case studies of satisfied customers. In some situations, such as accountancy, consulting, and IT services, many organizations provide qualified teams designated to work with the client in an attempt to generate trust and reduce uncertainty.

1 Think of four reasons why service quality might vary in the car recovery market.

2 Why do organizations such as Cisco, Dell, and IBM offer different maintenance contracts?

3 Visit the following websites and make notes about the different services offered by these competitors: www.greenflag.co.uk/ and www.theaa.com/.

opportunity to influence the perceived quality of the experience. Audiences create atmosphere and this may be positively or negatively charged. A good production can involve audiences in a play and keep them focused for the entire performance. However, a poor performance can frustrate audiences leading to some members walking out and hence influencing the perception others have of the performance and experience of the play.

Interaction within the solo experience (doctor–patient) allows for greater control by the service provider, if only because they can manage the immediate context within which the interaction occurs and not be unduly influenced by wider environmental issues. Opportunities exist for flexibility and adaptation as the service delivery unfolds. For example, a check-in operator for an airline operates within a particular context, is not influenced by other major events during the interaction, and can adapt their tone of voice, their body language, and their overall approach to meet the needs of particular travellers.

One final aspect of variability concerns the influence arising from the mixture of customers present during the service delivery. If there is a broad mix of customers service delivery may be affected as the needs of different groups have to be attended to by the service provider. Such a mixture may dilute the impact of the service actually delivered.

Lack of Ownership

The final characteristic associated with services marketing arises naturally from the other features. Services cannot be owned as nothing is transferred during the interaction or delivery experience. Although a legal transaction often occurs with a service there is no physical transfer of ownership as there is when a product is purchased. The seat in a theatre, train, plane, or ferry is rented on a temporary basis in exchange for a fee. The terms associated with the rental of the seat determine the time and use or experience to which the seat can be put. However, the seat remains the property of the theatre owner, rail operator, airline, and ferry company respectively as it needs to be available for renting to other people for further experiences.

One last point concerns loyalty schemes such as frequent flyer programmes and membership clubs, where the service provider actively promotes a sense of ownership. By creating involvement and participation, even though there is nothing to actually own, customers can develop an attitude based on their perceived right to be a part of the service provider.

The Service Mix

Previously we looked at the product/service spectrum and identified that there were a range of services. These ranged from services that were attached directly to a product and some which consisted of a pure stand-alone service. From this and an understanding of the various characteristics of services, it is possible to identify a **services mix**.

- Pure product—here there are no services, the offering is purely a product. Examples include salt, sugar, foot cream, and shower gel.

- Product with some services—here the product is supported with a range of one or more services. The more technologically sophisticated the product the more likely that it needs to be supported by services (Levitt, 1972). For example, cars require showrooms, delivery, warranties, and repair facilities, as without them, 'sales will shrivel'.

- Combination—here products and services are used in equal proportion in order that customers' expectations are met. So, in restaurants, service is expected as a complement to the food.

- Service with some products—here the emphasis is on the service but some products are a necessary part of the mix. For example, hotel guests rent a room, use leisure facilities, and seek relaxation, but in order that these are experienced, some products, such as food, drink, internet connections, and perhaps complimentary stationery, are necessary to complete the experience.

- Pure service—here no products are involved in the service experience. Examples include dog walking, tax advice, and counselling.

This interpretation of the service mix has been developed from Kotler (1997) and is useful because it demonstrates the wide range of services that are available, their complexity in terms of their variability, and the difficulty of defining and categorizing them.

Services can also be understood in terms of other variables. One important variable concerns the significance and intensity of the equipment that is required to provide the service, as opposed to the intensity of people's contribution to the delivery of a service. So, at one extreme, vending machines are examples of equipment-intensive services and window cleaning an example of people-intensive services.

Other variables include the degree to which customers need to be present at the time a service is delivered, for example a haircut against a car repair. Is the service directed at consumers (personal service) or businesses (business services)?

Service Processes

Services are considered to be processes and indeed a substantial part of the academic literature on services is based on a process perspective. A process is a series of sequential actions that lead to predetermined outcomes. So, a simple process might be the steps necessary to visit a dentist whereas a complex process might be the actions necessary to manage passengers on a two-week luxury cruise.

If processes are an integral part of the operations performed by service organizations, in the general sense, what are they processing? Lovelock, Vandermerwe, and Lewis (1999) argue that these processes are directly related to the equipment/people dimension referred to above. On the one hand, a haircut is people intensive but the failure of a network server is intensely equipment oriented. Lovelock,

Vandermerwe, and Lewis present a four-cell categorization of services based on tangible and intangible actions on people's bodies, minds, and physical assets. The categories involve four different processes: people processing, possession processing, mental stimulus processing, and information processing.

People Processing

In this type of processing people have to physically present themselves so that they become immersed within the service process. This involves them spending varying amounts of time actively cooperating with the service operation. So, people taking a train have to physically go to the station and get on a train and spend time getting to their destination. People undergoing dentistry work will have made an appointment prior to attending the dentist's surgery, will sit in the chair and open their mouths and cooperate with the dentist's various requests. They have physically become involved in the service process offered by their dentist.

From a marketing perspective consideration of the process and the outcomes arising from participation in the service process can lead to ideas about what benefits are being created and what non-financial costs are incurred as a result of the service operation. For the dentistry example, a comfortable chair, background music, a non-threatening or neutral to warm décor, and a pleasant manner can be of help.

Possession Processing

Just as people have to go to the service operation for people processing, so objects have to become involved in possession processing. Possessions such as kitchen gadgets, gardens, cars, and computers are liable to breakdown or need maintenance. Cleaning, storing, repairing, plus couriering, installation, and removal services are typical possession-processing activities.

In these situations people will either take an item to the service provider, or invite someone in to undertake the necessary work. In possession processing the level of customer involvement is limited compared to people processing. In most cases the sequence of activities is as follows. In order that the object will be attended to a telephone call is often required to fix an appointment. Then the item either needs to be taken to the service provider or you must wait for an attendant to visit. A brief to explain the problem/task/solution is given before returning at an agreed time/location to pay and take away the renewed item. This detachment from the service process enables people to focus on other tasks. The key difference here is that the quality of the service is not dependent on the owner or representative of the possession being present whilst the service operation takes place.

Mental Stimulus Processing

These types of services try to shape attitudes or behaviour. In order to achieve this, these services have to be oriented to people's minds, hence the expression mental stimulus processing. So, examples of these types of services include education, entertainment, professional advice, and news. In all of them people have to become involved mentally in the service interaction and give time in order that they experience the benefits of this type of service.

Service delivery can be through one of two locations. First, services can be created in a location that is distant to the receiver. In this case media channels are used to deliver the service. Alternatively, they can be delivered and consumed at the point where they originate, that is, in a studio, theatre, or hall. One of the key differences here is the form and nature of the audience experience. The theatre experience is likely to be much richer than the distant format. Digital technology has enabled opportunities for increased amounts of interactive communication, even though the experience will be different from the original. In the same way, online or e-learning in its purest form has not yet become an established format, due perhaps to learners' needs to spend some of their learning time through interaction with their co-learners and in the presence of the tutor.

Information Processing

The final type of service concerns the huge arena of information processing, the most intangible of all the services. Transformed by advances in technology, and computers in particular, information processing has become quicker, more accurate, and more frequent. The use of technology is important but we should not exclude people as individuals have a huge capacity to process information.

One key question that arises concerns the degree to which people should become involved in information processing. Some organizations deliberately route customers away from people processing and into information processing. EasyJet makes it difficult for customers to telephone the company and seek advice from expensive staff. Their approach is to drive people to their website and use the FAQs to answer customer queries.

The Service Marketing Mix

As explained in Chapter 1 the traditional 4Ps marketing mix was developed at a time when product marketing was prevalent and the role of services was insignificant. As services marketing has become increasingly important certain limitations regarding the utility of the 4Ps approach have become apparent. For example, the intangibility of services is normally ignored while promotion fails to accommodate the inseparability issue between the production and consumption of services.

As a result of these and other shortcomings an extended marketing mix of 7Ps has emerged. The three additional Ps have been included in order to meet the express needs of the service context. These are People, Physical Evidence, and Processes. The 7Ps mix can also be applied to business-to-business and relationship marketing, the subjects of the next two chapters.

Product

Products are used to meet and satisfy customer needs and today this can incorporate anything tangible or intangible. Services are now commonly referred to as products in the widest sense. So, holidays, insurance policies, and bank accounts are referred to as products and they can all be categorized within a product mix.

Price

Because of the intangibility of services price often becomes a means by which customers make a judgement about the quality of service. As there is nothing to touch or feel, making considered opinions about the costs and benefits arising from a service interaction can be problematic.

Price can be an important instrument in managing demand. By varying price across different time periods it is easier to spread demand and ease pressure on the busiest of times. This also enables service providers to reach those customer segments who are willing and able to pay full price and in doing so deliver a service that meets the expectations of this type of customer.

Place

Place, in a traditional product-only context, refers to the way in which products are distributed in order that customers can access them at a time and place that is most convenient to them. In terms of services place refers to two issues. The first concerns the reservation and information systems necessary to support the service proposition. Increasingly this is undertaken remote from the service delivery point. The second refers to the simultaneous nature of the production/consumption interaction. Here the service should be regarded as a function of direct supply and would suggest that place has little relevance in a service context. These interactions can occur at a customer's house or business location or at the provider's location, such as a beautician's salon, an accountant's office, or a cinema. Other interactions take place remotely over the internet or telephone. One problem that arises for the provider is that this limits them in terms of their geographic coverage and the number of customers they can manage without suffering a decline in service performance.

Promotion

Promotion is concerned with the presentation of the marketing offer (products and services) to target audiences. However, the promotion of services is essentially more challenging than that for products, simply because of the intangibility issue. So, promotion cannot convey size or volume, whilst images of the packaging or in-use pictures are also ruled out. In its favour it is possible to depict or explain the benefits arising from the purchase of a service and it is also possible to show the physical evidence of people enjoying the service.

Perhaps the main goal of services-based promotional activity is to reduce the perceived uncertainty associated with the intangibility of a service. This can be achieved by providing tangible clues concerning the nature and quality of the service. First, make the service easy to recognize by providing a logo or brand identifier consistently in all communications. Lloyds Bank used the Black Horse for many years whilst Scottish Widows use an iconic black-caped young widow to

MARKET INSIGHT 15.4

Promoting Group Service

The Classic British Hotels consortium gives high-quality independent hotels the opportunity to maintain their independence or individual identity, yet enjoy similar benefits to those provided by national and global chain hotel brands.

Classic British Hotels: a consortium of high-quality independent hotels

Classic British Hotels

This network of quality independent hotel properties aims to generate referral business, provide a comprehensive conference placement operation, a reservations system, and enable members to tender for major room night volume business. In addition, the network provides extensive promotional exposure in a huge number of leisure brochures/magazines and on major websites around the world.

To join the network all hotels have to undergo a thorough quality audit because they all need to meet (and maintain) exacting quality standards. In return hotels are awarded the Classic British Hotels hallmark, a means of identification, status, and prestige designed to reinforce the positioning of the group.

To help customers understand the various types of hotel in the group, properties are classified by style and quality levels. These are used to help shape customer expectations and enable the group to generate high levels of customer satisfaction.

Five styles: Contemporary, Country House, Townhouse, Heritage, and Period Elegance.

Four quality levels: First Class, Superior First Class, Deluxe, and Luxury.

Source: Adapted from www.classicbritishhotels.com/.

1 How does the Classic British group communicate their high quality and positioning?

2 How do Classic British hotels use segmentation to assist their communications?

3 Visit the following websites and compare the services offered: www.classicbritishhotels.com/ and www.travelodge.co.uk/.

represent their brand. From this point it should be possible to develop a reputation for trust, reliability, and quality that hopefully will spur positive word-of-mouth communication. (See Market Insight 15.4 for the promotion of service on a group basis in the hotel industry.)

People

In the production of goods and manufactured items, the people element is removed from the customer at the point when the product is purchased. It does not matter what the engineers look like, how they speak to one another in the factory, or how they dress. In service industries this is an extremely important factor as people representing the service provider have a direct impact on the perceived quality of the service itself.

Staff represent the service and should deliver the service consistently to a level that matches the desired positioning and service blueprint. The recruitment, training, and rewarding of staff is an imperative if the required standards and expectations associated with customer interaction are to be achieved.

One final aspect concerning people in the services mix concerns the management of the atmosphere and interaction among customers. Ensuring that the right physical environment is in place, for example, comfortable seats, warmth, low beams, open fireplace, etc. in a pub, plus making sure that the right segments are attracted, is an important part of service marketing.

Physical Evidence

As mentioned previously the intangibility of a service means that it is important to provide tangible cues for potential customers to deduce the product quality. One of the more common approaches is to use sales literature and brochures to give signs about the quality and positioning of the service. Staff deportment and dress also provide clues about a service provider's attitude and attention to tidiness, routines, safety, and customer orientation.

Shostack (1977) suggests that physical evidence can take one of two forms; essential evidence and peripheral evidence. Essential evidence refers to those few, key elements that are important criteria when customers make purchasing decisions. For example the quality of cars used by a car rental company, the newness of planes, or the location and architecture of cinemas provide essential information. Peripheral evidence is, by definition, less important to a customer's evaluation of the overall quality of the service provision. Very often these items, such as sales literature, can be taken away by the customer and used as a reminder of the service brand.

Processes

Understanding service-related processes is important because customers are an integral part of service production. Processes include all the tasks, schedules, activities, and routines that enable a service to be delivered to a customer. If the marketing of services is to be successful then it is crucial that the processes customers use work effectively and appropriately.

The processes involved in getting a haircut involve making an appointment by phone, arriving at the salon, waiting for attention once booked in, being shampooed by the junior, discussing style and requirements, drinking tea/coffee, having hair cut and styled, drying, paying and tipping, collecting belongings, and leaving. This is a relatively straightforward process; others, as mentioned earlier, can be complex. Knowing these steps means that marketers can build benefits into key steps to avoid boredom or enhance the experience. It is also an opportunity to provide differentiation and reposition service brands.

Service Encounters

The development of service marketing strategies involves understanding the frequency and the ways in which customers contact service providers. Once this is understood strategies can be developed that maintain required levels of service, but the processes and linkages that bring the elements of the services marketing mix and associated systems together can be reformulated. Service marketing strategy, therefore, should be based on insight into the ways in which customers interact or contact a service. The form and nature of the customer encounter is of fundamental importance.

A service encounter is best understood as a period of time during which a customer interacts directly with a service (Shostack, 1985). These interactions may be short and encompass all the actions necessary to complete the service experience. Alternatively they may be protracted, involve several encounters, several representatives of the service provider, and indeed several locations, in order that the service experience be completed.

Originally the term 'encounter' was used to describe the personal interaction between a service provider and customers. A more contemporary interpretation needs to include all those interactions that occur through people and their equipment and machines with the people and equipment belonging to the service provider (Glyn and Lehtinen, 1995). As a result three levels of customer contact can be observed; high-contact services, medium-contact services, and low-contact services. See Table 15.2 on p 607.

One of the interesting developments in recent years is the decision by some organizations to move their customers from high-contact services to low-contact services. Clear examples of this are to be found in the banking sector with first ATMs, then telephone, and now internet banking, all of which either lower or remove personal contact with bank employees. Further examples are vending machines, self or rapid checkout facilities in hotels, and online ticket purchases. (See also Market Insight 15.5.)

This demarcation of customer contact levels is necessary because it provides a sound base upon which to develop services marketing.

Service Quality and Performance

Measuring the quality of a service encounter has become a major factor in the management of service-based organizations. Service quality is based on the idea that customer's expectations of the service they will receive shape their perception of the actual service encounter. In essence, therefore, customers compare the perceived service with the expected service.

So, if the perceived service meets or even exceeds expectations then customers are deemed to be satisfied and are much more likely to return at some point in the future. However, if the perceived service falls below what was expected then they are more likely to feel disappointed and unlikely to return.

In order to help organizations manage and provide a consistent level of service various models have been proposed. Primarily these have been based on performance measures, disconfirmation (the gap between expected and perceived service encounter), and importance-performance ideas (Palmer, 2005). See Table 15.3.

Each of these approaches has strengths and weaknesses but the one approach that has received most attention is **SERVQUAL** developed by Parasuraman, Zeithaml, and Berry (1988). For some it represents the benchmark approach to managing service quality.

SERVQUAL is a disconfirmation model and is based on the difference between the expected services and the actual perceived service. Inherently this approach assumes that there is a gap between these variables, and five particular types of GAP have been established across service industries. These are:

● GAP 1: the gap between the customer's expectations and management perception.

By not understanding customers' needs correctly, management direct resources into inappropriate areas. For example, train service operators may think that customers want places to store bags whereas they actually want a seat in a comfortable, safe environment.

Table 15.3
Three approaches to service quality measurement

Contact level	Explanation
Performance measures	Derived from the manufacturing sector this approach simply asks customers to rate the performance of a service encounter. SERVPERF is the standard measurement technique.
Disconfirmation	This approach is based on the difference between what was expected from a service and was delivered, as perceived by the customer. SERVQUAL is the standard measurement technique.
Importance-performance	Seeks to compare the performance of the different elements that make up a service with the customer's perception of the relative importance of these elements. IPA (importance-performance analysis) is the standard measurement technique.

- GAP 2: the gap between management perception and service-quality specification.

In this case management perceive customer wants correctly but fail to set a performance standard, fail to clarify it, or set one that is not realistic and hence unachievable. For example, the train operator understands customers' desire for a comfortable seat but fails to specify how many of them should be provided relative to the anticipated number of travellers on each route.

- GAP 3: the gap between service-quality specifications and service delivery.

In this situation the service delivery does not match the specification for the service. This may be due to human error, poor training, or a failure in the technology necessary to delivery parts of a service. For example, the trolley-buffet service on a train may be perceived as poor because the trolley operator was impolite because they had not received suitable training or because the supplier had not delivered the sandwiches on time.

- GAP 4: the gap between service delivery and external communications.

The service promise presented in advertisements, on the website, and in sales literature helps set customer expectations. If these promises are not realized in service delivery practice, customers become dissatisfied. For example, if an advertisement shows the interior of a train with comfortable seats and plenty of space yet a customer boards a train only to find a lack of space and hard seating, the external communications have misled customers and distorted their view of what might be realistically expected.

- GAP 5: the gap between perceived service and expected service.

This gap arises because customers misunderstand the service quality relative to what they expect. This may be due to one or more of the previous gaps. For example, a customer might assume that the lack of information when a train comes to a standstill for an unexpectedly long period of time is due to ignorance or 'they never tell us anything' attitude. In reality this silence may be due to a failure of the internal communication system.

Using this GAPS approach five different dimensions of service quality have been established. These are:

1 Reliability—the accuracy and dependability of repeated performances of service delivery.

2 Responsiveness—the helpfulness and willingness of staff to provide prompt service.

3 Assurance—the courtesy, confidence, and competence of employees.

4 Empathy—the ease and individualized care shown towards customers.

5 Tangibles—the appearance of employees, the physical location and any facilities and equipment, and the communication materials.

The SERVQUAL model consists of a questionnaire containing twenty-two items, based on these five dimensions. When completed by customers it provides management with opportunities to correct areas where service performance is perceived to be less than satisfactory and learn from and congratulate people about the successful components.

Although SERVQUAL has been used extensively there are some problems associated with its use. These difficulties concern the different dimensions customers use to assess quality, which varies according to each situation. In addition there are statistical inconsistencies associated with measuring differences and the scoring techniques plus reliability issues associated with asking customers their expectations after they have consumed a service (Gabbott and Hogg, 1998).

Service Failure and Recovery

Dealing with service quality and ideas about customer satisfaction equating or exceeding expectations should not mask sight from those occasions, and all organizations have them, when things go wrong. There is an inevitability that where there is intangibility, inseparability, and variability then service performance may sometimes fall short of the required standard. Where a customer's expectations are not met then the result is service failure.

Service failures, according to Bitner, Booms, and Tetreault (1990), arise from one of three main areas. These are failures in the delivery system, failure in response to customer requests, and failure through employee actions. Table 15.4 provides a brief explanation of these three types of service failure.

The problem with service failure is not the failure itself but how the customer reacts. Whilst some customers will tell a few people about exceptional service performance, service failure can result in a disproportionate number of people hearing about the lost bag, the slow service, or the cold food. Dissatisfied customers are unlikely to come back so it is really important to ensure that service performance is correct in the first place. Should a failure occur steps have to be taken immediately to correct the situation and turn a potentially negative situation into a one that leads to positive outcomes for all involved. This is known as **service recovery**.

Table 15.4

Sources of service
failure

Type of service failure	Explanation
Failures in the delivery system	Here links between service personnel and service process break down. This is due to service unavailability (e.g. swimming pool closed), slow service (e.g. airport queues and delays), and core service failure (e.g. undercooked food).
Failure in response to customer requests	Explicit customer requests (e.g. a room with a sea view) or implicit customer requests (e.g. that children be excluded from quiet areas). Alternatively customers make errors (e.g. forgotten PIN number).
Failure through employee actions	Unexpected, non-standard employee actions where delivery of the service is perceived to be rude, dismissive, or unfair.

Source: Adapted from Bitner, Booms, and Tetreault (1990).

Service recovery is concerned with an organization's systematic attempt to correct a problem following service failure and to retain a customer's goodwill (Lovelock, 2001). By acting quickly, demonstrating empathy with the customer's perception of the failure, and enabling employees to instigate corrective actions and award appropriate compensation, well-managed organizations are able to overcome service failure and develop positive reputations.

One of the ways in which organizations manage service failure, especially those failures that are not reported formally to the service provider but informally to family and friends, is to actively encourage customers to provide written feedback through questionnaires. By reacting promptly to the feedback and offering additional services free of charge, or financial compensation against the current or future service opportunities, organizations are more likely to retain customers, prevent negative word of mouth, and may enhance their reputations.

RESEARCH INSIGHT 15.4

To take your learning further, you might wish to read this influential paper.

Lewis, B. R., and Clacher, E. (2001), 'Service failure and recovery in UK theme parks: the employees' perspective', *International Journal of Contemporary Hospitality Management*, 13, 4, 166–75.

This is an interesting paper because it concerns research into fraudulent customer complaints, and explores the motivations and forms of such deliberate 'illegitimate' customer complaints. The paper identifies four distinct forms of customer complaints and six main motives for making fraudulent complaints.

Characteristics of Business Markets

Business markets are characterized by a number of factors but the main ones are: the nature of demand, the buying processes, international dimensions, and, perhaps most importantly, the relationships that develop between organizations in the process of buying and selling. These are shown in Figure 16.1 and are examined in turn.

The Nature of Demand

There are three aspects of demand in business markets: derivation, variance, and elasticity. Demand in business markets is ultimately **derived** from consumers. This may seem a little odd but consider the demand for building trains. When Virgin Trains considered ordering the high-speed Pendolino trains for the west coast route in the UK, for example, part of Virgin's calculation was based on their estimation of the number of people prepared to make that train journey and what they are prepared to pay. Even though each train is the result of hundreds of organizations interacting with one another it is train passengers (consumers) who actually stimulate demand for the construction of trains.

Demand is **variable** because consumer preferences and behaviour fluctuate. The demand for rail journeys, for example, invariably declines following a major train accident or a significant increase in fares. The subsequent impact could be felt on rail operators, support services, train manufacturers, and the whole array of suppliers and subcontractors in the market. All of this suggests that organizations should monitor and anticipate demand as cycles unfold. See Market Insight 16.1 for an example.

Demand is essentially **inelastic.** If suppliers raise their prices, most manufacturers will try to absorb the increases into their own cost structures to prevent

Figure 16.1
Key characteristics of business markets

Fluctuating Demand for Computers

Multinational personal computer companies are typical original equipment manufacturers (OEMs). Companies such as IBM, Dell, and Hewlett Packard assemble their own equipment from components that are largely bought from other manufacturers. However, the computer business is intensely competitive and dynamic mainly because demand is influenced by three main factors.

Falling prices. The price of computers has fallen dramatically in the past twenty-five years. In addition to aggressive price-cutting strategies all the major companies operate 'just-in-time' stocking systems designed to keep only a few days' supplies of components in their warehouses. This has allowed them to cut prices.

Rapid technological change. The pace of technological change has been enormous. As chip capacity doubles every 18 to 24 months so computer processing power has increased by a factor of 100 over the past decade. One result of this is that many consumers want the latest designs and often reject technology that is just six months old. Consumers therefore can create huge fluctuations in demand.

Volatility. Fast technological development and fluctuating market demand often combine to cause great instability in the computer supply chain. Frequent variation in product demand can cause these companies to swing between stock-outs to periods of overproduction and surplus capacity. This in turn can impact on the rate and size of investment made by organizations as they flex themselves in anticipation of 'foreseeable' demand. For example, Dell hit a crisis in 1989 when chip capacity went from 256K to 1Mb virtually overnight and the company was left with millions of dollars' worth of unsaleable stock.

Source: Adapted from www.cafod.org.uk/policy_and_analysis/public_policy_papers/.

1 From where is the demand for PCs derived?

2 Is demand in the personal computer market elastic or inelastic?

3 How could a marketing manager overcome the volatility of this market?

letting their customers down in the short term, or because they are tied into fixed priced contracts. Incorporating these price increases, at least over the short to medium term, means that there is price inelasticity. In the medium term manufacturers can either eliminate the original parts, redesign the product, or search for new suppliers.

International Aspects

In comparison to consumer markets, B2B marketing is much easier to conduct internationally. This is because the needs of businesses around the world are far more similar to one another than the needs of consumers, whose preferences, tastes, and resources vary. As a result an increasing number of B2B organizations are moving into international markets. This is often enabled by advances in technology, most notably the internet, which permit organizations enormous geographic coverage.

In comparison to B2C markets, B2B organizations benefit from a lower variety of product functionality and performance. This is partly because the various trading associations across the world have agreed standards relating to content and performance. What this means is that buying and selling of products and services, wherever located, is relatively simple and the trading environment reasonably well regulated and controlled. Many industries, for example, the steel, plastic, chemicals, and paper industries, all have common agreed standards, which facilitate inter-organizational exchange processes. In B2C markets there are numerous issues concerning consumer culture and values and the adaptation of products and promotional activities to meet various colour, ingredient, stylistic, buying processes, packaging, and language requirements.

Relationships

If there is one characteristic that separates business marketing from consumer marketing it is the importance of relationships. In B2C markets the low perceived value of the products, and the competitive nature of the market, which makes product substitution relatively easy, makes relationships between manufacturers and consumers relatively difficult to establish. In business marketing the interaction between buyers, sellers, and other stakeholders is of major significance. The development and maintenance of relationships between buying and selling organizations is pivotal to success. Interdependence, collaboration, and in some cases partnership, over the development, supply, and support of products and services, is considered a core element of B2B marketing.

The importance of this aspect of B2B marketing cannot be underestimated and is explored in greater depth in Chapter 17.

RESEARCH INSIGHT 16.1

To take your learning further, you might wish to read this influential paper.

Dwyer, R. F., Schurr, P. H., and Oh, S. (1987), 'Developing buyer–seller relationships', *Journal of Marketing*, 51 (April), 11–27.

This paper is one of the most cited by other researchers in the subject area. Its popularity is based on the critical observation that buyer–seller exchanges are not discrete activities or events, but a part of ongoing relationships. The authors present a framework for developing buyer–seller relationships that links into marketing strategy.

Types of Organizational Customers

Once referred to as industrial marketing, the term B2B marketing has been adopted because it recognizes the involvement of a range of other, non-industrial suppliers, agents, and participants. The government, the non-profit sector, and both charities and institutions in most countries are responsible for a huge level of B2B activity. Consider the transactions necessary to support various government functions. For example, the huge range of products and services necessary to support the pharmaceutical and medical supplies in the health service, the products and infrastructure necessary to maintain the prison and military services, all represent a major slice of B2B activity.

It is possible to categorize organizations by their size (revenue or number of employees), namely large, medium, and small-sized organizations. Macfarlane (2002) refers to global and national organizations, the public sector, small and medium-sized enterprises (SMEs), and small office/home office (SOHOs). However, this approach is too general and fails to accommodate different buyer needs and purchasing procedures. Here, three broad types of B2B organizations are identified: commercial, government, and institutional organizations.

Commercial Organizations

There are a huge number of different types of commercial organization and it is important to appreciate the different roles that they fulfil in the commercial sector. Four types of commercial organizations are considered here: **distributors**, **original equipment manufacturers** (OEMs), **users**, and **retailers**. Each of these sectors uses products and services in different ways but they all share common buyer behaviour characteristics and communications.

Distributors

The marketing channel consists of various organizations, referred to as distributors or intermediaries, who play an important role in the transfer of products from manufacturers to the final end user customers. Distributors should not only smooth the progress of products through the marketing channel but they should also add value to them by providing storage (through distribution centres), services (such as training), or financial support (such as credit facilities).

In most cases distributors will take ownership and physical possession of the goods but there are occasions when this might not be true. For example, the involvement of an agent in negotiations may mean that ownership passes over them, rather than through them, to the next intermediary or customer.

Some of the more common types of distributor are: **wholesalers**, **value added resellers**, and distributors/dealers.

Wholesalers fulfil a number of roles but their principal contribution is to add value to the distribution process. They can do this in a number of ways and one

Racing to Win

HONDA
The Power of Dreams

Honda Racing

P1

JAMES TOSELAND

SBK ROUND 1

LOSAIL QATAR

25 02 2006

HONDA CBR1000RR

www.honda.co.uk
Honda Contact Centre : 0800 1234567

of these is referred to as 'breaking bulk'. Manufacturers produce large quantities of product but customers only consume relatively small quantities. Wholesalers strip down large containers, pallets, or quantities of goods and redistribute them to retailers or customers in quantities that they want to buy, store, and consume them in. This allows manufacturers to concentrate on their core activities and leave the skills associated with distribution to others, namely the dealers and distributors.

Value added resellers fulfil a similar role to those of retailers in consumer markets. Their role is to bring together a variety of software and hardware products and design customized systems solutions for their business customers. They provide integrated systems by drawing on a network of providers and, in doing so, create a value network at the business customer level.

Distributors/dealers supply both end user business customers and original equipment manufacturers (see below). They play the important role of providing a wide range of products from a number of different manufacturers and provide their customers with easy access to them. They take full ownership of the goods they purchase for resale and provide advice, repair, and credit facilities where necessary. (See Market Insight 16.2 below for Honda's use of deals in various market.)

MARKET INSIGHT 16.2

Dealing in Motorbikes

Honda sells over 12 million motorcycles in the Asia Oceania region alone and the management of its distribution networks is a vital element in maintaining customer access and satisfaction. Honda produces a wide range of motorcycles, ranging from the 50 cc class to the 1,800 cc class, and is the largest manufacturer of motorcycles in the world, in terms of annual units of production. In the region, Honda's motorcycles are produced at sites in Japan, Indonesia, Philippines, Pakistan, and India.

In Japan, sales of Honda motorcycles (and automobiles, and power product) are made through different distribution networks. Honda's products are sold to consumers primarily through independent retail dealers, and motorcycles are distributed through approximately 11,600 outlets, including approximately 1,400 PROS authorized dealerships. PROS dealerships sell all Honda's Japanese motorcycle models, not just selected models.

Most of Honda's overseas sales are made through its main sales subsidiaries, which distribute Honda's products to local wholesalers and retail dealers. In Indonesia, Honda has recently developed its dealer network of 4,000 dealers and service shops to support sales and provide excellent after-sales service. In the USA, Honda's wholly owned subsidiary markets Honda's motorcycle products through a sales network of approximately 1,260 independent local dealers. Many of these motorcycle dealers also sell other Honda products.

In Europe, subsidiaries of the company in the United Kingdom, Germany, France, Belgium, the Netherlands, Spain, Switzerland, Austria, Italy, and other European countries distribute Honda's motorcycles through approximately 1,600 independent local dealers.

One core element of Honda's dealer strategy, worldwide, is its comprehensive 4S support system. This covers Sales, Service, Spare parts, and Safety. For example, in 2006, Honda provided its dealers in Thailand, Indonesia, Vietnam, and India with an easy-to-use riding simulator, called 'Riding Trainer', through which riders can get an opportunity to receive risk awareness training and riding practice and, of course, engagement with the Honda brand.

Recently a fifth S has been added, 'Second-Hand (or used)' business. In Thailand, for example, the second-hand motorcycle business has been deliberately strengthened as a means of developing business. The strategy encourages potential motorcycle owners and those ready for an upgrade to purchase pre-owned Honda models. This draws this segment into the brand.

Sources: www.world.honda.com/; www.findarticles.com/p/articles/; http://sec.edgar-online.com/.

1 Why does Honda set up subsidiary organizations in each overseas region or country?

2 What do you think are the benefits of the 4S support system?

3 What might affect Honda's dealer network (marketing channel) in the future?

Original Equipment Manufacturers

Original equipment manufacturers, or OEMs as they are commonly referred to, purchase materials such as parts, finished and partly finished goods, and even sub-assemblies that have been outsourced, and build them directly into the products that they offer to their customers. The term OEM specifically refers to one company relabelling a product, incorporating it within a different product, in order to sell it under their own brand name.

For example, Toyota may have a contract with a headlight manufacturer to supply them with a certain quantity of headlight assemblies. Toyota are the OEM because they build these headlight assemblies into their different cars and sell the car as a Toyota, without identifying the manufacturer of the headlight assembly.

SanDisk, the inventor of flash data storage, claim that the growth of flash memory is the direct result of increased consumer demand (remember derived demand mentioned earlier?) for ever-smaller, feature-packed portable digital devices such as digital cameras and multimedia mobile phones. SanDisk claim that OEMs, the manufacturers of these devices, can rely on SanDisk for supplying the right flash memory products.

Users

Users are organizations that purchase goods and services that are consumed as part of their production and manufacturing processes. Users, therefore, consume these parts and materials and they do not appear in the final product offering but do contribute to its production.

Toyota will purchase many support materials, for example, machine tools, electrical manufacturing equipment, vending machines, office furniture, and stationery. None of these can be identified within the cars they produce.

Retailers

The final type of commercial organization is retailers. Retailers are an important aspect of B2B marketing, even though a retailer's customer is a consumer. Retailers need to purchase goods in order to resell them just as other organizations do. However, the buying processes are not always as complex or as intricate as those normally associated with organizational buying and the group of people who make purchase decisions (the **decision-making unit** or DMU).

Just as retailers need to buy products to sell so suppliers need to sell on to retailers. To do this successfully suppliers need to understand their retailers and their markets. Retailing is a specialist activity and retailers' various roles and tasks are considered in Chapter 14.

Government

Governments are responsible for an enormous amount of business purchases. Not only do they undertake a huge volume of business purchases but the value of the business undertaken by governments is also high. Health, policing, education, transport, environmental protection, and national defence and security are a few of the areas that require public investment.

Many of the larger projects that concern governments and associated ministries are large and complex and involve a huge number of stakeholders. Very often many projects end up over budget and past the planned completion date. Many people attribute this to the financial policies and accounting practices insisted on by government.

The procedures and guidelines relating to government purchasing policies and the buying behaviours they exhibit are not that different from those experienced by commercial organizations. However, there are some major differences, namely factors relating to political objectives, budget policies, accountability, and EC Directives (van Weele, 2002).

Institutions

Institutions include not-for-profit organizations such as churches and charities, community-based organizations such as housing associations, and government-related organizations such as hospitals, schools, museums, libraries, and universities.

In many ways these organizations reflect some of the characteristics associated with both commercial and government markets. For example, purchasing in some institutional markets can be significantly constrained by political influences such as the pressure some schools experience from the direct control of local education authorities, and various social influences experienced by faith and religious groups. However, all these organizations need to purchase a wide range of goods, parts, materials, and services in order to: function properly; meet their customers' needs; and achieve their organizational objectives and performance targets.

One of the interesting ways in which these institutions influence their environment is their willingness to form large buying groups. Through collaboration the group is able to negotiate greatly reduced prices and much larger discounts, usually related to bulk purchases. See Market Insight 16.3.

MARKET INSIGHT 16.3

Grouping to Buy Health Supplies

At one time doctors in hospitals and general practice used to buy medicines and health supplies on a local basis, each negotiating directly with healthcare and pharmaceutical companies. Now general practices and hospitals are organized into larger groups referred to as NHS primary trusts. Each trust works together to agree a list of supplies and suppliers from which all doctors in the trust must buy and prescribe.

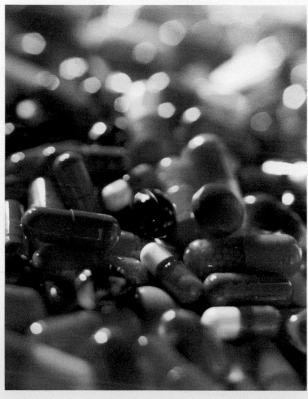

Group buying medicines can improve value for the customer

Photodisc

This is known as a 'formulary list' and it specifies the range of suppliers and the items that can be purchased in each therapeutic area. Not only does this procedure generate discounts and lower costs but it also saves doctors' time as they no longer have to spend time purchasing materials. Group buying in this case can represent better value for the public they serve.

1 What do you think a doctor might do if a preferred drug is not included on the formulary list?

2 How might collaboration with the NHS primary trusts work against the public interest?

RESEARCH INSIGHT 16.2

To take your learning further, you might wish to read this influential paper.

Achrol, R. S. (1997), 'Changes in the theory of interorganizational relations in marketing: toward a network paradigm', *Journal of the Academy of Marketing Science*, 25, 1, 56–71.

Achrol sets out how the then established vertically integrated, multidivisional type of organization is being replaced by new forms of network organization consisting of large numbers of functionally specialized firms tied together in cooperative exchange relationships. He considers four main types, the variables involved, the economic rationale, and the types of coordination and control mechanisms necessary for organizations to adapt to the new environment.

The impact of group buying on supplier organizations is that they have had to adapt their marketing strategies. In the case of formulary lists, set out in Market Insight 16.3, rather than sell into individual doctor's surgeries using the local and largely individual buying procedures, suppliers have had to adapt to group buying behaviours and associated negotiation processes. This requires knowledge and understanding of the different people who make up the purchasing team. Although price is an important factor in this environment, to be successful supplying organizations have recognized the need to develop relationships with each of the key members of the purchasing team. This means adapting their communications strategy and at the same time developing their delivery and supply chain procedures (the logistics) in order to meet the variety of delivery requirements of the purchasing group.

All of these types of B2B organizations, commercial, government, and institutions, buy goods and services on an inter-organizational basis. Consumers are only involved through their interaction with retailers or as end users of health treatments, education, or policing for which no direct financial exchange occurs. The type of marketing activities used in order to encourage repeat exchanges between these various types of organization can be considerable. However, one common strategy has been the more overt approach to developing relationships through cooperation and collaboration.

Types of Business Goods and Services

Just as there is a variety of types of organizations in the business sector so the products and services offered are equally varied and complex. Table 16.1 sets out the three principal business types of goods and services.

Most organizations, at various points in their development, have to decide whether to make/supply their own products and services or buy them in from

Table 16.1

Types of business
goods and services

Type of goods	Explanation
Input goods Raw materials, semi-manufactured parts, and finished goods	Input goods have been subjected to different levels of processing (*raw materials*, *semi-manufactured parts*, and *finished* goods), and they lose their individual identities and become part of the finished item.
Equipment goods Otherwise known as capital or investment goods	These are necessary for manufacturing and operations to take place. Land and buildings, computer systems, and machine tools are all necessary to support the production process, but they cannot be identified in the finished product.
Supply goods Otherwise known as maintenance, repair, and operating materials (MRO) items	These goods and services are 'consumables' as they are necessary to keep production processes and the organization running. For example, lubricants, paints, screws, and cleaning materials may all be necessary to maintain a firm's operations. Computer or IT servicing is necessary to maintain operations and to avoid down time, whilst accounting audits are a legal requirement.

outsourced providers. This 'make or buy' decision can have far-reaching effects not just on the strategic and operational aspects of an organization, but on the purchasing function and its role within an organization as well.

Outsourcing is an increasingly popular activity practised by a wide range of organizations. As a result, purchasing behaviours have had to adapt accordingly, which in turn has impacted on business marketing. Hines (1996) argues that the development of 'lean management' in the 1990s became a common strategy in which organizations concentrated on their core processes and then outsourced all other activities. He argues that as organizations become 'leaner', so the importance of purchasing increases.

The Role of Purchasing in Organizations

Whether products and services are outsourced or developed internally, all organizations have to buy a variety of products and services in order to operate normally and achieve their performance targets. Professional purchasing is not only an important (if not critical) feature, it should also be an integral part of an organization's overall operations and strategic orientation (Ryals and Rogers, 2006).

In the past, an organization's purchasing activities could have been characterized as an 'order-delivery response function'. Purchasing departments signed orders and the right deliveries were made at the right place, at the right time, and then invoiced correctly. The goal was to play off one supplier against another, and as a result reduce costs and improve short-term profits. Purchasing departments used to be regarded as an isolated function within organizations, a necessary but uninteresting aspect of organizational performance.

That perspective changed towards the end of the last century. Now organizations reduce the number of their suppliers, sometimes to just one, and strategic procurement (as it is often termed) is used to negotiate with suppliers on a cooperative basis, in order to help build long-term relationships. Purchasing has become an integral part of an organization's operations. One of the main reasons for this changed approach was research that showed that business performance improves when organizations adopt a collaborative, rather than adversarial, approach to purchasing and account management (Swinder and Seshadri, 2001). However, there are several other related issues that have changed the role of purchasing, namely, customer sophistication, increasing competition, and various strategic issues.

Customer Sophistication

Due to increasing customer sophistication, organizations are trying to differentiate their offerings and become more specialized. Organizational purchasing has to follow this movement and also become more specialized, otherwise the organization will become increasingly ineffective in meeting customer needs.

Increasing Competition

With increasing competition, margins have been eroded. As a result more attention has been given to internal costs and operations. By influencing purchasing costs and managerial costs associated with dealing with multiple suppliers, the profitability of the organization can be directly impacted. Consequently the importance of purchasing polices, processes, and procedures within organizations has increased.

Strategic Issues

There are several strategic issues related to the purchasing activities undertaken by organizations. First, there is the 'make or buy' decision. Should organizations make and/or assemble products for resale, or outsource or buy in particular products, parts, services, or sub-assemblies and concentrate on what is referred to as core activities or competences? Second, the benefits that arise through closer cooperation with suppliers and the increasing influence of buyer–seller relationships and 'joint value creation' have inevitably led to a tighter, more professional and integrated purchasing function. The third strategy-related issue concerns the degree to which the purchasing function is integrated into the organization. New IT systems have raised the level of possible integration of purchasing and operations to the extent that possible disruptions to production and output can be minimized, and the competitive strength of the organization enhanced (Laois and Moschuris, 2001).

Organizational Buyer Behaviour

Whether an organization operates a centralized or decentralized purchasing system does not remove the importance of understanding the way in which a potential customer organization buys products and services. Only by appreciating the particular purchasing systems, people, and policies used by an organization can suitable marketing and selling strategies be implemented. This next section builds on the **organizational buyer behaviour** information introduced in Chapter 6 and considers some of the key issues associated with the subject.

Two definitions of organizational buyer behaviour reveal two important aspects of this subject. First, Webster and Wind (1972) defined organizational buying as 'the decision making process by which formal organisations establish the need for purchased products and services and identify, evaluate and choose among alternative brands and suppliers'.

This adopts a buying organization's perspective and highlights the important point that organizational buying behaviour involves processes rather than a single, static, one-off event. There are a number of stages, or phases, associated with product procurement, each one often requiring a key decision to be made. These are considered later.

A second definition, by Parkinson and Baker (1994: 6), cited by Ulkuniemi (2003), states that organizational buying behaviour concerns 'the purchase of a product or service to satisfy organisational rather than individual goals'. This takes a neutral perspective but makes the point that organizational buyer behaviour is about satisfying organization-wide needs and hence requires marketers to adopt processes which take into account the needs of different people, not a single individual.

Organizational buying behaviour is about three key issues:

- The functions and processes buyers move through when purchasing products for use in business markets.

- Strategy, where purchasing is designed to assist competitive advantage and to influence supply chain activities.

- The network of relationships that organizations are part of when purchasing. The placement of orders and contracts between organizations can confirm a current trading relationship, initiate a new set of relationships, or may even signal the demise of a relationship.

What should be clear is that organizational buying behaviour is not just about the purchase of goods and services. In addition to this fundamental task, it is concerned with the strategic development of the organization and the management of inter-organizational relationships, both key issues in B2B marketing. These three issues overlap each other and are not discrete items.

Decision-Making Units: Characteristics

Although organizations usually designate a 'buyer' who is responsible for the purchase of a range of products and services, in reality a range of people are involved in the purchasing process. This group of people is referred to as either the decision-making unit (DMU) or the **buying centre**. In many circumstances these are informal groupings of people who come together in varying ways to contribute to the decision-making process. Certain projects, usually of major significance or value, require a group of people to be formally constituted and who have express responsibility to oversee and complete the purchase of a stipulated item or products and services relating to a specific project.

DMUs vary in composition and size according to the nature of each individual purchasing task. Webster and Wind (1972) identified a number of people who undertake different roles within buying centres and these are set out in Figure 16.2.

Initiators start the whole process by requesting the purchase of an item. They may also assume other roles within the DMU or wider organization.

Users literally use the product once it has been acquired and they will also evaluate its performance. Users may not only initiate the purchase process but are sometimes involved in the specification process. Their role is continuous, although it may vary from the highly involved to the peripheral.

Influencers very often help set the technical specifications for the proposed purchase and assist the evaluation of alternative offerings by potential suppliers. These may be consultants hired to complete a particular project. This is quite common in high-technology purchases where the customer has little relevant expertise. (See Market Insight 16.4.)

Deciders are those who make purchasing decisions and they are the most difficult to identify. This is because they may not have formal authority to make

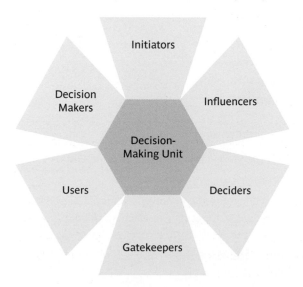

Figure 16.2
Membership of the decision-making unit

Source: Fill and Fill (2005). Reproduced with the kind permission of Chris Fill and Karen Fill.

a purchase decision, yet are sufficiently influential internally that their decision carries the most weight. In repeat buying activities the buyer may also be the decider. However, it is normal practice for a senior manager to authorize expenditure decisions involving sums over a certain financial limit.

Buyers or purchasing managers select suppliers and manage the process whereby the required products are procured. Buyers may not decide which product is to be purchased but they influence the framework within which the decision is made. They will formally undertake the process whereby products and services are purchased once a decision has been made to procure them. For example, they may be formal buyers and kick-start the purchase of a type of lubricant because the stock figures have fallen to a threshold level that indicates that current supplies will be exhausted within three weeks. They will therefore assume both an initiator's and a buyer's role.

Gatekeepers have the potential to control the type and flow of information to the organization and the members of the DMU. These gatekeepers may be assistants, technical personnel, secretaries, or telephone switchboard operators.

The size and form of the buying centre is not static. It can vary according to the complexity of the product being considered and the degree of risk each decision is perceived to carry for the organization. Different roles are required and adopted as the nature of the buying task changes with each new purchase situation (Bonoma, 1982). All of these roles might be subsumed within one individual for certain decisions. It is vital for seller organizations to identify members of the buying centre and to target and refine their messages to meet the needs of each member of the centre.

Membership of the DMU is far from fixed, and this sheer fluidity poses problems for selling organizations simply because it is not always possible to identify key members or shifts in policy or requirements. As Spekman and Gronhaug (1986) point out, the DMU is a 'vague construct that can reach across a number of different functional roles with any number of individuals participating or exerting influence at any one time'. It is worth noting, therefore, that within this context the behaviour of DMU members is also largely determined by the interpersonal relationships of the members of the centre.

RESEARCH INSIGHT 16.3

To take your learning further, you might wish to read this influential paper.

Johnson, W. J., and Lewin, J. E. (1996), 'Organizational buying behavior: toward an integrative framework', *Journal of Business Research*, 35 (January), 1–15.

Although written in 1996 this paper is important because it brings together twenty-five years of research into organizational buying behaviour. It includes critical contributions by the leading researchers including the work of Robinson, Faris, and Wind (1967), Webster and Wind (1972), and Sheth (1973). It concludes by developing a model of buying behaviour drawing on a number of constructs developed since these three leading models were published.

The Decision-Making Unit: Processes

Organizational buying decisions vary in terms of the nature of the product or service, the frequency and the relative value of purchases, their strategic impact (if any), and the type of relationship with suppliers. These, and many other factors, are potentially significant to individual buying organizations. However, there are three main types of buying situations. Referred to by Robinson, Faris, and Wind (1967) as **buyclasses** these are: **new task**, **modified rebuy**, and **straight rebuy**. These are summarized in Table 16.2.

Buyclasses

New Task

As the name implies, the organization is faced with a first-time buying situation. Risk is inevitably large at this point as there is little collective experience of the product/service or of the relevant suppliers. As a result of these factors there are normally a large number of decision participants. Each participant requires a lot of information and a relatively long period of time is needed for the information to be assimilated and a decision to be made.

Modified Rebuy

Having purchased a product, uncertainty is reduced but not eliminated, so the organization may request through their buyer(s) that certain modifications be made to future purchases. For example, adjustments to the specification of the

Buyclass	Degree of familiarity with the problem	Information requirements	Alternative solutions
New buy	The problem is fresh to the decision makers	A great deal of information is required	Alternative solutions are unknown, all are considered new
Modified rebuy	The requirement is not new but is different from previous situations	More information is required but past experience is of use	Buying decision needs new solutions
Rebuy	The problem is identical to previous experiences	Little or no information is required	Alternative solutions not sought or required

Source: Marketing Communications, 4th edn., Fill, C., Pearson Education Limited (2006). Reproduced with the kind permission of Pearson Education Limited.

Table 16.2
Main characteristics of the buyclasses

product, further negotiation on price levels, or perhaps an arrangement for alternative delivery patterns. Fewer people are involved in the decision-making process than in the new task situation.

Straight Rebuy

In this situation, the purchasing department reorders on a routine basis, very often working from an approved list of suppliers. These may be products that an organization consumes in order to keep operating (e.g. office stationery), or may be low-value materials used within the operational, value added part of the organization (e.g. the manufacturing processes). No other people are involved with the exercise until different suppliers attempt to change the environment in which the decision is made. For example, a new supplier may interrupt the procedure with a potentially better offer. This may stimulate the emergence of a modified rebuy situation.

Straight rebuy presents classic conditions for the use of automatic reordering systems. Costs can be reduced, managerial time redirected to other projects, and the relationship between buyer and seller embedded within a stronger framework. One possible difficulty is that both parties perceive the system to be a significant exit barrier should conditions change, and this may deter flexibility or restrict opportunities to develop the same or other relationships.

The use of electronic purchasing systems at the straight rebuy stage has enabled organizations to empower employees to make purchases although control still resides with purchasing managers. Employees can buy direct online, from a catalogue list of authorized suppliers. The benefits are that employees are more involved, the purchasing process is speeded up, costs are reduced, and purchasing managers can spend more time with other higher-priority activities.

Buyphases

Organizational buyer behaviour (OBB) consists of a series of sequential activities through which organizations proceed when making purchasing decisions. Robinson *et al.* (1967) referred to these as buying stages or **buyphases**. The following sequence of buyphases is particular to the new task situation just described. Many of these buyphases are ignored or compressed according to the complexity of the product and when either a modified rebuy and straight rebuy situation is encountered.

Need/Problem Recognition

The need/recognition phase is about the identification of a gap. This is the gap between the benefits an organization is experiencing now and the benefits it would like to have. For example, when a new product is to be produced there is an obvious gap between having the necessary materials and components and being out of stock and unable to build. The first decision therefore is about how to close this gap and there are two broad options: outsourcing the whole or parts of the production process, or building or making the objects oneself. The need has been recognized and the gap identified. The rest of this section is based on a build decision being taken.

Product Specification

As a result of identifying a problem and the size of the gap, influencers and users can determine the desired characteristics of the product needed to resolve the problem. This may take the form of either a general functional description or a much more detailed analysis and the creation of a detailed technical specification for a particular product. What sort of photocopier is required? What is it expected to achieve? How many documents should it copy per minute? Is a collator or tray required? This is an important part of the process, because if it is executed properly it will narrow the supplier search and save on the costs associated with evaluation prior to a final decision. The results of the functional and detailed specifications are often combined within a purchase order specification.

Supplier and Product Search

At this stage the buyer actively seeks suppliers who can supply the necessary product(s). There are two main issues at this point. First, will the product match the specification and the required performance standards? Second, will the potential supplier meet the other organizational requirements such as experience, reputation, accreditation, and credit rating? In most circumstances organizations review the market and their internal sources of information and arrive at a decision that is based on rational criteria.

Organizations work, wherever possible, to reduce uncertainty and risk. By working with others who are known, of whom the organization has direct experience, and who can be trusted, risk and uncertainty can be reduced substantially. This highlights another reason why many organizations prefer to operate within established networks that can provide support and advice when needed.

Evaluation of Proposals

Depending upon the complexity and value of the potential order(s), the proposal is a vital part of the process and should be prepared professionally. The proposals from the shortlisted organizations are reviewed in the context of two main criteria: the purchase order specification and the evaluation of the supplying organization. If the potential supplier is already a part of the network, little search and review time is needed. If the proposed supplier is not part of the network, a review may be necessary to establish whether it will be appropriate (in terms of price, delivery, and service) and whether there is the potential for a long-term relationship or whether this is a single purchase that is unlikely to be repeated.

Supplier Selection

The DMU will normally undertake a supplier analysis and use a variety of decision criteria, according to the particular type of item sought. This selection process takes place in the light of the comments made in the previous section. A further useful perspective is to view supplier organizations as a continuum, from reliance on a single source to the use of a wide variety of suppliers for the same product.

Jackson (1985) proposed that organizations might buy a product from a range of different suppliers, in other words maintain a range of multiple sources (a practice of many government departments). She labelled this approach 'always a share', as several suppliers are given the opportunity to share the business available to the buying centre. The major disadvantage is that this approach fails to drive cost as low as possible, as the discounts derived from volume sales are not achieved. The advantage to the buying centre is that a relatively small investment is required and little risk is entailed in following such a strategy.

At the other end of the continuum are organizations that only use a single source supplier. All purchases are made from the single source until circumstances change to such a degree that the buyer's needs are no longer being satisfied. Jackson referred to these organizations as 'lost for good', because once a relationship with a new organization has been developed they are lost for good to the original supplier. An increasing number of organizations are choosing to enter alliances with a limited number or even single source suppliers. The objective is to build a long-term relationship, to work together to build quality and help each other achieve their goals. Outsourcing manufacturing activities for non-core activities has increased, and this has moved the focus of communications from an internal to an external perspective.

Evaluation

The order is written against the selected supplier which is then monitored and evaluated against such diverse criteria as responsiveness to enquiries, modifications to the specification, and timing of delivery. When the product is delivered it may reach the stated specification but fail to satisfy the original need. In this case, the specification needs to be rewritten before any future orders are placed.

Developments in the environment can impact on organizational buyers and change both the nature of decisions and the way they are made. For example, the decision to purchase new plant and machinery requires consideration of the future cash flows generated by the capital item. Many people will be involved in the decision, and the time necessary for consultation may mean that other parts of the decision-making process are completed simultaneously.

RESEARCH INSIGHT 16.4

To take your learning further, you might wish to read this influential paper.

Jackson, B. (1985), 'Build customer relationships that last', *Harvard Business Review*, 63, 6, 120–8.

This paper discusses the outcomes of research into long-term customer–seller relationships. It considers the circumstances in which long- or short-term relationships are formed and the varying patterns of behaviour between the parties. Perhaps the paper is best known for the models 'Always a share' and 'Lost for good'. Quite readable.

Influencing the Influencers

In B2B marketing, the role of the influencer should not be overlooked

Photodisc

Just as decision makers are important in the B2B buying process, the role of influencers should not be overlooked. When faced with risk, decision makers buy from familiar companies and influencers. By sending appropriate information to known influencers, opportunities can arise for building credibility and providing a sound platform for a long-term relationship with individual influencers.

Influencers need not be employees or other people internal to an organization. For example;

- a company which sells printing and computer-imaging services: the purchase decision maker is the advertising manager at a cosmetics, food, or beverage company. The influencers may include the creative director at the customer's advertising agency.

- A computer services firm's decision makers are often information technology (IT) managers but the influencers are those that shape the IT managers' view of technology and products, i.e. third-party IT consultants.

- A sales training firm might identify the director or vice president of training and development as the key decision maker but the key influencer is the sales manager who knows how much the sales force could benefit from the marketer's training programmes and who conveys that perception to the VP of training.

- An office furniture manufacturer will see office managers as key decision makers but understand that specifiers such as office designers and architects influence the office manager's decision about furniture decisions.

Source: Adapted with kind permission from M. H. 'Mac' McIntosh, 'Target influencers to sway B2B sales', available at www.sales-lead-experts.com/tips/articles/influencers.cfm, accessed 27 August 2006.

1 What do you think is the main difference between an influencer and an opinion former?

2 Think of an industry or sector with which you are familiar and try to determine possible influencers.

Table 16.3
The buygrid
framework

Buyphases	Buyclasses		
	New task	**Modified rebuy**	**Straight rebuy**
Problem recognition	Yes	Possibly	No
General need description	Yes	Possibly	No
Product specification	Yes	Yes	Yes
Supplier search	Yes	Possibly	No
Supplier selection	Yes	Possibly	No
Order process specification	Yes	Possibly	No
Performance review	Yes	Yes	Yes

Buygrids

When the buyphases are linked to the buyclasses, a buygrid is determined. This grid is shown in Table 16.3.

The buygrid serves to illustrate the relationships between these two main elements. The buygrid is important because it highlights the need to focus on buying situations or contexts, rather than on products. Even though this approach was developed over forty years ago, it is still an important foundation for this topic.

According to the buyphase model, buyers make decisions rationally and sequentially, but this does not entirely match with practical experience. For example such a long and complex process is not evident in every buying situation and differs according to the kind of products and services bought, the experience and resources available to organizations, and the prevailing culture. In other words there are many variables that can influence organizational buying behaviour.

Influences Shaping Organizational Buying Behaviour

As suggested, there are a number of forces that shape the way in which organizations purchase products. Organizational buying behaviour is contextually bound. This means that buying behaviour is influenced by the immediate surroundings and the dynamics of the environment, which can of course change quickly and dynamically. Sellers should understand the nature of the changes and either anticipate or react in appropriate ways. Four main areas of influence can be

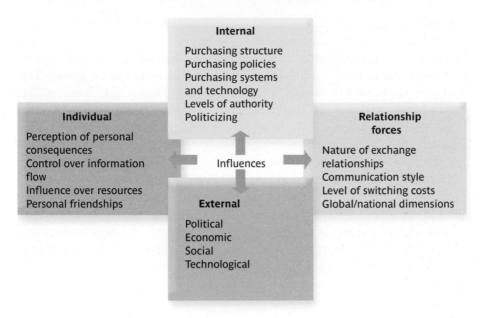

Internal
Purchasing structure
Purchasing policies
Purchasing systems
and technology
Levels of authority
Politicizing

Individual
Perception of personal
consequences
Control over information
flow
Influence over resources
Personal friendships

Influences

External
Political
Economic
Social
Technological

**Relationship
forces**
Nature of exchange
relationships
Communication style
Level of switching costs
Global/national dimensions

Figure 16.3
Major influences on
organizational buying
behaviour

Source: Fill and Fill (2005).
Reproduced with the kind
permission of Chris Fill and
Karen Fill.

identified: these are internal, external, individual, and relationship forces and are
depicted in Figure 16.3.

Internal Influences

An organization can decide to make all of its purchases from one central location and, in doing so, exert tighter control, reduce its costs, and provide greater
consistency. Alternatively it can decentralize its buying to geographically dispersed operating divisions or departments. This helps meet local needs, provides
flexibility, and promotes a sense of empowerment.

Other internal pressures spring from purchasing policies (for example, a move
towards lean manufacturing); changes to the levels of authority and responsibility for purchasing activities; enhancements to purchasing systems; and use of
technology. In addition organizational changes arising from restructuring, a change
in ownership (or merger and acquisition activities), or any politicizing can all influence purchasing activities.

External Influences

Using the PESTLE framework discussed in Chapter 2, it becomes possible to see
the many ways in which the external environment can affect purchasing. For
example, **economic** factors and overall confidence in the stock market can impact
on purchase behaviour. Movements in interest rates can influence confidence
and the volume of purchases made. For example, higher interest rates will lead to
mortgage rate increases, depress the amount of disposable income, and impact
building materials, financial services and labour market employment, travel,

and even the types of food purchased in supermarkets. **Social** changes can also affect organizational buying behaviour. The recent publicity about obesity and health has resulted in some food producers losing sales and market share because increasing numbers of the public are reducing their salt and fat intake. This impact is passed back to the suppliers of these food producers as they reformulate their product portfolios. **Technological** changes (systems, technology, and communications) have had a dramatic impact on organizational buying behaviour. The internet has changed the ways organizations communicate, do business, and interact with one another. Technological changes have given rise to new types of intermediaries and suppliers in the marketing channels which means that the nature and form of the supply chain has also changed and has required organizations to appraise and review their purchasing procedures.

One particular aspect of technological progress is e-procurement or electronic organizational purchasing. De Boer, Harink, and Heijboor (2002: 2) define e-procurement as 'using Internet technology in the purchasing process' and describe it as having six principal forms:

1 e-MRO—systems used to create and place purchase orders for maintenance, repair, and operating supplies, electronically.

2 web-based ERP—systems used to create and place purchase orders for replenishing products (goods and services).

3 e-sourcing—to identify/compare potential suppliers.

4 e-tendering—to request/receive information and prices.

5 e-reverse auctioning—to buy goods and services (see more on e-auctions below).

6 e-informing—to exchange information internally and externally.

The use of digital technology in the form of websites, e-auctions, e-collaboration activities, and web-based portals have led to a number of benefits for both suppliers and buyers. Suppliers who allow web-based access to an extranet and online catalogues can reduce printing and distribution costs and minimize delays, help introduce and market new products, and reduce the number of incoming telephone calls and associated problem-solving activities.

Buyers can access up-to-date product and price data, get quicker, more accurate cross-company comparisons, make fewer outgoing telephone calls, and make order processing faster and more accurate than it is when provided by manual systems. The disadvantages of e-procurement are largely felt by suppliers and include the heavy costs associated with information systems and technology (IST); downward pressure on prices; and the ease with which customers can compare and switch suppliers. Both suppliers and buyers may welcome or regret the decreased personal contact of sales visits, telephone calls, and face-to-face competitive tendering.

Individual Influences

Participation in the buying centre is influenced by individual perceptions of the personal consequences of their contribution to each of the stages in the buying process. The more that individuals think they will be blamed for a bad decision or praised for a good one, the greater their participation, influence, and visible DMU-related activity (McQuiston and Dickson, 1991). The nature and dispersal of power within the unit can influence the decisions that are made. Certain individuals are able to control the flow of information and/or the deployment of resources (Spekman and Gronhaug, 1986). This assertiveness can enable individuals to have undue influence within a DMU.

Individuals may develop personal friendships with suppliers and buyers. Such personal relationships overlay inter-organizational relationships and work perfectly smoothly but they can also give rise to conflict, for example when inter-organizational relationships change.

Relationship Influences

The importance of inter-organizational relationships is explored in depth in the following chapter (Chapter 17). However, the nature of the exchange relationships, the style of communications, and the overall atmosphere in which organizations share in a relationship, all influence buying decisions. So, if a relationship between organizations is trusting, mutually supportive, and based upon a longer-term perspective, then the behaviour of the buying centre may be seen to be cooperative and constructive. However, if the relationship is formal, regular, unsupportive, and based upon short-term convenience, then the purchase behaviour may be observed as courteous yet distant.

Organizations invest in time, people, assets, and systems when a relationship develops. Should the relationship fail to work satisfactorily then a cost is incurred in switching to another supplier. These so-called **switching costs** can have a severe impact on buying decisions. High switching costs can help organizations try to make the relationship work right from the beginning whereas low perceived switching costs can lead some organizations not to want to invest in relationships with suppliers.

Customer Portfolio Matrix

Most organizations have a mixture of different types of customers or accounts. Each account varies in terms of their frequency of purchase, the types of products and services bought, prices paid, delivery cycles, time taken to pay, the level of support required, and many other factors. These variables are a reflection of the strength of the relationship between buyer and seller and they impact on the profitability each account represents to the seller.

It makes sense, therefore, to categorize customers in order to determine their relative profitability. This in turn enables sellers to allocate resources to customers according to their potential to deliver profits in the future. One useful approach, called a customer (or account) portfolio matrix, brings together the potential attractiveness and the current strength of the relationship between seller and buyer. See Figure 16.4.

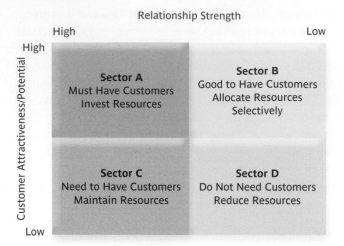

Figure 16.4
Customer portfolio
matrix

The relationship dimension incorporates the strengths from a customer's perspective relative to competitors. A strong relationship, for example, is indicative of two organizations working closely together whereas a weak relationship suggests that there is little interest in each other. Customer attractiveness refers to total revenue spend, average rate of growth, and the opportunities a buyer represents to the seller in terms of their profit potential. These calculations can be complicated and involve a measure of management judgement. For reasons of clarity, these scales are presented as either high or low, strong or weak. However, they should be considered as a continuum and accounts can be positioned on the matrix, not just in a sector but at a particular position within a sector. As a result strategies can be formulated to move accounts to different positions, which in turn necessitates the use of different resources.

'Must Have Customers' in Sector A enjoy a close business relationship and are also attractive in terms of their profit potential. Many of these customers are assigned key account status (see next section in this chapter) but all of them represent investment opportunities and resources should be allocated to develop them all.

'Good to Have Customers' in Sector B are essentially prospects because although they are highly attractive, their relationship with the seller is currently weak. In this situation marketing resources should be allocated on a selective basis, one that is proportional to the value that each prospect represents: high investment for good prospects and low for the others.

Relationships with customers in Sector C are strong but they do not offer strong potential. Therefore, these 'Need to Have Customers' are important because they provide steady background business that is marginally profitable, so resources need to be maintained. Where it is identified that some of these customers are supported by an relatively large sales team, significant cost savings can be achieved relatively quickly. There is little reason to invest in the 'Do Not Need Customers' in Sector D. Relationships with these customers are weak and as they are relatively unattractive in terms of profit potential, many of these customers should be 'let go' and released to competitors. They represent a net drain on

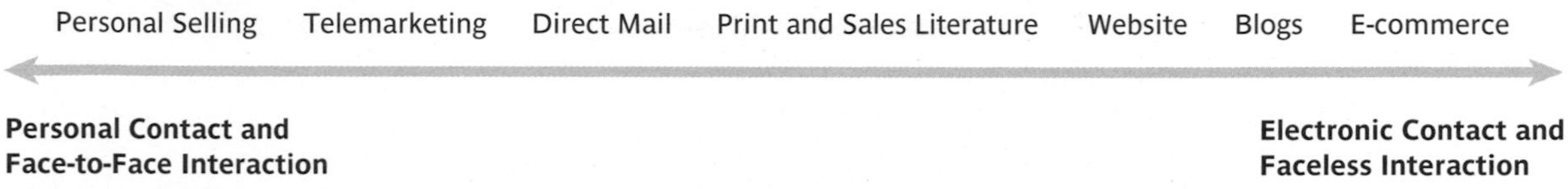

| Personal Selling | Telemarketing | Direct Mail | Print and Sales Literature | Website | Blogs | E-commerce |

<--->

**Personal Contact and
Face-to-Face Interaction**   **Electronic Contact and
                                                              Faceless Interaction**

Figure 16.5 A spectrum of multi-channel strategies

---

the selling organization. Therefore, customers in this sector should receive little support and freed-up resources be directed to customers in sectors A and B, as previously established.

One of the benefits of developing a **customer portfolio matrix** is that it becomes easier to allocate sales channels to customers. Multichannel marketing decisions are important and should be rooted within the customer portfolio matrix. A range of channel strategies that relate to the channel needs of business customers and to any end user target consumer segments can be identified (Payne and Frow, 2004). These can be considered to be part of a spectrum. At one end, channels can consist of a dedicated personal key account manager (highly personalized sales channel) and at the other end, the channel can be purely electronic with no personal contact at all. In the middle there will be a range of different combinations of personal and electronic channels. See Figure 16.5.

In reality most business customers will use a mixture of online and offline resources wherever possible and according to their specific needs. It is important, therefore, for selling organizations to identify and allocate the most appropriate set of channels for their customers, based on the business potential each customer represents. These channels can be changed as the intensity of a customer relationship and their attractiveness develops over time.

Key Account Management (KAM)

It should be clear from the previous section that not all customers represent the same potential and profitability. However, it is quite common for a small number of customers to contribute to a disproportionately large part of an organization's income and profitability. As a result, these organizations often become essential to the firm's survival. As discussed in Chapter 12, the term 'key accounts' has become the established term to refer to those customers who are considered to be strategically important. A key account might offer the supply side company opportunities to learn about new markets or types of customers. It might provide access to new and valuable resources, offer involvement with other key organizations, or just be symbolically valuable in terms of influence, power, and stature. Size alone is not important for key account status. (See Market Insight 16.5.)

Establishing key accounts and the supporting infrastructure represents a significant investment for organizations and an opportunity cost. So, why have so many organizations established and formalized their key account strategies? There are many reasons, some particular to each organization; however, the main ones relate to changes in the competitive environment and to changes in industry structure.

Changes in the Competitive Environment

In an increasingly complex and competitive environment, where product life-cycles appear to be getting shorter, and differentiation difficult to sustain, the need to find new ways of enhancing business performance has intensified. One of the ways in which this can be achieved is to provide a range of services that are tailored to the needs of each customer. Many types of service can be custom-ized, for example customized training, advantageous financial arrangements, extranets, customer-driven delivery routes and timings, product support, and advice facilities. However, it is through the provision of added value services that relationships are often developed and maintained. Establishing key accounts is a natural extension of providing particular services for key customers. Not only does this enhance the profile of these customers, both internally and externally, but it also helps to focus resources on particular customers and their individual needs.

Changes in Industry Structure

Many organizations have centralized their purchasing activities, a move driven by two main factors. First, the amount of industry consolidation, a process by which a few organizations grow larger by merging or acquiring their competitors, so that the industry is concentrated around a small number of large organizations. Industry consolidation has increased substantially in the past decade. Second, in industries where consolidation has not been significant, many organizations have moved towards centralizing their purchasing departments, processes, and functions as a means of achieving cost savings, improving effectiveness and efficiencies, and in doing so improving profits.

The result of both of these actions is that there are a smaller number of pur-chasing units responsible for a larger proportion of business. For business mar-keters and suppliers generally, these trends towards industrial concentration and purchasing centralization mean that competition is increased and marketing strategies need to be much more customer specific. Key account programmes are used with the deliberate intention of building relationships, often achieved by influencing levels of trust and commitment in order to generate more business. However, in relationships between manufacturers and retailers (for example the grocery business), the presence of a key account relationship does not appear to have any significant benefit on the amount of resources allocated to the supplier's products (Verbeke, Bagozzi, and Farris, 2006).

Collaborative Packaging

Sonoco, a packaging supplier, worked hard with its customer Lance, a snack food maker, to determine the ideal packaging for its product lines. One improvement involved the use of flexographic printed packaging film in Lance's single and multiserving Home Pack snacks brands. This collaboration drastically reduced Lance's packaging costs, and the company made Sonoco its 'Supplier of the Year'. In an industry where most players were growing slowly or shrinking, Sonoco grew 7% and margins grew 18% over three years.

Collaboration between organizations appears to work better if senior management leads and focuses on key customer relationships. For example:

- At Bosch, each of the top eleven executives is linked to a major OEM customer.

- Senior management at Alcoa play an active account management role and have created the role of chief customer officer, a position with oversight of all its business units.

- IBM have a separate group, led by a senior executive, that focuses on significant customers.

- When Jeff Immelt was at GE Plastics, he made a point of visiting one major customer each week. Immelt's involvement sent a signal to customers that they mattered and to internal teams that collaborative efforts were important. It also kept him closely connected with the day-to-day challenges of sales teams and helped remove any barriers to their progress.

Source: Hancock, John, and Wojcik (2005).

1 In addition to packaging, think of three different areas in which organizations might collaborate.

2 Discuss the view that KAM is just a supplier's way of retaining their most profitable customers.

Key Account Relationship Cycles

Key accounts do not just appear and flourish, they are the result of careful management, nurturing, and time. Key accounts represent a particular strength of relationship and, as with good wine, need time to develop to reach full potential. Consequently, each key account will, at any one moment in time, be at a particular stage of relationship development (Millman and Wilson, 1995). Key accounts can be plotted through various stages of a development cycle. One such cycle is shown in Table 16.4.

The time between stages is not fixed and varies according to the nature and circumstances of the parties involved. The stages can be negotiated quickly in some cases, or may become protracted. The titles to each of the stages reflect the relationship status of both parties rather than of the selling company (e.g. prospective) or buying company (e.g. preferred supplier).

Table 16.4

KAM development
stages

Development stages within a cycle	Explanation
Exploratory	Suppliers identify and isolate those customer accounts that have key account potential.
Basic	In this transactional period exchanges are used by both parties to test each other as potential long-term partners.
Cooperative	An increasing number of people from both parties become involved in the relationship.
Interdependent	Mutual recognition of each other's importance. Very often single supplier status is conferred.
Integrated	Both parties share sensitive information and undertake joint problem solving. The relationship is regarded as a single entity.
Disintegrated	The termination or readjustment of the relationship can occur at any time.

Managing Key Accounts

Key account managers provide the main link between their employer and their key account customers. They provide a route through which information flows, preferably in both directions. They must be capable of dealing with organizations where buying decisions can be both protracted and delayed (Sharma, 1997) and quick and demanding. However, key account managers do not operate alone and are not the sole point of contact between organizations. Normally there are a number of levels of interaction between the two organizations, to the extent that there could be 'an entire team dedicated to providing services and support to the key account' (Ojasalo, 2001: 109). Therefore, key account managers assume responsibility for all points of contact within the customer organization.

Key account managers have an important role and it is crucial to select the right individual (Napolitano, 1997) with the right array of skills. This person should possess particularly strong interpersonal and relationship skills and be capable of managing larger, significant, and often complex customers (Abratt and Kelly, 2002).

The degree of impact a particular product has on a customer's business will have a significant influence on the level of attention given by the buyer to the supplier's programme (Pardo, 1997). Further, the level to which an organization uses centralized buying procedures will also impact on the effectiveness of a KAM programme. Unsurprisingly, key account sales behaviours cannot be the same as those used in field sales roles. So, as the majority of key account

To take your learning further, you might wish to read this influential paper.

Millman, T., and Wilson, K. (1995), 'From key account selling to key account management', *Journal of Marketing Practice: Applied Marketing Science*, 1, 1, 9–21.

This paper is interesting because it was one of the first to focus attention on key account management (KAM) systems by taking into consideration the issues faced by buyers, when developing buyer–seller relationships. Previous research had adopted a sellers only perspective. The authors examine the nature of KAM in industrial markets structured around several strategic issues.

managers are drawn internally from the sales force (Hannah, 1998, cited by Abratt and Kelly, 2002), it is necessary to ensure that they have the correct skills mix, or are trained appropriately. Abratt and Kelly found six factors that were of particular importance when establishing a KAM programme. These were the 'suitability of the key account manager, knowledge and understanding of the key account customer's business, commitment to the KAM partnership, delivering value, the importance of trust and the proper implementation and understanding of the KAM concept'.

In addition to the interpersonal relationships that exist between the customer's contact person and the supplier's key account manager, there are also inter-organizational relationships that may concern system and policy issues. These will vary in strength and some may not be compatible with the tasks facing the key account manager (Benedapudi and Leone, 2002).

A Comparison of B2B and B2C Buying Characteristics

So far in this chapter, we have considered various characteristics of the business market. These include the different types of products and services, the variety of customers, the processes used to buy business products and services, and the key account management systems used by suppliers to reach and develop relationships with business customers. What do these factors contribute to our understanding of B2B marketing?

Well, overall, the marketing of goods and services between organizations is not the same as consumer goods marketing and, because there are a number of fundamentally different characteristics, diverse marketing strategies and operations need to be implemented to meet the needs of business customers.

Differences

Business marketing can be distinguished from consumer marketing by two main ideas: first the intended customer, which is an organization not an individual; secondly, the intended use of the product, which is to support organizational objectives. As a result, different marketing programmes are required to reach and influence organizational buyers as opposed to consumers.

In the business sector, organizations buy a range of products and services to either make new products or enable production processes to operate successfully. Defined processes and procedures are used to buy products and services, and the decisions attached to securing the necessary materials, unlike consumer-based decisions, very often involve a large number of people.

Many of the key differences between consumer and business marketing are rooted in the principal characteristics associated with the respective buying behaviours. These are set out in Table 16.5.

Table 16.5

A comparison of buying characteristics in organizational and consumer markets

	Consumer buying characteristics	Organizational buying characteristics
No. of buyers	Many	Few
Purchase initiation	Self	Others
Evaluative criteria	Social, ego and level of utility	Price, value, and level of utility
Information search	Normally short	Normally long
Range of suppliers used	Small number of suppliers considered	Can be extensive
Importance of supplier shoice	Normally limited	Can be critical
Size of orders	Small	Large
Frequency of orders	Light	High
Value of orders placed	Light	Heavy
Complexity of decision making	Light to moderate	Moderate to high
Range of information inputs	Moderate	Moderate to high

Source: Fill and Fill (2005). Used with permission.

One of the main characteristics is that there are far fewer buyers in organizational markets than in consumer markets. Even though there may be several people associated with a buying decision in an organization, the overall number of people involved in buying packaging products or road construction equipment (for example) is very small compared with the millions of people that might potentially buy a chocolate bar.

The financial value of organizational purchase orders is invariably larger and the frequency with which they are placed is much lower. It is quite common for agreements to be made between organizations for the supply of materials over a number of years. Similarly, depending upon the complexity of the product (for example, photocopying paper or a one-off satellite), the negotiation process may also take a long time.

Although there are differences, many of the characteristics associated with consumer decision-making processes can still be observed in the organizational context. However, organizational buyers make decisions that ultimately contribute to the achievement of corporate objectives. To make the necessary decisions, a high volume of pertinent information is often required. This information needs to be relatively detailed and is normally presented in a rational and logical style. The

MARKET INSIGHT 16.6

Airways to Sales Heaven

LMA manufacture and distribute a range of surgical airways used by anaesthetists. A campaign was developed to drive attention to a new product that was still in production and to raise the profile of the organization prior to a stock market flotation.

The development of the new product involved a range of specialist engineers as well as various anaesthetists and took several years to bring to the market. The premium prices reflected the investment, the product attributes, and the benefits brought to users, and of course patients.

As in many other industries, the users were not the buyers so it was important that communication with the users was sufficiently compelling so that users influenced buyers to purchase the product when it was released. A direct mail piece was sent to a list of customers, covering 22 countries, taken from various databases and suitably cleaned. This was followed by a phone call 48 hours later. The mailer was designed to not only attract the attention of anaesthetists but also to pass through internal postal systems and not fall out of pigeon holes. Prospects were offered the opportunity to meet an LMA representative and of the 912 packs sent out 76% requested a meeting. These leads were passed to the local distributors and as a result all the available stock was sold out. What really surprised LMA was that the sell-out was achieved without any price negotiation.

Source: Adapted from www.b2bmarketingawards.co.uk.

1　Find out how lists from databases can be cleaned.

2　What role did 'place' have in LMA's marketing mix?

3　How do you think a B2B marketing mix differs from its B2C counterpart?

needs of the buyers are many and complex, and some may be personal. Goals, such as promotion and career advancement within the organization, coupled with ego and employee satisfaction, combine to make organizational buying an important task. It is one that requires professional training and the development of expertise if the role is to be performed optimally. (See Market Insight 16.6.)

Similarities

Although there are many differences between the B2C and B2B sectors, there are also an increasing number of areas where the two converge. Two of the most important similarities emerge through market orientation, regardless of the sector in which an organization operates.

Both have a customer orientation and work backwards from an understanding of customer needs. Both need the ability to gather, process, and use information about customers and competitors in order to achieve their objectives.

In addition both types of supplier desire positive relationships with their customers. It does not matter whether they are consumers or organizations, what is wanted is that the relationship is continued for mutual benefit.

The fundamental notion that organizational decision making is basically rational in nature and that consumer decision making is more unstructured and emotionally driven is questionable. For example, many personal purchases are of such technical complexity (e.g. financial services) that consumers need to adopt a more rational, factual-based approach to their buying. Some business-oriented decisions are made on the basis of social contacts, consisting mainly of family and friendship networks.

Wilson (2000) explores some of these issues of similarity and observes that consumers use a wide range of inputs from other people and not just those in the immediate family environment when making product-related purchase decisions. This is similar to group-buying dynamics associated with the DMU. He also suggests that the rationality normally associated with organizational decision making is misplaced, because in some circumstances the protracted nature of the process is more a reflection of organizational culture and the need to follow bureaucratic procedures and to show due diligence. In addition, issues concerning established behaviour patterns, difficulties and reluctance to break with traditional purchasing practices, intra- and inter-organizational politics and relationships, and the costs associated with supplier switching all contribute to a more interpretative understanding of organizational decision making. Further support for this view is given by Mason and Gray (1999) who refer to the characteristics of decision making in the air travel market and note some strong similarities between consumers and business passengers.

It is also interesting to observe the similarities between the extended problem-solving, limited problem-solving, and routinized response behaviour phases of consumer buying and the new task, modified rebuy, and rebuy states associated with organizational buying. There is a close match between the two in terms of the purpose, approach, and content. Risk and involvement are relevant to both categories and, although the background to both may vary, the principles used to manage the various phases and conditions are essentially the same, just deployed in different ways.

One further area of similarity concerns branding. In consumer markets, branding is common practice and for a long time was not thought to be of direct concern to business marketers. Now, however, B2B organizations use a variety of branding approaches. Ingredient branding (Intel Inside and Lycra mentioned earlier), cause-related branding, cooperative advertising, dual branding, in addition to joint advertising and sales promotion activities, are all used to raise the perceived value (Bengtsson and Servais, 2005). Traditionally, trucking companies have not paid much attention to the way they present themselves. When Eddie Stobart recognized this in the UK trucking market he used it as a branding opportunity. In addition to the distinctive livery he ensured his trucks were always clean, that his drivers wore the company's green shirt and tie, and that his operation ran efficiently and always on time. As a result the Eddie Stobart brand stands out and helps justify a substantial price premium (Hague, 2006).

It is important to recognize that although there are some substantial differences between consumer and business marketing there are also several areas where there are distinct similarities. This suggests that the principles of marketing apply equally to the consumer and business markets and that when planning and implementing marketing programmes, particular care should be given to understanding the nature and characteristics of the buying processes and procedures of the target market.

Eddie Stobart takes branding particularly seriously

Eddie Stobart Ltd

Electrical Exchanges

Philips, Hotpoint, and Samsung are manufacturers of electrical equipment such as toasters and kettles. They do not sell their products to individual consumers because consumers are relatively infrequent buyers of these products and when they do buy from a retailer, online or offline, it is normally a one-off or market exchange.

Electrical equipment manufacturers normally develop collaborative exchanges with their key distributors and retailers. These organizations tend to buy large quantities of kettles on a regular basis, and sell them through their various offline (shops and catalogues) and online retail channels. Communications and interaction between the parties tend to be continuous and designed to support the relationship over the longer term.

Electrical equipment manufacturers sell batches of each type of product to their appointed retailers at pre-agreed dates. However, it would be incorrect to assume that all of these exchanges are collaborative. Some are transactional exchanges where the goal of the manufacturer is to 'turn' stock and their decisions are not always based on the financial or marketing situation facing each of their distributors or retailers. The element of collaboration and mutual self-help characteristic of collaborative exchanges may be missing within these relationships.

1 How might electrical goods manufacturers develop more collaborative relationships with all of their retailers? Should they even try to do so?

2 Name one electrical manufacturer you consider to be successful.

3 How might environmental issues be part of a manufacturer's selection of parts and items for their kettles?

partnership and mutual support. Trust and commitment underpin these relationships and these variables become increasingly important as stronger relational exchanges become established. The prime goal therefore shifts from initial attraction to retention and to mutual understanding of each other's needs. (See Market Insight 17.2 above.)

To take your learning further, you might wish to read this influential paper.

Day, G. (2000), 'Managing market relationships', *Journal of the Academy of Marketing Science*, 28, 1 (Winter), 24–30.

Day considers that the basis of competitive advantage rests with an organization's ability to create and maintain relationships with their most valuable customers. Part of this advantage rests with the value generated and he presents a continuum of exchanges to express the possible range of values.

Nature and Characteristics of Relationship Marketing

The continuum of value exchanges provides a visual expression of the diversity of organizational transactions, from the one-off, short-term exchange to those that are long term and based upon collaboration and partnership.

Founding ideas about industrial (now termed business) marketing were based on market exchanges between organizations, where there was no prior history of exchange and no future exchanges expected. These paired organizations were considered to enter into transactions where products were the main focus and price was the key mechanism to exchange completion. Organizations were perceived to be adversarial and competition was paramount. These undertakings are referred to as market (or discrete) exchanges and often termed 'transactional marketing'.

In contrast, relationship marketing is based on the principles that there is a history of exchanges and an expectation that there will be exchanges in the future. Furthermore, the perspective is on the long term, envisioning a form of loyalty or continued attachment by the buyer to the seller. Price as the key controlling mechanism is replaced by customer service and quality of interaction between the two organizations. The exchange is termed collaborative because the focus is upon both organizations seeking to achieve their goals in a mutually rewarding way and not at the expense of one another. See Table 17.1 for a more comprehensive list of fundamental differences between transactional and collaborative exchange-based marketing.

Although market exchanges focus on products and prices, there is still a relational component, if only because interaction requires a basic relationship between

Attribute	Market exchange	Collaborative exchange
Length of relationship	Short term Abrupt end	Long term A continuous process
Relational expectations	Conflicts of goals Immediate payment No future problems (there is no future)	Conflicts of interest Deferred payment Future problems expected to be overcome by joint commitment
Communication	Low frequency of communication Formal communication predominates	Frequent communication Informal communication predominates
Cooperation	No joint cooperation	Joint cooperative projects
Responsibilities	Distinct responsibilities Defined obligations	Shared responsibilities Shared obligations

Table 17.1
Characteristics of market and collaborative exchanges

both buyer and seller begin to understand each other's requirements and goals in greater detail. It is also during this stage that the seller develops a better understanding of the wider array of stakeholder relationships that the buyer interacts with. This can have a significant influence on the nature of the supplier's relationship with the buyer, often indicating the depth to which the relationship will aspire.

Customer Retention

The retention phase is characterized by greater relationship stability and certainty. As a result the relationship becomes stabilized, displaying greater levels of trust and commitment between the partners. This in turn allows for increased cross-buying and product experimentation, joint projects, and product development. More commonly, suppliers provide customer loyalty schemes in order to increase the volume and value of products and services bought, and to lock in their customers by creating relationship exit barriers. Customer loyalty schemes are explored in more detail later in this chapter.

Customer Decline

In many cases relationships become destabilized and higher levels of uncertainty emerge. This might occur after a long period of relationship stability or after a short period immediately after acquisition. The reasons for this are many and varied and range from purchasing agreements and loyalty programmes that are not sufficiently attractive to continue to lock in the customer to changes in the wider environment such as legislative, climatic, or economic developments. As a result, this period is concerned with the demise of the relationship and termination becomes a serious problem or episode for the parties to manage. The likely process is that the buying organization decides to reduce its reliance on the seller and either notifies them formally or begins to reduce the frequency and duration of contact and moves business to other, competitive organizations. Customer recovery strategies are required at the first sign that the relationship is waning. These are examined later.

Loyalty, Retention, and Customer Satisfaction

The customer relationship cycle implies that customers who keep coming back to buy from a particular supplier are loyal. One problem with this suggestion is that what is understood to be 'loyalty' may actually be nothing more than pure convenience. A person who regularly attends the same supermarket is not necessarily consciously loyal to the supermarket brand but happy with the convenience of the location and the overall quality and value of the products and

Partner: someone who has the relationship of a partner with you

Advocate: someone who actively recommends you to others, who does your marketing for you

Supporter: someone who likes your organisation, but only supports you passively

Client: someone who has done business with you on a repeat basis but may be negative, or at best neutral, towards your organisation

Purchaser: someone who has done business just once with your organisation

Prospect: someone whom you believe may be persuaded to do business with you

Figure 17.7
The relationship marketing ladder of loyalty

Source: Christopher, Payne, and Ballantyne (2002). Reprinted from *Relationship Marketing Creating Stakeholder Value*, p 48 (2002) with permission from Elsevier.

services offered. Loyalty might be better appreciated in the context of a football supporter who travels to all away and home fixtures (regardless of domestic commitments), is a member of the club, buys into the merchandise and credit card offerings, and defends their club, even when they are relegated at the end of the season.

Various writers have used a ladder to depict ascending levels of loyalty. One of the better known is entitled the relationship marketing ladder of loyalty (Christopher, Payne, and Ballantyne, 2002) and is shown in Figure 17.7.

Following an initial transaction, a prospect becomes a purchaser. These purchasers or customers are designated as clients following several completed transactions but are still ambivalent towards the selling organization. Customers who enter into regular purchases may still be passive about the organization but are said to be supporters. Advocates are an important group because not only do they support an organization and/or its products but they actively recommend it to others through positive word-of-mouth communications. At the top of this ladder are partners. Their key characteristic is the complete trust and support for an organization. This strength of feeling is reciprocated by the organization and in doing so provides partnership status. Partnership is the essence of relational exchanges and inter-organizational collaboration.

The simplicity of the loyalty ladder concept illustrates the important point that customers represent different values to other organizations. That perceived value (or worth) may or may not be reciprocated, thus establishing the basis for a variety and complexity of different relationships.

This cycle of customer attraction (acquisition), development, retention, and eventual decline represents a major difference from the 4Ps approach. The relationship approach is customer centred and therefore complements marketing values more effectively than the 4Ps model. However, although the focus has moved from product and prices to relationships, questions remain about whose relationship it is that is being managed. Early interpretations of relationship marketing focused on suppliers' attempts to develop relationships with customers. In other words they were 'customer relationships' and this meant there was an imbalance or one-sidedness within the relationship. Today relationship marketing recognizes the need for balanced customer–supplier relationships in which participants share the same level of interest, goodwill, and commitment towards each other.

Types and Levels of Loyalty

The concept of loyalty has attracted much research attention if only because of the recent and current popularity of this approach. Table 17.2 represents some of the more general types of loyalty that can be observed.

These hierarchical schemes suggest that consumers are capable of varying degrees of loyalty. This type of categorization has been questioned by a number of researchers. Fournier and Yao (1997) doubt the validity of such approaches and Baldinger and Rubinson (1996) support the idea that consumers work within an evoked set and switch between brands. This view is supported on the grounds that many consumers display elements of curiosity in their purchase habits, enjoy variety, and are happy to switch brands as a result of marketing communication activities and product experience.

Loyalty at one level can be seen to be about increasing sales volume, that is, fostering loyal purchase behaviour. High levels of repeat purchase, however, are not necessarily an adequate measure of loyalty, as there may be a number of situational factors determining purchase behaviour, such as brand availability (Dick and Basu, 1994). At whichever level of loyalty, customer retention is paramount and neither behavioural nor attitudinal measures alone are adequate indicators of true loyalty. O'Malley (1998) suggests that a combination of the two is of greater use and that the twin parameters of relative attitudes (to alternatives) and patronage

Table 17.2
Types of loyalty

Type of loyalty	Explanation
Emotional loyalty	This is a true form of loyalty and is driven by personal identification with real or perceived values and benefits.
Price loyalty	This type of loyalty is driven by rational economic behaviour and the main motivations are cautious management of money or financial necessity.
Incentivized loyalty	This refers to promiscuous buyers: those with no one favourite brand who demonstrate through repeat experience the value of becoming loyal.
Monopoly loyalty	This class of loyalty arises where a consumer has no purchase choice owing to a national monopoly. This, therefore, is not a true form of loyalty.

behaviour (the recency, frequency, and monetary model), as suggested by Dick and Basu, offer more accurate indicators of loyalty when used together.

Loyalty and Retention Programmes

The number of loyalty programmes offered by organizations has grown significantly in recent years. These range from supermarket-based points schemes and frequent flyer reward programmes offered by airlines to attract and retain high-margin business customers to discounts and loyalty bonus formats designed to retain contract-based customers such as those associated with mobile phones and financial services, for example, car insurance. One of the more visible schemes has been the Clubcard offered by Tesco, which has been partly responsible for Tesco dominating the UK grocery market. The response of its nearest rival Sainsbury's, at the time, was to publicly reject loyalty cards, but some 18 months later it launched its Reward Card and then subsequently joined the group scheme Nectar.

The increasing use of loyalty schemes has been propelled by technological developments, one of which was the swipe card. Users are rewarded with points each time a purchase is made. This is referred to as a 'points accrual programme', whereby loyal users are able to build up the necessary points, which are stored (often) on a card, and 'cashed in' at a later date for gifts or merchandise. The benefit for the company supporting the scheme is that the promised rewards motivate customers to accrue more points and in doing so increase their switching costs, effectively locking them into the loyalty programme and preventing them from moving to a competitor brand. See Market Insight 17.5 for an example of how the Nectar loyalty programme has been developed to help reward customers.

Swipe cards, although still prevalent, have been superseded by smart cards. These cards contain a small microprocessor and can record massive amounts of information, which is updated each time a purchase is made. Smart cards can be used to update database records in order to provide improved product availability and stocking plus improved marketing communications messages and timely offers and incentives. They are also used as a payment facility for use in transportation systems, such as the Octopus Card in Hong Kong, the Easyrider card in Nottingham, and the Tcard in Sydney.

The potential number of applications for smart cards is remarkable. However, just like swipe cards, the targeting of specific groups of buyers can be expected to become more precise and efficient, and it is also easier to track and target individuals for future promotional activities.

These schemes can be important not only because they help retain customers but also because they allow for the collection of up-to-date customer information. This data can then be used to target marketing communication campaigns and to make product purchase decisions, volumes, and scheduling, in order to make savings in the supply chain.

There has been a proliferation of loyalty cards, reflecting the increased emphasis upon keeping customers rather than constantly finding new ones, and there is some evidence that sales lift by about 2–3 per cent when a loyalty scheme is launched. Yet there is little evidence to support the notion that sales promotions

Nectar Brings Sweet Rewards

Loyalty Management UK, the company behind the air miles scheme, operates the UK's largest customer loyalty programme, the Nectar programme.

Nectar card

Nectar's logo

Nectar points are collected when purchases are made at designated retailers. Customers store these points on individual cards and can redeem them to achieve a range of rewards. These range from high street savings, treats, and gifts through to leisure and travel rewards. Major rewards suppliers include Sainsbury's (groceries), Argos (general merchandise), Odeon (cinemas), Blockbuster (video rental), Thomson (money off holidays), ebookers (flights), CDWOW (CDs, DVDs, and games), and Tussauds (theme parks).

In January 2005 Nectar for Business was launched, enabling businesses to collect points associated with their business purchases. These ranged from stationery and catering supplies to van hire and decorators' materials.

The Nectar scheme was extended again in October 2005 with the launch of Nectar eStores—an online shopping site with over 60 online retailers including Ebay, Amazon, CDWOW, and Game. Collectors earn Nectar points when making purchases at any of the eStores. The success and extension of this reward scheme from consumer to business and then into eStores indicates that this form of reward scheme is of value to a wide variety of customers across different contexts.

Sources: www.loyalty.co.uk/about_lmuk.html; www.nectar.co.uk.

1 Do you think reward schemes are a suitable measure of customer loyalty? If not why not?

2 Name a loyalty scheme you are aware of or even a member of. What do you think they know about you?

3 Think about the reasons why you choose to visit a particular nightclub or bar. Are these because you feel loyalty or are there other reasons for your patronage?

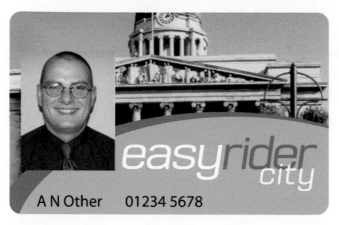

Easyrider

The Easyrider card in
Nottingham, UK

Easyrider

Octopus Card

The Octopus Card in
Hong Kong

Octopus Card

are capable of encouraging loyalty. Schemes do enable organizations to monitor and manage stock, use direct marketing to cross and up-sell customers, and manage their portfolio in order to increase a customer's spending. However, questions still exist about whether 'loyalty' is developed by encouraging buyers to make repeat purchases or whether these schemes are merely sales promotion techniques that encourage short-term retention purchasing patterns.

There has been a proliferation of loyalty programmes to the extent that Capizzi, Ferguson, and Cuthbertson (2004) suggest that the market is mature. They also argue that five clear trends within the loyalty market can be identified. These are set out in Table 17.3 on p 697.

These trends suggest that successful sales promotions schemes will be those that enable members to perceive significant value linked to their continued association with a scheme. (See Market Insight 17.6.) That value will be driven by schemes run by groups of complementary brands, which use technology to understand customer dynamics and communications that complement their preferred values. The medium-term goal might be that these schemes should reflect customers' different relationship needs and recognize the different loyalty levels desired by different people.

Bagging Points at Tesco

In an attempt to address a number of environmental issues, Tesco announced a ten-point plan in May 2006. One of these concerned their approach to the growing litter problem associated with the 17 billion plastic bags used by UK consumers each year (Tran, 2006).

Tesco's goal is to cut the number of bags it hands out by 25% over two years. This is equal to 1bn bags a year. To achieve this Tesco offers its 13 million Clubcard holders points for every bag they don't take away from their stores. Points are awarded to shoppers who reuse old plastic bags or bring other bags into store. Checkout staff are empowered to use their discretion in deciding how many Clubcard points they give out. In line with the French government's policy, which has banned supermarkets from using plastic bags, Tesco have introduced biodegradable bags.

Tesco Clubcard holders are offered points if they use fewer bags when they shop

Tesco

Ikea, which gave away 32 m bags in 2005, now charges 10p for plastic bags and is hoping to more than halve that number.

Sources: Various.

1 Do you think that using environmental issues to retain customers is a good idea?

2 Name one organization you consider to have been successful using environmental issues to retain customers.

3 Would it be better if supermarkets were forced by government to charge for plastic bags or would it be better not even to provide them?

Managing Relationships

The next sections of this chapter concern issues associated with the management of relationships. The first section considers ideas about trust and commitment and is followed by related issues concerning customer satisfaction. The next section

Table 17.3
Five loyalty trends

Trend	Explanation
Ubiquity	The proliferation of loyalty programmes in most mature markets. Many members have little interest in them other than the functionality of points collection.
Coalition	Schemes run by a number of different organizations in order to share costs, information, and branding (e.g. Nectar) appear to be the dominant structure industry model.
Imagination	Opportunities to exploit technologies and niche markets will depend on creativity and imagination in order to get customer data to feed into the loyalty system.
Wow	To overcome consumer lethargy and boredom with loyalty schemes, many rewards in future will be experiential, emotional, and unique in an attempt to appeal to lifestage and aspirational lifestyle goals—wow them.
Analysis	To be competitive the use of customer data analytics and business intelligence is becoming critical, if only to feed CRM programmes. Collect and analyse customer information effectively.

Source: Adapted from Capizzi, Ferguson, and Cuthbertson (2004).

deals with ideas about power and the way in which conflict can arise between organizations. The final section deals with ways in which these important relationships can be managed and in particular considers customer service systems and processes such as CRM and customer recovery issues.

Trust, Commitment, and Satisfaction

Many writers contend that one of the crucial factors associated with the development and maintenance of inter-organizational relationships is trust (Morgan and Hunt, 1994; Doney and Cannon, 1997). However, these concepts, although important, are difficult to define and many authors fail to specify clearly what they mean when using them (Cousins and Stanwix, 2001). A review of the literature indicates that trust is an element associated with personal, intra-organizational, and inter-organizational relationships, and is necessary for their continuation. As Gambetta (1988) argues, trust is a means of reducing uncertainty in order that effective relationships can develop.

Cousins and Stanwix also suggest that, although trust is a term used to explain how relationships work, often it actually refers to ideas concerning risk, power, and dependency, and these propositions are used interchangeably. From their research of vehicle manufacturers, it emerges that B2B relationships are about the creation of mutual business advantage and the degree of confidence that one organization has in another.

Trust is based on two main dimensions; credibility and benevolence. Credibility concerns the extent to which one party believes (is confident) that another organization will undertake and complete its agreed roles and tasks. Benevolence is concerned with goodwill, that the other party will not act opportunistically, even if the conditions for exploitation should arise (Pavlou, 2002). In other words, trust involves judgements about reliability and integrity and is concerned with the degree of confidence that one party to a relationship has that another will fulfil their obligations and responsibilities.

The presence of trust in a relationship is important because it reduces both the threat of opportunism and the possibility of conflict, which in turn increases the probability of buyer satisfaction. It has been claimed that the three major outcomes from the development of relationship trust are satisfaction, reduced **perceived risk**, and continuity (Pavlou, 2002).

- Perceived risk is concerned with the expectation of loss and is therefore tied closely with organizational performance.

- Trust that a seller will not take advantage of the imbalance of information between buyer and seller effectively reduces risk.

- Continuity is related to business volumes, necessary in online B2B marketplaces, and the development of both on- and offline enduring relationships. Trust is associated with continuity and when present is therefore indicative of long-term relationships.

Trust within a consumer context is important as it can reduce uncertainty. For example, brands are an important means of instilling trust mainly because they are a means of condensing and conveying information. Strong brands provide sufficient information for consumers to make calculated purchase decisions in the absence of full knowledge. In a sense, consumers transfer their responsibility for brand decision making, and hence brand performance, to the brand itself. Through regular brand purchases, habits or 'routinized response behaviour' develop. This is important not just because complex decision making is simplified but because the amount of communication necessary to assist and provoke purchase is considerably reduced.

One particular aspect of this topic is called institutional trust, that is, trust in organizations rather than individual people or product/service brands. This is important, not only in B2B markets where the overall reputation of the organization is important when dealing with other organizations, but it can also be critical in B2C markets. In these markets the development of trust to encourage safe purchasing can be vital. Airlines and financial services organizations use corporate branding to instil trust while online consumer purchasing requires that risk of credit card fraud and deception be minimized. To achieve this organizations use a variety of techniques to lower perceived risk.

Pavlou (2002) argues that there are six means by which institutional trust can be encouraged. These are reproduced in Table 17.4.

The presence of trust within a relationship is influenced by four main factors (Young and Wilkinson, 1989). These include the duration of the relationship; the relative power of the participants; the presence of cooperation; and various environmental factors that may be present at any one moment. Although pertinent,

Table 17.4

Elements of
institutional trust

Element of institutional trust	Key aspect
Perceived monitoring	Refers to the supervision of transactions by, for example, regulatory authorities or owners of B2B market exchanges. This can mitigate uncertainty through a perception that sellers or buyers who fail to conform with established rules and regulations will be penalized.
Perceived accreditation	Refers to badges or symbols that denote membership of externally recognized bodies that bestow credibility, authority, security, and privacy on a selling organization.
Perceived legal bonds	Refers to contracts between buyers, sellers, and independent third parties, so that the costs of breaking a contract are perceived to be greater than the benefits of such an action. Trust in the selling organization is therefore enhanced when bonds are present.
Perceived feedback	Refers to signals about the quality of an organization's reputation, and such feedback from other buyers about sellers, perhaps through word-of-mouth communication, can deter sellers from undertaking opportunistic behaviour.
Perceived cooperative norms	Refers to the values, standards, and principles adopted by those party to a series of exchanges. Cooperative norms and values signal good faith and behavioural intent, through which trust is developed.

Source: Reprinted from Pavlou (2002) with permission from Elsevier.

these are quite general factors and it is Morgan and Hunt (1994) who established what are regarded today as the key underlying dimensions of relationship marketing. In their seminal paper they argued that it is the presence of both commitment and trust that leads to cooperative behaviour, customer satisfaction, and ultimately successful relationship marketing.

Commitment is important because it implies a desire that a relationship continues and is strengthened because it is of value. Morgan and Hunt proposed that commitment and trust are the key mediating variables between five antecedents and five outcomes. See Figure 17.8.

According to the **KMV** model, the greater the losses anticipated through the termination of a relationship the greater the commitment expressed by the exchange partners. When relationship partners share similar values, commitment increases. Morgan and Hunt proposed that building a relationship based on trust and commitment can give rise to a number of benefits. Some of these include developing a set of shared values, reducing costs when the relationship finishes, and increasing profitability as a greater number of end user customers are retained because of the inherent value and satisfaction they experience. Cooperation arises from a relationship driven by high levels of both trust and commitment (Morgan and Hunt, 1994).

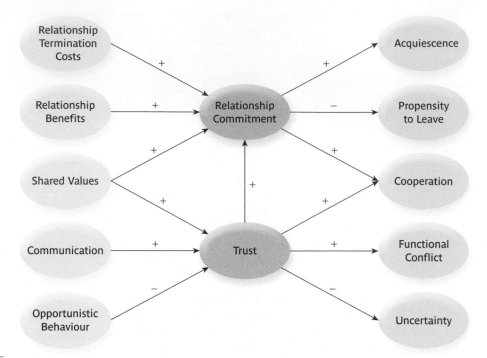

Figure 17.8

The KMV model of relationship marketing

Source: Morgan and Hunt (1994). Reprinted with permission from *The Journal of Marketing*, published by the American Marketing Association, Morgan and Hunt, July 1994, p 22.

Ryssel, Ritter, and Gemunden (2004: 203) recognize that trust (and commitment) has a 'significant impact on the creation of value and conclude that value creation is a function of the atmosphere of a relationship rather than the technology employed'. Trust and commitment are concepts that are central to relationship marketing.

Customer Satisfaction

A natural outcome from building trust and developing commitment is the establishment of customer satisfaction. This is seen as important because satisfaction

---

RESEARCH INSIGHT 17.4

To take your learning further, you might wish to read this influential paper.

Morgan, R. M., and Hunt, S. D. (1994), 'The commitment–trust theory of relationship marketing', *Journal of Marketing*, 58 (July), 20–38.

This well-known paper examines the role of trust and commitment in buyer–supplier relationships. The authors present the KMV model to explain various behavioural and cognitive aspects associated with exchange partnerships. Using social exchange theory, it is argued that through mutually beneficial exchanges, trust and commitment develop which in turn leads to longer-lasting relationships.

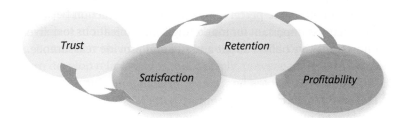

Figure 17.9
Trust/profitability
sequence

is thought to be positively related to customer retention which in turn leads to an improved return on investment and hence profitability. Unsurprisingly many organizations seek to improve levels of customer satisfaction, with the intention of strengthening customer relationships and driving higher levels of retention and loyalty (Ravald and Grönroos, 1996).

So, the simple equation is build trust, drive satisfaction, improve retention, and increase profits. See Figure 17.9.

However, customer satisfaction is not driven by trust alone. Customer expectations play an important role and help shape a customer's perception of product/service performance. Customers compare performance against their expectations and through this process feel a sense of customer satisfaction or dissatisfaction. More recent ideas suggest that the perceived value of a relationship can be more important than trust when building customer satisfaction (Ulaga and Eggert, 2006).

So, if expectations are met then customer satisfaction is achieved. If expectations are exceeded then customers are delighted but if expectations are not met then customers are said to be dissatisfied. This simplistic interpretation can be misleading because satisfaction does not always imply loyalty (Mittal and Lasson, 1998). As noted earlier, what may be seen as loyalty may be nothing more than convenience or even inertia, and dissatisfaction need not result in brand desertion (O'Malley, 1998).

Cumby and Barnes (1998) provide a useful insight into what contributes to customer satisfaction:

- Core product/service—the bundle of attributes, features, and benefits which must reach competitive levels if a relationship is to develop.
- Support services and systems—the quality of services and systems used to support the core product/service.
- Technical performance—the synchronization of the core product/services with the support infrastructure to deliver on the promise.
- Elements of customer interaction—the quality of customer care demonstrated through face-to-face and technology-mediated communications.
- Affective dimensions of services—the subtle and non-core interactions that say something about the way the organization feels about the customer.

This is a more useful insight into what it is that drives customer satisfaction because it incorporates a wide range of factors and recognizes the importance of personal contact. Customer satisfaction and the quality of customer relationship are related, in differing ways, among differing people and contexts. However, one

contact centres enable customers to complain about a product performance and related experience, seek product-related advice, make suggestions regarding product or packaging development, and comment about an action or development concerning the brand as a whole. Very often this access is referred to as a 'careline': a dedicated telephone and email connection. In addition, organizations can use contact centres to provide outbound calls, often to generate sales leads or to provide market information.

Carelines and contact centres have enormous potential to support brands. The majority of careline calls are not about complaints but are from people seeking advice or help about products. Food manufacturers provide cooking and recipe advice; cosmetic and toiletries companies provide healthcare advice and application guidelines; while white goods and service-based organizations can provide technical and operational support. By dealing with complaints in a prompt, courteous, and efficient manner, people are more likely to repurchase a brand than if the service was not available. Carelines are essentially a post-purchase support mechanism, which facilitates feedback and intelligence gathering. They can warn of imminent problems (product defects), provide ideas for new products or variants, and of course provide a valuable method to reassure customers and improve customer retention levels.

CRM Systems

The development of customer relationship management (CRM) systems has been a significant development in the way organizations have attempted to manage their customers. CRM applications were originally developed as sales force support systems (mainly sales force automation) and later applications were designed for supplier organizations to enable them to manage their end user customers. They have subsequently evolved as a more sophisticated means of managing direct customers and are an integral part of customer contact centres, discussed in the previous section.

The principal aim of CRM systems is to provide relationships with superior value by enabling suppliers' access to real-time customer information. This helps suppliers to anticipate and satisfy customers' needs effectively, efficiently, and in a timely manner. To make this happen, a complete history of each customer needs to be available to all staff who interact with customers. This is necessary in order to answer two types of questions. First, there are questions prompted by customers about orders, quotations, or products, and secondly questions prompted by internal managers concerning, for example, strategy, segmentation, relationship potential, sales forecasts, and sales force management. (Market Insight 17.8 discusses the Carphone Warehouse's use of CRM systems.)

CRM applications typically consist of call management, lead management, customer record, and sales support and payment systems. Ideally, they should be incorporated as part of an overall strategic approach (Wightman, 2000). However, such systems are invariably treated as add-on applications that are expected to resolve customer interface difficulties. Unsurprisingly, many clients have voiced their dissatisfaction with CRM as many of the promises and expectations have not been fulfilled.

Sood (2002) suggests that problems have arisen with CRM implementation because technology vendors have not properly understood the need to manage all relationships with all major stakeholders. Disappointment with CRM systems can also be regarded as a failure to understand the central tenets of a customer-focused philosophy and the need to adopt a strategic business approach to managing customer relationships. If the centrality of concepts such as trust and commitment is not understood, nor a willingness displayed to share information and achieve a balanced relationship, the installation of databases and data warehouses will not, and to date has not, changed the quality of an organization's relationships with its customers.

O'Malley and Mitussi (2002) also refer to the failure of CRM systems in terms of internal political power struggles and associated issues about who owns particular systems and data. Where an organization has not established a customer-oriented culture nor begun to implement enterprise-wide systems and procedures, it is probable that access to certain data might be impeded or at least made problematic.

MARKET INSIGHT 17.8

Talking to Customers at Carphone Warehouse

A part of the Carphone Warehouse's strategy to become the largest independent retailer of mobile communications in Europe required that they became a customer- rather than a product-focused organization.

All customer-facing staff had to be able to support a consultative sell but they did not have the customer information necessary to do this. Customer information was stored in several different product-based databases and so it was necessary to integrate the data into a CRM system that provided all staff with a single customer view, whether accessed by call centres, retail stores, or other marketing formats.

Using Trillium Software, the data was cleaned (e.g. old contacts and addresses were removed), de-duplicated, and migrated to a new database. As a result staff now have a comprehensive, accurate, and up-to-date view of their customers and can see viable cross-selling opportunities. Whilst marketing communication campaigns are generating substantially improved revenues, perhaps the most important benefit has been the improvement in the customer experience.

Source: www.trilliumsoftware.com/.

1 Do you think CRM systems provide customers with added value or are they just a means by which organizations can achieve their business goals?

2 Search the web and identify two CRM systems offered by software houses. What are the main differences between the systems?

3 Is the outsourcing of customer contact centres to a different country in the customers' best interests?

McLoughlin, D., and Horan, C. (2000), 'Perspectives from the markets-as-networks approach', *Industrial Marketing Management*, 29, 4, 285–92.

Menon, A., Bharadwaj, S. G., and Howell, R. (1996), 'The quality and effectiveness of marketing strategy: effects of functional and dysfunctional conflict in intraorganisational relationships', *Journal of Academy of Marketing Science*, 24, 4, 299–313.

—— Homburg, C., and Beutin, N. (2005), 'Understanding customer value in business-to-business relationships', *Journal of Business to Business Marketing*, 12, 2, 1–38.

Mittal, B., and Lassar, W. M. (1998), 'Why do consumers switch? The dynamics of satisfaction versus loyalty', *Journal of Services Marketing*, 12, 3, 177–94.

Morgan, R. M., and Hunt, S. D. (1994), 'The commitment–trust theory of relationship marketing', *Journal of Marketing*, 58 (July), 20–38.

O'Malley, L. (1998), 'Can loyalty schemes really build loyalty?', *Marketing Intelligence and Planning*, 16, 1, 47–55.

—— and Mitussi, D. (2002), 'Relationships and technology: strategic implications', *Journal of Strategic Marketing*, 10, 225–38.

Packard, V. (1958), *The Hidden Persuaders*, London: Penguin.

Palmer, R., Lindgreen, A., and Vanhamme, J. (2005), 'Relationship marketing: schools of thought and future research directions', *Marketing Intelligence and Planning*, 23, 2, 313–30.

Pavlou, P. A. (2002), 'Institution-based trust in interorganisational exchange relationships: the role of online B2B marketplaces on trust formation', *Journal of Strategic Information Systems*, 11, 3–4 (December), 215–43.

Pondy, L. R. (1967), 'Organisational conflict: conflict and models', *Administrative Science Quarterly*, 12 (September), 296–320.

Porter, M. E. (1985), *Competitive Advantage: Creating and Sustaining Superior Performance*, New York: The Free Press.

Ravald, A., and Gronroos, C. (1996), 'The value concept and relationship marketing', *European Journal of Marketing*, 30, 2, 19–33.

Reichheld, F. F., and Sasser, E. W. (1990), 'Zero defections: quality comes to services', *Harvard Business Review*, September, 105–11.

Reinartz, W. J., and Kumar, V. (2002), 'The mismanagement of customer loyalty', *Harvard Business Review*, July, 86–94.

Rose, G. M., and Shoham, A. (2002), 'Interorganisational task and emotional conflict with internationals channels of distribution', *Journal of Business Research*, 57, 9 (September), 942–50.

Rosenberg, L. J., and Stern, L. W. (1970), 'Toward the analysis of conflict in distribution channels: a descriptive model', *Journal of Marketing*, 34, 4 (October), 40–6.

Rosenbloom, B. (1973), 'Conflict and channel efficiency: some conceptual models for the decision maker', *Journal of Marketing*, 37 (July), 26–30.

—— (1978), 'Motivating independent distribution channel members', *Industrial Marketing Management*, 7 (November), 275–81.

Ryssel, R., Ritter, T., and Gemunden, H. G. (2004), 'The impact of information technology deployment on trust, commitment and value creation in business relationships', *Journal of Business and Industrial Marketing*, 19, 3, 197–207.

Sahedev, S. (2005), 'Exploring the role of expert power in channel management: an empirical study', *Industrial Marketing Management*, 37, 487–94.

Sharma, A., Krishman, R., and Grewal, D. (2001), 'Value creation in markets: a critical area of focus for business-to-business markets', *Industrial Marketing Management*, 30, 4 (May), 341–402.

Sheth, J. (1973), 'A model of industrial buyer behaviour', *Journal of Marketing*, 37 (October), 50–6.

Simpson, P. M., Sigauw, J. A., and Baker, T. L. (2001), 'A model of value creation: supplier behaviors and their impact on reseller-perceived value', *Industrial Marketing Management*, 30, 2 (February), 119–34.

Sood, B. (2002), *CRM in B2B: Developing Customer-centric Practices for Partner and Supplier Relationships*, available at www.intelligentcrm.com/020509/508feat2_2.shtml, accessed December 2007.

Southam, A. G. (2002), 'Understanding channel conflict', available at www.reshare.com, accessed December 2007.

Spekman, R. E., and Carroway, R. (2005), 'Making the transition to collaborative buyer–seller relationships: an emerging framework', *Industrial Marketing Management*, 35, 1 (January), 10–19.

Stern, L. (2006), *Dealing with Justice*, available at www.viaint.com/article.php/articleid/14, accessed December 2007.

—— El-Ansary, A. I., and Coughlan, A. T. (1996), *Marketing Channels*, 5th edn., Englewood Cliffs, NJ: Prentice Hall.

—— and Heskett, J. L. (1969), 'Conflict management in interorganisational relations: a conceptual framework', in L. W. Stern (ed.), *Distribution Channels: Behavioural Dimensions*, Boston: Houghton-Mifflin.

Stone, M. (2002), 'Managing public sector customers', *What's New in Marketing*, October, www.wnim.com/, accessed December 2007.

Tran, M. (2006), 'Sainsbury's introduces compostable packaging', Guardian Unlimited, 8 September, available at www.guardian.co.uk/environment/2006/sep/08/supermarkets.business, accessed 23 September 2007.

Ulaga, W., and Eggert A. (2006), 'Relationship value and relationship quality', *European Journal of Marketing*, 40, 3–4, 311–27.

Webb, K. L. (2002), 'Managing channels of distribution in the age of electronic commerce', *Industrial Marketing Management*, 31, 2, 95–102.

—— and Hogan, J. E. (2002), 'Hybrid channel conflict: causes and effects on channel performance', *Journal of Business and Industrial Marketing*, 17, 5, 338–56.

Webster, F. E., and Wind, Y. (1972), 'A general model for understanding organisational buying behaviour', *Journal of Marketing*, 36 (April), 12–14.

Wightman, T. (2000), 'e-CRM: the critical dot.com discipline', *Admap*, April, 46–8.

Worthington, S., and Horne, S. (1998), 'A new relationship marketing model and its application in the affinity credit card market', *International Journal of Bank Marketing*, 16, 1 (February), 39–44.

Young, L. C., and Wilkinson, I. F. (1989), 'The role of trust and co-operation in marketing channels: a preliminary study', *European Journal of Marketing*, 23, 2, 109–22.

Part 5

Contemporary Marketing Practice

Part 5 introduces you to contemporary marketing practice. From new technology issues to post-modern marketing and marketing ethics, it provides an overview of the latest developments in the field.

Part 1: Marketing Fundamentals

1 Marketing Principles and Society
2 The Marketing Environment
3 Marketing Psychology and Consumer Buying Behaviour
4 Marketing Research and Marketing Information Systems

Part 2: Principles of Marketing Management

5 Marketing Strategy
6 Market Segmentation and Positioning
7 Market Development and International Marketing
8 Marketing implementation and Control

Part 3: The Marketing Mix Principle

9 Products, Services, and Branding Decisions
10 Price Decisions
11 An Introduction to Marketing Communications
12 Marketing Communications: Tools and Techniques
13 Managing Marketing Communications: Strategy, Planning, and Implementation
14 Channel Management and Retailing

Part 4: Principles of Relational Marketing

15 Services Marketing and Non-Profit Marketing
16 Business-to-Business Marketing
17 Relationship Marketing

❯ **Part 5: Contemporary Marketing Practice**

18 New Technology and Marketing
19 Postmodern Marketing
20 Marketing Ethics

Creating Community with MySpace!

Two guys in Los Angeles came up with the idea of hitting a grocery store, loading up on tortillas, rice, and beans, going home to make burritos, and distributing them to the homeless. Becoming known as the Burrito Project, they felt this was an immediate way to feed hungry people. To share their idea and work with others they created a MySpace page (www.myspace.com/burritoproject). MySpace is a popular social networking website with 130 million users and increasing by 8 million more each month, which offers an interactive, user-submitted network of friends, personal profiles, blogs, groups, photos, music, and videos internationally. Without spending a dime on advertising, their MySpace community grew to 4,800, and word spread to other cities. In short order, Burrito Projects were launched in nearby San Bernardino, California and across the country in Charlotte, North Carolina.

It wasn't long before this project was nominated for the MySpace Impact Awards (www.myspace.com/impactawards), a programme honouring individuals and organizations having a positive effect on the world through the site. In just days tens of thousands of nominations for deserving groups were made, with the Burrito Project being the landslide winner, taking home a $10,000 cheque and a hefty package of promotion on the site. As a consequence the Burrito Project has gone global. There are now projects not only in Phoenix, Detroit, and Denver, but also in Mexico City and Damascus, Syria, where MySpace users created a Falafel Project (www.myspace.com/falafelproject).

People have come to expect stories about musicians or film-makers who get the big breaks because they were discovered on MySpace. However, MySpace increasingly serves as a platform for doing good and for building community. The generation that has flocked to MySpace is thought by many to be so self-involved that it has no idea what's happening in the rest of the world. These consumers are interested in building communities and creating experiences that are different or special. It's not just about wearing the brand as a badge anymore; it is all about feeling connected to it. They care about community, and they're actively engaged in civic causes. Young people balance their interests in the latest fashions and the hottest dubs with intrigue about going carbon neutral and concern for entire villages being wiped out.

MySpace.com is a site and a community that offers a truly level playing field. It's free, it's easy, and it has an equal chance to work for everyone. It offers a democracy of ideas and tools to communicate them. The most important thing to take from MySpace is that it is a community where people can interact with each other. As consumers become more detached from traditional ways of life, they are looking to find communities in other places or virtual spaces.

Sources: Hof (2006); Anon. (2007); Dewolfe (2007); Hamm (2007).

1 Do you have a MySpace site? If so in what way do you use the site? Can your friends download music or view pictures? Are you promoting a band you're in or your views on politics and society? Do you use your MySpace site to communicate with friends through your blog or chat?

2 How much interactivity does your MySpace site facilitate? Is it really interactive or can your friends just read information?

3 List ways in which you could use your MySpace site to create more of a sense of community with your friends—what project could you do!

To take your learning further, you might wish to read this influential paper.

Hoffman, D. L., and Novak, T. P. (1996), 'Marketing in hypermedia computer-mediated environments: conceptual foundations', *Journal of Marketing*, 60 (July), 50–68.

This article addresses the role of marketing in hypermedia computer-mediated environments (HCMEs) of which the world wide web on the internet is the first and current global implementation. The authors introduced marketers to various unique characteristics of this medium and proposed a structural model of consumer behaviour in a HCME.

New Technology and Marketing Activities

Electronic resources are increasingly used by marketers for the conduct and management of marketing activities. The implications of electronic resources for marketing are not just in their existence or development, or even the presence of new 'never been seen before' features, but in how they are used to effectively and efficiently improve the management and implementation of marketing activities. Think about how the television changed the way information was communicated to consumers, or how the internet gives you better access to the latest music, or how automatic teller machines now mean you can access cash 24/7. Many new electronic technologies are making it easier, quicker, cheaper, and more creative for us to conduct marketing activities.

The **electronic marketing activity management** (EMAM) framework is a framework that can assist the classification of how electronic technologies are influencing marketing activities (Page-Thomas, 2005). EMAM outlines five core marketing activities which electronic resources are influencing (see Figure 18.1). These include:

- how we can provide information to our customers (information provision);

- how we access information about our customers (data and information acquisition);

- how we personally communicate with our customers (communication and relationship management);

- how we manage the payment for our products (transaction management); and

- how we deliver our product to our customers (distribution and logistics management).

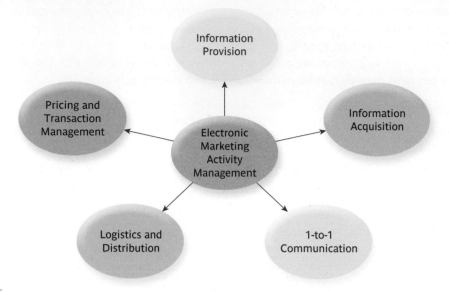

Figure 18.1
EMAM framework

The content of these marketing activities, the context in which these activities occur, and the process of managing them will change based on the technology used, the objectives set down, and other resources (e.g. personnel).

Information Provision Activities

Electronic resources are having a deep impact on the way marketing information is delivered, or transmitted to stakeholders. In short, developments in electronic tools and technologies are:

* increasing the speed with which information is transferred;
* increasing the amount of information that can be stored, processed, and transferred in a given time period;
* supporting new patterns of information organization and accessibility.

Key trends affecting information provision activities as a result of new technology include **audience fragmentation**, **channel convergence**, and **interactive integrated marketing communications (IMC)**:

Audience fragmentation—Market and audiences sizes are breaking up and getting smaller due to the increased number of media channels now available, raising the complexity of media and technology audience usage behaviour.

Channel convergence—Media channels are converging in that channels are developing that combine the characteristics of numerous traditional channels (e.g. video content through the mobile phone or radio airtime accessible through the web). This is making it more and more necessary to adopt an integrated approach to information provision with marketers requiring an increased understanding of the delivery channel, the message, and the needs and technology behaviour of the target audience (Peltier, Schibrowsky, and Schultz, 2003).

Interactive integrated marketing communications (IMC) is rising given the unique ability of newer forms of electronic media to provide two-way, user-controlled, customized, one-to-one information exchange. As such, developments in electronic technologies are providing marketers with numerous tools with which to manage and implement the activities of the promotional mix.

Advertising

New electronic technologies are increasing the range of media channel options for advertisers, the way content is displayed, and how an audience can respond.

The Website

The commercialization of the World Wide Web has brought the use of the website for the promotion and delivery of interactive and customizable information to the forefront of marketing activities. Take the website launched in France by RATP (public transportation company in Paris). The site is called 'Objectif-Respect' and aims at educating Parisians on how public transportation should be used, respecting other passengers, not destroying the seats, regularly paying for the tickets, etc. The site is divided into several sections, each explaining a concept both through an advertainment piece (i.e. a cartoon, an advergame, a quiz, etc.) and through a video documentary containing interviews with public transportation users and workers. This site combines the use of the internet as a promotional tool for increasing awareness, education, and changing user behaviour through interactive multimedia advertising content.

The internet is increasingly used to reach younger generations with their advertising messages that were once limited to television and cinema media channels. Market Insight 18.2 provides a snapshot as to how leading brands are using YouTube to reach younger generations.

Online Advertising

Specific online advertising includes many formats such as display advertising (e.g. static banner ads); rich media ads (e.g. embedded multimedia ads, pop-up ads, **interstitials**, video streaming); **search engine marketing**, sponsored sites, email advertising, blogging, classified listings, and so on. These forms of advertising help marketers to drive traffic to websites ('click-through rate') and also encourage trial, purchase, or repeat-purchase activity ('conversion rate').

In the first half of 2005, online advertising took a 5.8 per cent share of all UK adspend, exceeding outdoor advertising's 5.1 per cent and radio at 3.6 per cent (IAB-PwC, 2005). With a total adspend of £490.8 m, online advertising has come of age as it continues to be the fastest-growing advertising medium in history. Such figures highlight the fact that online media is growing in significance in its own right, as well as being an increasingly important component of the media mix. The online industry in the UK has experienced strong growth across all advertising formats (IAB-PwC, 2005). However, the main three formats receiving

Getting Creative with YouTube

Generation X and Generation Y grasp that media choices can and must be customized to reach individual decision makers. To them it is all about creativity, customization, and user-generated content. The short of it is, if you want to talk to young consumers these days, you'd better be on YouTube. It has always been difficult to reach young men and women through mass media like TV. Teenagers in particular are very fragmented in their media choices and they are increasingly spending enormous amounts of time online and on sites where they have increased choice like YouTube.

The sheer fact that young people can decide for themselves what videos they want to watch and can share them with their friends helps drive Youtube's popularity. YouTube is on demand, which is seen as the future of communication. People don't want to be told what to watch, and they want ideas to be shared. They want to pick and choose and not be forced to watch things. YouTube becomes a campfire where everybody wants to hear stories, find out stories, and share stories. It attracts millions.

According to Media Metrix, YouTube had 160.8 million unique visitors worldwide in March 2007, a sixfold increase from 22.3 million visitors worldwide in March 2006. Youtube has enjoyed such large increases in audience size that the video-sharing site now commands more visitors than the next 64 portals of its type combined. YouTube's total share of the online video market rose to 60.2% in May 2007, followed by News Corp's MySpace video with 16.08%, Google's video at 7.81%, and Yahoo's video with 2.77%. The demand is so great that even big brands are getting on YouTube in an attempt to reach the younger generation.

Brands ranging from Gap to Victoria's Secret, Ralph Lauren, Calvin Klein, Nike, and Adidas are increasingly finding a home on YouTube, MySpace, and similar sites, where their videos, commercials, behind-the-scenes footage, and fashion shows are posted for free. These sites have the potential to transform the way fashion brands reach their current and future customers since hundreds of thousands of people can view a single spot—with humorous ones scoring the most hits. The keys to unlocking the generational secrets are creativity, language, and formats. The internet and associated applications are dominant media sources in their lives.

These generations are not static consumer audiences like their predecessors were. If they don't like a ringtone, they'll make one themselves. If they don't like news coverage, they'll write their own stories and shoot their own videos. So, to keep connected with these generations marketers are forced to get creative, customized, and enable user-generated content in their own way.

Sources: Hamm (2007); Lockwood (2007); Dye (2007); Dickey and Sullivan (2007).

1　Why is YouTube.com so popular amongst internet users, especially the younger generations?

2　Why is YouTube.com so attractive to advertisers as a media channel?

3　What are the negatives of advertisers increasingly using YouTube as a channel to reach younger audiences? What effect might it have on the popularity of YouTube?

significant growth in the first half of 2005 include search advertising (or search engine marketing) and classifieds.

Search Engine Marketing

Given the plethora of information accessible on the web, interactive decision aids are increasingly used to help locate websites. The main two types of decision aids include search engines and search directories (e.g. Google, Yahoo!). Advertising with these decision aids helps drive traffic to a vendor's website, and is more commonly known as search engine marketing (SEM) (also known as search advertising). Formally defined, SEM is a set of marketing methods to increase the visibility of a website in search engine results pages (SERPs).

The three main methods of SEM include:

- **Search engine optimization (SEO)** attempts to improve rankings for relevant keywords in search results by improving a website's structure and content;

- **Pay-per-click (PPC)** advertising uses sponsored search engine listings to drive traffic to a website. The advertiser bids for search terms, and the search engine ranks ads based on a competitive auction as well as other factors.

- **Paid inclusion** can provide a guarantee that the website is included in the search engine's natural listings.

The most common methods to improve search engine listings include advertising by keyword and advertising by website content.

Advertising by keywords: Advertising based on a keyword search could take place through a search engine such as google.com, or a search engine partner site, such as shopping.com. For example, Google uses Google Adwords™. With Google AdWords you can reach people when they are actively looking for your products and services. In essence, when a user enters a query for a florist or flowers on Google (UK) for example, websites or text advertisements appear in the list of results. The idea is about getting an advertiser's listing to the top of search results on the keywords relevant to the advertiser's business. Some sites make the advertisement separate like Google which also uses text-only messages adjacent to a list of results.

Advertising by site content: Many search engines (e.g. Google, Ask.com, Yahoo! Search) have partner websites with specific content and ad-serving technology. The websites agree to let the search engines place content-specific advertising on their website, in return for a fee. The search engine then finds companies interested in advertising on websites with their desired content. For example, a real estate agent might have an advertisement for house insurance. Generally these advertisements are paid for based on either a pay-per-click campaign or an impression-based campaign.

Both of these search engine marketing techniques allow advertisers to target specific users with certain interests; however every search engine takes a different approach. But one thing unites them—selling traffic is big business because it works.

As shown in Figure 18.2 SEM is of increasing importance to the online advertising industry, in fact 76 per cent of marketing executives who use search engines to market say that buying clicks is more successful than banner advertisements

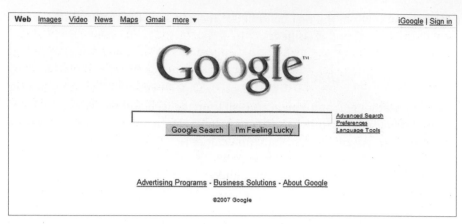

Google Inc.

You may well recognize the Google search engine

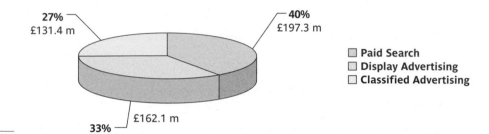

27%
£131.4 m

40%
£197.3 m

☐ **Paid Search**
☐ **Display Advertising**
☐ **Classified Advertising**

£162.1 m

33%

Figure 18.2

Online advertising spend (Q1&2 2005)

Source: IAB-PwC (2005).

(Arnold, 2003). This is supported by the fact that paid search advertising is also not perceived as being as invasive as other forms of online advertising heavily disliked by online consumers like pop-up ads (Nail, Charron, and Cohen, 2005). Forrester (2007) estimates that the value of European online marketing—including email, search, and display advertising—will more than double from around €7.5 billion in 2006 to more than €16 billion in 2012, 18 per cent of total media budgets. Firms will raise their online budgets primarily to better reach the growing net audience that relies on the web for a widening range of decisions. After five years of dipping their toes into the online marketing waters, firms have come to realize that the internet is a valuable medium for client acquisition, retention, and market expansion.

SMS Advertising and Podcasting

Mobile technology is also increasingly influencing advertising and marketing communications. Mobile marketing is the use of the mobile medium as a communications and entertainment channel between a brand and an end user and is the only personal channel enabling spontaneous, direct, interactive, and/or targeted communications, any time, any place. Growth in penetration levels sees Europe's mobile phone penetration plateauing at around 80 per cent (Herzog, Reitsma, and de Lussanet, 2005). Given the growth in mobile phone adoption and the use of SMS, mobile phones are the next natural marketing channel. As a result, marketing investment in the channel has increased significantly over the last few years, growing by 34 per cent from €155.3 million in 2003 to €208.7 million in 2004 (Smith, 2005). This growth has provided for an attractive advertising channel for media buyers, with the added benefits of store-and-send technology giving the option of message storage; it is quick, inexpensive, and reaches audience wherever they are. However, the message content is limited. Amongst the top ten business users of SMS advertising are recruitment agencies, clubs and bars, internet service providers, couriers, hair salons, dentists, and charities. We will discuss more about SMS and sales promotions later in this chapter.

Similar to SMS, podcasts, audio feeds downloaded at audience request to MP3 players (e.g. iPod), have the commercial potential to carry targeted advertising. Although currently limited to audio content, audiences download content-specific information such as travel guides, news and entertainment, finance, or technologies to listen to at their convenience. No longer are advertising messages limited to a few electronic delivery options, they are now prevalent across a large number of electronic channels.

Public Relations

The development of electronic technologies has many implications for the management and conduct of public relations activities. More specifically:

- **Analysis and PR management**: Specialist analyst software aids the analysis, planning, and evaluation functions of public relations (e.g. www.vocus.com/).

- **Press release publication**: Web posting of press releases from external, independent sources or the internal company news and information can increase awareness of and interest for a product, and can reinforce a customer's 'post-purchase decision' (e.g. www.ibm.com/news/us).

- **News monitoring services**: PR professionals use automated internet monitoring and web clipping services, such as Cyberalert (www.cyberalert.com) or PR Newswire (www.prnewswire.com), to find and/or distribute 'newsworthy' information.

- **Stakeholder feedback and interaction**: Developing interactive communication technologies like email, chat rooms, newsgroups, and more recently blogs are further providing PR professionals with customer reviews, feedback, and insight to inform corporate activities.

A more recent addition to the PR toolbox for stakeholder feedback and interaction is the use of **blogs**, a frequent web-based publication of personal thoughts and web links made accessible to a wider online audience that support audience feedback. They can range in scope from individual diaries to arms of political campaigns, media programmes, and corporations. They can also range in scale from the writings of one occasional author (known as a blogger), to the collaboration of a large community of writers. Although many consumers use blogs as diaries, companies also use them to provide internal teams with frequent project updates, or to deliver product support information or company news to customers and external stakeholders. Blog use has grown significantly in the past year.

Table 18.3

Advantages and
disadvantages of
blogs

Advantages	Disadvantages
The consumer and citizen are potentially better informed.	Most people are unable to write down their ideas in a compelling and clear manner.
Blogs have potential to help the organization develop stronger relationships and brand loyalty with its customers, as they interact with the 'human face' (i.e. employees) of the organization through blogs.	Blogs are easy to start and hard to maintain. Writing coherently is one of the most difficult and time-consuming tasks for a human being to undertake. So, far from blogs being a cheap strategy, they are a very expensive one, in that they eat up time. As a result, many blogs are not updated, thus damaging rather than enhancing the reputation of the organization.
Blogs, in an intranet environment, can be an excellent way of sharing information and knowledge within the organization.	People who have most time to write have least to say, and the people who have most to say don't have enough time to write it. Thus, the real expertise within the organization lies hidden.
Blogs can be a positive way of getting feedback from differing stakeholder groups. Blogs can build the profile of the writer, showcasing the organization as having talent and expertise.	Organizations are not democracies. The web makes many organizations look like disorganizations, with multiple tones and opinions, not delivering a consistent image or message.

Source: Adapted from McGovern (2004). Reproduced with the kind permission of Gerry McGovern, internet author, and consultant: www.gerrymcgovern.com/nt/2004/nt_2004_08_23_blogging.htm.

A new blog is created every second, over 70,000 daily, somewhere in the world, with the blogosphere now over thirty times as big as it was three years ago (Sifry, 2005). It is also estimated that 10 per cent of consumers read blogs once a week or more, compared with 5 per cent in 2004 (Li, Bernoff, and McHarg, 2004). As such, at a minimum, companies should monitor blogs to learn what is being said about their products and services. A list of advantages and disadvantages of blogs from an organizational perspective is provided in Table 18.3. See also Market Insight 18.3 for an example of the use of blogs in marketing.

Sales Promotions

Electronic technologies are also used to enhance the delivery and management of rewards and incentives such as sales promotions. For example:

- Database technology is central to the management of sales promotion activities by helping to store and track responses and redemption of promotions, assess the impact of different types of incentives, and refine promotional offers.
- The delivery of sales promotions, particularly competitions, can be improved by a range of electronic devices, including the use of barcodes on entry forms; automated voice recognition data entry via the telephone; direct database entry of competition forms via the internet; and entry details or offers of redemption through mobile technologies (i.e. SMS) and online.

Toyota Keeps it Real!

Word-of-mouth (WOM) marketing is a global phenomenon that packs a powerful punch in influencing consumer purchases. Increasingly we are seeing WOM marketing campaigns facilitated by the internet. From blogs, viral campaigns, and other tools, you can spread word of mouth faster and to a larger audience than ever before. Although the web did not invent word-of-mouth marketing, it has increased its spread and impact, especially with the rise in consumer-generated media (CGM) vehicles.

CGM vehicles can be as diverse as blogs, podcasts, MySpace pages, video clips, or, more prosaically, customizable online ads. In all, the consumer creates and distributes the brand message. To leveraging the power of active consumers and maximizing CGM, the following are key considerations:

- Make participation simple.
- Target niche first, mass later.
- Make it authentic, transparent.
- Make word of mouth relevant.
- Step up after going live.
- Think beyond campaigns.

An excellent example that adopts most of these considerations is the use of blogs in the automotive industry to share consumer experiences of new car test drives. Test driving a new car is a powerful trigger for reappraisal, positive perceptions, and ultimately purchase of a new car model. To try and tap into the powerful influence of WOM communication and the sharing of experiences of new car test drives, bloggers in Greece were invited to test drive the new Auris for a week and post their findings on http://www.aurisblog.gr. Participation was simple, targeting a niche audience to share real experiences while test driving the car.

The site received 52,000 visits by 41,000 unique visitors and overall response rate of the banner campaign was at 4.75%. More importantly, 2,000 test drive requests were submitted from this campaign, accounting for 50% of the total test drive requests received through all channels (phone, in-store, events, or promotions).

Sources: Wasserman (2005); Mitch (2006); adverblog (2007); Guegan (2007).

1 Why do you think consumers who had test driven the Toyota Auris would participate in the blog?

2 What benefit does the blog offer Toyota?

3 What are some of the problems that could have occurred for Toyota as a result of this blog?

- The trial of goods like software, digital books, or music prior to purchase provides an incentive to buy as it reduces the perceived risk of purchase. For example iTunes provides a snapshot of songs and video clips prior to purchase and download.

- Other electronic sales promotions include online advergames and competitions, product edutainment on CD or DVD, electronic business cards, PC screensavers, and so on.

The successful Orange Wednesdays promotion

Orange

Mobile technology is of significant interest to marketers in the management and delivery of sales promotions. An example of a very successful SMS campaign and the first attempt at mobile coupons is the renowned 'Orange Wednesdays' campaign. Orange wanted to increase brand association with film by leveraging its sponsorship relationship with the UK cinema industry. It also wanted to promote loyalty and reward Orange customers, attract new subscribers over the course of the campaign, and learn about subscriber preferences by capturing data on film viewing habits by geography, film genre, mobile usage, and other customer segments. Orange Wednesdays, a three-year programme, offering Orange customers a 2–4–1 deal on any cinema ticket, at any cinema nationwide, was therefore devised as the core promotional element of Orange's sponsorship programme.

With such a wide target audience, Orange wanted to make it simple to distribute the 2-4-1 vouchers. Orange customers simply request vouchers by texting 'film' to 241, by browsing Orange's WAP site, or by calling 241 and linking to an interactive voice response interface. They then receive a mobile voucher by SMS directly to their handset, containing a unique code. Redemption occurs at the point of purchase (in the cinema), with more than 2,000 voucher redemption terminals, powered by RAPOS™, installed in cinemas to check vouchers for validity. This end-to-end tracking of vouchers requested and redeemed allowed for segmenting data in real time on its customers and their film and cinema habits (Campaign, 2004; New Media Age, 2004). The campaign has been industry shaping and now Wednesdays have the highest weekday traffic at the cinemas and the campaign has built strong brand recognition for Orange Wednesdays.

Two other forms of online promotions that move well beyond traditional methods and provide rewards in terms of novel and fun entertainment, are **advergaming** and **viral marketing**. Advergaming is the use of online computer games for advertising. Viral marketing is a strategy based on consumers motivated to pass along marketing messages to friends or colleagues, a virtual word of mouth. Advergames rely on a viral element for the concept to be passed on from user to user on the web. Most require users to register, allowing for the collection of data for marketing research and other marketing initiatives, and mix interactivity, gaming, and advertising in a novel and innovative way. Examples of advergames are presented in Market Insight 18.4.

Another growing trend in sales promotions is the use of online media for competitions and sweepstakes. In Italy, Gillette started a mobile competition targeting football fans. On the Gillette gels and razors packaging buyers find a code to be texted to a special number with the answer to a quiz question. Winners are notified immediately and will receive a FIFA World Cup 2006 football ball. The competition then goes a step further: by visiting the website gillettem3power. com users can enter a draw to win a trip to Madrid with the chance to meet David Beckham, Gillette's endorser. In Spain, Carlsberg beer ran an online competition which allowed a lucky winner to get seven days, travel with seven friends on board a private jet. To enter the draw, people just have to buy a Carlsberg, get the code, and text it via SMS or online. The competition also includes immediate prizes such as Canon digital cameras, iPods, and Sony Ericsson mobile phones. The benefit of online competitions is that they create brand awareness, build consumer interaction with the brand, and enable the expansion of a brand's opt-in email database.

Direct Marketing

Developments in digital and interactive media technologies have had a positive influence on the growth of direct response advertising and audience participation. Despite non-electronic resources such as catalogues and mail order being the main direct marketing delivery vehicles, electronic databases underpin the effectiveness of direct mail campaigns (Linton, 1995; Peltier, Schibrowsky, and Schultz, 2003). For example, through advancements in call centre technology and the web, mass advertising channels can now promote opportunities for real dialogue by providing phone numbers or website/email addresses. This is evidenced by the rise in reality TV shows such as *Big Brother* and *Pop Idol* and *I'm a Celebrity Get Me Out of Here!*, all of which encourage audience participation in programme content.

Table 18.6

Advantages and
disadvantages of
internet surveys

Advantages	Disadvantages
High response rates	Sample self-selection
Greater response accuracy	Unrepresentativeness of the general population
More enjoyable and aesthetically pleasing questionnaires	Anonymity
	Multicultural considerations
Less expensive	Shorter attention span of respondents
Faster turnaround	Lack of interpersonal nuances
Customized surveys	Untruthfulness of respondents
	Multiple entries

Observation

Observation is another form of primary data collection method that over the years has been dramatically influenced by changes in electronic technologies. Electronic devices that record behaviour include electronic turnstiles, traffic counters, optical mark scanners, geographical information systems, tracking devices such as RFID, and cookies on the internet. These are increasingly providing marketers with an extraordinarily powerful way to track behaviour, such as purchase or usage behaviour, and acquire rich data to be used for marketing decision making.

One of the major forms of observational research conducted on the internet is the use of cookies. A **cookie** is a small text file found on your hard drive that allows information about your web activity patterns to be stored in the memory of your browser. From this file organizations are able to gain a more detailed understanding of the browsing patterns and even purchasing behaviours of their online audience. In light of this they are able to tailor offerings and customize pages and advertising specifically to each site visitor.

For example, have you ever purchased something from Amazon.com and on returning to the site days later been greeted by 'Hi [your name]', received personal recommendations for future purchases, or come across a banner ad that was just what you were looking for? Or found, after filling in a questionnaire at a MySpace, MyYahoo! or Excite website about your interests and information needs, that on your next visit the site had been tailored to those needs? Welcome to the world of cookie technology. Cookies are currently being used in three different ways:

1 To add **functionality and simplicity** to a website by facilitating site access and interaction. For example, Amazon.com uses cookie technology in such a way that users can store their names and passwords and facilitates virtual shopping by permitting the maintenance of shopping baskets between visits.

2 To **track a user's travel** within a website, allowing the site provider to learn what visitors are interested in and whether they are having problems navigating the site. For example, the DoubleClick ad-serving network (www.doubleclick.net) uses cookie technology to track users and deliver targeted banner advertising.

3 To **customize** a website to each visitor's needs, as in the example above of MyYahoo! (http://my.yahoo.com) and Excite (www.excite.com).

From a marketing point of view, cookies aid targeted advertising on the web, enable marketers to build customized websites, and increase control over promotional offers. In addition, they are an excellent means of gathering stakeholder intelligence.

1-to-1 Communication Activities

New electronic technologies are continuing to have a profound effect on customer service and personal selling and personal exchanges between customers with developments in voice over internet protocol or VoIP technologies. One of the hottest trends to hit the online world is social networking through VoIP (see Market Insight 18.5).

Customer Service

Interpersonal communication has always been a central component of an organization's customer service functions. Increasingly we are seeing technology being used to help manage all customer touch points (i.e. 'moments of truth') and deliver and manage customer service. Three types of technologies we discuss include customer service management technologies, live customer call technologies, and self-service technologies.

Customer Service Management Technologies

With developments in computing and database technology, and customer interaction centres (CIC) (i.e. call centres), using computer–telephone integration has streamlined help desk operations, increased the quality and degree of

MARKET INSIGHT 18.5

It's Only Human!

One of the hottest trends on the internet is social networking and the use of voice over internet protocol (VoIP) and videoconferencing. What Skype has been to internet calling and YouTube is to video sharing, Paltalk want to be to a new generation of companies that allow users to see multiple people transmitting video. By all indications, humans enjoy interacting online. Social networking and video-sharing sites such as MySpace and YouTube are among the most trafficked on the web. But communication on the internet is still largely dependent on text via instant message or email. Two leading companies are trying to change this, Skype and Paltalk.

Skype have
revolutionized free
calling over the
internet

Skype

Skype is an internet communications software that lets users have free voice and video calls, as well as text chats. Skype has always focused on making it easy for people to have conversations for as long as they like, anywhere in the world, for free. 'We want to make internet calling incredibly straightforward so people can effortlessly stay in touch,' said Skype CEO Niklas Zennstrom. In 2006, Skype introduced Skypecasts, live moderated conversations that allow groups of up to 100 people to talk to one another from anywhere in the world. For some time, Skype has enabled one-to-one video calls helping people to interact online more like they do in face-to-face discussions. Paltalk has taken that concept to a one-to-one or many-to-many scale and has created a group video application. Online videoconferencing has been around for years; however, big corporations were typically the only ones that could afford to pay for the service. Until now it hasn't been applied on a wide scale to social networking.

'Voice is OK, but it lacks the richness of sight,' Smernoff said. 'Humans like to see faces and expression.'

Sources: LeClaire (2006); Sandoval (2006).

1 Why are synchronicity, interactivity, and the mode of communication transfer so important to services such as those offered by Skype and Paltalk?

2 Which service provider is providing a more vivid service offering for their users? Do you think vividness is important?

3 How do email and chat services compare to Skype and Paltalk for social-networking activities?

Table 18.7

Classification of customer service management technologies

Application	Description	Example
Customer-facing	Customers interact with the company representatives; however, technologies support employees in information flow, service delivery, and customer interaction.	• Customer interaction centres (CIC) using computer-telephone integration • Automated email responses • Sales force automation (SFA) • Field service automation (FSA)
Customer-touching	Customers interact directly with technologies.	• Self-service technologies • Personalized/customerized web pages • E-commerce applications • Automated/interactive voice response (AVR/IVR) systems • Interactive kiosks (e.g. ATMs etc.)
Customer-centric intelligence	Technologies are used to analyse the results of operational processing; the results are used to improve management of customer service delivery and management.	• Data reporting and warehousing • Data analysis and mining • e.g. SPSS, SAS, MS Excel
Online networking	Methods provide the opportunity to build personal relationships between stakeholders (e.g. employees, customers).	• Forums • Chat • Newsgroups • Blogs • Email

standardization of services delivered, and cut operational costs. Many differing applications and tools are being used to manage customer relationships and service delivery. These can be categorized into four types: customer facing, customer touching, customer-centric intelligence, and online networking (Table 18.7).

Another telecommunications technology also used for customer service delivery is SMS. Many companies use SMS as a marketing tool or to generate revenue, but the AA Roadside Assistance in the UK uses text messaging as a powerful customer service tool. The AA Roadside Assistance Alert service is designed to reassure customers who are waiting for an AA vehicle to arrive by sending customers a text message after they have logged a call with the AA, informing them that a patrol is on the way, with further text messages sent until the vehicle arrives. The AA estimates that it saves around £288,000 a year using text messaging as opposed to ringing customers (Smith, 2005).

Live Customer Service Technologies

With the addition of internet-based technologies and especially VoIP, live customer service solutions are taking customer service to much higher levels. Click-to-chat, instant messaging, and live voice or click-to-call technologies are increasingly being trialled and adopted. However, success of the two-way communication is dependent on user connection speed, the technology used, and faces regional time constraints due to real-time interaction.

Click-to-call buttons are popping up everywhere, on corporate websites, emails, interactive ads, and search engine directory ads. Even media buzz has recently focused around click-to-call, with internet search giants Google and Yahoo! testing ways to enable immediate web-to-phone connections between buyers and sellers through their local search ads. Savvy marketers have proved you can drive material benefits from the technology, but many others are wondering how and when one should implement click-to-call. Click-to-call services let users click a button and immediately speak with a customer service representative. Customers can either place a call over the computer using VoIP technology or request an immediate call back from the advertiser by entering their phone number. Unlike a toll-free phone number, click-to-call services enable companies to monitor and control when and where online visitors migrate from the web to the phone sales channel.

The reality is that self-service cannot always be achieved online, particularly when making complex purchasing decisions. For high-value transactions, there's nothing like the power of voice for closing the deal. Jupiter Research has found that when it comes to questions about payment and delivery, product support, or service and general order enquiries, the relative majority of consumers prefer phone contact over any other alternative, including email, self-service tools, and text chat. Click-to-call technology is driving benefits for companies from Amazon. com to DaimlerChrysler. Using click-to-call services, companies have found, on average (Federman, 2006):

- A 22 per cent to 25 per cent reduction in website abandonment from website pages with click-to-call services;
- As much as a 100 per cent increase in transaction conversions from click-to-call users versus toll-free callers; and
- 88 per cent of click-to-call users say they are more likely to contact a company that offers a click-to-call service than one that does not.

Self-Service Technologies

Services have traditionally relied on personal contact between customers and employees, but increasingly we are seeing the use of **self-service technologies (SSTs)** to facilitate service delivery. Self-service technologies are technological tools that enable customers to produce services for themselves without assistance from firm employees. Examples include telephone banking using automated voice response (AVR) systems, automated hotel checkout and flight check-in, pay-at-the-pump terminals, internet transactions, and automatic teller machines (ATMs), to name a few. Within this growing self-service culture, it is estimated that British adults now spend about 30 minutes every day performing tasks previously undertaken by business providers (Kennedy, 2005). The primary motivation for business to adopt SSTs is to reduce costs in service delivery and to try and standardize the service delivered. From a consumer perspective, convenience, speed of service delivery, and customer control are some of the core benefits of SST usage (Meuter *et al.*, 2005).

To take your learning further, you might wish to read this influential paper.

Meuter, M. L., Bitner, M. J., Ostrom, A. L., and Brown, S. W. (2005), 'Choosing among alternative service delivery modes: an investigation of customer trial of self-service technologies', *Journal of Marketing*, 69, 2 (April), 61–83.

For many firms, often the challenge is not managing a SST but rather getting consumers to try the technology. In this article the authors research why customers decide to try SSTs and why some SSTs are more widely accepted than others in the marketplace. The authors specifically focus on actual behaviour in situations in which the consumer has a choice among delivery modes.

An industry where electronic technologies and increasingly SST have had a dramatic impact is that of financial retailing services. Financial services began to open up alternative transaction/distribution channels as credit cards started appearing. Following this were early experiments with telephone banking and cash dispensers that evolved into automated teller machines (ATMs or cashpoints). These developments provided a bridge into the new phase of banking—internet banking and the growth in use of self-service technologies (Liao *et al.*, 1999). In financial services, AVR (automated voice recognition) systems, the internet, and interactive kiosks such as ATMs are primarily used for the provision of customer services, for the conduct of transactions, and to provide information and educate customers about the vendor's products (Bitner, Ostrom, and Meuter, 2002).

Sales Force Communication, Automation, and Management

Early efforts to apply electronic technology in personal selling, such as by using the telephone to reach interested stakeholders in offices and homes, initially met with a lot of resistance. Mobile telecommunications, teleconferencing, and videoconferencing are now part of everyday communication channels used to mediate and enhance personal selling activities. These channels are further being enhanced by internet-based technologies such as email, chat, and VoIP.

Electronic technologies are further having an impact on the management of sales force activities through **sales force automation (SFA)**. SFA includes communication technologies (e.g. cell phones, beepers, car faxes, wireless devices, and email), customer relationship management (CRM), and knowledge management technologies. The aims of these systems are to reduce time spent on support activities and thereby increase time spent on sales activities; and to provide faster access to timely information (Rivers and Dart, 1999). However, not only are these increasing the accountability and contactability of sales staff, but given SFA can be applied to diverse range of sales activities, management expectations of sales management efficiency are increasing. For example, SFA can be used to manage order processing, contact management, scheduling, information management, forecasting, territory and route mapping, prospecting, sales forecast analysis, and employee performance evaluation (Honeycutt *et al.*, 2005).

Distribution and Channel Management

In the last decade of the twentieth century, electronic resources revolutionized the management and conduct of distribution activities. Developments in technologies have influenced and will continue to influence the:

- structure of distribution channels and the role of intermediaries in the delivery of the product offering (see discussion in Chapter 14);
- management of the logistical functions of order processing, inventory control, warehousing, and the physical transportation of the product offering; and
- electronic distribution of goods and services through electronic information and communication networks.

Logistics Management

New electronic technologies are having a tremendous effect on the logistical functions of order processing, inventory control, warehousing, and transportation. The key logistics technologies can be classified into three categories based on financial cost and the degree of impact on logistical functions (see Table 18.8).

Electronic technologies have increased the efficiency and effectiveness with which orders can be received, processed, and executed. Orders can now be submitted in many ways: by mail, by telephone, through salespeople supported by

Table 18.8
Distribution and logistics technologies

High-cost and revolutionary technology	Robotics; automated material handling equipment; automated storage and retrieval equipment
Medium-cost and medium-revolutionary technology	Handling hardware—RFID, barcodes, optical scanners, local area networks, hand-held data entry devices; and software—EDI, direct product profitability
Low-cost, incremental technology	Software applied to inventory control—order selection, short interval scheduling; as well as other functions—sales forecasting, financial support

Source: Adapted from Sum, Teo, and Ng (2001). Reproduced with the kind permission of Emerald Group Publishing Limited.

a laptop or mobile technologies, or via a computer using the internet, electronic data interchange (EDI), or extranets. Electronic technologies have increased product ordering speed, accuracy, and efficiency, providing benefit to both producer and customer.

Many organizations have greatly reduced their inventory levels and related costs through just-in-time (JIT) systems, EDI, and extranet technologies (Yao and Carlson, 1999). Electronic warehousing systems or database systems are being used more and more for the storage of digital products (Alshawi, Saez-Pujol, and Irani, 2003). These systems can be searched or browsed electronically, providing the user with immediate electronic delivery options. For example Apple has thousands of music and video titles accessible from advanced database systems.

As it is more cost effective and efficient to exchange information between members of a supply chain, electronic technologies are also changing where products move, the size of typical shipments, and the time periods within which goods must be delivered. For example, load-matching systems accessible through the web help freight carriers to find loads, and online auctions help to match freight to carriers and automate the bidding process. Tracking and tracing technologies for containers and packages such as scanners, coupled with universal product codes (UPC), and more recently Radio frequency identification data (RFID), are

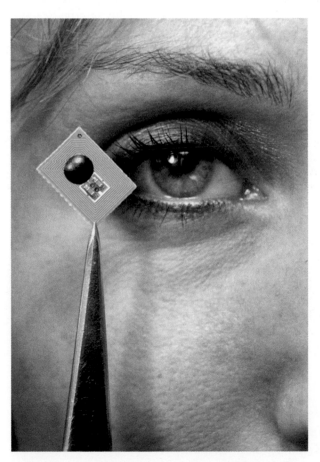

RFID

It is anticipated that the RFID tag market will continue to grow rapidly also gaining widespread use, reporting information to customers about where their products are in real time (i.e. via email, telephone, or web-based automatic response system). RFID technology has now been developed to the point at which it can provide suppliers, manufacturers, distributors, and retailers with precise real-time information on where their products are in the supply chain. It is estimated that the worldwide RFID tag market will grow nearly tenfold from $300 million in 2004 to $2.8 billion in 2009 (McGann, 2005).

Another notable electronic channel development of the late twentieth century has been the internet as a retail channel. Retail services such as travel and financial services have quickly made use of differing technologies like the telephone, facsimile, ATMs, and the internet to electronically distribute their product offering to more customers more efficiently and cost effectively. These are discussed in more detail in Chapter 14.

Pricing and Transactional Management

Over the past few decades, electronic technologies such as marketing information systems (MkIS), database technologies, and more recently internet-enabled technologies, have been changing the rules of strategic pricing and pricing decisions. Pricing strategies such as 'real-time' or 'dynamic' pricing have increasingly developed in both B2C and B2B markets through online price comparison decision aids and online auctions. We are also seeing electronic technologies influence how retailers manage stock pricing and how we actually buy or conduct a financial transaction—bringing into reality the idea of the cashless society.

Price Comparisons

With the ease with which information can be exchanged, we are also seeing the proliferation of web-based information brokers with information offerings of product and price comparisons. In the internet age, price comparison websites are an increasingly common feature of the electronic landscape. Examples include pricewatch.com and kelkoo.co.uk. Companies with strong sales in this channel need to consider competitors' prices, even if they do not meet those prices.

The British price comparison website moneysupermarket.com provides price comparison information across a broad range of products and services. Like its counterparts in the USA (e.g. Pricescan.com) and France (e.g. Monsieurprix.com), it is rapidly developing a large customer database. Examples of compared services on Moneysupermarket include complex services such as gas and electricity supply, insurance, mobile phone packages, and travel, as well as standard products like cars and car breakdown cover. The implication for large companies is clear. Marketers now work in a much more price-transparent environment, where both on- and offline customers want to know what the prices are, presented as simply as possible. Price comparison websites are having a dramatic impact on business for some of the organizations whose prices they are comparing against, since they are coming to be seen as overpriced compared to their competitors.

Online Auctions

With the internet we are seeing the increasing rise of online auctions because it is extremely easy to bring together a large number of buyers and sellers spanning various geographic regions and backgrounds. Within consumer markets as well, the internet has revolutionized how consumers purchase goods, bringing about the development of an entirely new market channel, i.e. consumer-to-consumer commerce through online sites such as Ebay.com and Amazon Exchange. These organizations take advantage of large customer and product databases to allow consumers to sell second-hand items to one another, and to allow people to develop entrepreneurial online businesses selling new and used items.

On Ebay, consumers and businesses list their items for sale by posting a photo of their product within a relevant category for that item. Ebay charge a set service fee for posting each single item. If you want your item to be more visible, Ebay offer the choice of multiple category listings and other services at extra cost. When the item is sold, there is no extra charge from Ebay. The seller sets the starting bid price and the item is made available to all bidders for a specified period of time (e.g. 3, 5, 7, 10 days). If the item is not sold, the seller will have to re-list, probably at a lower price, and pay the listing fee again. Individual bidders compete to purchase the item through the offering of incremental prices above

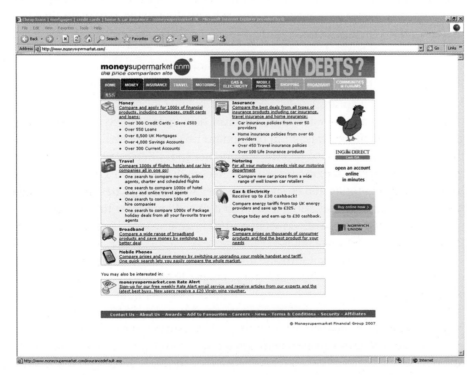

Moneysupermarket.com

Moneysupermarket.com is one of the price comparison sites available the original set bid price. The highest price at the end of the bid period wins the item at their final bid price.

In a typical commercial and consumer transaction, price is defined at a set level at which we do not usually go beyond in most transactions in Western markets. Haggling, where buyers and sellers argue over the price of the transaction, should be the norm only for a small range of transactions. In the auction, there is no such price ceiling. We define the notion of what consumers actually pay and what they may be willing to pay as consumer surplus. Auctions function to remove these consumer surpluses, since customers pay what they are prepared to, rather than what they have to, providing the original set bid price is reasonable. Ebay, the auction house, is happy because they have hundreds of millions of consumers listing their items worldwide on a daily basis. There are other types of auction, e.g. Dutch auctions where the price is set at a higher level and slowly reduced until someone decides to buy. In a reverse auction, the price is set by the customer rather than the seller.

Retail Revenue Management

Electronic technologies are further aiding management decision making by providing advanced tools for price modelling. In most cases, retail revenue management (RRM) systems replace manual decision-making processes based on reams of paper, educated guesses, and subjective rules of thumb. Retailers looking to implement more scientific processes use vendor systems and complex mathematical modelling tools which sort through volumes of sales and inventory data, and present retailers with suggested pricing tactics and estimated profit margins that can be achieved if those tactics are followed. The goal is to help retailers understand the financial effects of their pricing decisions.

The stakes are high: drug and grocery retailers spend billions of dollars each year on short-term promotions in which every nickel counts. A typical grocery chain that relies heavily on promotions could have 3,000 to 4,000 items on some kind of promotion in any given week. Even organizations that don't promote heavily are taxed by promotions. For example, a company which might only generate 20 per cent of their sales from promotions might outlay about 80 per cent of their weekly budget to manage these promotions. In fashion retailing markdowns are big business. ProfitLogic cites market research that estimates that 78 per cent of all apparel sold today at national chains has been discounted, up from 35 per cent in 1996. Retailers are losing more than $200 billion a year because of markdowns, according to analysis of retail and economic trends reported by the US Census Bureau and National Retail Federation.

With help from analytical software from companies such as DemandTec, retailers can design pricing strategies at a store or regional level, rather than apply consistent pricing and markdowns across all properties. Without automated tools, such customized pricing was not possible, observers say. The trend to invest in pricing and promotions optimization technology is catching on, AMR Research reports. The market for retail revenue management software should grow from about $475 million in 2002 to at least $500 million by 2005, the research firm says (Bednarz, 2003).

Transaction Management

A transaction occurs when buyers accept a price, and sellers receive payment in the form of something that both they and the buyers value. Therefore, when we talk about transactions here we are referring to the 'how, when, and where' aspects of the transaction process. Like so many other marketing activities, the 'how, when, and where' aspects of both business and consumer transactions have been influenced by developments in electronic systems and technologies. These include but are not limited to:

- Electronic payment systems (EPS);
- Electronic data interchange (EDI);
- Electronic funds transfer (EFT);
- Electronic funds transfer at point of sale (EFTPOS/EPOS);
- Network systems such as VANS and IVANS;
- Open buying on the internet: internet EDI (OBI);
- Banking internet payment systems (BIPS);
- Credit cards and stored value cards (SVCs); and
- Facsimile machines, telephones, and of course, the internet (Yu, Hsi, and Kuo, 2002; O'Connor, Galvin, and Evans, 2004).

Think about how often you use EFTPOS/EPOS to make an in-store purchase; how often you present a retailer loyalty card to a cashier to receive free or discounted promotional offers (e.g. fly-buys, coupons); how often you visit your local ATM to withdraw cash or check account balances; how often you purchase goods on the internet or pay your bills online; how often you use your credit card to pay for goods or do your banking via the telephone; or use the web to search for purchase-related information. As you can see, today, as a consequence of their increasing affordability and functionality, electronic technologies greatly facilitate consumer transactional activities, especially more recently with internet-based applications such as the web. For example, online retailing sales in Europe will more than double

RESEARCH INSIGHT 18.4

To take your learning further, you might wish to read this influential paper.

Jap, S. D. (2007), 'The impact of online reverse auction design on buyer–supplier relationships', *Journal of Marketing*, 71, 1, 146.

This article provides a useful discussion of online reverse auctions in industrial sourcing activities and their impact on inter-organizational performance. This research examines how the buyer's auction design (i.e. the number of bidders, the economic stakes, and price visibility) and the price dynamics over the course of the auction affect its relationship with suppliers.

in the next five years, to €263 billion in 2011, according to Forrester Research, as the number of online shoppers grows to 174 million (Forrester, 2006). Growth is also evident in B2B transactions with technologies facilitating sales transactions between businesses through EDI/VANs, websites, and extranets.

Key Considerations for Electronic Marketing

With the rise in electronic technologies, and their increasing use for marketing activities, come complications and changes to legislation and regulated business practices. The sorts of legal and regulatory issues that marketers need to increasingly consider include the following:

- Where does the marketing takes place? Commercial law is based on transactions within national boundaries, but electronic marketing (call centres handling phone enquiries or orders from one country to another, internet customers, etc.) exposes both customers and suppliers to risks outside these boundaries.

- Who owns the content? Copyright law is a national issue, and the copyright laws (what can and cannot be used without the originator's permission) differ from one country to the next. Some countries don't have copyright or intellectual property protection and so ideas, designs, etc. sent to those countries can be taken and used without the agreement of the copyright holder.

- Do you have the right permissions? Privacy legislation is also national, and the right of the organization to use information given to it via its electronic marketing efforts will be subject to this legislation. While some countries have no privacy legislation, at the time of writing the EC Privacy and Electronic Communications Directive governed the electronic collection, management, communication, and use of personal identifiable data in Europe.

- How secure is the data and information? Information and transaction security and protection from fraud is another area of increasing change. Legislation varies from country and region, with further differences evident in the laws that govern and protect consumer and business interests (e.g. distance selling regulations, consumer protection (e-Commerce) regulations).

- Does everyone have access? Disability and discrimination legislation also needs management consideration with the right to access for all becoming an important agenda item for the dissemination of information and services electronically.

Chapter Summary

To consolidate your learning, the key points made throughout this chapter are summarized below:

- Define what we mean by 'electronic marketing'.

  Electronic marketing is the process of marketing accomplished or facilitated through the application of electronic devices, appliances, tools, techniques, technologies, and or systems. This definition acknowledges the use of a wide array of electronic resources to improve the effectiveness and efficiency of the marketing process by aiding the management and implementation of marketing activities.

- Compare and contrast electronic marketing with other frequently used terms such as interactive and internet marketing.

  Interactive marketing is described as creating a situation or mechanism through which a marketer and a customer (or stakeholders) interact usually in real time. As such not all interactive marketing is electronic (e.g. face-to-face sales); not all direct marketing is electronic (e.g. print direct mail). In contrast, internet or online marketing is a form of electronic marketing limited in technical context and is thus a tool-based definition denoting the use of only internet-based technologies (e.g. web, email, intranet, extranets). This excludes the use of electronic broadcast media and stand-alone management information systems, amongst others. These terms are in contrast to electronic marketing as defined above, as encompassing a broader definition.

- Discuss and evaluate the key technology characteristics across which electronic technologies may differ.

  The characteristics of technology which marketing practitioners increasingly need to take into consideration when planning the adoption and use of electronic resources include vividness, synchronicity, pacing, interactivity, and mode of transfer. These structural properties across which electronic resources may differ and can be compared have an impact on the nature of the user experience, and the achievement of marketing objectives. As such, marketers need to be increasingly aware of their effect and their marketing implications.

- Consider the use of electronic technologies to achieve marketing objectives through the management and implementation of core marketing activities.

  Given the rapid development of electronic resources, and their use by the marketing profession, marketers further need to refrain from concentrating on specific technologies (e.g. web marketing, SMS marketing, mobile marketing), and focus on the activities for which these technologies are used. The electronic marketing activity management (EMAM) framework is one such approach that can assist the classification of electronic resources when planning what electronic resources to use for certain tasks, in order to achieve certain marketing objectives. EMAM outlines five core marketing activities for which we use electronic resources; these activities include: data acquisition; information provision, communication, and relationship management; transaction management; and distribution and logistics management. In essence, the most important aspect of electronic technology for marketing is not how innovative and unique technologies are, but rather what they will allow you to do differently, more effectively, and/or more efficiently.

Visit the **Online Resource Centre** that accompanies this book to read more information relating to new technology and marketing: www.oxfordtextbooks.co.uk/orc/baines/

❓ Review Questions

1 In your own words, define how electronic marketing differs from interactive and internet marketing.

2 Why is new technology of growing importance to marketing?

3 What do vividness, synchronicity, pacing, and interactivity entail and why are they important technology characteristics marketers should be aware of?

4 What are the three main modes of transfer?

5 What do we mean by electronic marketing activity management or EMAM?

6 What is search engine marketing (SEM) and why is it of growing importance?

7 What do we mean by observational data collection methods, and what role do cookie technologies or 'cookies' play in internet-based user observation?

8 Self-service technologies (SST) are dramatically changing the interaction between businesses and their customers. What impact are SSTs having on the provision of customer service for financial services?

9 What are retail revenue management (RRM) systems and why are they increasingly being adopted by large retailers?

10 Explain in your own words what are the key considerations marketers should be aware of in the implementation of electronic marketing activities.

❓ Discussion Questions

1 Having read the Case Insight at the beginning of this chapter, how would you advise the National Trust to develop their use of electronic technologies in their marketing?

2 Visit www.myspace.com and create your own MySpace if you don't already have one. Think of your use of MySpace. Who has control over how the content is viewed—you or your online friends? How fast is information exchanged? What type of interactivity does MySpace facilitate?

3 Discuss how the following technologies have influenced advertising and sales promotions activities:

(a) Database;

(b) Website;

(c) SMS;

(d) Cookies;

(e) Blogs.

4 You have been approached by Unilever, a leading manufacturer of fast-moving consumer goods. You have been asked to design an online survey for the testing of a new product concept. Discuss the use of online surveys for market research, their advantages and disadvantages.

5 Discuss the effect electronic technologies could have on the distribution of the following products:

(a) Music and/or video;

(b) Financial services;

(c) Fast-moving consumer goods.

📖 References

adverblog (2007), 'Toyota challenges Greek bloggers', *Blog*, 31 May, available at www.adverblog.com/archives/003088.htm, accessed June 2007.

Alshawi, S., Saez-Pujol, I., and Irani, Z. (2003), 'Data warehousing in decision support for pharmaceutical R&D supply chain', *International Journal of Information Management*, 23, 259–68.

Anon. (2007), 'Opinion: building a community spirit around your brand', *Brand Strategy*, 9 May, 10.

Arnold, S. (2003), 'The new Internet gold rush is search marketing', *Information World Review*, 193, 14.

Bednarz, A. (2003), 'New software helps retailers grow', *Network World*, 9 June, 25, 28.

Bitner, M. J., Ostrom, A. L., and Meuter, M. L. (2002), 'Implementing successful self-service technologies', *Academy of Management Executive*, 16, 4, 96–108.

Campaign (2004), 'The 10 best mobile campaigns', *Campaign*, 17 December.

Dewolfe, C. (2007), 'The MySpace generation', *Forbes*, 179 (7 May), 72–4.

Dickey, J., and Sullivan, J. (2007), 'Generational shift in media habits', *Mediaweek*, 17 (12 February), 10.

Dye, J. (2007), 'Meet Generation C: creatively connecting through content', *EContent*, 30 (May), 38–44.

Federman, J. (2006), 'Click-to-call can boost conversions', 6 March, available at www.imediaconnection.com/content/8524.asp, accessed 11 January 2007.

File, K. M., Judd, B. B., and Prince, R. A. (1992), 'Interactive marketing: the influence of participation on positive word of mouth and referrals', *Journal of Services Marketing*, 6, 4 (Fall), 5–13.

Forrest, E. (1999), *Internet Marketing Research*. Sydney: McGraw-Hill.

Forrester (2006), 'European net retail crosses the €100 billion mark—and keeps growing', *Forrester Research European eCommerce Forecast: 2006 to 2011*, 4 July, accessed 11 January 2007.

—— (2007), 'European online marketing tops €16 billion in 2012', 12 July, www.forrester.com/Research/Document/0,7211,41451,00.html, accessed December 2007. See Figure 8: Forecast: European internet advertising spend by type, 2007 to 2012.

Peltier, J. W., Schibrowsky, J. A., and Schultz, D. E. (2003), 'Interactive integrated marketing communication: combining the power of IMC, the new media and database marketing', *International Journal of Advertising*, 22, 1, 93–116.

Peterson, R. A. (ed.) (1997), *Electronic Marketing and the Consumer*, Berkeley: Sage.

Philips, S. (2005), 'Look to gaming promos to target youth market', *Promotions & Incentives*, November–December, 18.

Postini (2005), 'Spam activity report (October 2005)', 10 October, available at www.postini.com, accessed December 2007.

Rivers, L. M., and Dart, J. (1999), 'The acquisition and use of sales force automation by mid-sized manufacturers', *Journal of Personal Selling & Sales Management*, 19, 2, 59–74.

Sandoval, G. (2006), 'Social networking melds with videoconferencing', *CNET News.com*', 17 November, available at http://news.com.com/Social+networking+melds+with+videoconferencing/2100-1038_3-6136645.html, accessed 2 January 2007.

Sifry, D. (2005), 'State of the blogosphere, October 2005, part 1: on blogosphere growth', 17 October, available at www.technorati.com/weblog/2005/10/53.html, accessed December 2007.

Smith, J. (2005), 'Mobile marketing: Europe offers inspiration and ideas', 6 September, available at www.clickz.com/features/insight/article.php/3532366, accessed December 2007.

Strategies, I. (1999), 'Permission email: the future of direct marketing', available at http://whitepapers.zdnet.co.uk/0,1000000651,260013385p,00.htm, accessed December 2007.

Sum, C., Teo, C., and Ng, K. (2001), 'Strategic logistics management in Singapore', *International Journal of Operations and Production Management*, 21, 9, 1239–60.

Waring, T., and Martinez, A. (2002), 'Ethical customer relationships: a comparative analysis of US and French organisations using permission-based e-mail marketing', *Journal of Database Marketing*, 10, 1, 53–70.

Wasserman, T. (2005), 'Blogs cause word of mouth business to spread quickly', *Brandweek*, 3 October, 9.

Yao, A. C., and Carlson, J. G. (1999), 'The impact of real-time data communications on inventory management', *International Journal of Production Economics*, 59, 213–19.

Yu, H.-C., Hsi, K.-H., and Kuo, P-I (2002), 'Electronic payment systems: an analysis and comparison of types', *Technology in Society*, 24, 3, 331–47.

19

Postmodern Marketing

Q. What's the difference between a postmodernist and the Mafia? A. The postmodernist makes you an offer you can't understand!

Stephen Brown

Learning Outcomes

After reading this chapter, you will be able to:

✔ Explain possible meanings of the term postmodern.

✔ Explain the key features of postmodern marketing.

✔ Explain how markets are becoming increasingly fragmented.

✔ Recognize that in the postmodern context, production and consumption are reversed.

✔ Explain the role of semiotics in consumption.

✔ Deconstruct marketing 'texts'.

✔ Debate whether marketing is based more on science or art.

Livity is a youth marketing agency set up with the core aim to be socially responsible. It communicates sensitive messages to hard-to-reach audiences. We speak to Michelle Clothier and Sam Conniff to find out more.

Michelle Clothier and Sam Conniff for Livity

How should a marketing agency work with a government client to communicate sensitive sexual health messages (e.g. promoting condom use and safer sex) to a typically disaffected and hard-to-reach youth audience? This was the challenge facing Livity, set up in 2001 by co-founders Michelle Clothier and Sam Conniff.

We wanted the agency to harness the awesome power of marketing to good effect rather than just ruthless profit making, and early briefs from O2 and Lambeth Council allowed us to grow and develop expertise in this area.

> *kids…don't generally read magazines, listen to commercial radio, or access media in the ways that people are used to*

Part of the difficulty for us at Livity is that kids—particularly those in the target audience—don't generally read magazines, listen to commercial radio, or access media in the ways that people are used to. Our challenge was to determine how the sexual health message could be brought to life in their worlds.

Government attempts at getting teenagers to comply with societal rules, including drinking and driving, speeding, the 'Just Say No' drug campaigns of the 1980s and 1990s, and sexual health campaigns, for example, tended to use a hard-hitting fear appeal outlining the consequences of these activities, and therefore had limited effect as the audience switched off. We don't believe in scaring teenagers, who believe themselves to be impervious to all danger and that they are going to live forever anyway. They are used to being bombarded with messages telling them what to do and what not to do, and it's in every way natural and right for a teenager to do the opposite of what they are told, especially if it's being told to them by an institution or organization like the government. We say no to 'Just Say No' campaigns!

The difficulty is in getting across what is a very serious message, to respect yourself by engaging in safer sex when the time is right and to make an informed choice about sexual partners. We needed something symbolic, since symbolism plays an important part in young people's lives. We chose lyrics because lyrics symbolize

The Rhyme 4 Respect lyrics challenge
Livity

an everyday phenomenon to young people, a truly democratic medium; something everyone understands; something that everyone can be part of. Lyrics allowed us to benefit from the association with major pop artists to cut through possible cultural and literary barriers and overcome typical teenage resistance to 'broadcast' messages regarding sexual health. Essentially, music is the symbol of success and empowerment for our target audience.

We wanted to develop a campaign which was fun at the same time as being serious, to make it easier to deal with taboos like sexual health. Nevertheless, developing an advertising campaign which used lyrics to convey the message isn't enough in itself either. We needed something else. An approach which really engaged the audience, an audience with a developing appetite for X-factor type talent shows, competitions, and a desire to rate their peers.

Given the fragmented nature of the youth group, their disengagement with mainstream media and marketing vehicles, their age, and their roots in popular culture, how would you design the campaign?

Introduction

Have you ever seen an advertisement and wondered what it is trying to tell you? Have you seen any advertisements in which you were convinced that they were saying something very deep but you couldn't work out quite what? Have you ever enjoyed the process of purchasing something more than the use of it, without being disappointed? Why do some brands manage to build up a cult following while others can't? We discuss some of the answers to these questions and more in this chapter on postmodern marketing.

This chapter is written in a very different style and tone from the other chapters in the book, principally because **postmodernism** is a very different topic from other mainstream marketing topics and does not lend itself to orthodox, conventional explanation. In fact, not only is it an unconventional topic but it uses an unconventional tone. For that reason, to explain postmodernist concepts requires that we use a postmodern tone (otherwise we would be explaining postmodernism in a **modernist** style, which would be entirely against what postmodernism stands for). We explain as many of the words that we use as possible within the text to make the text flow better, and as these may not be familiar to you because they originate mainly from French cultural philosophy. Consequently, you should visit the glossary at the end of the book as often as is necessary to understand the concepts better.

But do not let the need to refer to the glossary deter you! Postmodern marketing is an excitingly different, yet demanding, subject. In a subtle way, it pokes fun at the received ideas of major foundational thinkers. What postmodernist thinkers do is remind us of the cultural context in which marketing operates, particularly associated with advertising and marketing communication, because mediated images are dominant in these contexts. Nevertheless, because postmodernist thinkers regard any work projected to an audience as a statement (not just communications but buildings, art, etc.), postmodern concepts are not exclusively linked with advertising and marketing communications, but with any marketing **artefact**.

We begin by defining first modernism, then its antithesis, its opposite, postmodernism, because postmodernism is really a rejection of modernist thought. We extend your understanding by applying postmodernism and its cultural implications to marketing, discussing ideas such as **fragmentation**, **hyperreality**, the self, and **inverted production/distribution** mechanisms, which may seem strange now but will become clearer later once they are described. In order to culturally ground the marketing discipline, we look at the changing nature of values within society, to provide evidence of movement in values among citizen-consumers in Western markets from materialist to post-materialist societies and so indicate the usefulness of postmodern concepts in marketing. In addition, we consider how **semiotics**—the so-called science of signs—can be used to help marketers understand the cultural grounding employed in adverts. We consider whether marketing is a **science** or an **art**, concluding in postmodern style that it is both but the science component has for too long been overemphasized. Finally, we take a brief look at green marketing and sustainability, providing further evidence of this paradoxical shift towards branded anti-consumption among consumers in the postmodern world.

The Concepts of Modernism and Postmodernism

Many writers do not bother defining postmodernism *per se*, or define it in relation to its exact opposite, modernism. Or they go on to describe it in such detail, and with such a diverse range of other terms, to render it almost indecipherable and meaningless to the common reader. For some, postmodernism is 'impervious to definition' (Heartney, 2001). The postmodern movement has gained popularity in the latter part of the twentieth century in a diverse range of areas including contemporary philosophy, art, critical theory, literature, architecture and design, marketing, business, history, cultural studies, and no doubt many others. The term postmodern is said to have first gained currency in architecture, where it denotes 'a rejection of the functionalism and brutalism of modern architecture (high-rise slums, impersonal box-like office blocks)' (Mautner, 1999). So postmodernism is first and foremost reactionary. As a movement, it disputes the way things are, and should be, and strives to be different in its approach. But this is not all that it is.

'Whereas modernism assumes that there is hidden meaning and truth and is engaged in a search for it, post-modernism, able to recognise absurdity when it sees it, has recourse to **pastiche**, many-layered **irony**, **flippancy**' (Mautner, 1999). So, postmodernism is essentially **anti-foundational** and certainly irreverent. In other words, it aims to show up, and poke fun at, our established beliefs. In typical obscure explanation, postmodernism has been defined as 'an incredulity towards **metanarratives**' (Lyotard, 1984), which means that postmodernists are critical and disbelieving of the overarching belief systems—metanarratives—often taken for granted and inherent in any discipline. Such metanarratives in Western society include beliefs in capitalist economic progress, the importance of scientific advancement, the idea of an objective reality, and the independent subject (or man as an unbiased rational observer).

However, we should understand that in order for something to be modern, that something must first have been postmodern. Consequently, postmodernism can be regarded as both the end of the evolution of one form of concept and the beginning of the evolution of another concept, with both in constant flux (Lyotard, 1984). As a result of this shifting between old and new, postmodernism represents a crisis of representation (i.e. is it old or is it new?), by which we mean that postmodernism indicates a break with the old ways of thinking and the re-enchantment, or resurrection, of new ways of thinking. We say resurrection here because postmodernism typically conjures up old associations and re-places them in a new light, providing us with new insights into old ideas. In art, for example, French artist Michel Duchamp's urinal, a piece of work he entitled *Fountain*, complete with his signature, rocked the art world in 1917. In suggesting that the signed urinal was a work of art, Duchamp was making a statement about the quality of existing art while at the same time questioning why urination was such a taboo in French society. His work was voted the most influential modern art work of the twentieth century by a survey of 500 art experts in 2004 (BBC, 2004), ahead of Picasso's *Guernica* and Andy Warhol's *Marilyn Diptych*.

Duchamp's work inspired that of influential English artist Tracy Emin, whose unmade bed 'work of art' created a media furore when it was shortlisted for the Turner Prize in 1999.

Postmodern Marketing

But how does the concept of postmodernism manifest itself in the way consumers consume? Whereas modern marketing is concerned with marketing to individual consumers, postmodern marketing is concerned with marketing to 'tribes' (building customers into communities of consumers). Whereas modern marketing is concerned with building the image of the company and the brand, postmodern marketers are concerned with building customer experiences. Postmodern marketing emphasizes the value of linking with a product/service rather than simply using it, focusing on co-creation of meaning in its use, rather than simply a transference of meaning from the producer to the consumer. For the postmodern marketer, the consumer actively participates in the brand experience, not simply acting as a passive recipient of advertising messages (see Cova, 1996).

There is increasingly a belief amongst consumer researchers that postmodern consumers are incapable of being grouped and segmented according to their needs (see Chapter 6). The postmodern consumption era is defined by the celebrated late French cultural critic and philosopher Jean Baudrillard (1995) as characterized by the fragmentation and trivialization of our values, images, and symbols. Fragmentation occurs in everyday life experiences and results in a loss of commitment to a single lifestyle (Firat and Shultz, 1997). In these circumstances, the consumer consumes (rather than just purchases), becoming both a customizer and producer of (self-) images in each consumptive experience (Dittmar, 1992; Firat, Dholakia, and Ventakesh, 1995; Gabriel and Lang, 1995).

Modern, as opposed to postmodern, marketing suggests that value for the consumer is materialized in the prescribed benefits of the bundle of product attributes offered to the consumer, and from value inherent in this bundle, customer satisfaction is obtained. But in postmodern markets, production and consumption are reversed. By this, we mean that there is emphasis on the consumption experience, as opposed to what it is that is actually being consumed or purchased. (See Market Insight 19.1.) In service-based markets, this linkage between production and consumption is pronounced further as production and consumption are considered to be inseparable (see Chapter 15). In postmodern service markets, the emphasis leads to an exaggeration of the importance of process in some cases: of the importance of form over content. For example, in both American and British political campaigns, the increasing use of marketing has led to a perceived slickness of the electoral machinery, a development of the form of citizen politics but not a corresponding development in the substance, the policy, of politics. But politics is just one example.

As a distinct area of thought in marketing, postmodernism has a set of central conditions and key features which focus on the following concepts (Firat and Shultz, 1997):

Who's Watching Whom? *Big Brother* and the Birth of Reality Television

A more obvious example of the phenomenon of the reversal of production and consumption is the movement in television generally towards reality ('living soap') TV shows, where the audience is actually taking part both in voting for the outcomes of the show, and quite often in actually appearing on the show itself as contestants. Examples of such shows include *Big Brother*, first developed by producer John de Mol, and his production company Endemol, in the Netherlands in September 1999, copied quickly in the UK, and exported to many countries around the world including Australia, Russia, countries of the Middle and Far East, and many more, and *Pop Idol*, developed in the UK but successfully exported to the USA as *American Idol* and elsewhere albeit with slightly different formats.

In *Big Brother*, 'housemates'—a motley crew of less than fifteen or so people from the general public and/or sometimes so-called celebrities—are housed in a specially designed studio apartment, kitted out with CCTV in all rooms, so that TV audiences can watch as the housemates interact with each other, sometimes in erotic, disastrous, and humorous circumstances. The housemates are kept in the apartment for a fixed length of time, without any contact with anybody else, except those in the house and Big Brother—a voice which booms over the microphones in the apartment tasking housemates to keep them busy for the audience's amusement. At set intervals, the housemates are asked to divulge their feelings on being in the house and to give their views on who of their housemates should be nominated for eviction. The general public is then asked to vote to 'evict' a particular contestant with the most nominations from the housemates. The housemate remaining at the end is the winner of a substantial cash prize.

Sources: www.bigbrother.com; www.wikipedia.org; http://www.channel4.com/bigbrother/.

1 In what ways are production and consumption reversed in this example, from the perspective of the TV audience?

2 Why do you think the format of this show is so successful? What has been the secret of its marketing success?

3 Can you think of other areas of entertainment where we co-produce the final product?

• Hyperreality—postmodern markets are hyperreal where illusory and fantastical experiential components of brands are represented to us instead of the functional concrete attributes of brands. Reality is constituted through hype and simulation.

• Fragmentation of markets—in postmodernity, there is recognition that we are individuals with multiple or **multiphrenic** (from 'multi' meaning many and 'phrenia' meaning mind) personalities without commitment to a single lifestyle, acting in different ways in different circumstances, at different times, with different people, in different cultures. Experiences with products and services are disjointed and disconnected as a result.

- Reversal of production and consumption—in postmodern times, when produce is plentiful, we no longer satisfy our needs but our desires. This change in emphasis requires a complete change in focus on production and consumption. Instead of producing what we need, manufacturers have shifted marketing emphasis to produce what we desire, a level of product and particularly service development more focused on experiential phenomena. Instead of simply passively accepting a product or service, consumers have shifted to actively interpreting brands and how they are used.

- Decentred subject—consumers are becoming dominated by the things they consume and the experiences they have. Instead of simply having one self operating in different purchase situations, consumers have many selves operating in different consumption experiences.

- **Juxtaposition** of opposites—whereas the modern world can be described in extremes using unipolar and black and white differentials, such as good *or* evil, for example, or nice *or* nasty, in the postmodern world, we use bipolar dimensions, known as **dialectics**, such as good *and* evil, nice *and* nasty, to explain events, things, places, or other phenomena.

Elliot (1997) argues that consumption in the postmodern era has changed over the latter part of the twentieth century across five such dialectics, which he states include the following:

1 The material versus the symbolic;

2 The social versus the self;

3 Desire versus the satisfaction;

4 Rationality versus irrationality; and

5 Creativity versus constraint.

We consider each of these in the following sections.

The Material versus the Symbolic

Consumption experiences have moved from the satisfaction of mere needs to the realms of the symbolic. Consumers are consuming not only the material

RESEARCH   INSIGHT 19.1

To take your learning further, you might wish to read this influential paper.

Elliot, R. (1997), 'Existential consumption and irrational desire', *European Journal of Marketing*, 31, 3/4, 285–96.

This article considers marketing in the contemporary world from the perspective of five dialectics—material/symbolic, social/self, desire/satisfaction, rationality/irrationality, and creativity/constraint—to provide insights into consumption from cultural, social, and psychological perspectives. Elliot argues that the consumption process is an end in itself and that consumers derive personal meaning and identity from the consumption process, not just from obtaining the offering.

components of the products but the actual meaning that they represent to them. We shift as consumers, not merely as purchasers of petrol from, say, a Shell petrol station, but as purchasers of petrol from a company that we may, or may not, believe is a worldwide environmental leader. As postmodern consumers, we are (not) buying corporate image and activism, just as much as we are consuming their products.

Luxury goods, for example, Prada handbags, Mont Blanc pens, and Vertu's exclusive mobile phone range, are products which sell at very high retail price points. They are sold not purely on their functionality but on their **aesthetic**—visual and sensory—value. The Prada handbag is the epitome of chic, the Mont Blanc pen the epitome of design and sophistication, and the Vertu phone the epitome of arrival and style. But although we might expect luxury goods to be sold on the basis of their symbolism, there is an increasing shift towards marketing any product on its symbolism. Witness the movement by some companies towards ethical branding, e.g. Ben & Jerry's ice cream, the Co-operative Bank and The Body Shop in Britain, and the Italian retailer Benetton. These companies are not simply selling their products, but also their stance on particular issues. For instance, Ben & Jerry's are famous for their positive stance towards the alleviation of world social and environmental problems. The Co-operative Bank has a policy of ethical investment, and so does not bank arms manufacturers, tobacco companies, and other contentious business organizations. Benetton is perhaps the most famous and controversial example, having used high-profile advertisements to raise awareness of social problems and issues in the late 1980s and early 1990s. Similarly, The Body Shop has also embraced, not uncontroversially, the idea of not testing cosmetics on animals (since it was alleged that its suppliers of cosmetic components had tested their products on animals!).

A key feature of postmodern marketing is the development of products and services which feature a new theme on an old product. Brown (2001) defines this as retromarketing or 'the revival or relaunch of a product or service brand from a prior historical period, which is usually but not always updated to contemporary standards of performance, functioning, or taste'. Such examples include the iconic Volkswagen (VW) Beetle relaunched in 1998 and the New Mini, which attempt to recreate and conjure up associations associated with the past for a new set of consumers. More recently, Michelin, the French tyre maker, travel assistance, and lifestyle product manufacturer, recast Bibendum, also known as 'the Michelin man', back in its adverts. First created in 1898, Bibendum has gone from being rather overweight in form to being spritely and dynamic in his modern incarnation. Go to http://bibendum-in-museums.michelin.com/indexen.htm to see more on Bibendum as he has evolved over the twentieth century. (See also Market Insight 19.2.)

Retromarketing attempts to induce feelings of pseudo-nostalgia. We mean pseudo-nostalgia because many consumers may not have experienced the original brand. So postmodern marketers try to reproduce an 'authentic' version of the previous model but enhance it in some way to bring it into the present. The fact that the product is really a copy however makes it inauthentic.

The fact that some consumers will not have encountered the original version makes the new version, to that group of consumers at least, a copy without an original. This is what Baudrillard (1995) refers to as a **simulacrum**.

Back to the Future: The Royal Enfield Bullet Electra

Royal Enfield

Back to the future with
the Royal Enfield Bullet

Perhaps the most famous of the original Royal Enfield brands was the Bullet, first built in 1931, which typified the company's logo 'built like a gun, goes like a bullet'. In 1949, an updated model, the 350 cc Bullet, was launched in India, sold to Madras Motors, to cater for an order won from the Indian Army. The original Bullet model was so successful that its design remained unchanged for over thirty years. In 1955, Royal Enfield, the motorcycle maker based in Redditch in the UK, decided to sell Indian manufacturers a licence to produce its single-cylinder motorcycle, not least because the Indian Army refused to buy motorcycles from non-domestic motorcycle manufacturers in the post-colonial period after India won its independence from the United Kingdom. So the Enfield India Company was born.

By 1970, demand in the UK for Enfield motorcycles had bottomed out and whereas the UK company was forced to close, the Indian company went from strength to strength. It now sells around 30,000 motorcycles per year. In March 1994, the Eicher group acquired Enfield, changing its name to Royal Enfield Motors Limited. In 1999, Watsonian-Squire, Britain's oldest maker of motorcycle sidecars, acquired the licence to sell the Indian-made Enfield in the UK, which now represents the Indian company's largest export market. The Bullet Electra, the flagship model, is not a particularly fast bike, with a top speed of 78 miles per hour, but is very economical at 87 miles per gallon and requires little maintenance, so appealing to the first-time buyer. So what was good for the Indian Army, travelling up the Khyber Pass, is still good for the Brits. Plus ça change!

Sources: www.royal-enfield.com; Jaggi (2006).

1 Why do you think the Enfield Bullet is proving to be a successful export to the UK?

2 To what extent does the Bullet's Anglo-Indian heritage impact on the consumer, do you think?

3 What other retro products have you come across recently? Did you feel any degree of nostalgia for the brands?

A simulacrum is a copy without an original. A simulacrum develops through successive evolutionary image-phase-changes comprising different stages of (mis)representation:

1 An image which reflects a profound reality (a *good* likeness);

2 An image which masks and denatures a profound reality (a *bad* likeness);

3 An image which masks the absence of a profound reality (something which plays at being an appearance); and

4 An image which has no relation to any reality whatsoever (a simulacrum, a copy without an original or a simulation).

The concept of the simulacrum helps us to understand how images are produced, and reproduced, in postmodern times, particularly through our electronic media culture.

When numerous simulacra come together, we encounter a play of illusion and phantasm (i.e. ghostlike, fleeting appearance), effectively a theme park. One example of such inauthenticity and simulation is the inauthentic 'authentic' Irish theme pubs, supposedly made to resemble original Irish drinking dens, and deliberately made to look as if they have heritage by appearing older in décor than they really are. For Baudrillard, Disneyland and Las Vegas are the perfect examples of places incorporating simulacra. Using fake fantastic worlds, with no reference to any myth or children's folklore (unlike in Europe, for example, where some theme parks conveyed the fantastical worlds of celebrated Danish author Hans-Christian Andersen), Disney for example quite literally created a Mickey Mouse world, complete with its own fantastical themes. This use of fantasy and illusion, with no real basis in reality, produces a hyperreality.

The Social versus the Self

Consumer goods have always meant more to us as consumers than for what they can do, functionally. But in the postmodern environment, goods and services not only affirm who we are to ourselves but who we are to others. There is social status in owning particular kinds of goods or using particular kinds of services. Our possession of these goods and services projects meaning about us to others within a cultural context. What is particularly different in postmodern environments is how easy it is to change ourselves, to be someone different. For example, in cyberspace, our anonymity—consuming unknown from behind a computer screen—means that we behave differently because we can operate as multiple selves, consuming in different patterns on different sites than we might otherwise if we were to buy the same things in person. (See Market Insight 19.3.) But this pattern of buying is increasingly transgressing the real as well as the virtual world, as consumers' individual identities become fragmented, as they become isolated from existing communities, knowing fewer people within the area where they live, but more people across the world, and across cyberspace.

Whereas marketers in the past may well have focused on rational consumer buying motives, there is an increasing acceptance and movement towards the idea that consumers purchase things not because of what they want, but what

RESEARCH INSIGHT 19.2

To take your learning further, you might wish to read this influential paper.

Firat, A. F., and Shultz II, C. J. (1997), 'From segmentation to fragmentation: markets and modern marketing strategy in the postmodern era', *European Journal of Marketing*, 31, 3–4, 183–207.

Firat and Shultz's article provides a definitive understanding of how postmodern conditions in the market environment, what the authors call a 'social phenomenon', affect marketing strategy. Particular focus is devoted to the concept of fragmentation, in terms of images, identity, and customer commitment, demonstrating the increasing need consumers have to be, rather than to have, to experience rather than to acquire, to co-produce goods and services rather than to simply receive goods.

they do not want. Cova (1997) talks of deconsumption, where consumers reject virtual satisfaction through purchasing and repurchasing activity because the acquisition of material possessions is no longer a new or exciting phenomenon for them. Whereas families in the 1800s may have had 150 to 200 possessions in their home, a typical family at the beginning of the twenty-first century may have many thousands of possessions. As the postmodern consumer loses contact with the community in the traditional sense, time-starved as he or she is, they increasingly crave satisfaction through **emotion** shared with others, and particularly through experiences.

MARKET INSIGHT 19.3

Marketing in the Community: Ebay.com

First set up in 1995, Ebay—the innovative online auctioneer—sells everything to everyone, from comics and cars, to tools and TVs and lots more besides. In addition to its consumer-to-consumer offerings, where members trade with each other, Ebay offers online 'stalls' to businesses, and has created millions of online millionaire entrepreneurs over the years since it started. Ebay operates as an online marketplace bringing together buyers and sellers, and taking a fee for each product or service sold on the site, charging extra fees for advertising and other services.

Over a relatively short period of time, Ebay has gone from strength to strength to become the world's 47th largest brand in 2006 (note: the brand, not the company) valued at US$6.7 bn, according to Interbrand's survey of the world's top 100 brands. Such phenomenal growth has occurred through the development of the Ebay community where members join the site and interact with one another during auctions. In 2005, Ebay acquired the peer-to-peer, voice over internet protocol (VOIP) provider Skype, as a means by which Ebay members could communicate with each other more easily and free of charge, across often large geographic boundaries.

The UK division of Ebay, Ebay.co.uk, has enjoyed much the same rise in reputation. In 2006, Douglas McCallum, ebay.co.uk CEO, announced at the Institute of Directors' Convention that it had become the nation's largest

Glass, K. (2006), 'Top 10 tips for targeted email marketing', *B&T Weekly*, 3 November, 21.

Guegan, P. (2007), 'Keep it simple, honest and focused', *Advertising Age*, 23 April, 23.

Hamm, S. (2007), 'Children of the web: how the second-generation internet is spawning a global youth culture and what business can do to cash in!', *Business Week*, 2 July, 50.

Hein, K. (2006), 'Advergaming attracts large A-list players', *BrandWeek*, 11 September, 47, 15.

Herzog, C., Reitsma, R., and de Lussanet, M. (2005), 'Europe's mobile consumer', 16 June, available at www.forrester.com/Research/Document/Excerpt/0,7211,36954,00.html, accessed December 2007.

Hof, R. D. (2006), 'There is not enough me in MySpace', *Business Week* (New York), 4 December, 40.

Honeycutt, E. D. J., Thelen, T., Thelen, S. T., and Hodge, S. K. (2005), 'Impediments to sales force automation', *Industrial Marketing Management*, 34, 4 (May), 313–22.

IAB-PwC (2005), 'H1 2005: Online adspend grows 62%', July, available at www.iabuk.net/media/images/IABPwCadspendstudyfactsheetH12005_409.pdf, accessed December 2007.

IMT (1999), 'permission email: the future of direct marketing', available at http://whitepapers.zdnet.co.uk/0,1000000651,260013385p,00.htm, accessed December 2007.

Kennedy, C. (2005), 'In search of excellence', *Director*, 59 (September), 22.

LeClaire, J. (2006), 'Skype extends social networking to VoIP', *TechNewsWorld*, 3 May, available at www.technewsworld.com/story/50318.html, accessed 2 January 2007.

Li, C., Bernoff, J., and McHarg, T. (2004), *Blogging: Bubble or Big Deal? When and How Businesses Should Use Blogs*, New York: Forrester Research Ltd.

Liao, S., Shao, Y. P., Wang, H., and Chen, A. (1999), 'The adoption of virtual banking: an empirical study', *International Journal of Information Management*, 19, 63–74.

Linton, I. (1995), *Database Marketing: Know What your Customer Wants*, London: Pitman.

Lockwood, L. (2007), 'Talking to a generation: brands turn to YouTube to spread the message', *WWD: Women's Wear Daily*, 193 (29 May), 1–9.

McGann, R. (2005), 'RFID tag market to swell tenfold by 2009', 18 January, available at www.clickz.com/showPage.html?page=3460851, accessed September 2007.

McGovern, G. (2004), 'Blogs and blogging: advantages and disadvantages', 23 August, available at www.gerrymcgovern.com/nt/_2004_08_23_blogging.htm, accessed December 2007.

Meuter, M. L., Bitner, M. J., Ostrom, A. L., and Brown, S. W. (2005), 'Choosing among alternative service delivery modes: an investigation of customer trial of self-service technologies', *Journal of Marketing*, 69, 2 (April), 61–83.

Mitch, J. (2006), 'Building le buzz', *Marketing*, 10 April, 19.

Morrissey, B. (2002), 'Spam under the tree: internet advertising report', 24 December, available at www.clickz.com/news/article.php/1561201, accessed December 2007.

Nail, J., Charron, C., and Cohen, S. (2005), *The Consumer Advertising Backlash Worsens*, New York: Forrester Research.

New Media Age (2004), 'Best use of wireless winner', *New Media Age*, 11 November, 29.

Norman, D. (1990), *The Design of Everyday Things*, New York: Doubleday.

O'Connor, J., Galvin, E., and Evans, M. (2004), *E-marketing: Theory and Practice for the Twenty-First Century*, Harlow: Pearson Education Ltd.

Page-Thomas, K. L. (2005), 'Electronic marketing: the bigger picture', *Marketing Review*, 5, 3 (Autumn), 243–62.

To take your learning further, you might wish to read this influential paper.

Firat, A. F., and Shultz II, C. J. (1997), 'From segmentation to fragmentation: markets and modern marketing strategy in the postmodern era', *European Journal of Marketing*, 31, 3–4, 183–207.

Firat and Shultz's article provides a definitive understanding of how postmodern conditions in the market environment, what the authors call a 'social phenomenon', affect marketing strategy. Particular focus is devoted to the concept of fragmentation, in terms of images, identity, and customer commitment, demonstrating the increasing need consumers have to be, rather than to have, to experience rather than to acquire, to co-produce goods and services rather than to simply receive goods.

they do not want. Cova (1997) talks of deconsumption, where consumers reject virtual satisfaction through purchasing and repurchasing activity because the acquisition of material possessions is no longer a new or exciting phenomenon for them. Whereas families in the 1800s may have had 150 to 200 possessions in their home, a typical family at the beginning of the twenty-first century may have many thousands of possessions. As the postmodern consumer loses contact with the community in the traditional sense, time-starved as he or she is, they increasingly crave satisfaction through **emotion** shared with others, and particularly through experiences.

Marketing in the Community: Ebay.com

First set up in 1995, Ebay—the innovative online auctioneer—sells everything to everyone, from comics and cars, to tools and TVs and lots more besides. In addition to its consumer-to-consumer offerings, where members trade with each other, Ebay offers online 'stalls' to businesses, and has created millions of online millionaire entrepreneurs over the years since it started. Ebay operates as an online marketplace bringing together buyers and sellers, and taking a fee for each product or service sold on the site, charging extra fees for advertising and other services.

Over a relatively short period of time, Ebay has gone from strength to strength to become the world's 47th largest brand in 2006 (note: the brand, not the company) valued at US$6.7 bn, according to Interbrand's survey of the world's top 100 brands. Such phenomenal growth has occurred through the development of the Ebay community where members join the site and interact with one another during auctions. In 2005, Ebay acquired the peer-to-peer, voice over internet protocol (VOIP) provider Skype, as a means by which Ebay members could communicate with each other more easily and free of charge, across often large geographic boundaries.

The UK division of Ebay, Ebay.co.uk, has enjoyed much the same rise in reputation. In 2006, Douglas McCallum, ebay.co.uk CEO, announced at the Institute of Directors' Convention that it had become the nation's largest

Ebay: the innovative
online auctioneer

Ebay

second-hand car retailer, beating long-established automotive trading companies, without having to advertise for buyers. For its phenomenal development, Ebay has relied on the principle of word of mouth, that people will tell their friends when they've managed to get a good deal, whether they're in cyberspace or not.

Source: http://www.interbrand.com.

1   Why do you think people want to become part of an online marketplace community like Ebay?

2   Do you think your own identity in terms of the purchases you make is different when you are shopping online compared with when you are offline? How is it different?

3   What are other examples of strong communities developed online? Have you joined any of these? Why did you do so?

Cova (1997) refers to the process of like-minded (de)consumers gathering together as tribalism. Its effects in the postmodern world are clear for all to see and result in the kind of mass demonstrations, organized by anti-consumer activists, that we saw in Seattle in the USA at the beginning of the millennium. These kinds of events tend to occur on a much more frequent basis in today's world.

Table 19.1

Percentage of
population who
have taken part in a
consumer boycott

Country	1974 (%)	1981 (%)	1990 (%)	1995 (%)	2000 (%)	Net shift 1974–2000 (%)
Britain	6	7	14	n/a	17	+11
West Germany	5	8	10	18	10	+5
Italy	2	6	11	n/a	10	+8
The Netherlands	6	7	9	n/a	22	+16
United States	16	15	18	19	25	+9
Finland	1	9	14	12	15	+14
Switzerland	5	n/a	n/a	11	n/a	+6
Austria	3	n/a	5	n/a	10	+7
Mean	6	8	11	12	15	+9

Source: Inglehart and Welzel (2005: 122). Inglehart, Ronald F., and Christian Welzel. *Modernization, Cultural Change and Democracy*. Cambridge University Press, 2005.

Table 19.1 provides some interesting data from the World Values Survey providing an insight into the shift in Western Europe and the United States towards consumer activism, or what is often termed **consumerism**, in the last quarter of the twentieth century. Consumer activism, a key component of the anti-globalization movement, has particularly risen in the Netherlands and Finland but in Britain as well, although, in general, consumerism remains the highest in the USA over the period 1974–2000.

MARKET INSIGHT 19.4

The Tribe of Harley-Davidson

In 2005, Harley-Davidson Inc. celebrated its twentieth consecutive year of record revenue and earnings. Consolidated revenue was $5.34 billion and net income was $959.6 million. The Harley-Davidson company not only sells its now eponymous brand of motorcycles that Dennis Hopper and Peter Fonda rode in the classic 1960s Hollywood road film *Easy Rider*, but it also sells customized accessories and merchandise, financial services, and motorcycle hire and training, through Rider's Edge®—the Harley-Davidson® Motorcycle Training Academy—around the globe.

Harley-Davidson not only sells its eponymous brand of motorcycles

Harley-Davidson

Harley-Davidson operates a strategy of super customer engagement, recognizing the importance of its customers and its employees, working hard to make it easy for new owners to purchase their dream bike, and for existing customers to upgrade to a new model, at the same time as retaining links with them in the biking community through the Harley Owners Group®, which aims to build and reinforce a biker's identity with both Harley-Davidson and the free-spirited romantic thinking associated with motorcycling in the *Easy Rider* film. With more than a million members, HOG®, is a unique organization of consumers, 'brothers and sisters', organized into 'local chapters', representing the world's largest factory-sponsored organization in the world.

In testament to the importance of customer retention, nearly 5 in 10 (49%) Harley-Davidson® purchasers in 2006 already owned a Harley-Davidson® motorcycle although 1.4 in 4 (14%) were new to motorcycling and the remaining customers, nearly 4 in 10 (37%), moved away from competitors' motorcycles. In 2006, nearly 9 in 10 buyers were male, although just more than 1 in 10 were female, a statistic which has increased somewhat for the last five years. The median buyer was around 47 years old and earned around $80 k, so this is a high-earning, predominantly male, tribe. Harley-Davidson's mission statement explains it all: 'We fulfil dreams through the experiences of motorcycling by providing to motorcyclists and the general public an expanding line of motorcycles, branded products and services in selected market segments.'

Sources: Harley-Davidson, Annual Report, 2004. www.harley-davidson.com.

1 Why do you think motorcyclists want to become part of the Harley-Davidson 'tribe' of consumers?

2 Have a look at the company's website. How has it developed this cult following?

3 Consider other cult brands with a tribe of followers. What product categories do they come from?

Others argue that although there are a few examples of such tribes of consumers, as in the Harley-Davidson example in Market Insight 19.4, in actual fact such examples are few and far between, and in the main where they do exist, they exist not because they have subverted the product aimed at them but are actually responding to the marketing (Firat, 2005).

Desire versus Satisfaction

Whereas in the modern era, the focus was upon satisfying the consumer, particularly through functional appeals, in the postmodern era, the focus shifts to consumer desire. Not so much satisfying desire, because desire can never be satisfied, but simply allowing the consumer to recognize that desire exists and to experience its effects. Much post-war American advertising has tended to focus on functional appeals, particularly in print advertising, where wordy adverts outline how a particular product satisfies a particular consumer need.

For Baudrillard ([1968] 2005: 195), such rational appeal to consumer choice (see Chapter 3) fails to explain why particular brands and commodities are so in demand. For him, economic concepts of consumer decision making needed to be replaced with a theory of the value of signs, which recognizes the importance of symbolism, and desire, as opposed to need (Cherrier and Murray, 2004). Postmodern marketers recognize the consumer shift away from simply satisfaction of functional needs. Although advertising has long fed our desires as consumers, in postmodern environments, as consumers, we want others to see our desires met also.

In postmodern markets such desire, for its own sake even, is both accepted and acceptable. The consumer is left with the message that it is good to desire something just for the sake of experiencing it, and not because one actually needs it. Consequently, appeals to consumer desire as opposed to consumer rationality are persuasive because they appeal to the subconscious, often through sexual appeal and the satisfaction of previously taboo desires (Elliot, 1999). For some marketing commentators, this shift towards satisfying consumer desire is a step too far. For them, marketing is increasingly being used to increase consumption to the benefits of capitalist exploitation 'by creating a logic of signs and codes that has no other virtue but to serve a system of competitive power where consumer needs are purely dominated' (Cherrier and Murray, 2004).

Rationality versus Irrationality

Consumers buy and consume products and services because they have fun with them, enjoy their use, and gain pleasure from them. These are outcomes of our consumption experience. But although this might seem common sense to you, for many years consumer behaviourists have stressed that consumers consider functionality, the results of the use of the product/service, as primary customer considerations.

But our evaluative criteria for brand selection are also psychosocial (e.g. aestheticism, play) rather than simply economic. Inputs to the purchasing decision are based on considerations of time, as well as money, hedonism as opposed to

To take your learning further, you might wish to read this influential paper.

Holbrook, M. B., and Hirschmann, E. C. (1982), 'The experiential aspects of consumption: consumer fantasies, feelings and fun', *Journal of Consumer Research*, 9 (September), 132–40.

This definitive article was the first to really challenge the received impression that consumers buy goods purely on a rational basis. Holbrook and Hirschmann have suggested that existing consumer behaviour models do not take account of irrational and experiential considerations. They stress the experiential process of consumer purchasing. Our **cognitions** of, thoughts about, the brand may not only encompass our current memories but information from our subconscious, imagery rather than simply knowledge and structure, and fantasies and daydreams.

problem solving, right-brain thinking as opposed to left-brain thinking, exploratory behaviour as opposed to information-acquisitive behaviour, and personality type rather than customer characteristics such as lifestyle or social class. Environmental inputs into this experiential consideration of consumer decision making stress the following:

- Syntactic forms of communication—how something is said—as opposed to semantic forms—what is actually said;
- Non-verbal as opposed to verbal stimuli; and
- Subjective features, as opposed to objective functions, of a product or service.

The experiential consumer decision-making process is particularly appropriate to buying situations involving consumer experiences of entertainment, arts, and leisure products, for example, visits to museums (Goulding, 1999). Other such experiences might include visits to dry ski slopes, travel and leisure generally, and so on.

In making decisions about what we consume, we may use different frames of reference at different points in time to evaluate our experiences. Postmodernists suggest that we are 'multiphrenic', a kind of consumer multiple personality (dis)order where we may simultaneously want something and not want it at the same time, or want very different things at the same time, or want very different things at different times for the same purpose, and so on.

Creativity versus Constraint

In the postmodern world, opposing social forces exist. By this we can question whether advertising reflects reality or reality reflects advertising. In other words, are our needs reflected in the advertising or is the advertising reflected in our needs? There is to some extent a backlash by many citizen-consumers against the kind of materialism that advertising has long implicitly put forward. Constant advertising of a good or service leads to the development of the idea that materialism in society is a good thing, that the feeding of our materialistic desires is

The multiphrenic consumer

Reproduced with the kind permission of Mark Silver, www.marksilver.co.uk

something worthy of our attention and action. In many, this creates a kind of **psychological reactance** (see Chapter 3), and a desire to adopt a different and opposing frame of reference. Consumption from this new frame of reference, in a creative way, is a way of restoring the freedom those postmodern consumers feel that they are in danger of losing. This leads to the development of a new form of tribal behaviour (Cova, 1997), where consumers develop entire communities around the symbolic consumption of goods and services. Examples of such communities include the Harley Owners Group, and owners of the Volkswagen Beetle.

People's values are defined in marketing as 'consensual views about the kind of life individuals should follow, formal and informal rules specifying the goals they should pursue and how they should pursue them' (Foxall, Goldsmith, and Brown, 1998). Values tend to change and differ from one country to another. In the 2005 World Values Survey (Inglehart and Welzel, 2005), numerous countries around the world were organized into eight distinct socio-cultural zones as follows:

1 *Protestant Zone* (excluding English-speaking countries): Denmark, Estonia, Finland, Germany, Iceland, Latvia, the Netherlands, Norway, Sweden, Switzerland.

2 *English-Speaking Zone*: Australia, Canada, Great Britain, Ireland, New Zealand, USA.

3 *European Catholic Zone*: Austria, Belgium, Croatia, Czech Republic, France, Hungary, Italy, Lithuania, Luxembourg, Malta, Poland, Portugal, Slovakia, Slovenia, Spain.

4 *European Orthodox and Islamic Zone*: Albania, Armenia, Belarus, Bosnia-Herzegovina, Bulgaria, Georgia, Macedonia, Moldova, Romania, Russia, Turkey, Ukraine, Yugoslavia.

5 *Confucian Zone*: China, Japan, South Korea, Taiwan, Vietnam.

6 *Latin American Zone (plus the Philippines)*: Argentina, Brazil, Chile, Colombia, Dominican Republic, El Salvador, Mexico, Peru, Philippines, Uruguay, Venezuela.

7 *Islamic Zone (plus India, excluding European Islamic societies)*: Algeria, Azerbaijan, Bangladesh, Egypt, India, Indonesia, Iran, Jordan, Morocco, Pakistan.

8 *Sub-Saharan African Zone*: Nigeria, Tanzania, Uganda, Zimbabwe.

The survey is highly useful to marketers, since it provides an indication of how different countries have similar socio-cultural approaches and their relative differences in values, which helps marketers in developing their international marketing strategies and understanding further their own cultures. Generally, throughout the world, people's values are shifting from **materialist** goals to **post-materialist** goals, emphasizing self-expression and quality of life, similar to what Maslow (1943) called self-actualization needs (see Chapter 3), as opposed to economic and physical security, or what Maslow called safety needs.

As we see increasing conflict between the Middle East and the West, there is a rise in Muslim brands aimed specifically at the Muslim **diaspora** around the world. In Britain, Qibla Cola has launched itself as a Muslim alternative to Coca-Cola, with the wonderful tagline 'liberate your taste' (Hall and Wentz, 2003), with all its associations to anti-American imperialism. Al-Jazeera, the pan-Arab Qatari-based television broadcaster, has also set its sights on Western markets, targeting non-Arab Muslims and covering more than just issues of Islamic interest (Mutel, 2004).

Researching Fragmented Markets

Because of the experiential components of consumption behaviour, the analysis of postmodern consumer buyer behaviour requires the use of research approaches from **cultural anthropology** and **ethnography**. While modern consumer research has used experiments and surveys, postmodern consumer research uses ethnographies, study of the behaviour of specific groups from within the group. It adopts qualitative forms of research as opposed to quantitative research (see Chapter 4) and is focused on developing theories of consumer behaviour using the emerging data rather than with testing theories developed prior to the data collection.

Although modern consumer research tends to be economic/psychological and micro/managerially focused, postmodern research focuses much more on socio-logical/anthropological paradigms. Postmodern researchers are concerned with

making as the world, and the European Union in particular, frets over the issue of how industrialization is causing unwanted climate change. Some critics have suggested that climate change will cause the melting of polar ice caps, freak tsunamis like the one that devastated Indonesia, Thailand, and India in December 2005, and other freak weather events.

Chapter Summary

To consolidate your learning, the key points from this chapter are summarized below:

- Explain possible meanings of the term postmodern.

  Postmodernism can be described as the artform of society (Scott, 1992). It is first and foremost a reactionary movement. It disputes the way things are, and should be, and strives to be different in its approach. The postmodern movement gained popularity in the latter part of the twentieth century in a diverse range of areas including contemporary philosophy, art, critical theory, literature, architecture and design, marketing, business, history, and cultural studies. The concept first gained currency in architecture. As a philosophical concept, it indicates a break with past ideas regarded as received wisdom (what Lyotard calls metanarratives) and the development of new ideas based on a rejection of the old ones.

- Explain the key features of postmodern marketing.

  In the marketing context, a postmodernist application would indicate that marketers need to think more about how we go about segmenting our markets, since markets are fragmenting, about how our consumers choose goods and services, because they are irrational as well as rational beings, being careful not to characterize them as being of one type since we display different selves in purchasing and consumption. Postmodernism in marketing is an orientation, a way of thinking and rethinking, about how we experience the marketing world around us. It denotes a break with the past, with the old concepts of marketing described above, towards a new theory of how marketing should interact with customers in the future. To do this, postmodern marketers will accept the multiphrenic nature of the consumer, experiencing and co-creating the brand, rather than simply consuming it, as the modernist marketers might assert. Postmodern markets are hyperreal, or simulated environments, which are increasingly fragmented in terms of their customer bases and the identities of those customers. Increasingly, customers are more involved with the process of production and consumption and co-produce those consumer products and experiences in a situation where product/service development begins from the perspective of consumption first with production secondary. The customer becomes dominated or owned by his or her experiences rather than the reverse where in the past customers might have been more likely to have dominated and owned their products. Marketing in the postmodern world has dialectical features with seemingly opposite characteristics existing simultaneously, focusing on the material/symbolic, social/self, desire/satisfaction, rational/irrational, and creativity/constraint dimensions.

- Explain how markets are becoming increasingly fragmented.

  In contemporary society, there has been a fragmentation and trivialization of our existing values over the course of the late twentieth century as we have moved from a materialist to a post-materialist society. This fragmentation has also taken place in markets, as consumers as individuals develop apparently multiple personalities in consumption contexts and weak commitment to a single lifestyle. We act in different ways in different circumstances, at different times, with different people, in different cultures, defying market segmentation and positioning programmes which seek to categorize us within groups of consumers.

- Recognize that in the postmodern context, production and consumption are reversed.

  In postmodern times, when produce is plentiful, we no longer simply satisfy our needs but also our desires. The change in emphasis has required a complete shift in focus from production to consumption. Instead of producing what consumers need, manufacturers have shifted marketing emphasis to producing what they desire, a level of product and particularly service development more focused on experiential phenomena. Instead of simply passively accepting a product or service, consumers have shifted to actively interpreting brands and how they are used, and are increasingly involved in the co-creation of the products/services in a metaphorical, symbolic, as well as a literal sense.

- Explain the role of semiotics in consumption.

  Semiotics is the science of signs. A sign can be anything which represents meaning and includes sensory information such as visuals/pictures, sound/music, taste, smell, touch/pain, and cultural forms such as film, dance, gesture, mime, and architecture. In analysing signs, we use linguistic concepts developed by Saussure to determine what is signified by a signifier. Peirce took the concept a stage further by identifying a concept which he called the 'interpretant' which indicates the shared cultural meaning that derives as a result of the image projected from the object. Semiotics is used by marketers to understand such image-meanings, to embed the macro-analysis of consumer decision making into a theory of cultural interaction. As a result, we can link the consumer to his or her purchasing context to determine how the two interact with each other. Semiotic analysis is particularly useful as a technique to analyse the intended strategy behind competitors' advertising approaches as an alternative to positioning studies.

- Deconstruct marketing 'texts'.

  Semioticians often talk of 'texts' and anything that conveys meaning as a 'text'. Approaches to analysis of 'texts' include the use of the deconstruction linguistic technique, mostly commonly associated with French philosopher Jacques Derrida. In deconstruction, the aim is to determine what the 'text' is trying to convey by revisiting its meanings. The reader searches for gaps, inconsistencies, and underlying 'absences' in the text (Derrida, 1967). The textual analysis breaks the text down into privileged themes, and then determines a series of 'binary opposites' (e.g. man/woman, white/black, right/wrong) of those privileged themes as the hidden or absent meaning of the work. Once these binary opposites have been determined, the deconstruction technique proposes that the lesser non-privileged binary opposite is what the focus of the work was *really* about.

- Debate whether marketing is based more on science or art.

  According to Brown (1996), the intellectual development of marketing has been hindered over the course of the latter half of the twentieth century as the discipline has remained wedded to modernist concepts of scientific application. The discipline would benefit from a concentration on a subjective, rather than an objective, orientation, from a focus on experience and imaginative self-expression, and the use of multiple approaches to research methodology, as opposed to rigid scientific (i.e. empirical) approaches only. Marketing research should aim to create meaning and generate understanding of marketing phenomena to alter managers' and consumers' perceptions, rather than to discover 'truth'. Although marketers have always tried to increase the effectiveness of marketing by linking it with popular culture, marketing artefacts are increasingly coming to be seen as art in themselves and so marketing is itself becoming popular culture.

 Visit the **Online Resource Centre** that accompanies this book to read more information relating to postmodern marketing: www.oxfordtextbooks.co.uk/orc/baines/

❓ Review Questions

1 Try to define postmodernism in your own words.

2 Explain the contexts in which postmodern marketing operates.

3 What are the key features of postmodernism in marketing according to Elliot?

4 What is a simulacrum?

5 How are postmodern markets becoming increasingly fragmented?

6 When postmodernists say that production and consumption are reversed, what do they mean?

7 What is the juxtaposition of opposites?

8 What is the discipline of semiotics?

9 What are the three components of the positioning triad?

10 Is marketing more of a science or an art discipline?

❓ Discussion Questions

1 Having read the Case Insight at the beginning of this chapter, how would you advise Livity to devise its next sexual health campaign to teenagers? Given the fragmented nature of youth, their disengagement with mainstream media and marketing vehicles, their age, and their roots in popular culture, how would you design the campaign?

2 Explain how each of the following dialectic postmodern concepts is relevant in marketing the following three service offerings: (1) material versus symbolic, (2) social versus self, (3) desire versus satisfaction, (4) rationality versus irrationality, and (5) creativity versus constraint.

   (a) A newly themed Irish pub.

   (b) The Harley-Davidson motorcycle.

   (c) A L'Oréal designer perfume, such as Viktor and Rolf's men's fragrance Antidote.

3 Analyse a postmodern advertisement of your choice with which you are familiar. In order to select your postmodern advertisement, remember that they tend to be parodies, poking fun at existing ways of doing and seeing things. They might also be surreal. They can appear both in print form in magazines and newspapers and on TV. If in doubt, ask your tutor to help you select an appropriate one. Use Derrida's deconstruction method to determine what the advertisement is really trying to say.

📖 References

Baudrillard, J. ([1968] 2005), *The System of Objects*, trans. James Benedict, London: Verso Books.

——(1995), *Simulacra and Simulation*, trans. Sheila Faria Glaser, Ann Arbor: University of Michigan Press.

BBC (2002), 'Century of the self part 1: happiness machines', aired Monday, 29 April, BBC4, London: British Broadcasting Corporation.

——(2004), 'Duchamp's urinal tops art survey', 1 December, available at http://news.bbc.co.uk/1/hi/entertainment/arts/4059997.stm, accessed 4 March 2007.

Belk, R W. (1995), 'Studies in the new consumer behaviour', in D. Miller (ed.), *Acknowledging Consumption*, London: Routledge, 58–95.

Brown, S. (1995), *Postmodern Marketing*, London: Routledge.

——(1996), 'Art or science: fifty years of marketing debate', *Journal of Marketing Management*, 12, 243–67.

——(2001), *Marketing: The Retro Revolution*, London: Sage Publications.

Brownlie, D., Saren, M., Wensley, R., and Whittington, R. (1999), *Rethinking Marketing: Towards Critical Marketing Accountings*, London: Sage Publications.

Cherrier, H., and Murray, J. B. (2004), 'The sociology of consumption: the hidden facet of marketing', *Journal of Marketing Management*, 20, 509–25.

Cova, B. (1996), 'The postmodern explained to managers: implications for marketing', *Business Horizons*, November–December, 15–23.

——(1997), 'Community and consumption: toward a definition of the "linking value" of products or services', *European Journal of Marketing*, 31, 3–4, 297–316.

Derrida, J. (1967), *Of Grammatology*, trans. Gayatri Chakravorty Spivak, Baltimore: Johns Hopkins University Press.

Dittmar, H. (1992), *The Social Psychology of Material Possessions*, Hemel Hempstead: Harvester Wheatsheaf.

Elkington, J. (2007), 'Switch on the value blender', *The Marketer*, January, 17–19.

Elliot, R. (1997), 'Existential consumption and irrational desire', *European Journal of Marketing*, 31, 3–4, 285–96.

——(1999), 'Symbolic meaning and postmodern consumer culture', in D. Browlie, M. Saren, R. Wensley, and R. Whittington (1999), *Rethinking Marketing: Towards Critical Marketing Accountings*, London: Sage Publications.

Firat, A. F. (2005), 'Meridian thinking in marketing: a comment on Cova', *Marketing Theory*, 5, 2, 215–19.

——Dholakia, N., and Ventakesh, A. (1995), 'Marketing in a postmodern world', *European Journal of Marketing*, 29, 1, 239–67.

——and Shultz II, C. J. (1997), 'From segmentation to fragmentation: markets and modern marketing strategy in the postmodern era', *European Journal of Marketing*, 31, 3–4, 183–207.

Foxall, G., Goldsmith, R., and Brown, S. (1998), *Consumer Psychology for Marketing*, 2nd edn., London: International Thomson Business.

Freud, S. (1927), *The Ego and the Id*, Richmond: Hogarth Press.

Gabriel, I., and Lang, T. (1995), *The Unmanageable Consumer: Contemporary Consumption and its Fragmentations*, London: Sage Publications.

Goulding, C. (1999), 'Contemporary museum culture and consumer behaviour', *Journal of Marketing Management*, 15, 647–71.

Hall, E., and Wentz, L. (2003), 'Qibla cola takes traditional tack', *Advertising Age*, 74, 44 (3 November), 20.

Harvey, M., and Evans, E. (2001), 'Decoding competitive propositions: a semiotic alternative to traditional advertising research', *International Journal of Market Research*, 43, 2, 171–87.

Heartney, E. (2001), *Movements in Modern Art: Postmodernism*, London: Tate Publishing.

Holbrook, M. B., and Hirschmann, E. C. (1982), 'The experiential aspects of consumption: consumer fantasies, feelings and fun', *Journal of Consumer Research*, 9 (September), 132–40.

Inglehart, R., and Welzel, C. (2005), *Modernisation, Cultural Change and Democracy: The Human Development Sequence*, Cambridge: Cambridge University Press.

Jaggi, R. (2006), 'Let's do the time warp again', *Financial Times*, 23–4 September.

Lawes, R. (2002), 'Demystifying semiotics: some key questions answered', *International Journal of Market Research*, 44, 3, 251–64.

Lyotard, J.-F. (1984), *The Postmodern Condition*, Paris: Les Éditions de Minuit.

Maslow, A. H. (1943), 'A theory of motivation', *Psychological Review*, 50, 370–96.

Mautner, T. (1999), *Dictionary of Philosophy*, London: Penguin.

Mick, D. G. (1986), 'Consumer research and semiotics: exploring the morphology of signs, symbols and significance', *Journal of Consumer Research*, 13, 196–213.

Mutel, G. (2004), 'Al-Jazeera to go global and broadcast in English', *Campaign* (UK), 41 (8 October).

Peirce, C. S. (1931–58), *Collected Papers*, ed. Charles Hartshorne, Paul Weiss, and Arthur W. Burks, Cambridge, Mass: Harvard University Press.

Proctor, S., Papasolomou-Doukakis, I., and Proctor, T. (2001), 'What are television advertisements really trying to tell us? A postmodern perspective', *Journal of Consumer Behaviour*, 1, 3, 246–55.

Scott, L. M. (1992), 'Playing with pictures: postmodernism, poststructuralism, and advertising visuals', *Advances in Consumer Research*, 19, 596–611.

Zakia, R. D., and Nadin, M. (1987), 'Semiotics, advertising and marketing', *Journal of Consumer Marketing*, 4, 2 (Spring), 5–12.

20

Marketing Ethics

A business that makes nothing but money is a poor kind of business.

Henry Ford (1863–1947)

Learning Outcomes

After reading this chapter, you will be able to:

✔ Define the term ethics and apply the discipline to marketing.

✔ Explain the common ethical norms applied in marketing.

✔ Describe the role of ethics in marketing decision making.

✔ Analyse situations to determine the kind of ethical approaches that might be adopted.

✔ Recognize how to apply an understanding of ethics to a company's marketing programmes.

✔ Explain the difficulties associated with developing the socially responsible company.

The Co-operative Bank was the first and remains the only UK high street bank with a customer-led Ethical Policy which gives customers a say in how their money is used. We speak to Kelvin Collins to find out more.

Kelvin Collins for The Co-operative Bank

In a recent customer panel over 60% of customers said, 'Well of course we expect you to offer a green mortgage!' Our customers have high expectations from us.

I believe that 'Green' shouldn't be dull, or a sacrifice. Whatever industry we're in, I believe we should seek out ways to deliver what we all need, then make it better with environmental benefits. I call this Bright Green.

> ### I believe that 'Green' shouldn't be dull, or a sacrifice

Yet look at our industry—we're rate crazy. A quick scan of the newspapers would leave anyone thinking the whole country buys on rate alone. However, a recent *Guardian* survey indicates that less than 40% of us are with our financial services provider just because of price. Ethics—in all its varied forms—recruits our customers and keeps them with us.

The origins of our parent company, The Co-operative Group, lie in social banking: in other words, concern for our customers. We have our roots in The Co-operative Movement of the late eighteenth century, which was based on a philosophy that businesses should be run for the benefit of customers, the people who work in them, their families, and the wider community—not a privileged few. In our long life, we have introduced many innovations into the banking sector, including such headline-grabbing moves as being the first high street bank to introduce free banking and internet banking.

The year 1992 was a particularly exciting one for us: we built on our achievements by introducing a customer-led Ethical Policy. What's unique about our policy is that it is based on the issues that matter most to our customers. It covers issues as diverse as the arms trade, the environment, genetic modification, and much more. And it's not just hot air—since we launched the policy we've turned away over £700 million of loans that have conflicted with our policy.

We also offer different levels of engagement to suit our customers. They all contribute to our Customers Who Care campaign through spending on their credit or debit cards. But they can also join our campaigning activity and lobbying government, if that's what they want. One of the first campaigns called for a ban on landmines—now outlawed in 144 countries—since then we've campaigned on a wide range of issues from third world debt to human rights, biodiversity to safer chemicals, and trade justice. We are passionate about ethical banking; our commitment is genuine and we have to convey this to our customers. They expect us to deliver. Every time.

But marketing can sometimes be more about perceptions than substance. Although we were one of the pioneers of ethical business in the UK, the broader marketplace has now finally recognized that consumers do care about social responsibility, and the environmental impact on business, and so other brands have started to adopt ethics and green issues as part of their brand values.

The question is how do we continue to differentiate ourselves from these newcomers in the marketplace, remain true to our history, and take our business forward at the same time?

The **co-operative** bank
good with money

Make a tiny difference to the world. Every day.

I made a choice to be with a bank that stands up for the issues I care about – such as global climate change. It means I never have to worry how my money is invested. It's why they're the right bank for me – they're good with money.

Are you with us?
co-operativebank.co.uk

Part of The **co-operative** financial services

Introduction

Does your bank charge you huge penalty fees if you go above your overdraft limit? Do you have to pay more for a coffee on campus than at the local Starbucks? What is an acceptable level of profit for a company to make? How much should non-profit organizations make above and beyond their costs? When should companies give back to their communities? What is 'good' marketing behaviour and what is 'bad' marketing behaviour? Are corporate social responsibility initiatives a good idea or are they cynically used by organizations to further their own ends or to suck up to consumers? These are some of the questions we consider in this chapter.

We begin by explaining what ethics is before applying ethics to the marketing context. We outline how ethical situations impact on the marketing decision-making process. Four main ethical approaches to marketing decision making are outlined. Ethical situations arising in product, promotion, price, and distribution programmes are also explained. We consider ethical issues in international marketing, i.e. whether or not different cultures should have different moral rules. Finally, we give some consideration to what the socially responsible company might look like.

Understanding marketing ethics is important to business students because there is a need to understand ethical, legal, and social dimensions of marketing decision making and develop analytical skills for considering ethical marketing problems. Since the financial scandals of Enron and WorldCom, when major multinational American companies misreported their financial status to inflate their companies' values, there has been an increased interest in business ethics and the socially responsible company worldwide. But this is not the only driver for increased interest; other drivers include:

- An increasing belief that corporate social responsibility leads to increased business performance.

- Government legislation, e.g. the American Sarbanes–Oxley Act 2002, which set up an oversight board for the US accounting profession, strengthened auditor independence rules, increased accountability of officers and directors of companies, enhanced the timeliness and quality of finance reports of public companies, and placed restrictions on the selling of shares in certain situations.

- The increase in global trade and the rise of the multinational company with interests across country boundaries, particularly in developing countries.

- The rise of global media companies, operating on a continual 24 hour/7 days a week basis, such as the BBC World Service, CNN, and Asia News, with the potential to damage corporate reputations among large sections of the public around the world.

(opposite)

A Co-op poster displaying marketing ethics

Co-operative Bank

The Origins of Ethics

Ethics as an academic discipline has been around for over 2,000 years. It is a well-developed system of thinking within the discipline of philosophy. The *Oxford English Dictionary* defines ethics as follows:

- The science of morals, the department of study concerned with the principles of human duty;
- The moral principles or system of a particular leader or school of thought; and
- The whole field of moral science, including the science of law whether civil, political, or international.

Ethics is concerned with morality (from the Latin *moralis*), with doing 'good' in the realms of civil, political, and international life. The word ethics was originally derived from the Greek *ethos*, meaning habit or custom. Ethics can be divided into the following types:

- **Normative ethics**—concerned with the rational enquiry into standards of right and wrong (i.e. norms), good or bad, in respect of character and conduct and which *ought to be* accepted by a class of individuals.
- **Social or religious ethics**—concerned with what is right and wrong, good and bad, in respect of character and conduct. It does not claim to be established merely on the basis of rational enquiry and makes an implicit claim to general allegiance to something (e.g. God).
- **Positive morality**—a body of knowledge that is generally adhered to by a social group of individuals, concerning what is right and wrong, good and bad, in respect of character and conduct.
- **Descriptive ethics**—concerned with the study of the system of beliefs and practices of a social group from the perspective of being outside that group.
- Metaethics—a form of philosophical enquiry which treats ethical concepts and belief systems as objects of philosophical enquiry in themselves.

The study of ethics is concerned with answering Aristotle's age-old question, 'what is the good life for man?' But such a question brings a further question of what is 'good'? The *Oxford English Dictionary* defines good as 'implying the existence in a high, or at least satisfactory, degree of characteristic qualities which are either admirable in themselves or useful for some purpose'. Good implies something is either 'fit for purpose' or possesses admirable characteristics. But what is 'fit for purpose' and for whom should this action be admirable?

Ethics and Marketing

When Western people think of ethics they might think of the Ten Commandments, said to have been passed down to Moses from God on Mount Sinai and carved onto two stone tablets, according to Judaeo-Christian doctrine, proposing that man must not kill, commit adultery, take another God, blaspheme, and the importance of observing the Sabbath day, for instance, among other prescriptions. Muslim readers may well believe that the Ten Commandments were corrupted over the years and are only revealed in the Qur'an, and the practices of the Holy Prophet, which added dimensions such as the importance of not approaching lewd behaviour in open or secret, the importance of keeping one's word, looking after orphans, and not taking life except in the name of law and justice. These two sets of codified ethics are normative, therefore they are prescriptive. They provide for how we *ought to* behave.

Buddhists might think of ethics from the perspective of the Buddha's Five Precepts (i.e. principles), including the need to refrain from harming living creatures, to refrain from taking that which is not freely given, to refrain from sexual misconduct, to refrain from idle speech, and to refrain from intoxicants which lead to loss of mindfulness and to follow the Noble Eightfold Path, with prescriptions about how to attain wisdom, virtue, and develop mental concentration. Other world religions have their own, and different, prescriptions emphasizing particular concerns. We mention the religions above because it is from this point that many people understand and analyse ethical behaviour, i.e. from a religious perspective, even if they do not believe in God. But religious belief is not a necessary condition to evaluate one's actions ethically. So, how does ethics relate to marketing?

Earlier, we defined ethics as the study of morality in order to determine how the 'good' person should behave. In order to determine how to apply ethics to marketing, we must first redefine what marketing is. Although there are numerous definitions in Chapter 1, we shall take the Chartered Institute of Marketing's (CIM) definition here as 'the management process responsible for identifying, anticipating and satisfying customer requirements profitably'. So how does ethics relate to marketing? We could perhaps suggest that marketing ethics is concerned with how we go about that management process of identifying, anticipating, and satisfying customer requirements. The application of ethical principles also should consider what meaning is given to the term profitable. Islamic readers

RESEARCH INSIGHT 20.1

To take your learning further, you might wish to read this influential paper.

Hunt, S. D., and Vitell, S. (2006), 'The general theory of marketing ethics: a revision and three questions', *Journal of Macromarketing*, 26, 2, 143–53.

Probably the most highly cited paper in marketing ethics, Hunt and Vitell's original article, 'A general theory of marketing ethics' in the *Journal of Macromarketing* in 1986, defined and gave momentum to the study of marketing ethics. This updating paper suggests that the original 1986 theory required revision because the model was applicable in any ethical decision-making situation, not just in business and management contexts, and required empirical testing. The authors argue that ethical judgements lead to intentions and on to behaviour. Our intentions are made on the basis of whether an action is right in itself (i.e. deontological ethics) and whether our intentions are right (i.e. **teleological ethics**).

may not be entirely happy with the ultimate objective of a firm being to achieve profit. They might well feel that it is more worthy for a firm to aspire to value maximization (Saeed, Ahmed, and Mukhtar, 2001). Because there are both prescriptive and descriptive components of ethics, we define marketing ethics as: *'The analysis and application of moral principles to marketing decision making and the outcomes of these decisions.'*

Marketing Ethics in the Profession

Professional marketing organizations typically have a code of professional practice which requires members to behave and act in a manner consistent with their professional status. The Chartered Institute of Marketing, the world's largest member-based marketing organization, require their members to:

- Demonstrate integrity, bringing credit to the profession of marketing;
- Be fair and equitable towards other marketing professionals;
- Be honest in dealing with customers, clients, employers, and employees;
- Avoid the dissemination of false or misleading information;
- Demonstrate current knowledge of the latest developments and show competence in their application;
- Avoid conflicts of interest and commitment to maintaining impartiality;
- Treat sensitive information with complete confidence;
- Negotiate business in a professional and ethical manner;
- Demonstrate knowledge and observation of the requirements of other (professions') codes of practice;
- Demonstrate due diligence in using third-party endorsement which must have prior approval; and
- Comply with the governing laws of the relevant country concerned (CIM, 2005).

Ethical Norms in Marketing Decision Making

Norms are suggestions about how we *ought to* behave. In ethics, these typically include four general approaches: (1) managerial egoism, (2) deontological ethics, (3) utilitarianism, and (4) virtue ethics (see Table 20.1). Each of these main approaches is outlined in further detail below. Do not be overly concerned about determining the differences between each of these approaches at this stage. As you read through each section and the associated examples, you will begin to understand the differences. If necessary, read through this section several times before moving on to the next section.

Ethical approach	Explanation
Managerial egoism	A form of ethical approach which recognizes that a manager ought to act in his or her own best interests and that an action is right if it benefits the manager undertaking that action.
Utilitarianism	An ethical approach originally developed by English philosopher and social reformer Jeremy Bentham which suggests that an action is right if, and only if, it conforms to the principle of utility, whereby utility is maximized (i.e. pleasure, happiness, or welfare)—and pain or unhappiness minimized—more than any alternative.
Deontological ethics	A form of ethical approach where the rightness or wrongness of an action or decision is not judged to be exclusively based on the consequences of that action or decision.
Virtue ethics	A form of ethical approach associated with Aristotle, which stresses the importance of developing virtuous principles, with developing 'right' character, and the pursuit of a virtuous life.

Table 20.1
The main normative approaches to ethical decision making

Managerial Egoism

The rationale for egoism is the pursuit of our own interests, or self-interest. In relation to marketing, we have to assume that the interests of marketing managers in an organization are in agreement with the interests of the organization's owners or directors, which they may not be. Nevertheless, if they are, then the ethical principle of **managerial egoism** is the maximization of shareholder value or stakeholder value (for a non-profit). Equally, in the marketing-driven firm, the goal might be the maximization of customer equity, or customer value, which is linked to shareholder value (Doyle, 2000).

If managers aim to maximize their own self-interest within the free market, economic welfare is maximized across the population, according to Adam Smith (1776). If we adopt the managerial egoist principle, then we would conclude that companies should set their marketing programmes so as to maximize shareholder or stakeholder value. There is some evidence to suggest that companies offering services rather than goods might require employees to be more ethical since there is a greater opportunity for unethical behaviour due to the greater interaction between company and customer and the trust generated from this interaction (Rao and Singhapakdi, 1997).

Milton Friedman suggested that managers should only have responsibility to maximize shareholder returns since they 'lack the wisdom and ability to resolve complex social problems' (1979: 90). He argued that managers' limited understanding meant that they are unsuitable for ethical problem decision making. Economists have long suggested that markets are amoral, i.e. without any particular moral stance. The free market mechanism does not work to promote ethical decisions by marketers or managers alike, but it does work in such a way as to supply the optimal amount of goods and services in a society.

There is a view that marketers should not concern themselves with ethics, as long as they uphold the law and manage their own self-interest, since unethical behaviour is subject to sanction in the marketplace in any case. Firms will pursue their own self-interest and act ethically anyway (Gaski, 1999). However, although consumer wants exert a powerful control on marketing behaviour, consumers' veto or boycott power alone is not enough to properly regulate a market (Clasen, 1967).

Some have argued that if marketers act according to the law or a company's self-interest this is merely a moral minimum. Most societies would require companies to go beyond these, e.g. the American pharmaceutical company Merck produces and distributes Mectizan, a treatment for river blindness, for a market which was unlikely to be profitable but could substantially improve the lives of many people (Smith, 2001).

It is not always possible to determine whether a company is pursuing a managerial egoist approach (i.e. acting in their own self-interest because ultimately this will benefit others), or a shareholder value maximization approach. The two can seem to be the same. The cynical person will wonder whether a company which goes beyond its legal duties and apparently acts according to higher morals (e.g. The Body Shop, Benetton, the Co-operative Bank) is simply trying to win over public opinion and maximize long-term shareholder value rather than truly be ethical.

This charge is frequently aimed at companies running corporate social responsibility (CSR) programmes. Where the views of the stakeholders are considered important, e.g. the mass media, it makes sense for the company to clearly outline its ethical standpoint and why they are pursuing this approach, as GSK and other pharmaceutical companies realized in the South African pharmaceutical market for anti-retroviral drugs (see Chapter 10), and Nestlé found out in the African baby milk market.

Utilitarianism

An ethical approach originally developed by English philosopher and social reformer Jeremy Bentham, **utilitarianism**, suggests that an action is right if, and only if, its performance will be more productive of pleasure or happiness or welfare, or more preventive of pain or unhappiness, than any alternative (Mautner, 1999). Utilitarian arguments are concerned with the *consequences* of an action. Most ethical arguments put forward by marketers are utilitarian. Indeed, the very concept of marketing could be argued to be utilitarian since it is typically concerned with satisfying consumer needs and wants at the market level (Nantel and Weeks, 1996).

Generally, utilitarianism is concerned with 'producing the greater good for the greatest number of people'. The problem with utilitarian ethical decision making is that the maximization of one group's utility can sometimes lead to the minimization of another group's utility. In order to determine the utility associated with a particular decision, it is necessary to determine the 'costs' and 'benefits' which, quite often, are more or less impossible to quantify. Where products may save lives, such as with life-saving drugs or health treatments, it is possible that the losers will pay with their lives and the gainers will survive, particularly where that product is in scarce supply.

The concept of utilitarianism is easily explained if we consider how a train operating company determines how to improve its health and safety record, for instance, when deciding how much to spend on safety instrumentation (i.e. signalling and track equipment). In such a situation, the company has to decide exactly how much to spend on protecting passengers' health and safety needs. The costs of purchasing and fitting equipment to reduce what industrial safety engineers call the **fatal accident rate** (FAR) are typically passed on to the customer. A decision over whether or not to fit the equipment, and how much to spend on it, requires a calculation of the likely reduction in risk of accidents against how likely the passengers are to pay the increased prices, or the company alternatively will have to absorb the extra costs. This might be the decision-making process for a train company considering its health and safety requirements from a utilitarian perspective. The question is, is it an acceptable approach? Many would argue not, stating that if even one life lost or damaged could be avoided then the company has a duty to improve the health and safety of all passengers regardless. The decision to ration supplies is an extreme example of utilitarianism, as has occurred with electricity in Chile in 1999, with food and some household goods in many parts of Europe during the Second World War, and with petrol in Iran in 2007.

Deontological Ethics

Deontological ethics proposes that the rightness of an action is not determined by the consequences of that action (Mautner, 1999). The opposite of deontology is concerned with the consequences of a moral decision, and is known as teleology. Deontological ethics tend to emphasize the importance of codes of ethics, e.g. those outlined by the Market Research Society (MRS) governing market research in Britain, or by ESOMAR (European Society for Market and Opinion Research) in Europe.

Deontological approaches to marketing ethics propose that we have not only a moral duty to ensure the satisfaction of our customers and consumers through the finished product or service but also a duty to ensure integrity in the way that the product or service is manufactured and marketed to them. The Co-operative Bank prides itself on the fact that it is against animal testing, fur trading, investment in defence companies, and acts to advance many other social causes.

In Rawls' *Theory of Justice* (Rawls, 1972), he argues that in a just society the following two conditions must be met:

1 'Each person is to have an equal right to the most extensive total system of equal basic liberties compatible with a similar system of liberty for all' (Liberty Principle).

2 'Social and economic inequalities are to be arranged so that they are both:

   (a) to the greatest benefit of the least advantaged; and

   (b) attached to offices and positions open to all under the conditions of fair equality of opportunity' (Difference Principle).

The application of the principle to marketing situations suggests that vulnerable groups in society should not be disadvantaged further by management and marketing decisions. Indeed, they should be positively helped. It is to this principle that the international media implicitly appeal when criticizing international pharmaceutical companies, oil and gas companies, and banks for what they term to be excessive profiteering. This approach to ethical decision making would suggest that we have a duty to help the disadvantaged, particularly where they are likely to be adversely affected by our actions.

Virtue Ethics

The ethical theories outlined above, managerial egoist, utilitarian, and deontological, provide the marketer with ethical decision-making approaches that can be used to choose between alternative courses of 'right' action. In direct contrast, **virtue ethics** stresses the importance of developing virtuous principles, with 'right' character, and the pursuit of a virtuous life. This branch of ethics is associated principally with Aristotle (Mautner, 1999). Virtue ethics is an approach which proposes the development of good character, suggesting that in this context, we should aim to develop the virtuous marketing organization within a company. But what virtues should a company strive to develop? The idea behind this approach is that if we live a virtuous life, then virtuous decision making will develop naturally.

Many companies claim that they are virtuous. The values statements of some pharmaceutical and oil and gas companies emphasize the importance of 'integrity'. But exactly what does this mean and how is it operationalized within the company? Such an approach to marketing ethics requires a company to consider exactly what kind of values it really wants to promote and then requires the company to act in accordance with those values.

Aristotle, in *Nicomachean Ethics*, defines virtue as 'a settled disposition of the mind which determines choice, and essentially consists in observing the mean relative to us, a mean rationally determined, that is, as a man of practical wisdom would determine it' (Mautner, 1999). He goes on to define eleven virtues comprising bravery, self-control, generosity, magnificence, self-respect, balanced ambition, gentleness, friendliness, truthfulness, wittiness, and justice. It is more difficult to apply these concepts to a company, since a company does not have a character in the same way that a person does, although its employees do. Nevertheless, it is possible to consider how these virtues *might* relate to a company. For example, generosity might relate to the development of CSR programmes, or incentives given to employees. Table 20.2 provides an outline of each virtue and how it might be applied to an organization.

The Ethical Decision-Making Process

Now that we have defined the four main ways in which we analyse how an organization *ought* to behave, we turn to how organizations have actually gone about making ethical decisions. According to Hunt and Vitell (2006), a manager first

Table 20.2

Moral virtues applied
to companies

Moral Virtue	Application in business and marketing
Bravery, valour	Bravery in relation to innovation and new product/service development.
Self-control in respect of bodily pleasure	Not given to excessive pricing or profit taking.
Generosity	Development of CSR programmes or philanthropy, or in terms of discounted products/services or in relation to incentives given to employees or other stakeholders.
Magnificence	Aiming to build a large enterprise with a well-defined mission which serves its customers well.
Self-respect or pride	Openly communicating to stakeholders both the good and bad news associated with a company's operations.
Having some ambition but not in excess	Competitive but not at all costs and not combative within an industry.
Gentleness or good temper	The use of a balanced approach to dealings with stakeholder relations, e.g. industrial relations, consumer action.
Friendliness	The will to join forces with competitors in the same industry where necessary, e.g. for purposes of self-regulation, to develop industry standards, and an exemplary approach to customer service and satisfaction.
Truthfulness	Particularly in relation to financial integrity and other stakeholder communications.
Wittiness	Taken to mean intelligence and a company's ability to redefine the 'rules of the game' without taking itself too seriously.
Justice	Including the audit of one's own ethical approaches and the initiation of reward/punishment when these are disregarded.

has to perceive that there might be an ethical dilemma before undergoing the ethical decision-making process. Critically, if no ethical dilemma is seen to exist, no consideration of alternative sources of action can then take place. However, determining whether or not a situation has ethical content is specific to an individual culture. In other words, people in some cultures are more likely to perceive ethical breaches than others. Nevertheless, around the world there are some universal standards (for example, the OECD's Guidelines for Multinational Companies). Bribery is almost universally condemned around the world and most countries have laws making bribery of public officials illegal.

Early attempts to devise frameworks of how to act ethically involved asking ourselves reflective questions on the actions associated with the ethical dilemma.

Laczniak and Murphy (1993) provide typical examples. They suggested that we asked ourselves:

- Does the contemplated action violate the law (legal test)?

- Is this action contrary to widely accepted moral obligations (duties test)?

- Does the proposed action violate any other special obligations that stem from the type of marketing organization in focus (special obligations test)?

- Is the intent of the contemplated action harmful (motives test)?

- Is it likely that any major damage to people or organizations will result from the contemplated action (consequences test)?

- Is there a satisfactory alternative action that produces equal or greater benefits to the parties affected than the proposed action (utilitarian test)?

- Does the contemplated action infringe on property rights, privacy rights, or the inalienable rights of the consumer (rights test)?

- Does the proposed action leave another person or group less well off? Is this person or group already a member of a relatively underprivileged class (justice test)?

Murphy (2004) suggested that when we analyse cases involving ethical issues we should undertake the following process:

1 Determine the facts—what, who, when, and where;

2 Define the ethical issue;

3 Identify major principles, rules, values (in relation to ethical norms outlined earlier);

4 Undertake a stakeholder analysis;

5 Specify the alternative courses of action;

6 Compare principles, values, and consequences with alternatives; and

7 Make and justify the decision.

A more elaborate model of ethical decision making, which begins with the particular ethical issue or dilemma, is shown in Figure 20.1 (Ferrell and Gresham, 1985). The authors cite five key issues including bid rigging, price collusion, bribery, falsifying research data, and advertising deception. In **bid rigging**, this can arise where subcontractors submit false bids, perhaps offering goods and services that are too expensive in the knowledge that they will form part of the final contract, but are subcontracted to the winner as a condition of obtaining the contract. Sometimes, companies might agree not to submit a bid so that another company can successfully win a contract. **Collusion** may also occur in rotation with companies submitting bids for some competitions but not others. With price collusion, companies either conspire to set prices or limit production, which typically has the same effect.

Determining what to do when a person in an organization encounters such situations depends on their social and cultural environment. Although bribery is illegal in almost all countries around the world, it is still more likely to take place in some countries than others (see later section on bribery). In addition to cultural and social background, how an employee makes a decision on an ethical issue

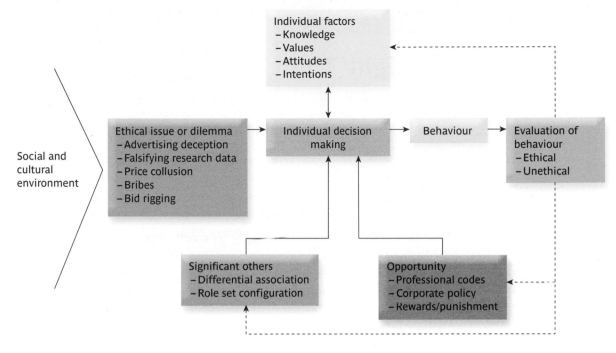

Figure 20.1 A contingency model of ethical decision making in a marketing organization

Source: Reprinted with permission from *Journal of Marketing*, published by the American Marketing Organization. Ferrell and Gresham (1985).

is affected by their own knowledge, values, attitudes, and intentions in addition to whether or not the company has a code of ethics, a corporate ethical policy, and guidelines on rewards/punishment for ethical and unethical behaviour (see Market Insight 20.1).

A person's ethical decision making is determined by how they interact with people who are part of their reference group. In other words, association with others who are perceived to be participating in unethical behaviour, combined with the opportunity to be involved in such behaviour oneself, is a major predictor of unethical behaviour (Ferrell and Gresham, 1985). Therefore, the behaviour of

RESEARCH INSIGHT 20.2

To take your learning further, you might wish to read this influential paper.

Ferrell, O. C., and Gresham, L. G. (1985), 'A contingency framework for understanding ethical decision making in marketing', *Journal of Marketing*, 49 (Summer), 87–96.

A highly cited, relatively short, and highly readable paper outlining how ethical marketing decisions are contingent on certain factors. The paper proposes that the factors that ethical decision making is influenced by include the ethical issue itself, the social and cultural environment, individual factors (such as attitudes and values), significant others, and the opportunity (i.e. professional codes with which one operates, corporate policy), focusing academic attention on the fact that ethical marketing decisions are dependent on the circumstances in which the decision making is occurring for the first time.

Doing the 'Right' Thing?

How would you react if you were in the following situations at work? Consider the ethical content of each of the following situations:

- You work for a Western defence company (i.e. USA, UK, France) and have just visited Saudi Arabia where you are likely to be awarded a multi-billion-dollar contract to supply the government with missile technology, which they state that they intend to use only for defence of their nation, rather than aggression against their neighbours. Your Saudi Arabian contact within the Saudi government asks for a large 'commission' equivalent to about 5% of the contract value for arranging the contract. If you do not arrange the 'commission', you will not get the contract and may lose your job. Do you pay the 'commission'?

- You work for a toy company selling a particularly fast-selling range of teddy bears. One of your two laboratory test reports—lab tests are required under EU guidelines—indicates that the eye in one of your bears easily comes loose and could therefore be swallowed by a child. However, you have already pre-sold 130,000 units to shops around the country. Do you go through the trouble of destroying or fixing the bears, and claiming the costs on your insurance or seeking compensation from your suppliers, or do you do nothing in the hope that there won't be any problems and no one will pick up the error anyway?

- A competitor is developing a vastly new improved version of their product according to some industry gossip you picked up at a recent trade fair, which may completely change the nature of your industry. Is it legitimate to hire a competitive intelligence professional, who would not operate illegally, to monitor their key new product development staff in the hopes of learning more details?

- You take on a competitor's buying manager within your company. Is it appropriate to request that they provide you with full details of their former employer's suppliers, including details of the contracts and prices that they negotiated?

- An advertising agency devises a sexual abuse awareness-raising campaign for the small charity that you work for as marketing director, with a hard-hitting campaign depicting scenes which infer sexual abuse is taking place, but without actually showing the sexual abuse itself. Research indicates that the audience, particularly those who have themselves suffered sexual abuse, find the advert extremely harrowing, but it does raise awareness more generally of your relatively little-known charity. Would you commission the campaign?

- You work for a supplier of electricity, in a regulated European market during an election year. You recognize that the leading political party in power is in a position once it forms government to allow you to substantially increase the unit price of electricity, but in order to obtain this representation you will need to donate a 'large gift' to the party. Do you make the donation?

1 Go through each one of the above situations and work out what you would do in the given circumstances. Why would you act in this way?

2 Can you think of other marketing situations with ethical content?

3 How important is it for a company to have clear ethical policies? Do you think they can provide guidelines for all situations that employees might find themselves in?

superiors is important in determining how employees behave and was found to be the most important factor influencing ethical/unethical decisions.

In the next section, we consider how ethics impacts upon major marketing considerations including distribution, promotion, products, and pricing decisions.

Distribution Management and Ethics

Distribution and production policy can have major ethical dimensions. Ethical breaches in distribution management can occur when, for example, companies collude over production quotas, when companies abuse their monopoly status, and when companies overcharge or exploit their supply chain partners. The following sections provide examples of companies or situations where ethical breaches have occurred.

Collusion

In 1996, Italian Antitrust Authorities (IAA) found its two largest dairy producers, high-value cheese producers Consorzio del Grana Padano (CGP) and Consorzio del Parmigiano Reggiano (CPR), guilty of uncompetitive behaviour. The IAA found that they were operating strict production quotas placed on each dairy designed to effectively co-manage each other's market share and drive overall prices up in the sector although the companies had argued that they were operating a coordinated policy in order to reduce the cyclical nature of the market and comply with Italian legislation covering product quality (Braga and Nardella, 2003).

Abuse of Monopoly Status

In March 2004, the European Union levied a half-billion-euro fine against Microsoft, the American software giant, for abusing its 'near monopoly' status. Mario Monti, the EU Competition Commissioner, stated that 'dominant companies have a special responsibility to ensure that the way they do business doesn't prevent competition . . . and does not harm consumers and innovation'. The EU anti-competition authority called for Microsoft to offer a version of Windows which did not contain its digital media player within three months and to release a 'complete and accurate' interface code to other software companies in the server market within four months to ensure interoperability between different competitor companies' products (Deutsche-Welle, 2004).

Supply Chain Exploitation

Perhaps the best example in Western markets of supply chain exploitation is that taking place between supermarkets and their suppliers, particularly those supplying multinational supermarket groups. Numerous European countries have brought in legislation to stop supermarkets from wielding excessive power. For instance, in France the 'Loi Galland' since 1996 forbids supermarkets selling at 'excessively low prices', and so-called **listing fees**—a fee charged by the supermarket to a supplier per unit item—are forbidden where no value is provided to the supplier. The French Competition Council/Office of Fair Trading was given the role of preventing abuse of positions of dominance and/or monopoly. Similarly, in Germany, the 1999 Restraints on Competition Act stops retailers from setting prices below the purchased price and allows companies to take others to court where there is abuse of a dominant position of either a supplier or a retailer without waiting for the German Cartel Office to investigate (Vorley, 2003).

Promotion and Ethics

There are numerous issues in advertising which prompt ethical consideration, especially since advertising is perhaps the most visible element of marketing practice. Some considerations include when to use shock and sexual appeals in advertising, the labelling of consumer products, the use of propaganda and advertising in political situations, and marketing to children.

The Use of Sexual and Shock Appeals

Emotional appeals in advertising are used because they capture our attention. We are persuaded by these types of messages because we are less likely to consider objections about why we might not agree with the message. For the celebrated French philosopher Jean Baudrillard (2005: 187), advertising has an erotic element to it anyway since through advertising, 'the product exposes itself to our view and invites us to handle it; it is, in fact, eroticised—not just because of the explicitly sexual themes evoked'.

The ethical question arises because a substantial proportion of adverts do use sexual themes explicitly, e.g. naked or semi-naked attractive models, sometime male, but more often than not women, to advertise their products. Many critics argue that this reduces women, and much less frequently men, to the status of sex objects. More recently, the fashion industry has finally decided not to use models younger than 16.

Equally, others might argue that this type of advert is appropriate for the product in question, i.e. a perfume, since this product is so closely linked with sexuality. The difficulty is in determining where to draw the line in the use of sexual appeals. For what products is it appropriate, in what countries, and targeted at people of what ages?

Shock advertising appeals can also create furore and controversy but depending on how they are executed, they make the receiver both more and less susceptible to persuasion. The NSPCC's (National Society for the Prevention of Cruelty to Children) Full Stop campaign in Britain has been a model example of how to

UNITED COLORS
OF BENETTON.

Benetton's Bloody Soldiers advert

Benetton Group SPA

execute a shock appeal, since it raised both awareness and funds, without creat-ing offence.

Perhaps the best example of a shock appeal used in advertising is that used by governments to reduce tobacco smoking. Under Canadian law, the top 50 per cent of the front and back of each cigarette pack depicts a full-colour, stark graphic warning. The pictures have included depictions of a lung tumour, a brain after a stroke, and a damaged heart. Nevertheless, it has been argued that shock appeals are limited in their effectiveness because viewers when encountering a dismaying image simply ignore the messages, in a process psychologists call 'emotional forgetting'. This is not forgetting in the usual sense but simply a form of selective exposure (see Chapter 3). It's a way of ignoring the message to filter out the unwelcome negative state of mind induced by the image. The ethical consideration for an advertiser is to determine what level of shock is appropriate to get the audience's attention about a particular issue or product. For this rea-son, shock advertising is more likely to be used by social marketing campaigners than product and service marketers since there is a greater fit with their message. Probably the best-known, most controversial user of shock advertising was the Italian clothing group Benetton's use of images of blood-stained trousers during the Kosovo War and a black woman breastfeeding a white baby to advertise its United Colours of Benetton clothing range in the mid-1990s.

A much more difficult ethical question surrounds the use of marketing tools and techniques in wartime. O'Shaughnessy (2004) outlines how Osama bin Laden, the Al Qaeda chief, has been particularly keen to use propaganda, which takes the form of visual rhetoric—video-recordings distributed through Qatari TV station Al Jazeera, and on the internet, displaying the man, his rifle, and his words of jihad and terror in the mythological form of a holy warrior-priest.

The American and British military have both used propaganda methods in their bid to justify the Iraq War, particularly the practice of **embedding** journalists in allied combat units, but also through press censorship and event staging (see Baines and Worcester, 2005). An understanding of marketing and public relations provides its user with the means to persuade mass groups of people. The question arises whether or not it is legitimate for governments to use these means to persuade electorates about the legitimacy of war before, during, and after the event.

Marketing to Children

Numerous scholars have commented on whether or not children should be targeted for advertising, in view of their immature concepts of time, money, and identity. In a research study on marketing to children in Britain, undertaken on Business in the Community's (BITC) behalf by Research International and Lightspeed Research, researchers found evidence that children were increasingly targeted in promotional campaigns and that parents were increasingly concerned by this. A summary of the report outlines:

• Children are more exposed to marketing than ever before and parents are increasingly feeling that they are losing control of the marketing directed at their children.

Children are more exposed to marketing than ever before

iStock

- Parents are particularly concerned about the newer marketing channels such as the internet and mobile phones which can target their children directly.

- Inappropriate marketing to children damages the brand, making it less likely that you will get past the parent as gatekeeper.

- More appropriate marketing methods are those that are informative and help parents to feel more in control.

- Consumers are willing to support companies that communicate with children in a responsible way.

- It is up to marketers, especially advertisers, to use the means of communication appropriately and to educate parents and children alike on newer and less traditional communication mediums. Ensuring the responsible use of these less traditional mediums is paramount (Daniels and Holmes, 2005).

One company that has come under increasing pressure in relation to its promotion to children is McDonald's, since its products particularly appeal to children, particularly through the use of licensed characters and celebrity endorsement. Child obesity is regarded as an increasing problem in many countries (e.g. New Zealand, Britain, America) and is seen to be a problem at least partly caused by food advertising to children although the evidence is unclear since it could also be linked to inactive lifestyles and a lack of exercise in general. In Britain, the Department of Health has announced that it is set to monitor food promotion to children for a year with a view to determining its effect on child obesity. As a result, fast food retailers such as McDonald's, KFC, and Burger King are coming under increasing pressure to make their menus healthier around the world.

Products and Ethics

An important consideration in marketing ethics is whether or not a good or service complies with industry health and safety standards. Most multinational companies have guidelines on the quality of their offerings. Where consumers have concerns about a particular company's product quality, they can inform a government body that will then be charged with looking into the case on the consumer/customer's behalf. For instance, the US Product Safety Commission, the UK's Office of Fair Trading, Sweden's National Consumer Agency, New Zealand's Ministry of Consumer Affairs, Korea's Consumer Protection Board, and the EU's Health and Consumer Protection Directorate-General all perform this role.

It is interesting to note that while most countries have organizations charged with ensuring product quality, the same degree of protection for ensuring service quality does not seem to exist, presumably because it is much more difficult to monitor service quality, decide on minimum standards of service quality, and determine whether or not breaches have been made. Nevertheless, the above agencies do provide consumer information. For instance, the UK's Office of Fair Trading provides information on such services as buying warranties for electrical

Durex: A Touchy-Feely Subject

The UK retail condom market was valued at £56 m (€84 m) in 2005. The condom maker SSL International distributes condoms under the brand name Durex, and takes about 82% market share, by value. The nearest competitor is Ansell Health Care, who distribute the brand Mates. Since condoms are designed to reduce the incidence of sexually transmitted diseases and as a form of birth control, sales are dependent on trends in sexual activity. The manufacturers of condoms therefore have a strong role to play in discouraging sexually promiscuous behaviour and teenage pregnancy. The UK also has the highest rate of teenage pregnancies in Europe.

Operating in such a sensitive market, it is necessary to have clearly defined ethical marketing standards. As a result, SSL International (2005) have outlined a clear ethical statement as follows:

'As part of its ongoing commitment to excellence, SSL International plc (SSL) is committed to producing the highest quality products across all the company's business areas. By consistently providing products that please customers and meet or exceed international standards, we will develop user loyalty and so achieve strong business performance. All employees are expected to help the company attain high quality standards. It is company policy to:

- maintain and keep records of a quality management system in accordance with international standards, regulations and directives;
- ensure all staff are fully trained and understand their role providing quality products and good customer service;
- provide products which fully meet customer requirements;
- develop or acquire products which are effective, safe and reliable;
- make sure the services and materials from suppliers are of consistent and sufficient quality;
- strive for continual improvement in performance, underpinned by the necessary financial resources, and highlight objectives and progress through internal and external communications.'

To demonstrate its commitment to highlighting safe sexual activity, Durex launched the 'He Says, You Say' initiative during National Condom Week in May 2006. The campaign was intended to make young people think more about safe sex. In particular, the campaign was designed to give women suitable answers to excuses that their partners may devise to avoid wearing condoms. In particular, Durex has shifted its positioning focus from a message of safer sex to one of better sex, and its product range now includes the Durex Play range of lubricants and personal sexual devices in addition to its range of condoms including the Fetherlite, Extra Safe, Avanti, Performa, Sensation, Select Flavours, and others.

Source: SSL International (2005); Mintel (2006).

1　The Fetherlite and Extra Safe products of the Durex range are reportedly the company's best-sellers. Why is it so important that product quality standards are of the highest levels possible in this product market?

2　Read the above company policy relating to product quality. How different is this policy from say that of a toy manufacturer?

3　What other products require strict adherence to product quality guidelines? Why?

goods, funerals, buying and selling your home, holidays, pawnbroking, ticket agents, private dentistry, and other industries where sharp practice seems to occur more often than usual.

Breaches in product quality can be extremely serious and lead to loss of life and grave injury, particularly in the food industry. For this reason, many countries have separate official bodies charged with ensuring food safety guidelines, e.g. the American Food and Drug Administration, Britain's Food Standard's Agency, France's Agence Française de Sécurité Sanitaire des Aliments (AFSSA), and the bi-national Food Safety Australia and New Zealand (FSANZ) organization which covers both territories. Four pertinent examples of defective products causing multiple death and injury include the following situations:

1 Thalidomide, a tranquillizer administered to pregnant women, was sold in the UK, under the brand name Distaval, by Distillers (Biochemicals) Limited. The drug caused limb deformity and death in around 10,000 babies throughout the world. The drug was withdrawn in 1961 but Diageo plc retains the moral responsibility to fund the Thalidomide Trust (until 2022), which makes compensation payments to Thalidomide victims in the UK.

2 The British government had to stop export sales of British beef when BSE (bovine spongiform encephelopathy)-infected beef caused over 74 human deaths in Britain by September 2000. Up to £3.5 bn in government subsidies was given to British farmers for disposal of infected and possibly infected cattle, and because of an EU-imposed four-year ban on exports, Britain probably suffered a further £2.5 bn in lost revenues.

3 Bridgestone/Firestone, the Japanese-owned, US-based tyre maker, and Ford, the US car maker (see Market Insight 20.3), had to recall and replace millions of tyres when accidents involving defective tyres on sports utility vehicles caused over 175 deaths and 700 injuries in more than 1,400 accidents around the world (Freitag, 2002).

4 Coca-Cola, the American global beverage manufacturer, was forced to recall 2.5 million bottles of Coca-Cola, Coca-Cola Light, Fanta, and Sprite in Belgium when bottles of the product were found to be contaminated with defective carbon dioxide and/or pesticide, resulting in the hospitalization of 100 children (Campbell, 1999).

Determining when to recall products is a difficult ethical problem. The recall of Hoodia, a weight loss supplement, by the Netherlands Food and Consumer Product Safety Authority (VWA) in 2005 was considered fundamental after concerns were raised over whether or not product safety had been properly evaluated. At the heart of the problem was a judgement call over what the likely risk was to the customer/consumer. Where there is considered to be a risk of injury, a product should be recalled. This might occur when:

• A serious consumer illness or injury is caused by contamination of products (the Belgian Coca-Cola case outlined above);

• There are similar complaints of illness or injury which apply to a specific product;

Ford and Bridgestone/Firestone: Tyre Blowout—Whose Fault Is it Anyway?

The Ford Motor Company and Bridgestone/Firestone, its US-based, Japanese-owned tyre supplier, both sustained considerable reputational damage when tyre blowouts on Ford Explorer sport utility vehicles (SUV) caused them to roll over. Over 175 people were killed and 700 injured in more than 1,400 accidents related to tyre blowout around the world.

They tackled the world's understandably irate media together initially. But over time and under considerable pressure, Ford eventually blamed the accidents on the Firestone tyre, and the fact that the tread became separated from the rest of the tyre. Bridgestone/Firestone argued that if the Ford Explorer had been designed properly—it had a low centre of gravity at the back causing instability under these circumstances—the accidents would not have been so serious. It noted that 60% of the accidents reported involved tyres placed in the left rear position of the vehicle. The rush to pass the blame onto the other party broke a relationship which had lasted over 100 years.

Yet passing the blame on to one another was not the only approach that they could have adopted. According to Coombs (1998), there are *seven* potential courses of action an organization can take to preserve its reputation in crisis circumstances, ranging from defensive to accommodative as follows:

1 Accuser persecution—in this case either attacking the media, e.g. their reporting methods, or, once recriminations with the partner began, attacking the partner.

2 Denial—essentially suggesting that the problem was not with the tyres or the SUV.

3 Responsibility avoidance—the suggestion that the reasons for the incident lie elsewhere and are the fault of others.

4 Salience reduction—involves an attempt to downplay the damage of the events that took place.

5 Ingratiation—an attempt to outline the good deeds that a company has done in order to direct the media spotlight elsewhere.

6 Corrective action—in this case, the recall of all tyres and their replacement at full cost to the company without necessarily accepting full responsibility.

7 Mortification—total acceptance of responsibility for the incident and the issue of a full apology and corrective action.

Sources: Freitag (2002); O'Rourke (2001); Coombs (1998).

1 Outline which of the above PR approaches Ford and Bridgestone/Firestone actually undertook.

2 If you were the CEO at Ford or Bridgestone/Firestone, which approach would you choose?

3 What are the ethical implications of adopting your particular strategy in question 2?

- A design or manufacturing failure could result in potential harm to consumers (as happened when Burger King, the fast food company, recalled 25 million Pokemon balls); or

- There is defective product labelling which could result in potential harm to consumers; or where a product has been tampered with.

Pricing and Ethics

An important consideration in marketing ethics is whether or not the price of a product or service is set at a 'fair' level. Key considerations concern price gouging, where the price of a good or service is far higher than what is considered reasonable; price discrimination, where the price of a good or service is set differently for certain groups of people, and price collusion, where competitors work together to set prices or distribution targets.

Price gouging

Price gouging occurs when a company charges more than governments perceive is fair for products and/or services. It occurs when companies operate a demand pricing formula (see Chapter 6) that leads to very high prices being charged to customers/consumers. One example was the pricing of anti-retroviral drugs in South Africa prior to 2002, when major global pharmaceutical companies charged very high prices for AIDS/HIV treatments despite generic versions being available at far lower prices. Of course, the issue was complicated by these companies holding global patents but the issue raised by the world's media was not the legality of the situation but the morality of it.

Price Discrimination

Price discrimination involves the setting of different prices for different groups of people. Thus, price discrimination is frequently linked to market segmentation (see Chapter 6). It is not unethical as a practice in itself, where the product is differentiated for different groups. The practice is more questionable though where there is no difference in product or other element of the offer, and the price remains the only difference. Nevertheless, price discrimination is a frequent occurrence. For instance, a sign at Ayutthaya Historical City, Thailand, shows the price to visit the monument for foreigners as 30 baht (about 42p at the time of writing), but (in Thai script) only 10 baht (about 14p at the time of writing) for Thai nationals (see overleaf).

Price discrimination occurs on airlines, e.g. EasyJet, since they use so-called yield management systems to sell airline tickets based on different prices dependent on time of booking. Women's haircuts are frequently more expensive than men's, although there is some scope for the argument that the service provided is more attentive and slightly different. Universities frequently offer discriminatory aid

Discriminatory Pricing
at the Ayutthaya
Historical City, Thailand

Paul Baines

and welfare packages and price their undergraduate and postgraduate courses differently dependent on whether or not you are a home or overseas student (see Chapter 10). Women are provided with cheaper car insurance than men, e.g. Diamond offer female-only car insurance although they will allow their male partners to go on their female customers' insurance policies as named second drivers!

In some markets, this concept goes further, with every customer potentially paying a different price through **haggling**, which is also a form of discriminatory pricing (see Kimes and Wirtz, 2003). Haggling is more common in some markets than in others, e.g. house and car buying in the UK, and in some countries compared with others, e.g. Middle Eastern and South-East Asian countries such as Egypt, Morocco, Thailand, and Indonesia as opposed to Western European countries like France, Germany, and the UK. Do you remember the last time you haggled when buying something? Where were you?

Price Collusion

Amazingly, some of the world's most well-known companies have been fined for price collusion. A good example is Swiss pharmaceutical giant Hoffmann-La Roche Ltd, who pleaded guilty and agreed to pay a $500 million criminal fine for heading a worldwide conspiracy to raise and fix prices and allocate market shares for certain vitamins sold in the United States and elsewhere. The US Department of Justice charged the company with conspiring to fix, raise, and maintain prices, and allocate sales volumes of vitamins sold by them and other unnamed co-conspirator companies in the USA and elsewhere. Federal officials also allege that the company allocated contracts for vitamin premixes for customers throughout the USA and rigged the bids for those contracts. The conspiracy, which lasted over nine years from January 1990 until February 1999, affected the vitamins most commonly used as nutritional supplements or to enrich human food and animal feed—vitamins A, B2, B5, C, E, and beta carotene (Mokhiber, 2005).

Another example was Japanese computer game and console maker Nintendo, which was fined €149 m (£92.1 m) by the European Commission for trying to rig the computer game market. The firm and seven distributors were found guilty of attempting to keep prices artificially high in some EU states over a seven-year period between 1991 and 1998. The fine, the fourth highest ever handed out by the EU for a single offence at that time, was justified by Nintendo's role as 'the driving force behind the illicit behaviour', the Commission said. Distributors, including Scotland-based retailer John Menzies, were fined €18 m (BBC News, 2002; European Commission, 2002).

A further example of price collusion occurred when Samsung Electronics, the world's largest computer memory chip maker, pleaded guilty and paid a US$300 million (€225 million) fine, on charges of conspiring to fix prices of dynamic random access memory (DRAM) chips between April 1999 and June 2002. At the time, it was the second-largest criminal antitrust fine ever levied by the US Justice Department, who spent more than three years investigating Samsung of South Korea, along with competitors Hynix Semiconductor of Korea and Infincon Technologies of Germany. Both Hynix and Infineon pleaded guilty to their roles in the conspiracy (Flynn, 2005).

Price collusion is regarded as unethical because of its inherent negative impact on consumers. It typically results in unfair, and higher, charges to consumers, and it can stifle innovation—since competitors do not need to develop better competing products—and consumers therefore do not benefit from improvements in product quality and/or performance.

International Marketing Ethics

Some cultures seem less likely than others to perceive ethical dilemmas. Ethicists consider how different groups of people see ethical situations from two perspectives. Under one perspective, ethicists suggest that universal codes of practice in ethics should exist because there are some things which are simply 'wrong' no matter what the colour or creed of the people concerned (e.g. murder, bribery, extortion). This is termed universalism. The opposite argument, termed cultural relativism, suggests that different groups legitimately consider ethical situations from different viewpoints and that there is nothing wrong with this (e.g. gifts, corporate entertainment). The debate in international marketing ethics concerns itself principally with this dichotomy, i.e. cultural relativism versus ethical universalism.

How should a manager of a head office consider the practices of a group of managers within the subdivision of its company operating in Africa using bribery to ensure access to certain African markets for its products, on the basis that if it didn't act this way, other companies would? The question is should managers within that subdivision be brought into line because the company's policy states that bribery is not acceptable and, in any case, is now illegal in all of the world's major countries? Looking at the problem from a cultural relativist perspective, we would tend to indicate that such practice was ethically unacceptable except under circumstances where such bribery might lead to a greater good, say widespread distribution of health-giving pharmaceuticals, whereas a universalist perspective would suggest that this was very clearly a fundamental ethical breach regardless of the circumstances.

In a study concerning American–Thai differences in ethical behaviour, American marketers were found to be more likely to perceive unethical marketing behaviours to be more serious than their Thai counterparts (Marta and Singhapakdi, 2005). In a separate study of how Thai managers made ethical decisions, Singhapakdi *et al.* (2000) stated that one approach to improve ethical decision making in Thai marketing managers would be to encourage idealism—the degree to which individuals 'assume that desirable consequences can, with the "right" action, always be obtained', rather than relativism—where 'an individual rejects universal moral rules' (Forsyth, 1980).

Idealism could be encouraged through training programmes and communication of clear company policies on ethical matters. In another study, Singhapakdi *et al.* (2000) found that there is a very strong positive relationship between a marketer's religiousness and their degree of idealism. In other words, the more religious you are, the more likely you are to hold universal ethical principles. Less religious marketers, according to these authors, tend to reject universal moral principles when evaluating situations with ethical content and the consequences of situations when examining them retrospectively.

In a study of marketing ethics in Korea, Kim and Chun (2003) found that Koreans perceived the seriousness of ethical problems in order of importance as follows:

1 Bribery;

2 Unfair price increases;

3 Exaggerated advertising;

4 Sexual discrimination.

They found in their research that younger Koreans were less likely to perceive situations as having ethical content generally, whereas the older generation perceived less ethical content in bribery situations. Overall, they felt that such a lack of ethical concern would have a negative impact on Korean business, affecting company performance, if there was no education on marketing ethics in Korea.

Micro-cultural differences do seem to have a big impact on perceived ethical problems, according to a study of the Javenese, Batak, and Indonesian-Chinese managers in Indonesia (Sarwono and Armstrong, 2001). Each subculture responded differently to situations with ethical content. As a result, the authors suggested that Indonesian managers and expatriates operating in Indonesia should undergo cultural training including ethical perceptions held by local managers, together with the establishment of formalized codes of conduct.

Bribery

Transparency International, the international organization with a mission to stamp out bribery and corrupt practices around the world, published a Bribe Payers Index based on survey data to determine the propensity to bribe public officials from twenty-one leading exporting nations shortly after the OECD Convention on Combating Bribery of Foreign Public Officials in International Business Transactions was introduced. In 2002, the worst perceived offender was Russia, followed closely by China. The top three countries least likely to pay bribes were considered to be Australia, Sweden, and Switzerland. The worst offending industries from which bribe payers were most likely to originate included public works/construction, arms and defence, and oil and gas. Companies in these industries have a greater need to provide ethical training, confidential helplines, and robust whistle-blowing procedures, where employees can highlight ethical breaches to senior managers without fear of penalty. In July 2003, Samsung Vice Chairman Lee Hak-soo was accused of bribery when local television station MBC reported a taped conversation in 1997 between Lee Hak-soo and Korean ambassador to the USA Hong Seok-hyun, then publisher of the Samsung-affiliated newspaper *JoongAng Ilbo*. The transcripts of the audio-tapes seemed to indicate that Samsung illegally offered around 10 billion *won* to Lee Hoi-chang, presidential candidate of the then ruling Grand National Party (GNP), ahead of the 1997 election (Tong-hyung, 2005). Exactly what Lee Hak-soo's motives were is unclear.

Where bribery occurs, it is typically used to attempt either to influence potentially adverse legislative programmes, or to obtain favourable contracts at another company's expense. In 1997, the OECD—the USA and thirty-three other countries—signed the OECD Convention on Combating Bribery of Foreign Public Officials in International Business Transactions. Britain passed the Bribery of Foreign Public Officials Bill in March 2001 to update and amend its own Prevention of Corruption Acts 1889 to 1916 and the Criminal Justice Acts 1987 and 1993 so that a bribing offence committed in respect of a public body, public office, person, agent, or principal outside the United Kingdom shall constitute an offence under those Acts just as if it was committed inside the United Kingdom.

The Socially (Ir)responsible Company

More recently, **corporate social responsibility** (CSR) initiatives have increased in importance amongst both business ethicists and directors of major corporations. Not surprisingly corporate social responsibility, or just corporate responsibility, is a concept which we would expect to fit within the marketing concept. After all, ensuring a company meets and exceeds its stakeholder concerns is the business of marketers as well (Maignan and Ferrell, 2004).

Many companies now publish annual CSR reports, e.g. BAT, GSK, SSL International. Increasingly, governments and supranational organizations have become

ExxonMobil: Statement on Bribery and Corruption

'Our policy is to comply with all governmental laws, rules, and regulations applicable to our business. We expect employee candour at all levels and adherence to the policy and controls. All employees are responsible for reporting any suspected violation of law or corporate policy to management. Each year, all managerial, professional, and technical employees are required to confirm that they have read and are familiar with the policies set forth in our *Standards of Business Conduct*. The company's foundation policies in the *Standards of Business Conduct* prohibit corruption of any type.

Our management framework to prevent bribery and corruption includes clear guidance on ethics, gifts and entertainment, conflict of interest, antitrust, and directorship policies. Sound financial control is fundamental to our business operating model. We have established effective control mechanisms for our worldwide operations. Responsibilities for authorizing, approving, and recording transactions are appropriately segregated to reduce risks of a single employee having exclusive knowledge, authority, or control over any significant transaction or group of transactions.

Approximately one-third of the Corporation's business activities and operating units are audited each year, and all operating units undergo regular self-assessments to provide assurance that operating standards are met. ExxonMobil employs more than 250 internal auditors, who are deployed throughout its facilities and business units at an annual cost of more than $50 million. Internal auditors have unrestricted access to all facilities, personnel, and records, and are specially trained to identify and report on control issues. They also conduct independent investigations of situations in which non-compliance with ExxonMobil's *Standards of Business Conduct* may have occurred. Significant matters are reported to the Audit Committee of the Board of Directors.

Every year, internal auditors and management conduct investigations of suspected violations of law, business practices, or internal control procedures. Such violations include conflicts of interest, exceeding transaction authority limits, excessive entertainment, falsified expense reports, misuse of company purchases and credit cards, or petty theft. Policy violations by employees lead to disciplinary actions up to and including separation from the company.

We provide a number of mechanisms for reporting suspected violations of law or the Corporation's business practices. Such complaints may be communicated by telephone or mail. Retaliation against any respondent is prohibited, and the anonymity of the respondent can be preserved if desired. All payments to third parties are expected to comply with the Foreign Corrupt Practices Act and Exxon Mobil *Guidelines for Payments to Third Parties*.'

Source: ExxonMobil (2004).

1 ExxonMobil spends more than US$50 m a year on internal auditors to check the compliance of its staff with its stated policy on bribery and corruption. Why?

2 Is it *always* unethical to offer bribes when doing business? Might there be a circumstance in which it is ethical to give the bribe?

3 When does a gift become a bribe? What are legitimate entertainment expenses when doing business in the oil and gas industry?

involved in the encouragement of CSR, for example, the UN Global Compact project encourages companies to join a corporate citizenship programme. The CSR movement is not endorsed by all, however. Until relatively recently, CSR practitioners and academics have focused on trying to demonstrate the commercial effectiveness of CSR programmes under the notion that 'good' business is good business. Of course, businesspersons have given philanthropically to charity for centuries. Famous cases include the John Paul Getty foundation in the USA, which has funded art and social projects around the world based on profits from the oil industry, and Sir Titus Salt in eighteenth-century Britain who provided social housing for the poor of Bradford based on profits from the textile industry. Despite these examples, the jury is still out on whether or not being a 'good' company means being a profitable company.

The central tenets of CSR initiatives are defined by Buchholz (1991: 19) as incorporating the following features:

- Corporations have responsibilities that go beyond the production of goods and services at a profit;
- These responsibilities involve helping to solve important social problems, especially those that they have helped to create;
- Corporations have a broader constituency than stockholders (shareholders) alone;
- Corporations have impacts that go beyond simple marketplace transactions;
- Corporations serve a wider range of human values than can be captured by a sole focus on economic values.

According to Kotler (2000), companies will increasingly differentiate themselves by sponsoring popular social causes in a bid to win the public's favour. Such an approach, known as **cause-related marketing**, is generally recognized to be a useful way to build a corporate personality since it builds not only customer loyalty, but also employee respect. In Britain, Tesco's popular Computers for Schools initiative first launched in 1992 has become the benchmark for cause-related marketing campaigns delivering over £84 million worth of Information Communications Technology (ICT) equipment to schools in Britain, including

RESEARCH INSIGHT 20.3

To take your learning further, you might wish to read this influential paper.

Maignan, I., and Ferrell, O. C. (2004), 'Corporate social responsibility and marketing: an integrative framework', *Journal of the Academy of Marketing Science*, 32, 1, 3–19.

A recent article outlining how marketing contributes to corporate social responsibility and demonstrating the conceptual fit between marketing and corporate social responsibility. CSR is seen principally as action used to conform to stakeholder and organizational requirements. The article concludes by asking a number of important questions such as 'how do stakeholder norms influence business practices?', 'which organizational processes can stimulate socially responsible corporate behaviours?', 'how do different stakeholders react to CSR practices?', and 'how should companies communicate their CSR practices?'

Corporate Disasters: Accidental or Irresponsible?

Over the last twenty-five years, there have been some spectacular corporate disasters, which in all cases have had major effects on human life and society because of the sheer scale of each company's actions. In many cases, the effects of these companies are still felt today as legal action continues in some of the examples outlined below:

- 1984: Union Carbide and Bhopal—when tonnes of toxic chemical gas, methyl isocyanate (MIC), were leaked from a Union Carbide plant at Bhopal, in the Indian state of Madhya Pradesh, causing 5,800 deaths and injury to many hundreds of thousands of people. In 1989, Union Carbide and Union Carbide India Limited (UCIL) eventually settled all claims arising from the incident with the Indian government for US$470 million, although victims are still seeking compensation from the Indian government.

- 1989: The *Exxon Valdez* affair—when Exxon's *Valdez* oil tanker accidentally dumped 10.8m gallons (approx. 42 litres) of crude oil in the waters around the Alaskan coastline, killing hundreds of thousands of seabirds and many other forms of local wildlife and ruining the livelihood of thousands of people whose employment depended on fishing. Exxon is still appealing against a $4.5 billion punitive fine placed on it in a federal court trial in 1994.

- 1991: The Swiss food giant Nestlé's marketing of baby milk formula in Africa has long been controversial. The General Synod of the Church of England called for its 1.3 m members to boycott Nescafe, the firm's best-selling coffee product, in 1991, as a result. A pressure group, the Baby Milk Action campaign, based in Cambridge, UK, continues to campaign against what it regards as irresponsible marketing practices since much of the water in Africa is contaminated and unsafe for babies to drink when compared with breast milk. Nestlé, as a result of adverse media coverage over the issue, has written its own Infant Formula Policy, promoting breastfeeding over the use of the bottle-feeding method except under certain circumstances.

- 1997: Nike's alleged tolerance of the use of sweatshops by its suppliers in Asia, often with the use of child labour in hazardous conditions, for the production of its sporting goods prompted media uproar in the mid-1990s and forced it to sign a high-profile code of conduct on global employment practices in 1997.

- 2001: Enron—one of the world's largest energy companies: improper financial accounting, including inflated turnover claims filed to the Securities and Exchange Commission, and fraudulent practices, which resulted in convictions for insider trading and securities fraud against senior employees, led to the collapse of a Fortune 500 company and its auditor, Arthur Andersen—at the time one of the world's largest accountancy firms.

Sources: Sen and Egelhoff (1991); Kumar (2004); AOSC (1990); Bayne (2005); Schwarz (1991); Usborne (1997); Swartz and Watkins (2003).

1 What do you think the effect of the crises is on each of the companies in terms of their corporate image? Consider particularly those companies which are still in existence today.

2 In two of these cases, Nestlé and Nike, the actions of the company led to a boycott of their products by selected consumers. How important is it to take account of your customers' views on matters of public policy such as these?

3 How important do you think it is for a company to act responsibly? Why is it so important?

RESEARCH INSIGHT 20.4

To take your learning further, you might wish to read this influential paper.

Dunfee, T. W., Smith, C. N., and Ross, W. T., Jr. (1999), 'Social contracts and marketing ethics', *Journal of Marketing*, July, 14–32.

The authors' intention was to build a best practice model for ethical decision making using social contract theory—which seeks to identify the extent to which people recognize the authority of the corporation in which they work. The authors produced a model process available to organizations which allows us to form ethical judgements only after a set of appropriate stakeholders have been consulted and clear criteria for evaluation of ethical problems have been determined and set.

over 52,000 computers and almost 550,000 items of additional ICT equipment by the end of 2003 (BITC, 2003). Activity of this kind generates consumer awareness of mainstream brands very early on in children's lives. Unfortunately, it is the schools in wealthier areas that tend to be more likely to find sponsorship and develop links of this kind; yet the schools in the deprived areas are likely to need the most resources (Bennett, 1999).

The socially responsible company has now become the model for major corporations because of concerns about the impacts of globalization and poor corporate governance, e.g. BCCI—Bank of Credit and Commerce International—in the UK, and Enron and WorldCom in the USA. There is an increased awareness of the reputational damage that can occur when companies do not act responsibly. Examples of irresponsible companies abound and some of the more famous cases are highlighted in the next section.

In Britain, the top ten corporate givers in 2003/4, according to the Charities Aid Foundation (CAF), were mainly banks, demonstrating their commitment to communities (see Table 20.3). Interestingly, this list of companies has changed substantially since 1999, when the top ten corporate givers included Diageo, the drink and food conglomerate; Reuters Group, the information and news company; Marks and Spencers, the clothing and food retailer; BAT, the tobacco company; Cable and Wireless, the telco; and Rio Tinto, the mining group.

A central theme of CSR is that corporations have some responsibility to wider society that goes beyond the pursuit of profit (Martin, 2002). Maitland (2002: 454) comments that drug manufacturers are now regarded as social outcasts, second only to big oil and defence contractors 'as the villains of contemporary populist folklore'. He went on to argue, contrary to the CSR agenda, that drug companies have no particular moral obligation to make drugs available cheaply. If there is a moral argument for making life-saving drugs available at little or no cost to patients who cannot afford them, then the cost of doing this should be shared widely among society, rather than foisted upon the companies that happen to manufacture them. By comparison, it is not considered the responsibility of food manufacturers to eradicate world hunger.

Another argument, against CSR, would suggest a laissez-faire approach to business against the fashion for CSR (i.e. 'live and let live'). The guiding principle

Table 20.3

Top ten corporate givers in the UK

Rank	Company	Donation as a % of pre-tax profits	Total worldwide community investment (£m, 2003/04)
1	GlaxoSmithKline plc	5.4	328
2	Royal Bank of Scotland plc	0.7	45.8
3	BP plc	0.4	45.8
4	HSBC Holdings plc	0.4	36.1
5	Barclays Bank plc	0.7	32.0
6	Lloyds TSB Group plc	0.9	31.6
7	Northern Rock plc	6.2	26.8
8	Anglo American plc	1.6	26.1
9	BHP Billiton plc	1.0	25.7
10	Vodafone Group plc	n/a (made a loss)	22.7

Source: Charities Aid Foundation (2005), www.cafonline.org. Reproduced with the kind permission of the Charities Aid Foundation.

behind this argument is that the market system is a uniquely good mechanism for allocating resources to satisfy the needs and wants of humanity, and that interference with the system, however well intentioned, could inevitably reduce the efficiency with which human needs are satisfied (see Chapter 1).

MARKET INSIGHT 20.6

CSR at Tata: Are Community Initiatives Good for Business?

The Tata Group is one of India's largest business conglomerates, with revenues in 2005–6 of US$21.9 billion (Rs 967,229 million), or the equivalent of about 2.8% of India's GDP, and a market capitalization of US$60.10 billion. As a conglomerate, its principal business interests lie in tea, steel, consultancy services, and the automotive sector, among others. Its separate businesses have always had an interest in the communities in which the group operates. Tata Steel, for example, established an eight-hour work day in 1912, free medical aid in 1915, a welfare department in 1917, leave with pay and a provident and compensation fund in 1920, and maternity benefit for women in 1928—all before these rights became statutory.

Recently, its steel division, Tata Steel, was presented with the 'Award for Corporate Social Responsibility in Public Health' by the US–India Business Council, Population Services International, and the Center for Strategic and International Studies, at an awards dinner held in Mumbai. The company's efforts to improve its employees' welfare, particularly around the steel works at the company's base in Jamshedpur, and its corporate leadership in working to prevent the spread of HIV/AIDS (since the 1990s), were the principal reasons for the coveted award. As a result of its pioneering work, Tata Steel is a member of the UN Global Compact.

But with social deprivation all around India, Ratan Tata, the company's CEO, feels his company has more of a duty to be socially responsible than perhaps Western companies might have within their countries, since the effects of deprivation are felt less.

Sources: Tata (2007a,b); Anon. (2007); Pandit (2005).

1 Does a company in a less developed country really have more responsibility to pursue a CSR agenda than a company in a wealthier country with less deprivation in the population?

2 Why do you think a steel company particularly needs to develop good relations with its communities?

3 What impact, if any, do you think CSR programmes have on Tata Steel's revenues?

Chapter Summary

To consolidate your learning, the key points from this chapter are summarized below:

- Define the term ethics and apply the discipline to marketing.

  Marketing ethics is concerned with how marketers *go about* the management process of identifying, anticipating, and satisfying customer requirements profitably. In particular, it is the application of moral principles to decision making in marketing and the consideration of the outcomes of those decisions.

- Explain the common ethical norms applied in marketing.

  Marketing ethics can be divided into normative and descriptive branches which distinguish between how we *ought* to act in a given marketing decision-making situation and how people *actually behave* when making marketing decisions.

- Describe the role of ethics in marketing decision making.

  Models of marketing decision making outline the importance of the ethical content of a situation, the importance of 'significant others', employees' values, and the ethical training given by a company in line with its own ethical policy. Hunt and Vitell's model (2006) of marketing decision making is perhaps the best known as it stresses the importance of considering what is the *right* thing to do (deontological norms) and what are the right intentions for us to follow (teleological norms).

- Analyse situations to determine the kind of ethical approaches that might be adopted.

  There are four main normative approaches to marketing decision making including managerial egoism (doing the *right* thing because it's the best thing to do), utilitarianism (doing the *right* thing for the largest number of people), deontological ethics (doing the *right* thing because it's the *right* thing to do), and virtue ethics (doing the *right* thing for everyone), each of which can be applied to any given ethical situation.

- Recognize how to apply an understanding of ethics to a company's marketing programmes.

  Ethical breaches can occur in all areas of an organization's marketing activity including distribution, pricing, promotion, and product policies. From a service's marketing perspective, the people and process components of the extended marketing mix are particularly appropriate since ethical breaches are often undertaken by employees who may or may not be following company ethical guidelines and codes of conduct appropriately.

- Explain the difficulties associated with developing the socially responsible company.

  There is an increasing movement towards developing a socially responsible agenda in marketing in companies around the world, where a proportion of profits is ploughed back into worthy causes, partly as a realization of the negative publicity that companies can obtain when they act socially irresponsibly and the damage this can cause their business.

 Visit the **Online Resource Centre** that accompanies this book to read more information relating to marketing ethics: www.oxfordtextbooks.co.uk/orc/baines/

? Review Questions

1 How do we define marketing ethics?

2 What are the common ethical norms applied in marketing?

3 What role does ethics in marketing play in the marketing decision-making process?

4 What are key ethical considerations when pricing goods and services?

5 What are key ethical considerations when promoting goods and services?

6 What are key ethical considerations when distributing goods and services?

7 What are key ethical concerns when developing the product offering?

8 What are the problems associated with developing the socially responsible company?

9 What are key examples of company irresponsibility in marketing?

? Discussion Questions

1 Having read the Case Insight at the beginning of this chapter, how would you advise The Co-operative Bank to continue to develop and promote its Ethical Policy? Think

about how it could differentiate itself within the marketplace when other banks are increasingly using CSR initiatives to promote their businesses.

2 Reread the section of the chapter on normative ethics. Consider SSL International plc's condom product, Durex, designed to reduce the proportion of people sustaining sexually transmitted diseases (STDs) and women having unwanted pregnancies. To what extent might it be appropriate for SSL International to promote condom usage to young children, particularly in (1) Catholic countries and (2) African countries?

Discuss this ethical problem using the following normative ethical approaches (check the definitions in the Glossary if necessary):

(a) Managerial egoism—the principle of managerial self-interest;

(b) Utilitarianism—the principle of the greater good for the greater number of people;

(c) Deontological ethics—the principle of duty-based ethics.

3 Consider whether or not it is unethical to act in the following ways in the following circumstances:

(a) You are a salesperson working for an American construction company trying to secure a natural gas plant building contract in Nigeria. You know that if you do not pay a 'commission' to the public official in charge of tendering for the project, you will not win the contract. Should you pay the 'commission' or do you have other choices of action?

(b) You are an international banker. A potential new client in New York insists on taking you to a very exclusive restaurant in Manhattan at her expense to discuss a loan she requires to purchase a new building for her rapidly expanding business. Should you accept?

(c) You are a farmer supplying a large chain supermarket in Britain with selected prime cuts of meat products. The supermarket requests an upfront 'listing' fee of £20k before they can accept you as a supplier. You can then expect orders of several hundreds of thousands of pounds. Should you pay the 'listing fee' to the supermarket? Would the situation be different in France? Why?

4 Which of the following schemes are examples of corporate social responsibility initiatives (be prepared to discuss your assumptions):

(a) A Turkish telecommunications company develops a programme to provide young women with free mobile telephone handsets in Istanbul.

(b) A British multiple retail grocer works with selected farmers for set meat, fruit, and vegetable products and charges each of them only £5,000 per product to list each of their products exclusively in its range.

(c) A crisp manufacturing company offers consumers the opportunity to save tokens on crisp packets so that they can collect enough tokens to donate special prizes to selected local schools.

(d) An ethical prescription drug manufacturing company offers selected drugs to very needy patients in African countries at an 80% discount on Western prices.

📖 References

AMA (2004), 'Code of ethics: ethical norms and values for marketers', available at www.marketingpower.com/content435.php, accessed 3 August 2006.

Anon. (2007), 'Tata Steel conferred with CSR award in public health', 14 March, available at www.moneycontrol.com, accessed 16 June 2007.

AOSC (1990), 'Spill, the wreck of the *Exxon Valdez*: implications for safe transportation of oil', Final Report, Juneau, Alaska: Alaska Oil Spill Commission.

Baines, P., and Worcester, R. (2005), 'When the British Tommy went to war, public opinion followed', *Journal of Public Affairs*, 5, 1, 4–19.

Bayne, K. (2005), 'The *Exxon Valdez* catastrophe', *The Times*, 26 May, 9.

BBC News (2002), 'Nintendo fined for price fixing', Wednesday, 30 October, available at http://news.bbc.co.uk/2/hi/business/2375967.stm, accessed 3 December 2005.

Baudrillard, J. (2005), *The System of Objects*, trans. James Benedict, London: Verso Books.

Bennett, R. (1999), 'Headteacher characteristics, management style and attitudes towards the acceptance of commercial sponsorship by state-funded schools', *Marketing, Intelligence and Planning*, 17, 1, 41–52.

BITC (2003), 'Tesco plc: the UK's biggest corporate giver', 19 December, available at www.bitc.org.uk, accessed 27 November 2005.

Braga, F., and Nardella, M. (2003), 'Supply chain management, agricultural policies and anti-trust: the case of Pamigiano Reggiano and Grana Padano', *International Food and Agribusiness Management Review*, 5, 4.

Brennan, R., and Baines, P. (2006), 'Is there a morally right price for anti-retroviral drugs in the developing world?', *Business Ethics: European Review*, forthcoming.

Buchholz, R. A. (1991), 'Corporate responsibility and the good society: from economics to ecology; factors which influence corporate policy decisions', *Business Horizons*, 34, 4, 19–31.

Campbell, T. (1999), 'Crisis management at Coke', *Sales and Marketing Management*, 151, 9, 14.

Charities Aid Foundation (2005), 'Banking sector dominates corporate giving', in *Charity Trends 2005*, available at www.cafonline.org, accessed 3 December 2005.

CIM (2005), 'Professional marketing standards: a guide for employers', available at www.cim.co.uk/standards, accessed 3 August 2006.

Clasen, E. A. (1967), 'Marketing ethics and the consumer', *Harvard Business Review*, January–February.

Coombs, W. T. (1998), 'An analytic framework for crisis situations: better responses from a better understanding of the situation', *Journal of Public Relations Research*, 10, 177–92.

Daniels, J., and Holmes, C. (2005), *Responsible Marketing to Children: Exploring the Impact on Adults' Attitudes and Behaviour*, London: Business in the Community.

Deutsche-Welle (2004), 'Microsoft slapped with biggest fine in EU history', 24 March 2004, http://www.dw-world.de, accessed 3 December 2005.

Doyle, P. (2000), *Value-Based Marketing: Marketing Strategies for Corporate Growth and Shareholder Value*, Chichester: John Wiley and Sons.

European Commission (2002), 'Commission fines Nintendo and seven of its European distributors for colluding to prevent trade in low-priced products', *European Commission Report IP/02/1584*, 30 October, available at http://europa.eu.int/, accessed 3 December 2005.

ExxonMobil (2004), 2004 Corporate Citizenship Report, available at www.exxonmobil.com/corporate/files/corporate/ccr04_full_report.pdf, accessed 14 September 2007.

Ferrell, O. C., and Gresham, L. G. (1985), 'A contingency framework for understanding ethical decision making in marketing', *Journal of Marketing*, 49 (Summer), 87–96.

Flynn, L. (2005), 'Samsung fined [AUS]$400m for part in price-fixing plot', *Sunday Morning Herald*, 15 October, available at www.smh.com.au/, accessed 3 December 2005.

Forsyth, D. R. (1980), 'A taxonomy of ethical ideologies', *Journal of Personality and Social Psychology*, 39, 1, 175–84.

Freitag, A. (2002), 'International coverage of the Firestone tyre recall', *Journal of Communication Management*, 6, 3, 239–56.

Friedman, M. (1979), 'The social responsibility of business is to increase profit', in T. Beanchamp and N. Bowie (eds.), *Ethical Theory and Business*, Englewood Cliffs, NJ: Prentice Hall.

Gaski, J. E. (1999), 'Does marketing ethics really have anything to say? A critical inventory of the literature', *Journal of Business Ethics*, 18, 315–34.

Hunt, S., and Vitell, S. J. (2006), 'The general theory of marketing ethics: a revision and three questions', *Journal of Macromarketing*, 26, 2, 143–53.

Kim, S. Y., and Chun, S. Y. (2003), 'A study of marketing ethics in Korea: what do Koreans care about?', *International Journal of Management*, 20, 3, 377–83.

Kimes, S. E., and Wirtz, J. (2003), 'Has revenue management become acceptable? Findings from an international study on the perceived fairness of rate fences', *Journal of Service Research*, 6, 2, 125–35.

Kofler, P. (2000), *Marketing Management: The Millennium Edition*, Englewood Cliffs, NJ: Prentice-Hall.

Kumar, S. (2004), 'Victims of gas leak in Bhopal seek redress on compensation', *British Medical Journal*, 329, 366.

Laczniak, G. R., and Murphy, P. E. (1993), *Ethical Marketing Decisions: The Higher Road*, Englewood Cliffs, NJ: Prentice-Hall.

Maignan, I., and Ferrell, O. C. (2004), 'Corporate social responsibility and marketing: an integrative framework', *Journal of the Academy of Marketing Science*, 32, 1, 3–19.

Maitland, I. (2002), 'Priceless drugs: how should life-saving drugs be priced?', *Business Ethics Quartely*, 12, 4, 451–80.

Marta, J. K. M., and Singhapakdi, A. (2005), 'Comparing Thai and US businesspeople: perceived intensity of unethical marketing practices, corporate ethical values and perceived importance of ethics', *International Marketing Review*, 22, 5, 562–77.

Martin, R. L. (2002), 'The virtue matrix: calculating the return on corporate responsibility', *Harvard Business Review*, 80, 5–11.

Mautner, T. (ed.) (1999), *Penguin Dictionary of Philosophy*, London: Penguin.

Mintel (2006), 'Contraceptives—UK', September, London: Mintel International Group, available at www.mintel.com, accessed 16 June 2007.

Mokhiber, R. (2005), 'Corporate crime reporter', available at www.corporatecrimereporter.com/top100.html, accessed 30 December 2005.

Murphy, P. E. (2004), 'Observations on teaching marketing ethics', *Marketing Education Review*, 14, 3 (Fall).

Nantel, J., and Weeks, W. A. (1996), 'Marketing ethics: is there more to it than the utilitarian approach?', *European Journal of Marketing*, 30, 5, 9–19.

O'Rourke, J. (2001), 'Bridgestone/Firestone Inc. and Ford Motor Company: how a product safety crisis ended a hundred year relationship', *Corporate Reputation Review*, 4, 3, 255–64.

O'Shaughnessy, N. J. (2004), *Politics and Propaganda: Weapons of Mass Seduction*, Manchester: Manchester University Press.

Pandit, R. (2005), 'What's next for Tata Group: an interview with its chairman', *McKinsey Quarterly*, 4.

Philips, Lord (2000), *BSE Enquiry: Findings and Conclusions*, vol. i, London: HMSO.

Rao, C. P., and Singhapakdi, A. (1997), 'Marketing ethics: a comparison between services and other marketing professionals', *Journal of Services Marketing*, 11, 6, 409–26.

Rawls, J. (1972), *A Theory of Justice*, Cambridge, Mass.: Harvard University Press.

Saeed, M., Ahmed, Z. U., and Mukhtar, S.-M. (2001), 'International marketing ethics from an Islamic perspective: a value-maximisation approach', *Journal of Business Ethics*, 32, 127–42.

Sarwono, S. S., and Armstrong, R. W. (2001), 'Microcultural differences and perceived ethical problems: an international business perspective', *Journal of Business Ethics*, 30, 41–56.

Schwarz, W. (1991), 'Nescafe boycott urged by synod', *The Guardian*, 16 July, 3.

Sen, F., and Egelhoff, W. G. (1991), 'Six years and counting: learning from crisis management at Bhopal', *Public Relations Review*, 17, 1, 68–93.

Singhapakdi, A., Marta, J. K., Rallapalli, K. C., and Rao, C. P. (2000), 'Towards an understanding of religiousness and marketing ethics: an empirical study', *Journal of Business Ethics*, 27, 305–19.

—— Salyachivin, S., Virakul, B., and Veerayangkur, V. (2000), 'Some important factors underlying ethical decision-making of managers in Thailand', *Journal of Business Ethics*, 27, 271–84.

Smith, A. (1776), *The Wealth of Nations*, London: Penguin.

Smith, N.C. (2001), 'Ethical guidelines for marketing practice: a reply to Gaski and some observations on the role of normative marketing ethics', *Journal of Business Ethics*, 32, 3–18.

SSL International (2005), available at www.ssl-international.com/copy/about/company/policies/quality.htm, accessed 14 September 2007.

Swartz, M., and Watkins, S. (2003), *Power Failure: The Inside Story of the Collapse of Enron*, London: Aurum Books.

Tata (2007a), *Tata Group Profile*, available at www.tata.com/0_about_us/group_profile.htm, accessed 16 June.

—— (2007b), *Corporate Social Responsibility*, available at www.tatatiscon.co.in/index.asp, accessed 16 June.

Tong-hyung, K. (2005), 'Justice minister hints at probe into Samsung chairman Lee', Asia Media, 22 September, available at www.asiamedia.ucla.edu/, accessed 3 December 2005.

United Nations (2004), *Report on the Global AIDS Epidemic*, Geneva: United Nations.

Usborne, D. (1997), 'Nike agrees code to ban sweated labour', *The Independent*, 15 April, 3.

Vorley, B. (2003), 'Corporate concentration from farm to consumer', *IIED/UK Food Group Report*, available at www.agribusinessaccountability.org/pdfs/247_Food%20Inc.pdf, accessed 31 December 2005.

Wall Street Journal (2001), 'Cost of developing drugs found to rise', 3 December.

Glossary

accessory equipment goods these support the key operational processes and activities of the organization.

account managers agency personnel who are responsible for representing the interests of the client within the agency and for ensuring that all those working on the client's account are fully informed, working to deadline and to budget. They have a key representational role in the client/agency relationship.

account planners agency personnel who undertake research to support a campaign. The research information is used to help the creative teams in order that a client's marketing goals are achieved.

adaptation orientation a firm believes that each country should be approached separately as a different market, buying or conducting market research into the particular country and developing specific market strategy for that particular market.

advertising a form of non-personal communication, by an identified sponsor, that is transmitted through the use of paid-for media.

aesthetic consideration of what is beautiful or in good taste, particularly in art.

affective a psychological term referring to our emotional state of mind. Values are affective because they are linked to our feelings about things.

agent (broker) a person who acts as a principal intermediary between the seller of a product or service and buyers without taking ownership of the product offering.

aggregated demand demand calculated at the population level rather than at the individual level.

AIDA a hierarchy of effects or sequential model used to explain how advertising works. AIDA stands for *awareness*, *interest*, *desire*, and *action* (a sale). It is no longer accepted as a valid interpretation.

AMA the American Marketing Association is a professional body for marketing professionals and marketing educators based in the United States, operating principally in the USA and Canada.

Ansoff matrix the product–market matrix provides a useful framework for considering the relationship between strategic direction and market opportunities.

anthropology the scientific discipline of observing, and recording, the behaviour of humans and animals.

anti-foundational a reaction against the development of something or an idea. An attempt to destroy the foundations of something, someone, or an idea.

anti-globalization a term most commonly ascribed to the political stance of people and groups who oppose certain aspects of globalization. Participants are united in opposition to the political power of large corporations, as exercised in trade agreements and elsewhere, which they say undermines democracy, the environment, labour rights, national sovereignty, the third world, and other concerns.

a priori method segments are predetermined using the judgement of the researchers beforehand.

art use of imitation, imagination, and creative flair, typically to make, draw, write, build, or develop something.

artefact a term derived from archaeology to denote man-made objects retrieved from dig sites but used in a metaphorical sense in marketing to indicate cultural meanings and brands.

asynchronous delays in interaction or information exchange ranging from a few seconds to even longer such as a few days or weeks.

atmospherics term denoting those components of a store which impact upon its atmosphere and which attract consumers to a store, including the merchandising plan, smells, lighting, architecture, product ranges and prices, access to the store and other sensory stimuli.

ATR a framework developed by Ehrenberg to explain how advertising works. ATR stands for awareness–trial–reinforcement.

attitudes refers to mental states of individuals which underlie the structuring of perceptions and guide behavioural response.

audience fragmentation the disintegration of large media audiences into many smaller audiences caused by the development of alternative forms of entertainment that people can experience. This means that to reach large numbers of people in a target market, companies need to use a variety of media, not just rely on a few mass media channels.

backward integration when a company takes over one or more of its suppliers, it is said to be backward integrating. Taking over a buyer is forward integrating.

bait and switch an American term, this occurs when a company, typically a retailer, promotes a low-priced product to engage customers but then persuades them to buy higher-priced product variants.

benefits sought by understanding the motivations customers derive from their purchases it is possible to have an insight into the benefits they seek from product use.

bid rigging when organizations conspire to determine which company or companies should win a particular contract.

blogs frequent web-based publication of personal thoughts and web links made accessible to a wider online audience that support audience feedback.

Boston Box a popular portfolio matrix commonly also referred to as the BCG, developed by the Boston Consulting Group.

brand comprehension refers to what we understand the brand to mean to us, both in functional terms, i.e. how it solves a particular problem, and in emotional terms. i.e. whether or not we like it and how we relate to it.

branded entertainment occurs when a brand becomes a constituent element of a film and the storyline is woven together with a brand. Derived from product placement.

brand equity this is a measure of the value of a brand. It is an assessment of a brand's physical assets plus a sum that represents their reputation or goodwill.

brand extensions a term used to refer to the process when a successful brand is used to launch a new product into a new market.

brands products and services that have been given added value by marketing managers in an attempt to augment their products with values and associations that are recognized by and are meaningful to their customers.

breakdown method the view that the market is considered to consist of customers which are essentially the same, so the task is to identify groups which share particular differences.

briefs written documents used to exchange information between parties involved with the development and implementation of a campaign.

build-up method considers a market to consist of customers that are all different, so here the task is to find similarities.

business markets characterized by organizations who consume products and services for use within the manufacture/production of other products or for use in their daily operations.

business-to-business marketing activities undertaken by one company which are directed at another.

buyclasses the different types of buying situations faced by organizations.

buyers people who select suppliers and manage the buying process whereby the required products and services are procured. They formally undertake the process whereby products and services are purchased once a decision has been made to procure them.

buying centre *see* decision-making unit.

buyphases a series of sequential activities or stages through which organizations proceed when making purchasing decisions.

call-to-action a part of a marketing communication message that explicitly requests the receiver to act in a particular way.

capital equipment goods buildings, heavy plant, and factory equipment necessary to build or assemble products.

capitalism the political system in which private (as opposed to governmental) capital and wealth is the predominant means of producing and distributing goods.

cartel when a union of manufacturers is developed to control prices. In most major world markets and countries, cartels are illegal.

category killer a large retail outlet typically positioned in out of town locations, specializing in selling one area of products with the aim of killing off the competition e.g. DIY stores such as Homebase in the UK, Toys R Us in the USA, France, and UK and other countries, for example. These stores are characterized by narrow but very deep product assortment, low prices, and few to moderate customer services.

causal research a technique used to investigate the relational link between two or more variables by manipulating the independent variable(s) to see their effect upon the dependent variable(s) and comparing these effects with a control group where no such manipulation takes place.

cause-related marketing a campaign where a company is linked to a charity or social cause with the express intention of building its own customer goodwill, providing the charity with an increase in resource, and the company with either a concomitant increase in sales of its product/service or a reputational dividend.

celebrity endorsement usually famous or respected members of the public, used by advertisers because they are perceived to be expert or knowledgeable or for their ability to display particular attractive qualities, to market specific goods and services.

channel conflict is where one channel member perceives another channel member to be acting in a way that prevents the first member from achieving its distribution activities.

channel convergence media channels are developing that combine the characteristics of numerous traditional channels (e.g. video content through the mobile phone or radio airtime accessible through the web).

channel power the ability of one organization to influence another in the marketing channel, to achieve their goals.

choice criteria denotes the principal dimensions on which we select a particular product or service. For a hairdresser, this might be price, location, range of services, level of expertise, friendliness, and so on.

CIM the Chartered Institute of Marketing is a professional body for marketing professionals based in the United Kingdom, with study centres and members around the world.

classical conditioning a theory of learning propounded by Russian physiologist Ivan Pavlov, who carried out a series of experiments with his dogs. He realized that if he rang the bell before serving food, the dogs would automatically associate the sound of the bell (conditioned stimulus) with the presentation of the food (unconditioned stimulus), and begin salivating. Classical conditioning occurs when the unconditioned stimulus becomes associated with the conditioned stimulus.

client brief a written document developed by clients to provide their appointed agencies with key information about their markets, goals, strategies, resources, and contacts. Client briefs should provide the agency with an insight into the client's task or communication problem that needs to be resolved.

co-branding the process by which two established brands work together, either on one product or service. The principle behind co-branding is that the combined power of the two brands generates increased consumer appeal and attraction.

coding in a survey when answers are assigned numbers in order to allow them to be more easily analysed. They can be either pre-coded (i.e. analysed before the questionnaire is completed, when answers are set) or coded afterward the questionnaire is filled in (when closed questions are used).

cognition knowing or perceiving something, typically as a result of rational thought.

cognitive a psychological term relating to the action of thinking about something. Our opinions are cognitive. Cognitions are mental structures formed about something in our minds.

cognitive dissonance a psychological theory proposed by Leon Festinger in 1957 which states that we are motivated to re-evaluate our beliefs, attitudes, opinions, or values if the position we hold on them at one point in time does not concur with the position held at an earlier period due to some intervening event, circumstance, or action.

collaborative exchanges a series of economic transactions between parties who have a long-term orientation towards and are primarily motivated by concern for each other.

collusion when a group of competitor companies conspire to control the market, often at the expense of the consumer/customer, and typically in relation to price fixing.

communication objectives goals related to the outcome of a marketing communications campaign. Normally set in terms of desired levels of awareness, perception, comprehension/knowledge, attitudes, and overall degree of preference for a brand.

communication the sharing of meaning created through the transmission of information.

competitive advantage achieved when an organization has an edge over its competitors on factors that are important to customers.

competitive intelligence the organized, professional, systematic collection of information, typically through informal mechanisms, used for the achievement of strategic and tactical organizational goals.

computer-assisted personal interviewing (CAPI) an approach to personal interviewing using a hand-held computer or laptop to display questions and record the respondents' answers.

computer-assisted telephone interviewing (CATI) an approach to telephone interviewing using a laptop or desktop computer to display the questions to the interviewer who reads them out and records the respondents' answers.

computer-assisted web interviewing (CAWI) an approach to online interviewing where the respondent uses a laptop or desktop computer to access questions in a set location to which the respondent must go. Questions are automatically set based on the respondents' answers.

conative a psychological term relating to our motivations to do something. Attitudes are conative because they are linked to our motivations to do things.

concentrated or niche marketing strategy recognizes that there are segments in the market; however a concentrated strategy is implemented by focusing on just one or two or a few market segments.

conceptual equivalence the degree to which interpretation of behaviour, or objects, is similar across countries.

conflict inter-organizational conflict concerns the disagreements and tensions that can arise between organizations. In particular, channel conflict can arise in distribution channels when one organization changes their role, scope, or strategy, which then has a negative impact on another organization.

consumer the user of a product, service, or other form of offering.

consumerism growing global movement concerned with countering the increasingly apparent symbolic importance of materialism and the consumption and purchase of consumer goods and capitalism more generally.

consumer juries consist of a collection of target consumers who are asked to rank in order ideas or concepts put to them and to explain their choices.

consumer marketing refers to marketing activities undertaken directly to influence consumers, as opposed to other businesses.

consumer surplus the difference between the price that the consumer is willing to pay for a product or service and the price that they actually end up paying, when the latter is lower than the actual price charged.

context analysis the first stage of the marketing communications planning process. It involves the analysis of four main contexts (or situations), the customer, business, internal, and external environmental contexts, in order to shape the detail of the plan.

contracting is where a manufacturer contracts an organization in a foreign market to manufacture or assemble the product in the foreign market.

control means achieving the optimum distribution costs without losing decision-making authority over the product offering and the way it is marketed and supported. This is therefore about maximizing your capacity to manage all the marketing mix decisions.

control group a sample group used in causal research which is not subjected to manipulation of some sort. *See* causal research.

convenience products non-durable goods or services, often bought with little pre-purchase thought or consideration.

convenience sampling a method used to select respondents where the criteria for selection are not restricted and the selection of the respondents is left entirely to the judgement of the researcher and the chance of selection beforehand is unknown.

convenience stores or corner shops offer a range of grocery and household items that cater for convenience and last-minute purchase needs of consumers. Key characteristics include: long opening times (e.g. 24/7), usually family run, and often belong to a trading group.

cookie an electronic 'token', a piece of data or record transmitted by a web server to a client computer. More simply put, a cookie is a small text file found on your hard drive that allows information about your web activity patterns to be stored in the memory of your browser.

corporate objectives the mission and overall business goals that an organization has agreed.

cost leadership a strategy involving the production of goods and services for a broad market segment, at a cost lower than all other competitors.

counter-implementation the behaviour employees exhibit when they resist tasks associated with the implementation of strategic programmes, whether intentionally or unintentionally, which is often motivated by anxiety.

coverage is about maximizing the amount of contact and value (or benefits) for the customer (in terms of product offering availability). This is the marketer's desire to have the product available to the maximum number of customers, in the maximum number of locations, across the widest range of times.

creative brief a written document, developed by the account manager to provide the creative team with relevant information necessary to develop messages and appropriate creative content.

creative team an advertising agency team composed of an art director and a copywriter. They are responsible for translating proposals and ideas, often embedded in the creative brief, into a finished advertisement.

credentials presentation a meeting between a potential client organization and a short-listed agency in an attempt to determine whether the agency is likely to 'fit' with the client's expectations and requirements.

CRM *see* customer relationship management.

CSR (corporate social responsibility) typically a programme of social and/or environmental activities undertaken by a company on behalf of one or more of its stakeholders to develop sustainable business operations, foster goodwill, and develop the company's corporate reputation.

cultural anthropology a branch of study concerned with observing and explaining cultural differences in human behaviour.

culture the values, beliefs, ideas, customs, actions, and symbols that are learned and shared by people within particular societies.

customer the person who purchases and pays for (or initially requests and specifies, in the case of a non-financial transaction) a product, service, or other form of offering from a company or organization.

customer acquisition all marketing activities and strategies used by organizations to attract new customers.

customer portfolio matrix a 2 × 2 grid that is used to reflect the strength of the relationships between a buyer and seller and the profitability each account represents to the seller.

customer relationship lifecycle the stages a customer moves through during their relationship

with an organization. These stages are customer acquisition, development, and retention.

customer relationship management (CRM) software systems that provide all staff with a complete view of the history and status of each customer.

customer relationship marketing all marketing activities and strategies used to retain customers. This is achieved by providing customers with relationship-enhancing products and/or services that are perceived to be of value and superior to those offered by a competitor.

customer retention all marketing activities and strategies used by organizations to keep current customers.

customer satisfaction a state of mind reached when the provision of goods or services meets or exceeds a customer's pre-purchase expectations of quality and service.

customized targeting strategy in which a marketing strategy is developed for each customer as opposed to each market segment.

deciders people who make organizational purchasing decisions, often very difficult to identify.

decision-making unit (DMU) a group of people who make purchasing decisions on behalf of an organization.

decision-making unit structure the attitudes, policies, and purchasing strategies used by organizations provide the means by which organizations can be clustered.

decoding that part of the communication process where receivers unpack the various components of the message, and begin to make sense and give the message meaning.

deconstruction a form of textual analysis, associated with French philosopher Jacques Derrida, used to uncover hidden or 'absent' meanings by breaking the text down into privileged themes, then determining the binary opposites of those privileged themes, as the hidden or absent meaning of the work, and essentially proposing that this is what the work was really trying to say.

demographic key variables concerning age, sex, occupation, level of education, religion, and social class, many of which determine a potential buyer's ability to purchase a product or service.

deontological ethics a form of ethical approach by which the rightness or wrongness of an action or decision is not judged to be exclusively based on the consequences of that action or decision.

department store a large-scale retailing institution that has a very broad and deep product assortment (both hard and soft goods), with the provision of a wide array of customer service facilities for store customers.

descriptive ethics concerned with the study of system of beliefs and practices of a social group from the perspective of being outside that group.

descriptive research a research technique used to test, and confirm, hypotheses developed from a management problem.

desk research *see* secondary research.

dialectics the art of investigating the truth of opinions by considering that which is said from opposing perspectives to determine which of the two opposite forces is dominant.

dialogue the development of knowledge that occurs when all parties to a communication event listen, adapt, and reason with one another, about a specific topic.

diaspora peoples dispersed, or those who have emigrated, from their homeland. Often used in relation to the Jewish peoples.

differentiated targeting approach recognizes that there are several market segments to target, each being attractive to the marketing organization. To exploit market segments, a marketing strategy is developed for each segment.

differentiation a strategy through which an organization offers products and services to broad particular customer groups, who perceive the offering to be significantly different from, and superior to, its competitors.

digital divide refers to the gap between those individuals and communities who own, access, and effectively use information and communication technologies (ICT) and those who do not.

digital value the means by which digital processes and systems can be used to provide customers with enhanced product and service value.

direct channel structure where the product goes directly from the producer to the final customer.

direct exporting involves the manufacturing firm itself distributing its product offering to foreign markets, direct to customers.

direct investment or foreign manufacture, thus some form of manufacture or production in the foreign or host country is sometimes necessary.

direct marketing a marketing communication tool that uses non-personal media to create and sustain a personal and intermediary-free communication with customers, potential customers, and other significant stakeholders. In most cases this is a media-based activity.

direct-response advertising advertisements that contain mechanisms such as telephone numbers, website addresses, email, and snail mail addresses. These are designed to encourage viewers to respond immediately to the ads. Most commonly used on television and known as DRTV.

direct selling is one of the oldest forms of retailing methods. Defined as the personal contact between a salesperson and a consumer away from the retailing environment, this type of retailing may also be called in-home personal selling.

discount retailers this type of retailer involves comparatively low prices as a major selling point combined with the reduced costs of doing business.

distribution *see* place.

distribution centres are designed to move goods, rather than just store them.

distribution channels can be defined as an organized network of agencies and organizations which, in combination, performs all the activities required to link producers and manufacturers with consumers, purchasers, and users to accomplish the marketing task of product offering distribution.

distributor brands brands developed by the wholesalers, distributors, dealers, and retailers who make up the distribution channel. Sometimes referred to as own-label brands.

distributors organizations that buy goods and services, often from a limited range of manufacturers, and normally sell them to retailers or resellers.

diversification a strategy that requires organizations to grow outside their current range of activities. This type of growth brings new value chain activities because the firm is operating with new products and in new markets.

divest a strategic objective that involves selling or killing off a product when products continue to incur losses and generate negative cash flows.

domain the area, field, or sphere in which an organization operates. There are four main elements; population, territory, roles, and issues.

dumping some organizations need to get rid of some excess stock and, with limited opportunity for sales in domestic markets, seek overseas markets in which to offload some of this stock.

durable goods goods bought infrequently, which are used repeatably, and which involve a reasonably high level of consumer risk.

dyadic essentially means two-way. A commercial relationship which is dyadic is an exchange between two people, typically a buyer and a seller.

early adopters a group of people in the process of diffusion who enjoy being at the leading edge of innovation and buy into new products at an early stage.

early majority a group of people in the process of diffusion who require reassurance that a product works and has been proven in the market before they are prepared to buy it.

ego a Freudian psychoanalytical concept which denotes the part of our psyche which attempts to find outlets for the urges in our id, moderated by the superego.

elasticity an economic concept associated with the extent to which changes in one variable are related to changes in another. If a price increase in a good causes a decline in volume of sales of that good, we say the good is price elastic and specify how much. If it causes no change or very little change, we say it is inelastic (see Chapter 6 for more on price elasticity).

electronic kiosks are being placed in shopping malls to assist the retailing experience. Mediated by hypermedia web-based interfaces, these computer-based retailing environments offer consumers increased self-service opportunity, wide product assortments, and large amounts of data and information aiding decision making.

electronic marketing the process of marketing accomplished or facilitated through the application of electronic devices, appliances, tools, techniques, technologies, and or systems.

electronic marketing activity management (EMAM) a framework that can assist the classification of electronic resources when planning what electronic resources to use for certain tasks, in order to achieve certain marketing objectives. EMAM outlines five core marketing activities for which we use electronic resources.

elicitation techniques a technique of disguising questioning so that information is obtained without the imparter recognizing what they are divulging.

embedding (journalists) refers to the practice of the government inviting selected journalists to report on military activity while based inside units involved in major combat operations. This provides the journalist with some degree of protection, but exposes them to the same risks as the soldiers from enemy combatants. Thus, it could be argued that their journalistic impartiality is compromised as a result.

emotion mental feeling or disturbance arising instinctually.

encoding a part of the communication process when the sender selects a combination of appropriate words, pictures, symbols, and music to represent a message to be transmitted.

environmental scanning the management process internal to an organization designed to identify external issues, situations, and threats which may impinge on an organization's future and its strategic decision making.

ethnocentric approach views the domestic market (home market) as the most important, and overseas markets as inferior with foreign imports not seen as representing a serious threat.

ethnographic studies involve an approach to research which emphasizes the collection of data through participant observation of members of a specific sub-cultural grouping and observation of participation of members of a specific sub-cultural grouping.

ethnography a sub-discipline derived from cultural anthropology as an approach to research which emphasizes the collection of data through participant observation of members of a specific sub-cultural grouping and observation of participation of members of a specific sub-cultural grouping.

evoked set a group of goods, brands, or services for a specific item which is brought up in a person's mind in a particular purchasing situation and from which he or she makes their decision of which product, brand, or service to buy.

exclusive distribution is where intermediaries are given exclusive rights to market the good or service within a defined 'territory', and thus you use a very limited number of intermediaries.

exhibitions events when groups of sellers meet collectively with the key purpose of attracting buyers.

exploratory research a research technique used to generate ideas to develop hypotheses based around a management problem.

exporting manufacturing goods in one country, but selling them to customers overseas in foreign markets.

expropriation confiscation of a firm's assets by a host government.

extensive problem solving occurs when consumers give a great deal of attention and care to a purchase decision where there is no previous or similar product purchase experience.

external pacing occurs where the speed, sequence, and content are controlled by the sender of the message/information.

face validity the use of the researcher's or an expert's subjective judgement to determine whether an instrument is measuring what it is designed to measure.

fatal accident rate (FAR) a term used in industrial safety engineering to denote how many people would be killed under certain hypothetical conditions. Typically, the FAR is calculated with a view to minimizing the number of fatalities in any given industrial scenario.

feedback a part of the communication process referring to the responses offered by receivers.

field marketing a marketing communications activity concerned with providing support for the sales force and merchandising personnel.

fixed capital the cost of plant, equipment, and machinery owned by a business.

fixed costs costs which do not vary according to the number of units of product made or service sold. For instance, fixed costs in the pharmaceutical market would include manufacturing plant costs. In a service business like the airline industry, fixed costs would include the cost of purchasing the plane.

flippancy lack of respect by treating something serious with less importance than others expect.

focus a strategy based on finding gaps in broad market segments or in competitors' product ranges.

focus group *see* group discussion.

fragmentation refers to the process of the trivialization of our value systems and corresponding break-up of associated market segments, the break-up of consumer identities, and a weak commitment to a single consumer lifestyle.

franchise where a company offers a complete brand concept, supplies, and logistics to a franchisee that invests an initial lump sum and

thereafter pays regular fees to continue the relationship.

franchising a contractual vertical marketing system in which a franchisor licenses a franchisee to produce or market goods or services to certain criteria laid down by the franchisor in return for fees and/or royalties.

full-service agencies refers to advertising agencies that provide their clients with a full range of services, including strategy and planning, designing the advertisements, and buying the media.

functional equivalence relates to whether or not a concept has the same function in different countries.

gatekeepers people who control the type and flow of information into an organization and in particular to members of the DMU.

generic brands brands sold without any promotional materials or any means of identifying the company.

geocentric approach sees the world as a single market – global, with the organization looking for global segments (e.g. ageing market) and global opportunities to rationalize communications, production, and product development.

geodemographic this approach to segmentation presumes that there is a relationship between the type of housing and location that people live in and their purchasing behaviours.

geographic in many situations the needs of potential customers in one geographic area are different from those in another area. This may be due to climate, custom, or tradition.

geographic proximity closeness of the market in physical terms to the domestic market.

global account management (GAM) the collaborative and centralized processes necessary to coordinate the worldwide buying and selling activities between global customers and global suppliers.

global capability the willingness and capability to operate anywhere in the world with a direct result in global brand recognition.

globalization refers to increasing global connectivity, integration, and interdependence in the economic, social, technological, cultural, political, and ecological spheres.

government the system of organization of a nation state.

grey marketing is the unauthorized sale of new, branded products diverted from authorized distribution channels or imported into a country for sale without the consent or knowledge of the manufacturer.

gross domestic product a measure of the output of a nation, the size of its economy. It is calculated as the market value of all finished goods and services produced in a country during a specified period, typically available annually or quarterly.

gross national product (GNP) total domestic and foreign added value claimed by residents of a state.

group discussions (or focus group) a group discussion on a pre-selected series of topics among 8–12 people introduced by a moderator where group members are encouraged to express their own views and interact with one another.

habit a repetitive form of behaviour, often undergone without conscious rational thought in a routine way. The processes underlying the routinization process are however voluntary (i.e. controllable) rather than reflexive (uncontrollable).

haggling when a customer argues with a supplier, usually a retailer, over the price to be paid for a good or service and is successful in obtaining a discount.

halal a term referring to what is permissible under sharia law and most typically used in Western societies when referring to permissible foodstuffs. For a food to be halal it must not contain alcohol, blood, or its by-products, or the meat of an omnivore or carnivore. In addition, where the food is from an animal, a Muslim must have pronounced the name of Allah before slaughtering the animal.

harvesting a strategic objective based on maximizing short-term profits and stimulating positive cash flow. Often used in mature markets as firms/products enter a decline phase.

hierarchy of effects (HoE) general sequential models used to explain how advertising works. Popular in the 1960s–1980s, these models provided a template that encouraged the development and use of communication objectives.

hold a strategic objective based on defending against attacks from aggressive competitors.

horizontal conflicts may arise between members of a channel on the same level of distribution.

host country a country where international marketing operations take place.

hybrid channel conflict conflict is bound to occur when producers compete with retailers by selling through their producer-owned stores.

hybrid channel structure where some products go directly from producer to customers and others go through intermediaries.

hyperreality a play of illusions and phantasms, an imaginary world, made up of simulacra.

id a Freudian psychoanalytical concept referring to the part of our psyche which harbours our instinctual drives and urges.

incredulity disbelief of someone, or towards something (e.g. an idea).

in-depth interview a qualitative research method used to identify hidden feelings, memories, attitudes, and motivations of the respondents using a face-to-face interview approach.

indirect channel structure where the product goes from the producer through an intermediary, or series of intermediaries, such as a wholesaler, retailer, franchisee, agent, or broker, to the final customer.

indirect exporting takes place where production and manufacture of the product offering occurs in the domestic market and involves the services of other companies (intermediaries) to sell the product in the foreign market.

industrial marketing and purchasing group (IMP) IMP represent a school of thought about relationship marketing.

industry type (SIC codes) standard industrial classifications (SIC) are codes used to identify and categorize all types of industry and businesses.

influencers people who help set the technical specifications for a proposed purchase and assist the evaluation of alternative offerings by potential suppliers.

information utility the provision of information about the product offering before and after sales; it can further provide information about those purchasing it.

initiators people who start the organizational buying decision process.

innovators a group of people in the process of diffusion who like new ideas, are most likely to take risks associated with new products.

inseparability a characteristic of a service, one that refers to its instantaneous production and consumption.

intangibility a characteristic of a service, namely that it does not have physical attributes and so cannot be perceived by the senses—cannot be tasted, seen, touched, smelt, or possessed.

integrated marketing communications (IMC) a process associated with the coordinated development and delivery of a consistent marketing communication message(s) with a target audience.

integrative a growth strategy based on working with the same products and the same markets but starting to perform some of the activities in the value chain that were previously undertaken by others.

intensity of channel coverage number of intermediaries to use when they want or need it.

intensive a growth strategy that requires an organization to concentrate its activities on markets or products that are familiar.

intensive distribution means placing your product or service in as many outlets or locations as possible, in order to maximize the opportunity for customers to find the good or service.

intention in the consumer context, this is linked to whether or not we intend, are motivated to, purchase a good or service.

interaction model the flow of communication messages that leads to mutual understanding about a specific topic.

interactive IMC the unique ability of especially newer forms of electronic media to provide two-way, user-controlled, customized, and one-to-one communication programs.

interactive marketing is more accurately described as creating a situation or mechanism through which a marketer and a customer (or stakeholders) interact usually in real time.

interactivity as such interactivity is about the interchange between two or more parties (i.e. people or machines) and the effect one party has on the other's response.

intermediary an independent business concern that operates as link between producers and ultimate consumers or end industrial users. It renders services in connection with the purchase and/or sale of the product offering moving from producers to consumers.

internal marketing the application of marketing concepts and principles within an organization. Normally targeted at employees with a view to encouraging them to support and endorse the organization's strategy, goals, and brands.

international marketing marketing activity that crosses national boundaries.

internet marketing (or online marketing) a form of electronic marketing limited in technical context and thus a tool-based definition denoting the use of only internet-based technologies (e.g. web, email, intranet, extranets, etc.) for marketing.

interstitials web pages that are displayed before an expected content page, often to display advertisements.

inverted production/consumption a concept indicating that the traditional pattern of consumption following production is changing in postmodern times, to a pattern of production following consumption, e.g. in reality television where the viewer votes on which contestants should enter/leave a particular show.

irony to say one thing and mean the opposite is to be ironic, often as a form of humour. To have something happen to you when the opposite was expected indicates an ironic event.

joint venture when two organizations come together to create a jointly owned third company. This is an example of cooperative as opposed to competitive operations in international marketing.

juxtaposition to place items beside each other, with connotations of contrast.

KAM development cycle the development stages experienced by organizations as relationships with key account customers develop.

key accounts business customers who are strategically significant and with whom a supplier wishes to build long-lasting relationships.

KMV The 'key mediating variables', commitment and trust, used within the Morgan and Hunt model of relationship marketing.

laggards a group of people in the process of diffusion who are suspicious of all new ideas and whose opinions are very hard to change.

late majority a group of people in the process of diffusion who are sceptical of new ideas and only adopt new products because of social or economic factors.

lead generation activities undertaken by a company or organization to develop lists of prospective customers.

licensing a commercial process whereby the trademark of an established brand is used by another organization over a defined period of time, in a defined area, in return for a fee, to develop another brand.

lifestage analysis is based on the principle that people need different products and services at different stages in their lives (e.g. childhood, adulthood, young couples, retired, etc.).

limited line retailers this type of retailer has a narrow but deep product assortment and customer services that vary from store to store.

limited problem solving occurs when consumers have some product and purchase familiarity.

listing fee when a retailer charges a supplier a fee to allow the supplier to supply the supermarket. This fee is not typically related to any discounts already provided to the retailer. Such fees are illegal in France.

logistics the process of transporting the initial components of goods, services, and other forms of offering, and their finished products, from the producer to the customer and then on to the consumer.

logistics management broadly the coordination of activities of the entire distribution channel to deliver maximum value to customers: from suppliers of raw materials to the manufacturer of the product, to the wholesalers who deliver the product, to the final customers who purchase it.

maintenance, repair, and operating (MRO) products, other than raw materials, that are necessary to ensure that the organization is able to continue functioning. Often referred to as consumables.

management problem a statement which outlines a situation faced by an organization requiring further investigation and subsequent organizational action.

managerial egoism a form of ethical approach to the effect that a manager ought to act in his or her own best interests and that an action is right if it benefits the manager undertaking that action.

manufacturer brands created and sustained by producers who seek widespread awareness and distribution because there is high demand for these brands.

market development strategy involves increasing sales by selling existing or 'old' products in new markets, either by targeting new audiences domestically or entering new markets internationally.

marketing communications mix the five key communication tools used by organizations to reach consumers and other organizations with product- and organization-based messages. These tools are advertising, sales promotions, public relations, direct marketing, and personal selling.

marketing communications planning framework (MCPF) a model of the various decisions and actions that are undertaken when preparing, implementing, and evaluating communication strategies and plans. It reflects a deliberate or planned approach to strategic marketing communications.

marketing information systems a system incorporating ad hoc and continuous market and marketing research surveys, together with secondary data and internal data sources, for the purpose of decision making by marketers.

marketing metrics a measure or set of measures which senior marketers use to assess the performance of their marketing strategies and programmes.

marketing mix the list of items a marketing manager should consider when devising plans for marketing products, including product decisions, place (distribution) decisions, pricing decisions, and promotion decisions. Later the mix was extended to include physical evidence, process, and people decisions to account for the lack of physical nature in service products.

marketing myopia a term coined by Harvard Business School professor Theodore Levitt to denote the mindset that some companies get into, when they completely fail to identify new competitors within their industry which result from the development of substitute products and services.

marketing objectives marketing goals to be accomplished within a particular period of time. Usually referred to in terms of market share, sales revenues, volumes, ROI (return on investment), and other profitability indicators.

marketing research the design, collection, analysis, and interpretation of data collected for the purpose of aiding marketing decision making.

market orientation refers to the development of a whole-organization approach to the generation, collection, and dissemination of market intelligence across different departments and the organization's responsiveness to that intelligence.

market segmentation the division of customer markets into group of customers with distinctly similar needs.

market segmentation approach designing product and service offerings around consumer demand.

market sensing an organization's ability to gather, interpret, and act upon strategic information from customers and competitors.

market separations where supply and demand, producers and consumers, are not matched (separated) in a given market but ought to be, because of market inefficiencies.

materialism a tendency to place superior value on physical things rather than spiritual or intellectual values.

measurement equivalence concerns the extent to which the methods by which the researcher collects and categorizes essential data and information from two or more different sources are comparable.

media facilities used by companies to convey or deliver messages to target audiences. Media is the plural of medium.

media brief a written document, often developed by the account manager, to provide media planners with relevant information necessary to select and buy media appropriate to the campaign.

media fragmentation the splintering of a few mainstream media channels into a multitude of media and channel formats.

media teams people responsible for media planning and media buying.

media usage data on what media channels are used, by whom, when, where, and for how long provides useful insight into the reach potential for certain market segments through differing media channels, and also insight into their media lifestyle.

media vehicle an individual medium or media vehicle, used to carry advertising messages.

merchant a merchant performs the same functions as an agent, but takes ownership.

metanarrative an overarching belief system, held by the majority. Might also be called the received wisdom. Examples in contemporary Western society are the belief in the need to maintain capitalist economic growth and the need for continual scientific advancement.

metric in a marketing sense, a measure or set of measures used to assess the performance of marketing strategies and programmes.

mission a statement that sets out an organization's long-term intentions, describing its purpose and direction.

mixed price bundling when a product or service is offered together with another typically complementary product or service which is also available separately in order to make the original product or service seem more attractive (e.g. a mobile phone package with text messages and international call packages included in the price).

mode of transfer a transmissive process is the method by which something travels from source or sender to a receiver.

modernist a style of thought based on logic and associated with the ideals and assumptions of the Enlightenment period advocating capitalist economic growth and the importance of scientific advancement among other ideals.

modified rebuy the organizational processes associated with the infrequent purchase of products and services.

multi-domestic competitive strategy an organization pursues a separate marketing strategy in each of its foreign markets while viewing the competitive challenge independently from market to market.

multiphrenic the many-minded consumer, who can want different kinds of consumer experiences all at the same time or at different times in the same sort of circumstances. A kind of consumer multiple personality disorder.

mystery shopping this form of research is designed to evaluate standards of customer service performance received by customers commissioned either within one's own organization or within a competitor's organization.

neoclassical economics refers to a meta-theory of economics predicated on delineating supply and demand based on rational individuals or agents each seeking to maximize their individual utility by making choices with a given amount of information.

new task the organizational processes associated with buying a product or service for the first time.

niche market a small part of a market segment that has specific and specialized characteristics that make it uneconomic for the leading competitors to enter this segment.

niche marketing strategy *see* concentrated.

noise influences that distort information in the communication process and which in turn make it difficult for the receiver to correctly decode and interpret a message.

non-durable goods low-priced products which are bought frequently, are used just once, and which incur low levels of purchase risk.

non-positivist a rejection of the idea that all knowledge can be gained only from genuine enquiry gleaned from observation.

non-probability sampling a sampling method used where the probability of selection of the sample elements from the population is unknown. Typical examples include quota, snowball, and convenience sampling approaches.

non-staple in the grocery context, grocery products which are not a main or important food.

non-store retailers retailing activities resulting in transactions that occur away from the retail store.

non-tariff barrier obstacle to international markets from a non-fiscal source (e.g. product safety legislation).

normative ethics concerned with the rational enquiry into standards of right and wrong, good or bad, in respect of character and conduct and which ought to be accepted by a class of individuals.

observation a research method which requires a researcher to watch, and record, how consumers or employees behave, typically in relation to either purchasing or selling activities.

observational study a study where behaviours of interest are recorded, e.g. mystery shopping and mass transit studies.

omnibus survey a regular survey which is made up of questions from several different clients at any one time, each buying one or more questions and spreading the cost of the survey between them.

online marketing *see* internet marketing.

operant conditioning a learning theory developed by B. F. Skinner which suggests that when a subject acts on a stimulus from the environment (antecedents), this is more likely to result in a particular behaviour (behaviour) if that behaviour is reinforced (consequence) through reward or punishment.

opinion followers people who turn to opinion leaders and formers for advice and information about products and services they are interested in purchasing or using.

opinion formers people who exert personal influence because of their profession, authority, education, or status associated with the object of the communication process. They are not part of the same peer group as the people they influence.

opinion leaders people who are predisposed to receiving information and then reprocessing it in order to influence others. They belong to the same peer group as the people they influence, they are not distant or removed.

opinions refer to observable, verbal responses given by individuals to an issue or question and are easily affected by current affairs and discussions with significant others.

opportunity cost the difference between the revenues generated from undertaking one particular activity compared with another feasible revenue-generating activity.

organization or corporate strategy the means by which the resources of the organization are matched with the needs of the environment in which the organization decides to operate.

organizational buyer behaviour the characteristics, issues, and processes associated with the behaviour of producers, resellers, government units, and institutions when purchasing goods and services.

organizational goals the outcomes of the organization's various activities, often expressed as market share, share value, return on investment, or numbers of customers served.

organizational size grouping organizations by their relative size (MNCs, international, large, SMEs) enables the identification of design, delivery, usage rates, or order size and other purchasing characteristics.

organizational values the standards of behaviour expected of an organization's employees.

original equipment manufacturers (OEMs) the process whereby one company purchases and relabels a product and then incorporates it within a different product in order to sell it under a different (their own) brand name.

overt search the point in the buying process when a consumer seeks further information in relation to a product or buying situation, according to the Howard–Sheth model of buyer behaviour.

ownership utility goods are available immediately from the intermediaries' stocks, thus ownership passes to the purchaser.

pacing the control of the speed and sequence of information transfer.

packaging activities associated with designing, protecting, and communicating a product's container or wrapper.

paid inclusion can provide a guarantee that the website is included in the search engine's natural listings.

panel study a study which uses information collected from a fixed group of respondents over a defined period of time.

pastiche something made up of different parts, especially in relation to music or picture, or a work of art composed in the style of another, often well-known, author.

pay per click (PPC) advertising which uses sponsored search engine listings to drive traffic to a website. The advertiser bids for search terms, and the search engine ranks ads based on a competitive auction as well as other factors.

penis envy a Freudian psychosexual development concept, often derided, particularly by feminist intellectuals, that girls switch from having the mother as love object to the father at the age of 4 years old, and consequently feel anxiety at not having their own penises.

perceived quality a relative subjective measure; we talk of perceived quality because there is no truly objective absolute measure of product or service quality.

perceived risk the real and imagined risks that customers consider when purchasing products and services.

perceived value a customer's estimate of the extent to which a product or service can satisfy their needs.

perception a mental picture in our heads based on existing attitudes, beliefs, needs, stimulus factors, and factors specific to our situation, which governs the way we see objects, events, or people in the world about us. Our perceptions govern our attitudes and behaviour toward whatever we perceive.

perceptual mapping a diagram, typically two-dimensional, of 'image-space' derived from attitudinal market research data, which display the differences in perceptions that customers, consumers, or the general public have of different products/services or brands in general.

performance environment organizations that directly or indirectly influence an organization's ability to achieve its strategic and operational goals.

perishability a characteristic of a service, one that recognizes that spare or unused capacity cannot be stored for use at some point in the future.

permission-based email marketing (opt-in) opt-in email or permission marketing is a method of advertising by electronic mail wherein the recipient of the advertisement has consented to receive it.

personal selling the use of interpersonal communications with the aim of encouraging people to purchase particular products and services, for personal gain and reward.

personality that aspect of our psyche that determines the way in which we respond to our environment in a relatively stable way over time.

PESTLE an acronym used to identify a framework which examines the external environment. PESTLE stands for the political, economic, socio-cultural, technological, legal, and ecological environments.

picking in the context of consumer behaviour, this word has a different meaning from the same term used in common parlance. It is the process of deliberative selection of a product or service from amongst a repertoire of acceptable alternatives even though the consumer believes the alternatives to be essentially identical in their ability to satisfy his or her need.

pitch a presentation, made by competing agencies, in order to win a client's account (or business).

place or distribution is essentially about how you can place the optimum amount of goods and/or services before the maximum number of members of your target market, at times and locations which optimize the marketing outcome, i.e. sales.

political environment that part of the macroenvironment concerned with impending and potential legislation and how it may affect a particular firm.

polycentric approach each overseas market is seen as a separate domestic market, each country seen as a separate entity, and the firm seeks to be seen as a local firm within that country.

positioning the way that an audience of consumers or buyers perceive a product or service, particularly as a result of the marketing communications process aimed at a target audience.

positive morality a body of doctrine that is generally adhered to by a social group of individuals, concerning what is right and wrong, good and bad, in respect of character and conduct.

positivist a theory of knowledge which ascertains that all genuine enquiry is concerned with the description and explanation of empirical (i.e. observable) facts.

post hoc method the segments are deduced from research.

postmaterialist emphasizes self-expression and quality of life, as opposed to economic and physical security.

postmodernism a rejection of modernist thought and approach which at its heart contravenes and pokes fun in an irreverent way at the existing received wisdom as a way to draw attention to itself and challenge the existing order.

pre-code in surveys, in order to speed up data processing answers to questions are assigned a unique code e.g. male 1, female 2, so that they can be easily analysed.

predatory pricing this occurs when organizations price their products or services at a lower level than the existing competition in certain markets, but maintain a higher price where competition is weaker or non-existent in other markets.

price the amount the customer has to pay to receive a good or service.

price collusion occurs when companies conspire to fix, raise, and maintain prices, and allocate sales volumes in their industries.

price discrimination involves the setting of different prices for different groups of people. Thus, price discrimination is frequently linked to market segmentation (see Chapter 11).

price elasticity the percentage change in volume demanded as a proportion of the percentage change in price, usually expressed as a negative number. A score close to zero indicates that a product or service price change has little impact on quantity demanded whilst a score of negative 1 indicates that a product or service price change effects an equal percentage quantity change. A value above −1 indicates a disproportionately higher change in quantity demanded as a result of a percentage price change.

price fixing when a group of competitor companies come together to either set prices or develop production quotas in order to control the overall prices at which they are sold. Such pricing mechanisms are illegal in most countries.

price gouging occurs when a company charges more than governments perceive is fair for products and/or services typically by taking advantage of demand pricing formulae where customers/consumers are reliant on a particular product/service and are therefore price insensitive.

price sensitivity the extent to which a company or consumer increases or lowers their purchase volumes in relation to changes in price. Thus, a customer is price insensitive when unit volumes drop proportionately less than increases in prices.

pricing cues proxy measures used by customers to estimate a product or service's reference price. Examples include quality, styling, packaging, sale signs, and odd-number endings.

primary activities the five direct activities within the value chain necessary to bring materials into an organization, to convert them into final products or services, to ship them out to customers, and to provide marketing and servicing facilities.

primary research a technique used to collect data for the first time that has been specifically collected and assembled for the current research problem.

probability sampling a sampling method used where the probability of selection of the sample elements from the population is known. Typical examples include simple random, stratified random, and cluster sampling methods.

process of adoption the process through which individuals accept and use new products. The different stages in the adoption process are sequential and are characterized by the different factors that are involved at each stage.

process of diffusion the rate at which a market adopts an innovation. According to Rogers, there are five categories of adopters; innovators, early adopters, early majority, late majority, and laggards.

procurement the purchasing (buying) process in a firm or organization.

product anything that is capable of satisfying customer needs.

product class a broad category referring to various types of related products. For example, cat food, shampoo, or cars.

product differentiation when companies produce offerings which are different from competing firms.

product lifecycle the pathway a product assumes over its lifetime. There are said to be five main stages; development, introduction, growth, maturity, and decline.

product lines groups of brands that are closely related in terms of their functions and the benefits they provide.

product mix the set of all product lines and items that an organization offers for sale to buyers.

search engine optimization (SEO) attempts to improve rankings for relevant keywords in search results by improving a website's structure and content.

secondary research a technique used to collect data that has been previously collected for a purpose other than the current research situation. The process is often referred to as desk research.

selective contestability the ability to disaggregate generic markets into meaningful sub-markets or segments, select those most attractive, and position the product offering appropriately.

selective distribution where some, but not all, available outlets for the good or service are used.

selective exposure the process associated with how consumers screen out that information that we do not consider meaningful or interesting.

self-referential drawing attention to oneself.

self-service technologies (SST) technological tools that enable customers to produce services for themselves without assistance from firm employees.

semantic differential a type of scale question used in market research studies, which asks respondents to rate each attitude object (e.g. brand) using a five- or seven-point item rating scale bounded at each end by bipolar (e.g. good–bad) or unipolar (e.g. good–not good) objectives or phrases.

semiotics the science of signs and how they convey meaning in their representation.

service encounter an event that occurs when a customer interacts directly with a service.

service failure an event that occurs when a customer's expectations of a service encounter are not met.

service guarantees when a service provider offers a minimum level of service or pays the customer a penalty as a consequence, e.g. a fast food company giving an order for free if the food was not delivered within 5 minutes.

service processes a series of sequential actions that lead to predetermined outcomes when a service is performed correctly.

service quality a measure of the extent to which a service experience exceeds customers' expectations.

service recovery an organization's systematic attempt to correct a service failure and to retain a customer's goodwill.

services any acts or performances offered by one party to another that are essentially intangible and where consumption does not result in any transfer of ownership.

servicescape the stimuli impacting upon the customer in the service environment. The concept is similar to the atmospherics present in a retail environment.

services mix a combination of different service elements, including products.

SERVQUAL a disconfirmation model designed to measure service quality. It is based on the difference between the expected service and the actual perceived service.

shopping product a type of consumer product that is bought relatively infrequently and which requires consumers to update their knowledge prior to purchase.

signified a term used in linguistics, developed by Ferdinand de Saussure to refer to something which is being discussed, e.g. French sparkling wine from the Champagne region of France (*see* signifier).

signifier a term used in linguistics, developed by Ferdinand de Saussure to refer to sound images used to represent something, e.g. the spoken word 'champagne' is used to refer to the signified French sparkling wine (*see* signified).

simple random sampling a method used to select respondents from a known population frame using randomly generated numbers assigned to population elements.

simulacrum the concept of a copy without an original, advanced by French philosopher Jean Baudrillard. A simulacrum comes into being through successive image-change phases, and after successive reproduction an end copy is so different from the original that it is no longer a copy but a simulated version only.

SMART an approach used to write effective objectives. SMART stands for 'specific, measurable, achievable, realistic, and timed'.

snowball sampling a method used to select respondents from rare populations where the criteria for selection are based on referral from an initial set of respondents typically generated through newspaper advertisements or some other method and this set of respondents refers another set of respondents and the process repeats.

social anthropology the scientific discipline of observing and recording the way humans behave in their different social groupings.

social class system of classification of consumers or citizens, based on the socio-economic status of the chief income earner in a household, typically into various sub-groupings of middle- and working-class categories.

social enterprise a business whose primary objectives are essentially social and whose surpluses are reinvested for that purpose in the business or in the community, rather than dispersed to the owners.

social learning social learning theory, advocated by Albert Bandura, suggests that we can learn from observing the experiences of others, and in contrast with operant conditioning we can delay gratification and even administer our own rewards or punishment.

social or religious ethics concerned with what is right and wrong, good and bad, in respect of character and conduct. It does not claim to be established merely on the basis of rational enquiry and makes a implicit claim to general allegiance to something (e.g. God).

society the customs, habits, and nature of a nation's social system.

spam unsolicited email, the junk mail of the twenty-first century, which clogs email servers and uses up much-needed bandwidth on the internet.

speciality products these are bought very infrequently, are very expensive, and represent very high risk.

sponsorship a marketing communications activity, whereby one party permits another an opportunity to exploit an association with a target audience in return for funds, services, or resources.

stakeholders people with an interest, a 'stake', in the levels of profit an organization achieves, its environmental impact, and its ethical conduct in society.

standardization orientation a firm operates as if the world were one large market (global market), ignoring regional and national differences, selling the same products and services the same way throughout the world.

storage warehouses store goods for moderate to long periods.

STP process the method by which whole markets are subdivided into different segments, for targeting and positioning.

straight rebuy the organizational processes associated with the routine reordering of good and services, often undertaken from an approved list of suppliers.

strategic business unit an organizational unit which for planning purposes is sufficiently large to exercise control over the principal strategic factors affecting its performance. Typically abbreviated to SBU, these might incorporate an entire brand and/or its sub-components, or a country region, or some other discrete unit of an organization.

strategic market analysis the starting point of the marketing strategy process, involving analysis of three main types of environment, the external environment, the performance environment, and the internal environment.

strategic market planning a process that involves identifying and defining target segments and markets and then setting out the direction and competitive approach that an organization wishes to take within these markets.

stratified random sampling a method used to select respondents from known homogeneous sub-groups of the population where sub groups are determined on the basis of specific criteria.

superego a Freudian psychoanalytical concept which denotes the part of our psyche which controls how we motivate ourselves to behave to respond to our instincts and urges in a socially acceptable manner.

supermarket a large self-service retailing environment which can be defined as a large-scale departmental retailing organization that offers a wide variety of differing merchandise to a large consumer base.

supply chains formed when organizations link their individual value chains.

support activities the indirect activities necessary to facilitate the primary activities within the value chain.

sustainable competitive advantage when an organization is able to offer a superior product to competitors which is not easily imitated and enjoys significant market share as a result.

switching costs the psychological, economic, time, and effort-related costs associated with substituting one product or service for another or changing a supplier from one to another.

SWOT analysis a methodology used by organizations to understand their strategic position. It involves analysis of an organization's strengths, weaknesses, opportunities, and threats.

synchronicity refers to the degree to which a user's input into a system/channel and the response they receive from the system/channel are simultaneous.

synchronous immediate or near so 'real-time' information exchange.

systematic random sampling a method used to select respondents from a known population using an initial random number generated to determine the first sample respondent but where each subsequent sample respondent is selected on the basis of the nth respondent proceeding, where n is determined by dividing the population size by the sample size and rounding up.

tangibility possessing the characteristics of something which is physical, i.e. it can be touched. As a result, it has form. When products are tangible they have physical presence.

tariff barrier a financial tax on imported goods.

telemarketing or telesales is a form of non-store retailing when purchase occurs over the telephone.

teleological ethics a form of ethical approach by which the rightness or wrongness of an action or decision is judged primarily on the intentions of the decision maker.

test marketing a stage in the new product development process, undertaken when a new product is tested with a sample of customers, or is launched in a specified geographical area, to judge customers' reactions prior to a national launch.

test markets regions within a country used to test the effects of the launch of a new product or service, typically using regional advertising to promote the service and pre- and post-advertising market research to measure promotional effectiveness.

time utility manufacture, purchase, and consumption might occur at differing points in time; time utility is bridging this gap.

transactional exchanges short-term economic transactions between parties who are primarily interested in products and prices. Participants are primarily motivated by self-interest.

transfer pricing typically occurs in large organisations and represents the pricing approach used when one unit of a company sells to another unit within the same company.

translation equivalence the degree to which the meaning of one language is represented in another after translation.

transvections a term proposed by Alderson and Miles to denote the relationships (transactions) that occur in the development of a product or service that cross between company (i.e. product/service)

ownership boundaries to produce a finished product or service. We would now consider such cooperation in manufacturing from the perspective of supply chain management as vertical integration or cooperation.

trust the degree of confidence that one person (or organization) has in another to fulfil an obligation or responsibility. Trust is achieved by reducing uncertainty, the threat of opportunism, and the possibility of conflict whilst at the same time building confidence, the probability of buyer satisfaction, and longer-term commitment, necessary for effective relationships to be sustained.

t-test a statistical test of difference used for small randomly selected samples with a size of less than 30.

two-step model a communication model that reflects a receiver's response to a message.

undifferentiated approach there is no delineation between market segments, and instead the market is viewed as one mass market with one marketing strategy for the entire market.

users people or groups who use business products and services once they have been acquired and who then evaluate their performance.

utilitarianism an ethical approach originally developed by English philosopher and social reformer Jeremy Bentham, which suggests that an action is right if, and only if, it conforms to the principle of utility, whereby utility—pleasure, happiness, or welfare—is maximized, or pain or unhappiness minimized, more than any alternative.

utility a measure of satisfaction or happiness obtained from the consumption of a specific good or a service in economic thought, typically measured as an aggregate.

validity the ability of a measurement instrument to measure exactly the construct it is attempting to measure.

value the regard that something is held to be worth, typically although not always in financial terms.

value chain a term determined by Michael Porter that refers to the various activities an organization undertakes and links together in order to provide products and services that are perceived by customers to be different and of superior value.

values consensual views formed on the basis of informal and formal societal rules which stipulate how individuals should live their lives.

variability a characteristic of a service, one that refers to the amount of diversity allowed in each step of service provision.

variable costs costs which vary according to the number of units of product made or service sold. For instance, variable costs in the pharmaceutical market would include plastic bottles to place the pills in. In a service business like the airline industry, variable costs would include airline meals.

vertical conflict conflict between sequential members in a distribution network such as producers, distributor, and retailers over such matters as carrying a particular range or price increases.

viral marketing the unpaid peer-to-peer communication of often provocative content originating from an identified sponsor using the internet to persuade or influence an audience to pass along the content to others.

virtue ethics principally associated with Aristotle, this branch of ethics stresses the importance of developing virtuous principles, with 'right' character, and the pursuit of a virtuous life.

vision how an organization sees its future and what it wants to become.

wholesalers stock products not services before the next level of distribution.

winner's curse terminology associated with the bidding process in commercial markets where a company ends up submitting a bid at a price which is unprofitable or not very profitable just to win the contract.

word of mouth a form of communication founded on interpersonal messages regarding products or services sought or consumed. The receiver regards the communicator as impartial and credible as they are not attempting to sell products or services.

working capital in accounting terms, this represents a company's short-term financial efficiency and is the difference between its current assets (what it owns) and its current liabilities (what it owes).

Wünderkind a German term referring in this context to an exceptionally bright (i.e. intelligent) person.

yield management a system for maximizing the profit generated from activities, which carefully manages price to ensure full utilization of capacity, while balancing supply and demand factors.

z-test a statistical test of difference used for large randomly selected samples with a size of 30 or more.

Index

A

Account management, 488
ACORN grouping
analysis of behaviour, 120–4
segmentation criteria, 230
Acquisition process
acquisition, 99–101
information gathering, 98–9
motive, 97–8
overview, 97
product selection, 99
re-evaluation, 101–4
Added value
exchanges, 677–8
meaning, 672–3
supply chains, 675–7
value chains, 673–5
Advertising
electronic marketing, 725
ethics
children, 808–9
propaganda and politics, 806–8
sexual material, 804–5
shock tactics, 804–5
legal environment, 63–5
meaning and scope, 473–4
media usage, 237–9
principal marketing tool, 471–2
strong theory, 475
weak theory, 475–6
Agencies
briefing, 537–40
industry changes, 530–1
personnel, 534–6
relationships, 536
remuneration, 540–1
selection criteria, 532–4
types, 531–2
Analysis of markets
competitors, 183–6
distributors, 187
planning, 187–8
suppliers, 187
SWOT analysis, 188–91
Anglo-Australian School, 685–6
Anti-globalization movement, 279–83
Attacking strategies, 202
Attitudes
analysis of behaviour, 118
international marketing, 296–7

B

Behaviour
business-to-business marketing, 642
diffusion theory, 93–6
influences on
business-to-business marketing, 650–3
customer perceptions, 398–404
management principles, 179–81
opinion leaders, 439–40
personal influencers, 439–41
social contexts, 118–20
strategy, 179–81
learning
classical conditioning, 107–8
operant conditioning, 108
social learning, 109
memory, 109–11
operational and socio-psychological contrasted, 92–3
perceptions, 105–7
personality
psychoanalytic approach, 111–12
self-conceptions, 116–18
trait approach, 112–15
post-modern marketing
creativity and constraint contrasted, 771–3
desire and satisfaction contrasted, 770
material and symbolic realms contrasted, 762–5
rationality and irrationality contrasted, 770–1
social and personal environments contrasted, 765–70
product acquisition
acquisition, 99–101
information gathering, 98–9
motive, 97–8
process, 97
product selection, 99
re-evaluation, 101–4
scope, 92
segmentation criteria, 234–9
social contexts
ethnicity, 126–7
grading, 120–4
group influences, 118–20
life cycle groups, 124–6
opinions, 118

Branding
brand entertainment, 501
equity as a measure of value, 382
meaning, 373–4
policies, 379–82
promotional factors, 461–2
rationale, 374–6
services, 608–10
strategies, 377–9
types, 376–7
Bribery, 817
Broadcasting *see* **Media**
Budgets
communication
determining allocations, 528–30
planning, 524
structural changes in industry, 527–8
costs
agency remuneration, 540–1
general marketing principle, 12–14
pricing approaches, 406–8
relationship with pricing, 393–5
delivery, 326–9
financial analysis, 83
Bundling of products, 403–4
Business-to-business marketing
B2C compared
differences, 660–2
similarities, 662–4
characteristics
demand, 630–1
international marketing, 631–2
relationship, 632
customer portfolio matrix, 653–5
customer types
commercial organizations, 633–7
government, 637
institutions, 637–9
decision-making
characteristics, 643–4
processes, 645–50
influences on behaviour, 650–3
key accounts
functions, 658–9
management, 655–7
relationship cycles, 657–8
meaning and scope, 628–9
organizational buyer behaviour, 642
pricing wars
tendering and bidding, 421–2
various approaches, 419–21

Business-to-business marketing
(*cont.*)
   product mix, 362–3
   products and services, 639–40
   requirement for different
      techniques, 32–4
   role of purchasing, 640–2
   segmentation
      customers, 243–6
      meaning and scope, 239–40
      organizational characteristics,
         240–3

C

Category killer stores, 578
Cause-related marketing, 620–1
Challengers, 200
Channel management
   disintermediation, 567–8
   electronic marketing, 744–6
   general marketing principle, 12–14
   grey markets, 570
   intensity of coverage, 563–7
   intermediaries, 554–6
   intermediary membership, 562–3
   logistics, 551–4
      importance, 570–1
      inventory management, 574
      order processing, 571–2
      transportation, 573–4
      warehousing, 572–3
   marketing mix, 14–17
   member functions, 557
   member incentives, 569–70
   overview, 550
   place, 551
   relationships, 568–9
   strategy, 557
   structure
      direct distribution, 558–9
      hybrid distribution, 560–2
      indirect distribution, 559–60
Charities, 619
Cinema, 497–8
Classical conditioning, 107–8
Co-operative strategies, 203–6
Communication
   agencies
      briefing, 537–40
      industry changes, 530–1
      personnel, 534–6
      relationships, 536
      remuneration, 540–1
      selection criteria, 532–4
      types, 531–2
   budgets
      determining allocations, 528–30
      structural changes in industry,
         527–8
   components, 447–9

defined, 445
evaluation, 541–2
influential ideas, 451–6
information acquisition, 736–44
integrated approach, 450–1
international marketing, 462–4
messages, 447
planning
   integrated approach, 525–7
   MCPC elements, 520–5
   systematic process, 518–19
role, 442–5
strategy
   3Ps, 511–12
   overview, 510
   profile strategy, 515–18
   pull strategy, 513–15
   push strategy, 513–15
   role, 510
tasks, 446–7
theory
   importance, 432–3
   interaction model, 439–40
   linear model, 434–7
   two-step model, 437–8
tools and techniques
   account management, 488
   advertising, 473–6
   direct marketing, 482–7
   media usage, 491–9
   other promotional methods, 500–2
   overview, 471–2
   personal selling, 487–8
   public relations, 478–82
   role, 472–3
   sales promotion, 476–8
   selecting the right mix, 489–91
   word-of-mouth, 449–50
Competition
   competitive advantage, 196–8
   competitive intelligence, 159–60
   competitive positioning, 199–201
   market analysis, 183–6
Conditioning
   classical conditioning, 107–8
   operant conditioning, 108
Consumers
   behaviour
      diffusion theory, 93–6
      learning, 107–9
      memory, 109–11
      operational and socio-
         psychological contrasted, 92–3
      perceptions, 105–7
      product acquisition, 97–104
      scope, 92
      social contexts, 118–27
   customers distinguished, 6
   personality
      psychoanalytic approach, 111–12
      self-conceptions, 116–18
      trait approach, 112–15

requirement for different
      techniques, 30–1
segmentation, 223–5
Context analysis, 520–1
Convenience stores, 579
Corporate social responsibility,
   817–23
Costs
   agency remuneration, 540–1
   general marketing principle, 12–14
   pricing approaches, 406–8
   relationship with pricing, 393–5
Culture *see* **Social environment**
Customers
   business segmentation, 243–6
   business-to-business marketing
      commercial organizations, 633–6
      government, 637
      institutions, 637–9
      portfolio matrix, 653–5
      role of purchasing, 641
   consumers distinguished, 6
   exchange process with sellers,
      17–18
   non-profit marketing, 617
   perceptions
      external influences, 398–404
      measurement, 397–8
      quality, 395–7
   performance environment, 76
   pricing policies, 415
   relationship marketing
      customer service, 704–8
      lifecycle, 687–90
      loyalty, retention and
         satisfaction, 690–6
      managing relationships, 696–704
   retailing
      customer value, 575–6
      defined, 575
      retailer types, 576–9
      store presence, 579–81
   satisfaction, 336

D

Data
   analysis and interpretation, 155–6
   business-to-business marketing, 244
   collection, 154–5
   costings, 395
   financial analysis, 83
   information processing, 110
   market orientation, 23–5
   market research, 137
   protection, 300
   sales forecasting, 341
   scanning the market environment,
      70–1
   technological environment, 57, 297
Deconstruction, 774–8

Defensive strategies, 203
Delivery
  budgets, 326–9
  essentials of marketing, 6–7
  implementation barriers, 251
  internal politics and negotiation,
    325–6
  market organization
    importance, 317–19
    team efforts, 324–5
    types of organization, 320–4
  market strategy
    competitive advantage, 196–8
    competitive positioning, 199–201
    generic studies, 198–9
  marketing metrics
    awareness, 333–4
    customer satisfaction, 336
    distribution and availability,
      336–7
    margins, 333
    market share, 334–5
    new products, 335
    prices, 335–6
    profitability, 332
    recognition, 329–31
    sales, 332–3
  overview, 316
  planning process, 316–17
  programme management, 337–41
  sales
    forecasting, 341–2
    variance analysis, 342–4
Demand
  business-to-business marketing,
    630–1
  elasticity, 408–9
Demographics
  lifestyles, 56–7
  market development strategy, 267
  marketing mix, 457
  origins of research, 137
  segmentation criteria, 221, 225–7
  social grading, 120
  sociological influences, 9
  technological environment, 297
Deontological ethics, 797–8
Department stores, 576–7
Design
  communication planning
    MCPC elements, 520–5
    systematic process, 518–19
  essentials of marketing, 6–7
  financial analysis, 83
  market analysis, 187–8
  marketing research, 152–4
    data analysis, 155–6
  new product mix, 370
  performance analysis, 72–9
  PESTLE analysis, 51
  positioning
    concept, 252–3

    importance, 251–2
    perceptual mapping, 253–4
    strategies, 254–8
  product portfolio analysis, 79–83
  segmentation
    consumers, 223–5
    meaning and scope, 217–21
    process, 221–3
    STP process, 216–17
  strategic market planning, 316–17
  strategy
    goals, 191–2
    growth, 193–5
    implementation, 196–201
    important influences, 179–81
    intent, 201–6
    market analysis, 183–91
    meaning and scope, 176–8
    planning, 180–2
  targeting
    importance, 246–8
    selected approaches, 248–9
Determination
  communications
    overall evaluation, 541–2
    planning, 524–5
  environment
    financial analysis, 83
    marketing audits, 83–4
    performance analysis, 72–9
    product portfolio analysis, 79–83
    scanning, 69–72
  essentials of marketing, 6–7
Development
  essentials of marketing, 6–7
  international marketing
    anti-globalization movement,
      279–83
    approaches to international
      markets, 271–5
    attitudes and values, 296–7
    changing world markets, 268–71
    competitive strategy, 275–9
    direct exporting, 306
    direct investment, 307
    driving forces, 283–7
    economic environment, 299
    entry methods, 302–3
    environment, 292
    global markets, 278–9
    indirect exporting, 303–4
    joint ventures and acquisitions,
      306
    legal environment, 299–301
    licensing, franchising and
      contracting, 304–5
    market selection, 287–91
    multi-domestic markets, 276–8
    political environment, 299–301
    selection criteria, 301–2
    social environment, 292–5
    technological environment, 297–9

    new product mix, 370–1
    overview, 266
    product–market matrix, 266–7
    relationship marketing, 681–4
    strategy, 267–8
Differentiation *see* **Segmentation**
Diffusion theory, 93–6
Digital media, 495
Direct marketing
  direct-response media, 484–7
  meaning and scope, 482–3
  principal marketing tool, 471–2
  role, 483–4
  technologies, 735–6
Discount retailers, 577–8
Disintermediation, 567–8
Distribution
  branding, 377
  business-to-business marketing,
    633–6
  channel management
    disintermediation, 567–8
    grey markets, 570
    intensity of coverage, 563–7
    intermediaries, 554–6
    intermediary membership,
      562–3
    logistics, 551–4, 570–5
    member functions, 557
    member incentives, 569–70
    overview, 550
    place, 551
    relationships, 568–9
    strategy, 557
    structure, 558–62
  ethics, 803–4
  market analysis, 187
Diversified growth, 194–5

E

Ecological environment, 65–9
Economic environment
  international marketing, 299
  key areas, 53–5
  relationship marketing, 686–7
Egoism, 795–6
Elasticity of demand, 408–9
Electronic marketing
  activity management, 723–4
  channel management, 744–6
  characteristics, 720–3
  direct marketing, 733–6
  importance, 718–19
  information acquisition, 736–44
  information provision, 723–4
  key considerations, 750
  meaning and scope, 719–20
  online auctions, 747–8
  price comparisons, 746–7
  promotional factors, 461

Electronic marketing (*cont.*)
  public relations, 729–30
  retail revenue management, 748
  sales promotions, 730–3
  SMS advertising and podcasting, 728–9
  transaction management, 749–50
Environment
  internal factors
    financial analysis, 83
    marketing audits, 83–4
    product portfolio analysis, 79–83
  international marketing, 292
  key areas
    ecology, 65–9
    economics, 53–5
    law, 59–65
    politics, 51–3
    social environment, 55–7
    technology, 57–9
  performance analysis, 69–72
    critical success factors, 77–9
    industries, 75–7
    scope, 72
  scanning, 69–72
Equivalence, 165–6
Ethics
  basic requirements, 794
  decision-making norms
    deontological ethics, 797–8
    managerial egoism, 795–6
    utilitarianism, 796–7
    virtue ethics, 798
  decision-making process, 798–803
  distribution, 803–4
  international marketing
    bribery, 817
    corporate social responsibility, 817–23
    overview, 815–16
  marketing research, 162–4
  meaning and scope, 792–4
  origins, 792
  overview, 791
  pricing, 813–15
  products, 809–13
  promotion
    children, 808–9
    labelling, 806
    propaganda and politics, 806–8
    sexual material, 804–5
    shock tactics, 804–5
Ethnicity, 126–7
Exhibitions, 501
Exporting. *see* **International marketing**

F

Fads and fashions, 365
Family branding, 379

Field marketing, 501
Financial analysis, 83
Followers, 200
Fragmented markets, 773–4
Full-service agencies, 531–2

G

Generic studies, 198–9
Geodemographics, 228–30
Geographics
  business segmentation, 241
  segmentation criteria, 227–8
Globalization
  anti-globalization movement, 279–83
  global markets, 278–9
  multi-domestic markets, 276–8
  overview, 265–6
Goals, 191–2
Goods *see* **Products**; **Services**
Government
  business-to-business marketing, 637
  non-profit marketing, 621
  propaganda and political advertising, 806–8
  public sector services, 618–19
Grey markets, 570
Group influences, 118–20
Growth
  diversified growth, 194–5
  integrated growth, 195
  intensive growth, 193–4
  meaning and scope, 193

I

Idea generation, 368–70
In-store media, 494–5
Indirect distribution, 559–60
Indirect exporting, 303–4
Industrial Marketing and Purchasing Group, 685–6
Influences on behaviour
  business-to-business marketing, 650–3
  customer perceptions, 398–404
  management principles, 179–81
  opinion leaders, 439–40
  personal influencers, 439–41
  social contexts, 118–20
  strategy, 179–81
Information
  gathering, 98–9
  processing, 601
  systems, 159–62
Infrastructure barriers, 250
Innovation
  diffusion theory, 93–6

marketing metrics, 335
pricing policies, 416–19
product mix
  commercialization, 371
  development and selection, 370–1
  idea generation, 368–70
  key concept, 367–8
  planning and analysis, 370
  screening, 370
  test marketing, 371
Inseparability, 596–8
Institutions
  business-to-business marketing, 637–9
  general marketing principle, 12–14
  promotional factors, 460
Intangibility, 593–5
Integrated growth, 195
Intensive growth, 193–4
Intermediaries
  channels of distribution, 554–6
  disintermediation, 567–8
  member incentives, 569–70
  membership, 562–3
  relationshipship management, 568–9
Internal environment
  financial analysis, 83
  marketing audits, 83–4
  product portfolio analysis, 77–9
International marketing
  anti-globalization movement, 279–83
  approaches to international markets, 271–5
  attitudes and values, 296–7
  business-to-business, 631–2
  changing world markets, 268–71
  communications, 462–4
  driving forces, 283–7
  economic environment, 299
  entry methods, 302–3
  environment, 292
  ethics
    bribery, 817
    corporate social responsibility, 817–23
    overview, 815–16
  indirect exporting, 303–4
  joint ventures and acquisitions, 306
  legal environment, 299–301
  licensing, franchising and contracting, 304–5
  market selection, 287–91
  political environment, 299–301
  research
    key issues, 164–6
    process, 166–8
  selection criteria, 301–2
  social environment, 292–5

strategy
  global markets, 278–9
    multi-domestic markets, 276–8
    overview, 265–6
  technology, 297–9
Internet
  digital media, 495
  direct marketing, 735–6
  electronic marketing, 725–7
  importance and scope, 719–20
  online auctions, 747–8
  online research, 157
  price comparisons, 746–7
  sales promotions, 730–3
  search engine marketing, 727–8
  social networking sites, 496–7
  transaction management,
    749–50
  warehousing of digital products,
    573
Inventory management, 574

K

Key accounts
  functions, 658–9
  management, 655–7
  relationship cycles, 657–8

L

Labelling
  ethics, 806
  marketing mix, 384–5
Leaders, 199–200
Learning
  classical conditioning, 107–8
  operant conditioning, 108
  social learning, 109
Legal environment
  advertising, 63–5
  international marketing,
    299–301
  safety, packaging and labelling,
    59–61
  wages and taxation, 61–3
Licensing
  brands, 380
  international marketing, 304–5
Life cycles
  effect on behaviour, 124–6
  product mix, 363–7
  relationship marketing, 687–90
  segmentation criteria, 227
Limited line retailers, 578
List pricing, 415
Logistics
  importance, 570–1
  inventory management, 574
  order processing, 571–2

transportation, 573–4
  warehousing, 572–3
Loss-leader pricing, 415

M

Management principles
  delivery
    budgets, 326–9
    internal politics and negotiation,
      325–6
    market organization, 317–25
    marketing metrics, 329–37
    overview, 316
    planning process, 316–17
    programme management, 337–41
    sales, 341–4
  development
    international marketing, 268–309
    overview, 266
    product–market matrix, 266–7
    strategy, 267–8
  positioning
    concept, 252–3
    importance, 251–2
    perceptual mapping, 253–4
    strategies, 254–8
  segmentation
    behavioural criteria, 234–9
    business-to-business marketing,
      239–46
    consumers, 223–5
    limitations, 250–0
    meaning and scope, 217–21
    profile criteria, 225–32
    process, 221–3
    psychological criteria, 232–4
    STP process, 216–17
  strategy
    goals, 191–2
    growth, 193–5
    implementation, 196–209
    important influences, 179–81
    intent, 201–6
    market analysis, 182–91
    meaning and scope, 176–8
    planning, 180–2, 206–9
  targeting
    importance, 246–8
    selected approaches, 248–9
Margins, 333
Marketing *see also* **Relationship
    marketing**
  4D phase, 6–7
  critical perspectives, 39–42
  defined, 4–6
  differing contexts
    consumer goods, 30–1
  exchange process between buyers
    and sellers, 17–18
  extended mix for services, 18–23

functions, 12–14
  general principles, 12–14
  history, 8–9
  impact on society, 34–9
  importance, 11–12
  orientation, 23–5
  requirement for different
    techniques
    business-to-business marketing,
      32–4
    overview, 29–30
    services, 32
  sales distinguished, 10
Marketing environment *see*
    Environment
Marketing metrics *see* **Metrics**
Marketing mix
  channel management
    disintermediation, 567–8
    grey markets, 570
    intensity of coverage, 563–7
    intermediaries, 554–6
    intermediary membership, 562–3
    logistics, 551–4, 570–5
    member functions, 557
    member incentives, 569–70
    overview, 550
    place, 551
    relationships, 568–9
    strategy, 557
    structure, 558–62
  communication agencies
    briefing, 537–40
    industry changes, 530–1
    personnel, 534–6
    relationships, 536
    remuneration, 540–1
    selection criteria, 532–4
    types, 531–2
  communication budgets
    determining allocations, 528–30
    structural changes in industry,
      527–8
  communication planning
    integrated approach, 525–7
    MCPC elements, 520–5
    systematic process, 518–19
  communication strategy
    3Ps, 511–12
    overview, 510
    profile strategy, 515–18
    pull strategy, 513–15
    push strategy, 513–15
    role, 510
  communication tools and
    techniques
    account management, 488
    advertising, 473–6
    direct marketing, 482–7
    media usage, 491–9
    other promotional methods,
      500–2

Marketing mix (*cont.*)
  overview, 471–2
  personal selling, 487–8
  public relations, 478–82
  role, 472–3
  sales promotion, 476–8
  selecting the right mix, 489–91
  communications evaluation, 541–2
  pricing
    approaches, 405–15
    business-to-business marketing, 419–22
    component parts, 392–3
    customer perceptions, 395–404
    new products and services, 416–19
    objectives, 404–5
    overview, 392
    policies, 415–22
    relationship with production costs, 393–5
  products
    adoption process, 373
    branding, 373–82
    business-to-business marketing, 362–3
    classification, 358–62
    innovation, 367–72
    labelling, 384–5
    levels, 355–8
    life cycles, 363–7
    packaging, 383–4
    ranges, 363
    tangibility, 354–5
  promotion
    communication components, 447–9
    communication defined, 445
    communication messages, 447
    communication tasks, 446–7
    communication theory, 432–9
    cultural aspects, 456–62
    influential ideas, 451–6
    integrated approach, 450–1
    international marketing, 462–4
    opinion followers, 438–9
    opinion leaders, 439–40
    overview, 430–2
    personal influencers, 439–41
    role of communications, 442–5, 442–5
    word-of-mouth, 449–50
  responsibilities of marketing managers, 14–17
  retailing
    customer value, 575–6
    defined, 575
    retailer types, 576–9
    store presence, 579–81
  services, 18–23, 601–5
  strategy planning, 209

Marketing research
  briefing document, 141–2
  commissioning, 139–41
  competitive intelligence, 159–60
  definitions, 137–9
  ethics, 162–4
  information systems, 159–62
  international research
    key issues, 164–6
    process, 166–8
  origins, 137
  overview, 136
  process
    overview, 143–4
    planning, 146–54
    problem definition, 144–5
  testing, 157
    online research, 157–8
Markets, 12–14
Media
  agency briefing, 538–9
  broadcasting, 494
  changing role, 498–9
  characteristics, 491–2
  cinema, 497–8
  direct marketing, 733–6
  importance and scope, 719–20
  in-store, 494–5
  internet
    digital media, 495
    social networking sites, 496–7
  outdoor media, 494
  overview, 471, 491
  print, 493–4
  segmentation, 237–9
  sponsorship, 497–8
Memory, 109–11
Mental stimulus processing, 600–1
Metrics
  awareness, 333–4
  customer satisfaction, 336
  distribution and availability, 336–7
  margins, 333
  market share, 334–5
  new products, 335
  prices, 335–6
  profitability, 332
  recognition, 329–31
  sales, 332–3
Mix *see* **Marketing mix**
MOSAIC segmentation, 230–1
Motive
  acquisition process, 97–8
  personality trait, 113–5
Multiple stakeholders, 616–17

N

Nichers, 200–1
Non-profit marketing, 616–21
Nordic School, 684

O

Odd-number pricing, 401
Online marketing, 495
Opinions, 118
Order processing, 571–2
Organizational forms, 317–25
Orientation
  meaning and scope, 23–5
Outdoor media, 494

P

Packaging, 383–4
People processing, 600
Perceptions
  added value
    exchanges, 677–8
    meaning, 672–3
    supply chains, 675–7
    value chains, 673–5
  behaviour, 105–7
  mapping, 253–4
Performance environment
  critical success factors, 77–9
  industries
    competitors, 77
    customers, 76
    new entrants, 73–5
    scope, 73
    substitutes, 75–6
    suppliers, 76–7
  scope, 72
Personal selling
  meaning and scope, 487
  principal marketing tool, 471–2
  role, 487–8
Personality
  psychoanalytic approach, 111–12
  self-conceptions, 116–18
  trait approach, 112–15
PESTLE analysis
  importance, 69
  meaning, 51
Placement, 551
Planning
  communication
    integrated approach, 525–7
    MCPC elements, 520–5
    systematic process, 518–19
  market analysis, 187–8, 207–8
  marketing research
    data collection, 154–5
    primary and secondary research contrasted, 146–7
    project design, 152–4
    qualitative and quantitative research contrasted, 147–52
    reporting, 157
    types of research, 147

new product mix, 370
strategic market planning, 316–17
strategy, 180–2, 206–9
PLC concept
meaning, 363–5
usefulness, 365–7
Podcasting, 728–9
Political environment
international marketing, 299–301
key areas, 51–3
Porter's generic studies, 198–9
Portfolio analysis, 77–9
Positioning *see also* **Segmentation;**
Targeting
concept, 252–3
importance, 251–2
perceptual mapping, 253–4
strategies, 254–8
Possession processing, 600
Post-modern marketing
art or science, 778–9
concepts, 759–60
key features
creativity and constraint
contrasted, 771–3
desire and satisfaction
contrasted, 770
material and symbolic realms
contrasted, 762–5
overview, 760–2
rationality and irrationality
contrasted, 770–1
social and personal
environments contrasted,
765–70
overview, 758
researching fragmented markets,
773–4
semiotics and deconstruction,
774–8
sustainable marketing, 779–82
Pricing
approaches
competitor-orientation, 409–11
cost-orientation, 406–8
demand-orientation, 408–9
value-orientation, 411–15
business-to-business marketing
tendering and bidding, 421–2
various approaches, 419–21
component parts, 392–3
customer perceptions
external influences, 398–404
measurement, 397–8
quality, 395–7
ethics, 813–15
internet comparisons, 746–7
marketing mix, 14–17
metrics, 335–6
new products and services, 416–19
objectives, 404–5
overview, 392

policies
overview, 415–16
relationship with production costs,
393–5
retail revenue management, 748
services market mix, 602
Print media, 493–4
Products
acquisition process
acquisition, 99–101
information gathering, 98–9
motive, 97–8
overview, 97
product selection, 99
re-evaluation, 101–4
bundling, 403–4
business-to-business marketing,
639–40
ethics, 809–13
marketing mix, 14–17
adoption process, 373
branding, 373–82
business-to-business marketing,
362–3
classification, 358–62
innovation, 367–72
labelling, 384–5
levels, 355–8
life cycles, 363–7
packaging, 383–4
ranges, 363
tangibility, 354–5
placement, 500–1
portfolio analysis, 77–9
product–market matrix, 266–7
services market mix, 602
strategic planning, 207
usage, 234–6
Profile strategy, 515–18
Profitability, 332
Programme management, 337–41
Promotion *see also under* **Sales**
communication components, 447–9
communication defined, 445
communication messages, 447
communication tasks, 446–7
communication theory
importance, 432–3
interaction model, 438–9
linear model, 434–7
two-step model, 437–8
cultural aspects
branding, 461–2
differing contexts, 456–8
institutions and groups, 460
multiple elements, 458–9
symbols, 459–60
technology, 461
ethics
children, 808–9
labelling, 806
propaganda and politics, 806–8

sexual material, 804–5
shock tactics, 804–5
influential ideas, 451–6
integrated approach, 450–1
international marketing, 462–4
marketing mix, 14–17
overview, 430–2
personal influencers
opinion followers, 440–1
opinion leaders, 439–40
pricing policies, 415
role of communications, 442–5
services market mix, 602–4
word-of-mouth, 449–50
Psychology
operational and socio-psychological
contrasted, 92–3
segmentation criteria, 232–4
Public relations
characteristics, 479–82
importance, 478
principal marketing tool, 471–2
role, 478–9
Public sector
non-profit marketing, 618–19
role of government, 621
Pull strategy, 512–13
Purchase behaviour, 236–7
Push strategy, 513–15
Psychoanalysis, 111–12

R

Re-evaluation, 101–4
Reference groups
analysis of behaviour, 118–20
profile criteria, 225–32
Reintermediation, 567–8
Relationship marketing *see also*
Business-to-business
marketing; Services
academic approaches
Anglo-Australian School, 684–5
Industrial Marketing and
Purchasing Group, 685–6
Nordic School, 684
business-to-business, 632
channel management, 568–9
co-operative strategies, 203–6
communication, 536
customer service
contact centres, 705–6
CRM systems, 706–8
importance, 704–5
customers
lifecycle, 687–90
loyalty, retention and
satisfaction, 690–6
development, 681–4
economic environment, 686–7
general marketing principle, 25–9

Relationship marketing (*cont.*)
  key accounts, 657–8
  managing relationships
    customer satisfaction, 700–2
    inter-organizational conflict, 703–4
    organizational power, 702–3
    overview, 696–7
    trust and commitment, 697–700
  nature and characteristics, 679–81
  perceived value
    exchanges, 677–8
    meaning, 672–3
    supply chains, 675–7
    value chains, 673–5
Research
  electronic marketing, 736–44
  environmental scanning, 69–72
  financial analysis, 83
  international marketing
    key issues, 164–6
    process, 166–8
  marketing
    briefing document, 141–2
    commissioning, 139–41
    competitive intelligence, 159–60
    definitions, 137–9
    ethics, 162–4
    information systems, 159–62
    international research, 164–8
    online research, 157
    origins, 137
    overview, 136
    process, 143–57
    testing, 157
  new entrants, 75
  post-modern marketing, 773–4
Resources *see* **Budgets**
Retailing
  customer value, 575–6
  defined, 575
  retailer types, 576–9
  revenue management, 748
  store presence, 579–81

S

Sales
  electronic marketing, 730–3
  forecasting, 341–2
  marketing distinguished, 10
  marketing metrics, 332–3
  promotion
    methods and techniques, 476–8
    principal marketing tool, 471–2
  signs, 401
  variance analysis, 342–4
Search engine marketing, 727–8
Segmentation *see also* **Positioning; Targeting**
  behavioural criteria, 234–9

business-to-business marketing
  customers, 243–6
  meaning and scope, 239–40
  organizational characteristics, 240–3
consumers, 223–5
meaning and scope, 217–21
pricing, 415
profile criteria, 225–32
process, 221–3
psychological criteria, 232–4
STP process, 216–17
Selection process, 99
Selective exposure, 105
Self-conceptions, 116–18
Self-service technologies, 742–3
Semiotics, 774–8
Services
  branding, 608–10
  business-to-business marketing, 639–40
  distinguishing characteristics
    inseparability, 596–8
    intangibility, 593–5
    lack of ownership, 598
    overview, 592–3
    variability, 595–6
  internal marketing, 610–11
  key dimensions, 607–8
  marketing mix, 18–23, 601–5
  meaning and scope, 590–1
  nature, 591–2
  non-profit marketing, 616–21
  processes, 599–601
  product mix, 362–3
  quality and performance, 612–15
  requirement for different techniques, 32
  role of government, 621
  service mix, 598–9
  strategy, 605–7
Share of market, 334–5
SMS advertising, 728–9
Social enterprise, 619–20
Social environment
  effect on behaviour
    ethnicity, 126–7
    grading, 120–4
    group influences, 118–20
    life cycle groups, 124–6
    opinions, 118
  international marketing, 292–5
  meaning, 55–7
  post-modern marketing, 765–70
  promotional factors
    branding, 461–2
    differing contexts, 456–8
    institutions and groups, 460
    multiple elements, 458–9
    symbols, 459–60
    technology, 461
Social networking sites, 496–7

Socially responsible companies, 817–23
Sponsorship, 497–8, 500
Standard Industrial Classification (SIC) codes, 241–3
Store presence, 579–81
STP process, 216–17
Strategy
  branding, 377–9
  business-to-business marketing, 641–2
  channel management, 557
  communication
    3Ps, 511–12
    overview, 510
    profile strategy, 515–18
    pull strategy, 513–15
    push strategy, 513–15
    role, 510
  development, 267–8
  goals, 191–2
  growth
    diversified growth, 194–5
    integrated growth, 195
    intensive growth, 193–4
    meaning and scope, 193
  implementation
    competitive advantage, 196–8
    competitive positioning, 199–201
    generic studies, 198–9
  important influences, 179–81
  intent
    attacking strategies, 202
    co-operation, 203–6
    defensive strategies, 203
    military analogies, 201–2
  international marketing
    global markets, 278–9
    multi-domestic markets, 276–8
    overview, 265–6, 265–6
  market analysis
    competitors, 183–6
    distributors, 187
    planning, 187–8, 207–8
    suppliers, 187
    SWOT analysis, 188–91
  meaning and scope, 176–8
  planning, 180–2, 206–9
  positioning, 254–8
  retailer types, 576–9
  services, 605–7
Supermarkets, 579
Suppliers, 187
Sustainable marketing, 779–82
SWOT analysis, 188–91

T

Tangibility, 354–5
Targeting *see also* **Positioning; Segmentation**

importance, 246–8
selected approaches, 248–9
Team efforts, 324–5
Technological environment
international marketing, 297–9
key areas, 57–9
Technology *see* **Electronic marketing**
Telephony
importance and scope, 719–20
information acquisition, 736–44
sales promotions, 730–3
SMS advertising and podcasting, 728–9
Texts, 774–8

Traits of personality, 112–15
Transaction behaviour, 236–7
Transparency, 618
Transportation, 573–4

U

Utilitarianism, 796–7

V

Values
analysis of behaviour, 118

international marketing, 296–7
perceived value
meaning, 662–4
supply chains, 675–7
value chains, 673–5
pricing approaches, 411–15
Variability, 595–6
Variance analysis, 342–4
Viral marketing, 501–2
Virtue ethics, 798

W

Warehousing, 572–3